ESSENTIALS OF

Business and Administrative Communication

CANADIAN EDITION

ESSENTIALS OF

Business and Administrative Communication

CANADIAN EDITION

Kitty O. Locker
The Ohio State University

Isobel Findlay
University of Saskatchewan

 **McGraw-Hill Ryerson**

Toronto Montréal Boston Burr Ridge, IL Dubuque, IA Madison, WI New York
San Francisco St. Louis Bangkok Bogotá Caracas Kuala Lumpur Lisbon London
Madrid Mexico City Milan New Delhi Santiago Seoul Singapore Sydney Taipei

Essentials of Business and Administrative Communication
Canadian Edition

ISBN: 0-07-087754-8

1 2 3 4 5 6 7 8 9 10 VH 0 9 8 7 6

Care has been taken to trace ownership of copyright material contained in this text; however, the publisher will welcome any information that enables them to rectify any reference or credit for subsequent editions.

Vice President, Editorial and Media Technology: Pat Ferrier
Executive Sponsoring Editor: James Buchanan
Sponsoring Editor: Karen Noxon
Senior Developmental Editor: Denise Foote
Marketing Manager: Marc Trudel
Editorial Coordinator: Marina Seguin
Senior Supervising Editor: Margaret Henderson
Copy Editor: Karen Rolfe
Senior Production Coordinator: Jennifer Wilkie
Composition: Greg Devitt Design
Cover Design: Dianna Little
Printer: Von Hoffman Press, Inc.

Library and Archives Canada Cataloguing in Publication

Locker, Kitty O.
    Essentials of business and administrative communication / Kitty O. Locker, Isobel Findlay. — 1st Canadian ed.

Includes bibliographical references and index.
ISBN 0-07-087754-8

    1. Business communication—Textbooks. 2. Communication in management— Textbooks. 3. Communication in organizations—Textbooks. I. Findlay, Isobel II. Title.

HF5718.L634 2006   658.4'5   C2006-900649-0

To Len, Andrew, and Nick—Isobel Findlay

In memory of...

Kitty O. Locker, associate professor of English at The Ohio State University in Columbus, Ohio, who coordinated the Writing Center and taught courses in business and technical discourse and in research methods. She also taught as Assistant Professor at Texas A&M University and the University of Illinois.

She wrote *The Irwin Business Communication Handbook: Writing and Speaking in Business Classes* (1993), co-authored *Business Writing Cases and Problems* (1980, 1984, 1987), and co-edited *Conducting Research in Business Communication* (1988). She twice received the Alpha Kappa Psi award for Distinguished Publication in Business Communication for her article "'Sir, This Will Never Do': Model Dunning Letters 1592–1873" and for her article "'As Per Your Request': A History of Business Jargon." In 1992 she received the Association for Business Communication's Outstanding Researcher Award.

Her research included work on the effect of commenting styles on student attitudes and performance, collaborative writing in the classroom and the workplace, and the emergence of bureaucratic writing in the correspondence of the British East India Company from 1600 to 1800.

Her consulting work included conducting tutorials and short courses in business, technical, and administrative writing for employees of URS Greiner, Ross Products Division of Abbott Laboratories, Franklin County, the Ohio Civil Service Employees Association, AT&T, the American Medical Association, Western Electric, the Illinois Department of Central Management Services, the Illinois Department of Transportation, the A.E. Staley Company, Flo-Con, the Police Executive Leadership College, and the Firemen's Institute. She developed a complete writing improvement program for Joseph T. Ryerson, the nation's largest steel materials service center.

She served as the interim editor of *The Bulletin of the Association for Business Communication* and, in 1994-1995, as president of the Association for Business Communication (ABC). She edited ABC's *Journal of Business Communication* from 1998-2000.

In 1998, she received ABC's Meada Gibbs Outstanding Teacher Award.

Isobel M. Findlay is an associate professor in the Department of Management and Marketing and a scholar, Centre for the Study of Co-operatives, University of Saskatchewan, where she teaches business communication, business and community, co-operative studies, and law and culture.

She has special research interests in communications, cultures, and communities; diversity in the workplace; Aboriginal and associative organizations; and corporate social responsibility, performance indicators, and reporting standards. She is just completing a three-year Social Sciences and Humanities Research Council of Canada (SSHRC) research project on Co-operative Membership and Globalization: Creating Social Cohesion through Market Relations, and beginning a five-year research project on Social Enterprises, Knowledgeable Economies, and Sustainable Communities.

In addition to writing communications course guides for Aboriginal Community Economic Development programs and essays on Aboriginal justice, economic development, and co-operatives in *Journal of Aboriginal Economic Development*, *Saskatchewan Law Review*, *Griffith Law Review*, and *Law, Social Justice, and Global Development*, she is editor, co-author, or co-editor of the following:

- Co-editor (with Warren Weir and Louise Clarke) of a special issue of the *Journal of Aboriginal Economic Development 4.1* (2004) on Value(s) Added: Sharing Voices on Aboriginal CED
- Editor, *Introduction to Literature*, 4th and 5th editions (2000, 2004)
- Co-author with James (Sakej) Youngblood Henderson and Marjorie L. Benson, *Aboriginal Tenure in the Constitution of Canada* (2000)
- Co-editor (with L. M. Findlay), *Realizing Community: Multidisciplinary Perspectives* (1995)

A member of the Canadian Communication Association and the International Association of Business Communicators, she has operated her own writing and editing business; facilitated workshops and consulted with the public and private sectors, profit and non-profit organizations; and written many successful grant applications and proposals. A proud recipient of a University of Saskatchewan Students' Union Teaching Excellence Award, she is also co-winner of the Saskatchewan Book Awards Scholarly Writing Award, 2000.

BRIEF CONTENTS

CONTENTS

13 Making Oral Presentations   327

PART FIVE   Job Hunting 347

---

14 Employment Communications   348

Appendix A   Designing Documents, Slides, and Screens   392

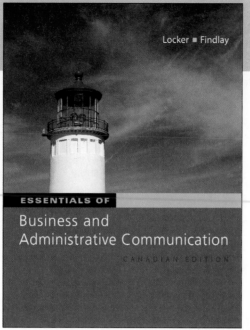

Locker/Findlay:

Your guide to business and administrative communication.

The first Canadian edition of *Essentials of Business and Administrative Communication* builds on the reputation of Kitty Locker, a major contributor to this field of study, and of her U.S. text, now in its seventh edition and a true leader in business communication. Beyond covering the broad scope of topics in both oral and written business and administrative communication, this brief edition uses a student-friendly writing style and strong design to hold student attention. Real-world examples and real business applications underscore the relevance and importance of the material to the classroom experience and to the students' careers. The text also conveys the best possible advice to students through its research base. I have taken care to continue the strong element of teachability and relevance from Locker's market-leading title while providing a true Canadian flavour.

New to the Canadian Edition

Brief

This Canadian edition has been fine-tuned into a comprehensive 14-chapter package, with Part One chapters reinforcing the writing process and guiding students through its stages.

Real-world Relevance

- All of the chapter-opening vignettes feature Canadian profiles of real business people to whom students can relate, discussing real business communication challenges they face in their careers.
- Canadian multiculturalism, diversity in the workplace, corporate social responsibility, reputation management, plain language, and plagiarism in academic and professional settings have been included.
- The text extends the range of businesses and organizations to big and small, corporate and cooperative, for-profit and non-profit, and Crown corporations.

Canadian Content

The inclusion of Canada's Conference Board Employability Skills 2000+ demonstrates that what students are learning in class is directly related to what they need to know in order to enter/stay in the workforce.

A GUIDED TOUR

AN INSIDE PERSPECTIVE

Each chapter is introduced with a real-world perspective. In many instances, real business professionals share on-the-job insight and advice relevant to the chapter's concepts. These opening statements set the stage for the chapter's goals and allow students a glimpse at how they contribute to effective business communication.

Essentials of Business and Administrative Communication, Canadian Edition, by Kitty O. Locker and Isobel Findlay, is a true leader in the business communications field. It is designed to teach students how to think critically, communicate effectively, and improve written and oral business communication skills. These skills will successfully prepare students to meet a variety of challenges they may face in their future careers.

We invite you to learn about this Canadian edition and its features by paging through this visual guide.

CHAPTER

5 Informative and Positive Messages

- Writing Letters, Memos, and E-Mails
- Organizing Informative and Positive Messages
- Choosing Subject Lines for Informative and Positive Messages
- Using Reader Benefits in Informative and Positive Messages
- Ending Informative and Positive Messages

- Distinguishing Varieties of Informative and Positive Messages
- Formatting Letters
- Formatting Envelopes
- Formatting Memos and E-Mails
- Solving a Sample Problem
- Summary of Key Points

AN INSIDE PERSPECTIVE

Informative and Positive Messages

Relationships built on a foundation of powerful and credible communications are key to the success of Canadian Tire Corporation. In an era of intense scrutiny and skepticism, the Canadian Tire communication team maintains a strong relationship with Canadians.

Communicating with 10 million households weekly and with more than 225 million annually, the communication teams presence is felt in decision-making and daily operations. Its ability to communicate with everyone and to mobilize and focus 45,000 team members is as essential to corporate success as any strategy or sales forecast.

Regulatory change, stakeholder demands, mandatory disclosure, and the need for transparency mean that a CEO's ability to communicate effectively with stakeholders is a leadership attribute that is taking on increasing importance. In fact, Wayne Sales often refers to himself as the Chief Communication Officer at Canadian Tire.

He is motivated by the words of aviation pioneer Anne Morrow Lindbergh who said that good communication is as stimulating as black coffee and just as hard to sleep after. If good communication is challenging, it's worth it. It is so powerful precisely because of the commitments of time and energy—and the attention to audience needs.

In the competition for audience attention, it's as well to remember that people forget as much as two-thirds of what they've heard or read in 24 hours. That is why there is a persuasive element in all writing. With nearly universal brand recognition, Canadian Tire clearly is getting its message across to Canadians.

Source: Wayne Sales, "A Seat at the Table," *Blitz Magazine*, 44, 1–5.

Wayne Sales, President and CEO, Canadian Tire Corporation, and winner of the 2005 Canadian Public Relations Society's Award of Excellence in Public Relations, promotes the value of informative and persuasive messages inside and outside the organization.
www.canadiantire.ca

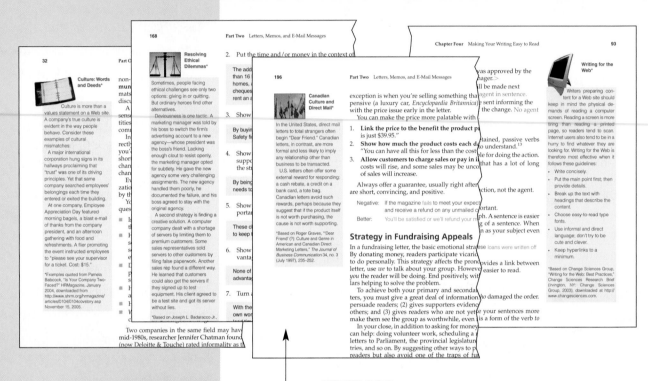

SIDEBARS

These novel and interesting examples effectively enhance student understanding of key concepts. Featured in the margins of every chapter, these sidebars cover four topic areas that include International, Legal/Ethical, Technology, and On the Job.

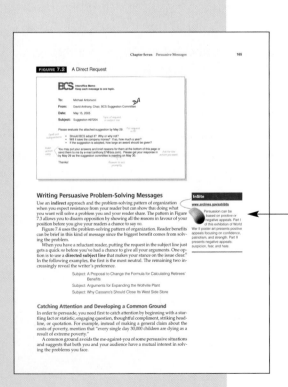

INSITE LINKS

These helpful URLs point to Web sites that include organizations and resources of effective business communication. They underscore the role of the Web in business communication and serve to motivate and enrich the student learning experience. They also cover a wide range of reference sources, including corporate, small business, non-profit, and government Web sites.

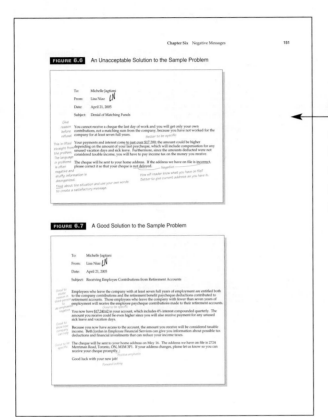

DOCUMENT EXAMPLES

A variety of visual examples featuring letters, memos, reports, and résumés are presented in the text. These actual examples include the authors' "handwritten" annotations, explaining communication miscues while offering suggestions for improvement.

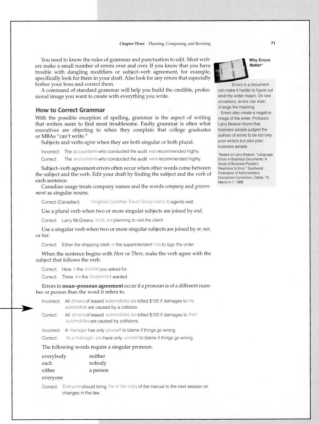

POSITIVE AND NEGATIVE EXAMPLES

Paired effective and ineffective communication examples are presented so students can pinpoint problematic ways to phrase messages so as to help improve their communication skills. Commentaries in red and blue inks indicate poor or better methods of message communication and allow for easy comparison.

CHECKLISTS

Checkpoints for important messages appear throughout the book. These helpful lists serve as a handy reference guide of items to keep in mind when composing and editing messages.

EXERCISES AND PROBLEMS

These hands-on exercises are flexible and can be used as in-class discussions or as individual and group assignments. They allow students to assume a role or perform a task in a variety of realistic business scenarios. Helpful "hints" provide structure and guidance to students for them to complete the exercises.

Supplements

For the Instructor:

- **Instructor CD-ROM** This all-in-one resource incorporates the Instructor's Manual, Computerized Test Bank, and Microsoft© PowerPoint© slides.
  - **Instructor's Manual** This supplement provides extensive chapter-by-chapter notes to help with classroom presentation, and useful suggestions for presenting key concepts and ideas. It also contains suggested answers for assignment material and bonus exercises and problems.
  - **Computerized Test Bank** Questions are organized by chapter and include true/false, multiple-choice, and essay questions. This product allows instructors to make different versions of the same test, change the answer order, edit and add questions, and conduct online testing. The Test Bank is also available in Word documents for added convenience.
  - **PowerPoint© Slides** Chapter-by-chapter slides offer a great visual complement for lectures. The complete set of slides is also available on the text's Web site.
- **Online Learning Centre (OLC)** This text-specific Web site provides vital support for learning and teaching, plus added sidebars and end-of-chapter material. The Instructor Centre also includes downloadable supplements such as the Instructor's Manual and PowerPoint® slides.

- **"Manager's Hot Seat" Videos.** These valuable video examples depict actual managers reacting unrehearsed to realistic business situations. There are four videos available discussing Negotiation and Cultural Differences, Communication in the Virtual Workplace, Active Listening, and Working in Teams.
- **PageOut** Visit **www.mhhe.com/pageout** to create a Web page for your course using our resources. PageOut is the McGraw-Hill Ryerson Web site development centre. This Web page–generation software is free to adopters and is designed to help faculty create an online course, complete with assignments, quizzes, links to relevant Web sites, and more—all in a matter of minutes. In addition, content cartridges are available for the course management systems **WebCT** and **Blackboard**. These platforms provide instructors with user-friendly, flexible teaching tools. Please contact your local McGraw-Hill Ryerson *i*Learning Sales Specialist for details.

Create a custom course Website with **PageOut**, free with every McGraw-Hill Ryerson textbook.

To learn more, contact your McGraw-Hill Ryerson publisher's representative or visit www.mhhe.com/solutions

- **Primis Online** Primis Online gives you access to our resources in the best medium for your students: printed textbooks or electronic e-books. There are over 350,000 pages of content available from which you can create customized learning tools from our online database at **www.mhhe.com/primis**.

i-Learning
ADVANTAGE
McGraw-Hill Ryerson

■ **Integrated Learning** Your Integrated Learning Sales Specialist is a McGraw-Hill Ryerson representative who has the experience, product knowledge, training, and support to help you assess and integrate any of our products, technology, and services into your course for optimum teaching and learning performance. Whether it is using our test bank software, helping your students improve their grades, or putting your entire course online, your *i*Learning Sales Specialist is there to help you do it. Contact your *i*Learning Sales Specialist today to learn how to maximize all of McGraw-Hill Ryerson's resources!

■ *i***Learning Services** McGraw-Hill Ryerson offers a unique *i*Services package designed for Canadian faculty. Our mission is to equip providers of higher education with superior tools and resources required for excellence in teaching. For additional information, visit us at **www.mcgrawhill.ca/highereducation/iservices**.

For the Student:

■ **Online Learning Centre (OLC)** The Student Centre is designed to offer guidance, direction, and tools to help students explore business and administrative communication. Course-wide content—including *Globe and Mail* headlines, practice exercises, plus memo, letter, and resume templates—complements chapter-specific content, such as learning objectives and quizzes.

■ **BComm Skill Booster.** This Internet-based learning reinforcement system, available as premium content on the OLC, delivers interactive lessons to help students practise what they learn in their course. Each lesson includes three action steps to help students master the skill—and these are reinforced through quizzes, exercises, tips, and Web links. Contact your *i*Learning Sales Specialist to learn more about making this valuable resource available to your students.

Trish Campbell, *Red Deer College*

Kendra Carmichael, *Acadia University*

Margie Clow-Bohan, *Dalhousie University*

Kathy Cocchio, *Northern Alberta Institute of Technology (NAIT)*

Grant Coleman, *Mohawk College*

Jana Comeau, *University of New Brunswick*

Valerie Creelman, *St. Mary's University College*

Terri Doughty, *Malaspina University-College*

Marissa Fleming, *Georgian College*

Helen Hornett, *Bow Valley College*

Susan Lieberman, *Grant MacEwan Community College*

Jean Mills, *Mt. Saint Vincent University*

Kathryn Pallister, *Red Deer College*

Brad Quiring, *Mount Royal College*

Donald Roberts, *Seneca College*

Melanie Rubens, *Seneca College*

Rhonda Sandberg, *George Brown College*

Michael Sider, *University of Western Ontario*

Ron Slavik, *Mohawk College*

Katherine Woodward, *Grant MacEwan Community College*

Joanne Wyatt, *Sheridan College*

The efforts of many people are needed to develop and improve a text. Among these people are the reviewers who point out areas of concern, cite areas of strength, and make recommendations for change. In this regard, the instructors named on this page provided feedback that was enormously helpful in preparing *Essentials of Business and Administrative Communication*, Canadian Edition.

ACKNOWLEDGEMENTS

I owe a particular debt to Kitty Locker whose work has inspired my own contributions to the field of business and administrative communication. I am also grateful to colleagues and students in the College of Commerce, University of Saskatchewan, and to organizations in the public and private sectors with whom I have consulted. All have added immeasurably to my own learning, to my sense of research opportunities, to my understanding of barriers to effective communication—and of models of professional communication.

To my editors at McGraw-Hill Ryerson I am especially grateful for their support, wise counsel, creativity, and compassion. The book has been greatly enriched by them: Leanna MacLean, Denise Foote, Margaret Henderson, and freelance editor Karen Rolfe. To the formatters and designers my sincere thanks for their work in transforming the manuscript into an eminently readable text.

To John Conway, friend and photographer extraordinaire, thanks so much. To my running partners Linda and Sue, thanks for continuing to listen long after you listened to the chapter-by-chapter production of my dissertation! And to dear friends and research partners Sakej Henderson and Marie Battiste, thanks for the support, the critical input, and the very necessary social diversions.

Finally, I want to thank my sons Andrew and Nick for their support, patience, and resilience in the face of my unusual hours and enthusiasm for my projects. My greatest debt I owe to my husband, Len Findlay, whose own scholarly engagement and intellectual rigour continue to inspire and sustain.

The Building Blocks of Effective Messages

1 Business Communication, Management, and Success

AN INSIDE PERSPECTIVE

Business Communication, Management, and Success

Myrna Bentley, President and CEO, Concentra Financial. Myrna leads by example and learns by listening to colleagues.

www.concentrafinancial.ca

Maintaining effective internal and external communications is at the heart of negotiating change in business today. President and CEO Myrna Bentley negotiated significant organizational change to launch in November 2004 Concentra Financial, a joint effort and amalgamation of Co-operative Trust Company of Canada and the commercial banking functions of Credit Union Central of Saskatchewan.

"We're very proud that we were able to accomplish this transition without any downsizing, said Ms Bentley. "This initiative is really about increasing the range of financial service options available to our clients."

Communicating with 400 employees in Regina, Saskatoon, and elsewhere in Canada "isn't much of a concern, what with modern e-mail and other communications technologies. We can video conference with our people in Regina," said Bentley.

In developing a new financial institution, Concentra effectively communicated goals and progress to internal and external stakeholders, while retaining "the heart and soul of a co-operative" and maintaining the Co-operative Trust record of excellence (four times one of Canada's Top 100 Employers and one of Canada's 50 Best Managed Companies in 2003).

Believing "the essence of an organization or company is its people," Bentley's company invests in management best practices, promoting an employee-led survey, involving all employees in strategic planning, and feeding business plan deliverables "through the organization from the front-line level."

In 2004 Concentra requalified for Canada's 50 Best Managed Companies thanks to "the dedication, hard work, and spirit" of employees that "are a testimony to what the 50 Best Managed Award represents."

Business depends on communication. People must communicate to plan products; hire, train, and motivate workers; coordinate manufacturing and delivery; persuade customers to buy; and bill them for the sale. Indeed, for many businesses and non-profit and government organizations, the "product" is information or services rather than something tangible. Information and services are created and delivered by communication. In every organization, communication is the way people get their points across and get work done.

Communication takes many forms: face-to-face or phone conversations, informal meetings, e-mail messages, letters, memos, and reports. All of these methods are forms of **verbal communication,** or communication that uses words. **Non-verbal communication** does not use words. Pictures, computer graphics, and company logos are non-verbal. Interpersonal non-verbal signals include smiles, who sits where at a meeting, the size of an office, and how long someone keeps a visitor waiting.

Communication Ability = Promotability

Even in your first job, you'll communicate. You'll read information; you'll listen to instructions; you'll ask questions; you may solve problems with other workers in teams. Even "entry-level" jobs require high-level skills in reasoning, mathematics, and communicating. As a result, communication ability ranks first among the qualities that employers look for in job and promotion candidates.

For the full text of the Conference Board of Canada's Employability Skills 2000+, see ➡ Figure 1.8 on p. 25. The employability skills are as relevant to entering, staying, or gaining promotion in the workplace as in our daily lives. And these valuable skills have become more, not less, important with the expansion of the Internet, where, author Charles Rubin argues, "you are what you write."[1]

According to Darlene Bailey, vice-president, human resources and field operations, WCG International Consultants, headquartered in Victoria, British Columbia, "If you have those [soft] skills, you have a better chance of getting a job and keeping the job. . . . Perhaps everyone knows a teacher has to be a good communicator, but it's a skill that many others have to call on, whether it's to deal with co-workers, customers, suppliers, or others they encounter even in the most solitary of positions."[2]

Richard Todd at the Federal Reserve Bank of Minneapolis tries to find people who can write and read critically:

> Good writing is one of two key abilities I focus on when hiring; the other is the ability to read critically. I can train people to do almost anything else, but I don't have time to teach this.[3]

Good communication skills are crucial if you want (or need) to change jobs. According to career counsellor Andrew Posner,

> Transferable skills—[the ability to] analyze, write, persuade, and manage—are what will facilitate a career change.[4]

As a result, good writers earn more. Linguist Stephen Reder has found that among people with two- or four-year degrees, workers in the top 20% of writing ability earn, on average, more than three times as much as workers whose writing falls into the worst 20%.[5]

Lessons from the Best*

When Watson Wyatt & Co. examined communications of 267 companies and their return to shareholders, study co-author Kathryn Yates found, "The bottom line is that employee communications is no longer a 'soft' function, but rather a business function that drives performance and contributes to a company's financial success."

"Open . . . lines of communication develop trust, encourage new ideas, eliminate intimidation and skepticism, and aid in building a brighter future for employees and the company," says Steve McGowen, Plant Manager, Halliburton Energy Services, Carrollton, TX (equipment for the oil and gas industries).

*Paragraph 1 based on "Better communication pays off for companies," *The Globe and Mail* November 7, 2003, C1; paragraph 2 from Michael A. Verespie, "Lessons from the Best," *Industry Week,* February 2, 1998.

No Substitute for Proofreading*

Computer software can make writing easier, but there's still no substitute for careful writing. Before you let your spell checker and grammar checker do your editing, consider these results from a University of Pittsburgh study. Researchers had graduate students proofread a business letter with or without their spell checker. When the students with the highest verbal SAT scores proofread on their own, they made, on average, 5 errors. Students with lower verbal SATs made an average of 12.3 errors.

Using the spell checker helped, right? On the contrary, when students turned on this tool, they made *more* mistakes. The students with the highest verbal SAT scores averaged 16 errors, and those with lower scores averaged 17 errors.

Considering that typos are a major turnoff to prospective employers and customers, it makes sense to practise your proofreading skills.

*Based on Jay Greene, "Spell-Cheque Nation," *BusinessWeek*, May 5, 2003.

"I'll Never Have to Write Because …"

Some students think that a secretary will do their writing, that they can use form letters if they do have to write, that only technical skills matter, or that they'll call rather than write. Each of these claims is fundamentally flawed.

Claim 1:   Secretaries will do all my writing.

Reality: Downsizing and voice mail have cut support staffs nationwide. Of the secretaries who remain, 71% are administrative assistants whose duties are managerial, not clerical.[6]

Claim 2:   I'll use form letters or templates when I need to write.

Reality: A **form letter** is a prewritten, fill-in-the-blank letter designed to fit standard situations. Using a form letter is OK if it's a good letter. But form letters cover only routine situations. The higher you rise, the more frequently you'll face situations that aren't routine, that demand creative solutions.

Claim 3:   I'm being hired as an accountant, not a writer.

Reality: In September 2001, the Canadian Institute of Chartered Accounts published its *Canadian CA Competency Map* as part of education reform for CA qualification. While technical skills are still required, they are valued at a lower level than performance in interpersonal communications, persuasive writing and presentations, listening and comprehending, ethics and the professional code of conduct, and skill development for lifelong learning. To be competitive in a global economy, accountants, like engineers, need these skills: "communications, team building, report writing and preparing presentations."[7]

Claim 4:   I'll just pick up the phone.

Reality: Important phone calls require follow-up letters, memos, or e-mail messages. People in organizations put things in writing to make themselves and their accomplishments visible, create a record, convey complex data, make things convenient for the reader, save money, and convey their own messages more effectively. "If it isn't in writing," says a manager at one company, "it didn't happen."

Many miscommunications arise not because people genuinely disagree but because they use symbols to mean different things and make different assumptions. **Communication theory** attempts to explain what happens when we communicate. **Semantics** is the study of the way our behaviour is influenced by the words and other symbols we use to communicate.

Communication theory and semantics both show why and where communication can break down, and what we can do to communicate more effectively.

Communication Channels in Organizations

Channels—formal and informal—vary in speed, accuracy of transmission, cost, number of messages carried, number of people reached, efficiency, and ability to promote goodwill. Depending on the audience, your purposes, and the situation, one channel may be better than another (➡ Chapter 2).

Oral channels are better for group decision making, allow misunderstandings to be cleared up more quickly, and seem more personal. Shorter communication channels are more accurate than longer chains. For important messages when the cost of miscommunication is high, managers usually use two different channels; for example, talking to someone about a written memo.

Channel choice may also be influenced by organizational culture. At Microsoft, e-mail is the preferred channel, and new employees have to learn to use it effectively.

A Model of the Communication Process

The model of the communication process (Figure 1.1) drastically simplifies what is perhaps the most complex human activity. Never merely a matter of transmitting information, the process is social, situational, and sophisticated. However, even a simplified model can give us a sense of the complexity of the communication process and of the communication context (from the immediate situation to the broader culture). And the model is useful in helping us see where and why miscommunication occurs at each stage from stimulus and **perception** to **encoding** the message to **transmission** to **decoding** and **feedback**.

Feedback may be direct and immediate or indirect and delayed; it may be verbal or non-verbal.

Noise can interfere with every aspect of the communication process. Noise may be physical or psychological. Physical noise could be a phone line with static, or handwriting that is hard to read. Psychological noise could include not liking a speaker, being preoccupied, or already having one's mind made up on an issue.

Channel overload occurs when the channel cannot handle all the messages that are being sent. A small business may have only two phone lines; no one else can get through if both lines are in use. **Information overload** occurs when more messages are transmitted than the human receiver can handle. Some receivers process information "first come, first served." Some may try to select the most important messages and ignore others. A third way is to depend on abstracts or summaries prepared by other people. None of these ways is completely satisfactory.

FIGURE 1.1   A Model of Two-Person Communication with Feedback

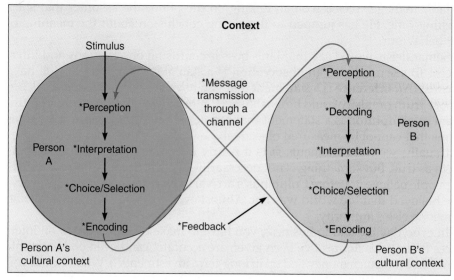

*Noise (and miscommunication) can occur here.

At every stage people may misperceive, misinterpret, choose badly, encode poorly, and choose inappropriate channels. Miscommunication can also occur because different people have different frames of reference. We always interpret messages in light of our personal experiences, our cultures (➡ Chapter 9) and subcultures, and even the point in history at which we live.

Principles of Semantics

Semantic principles offer eight guidelines for negotiating barriers and improving communication.

1. Perception Involves the Perceiver as Well as the Perceived.

What we see is conditioned by what we are able to see, what we have seen in the past, what we are prepared to see, and what we want to see.

Perception is also affected by what we expect or want to see. Most people have a tendency to attribute their own feelings to other people as well. We may tune out messages we think will challenge our own positions; we seek messages that support our positions.

Use these correctives to check the accuracy of your perceptions:

1. Recognize that everyone's perception will be in some measure biased.
2. Recognize that different positions cause us to view reality differently and to make different inferences from what we observe.
3. If a new idea comes along that does not fit neatly into your worldview, recognize that your worldview, not the challenging idea, may need rethinking.

2. Observations, Inferences, and Judgments Are Not the Same.

> Ten minutes before lunchtime, Jan is talking on the phone. Her manager thinks, "She's talking again. Doesn't she ever work?" Jan is talking to a potential customer; she sees the call as essential, since it may eventually lead to a sale. She can't understand why her manager doesn't think she's serious about her career.

Jan's manager sees a woman talking on the phone; he assumes that she's wasting time. He has jumped to the wrong conclusion about the meaning of her behaviour.

Semanticists would say that Jan's boss is confusing observations and inferences. To a semanticist, an **observation** is a statement that you yourself have verified. An **inference** is a statement that you have not personally verified, but whose truth or falsity could be established, either now or in the future. A **judgment** or an **opinion** is a statement that can never be verified, since it includes terms that cannot be measured objectively.

Usually, we call statements *facts* if nearly everyone in our culture accepts them as true. But something is not necessarily true just because large numbers of people believe it. Before Columbus's arrival in North America, nearly everyone believed that the world was flat. Almost everything we know we take on someone else's authority.

In everyday life and in business, you have to make decisions based on inferences ("The sales figures I've been given are accurate") and even on judgments ("We have too much money tied up in long-term investments"). What should you as a reader or writer do?

As both a reader and writer,

1. Check to see whether a statement is an observation, an inference, or a judgment.

2. Estimate the accuracy of the inference by comparing it to your experiences with the source and with this kind of situation. If the cost of making a mistake is high, try to get more information.

3. Label your inferences so that your audience can distinguish between what you know to be the case and what you think, assume, believe, or judge to be true. In the following example, the italicized words remind readers that the statements are inferences.

> *He predicts* that the stock market *could* move up an additional 10% to 20% during the next 12 to 18 months.

3. No Two Things Are Exactly Alike.

We make sense of the world by grouping things into categories. Once we have categories, we do not have to evaluate each new experience independently; instead, we simply assign it to a category and then make the response we find appropriate to that category.

Unfortunately, this convenient lumping can lead to **stereotyping** (➡ Chapter 9): putting similar people or events into a single category, even though significant differences exist.

To guard against stereotyping, you should

1. Recognize significant differences as well as similarities. The members of any one group are not identical.

2. Be sure that any analogy you use to make your point clear is accurate at the point of comparison.

4. Things Change Significantly with Time.

If you keep up with the stock market, with commodity prices, or with interest rates, you know that things (especially prices) change significantly with time.

People change too. The sales representative who was once judged too abrasive to make a good supervisor may have mellowed by now.

Someone who does not recognize that prices, situations, and people change is guilty of making a **frozen evaluation.** The following corrections help us remember not to freeze evaluations:

1. Date statements. The price of IBM stock on October 20, 1995, is not the price of IBM stock on January 3, 2005.

2. Provide a frame of reference so that your reader has some basis for comparing grades, profits, injuries, or percentages.

3. Periodically retest your assumptions about people, businesses, products, and services to make sure that your evaluations apply to the present situation.

5. Most *Either–Or* Classifications Are Not Legitimate.

A common logical fallacy is **polarization:** trying to force the reader into a position by arguing that there are only two possible positions, one of which is clearly unacceptable:

> Either the supervisor runs this department with a firm hand, or anarchy will take over and the work will never get done.

The Word Is Not Connected to the Object

- Oktoberfest is held in September.
- The Big 10 has 11 teams.
- The principal ingredient in sweetbread is neither sugar nor bread but the cooked pancreas or thymus of a young animal, usually a calf.
- Wild rice isn't necessarily wild. Nearly all the wild rice on grocery-store shelves is commercially cultivated in rice paddies and turned and watered by machines.

For centuries before Europeans came to North America, the Algonquin and Siouan peoples harvested wild rice, a seed from an aquatic grass rather than a member of the rice family. Canadian "Lake Wild Rice" is harvested from natural bodies of water rather than cultivated or paddy-grown as in the United States.*

*Adapted from Agriculture and Agri-Food Canada, "Canada's Wild Rice Industry," retrieved March 3, 2005, from http://www.agr.gc.ca.

Running a department "with a firm hand" is only one of several possible leadership styles; sharing authority with or even transferring it entirely to subordinates need not result in anarchy.

Even people who admit that there are more than two possible positions may still limit the options unnecessarily. Imposing limits that do not exist in reality is called **blindering,** after the blinders that horses wear. Blindering can lead to polarization.

Sometimes blindering is responsible for bad questions in surveys:

> Do you own _____ , rent _____ , or live with your parents _____ ?

What about someone who lives with a friend or with relatives other than parents?

Polarization sharpens divisions between people and obscures the common ground; blindering prevents our seeing creative solutions to the problems we face. Here are some correctives:

1. Recognize the complexities of a situation. Resist the temptation to oversimplify.
2. Whenever you see only two alternatives, consciously search for a third, and maybe even a fourth or fifth, before you make your decision.
3. Redefine the question or problem to get at the real issue.

    Don't ask: How can I as a manager show that I'm in control?

    Ask: How can we improve productivity in this unit?

6. A Statement Is Never the Whole Story.

It is impossible to know everything; it is impossible to tell someone everything. When we assume that a statement contains all the important information, or when the context is omitted (deliberately or inadvertently), meanings are inevitably twisted.

For example, some commentators argue that U.S. investments suffer because U.S. families save far less than do Japanese families. But, according to several economists, this statement overlooks differences in what counts as savings and as investments. Many U.S. families own their own homes, yet their equity isn't considered "savings." Few Japanese own homes; their "savings" are more likely to be in stocks and bonds. Economist Fumio Hayashi points out that Japanese accounting values depreciation at historical cost figures, thus understating the value of assets and making investments look higher. Furthermore, the United States counts government spending—even on schools, roads, and warships—as consumption. The Japanese system considers such expenditures to be investments.[8] When these differences are considered, the alleged gap between the two countries' savings and investment rates disappears.

What can we do to avoid misstatements by implication?

1. Recognize that the reports you get are filtered; you are not getting all the facts, and you are almost certainly getting inferences as well as observations.
2. Check the messages you send out to make sure you have provided the background information the reader needs to interpret your message accurately.

7. Words Are Not Identical to the Objects They Represent.

People perceive objects and think of ideas; they attach labels to those objects and ideas. Other labels could be substituted without changing reality. Indeed, the ability to attach a new label to an object—to attach a different meaning to it—is a key element of creative intelligence. People, who name things and use words, provide the only connection between the thing and the word.

We often respond to the label rather than to reality. Our degree of distress during a bleak economic period is likely to be as much a product of the label given the period as it is of the rate of unemployment: a *slowdown* doesn't sound as bad as a *recession,* and even that is better than a *depression.* Advertisers understand that labelling a book a *best-seller* is sure to increase sales.

Since we must use symbols to communicate, it's hard to avoid treating symbols as if they were reality. Try these correctives:

1. Support **claims** with specific **evidence** or **data**.
2. Check your own responses to make sure that your decisions are based not on labels but on valid, logical arguments.
3. If your claims cause others to produce a **counterclaim**, **limit** your claim or provide a **rebuttal** to be convincing.

8. Communication Symbols Must Stand for Essentially the Same Thing in the Minds of the Sender and the Receiver.

Communication depends on symbols; if those symbols mean different things to the people who use them, communication will fail. **Bypassing** occurs when two people use the same symbol to mean different things.

Bypassing creates misunderstandings. When employees hear communication skills described as "soft skills," they may assume that they are as easy, simple, and natural as the traditional label implies. They may understand communication as an elementary process of transmitting information and be impatient of and therefore not attentive to complex issues of audience, purpose, and context. They may fail to invest the sort of time, planning, and effort that effective communication takes. They may also blame themselves or become frustrated when they discover that communicating is among the most challenging and complex things we do in business.

Here are some measures that will help us avoid bypassing:

1. Be sensitive to contexts.
2. Consider the other person. Given his or her background and situation, what is he or she likely to mean?
3. Mirror what the other person has said by putting it into your own words, and let him or her check it for accuracy. Be sure to use different words for the key ideas.
4. Ask questions.

The Managerial Functions of Communication

According to McGill professor Henry Mintzberg, managers have three basic jobs: to collect and convey information, to make decisions, and to promote interpersonal unity.[9] Every one of those jobs is carried out through communication. Managers collect relevant information from conversations, the grapevine, phone calls, memos, reports, databases, and the Internet. They convey information and decisions to other people inside or outside the organization through meetings, speeches, press releases, videos, memos, letters, e-mail messages, and reports. Managers motivate organizational members in speeches, memos, conversations at lunch and over coffee, bulletin boards, and through "management by walking around."

Effective managers are able to use a wide variety of media and strategies to communicate. They know how to interpret comments from informal channels such as the company grapevine; they can speak effectively in small groups and in formal presentations; they write well.

Communication—oral, non-verbal, and written—goes to both internal and external audiences. **Internal audiences** (Figure 1.2) are other people in the same

The Payoff from Listening*

FIGURE 1.2   The Internal Audiences of the Sales Manager—West

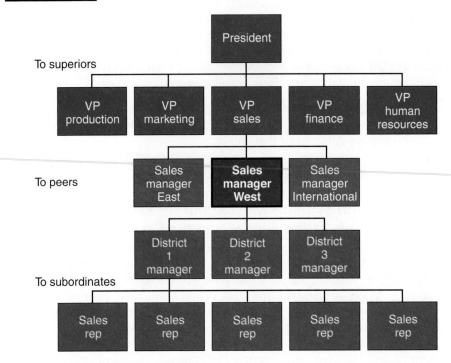

organization: subordinates, superiors, peers. **External audiences** (Figure 1.3) are people outside the organization: customers, suppliers, unions, stockholders, potential employees, government agencies, the press, and the general public.

The Importance of Listening, Speaking, and Interpersonal Communication

Informal listening, speaking, and working in groups are just as important as writing formal documents and giving formal oral presentations. As a newcomer in an organization, you'll need to listen to others both to find out what you're supposed to do and to learn about the organization's values and culture. Informal chat, both about yesterday's game and about what's happening at work, connects you to the **grapevine,** an informal source of company information. You may be asked to speak to small groups, either inside or outside your organization.[10] Networking with others in your office and your surroundings and working with others in workgroups will be crucial to your success.

These skills remain important as you climb the corporate ladder. In fact, a study of 15 executives judged good performers by their companies showed that these executives spent most of their time in informal contact with other people. These informal discussions, taking 76% of these executives' work time, enabled them to promote their agendas.[11]

The Documents That Writers in Organizations Write

People in organizations produce a large variety of documents. All of the documents in Figures 1.4 and 1.5 have one or more of the **three basic purposes of organizational writing:** to inform, to request or persuade, and to build goodwill. When you **inform,** you explain something or tell readers something. When you **request** or **persuade,** you want the reader to act. The word *request*

FIGURE 1.3 The Corporation's External Audiences

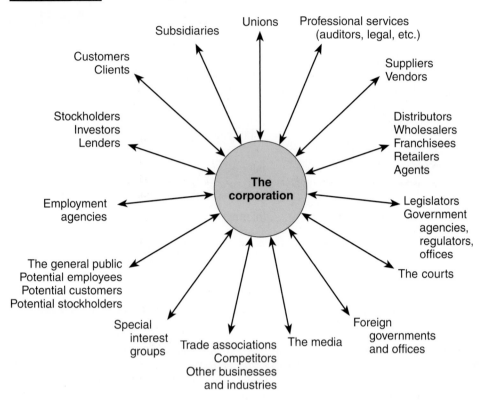

Source: Daphne A. Jameson

FIGURE 1.4 Internal Documents Produced in One Organization

Document	Description of document	Purpose(s) of document
Transmittal	Memo accompanying document, telling why it's being forwarded to the receiver	Inform; persuade reader to read document; build image and goodwill
Monthly or quarterly report	Report summarizing profitability, productivity, and problems during period. Used to plan activity for next month or quarter	Inform; build image and goodwill (report is accurate, complete; writer understands company)
Policy and procedure bulletin	Statement of company policies and instructions (e.g., how to enter orders, how to run fire drills)	Inform; build image and goodwill (procedures are reasonable)
Request to deviate from policy and procedure bulletin	Persuasive memo arguing that another approach is better for a specific situation than the standard approach	Persuade; build image and goodwill (request is reasonable; writer seeks good of company)
Performance appraisal	Evaluation of an employee's performance, with recommended areas for improvement or recommendation for promotion	Inform; persuade employee to improve
Memo of congratulations	Congratulations to employees who have won awards, been promoted, or earned community recognition	Build goodwill

FIGURE 1.5   External Documents Produced in One Organization

Document	Description of document	Purpose(s) of document
Quotation	Letter giving price for a specific product, fabrication, or service	Inform; build goodwill (price is reasonable)
Claims adjustment	Letter granting or denying customer request to be given credit for defective goods	Inform; build goodwill
Job description	Description of qualifications and duties of each job. Used for performance appraisals, setting salaries, and hiring	Inform; persuade good candidates to apply; build goodwill (job duties match level, pay)
10-K report	Report filed with the Securities and Exchange Commission detailing financial information	Inform
Annual report	Report to shareholders summarizing financial information for year	Inform; persuade shareholders to retain stock and others to buy; build goodwill (company is a good corporate citizen)
Thank-you letter	Letter to suppliers, customers, or other people who have helped individuals or the company	Build goodwill

suggests that the action will be easy or routine; *persuade* suggests that you will have to motivate and convince the reader to act. When you **build goodwill,** you create a good image of yourself and of your organization—the kind of image that makes people want to do business with you.

Most messages have multiple purposes. When you answer a question, you're informing, but you also want to build goodwill by suggesting that you're competent and perceptive and that your answer is correct and complete. In a claims adjustment, whether your answer is *yes* or *no,* you want to suggest that the reader's claim received careful consideration and that the decision is fair, businesslike, and justified.

Two of the documents listed in Figure 1.5 package the same information in different ways for different audiences. The 10-K report is informative, designed merely to show that a Canadian company trading in the United States is complying with SEC regulations. The annual report, in contrast, has multiple purposes and audiences. Its primary purpose is to convince shareholders that the company is a good investment and a good corporate citizen. Annual reports will also be read by employees, stockbrokers, potential shareholders, and job applicants, so the firm creates a report that is persuasive and builds goodwill as well as presenting information.

The Cost of Correspondence

Writing costs money. In 1996, according to the Dartnell Institute, a short one-page business letter cost between U.S.$13.60 and U.S.$20.52, depending on how it was produced.[12] But a consultant who surveyed employees in seven industries found that most of them spent 54 minutes planning, composing, and revising a one-page letter.[13] Her respondents, then, each spent over U.S.$84 at 1996 prices to create a one-page letter.

In many organizations, all external documents must be approved before they go out. A document may **cycle** from writer to superior to writer to another superior to writer again 3 or 4 or even 11 times before it is finally approved. The cycling process increases the cost of correspondence.

Longer documents can involve large teams of people and take months to write. An engineering firm that relies on military contracts for its business calculates that it spends $500,000 to put together an average proposal and $1 million to write a large proposal.[14]

Good communication is worth every minute it takes and every penny it costs. In fact, in a survey conducted by the International Association of Business Communicators, CEOs said that communication yielded a 235% return on investment.[15]

The Cost of Poor Correspondence

When writing isn't as good as it could be, you and your organization pay a price in wasted time, wasted efforts, and lost goodwill.

Bad writing has these costs:

- **Takes longer to read** (up to 97% of reading time involves trying to understand what we're reading)
- **Needs revision** (involving disproportionate managerial time on explaining how to revise)
- **Obscures ideas** and needlessly protracts discussions and decisions
- **Requires requests for further information** (and further delays)
- **Does not get results**—or the wrong results when reader guesses wrong
- **Undermines the image of the organization**
- **Loses goodwill**

Messages can also create a poor image because of poor audience analysis and inappropriate style. The form letter printed in Figure 1.6 failed because it was stuffy and selfish—and generated ill will. As the comments in red show, several things are wrong with the letter.

1. **The language is stiff and legalistic.** Note the obsolete (and sexist) "Gentlemen:" "Please be advised," "herein," and "expedite."
2. **The tone is selfish.** The letter is written from the writer's point of view; there are no benefits for the reader. (The writer says there are, but, without a shred of evidence, the claim isn't convincing.)

FIGURE 1.6   A Form Letter That Annoyed Customers

3. **The main point is buried** in the middle of the long first paragraph. The middle is the least emphatic part of a paragraph.
4. **The request is vague.** How many references does the supplier want? Would credit references, like banks, rather than vendor references work too? Is the name of the reference enough, or is it necessary also to specify the line of credit and/or the years credit has been established? What "additional financial information" does the supplier want? Bank balance? The request sounds like an invasion of privacy, not a reasonable business practice.
5. **Words are misused** (*herein* for *therein*), suggesting either an ignorant writer or one who doesn't care enough about the subject and the reader to use the right word.

Benefits of Improving Correspondence

Better writing helps you to

- **Save time.** Reduce reading and revision time and the time taken asking writers "What did you mean?"
- **Make your efforts more effective.** Increase the number of requests that are answered positively and promptly—on the first request. Present your points more forcefully.
- **Communicate your points more clearly.** Reduce the misunderstandings that occur when the reader has to supply missing or unclear information.
- **Build goodwill.** Build a positive image of your organization. Build an image of yourself as a knowledgeable, intelligent, capable person.

Criteria for Effective Messages

Good business and administrative writing meets five basic criteria: it's clear, complete, and correct; it saves the reader's time; and it builds goodwill.

1. **It's clear.** The meaning the reader gets is the meaning the writer intended. The reader doesn't have to guess.
2. **It's complete.** All of the reader's questions are answered. The reader has enough information to evaluate the message and act on it.
3. **It's correct.** All of the information in the message is accurate. The message is free from errors in punctuation, spelling, grammar, word order, and sentence structure.
4. **It saves the reader's time.** The style, organization, and visual impact of the message help the reader to read, understand, and act on the information promptly.
5. **It builds goodwill.** The message presents a positive image of the writer and his or her organization. It treats the reader as a person, not a number. It cements a good relationship between the writer and the reader.

Whether a message meets these five criteria depends on the interactions among the writer, the audience, the purposes of the message, and the situation. No single set of words will work in all possible situations.

Trends in Business and Administrative Communication

Both business and business communication are changing. Twelve trends in business, government, and non-profit organizations affect business and administrative communication: a focus on quality and customers' needs, entrepreneurship and outsourcing, teams, diversity, globalization, legal and ethical concerns, balancing work and family, corporate social responsibility, reputation management, the end of the job, the rapid rate of change, and technology.

Focus on Quality and Customers' Needs

In general, satisfaction with quality and customer service is falling.[16] That's a problem for companies, notes direct marketing expert James Rosenfield:

> Unhappy customers in industrialized countries historically tell 15 people about their experiences. [On the Internet] with one keystroke, you can now tell 150 or 1,500 or 15,000![17]

Superior customer service pays. Bank customers who described themselves as most satisfied were much more profitable for the company than were customers who were merely "satisfied."[18] Offering superior customer service doesn't always mean spending extra money. Learning from the example of Southwest Airlines in the United States, Clive Beddoe, President and CEO of WestJet, was determined to get people where they wanted to go on time and at the right price. And the passengers—or "guests"—bought his plan. WestJet was showing a profit within its first six months in 1996. According to Beddoe, "customer service is everything, and part of that is making sure people appreciate it whenever they fly with us. . . . I was just on the airplane now, and I stood at the exit and shook everybody's hand and thanked them." The corporate culture is informal, friendly, good humoured: the executive area at the Calgary headquarters is for the "Big Shots" and human resources is handled in the "People Department." But Beddoe can also be serious about his business—and about the public trust on which it depends. That's something he doesn't take lightly.[19]

Communication is at the centre of the focus on quality and customers' needs. Brainstorming and group problem solving are essential to develop more efficient ways to do things. Then the good ideas have to be communicated throughout the

Clive Beddoe, CEO of WestJet, fosters a corporate culture that nourishes customer satisfaction and employee loyalty.

Should Companies Care?*

As the world has become more virulently capitalist, it has also become more concerned about the environment, child labour, and human rights. . . .

A substantial number [of consumers] now base buying decisions on who made their Nike shoes or what McDonald's does with its paper waste. The trend is hardly universal—plenty of people still just want the lowest price—but it's utterly clear. You've seen it yourself, probably in your own family. . . .

Employees [also] care. One trend in business is that employees, especially the best young employees, want a sense of purpose in their work. . . . They want to know that what they do at work is good and right in some large sense. . . .

Consumers care and employees care. That means equity markets care. And that means CEOs care.

*Quoted from Geoffrey Colvin, "Should Companies Care?" *Fortune*, June 11, 2001, 60.

company. Innovators need to be recognized. And only by listening to what customers say—and listening to the silences that may accompany their actions—can an organization know what its customers really want.

Entrepreneurship and Outsourcing

Entrepreneurship is a fast-growing sector of the Canadian economy with women, youth, ethnic groups, and social entrepreneurs adding to the traditional players. Representing one-third of all self-employed Canadians in 1999, women owned half of all Canadian businesses by 2000. Predicted by a CIBC study to be one million by 2010, Canadian women entrepreneurs defy stereotypes about women and economic power, ranking first among the Organisation for Economic Co-operation and Development (OECD) countries.[20]

The Canadian Youth Business Foundation (CYBF), a non-profit, volunteer-based organization founded in 1996, provides mentoring and financing to support young Canadian entrepreneurs (18–34 years). Modelled on the U.K. Prince's Trust, CYBF's mission is to help fulfill the United Nations Millennium Development Goal to solve global youth unemployment and to contribute to sustainable economic development. Reaching over 860 local communities, it has created over 1,276 new jobs in the last three years.[21]

Although the participation of immigrant communities in entrepreneurship is well known, Aboriginal participation is perhaps less familiar. The 1996 Census identified over 20,000 North American Indians, Métis, and Inuit who now have their own businesses in primary and traditional industries as well as the knowledge economy. Between 1981 and 1996, this sector grew $2\frac{1}{2}$ times faster than the national increase, with marked growth among Aboriginal youth and women. This growth generated 48,502 new jobs.[22]

In the public, private, and non-profit sectors, social entrepreneurship responds to demands for corporate social responsibility and for answers to some complex social problems. Stressing hybrid models of activity, social entrepreneurship draws on the innovation, resourcefulness, and vision of traditional entrepreneurship "to combine the heart of business with the heart of the community through the creativity of the individual," in the words of Executive Director Gary McPherson, Canadian Centre for Social Entrepreneurship at the University of Alberta School of Business.[23]

Entrepreneurship is so popular that many business schools now offer courses, internships, or whole programs in starting and running a business.

Some established companies are trying to match the success and growth rate of start-ups by nurturing an entrepreneurial spirit within their organizations. Innovators who work within organizations are sometimes called **intrapreneurs.** Researchers at 3M can spend 15% of their time working on ideas that don't need management approval; Thermo Electron lets managers "spin out" promising new businesses; and Xerox employees write business proposals competing for corporate funds to develop new technologies.[24]

Some businesses have been forced to become entrepreneurial because of outsourcing. **Outsourcing** means going outside the company for products and services that once were provided by the company's employees. Companies can outsource manufacturing, customer service, and accounting (Virtual Growth provides accounting services for companies with 12–15 employees). Outsourcing is often a win–win solution: the company saves money, and the outsourcer makes a profit. Started in 1995, Virtual Growth grossed $12 billion in 1999.[25]

Outsourcing makes communication more difficult—and more important—than it was when jobs were done in-house. It's harder to ask questions, since people are no longer down the hall. And it's easier for problems to turn into major ones. Some companies now are creating a "chief resource officer" to monitor contracts with vendors so that lines of communication will be clear.

Teams

More and more companies are getting work done through teams. Teamwork brings together people's varying strengths and talents to solve problems and make decisions. Often, teams are cross-functional (drawing from different jobs or functions) and/or cross-cultural (including people from different nations or ethnic or cultural groups served by the company). Teams helped BC Biomedical Laboratories Ltd. meet client needs, enhance employee satisfaction—and become Canada's best employer three years running.

There's a "family feel" among the more than 650 employees of this Vancouver diagnostic testing service begun by Cam Coady in 1958 and now owned by 42 partner pathologists. The management structure is unusually flat (less hierarchical) in an organization where management and employees share goals and leadership. In a 90% female workforce, employees enjoy a "performance sharing plan," flexible scheduling, and the support of colleagues.

With about half the staff in 47 patient service centres and half at head office, Biomedical Laboratories relies on its strengths: its flexibility, culture of trust, strong communications, and network of team leaders.[26]

Teams put a premium on learning to identify and solve problems, to share leadership, to work *with* other people rather than merely delegating work *to* other people, to resolve conflicts constructively, and to motivate everyone to do his or her best job. To learn more about working in teams, see ➠ Chapter 10.

Diversity

Teams put a premium on being able to work with other people—even if they come from different backgrounds.

Diversity allows businesses to draw ideas from many traditions. At Xerox, co-workers "pass the rock" in a Native American talking circle. Only the person holding the stone can speak, forcing everyone to learn to listen.

Although women, Aboriginal people, persons with disabilities, and members of visible minorities have always been part of the workforce, they have not enjoyed equitable participation in the Canadian mainstream. Even when education became more accessible after World War II and women and other marginalized groups began to enter the professions in the 1960s and 1970s, few made it into management.

Professor Edward Harvey of the University of Toronto and researcher John Blakely have estimated the cost to the Canadian economy of the underemployment of these groups: a staggering $50 billion annually, or 5% of gross domestic product.[27] Now Canadian business is realizing that barriers to promotion are hurting the bottom line as well as individuals.

In the last decade, we have also become aware of other sources of diversity beyond those of gender and race: age, religion, class, regional differences, sexual orientation, disabilities. Helping each worker reach his or her potential requires more flexibility from managers as well as more knowledge about intercultural communication. And it's crucial to help workers from different backgrounds understand each other—especially when layoffs make many workers fear that increased opportunities for someone else will come only at a cost to themselves.

Treating readers with respect has always been a principle of good business and administrative communication. The emphasis on diversity simply makes it an economic mandate as well. To learn more about diversity and the workforce, read ➡ Chapter 9.

Globalization

In the global economy, importing and exporting are just the start. More and more companies have offices and factories around the world. To sell $200 million worth of appliances in India, Whirlpool adapts appliances to local markets and uses local contractors who speak India's 18 languages to deliver appliances by truck, bicycle, and even oxcart.[28]

Nezar Freeny, founder and president of Amanah Tech, has the intercultural competence and commands the trust—*Amanah* is Arabic for "trust"—to operate successfully in the global economy.

Born and raised in Sudan, North Africa, and educated in Canada, Nezar Freeny has made a virtue of his cross-cultural experience in shaping his success as an IT entrepreneur and owner of Amanah Tech Inc. in Saskatoon and Toronto. Ninety percent of the customers for his web-hosting and Internet solutions services are located in the Arabian Gulf. Freeny provides customer service and technical support in both Arabic and English 24 hours a day, seven days a week.[29]

All the challenges of communicating in one culture and country increase exponentially when people communicate across cultures and countries. Succeeding in a global market requires **intercultural competence,** the ability to communicate sensitively with people from other cultures and countries, based on an understanding of cultural differences. To learn more about international communication, see ➡ Chapter 9.

Legal and Ethical Concerns

Legal fees cost businesses hundreds of thousands of dollars. The price of many simple items, such as ladders, is inflated greatly by the built-in reserve to protect the manufacturer against lawsuits. Companies are finding that clear, open communication can reduce lawsuits by giving all the parties a chance to shape policies and by clarifying exactly what is and isn't being proposed.

Ethical concerns don't carry the same clear dollar cost as legal fees. But when the Internet stock bubble burst, the plunging stock prices and an overall economic slowdown were accompanied by a wave of news stories about unethical and illegal corporate practices. As investors and consumers heard the accusations of accounting fraud at WorldCom, Enron, and Adelphia Communications, many felt distrustful of businesses in general. The public outcry motivated the U.S. Congress to pass the Sarbanes-Oxley Act in 2002, requiring corporations to engage in much more careful control and reporting of their financial activities.[30]

The public distrust and government regulation that followed the recent scandals have renewed attention to corporate ethics. Some organizations have simply met Sarbanes-Oxley requirements. But many have gone further. A survey by accounting firm KPMG found that corporations are more aggressively taking action to investigate and report fraud by their employees. Such efforts may be bearing fruit. In a U.S. survey, the Ethics Resource Center found that employees in 2003 were more likely to report fraud than they had been in previous years, yet fewer of them had observed any misconduct.[31]

Canada has had its share of scandals. Both Nortel Networks and Hollinger International Inc. have become associated with unethical corporate practices. *Canadian Business*'s Matthew McClearn asks if "anybody even read" the code of ethics at Hollinger. As a result, Canadian companies now face new regulations and reporting standards as well as compliance with Sarbanes-Oxley if they trade on U.S. stock exchanges.

Their efforts to right wrongs have not always gone as planned. When Nortel CEO Bill Owens announced efforts to regain trust, he named his "first chief ethics officer" as "testimony to our commitment to the highest standards of ethics and integrity in all of our company's operations." Unfortunately, Susan Shepherd was not the first ethics officer at Nortel! Megan Barry had held that position from 1994 to 1999, though the department "grew increasingly invisible within the organization" under John Roth's leadership, according to *Maclean's* reporter Steve Maich.[32]

Whole issues of business magazines were devoted to accounting "tricks," including *Canadian Business*'s special on "Hide & Seek: 10 Accounting Warning Signs You Need to Know" (April 1, 2002), and business schools have been "scrambling to revamp curriculums on corporate governance and business ethics," reports Jane Gadd.

Pointing to gaps in educational offerings, the Association to Advance Collegiate Schools of Business (AACSB International) wants to see more done to teach about stewardship obligations, the concerns of stakeholders, and "the responsible use of power." To that end, Professor Tima Bansal at the Ivey School is teaching University of British Columbia professor Joel Bakan's *The Corporation*, showing the corporation as psychopath.[33]

As Figure 1.7 suggests, language, graphics, and document design—basic parts of any business document—can be ethical or manipulative. Persuasion and gaining compliance—activities at the heart of business and organizational life—can be done with respect or contempt for customers, co-workers, and subordinates.

Ethical concerns start with telling the truth and offering good value for money. Organizations must be concerned about broader ethical issues as well: being good environmental citizens, offering a good workplace for their employees, and contributing to the needs of the communities in which they operate.

Balancing Work and Family

The Wall Street Journal now runs a regular column on Work and Family. The Montgomery Work/Life Alliance reports that 78% of workers cited balancing

InSite

www.ethicsinaction.com/ recipients/index.html

The Ethics in Action Awards recognize businesses and individuals in British Columbia who are "doing the right thing."

FIGURE 1.7   Ethical Issues in Business Communication

Manner of conveying the message	Qualities of the message	Larger organizational context of the message
Language, Graphics, and Document Design • Is the message audience friendly? Does it respect the audience? • Do the words balance the organization's right to present its best case with its responsibility to present its message honestly? • Do graphics help the audience understand? Or are graphics used to distract or confuse? • Does the design of the document make reading easy? Does document design attempt to make readers skip key points? **Tactics Used to Shape Response** • Are the arguments logical? • Are the emotional appeals used fairly? Do they supplement logic rather than substituting for it? • Does the organizational pattern lead the audience without undue manipulation? • Are the tactics honest? That is, do they avoid deceiving the audience?	• Is the message an ethical one that treats all parties fairly and is sensitive to all stakeholders? • Have interested parties been able to provide input into the decision or message? • Does the audience get all the information it needs to make a good decision? • Is information communicated in a timely way, or is information withheld to reduce the audience's power? • Is information communicated in a schema the audience can grasp, or are data "dumped" without any context?	• How does the organization treat its employees? How do employees treat each other? • How sensitive is the organization to stakeholders such as the people who live near its factories, stores, or offices, and to the general public? • Does the organization support employees' efforts to be honest, fair, and ethical? • Do the organization's actions in making products, buying supplies, and marketing goods and services stand up to ethical scrutiny? • Is the organization a good corporate citizen, helpful rather than harmful to the community in which it exists? • Are the organization's products or services a good use of scarce resources?

work/life issues as their first priority. Companies are trying to respond. More than 60% of Fortune 500 companies offer flextime, telecommuting, or some other kind of flexible option. To make itself more family friendly, Ernst & Young tells people not to check their e-mail on weekends or vacations, limits consultants' travel, and tries to redesign work loads so people won't burn out.[34] Xerox is among companies that have found that taking workers' family needs into consideration produces clear gains in productivity and customer service.[35]

Balancing work and family requires using ways other than physical presence to demonstrate one's commitment to and enthusiasm for organizational goals. It may require negotiating conflicts with other workers who have different family situations or who raised children years ago when fewer companies were family friendly. The downside of this trend is that sometimes work and family life are not so much balanced as blurred. Many employees study training videos and CDs, write e-mail, and participate in conference calls on what used to be "personal time." Flexibility is necessary in an age of downsizing and doing business in many time zones, but it means that many managers are essentially on call all the time.

Corporate Social Responsibility

In the light of legal and ethical concerns, business schools like businesses are more and more preoccupied with issues of Corporate Social Responsibility—

the relationship between a corporation and all its stakeholders inside or outside the corporation. As recently as a generation ago, "few people would have had a very clear idea of what you were talking about had you mentioned corporate social responsibility (CSR)," says *The Globe and Mail*'s J. McFarland. They might even have thought it as oxymoronic as "socialist efficiency. . . . The responsibilities of a corporation . . . were seen by shareholders and management as absolutely focused on one thing: profit."[36]

According to one small business representative, "CSR is recognizing when you are in a position to do good." And many report "business benefits as a result of their CSR initiatives," the most reported benefit taking the form of a "competitive advantage."[37]

One commentator has warned about communications pitfalls for reporting CSR activities to financial communities: "Don't tell them about saving the Earth; they want to know about the value creation realized through sustainable development."[38]

For all the challenges of measuring and reporting performance, more and more organizations are making the effort. Some also recognize that clean water and air are "not strictly 'environmental' issues. They are *business* issues." In this context, taking care of the triple bottom line—economic, environmental, and social performance—"is key to success, even survival, in today's competitive business climate."[39] Indeed, a Pricewaterhouse-Coopers Global CEO Survey found that 70% of CEOs believe CSR programs enhance profitability.[40]

Reputation Management

Despite the diversity of size, shape, and structure of organizations, many have an interest in social accounting, reporting, and auditing to assess performance because they confront the same challenges of "reputation and legitimacy," especially in the face of media "judgement by anecdote."[41] If businesses used to think in terms of ethics *or* profits and some currently offer little more than window dressing—"a public relations device designed to throw sand in our eyes"[42]—many are increasingly recognizing that their own interests cannot be separated from those of all other stakeholders. In short, they recognize that ethics *are* profits.

Peri Lynn Turnbull, co-author of the Conference Board of Canada report *How Corporate Social Responsibility Can Affect Your Reputation*, reports that consumers are demanding more responsible behaviour from companies and value such behaviour over brand reputation and price. Still, linking reputation and CSR can be risky, especially for companies that do not live up to their claims. Bob Stamnes advises linking mission-based marketing to branding and a strategic stakeholder approach fully integrating social issues into corporate identity.[43]

In the context of shareholder activism and class-action lawsuits, reputation and crisis management are now high on "the boardroom agenda," in the view of reporters Janet McFarland and Elizabeth Church: "The costs of mishandling bad news have never been so high." David Beatty, managing director of the Canadian Coalition for Good Governance, agrees: Planning is now more proactive because the consequences are "more serious in terms of the financial consequences to the corporation, and potentially to the directors in terms of loss of reputation."[44]

The End of the Job

In traditional jobs, people did what they were told to do. Now, they do whatever needs to be done, based on the needs of customers, colleagues, and anyone else who depends on their work. At Sarasota Memorial Hospital, food service workers do more than bring food to patients; they open containers, resolve problems with meals, help patients read their menus, and adjust orders to meet patients'

Someone's Monitoring Your E-Mail*

E-monitors scan for keywords and note when something questionable is sent or viewed. Says Rob Spence of Ireland's Baltimore Technologies, "If I want to screen every outgoing e-mail that has the word 'résumé,' . . . I can do that."

Your home computer may not be private, either. In 2000, a U.S. federal judge ruled that a company had the right to copy the entire hard drive of the home computer of an employee suspected of organizing a sick-out.

*Paragraph 1 quoted from Ann Therese Palmer, "Workers, Surf at Your Own Risk," *BusinessWeek*, 2001, 14. Paragraph 2 based on Dana Hawkins, "Data on Home Computers Not Necessarily Your Own," *U.S. News & World Report*, February 28, 2000, 85.

preferences. This attentiveness not only serves the patients, but also is part of a team-spirited approach to patient care that in this case frees nurses to do other work.[45] And research suggests that the most effective workers don't see work as assigned tasks. Instead, they define their own goals based on the needs of customers and clients.[46]

With flatter organizations, workers are doing a much wider variety of tasks. Today's secretaries are likely to be researching, planning meetings, and keeping records of the department's expenses. Even as more bank customers use ATMs for deposits and withdrawals, banks keep tellers on hand to help with more complicated problems and to cross-sell financial products.

Your parents may have worked for the same company all their lives. You may do that, too, but you have to be prepared to job-hunt—not only when you finish your degree but also throughout your career. That means continuing to learn—keeping up with new technologies, new economic and political realities, new ways of interacting with people.

Rapid Rate of Change

The flexibility required for the modern job market is just one area in which change is defining the workplace. Jobs that are routine can readily be done in other countries at lower cost.

As any employee who has watched his or her job go overseas can testify, change—even change for the better—is stressful. Many people, especially those who have felt battered by changes in the workplace, fear that more change will further erode their positions. Even when change promises improvements, people have to work to learn new skills, new habits, and new attitudes. To reduce the stress of change, scholars suggest reducing the number of major, radical changes and relying more on frequent, small, incremental changes.[47]

Rapid change means that no college course or executive MBA program can teach you everything you need to know for the rest of your working life. You'll need to remain open to new ideas. And you'll need to view situations and options critically, so that you can evaluate new conditions to see whether they demand a new response. But the skills you learn can stand you in good stead for the rest of your life: critical thinking, computer savvy, problem solving, and the ability to write, to speak, and to work well with other people.

Technology

Technology is so pervasive that almost all office employees need to be able to navigate the Web and to use word processing, e-mail, spreadsheet, database, and presentation software. Most colleges and universities have short courses to help students master the fine points of these programs; take these courses or play around with the software to become proficient.

Technology provides new opportunities and saves companies money. On-line ticket sales have brought in new patrons and record receipts for the New York City Ballet and the San Francisco Opera.[48]

Intranets—Web pages just for employees—give everyone in an organization access to information. Ace Hardware started its message board to cut the cost of mailing out weekly newsletters to franchise owners and answering their phone questions. But an added benefit is that dealers share ideas with each other. One dealer wrote up his success in giving away a few cans of paint to attract corporate customers. Other dealers copied his idea, with equal success. Royal Dutch/Shell Group earned $5 million in new revenue when an engineering team in Africa was able to get the solution to a problem from teams in Europe and Asia that had already faced similar situations.[49]

Technology plays a large role in the changing face of business communication. Tools such as intranets, extranets, faxes, and e-mail have contributed to the efficiency of workplace communication. Meeting rooms are frequently equipped with laptops, pagers, and videoconferencing equipment, making it possible for people to have meetings across continents and time zones.

Extranets—Web pages for customers or suppliers—save time and money and improve quality. Two hours after dropping off a load of cranberries, growers can log on to Ocean Spray's extranet to find out how much they earned and how their berries compare to those of other growers. The information helps growers make decisions about harvesting the rest of the crop. Growers benefit by earning more money; Ocean Spray gets higher quality and cuts waste by 25%.[50]

Internet connections, faxes, and videophones allow employees to work at home rather than commute to a central office. Fax, e-mail, pagers, and text typewriter (TTY) telephones enable deaf and other hearing-impaired employees to fill a variety of jobs. Fax and e-mail make it easy to communicate across oceans and time zones. Teleconferencing makes it possible for people on different continents to have a meeting—complete with visual aids—without leaving their hometowns.

Technological change carries costs. Technology makes it easier for companies to monitor employees—even when they're out of the office. Acquiring technology and retraining workers requires an enormous investment. And the very ease of storing information and sending messages means more information and more messages to process. In the information age, time management depends in part on being able to identify which messages are important so that one isn't buried in trivia.

The technology of office communication also affects the way people interpret messages. Readers expect all documents to be well designed and error free—even though not everyone has access to a laser printer or even to a computer. E-mail and faxes lead people to expect instant responses, even though thinking and writing still take time.

Can Business Change the World?*

Joseph White, Dean of the University of Michigan Business School, says:

"The most moving experience that I've had in recent years was a meeting with Desmond Tutu in Cape Town. I asked him, 'What are your greatest concerns about the future of South Africa?' He said, 'We have 30 million people living on hope. If the economy and society don't deliver measurable improvements over the next five years, I don't know what's going to happen here.' Now, if you're a 25-year-old student and you're looking for a challenge, then look no further: Archbishop Tutu just delivered it to you.

"That opportunity reflects a fundamental difference between the current generation of business people and the previous generation. . . . If the dream 25 years ago was to join a big company and to pursue a career involving steady advancement, the dream now is to cultivate an economic entity that creates tremendous value, that provides opportunity for others, and that may even change the world."

*Quotation from Polly Labarre, ed., "Unit of One," *Fast Company*, January 1999, 74.

Understanding and Analyzing Business Communication Situations

In the face of such massive change impacting communications, the best communicators remain conscious of the context in which they make their choices; they're aware of options.

Ask yourself the following questions:

■ **What's at stake—to whom?** Think not only about your own needs but also about the concerns your boss and your readers will have. Your message will be most effective if you think of the entire organizational context—and the larger context of shareholders, customers, and regulators. When the stakes are high, you'll need to take into account people's emotional feelings as well as objective facts.

■ **Should you send a message?** Sometimes, especially when you're new on the job, silence is the most tactful response. But be alert for opportunities to learn, to influence, to make your case. You can use communication to build your career.

■ **What channel should you use?** Paper documents and presentations are formal and give you considerable control over the message. E-mail, phone calls, and stopping by someone's office are less formal. Oral channels promote group decision making, allow misunderstandings to be cleared up more quickly, and seem more personal. Sometimes you may need more than one message, in more than one channel.

■ **What should you say?** Content for a message may not be obvious. How detailed should you be? Should you repeat information that the audience already knows? The answers will depend on the kind of document, your purposes, audiences, and the corporate culture. And you'll have to figure these things out for yourself, without detailed instructions.

■ **How should you say it?** How you arrange your ideas—what comes first, second, and last—and the words you use shape the audience's response to what you say. A well-designed, visually attractive document enhances readability whether you are speaking for your organization or selling your skills to a potential employer.

Summary of Key Points

■ Communication helps organizations and the people in them achieve their goals. The ability to write and speak well becomes increasingly important as you rise in an organization.

■ People put things in writing to create a record, to convey complex data, to make things convenient for the reader, to save money, and to convey their own messages more effectively.

■ **Communication theory** attempts to explain what happens when we communicate. **Semantics** is the study of the way our behaviour is influenced by the words and other symbols we use to communicate. Communication theory and semantics both show why and where communication can break down and what we can do to communicate more effectively.

■ The best channel for a message will depend on the audience, the sender's purposes, and the situation. Channel choice may be shaped by the organizational culture.

■ **Channel overload** occurs when a channel cannot handle all the messages being sent. **Information overload** occurs when the receiver cannot process all the messages that arrive. Both kinds of overload require selection to determine which messages will be sent and which ones will be attended to.

FIGURE 1.8 Employability Skills 2000+

The skills you need to enter, stay in, and progress in the world of work—whether you work on your own or as a part of a team.

These skills can also be applied and used beyond the workplace in a range of daily activities.

Fundamental Skills

The skills needed as a base for further development.

You will be better prepared to progress in the world of work when you can:

Communicate
- read and understand information presented in a variety of forms (e.g., words,graphs,charts, diagrams)
- write and speak so others pay attention and understand
- listen and ask questions to understand and appreciate the points of view of others
- share information using a range of information and communications technologies (e.g., voice, e-mail, computers)
- use relevant scientific, technological and mathematical knowledge and skills to explain or clarify ideas

Manage Information
- locate, gather and organize information using appropriate technology and information systems
- access, analyze and apply knowledge and skills from various disciplines (e.g., the arts, languages, science, technology, mathematics, social sciences, and the humanities)

Use Numbers
- decide what needs to be measured or calculated
- observe and record data using appropriate methods, tools and technology
- make estimates and verify calculations

Think & Solve Problems
- assess situations and identify problems
- seek different points of view and evaluate them based on facts
- recognize the human, interpersonal, technical, scientific and mathematical dimensions of a problem
- identify the root cause of a problem
- be creative and innovative in exploring possible solutions
- readily use science, technology and mathematics as ways to think, gain and share knowledge, solve problems and make decisions
- evaluate solutions to make recommendations or decisions
- implement solutions
- check to see if a solution works, and act on opportunities for improvement

Personal Management Skills

The personal skill, attitudes, and behaviours that drive one's potential for growth

You will be able to offer yourself greater possibilities for achievement when you can:

Demonstrate Positive Attitudes & Behaviours
- feel good about yourself and be confident
- deal with people, problems and situations with honesty, integrity and personal ethics
- recognize your own and other people's efforts
- take care of your personal health
- show interest, initiative and effort

Be Responsible
- set goals and priorities balancing work and personal life
- plan and manage time, money and other resources to achieve goals
- assess, weigh and manage risk
- be accountable for your actions and the actions of your group
- be socially responsible and contribute to your community

Be Adaptable
- work independently or as a part of a team
- carry out multiple tasks or projects
- be innovative and resourceful; identify and suggest alternative ways to achieve goals and get the job done
- be open and respond constructively to change
- learn from your mistakes and accept feedback
- cope with uncertainty

Learn Continuously
- be willing to continuously learn and grow
- assess personal strengths and areas for development
- set your own learning goals
- identify and access learning sources and opportunities
- plan for and achieve your learning goals

Work Safely
- be aware of personal and group health and safety practices and procedures and act in accordance with these

Teamwork Skills

The skills and attributes needed to contribute productively

You will be better prepared to add value to the outcomes of a task, project or team when you can:

Work with Others
- understand and work within the dynamics of a group
- ensure that a team's purpose and objectives are clear
- be flexible: respect, be open to and supportive of the thoughts, opinions and contributions of others in a group
- recognize and respect people's diversity, individual differences and perspectives
- accept and provide feedback in a constructive and considerate manner
- contribute to a team by sharing information and expertise
- lead or support when appropriate, motivating a group for high performance
- understand the role of conflict in a group to reach solutions
- manage and resolve conflict when appropriate

Participate in Projects & Tasks
- plan, design or carry out a project or task from start to finish with well-defined objectives and outcomes
- develop a plan, seek feedback, test, revise and implement
- work to agreed quality standards and specifications
- select and use appropriate tools and technology for a task or project
- adapt to changing requirements and information
- continuously monitor the success of a project or task and identify ways to improve

The Conference Board of Canada

255 Smyth Road, Ottawa
ON K1H 8M7 Canada
Tel. (613) 526-3280
Fax (613) 526-4857
Internet:
http://www.conferenceboard.ca/education

Source: *Employability Skills 2000+* Brochure, 2000, EF (Ottawa: The Conference Board of Canada, 2000).

■ A sender goes through the following steps: **perception, interpretation, choice** or **selection, encoding,** and transmitting the message through a **channel.** The receiver perceives the message, **decodes** it, interprets it, chooses a response, encodes the response, and transmits it. The message transmitted to the original sender is called **feedback. Noise** is anything that interferes with communication. Miscommunication can occur at every point in the communication process.

■ Eight principles of semantics will help us avoid errors in perception, interpretation, choice, and encoding and decoding.

Perception

1. Perception involves the perceiver as well as the perceived.

Interpretation

2. **Observations** are statements you yourself have verified. **Inferences** are statements that have not yet been verified but that could be. **Judgments** can never be proven, since they depend not on measurable quantities but on values.

3. No two things are exactly alike.

4. Things change with time. Violating this principle produces **frozen evaluations.**

5. Most *either–or* classifications are not legitimate. Seeing only two alternatives is called **polarization.** Assuming limits that do not exist is called **blindering.**

Choice

6. A statement is never the whole story; it is impossible to know everything.

Encoding and Decoding

7. Words are not identical to the objects they represent.

8. The symbols used in communication must stand for essentially the same thing in the minds of the sender and the receiver. When the sender and the receiver use the same symbol to mean different things, **bypassing** occurs.

■ **Internal documents** go to people inside the organization. **External documents** go to audiences outside: clients, customers, suppliers, shareholders, the government, the media, and the general public.

■ The three basic purposes of business and administrative communication are **to inform, to request or persuade,** and **to build goodwill.** Most messages have more than one purpose.

■ Poor writing wastes time and effort, and jeopardizes goodwill.

■ Good business and administrative writing meets five basic criteria: it's clear, complete, and correct; it saves the reader's time; and it builds goodwill.

■ To evaluate a specific document, we must know the interactions among the writer, the reader(s), the purposes of the message, and the situation. No single set of words will work for all readers in all situations.

■ Twelve trends affecting business and administrative communication are a focus on quality and customers' needs, entrepreneurship and outsourcing, teams, diversity, global competition and opportunities, legal and ethical concerns, balancing work and family, corporate social responsibility, reputation management, the end of the job, the rapid rate of change, and technology.

- To understand business communication situations, ask the following questions:
  - What's at stake—to whom?
  - Should you send a message?
  - What channel should you use?
  - What should you say?
  - How should you say it?

CHAPTER 1 Exercises and Problems

Getting Started

1.1 Choosing a Channel to Convey a Specific Message

Assume that you're the campaign manager for a campus, municipal, or provincial election. What would be the advantages and disadvantages of each of the following channels as media to carry ads for your side?

a. Ad in the campus newspaper.
b. Posters around campus.
c. Ad in the local newspaper.
d. Ad on a local radio station after midnight.
e. Ad on the local TV station during the local news show.
f. Ads on billboards.
g. Ads on yard signs.
h. Flyers distributed door to door.
i. Ad on cable TV.

1.2 Explaining Bypassing

1. Show how the following statements could produce bypassing.
   a. The house needs painting badly.
   b. I made reservations for seven.
   c. If you think our servers are rude, you should see the manager.

2. Bypassing is the basis of many jokes. Find a joke that depends on bypassing and share it with the class.

1.3 Identifying Logos

Find four corporate logos. Do all your classmates recognize all the logos? Which logos seem to be especially effective symbols for their organizations? What makes them so effective?

1.4 Analyzing Arguments

Analyze the arguments in one or more of the following kinds of documents. For each, identify the claim and (if present) the evidence, the bridge, the foundation, rebuttals to counterclaims, and limiters. What additional parts (if any) are needed to make the argument convincing?

1. An article in a business periodical or Web site recommending that it is or is not a good idea to buy a particular company's stock.
2. A recruiting brochure or Web page explaining why a company is a good place to work.
3. The CEO's letter in an annual report arguing that the company is well positioned for the coming year.
4. A fundraising letter arguing that the organization is doing good work and is a deserving candidate for financial gifts.
5. A letter of recommendation recommending a candidate for a job or for a promotion.
6. Material from your city's chamber of commerce presenting your city as a good place to live and work.

Communicating at Work

1.5   Understanding the Role of Communication in Your Organization

Interview your supervisor to learn about the kinds and purposes of communication in your organization. Your questions could include the following:

■ What channels of communication (e.g., memos, e-mail, presentations) are most important in this organization?

■ What documents or presentations do you create? Are they designed to inform, to persuade, to build goodwill—or to do all three?

■ What documents or presentations do you receive? Are they designed to inform, to persuade, to build goodwill—or to do all three?

■ Who are your most important audiences within the organization?

■ Who are our most important external audiences?

■ What are the challenges of communicating in this organization?

■ What kinds of documents and presentations does the organization prefer?

As Your Professor Directs,

a.   Share your results with a small group of students.

b.   Present your results in a memo to your professor.

c.   Join with a group of students to make a group presentation to the class.

d.   Post your results online to the class.

Memo Assignments

1.6   Introducing Yourself to Your Professor

Write a memo (at least 1½ pages long) introducing yourself to your professor. Include the following topics:

Background: Where did you grow up? What have you done in terms of school, extracurricular activities, jobs, and family life?

Interests: What are you interested in? What do you like to do? What do you like to think about and talk about? What kind of writing have you done? Have you found different classes/instructors have different standards? What are your writing strengths and weaknesses?

Achievements: What achievements have given you the greatest personal satisfaction? List at least five. Include things that gave *you* a real sense of accomplishment

and pride, whether or not they're the sort of thing you'd list on a résumé.

Goals: What do you hope to accomplish this term? Where would you like to be professionally and personally five years from now?

Use complete memo format with appropriate headings. (See ➡ Chapter 5 for examples of memo format.) Use a conversational writing style; check your draft to polish the style and edit for mechanical and grammatical correctness. A good memo will enable your instructor to see you as an individual. Use specific details to make your memo vivid and interesting. Remember that one of your purposes is to interest your reader!

1.7   Introducing Yourself to Your Collaborative Writing Group

Write a memo (at least 1½ pages long) introducing yourself to the other students in your collaborative writing group. Include the following topics:

Background: What is your major? What special areas of knowledge do you have? What have you done in terms of school, extracurricular activities, jobs, and family life?

Previous experience in groups: What groups have you worked in before? Are you usually a leader, a follower, or a bit of both? Are you interested in a quality product? In maintaining harmony in the group? In working efficiently? What do you like most about working in groups? What do you like least?

Work and composing style: Do you like to talk out ideas while they're in a rough stage or work them out on paper before you discuss them? Would you rather have a complete outline before you start writing or just a general idea? Do you want to have a detailed schedule of everything that has to be done and who

will do it, or would you rather "go with the flow"? Do you work best under pressure, or do you want to have assignments ready well before the due date?

Areas of expertise: What can you contribute to the group in terms of knowledge and skills? Are you good at brainstorming ideas? Researching? Designing charts? Writing? Editing? Word processing? Managing the flow of work? Maintaining group cohesion?

Goals for collaborative assignments: What do you hope to accomplish this term? Where does this course fit into your priorities?

Use complete memo format with appropriate headings. (See ➡ Chapter 5 for examples of memo format.) Use a conversational writing style; edit your final draft for mechanical and grammatical correctness. A good memo will enable others in your group to see you as an individual. Use details to make your memo vivid and interesting. Remember that one of your purposes is to make your readers look forward to working with you!

Adapting to Audiences

- ■ Identifying Your Audiences
- ■ Ways to Analyze Your Audience
- ■ Choosing Channels to Reach Your Audience
- ■ Using Audience Analysis to Adapt Your Message
- ■ Reader Benefits
- ■ Writing or Speaking to Multiple Audiences with Different Needs

- ■ Goodwill
- ■ You-Attitude
- ■ Positive Emphasis
- ■ Tone, Power, and Politeness
- ■ Reducing Bias in Business Communication
- ■ Summary of Key Points

AN INSIDE PERSPECTIVE

Adapting Your Message to Your Audience

The first priority in any project is to analyze your audience. Only when you have a clear profile—nationality, culture, gender, age, abilities, socio-economic status, education, language, for example—and understand how their characteristics relate to particular messages can you effectively address audience needs, motivations, and benefits.

When you know who your audience is, you can identify what your audience knows and needs to know to respond to your message. What is your message purpose? Do you want readers to act, think, or feel? You may have multiple purposes: to inform your audience about a program, to persuade them yours is a program that will benefit them, and to consolidate the credibility of your organization as well as you as a writer.

What is the best channel for your purposes and budget? Internet, television, radio, print, or another medium?

Patrick Scissons, Vice-president, Associate Creative Director, BBDO Canada. Award-winning writer in several categories in the 2004 Marketing Awards, Scissons is as happy working on the pro bono as on the big accounts. In August 2004, he had a hand in the humorous spots for the ABC Canada Literacy Foundation campaign designed to encourage adult learners to seek help in literacy upgrading.

www.abc-canada.org

What information must your message include? Where and how should it be included for appropriate emphasis? What is the logic of your claims? What objections may the audience have? How can you de-emphasize the negative? How can you shift audience perspective by rephrasing and emphasizing the positive? How can you make clear what is in it for them? Putting yourself in your audience's shoes is key.

Writing for the ABC Canada Literacy Foundation to encourage adult learners to seek literacy upgrading, for example, meant persuading them they were not alone (five million Canadians or 22% of the adult population have serious literacy problems) and that others have much darker secrets.[1] One television spot portrays coworkers about to share their "dark secret" when a companion interrupts with a much more outrageous secret, making clear there's no reason to be ashamed. Using humour, the campaign encouraged people to share their "dark secrets" and subscribe.

Knowing to whom you're talking is fundamental to the success of any message. You need to identify your audiences, understand their motivations, and know how to reach them.

Identifying Your Audiences

Organizational messages have multiple audiences:[2]

1. The **initial audience** is the first audience to get your message. Sometimes the initial audience tells you to write the message.

2. A **gatekeeper** has the power to stop your message instead of sending it on to other audiences, including the primary audience. Sometimes the supervisor who assigns the message is also the gatekeeper; sometimes the gatekeeper is higher in the organization. In some cases, gatekeepers may exist outside the organization.

3. The **primary audience** will decide whether to accept your recommendations or act on the basis of your message. You must reach the primary audience to fulfill your purposes in any message.

4. The **secondary audience** may be asked to comment on your message or to implement your ideas after they've been approved. Secondary audiences also include lawyers who may use your message—perhaps years later—as evidence of your organization's culture and practices.

5. A **watchdog audience,** though it does not have the power to stop the message and will not act directly on it, has political, social, or economic power. The watchdog pays close attention to the transaction between you and the primary audience and may base future actions on its evaluation of your message.

As the following example shows, one person can be part of two audiences. Frequently, a supervisor is both the initial audience and the gatekeeper. Sometimes the initial audience is also the primary audience who will act on the message.

> Dawn is an assistant account executive in an ad agency. Her boss asks her to write a proposal for a marketing plan for a new product the agency's client is introducing. Her *primary audience* is the executive committee of the client company, who will decide whether to adopt the plan. The *secondary audience* includes the marketing staff of the client company, who will be asked for comments on the plan, as well as the artists, writers, and media buyers who will carry out details of the plan if it is adopted. Her boss, who must approve the plan before it is submitted to the client, is both the *initial audience* and the *gatekeeper.*

Ways to Analyze Your Audience

The most important tool in audience analysis is empathy. **Empathy** is the ability to put yourself in someone else's shoes, to feel with that person. In all probability, the audience is *not* just like you. Use what you know about people and about organizations to predict likely responses, and design your approach.

Analyzing Individuals

When you write or speak to people in your own organization and in other organizations you work closely with, you may be able to analyze your audience as individuals. It will usually be easy to get information by talking to members of your audience, talking to people who know your audience, and observing your audience.

InSite

www.2h.com/personality-tests.html

Before you analyze your audience, analyze yourself—so that you can see what you and your audience share and how you differ.

The **Myers-Briggs Type Indicator** uses four dimensions to identify ways that people differ.[3]

As Figure 2.1 suggests, you'll be most persuasive if you play to your audience's strengths. Indeed, many of the general principles of business communication reflect the types most common among managers. Putting the main point upfront satisfies the needs of judging types, and some 75% of managers are judging. Giving logical reasons satisfies the needs of the nearly 80% of managers who are thinking types.[4]

Analyzing the Organizational Culture and the Discourse Community

Be sensitive to the culture in which your audiences work and the discourse community or community of practice of which they are a part. **Organizational culture** is a set of values, attitudes, and philosophies. An organization's culture is revealed verbally in the organization's myths, stories, and heroes, and

FIGURE 2.1   Using Myers-Briggs Types in Persuasive Messages

If your audience is	Use this strategy	Because
An introvert	Write a memo and let the reader think about your proposal before responding.	Introverts prefer to think before they speak. Written documents give them the time they need to think through a proposal carefully.
An extravert	Try out your idea orally, in an informal setting.	Extroverts like to think on their feet. They are energized by people; they'd rather talk than write.
A sensing type	Present your reasoning step-by-step. Get all your facts exactly right.	Sensing types usually reach conclusions step by step. They want to know why something is important, but they trust their own experience more than someone else's say-so. They're good at facts and expect others to be, too.
An intuitive type	Present the big picture first. Stress the innovative, creative aspects of your proposal.	Intuitive types like solving problems and being creative. They can be impatient with details.
A thinking type	Use logic, not emotion, to persuade. Show that your proposal is fair, even if some people may be hurt by it.	Thinking types make decisions based on logic and abstract principles. They are often uncomfortable with emotion.
A feeling type	Show that your proposal meets the emotional needs of people as well as the dollars-and-cents needs of the organization.	Feeling types are very aware of other people and their feelings. They are sympathetic and like harmony.
A perceiving type	Show that you've considered all the alternatives. Ask for a decision by a specific date.	Perceiving types want to be sure they've considered all the options. They may postpone coming to closure.
A judging type	Present your request quickly.	Judging types are comfortable making quick decisions. They like to come to closure so they can move on to something else.

Culture: Words and Deeds*

Culture is more than a values statement on a Web site. A company's true culture is evident in the way people behave. Consider these examples of cultural mismatches:

A major international corporation hung signs in its hallways proclaiming that "trust" was one of its driving principles. Yet that same company searched employees' belongings each time they entered or exited the building.

At one company, Employee Appreciation Day featured morning bagels, a blast e-mail of thanks from the company president, and an afternoon gathering with food and refreshments. A flier promoting the event instructed employees to "please see your supervisor for a ticket. Cost: $15."

*Examples quoted from Pamela Babcock, "Is Your Company Two-Faced?" *HRMagazine*, January 2004, downloaded from http://www.shrm.org/hrmagazine/articles/0104/0104covstory.asp November 15, 2005.

InSite

www.gore.com/en_xx/aboutus/culture/index.html

W. L. Gore & Associates, Inc., maker of Gore-Tex, is one of many companies whose Web pages describe the corporate culture of the organization.

non-verbally in the allocation of space, money, and power. A **discourse community** is a group of people who share assumptions about what channels, formats, and styles to use for communication, what topics to discuss and how to discuss them, and what constitutes evidence.

A **community of practice** is a group of people who work together, share a sense of purpose, engage in learning together, produce meaning, develop identities, and add value to an organization. People may belong to more than one community of practice within an organization.

In an organization that values equality and individualism, you can write directly to the CEO and address him or her as a colleague. In other companies, you'd be expected to follow a chain of command. Some organizations prize short messages; some expect long, thorough documents. Messages, styles, and channels that are consistent with the organization's culture have a greater chance of succeeding—and of reshaping that culture.

Every organization—businesses, government agencies, non-profit organizations, even colleges—has a culture. An organization's culture is constructed by the people who found the organization, participate in it, and change it.

You can begin to analyze an organization's culture by asking the following questions:

- Is the organization tall or flat? Are there lots of levels between the CEO and the lowest worker, or only a few?
- How do people get ahead? Are the organization's rewards based on seniority, education, being well liked, making technical discoveries, or serving customers? Are rewards available only to a few top people, or is everyone expected to succeed?
- Does the organization value diversity or homogeneity? Does it value independence and creativity or being a team player and following orders? What stories do people tell? Who are the organization's heroes and villains?
- How important are friendship and sociability? To what extent do workers agree on goals, and how intently do they pursue them?
- How formal are behaviour, language, and dress?
- What are the organization's goals? Making money? Serving customers and clients? Advancing knowledge? Contributing to the community?

Two companies in the same field may have very different cultures. In the mid-1980s, researcher Jennifer Chatman found that employees of Touche Ross (now Deloitte & Touche) rated informality as the firm's number one value. At Arthur Andersen, informality was the last of 54 values. More recently, Chatman found that new hires who "fit" the company's culture were more likely to stay with the job, be more productive, and be more satisfied than those who did not fit the culture.[5]

Organizations, like nations, can have subcultures. For example, manufacturing and marketing may represent different subcultures in the same organization: they may dress differently and have different values.

To analyze an organization's discourse community, ask the following questions:

- What channels, formats, and styles are preferred for communication?
- What do people talk about? What topics are not discussed?
- What kind of and how much evidence is needed to be convincing?

A discourse community like a community of practice may be limited to a few people in an organization. However, some discourse communities span an entire

Companies that learn and laugh together succeed together. And in the case of Vancity everyone wins! Vancity's Chilliwack branch, like its other 42 branches in British Columbia, attracts employees committed to making a difference. And Vancity in 2004 contributed $7.4 million (or about 13% of earnings) in community donations.

organization or even everyone in the same field. You will be a member of several overlapping discourse communities.

In many organizational situations, then, you'll analyze your audience as members of a group: "taxpayers who must be notified that they owe more income tax," or "employees with small children." Focus on what group members have in common. In some cases, no research is necessary: in other cases, Statistics Canada and other databases may yield useful information. In still other cases, you may want to do original research.

If you know where your audience lives, databases enable you to map demographic and psychographic profiles of customers or employees. **Demographic characteristics** are measurable features that can be counted objectively: age, gender, race, religion, education level, income, and so on.

Sometimes demographic information is irrelevant; sometimes it's important. Does age matter? Sometimes. "Generational marketing" is helping manufacturers design and market products. Ford develops vehicles to meet the profile of each group of six generations.[6] But other marketers are finding that considering age alone is inadequate to sell to the "mature market."[7]

Psychographic characteristics are qualitative rather than quantitative: values, beliefs, goals, and lifestyles. Knowing what your audience finds important allows you to organize information in a way that seems natural to your audience and to choose appeals that the audience will find persuasive.

For example, a long-distance phone company used psychographics to understand the characteristics of people who are heavy users of long-distance service. This knowledge helped the company select a spokesperson the heavy users could relate to.[8] Tim Hortons diversified its menu to add to its client base by appealing to important weight-conscious customers—and is continuing to expand in Canada and the United States.[9]

Reading Levels*

- Only 52% of Canadian adults are fully literate.
- 22% (or five million) of Canadian adults have serious problems with reading, writing, and mathematics.
- Less than 10% of those Canadians who could benefit enrol in literacy programs.
- The Canadian Business Task Force on Literacy (1988) estimated poor reading skills cost Canadian business $4.1 billion annually: $1.6 billion lost to workplace accidents; $2.5 billion in lost productivity.

Increasingly complex workplaces—whether in mines equipped with complicated technology (and complicated instruction manuals) or in a factory or retail store—require higher communication skills than ever.

Research shows that investing in literacy is good for the bottom line, for enhanced health and safety, employee satisfaction, and a stronger culture.

*Adapted from ABC Canada Literacy Foundation Web site, retrieved March 12, 2005, from http://www.abc-canada.org; Andy Holloway, "Get a Proper Read: Workplace Literacy Is Way More Than It Used to Be," *Canadian Business* November 22–December 5, 2004, 105–106.

Choosing Channels to Reach Your Audience

Communication channels vary in speed, accuracy of transmission, cost, number of messages carried, number of people reached, efficiency, and ability to promote goodwill. Depending on the audience, your purposes, and the situation, one channel may be better than another.

A written message makes it easier to

- Present extensive or complex financial data.
- Present many specific details of a law, policy, or procedure.
- Minimize undesirable emotions.

Messages on paper are more formal than e-mail messages. E-mail messages are appropriate for routine interchanges with people you already know. Paper is better for someone to whom you're writing for the first time.

Oral messages make it easier to

- Use emotion to help persuade the audience.
- Focus the audience's attention on specific points.
- Answer questions, resolve conflicts, and build consensus.
- Modify a proposal that may not be acceptable in its original form.
- Get immediate action or response.

Scheduled meetings and oral presentations are more formal than phone calls or stopping someone in the hall.

Important messages should use more formal channels, whether they're oral or written. Oral and written messages have many similarities. In both, you should

- Adapt the message to the specific audience.
- Show the audience how they would benefit from the idea, policy, service, or product.
- Overcome any objections the audience may have (➡ Chapter 7).
- Use you-attitude (see ➡ page 43) and positive emphasis.
- Use visuals to clarify or emphasize material.
- Specify exactly what the audience should do.

Sometimes your channel choice is determined by the audience. Some organizations still post announcements and job openings on bulletin boards because the mail staff, cleaning people, and some clerical workers don't have computers and so can't check e-mail. Even people who have access to the same channels may prefer different ones. When a university updated its employee benefits manual, the computer scientists and librarians wanted the information online. Faculty wanted to be able to read the information on paper. Maintenance workers and carpenters wanted to get answers on voice mail.[10]

The bigger your audience, the more complicated channel choice becomes, since few channels reach everyone in your target audience. When possible, use multiple channels. For example, print ads and customer service materials should contain not only toll-free numbers but also street or e-mail addresses so that people who don't like to make phone calls or who have hearing impairments can contact the company.

Using Audience Analysis to Adapt Your Message

If you know your audience well and if you use words well, much of your audience analysis and adaptation will be unconscious. If you don't know your audience or if the message is very important, take the time to analyze your audience formally and to revise your draft with your analysis in mind.

As you answer these questions for a specific audience, think about the organizational culture in which the person works. At every point, your reader's reaction is affected not only by his or her personal feelings and preferences but also by the political environment of the organization, the economy, and current events.

1. How Will the Audience React to the Message?

Audiences will read and act on messages they see as important. When the audience may see your message as unimportant, you need to

- In a subject line or first paragraph, show your reader that this message is important and relevant.
- Make the action as easy as possible.
- Suggest a realistic deadline for action.
- Keep the message as short as possible.

The audience's experience with you, your organization, and the subject you're writing about shapes response to this new message. Someone who thinks well of you and your organization will be prepared to receive your message favourably.

When you must write to someone who has negative feelings about your organization, your position, or you personally, you need to

- Make a special effort to avoid phrases that could seem condescending, arrogant, rude, hostile, or uncaring.
- Use positive emphasis (➡ p. 47) to counteract the natural tendency to sound defensive.
- Develop logic and reader benefits fully.

2. How Much Information Does the Audience Need?

It's easy to overestimate the knowledge an audience has. Even people who once worked in your unit may have forgotten specific details now that their daily work is in management. People outside your organization won't know how *your* organization does things.

When some of your information is new to the audience, you need to

- Make a special effort to be clear. Define terms, explain concepts, use examples.
- Link new information to old information that the reader already knows.
- Use paragraphs and headings to break up new information into related chunks so that the information is easier to digest.
- Test your draft document with your reader or a subset of your intended audience to see whether the audience can understand and use what you've written.

Things we have learned through personal observation and experience always seem more real than things we've learned indirectly or from books. Other people may see our experience as an exception, an aberration, or a fluke; we see it as the best guide of what to expect in the future.

If you're trying to change someone's understanding of a policy or organization, you need to

- Acknowledge the audience's initial understanding early in the message.

- Use examples as well as theory or statistics to show the difference between short-term and long-term effects, or to show that the audience's experience is not universal.
- Allow the audience to save face by suggesting that changed circumstances call for new attitudes or action.

When the audience must think of background or old information to appreciate your points, you can

- Preface information with "As you know" to avoid suggesting that the reader does not know what you're saying.
- Put old or obvious information in a subordinate clause.
- Put lengthy background or reminder information in a separate section with an appropriate heading or in an attachment to your letter or memo.

3. What Obstacles Must You Overcome?

People who have already made up their minds are highly resistant to change. When the audience will oppose what you have to say, you need to

- Start your message with any areas of agreement or common ground that you share with your reader.
- Make a special effort to be clear and unambiguous.
- Make a special effort to avoid statements that will anger the audience.
- Limit your statement or request to the smallest possible area. If parts of your message could be delivered later, postpone them.
- Show that your solution is the best solution currently available, even though it isn't perfect.

Everyone has a set of ideas and habits and a mental self-image. If we're asked to do something that violates any of those, we first have to be persuaded to change our attitudes, habits, or self-image.

When your request is time consuming, complicated, or physically or psychologically difficult, you need to

- Make the action as easy as possible. Provide a form that can be filled out quickly; provide a stamped, self-addressed envelope if you are writing to another organization.
- Break down actions into a list, so the audience can check off each step as it is completed.
- Show that what you ask is consistent with what the audience believes.
- Show how the audience (not just you or your organization) will benefit when the action is completed.

4. What Positive Aspects Can You Emphasize?

Benefits help persuade the audience that your ideas are good ones. Make the most of the good points in your message.

- Put good news in the first paragraph.
- Use reader benefits that go beyond the basic good news of the first paragraph.

A sense of solidarity with someone can be an even more powerful reason to agree than the content of the message itself. Always use all the ethical strategies that are available to win support for your ideas.

When everyone in your audience shares the same experiences, interests, goals, and values, you can

- Consider using a vivid anecdote to remind the audience of what you share. If it is not vivid, you may seem to be lecturing the audience.
- Make a special effort to make your writing style friendly and informal.
- Use a salutation and close that remind the audience of their membership in this formal or informal group.

5. What Are the Audience's Expectations about the Appropriate Language, Structure, and Form for Messages?

Good writers adapt their style to suit the reader's preferences. A reader who sees contractions as too informal needs a different style from one who sees traditional business writing as too stuffy. As you write,

- Use what you know about your reader to choose a more or less distant, more or less friendly style.
- Use the reader's first name in the salutation only if you use that name when you talk to him or her in person or on the phone.

You don't have time to convince the audience that a term is broader or more neutral than his or her understanding. When you need agreement or approval, you should

- Avoid terms that carry emotional charges for many readers: for example, *criminal, fundamentalist.*
- Use your previous experience with an individual reader or listener to replace any terms that have particular meanings for him or her.

A message that does not give the audience the amount of or kind of detail he or she wants may fail. When you write to people you do not know well, you can

- Provide all the detail they need to understand and act on your message.
- Group chunks of information under headings so that readers can go directly to the parts of the message they find most interesting and relevant.
- Imitate the level of detail in similar documents to the same audience. If those documents have succeeded, you're probably safe in using the same level of detail that they do.

Individual personality or cultural background may lead someone to prefer a particular kind of structure. You'll be more effective if you use the structure and organization your audience prefers.

A document that meets the reader's expectations about length, number of visuals, and footnote format is more likely to succeed. If you can't meet those expectations, you need to

- Revise your document carefully. Be sure that a shorter-than-usual document covers the essential points; be sure that a longer-than-usual document is free from wordiness and repetition.
- Check with the audience to see whether the standards are flexible.
- Pretest the message on a subset of your audience to see if the format enhances or interferes with comprehension and action.

6. How Will the Audience Use the Document?

Reading a document in a quiet office calls for no special care. But suppose the reader will be reading your message on the train commuting home. Then the physical preparation of the document can make it easier or harder to use.

Write Your Way into the Discourse Community

You can learn a bit about your organization's discourse community by listening to people and reading the documents that other people write. But the best way to learn is to write.

The feedback you get from your supervisor will show you how to adapt your writing for the particular organization. To make the feedback most useful, categorize the comments and generalize.

Are you being asked to provide specific supporting details? To write so that people can understand what you say without having to reread? To use a more or less formal style? To include lots of charts or none at all?

Learning to adapt your content, structure, and style to the organization will make you a more effective writer and a more effective worker.

When the reader will use your document outside an office,

- Use lots of white space.
- Make the document small enough to hold in one hand.
- Number items so the reader can find his or her place after an interruption.
- Consider using plastic to protect the document.

Understanding how your audience will use the document will enable you to choose the best pattern of organization and the best level of detail. A memo within a company urging the adoption of pollution control equipment would need less information than one to a regulatory body. Different information would be needed for instructions by the manufacturer of the equipment explaining how to install and maintain it.

If the document will serve as a general reference,

- Use a specific subject line to aid in filing and retrieval. If the document is online, consider using several keywords to make it easy to find the document in a database search program.
- Use headings within the document so that readers can skim it.
- Give the office as well as the person to contact so that the reader can get in touch with the appropriate person some time from now.
- Spell out details that may be obvious now but might be forgotten in six months; check for accuracy, completeness, and friendliness.

If the document will be a detailed guide or contain instructions,

- Check to be sure that all the steps are in chronological order.
- Number steps or provide check-off boxes so that readers can easily see which steps they've completed.
- Group steps into five to seven subprocesses if there are many individual steps.
- Put any warnings at the beginning of the document; then repeat them just before the specific step to which they apply.

If the document will be used as the basis for a lawsuit,

- Give specific observations with dates and exact measurements as well as any inferences you've drawn from those observations.
- Give a full report with all the information you have. The lawyer can then decide which parts of the information to use in preparing the case.

Reader Benefits

Use your analysis of your audience to create effective reader benefits. **Reader benefits** are benefits or advantages that the reader gets by using your services, buying your products, following your policies, or adopting your ideas. In informative messages, reader benefits give reasons to comply with the policies you announce and suggest that the policies are good ones. In persuasive messages, reader benefits give reasons to act and help overcome reader resistance. Negative messages do not use reader benefits.

Good reader benefits meet four criteria. Each of these criteria suggests a technique for writing good reader benefits.

1. Adapt Reader Benefits to the Audience.

When you write to different audiences, you may need to stress different reader benefits. Suppose that you manufacture a product and want to persuade dealers to carry it. The features you may cite in ads directed toward customers—stylish colours, sleek lines, convenience, durability, good price—won't convince dealers. Shelf space is at a premium, and most dealers don't carry all the models of all the brands available for any given product. To be persuasive, talk about benefits from the dealer's point of view: turnover, profit margin, the national advertising campaign that will build customer awareness and interest, and the special store displays.

2. Stress Intrinsic as well as Extrinsic Motivators.

Intrinsic motivators come automatically from using a product or doing something. **Extrinsic motivators** are "added on." Someone in power decides to give them; they do not necessarily come from using the product or doing the action. Figure 2.2 gives examples of extrinsic and intrinsic motivators for three activities.

Intrinsic motivators or benefits are better than extrinsic motivators for two reasons:

1. You can't give a prize to every customer every time he or she places an order or to every employee who does what he or she is supposed to do.
2. Research shows that extrinsic motivators may actually make people *less* satisfied with the products they buy or the procedures they follow.

A 1999 survey found that having responsibility and autonomy, the respect and recognition of superiors, and the opportunity to have ideas adopted all were more important than salary and bonuses. Many family-friendly companies have discovered that a culture of care keeps turnover low. The higher salary that a competitor might pay just doesn't overcome the advantage of working at a supportive, flexible company that values its employees.[11]

Since money is not the only motivator, choose reader benefits that identify intrinsic as well as extrinsic motivators for following policies and adopting ideas.

3. Prove Reader Benefits with Clear Logic and Explain Them in Adequate Detail.

A reader benefit is a claim or assertion that the reader will benefit if he or she does something. Convincing the reader, therefore, involves two steps: making sure that the benefit really will occur, and explaining it to the reader.

If the logic behind a claimed reader benefit is faulty or inaccurate, there's no way to make that particular reader benefit convincing. Revise the benefit to make it logical.

FIGURE 2.2   Extrinsic and Intrinsic Motivators

Activity	Extrinsic motivator	Intrinsic motivator
Making a sale	Getting a commission	Pleasure in convincing someone; pride in using your talents to think of a strategy and execute it
Turning in a suggestion to a company suggestion system	Getting a monetary reward when the suggestion is implemented	Solving a problem at work; making the work environment a little more pleasant
Writing a report that solves an organizational problem	Getting praise, a good performance appraisal, and maybe a raise	Pleasure in having an effect on an organization; pride in using your skills to solve problems; solving the problem itself

Faulty logic:	Using a computer will enable you to write letters, memos, and reports much more quickly.
Analysis:	If you've never used a computer, in the short run it will take you *longer* to create a document using a computer than it would to type it. The real time savings come when a document incorporates parts of previous documents or goes through several revisions. Creating a first draft from scratch will still take planning and careful composing; the time savings may or may not be significant.
Revised reader benefit:	Using a computer allows you to revise and edit a document more easily. It eliminates retyping as a separate step and reduces the time needed to proofread revisions. It allows you to move the text around on the page to create the best layout.

Always provide enough detail to be vivid and concrete. You'll need more detail in the following situations:

a.   The reader may not have thought of the benefit before.
b.   The benefit depends on the difference between the long run and the short run.
c.   The reader will be hard to persuade, and you need detail to make the benefit vivid and emotionally convincing.

4. Phrase Reader Benefits in You-Attitude.

If reader benefits aren't in you-attitude (⮕ p. 43), they'll sound selfish and won't be as effective as they could be. A sales letter with strong you-attitude as well as reader benefits got a far bigger response than did an alternate version with reader benefits but no you-attitude.[12] In your final draft, check to be sure that you've used you-attitude.

Lacks you-attitude:	We have the lowest prices in town.
You-attitude:	At Havlichek Cars, you get the best deal in town.

Psychological description (⮕ Chapter 7) can help you make reader benefits vivid.

Brainstorm lots of reader benefits—perhaps twice as many as you'll need for the final letter or memo. Then you can choose the ones that are most effective for your audience, or that you can develop most easily.

When reader benefits are hard to identify or to develop, use the following three steps to identify and then develop good reader benefits.

1. Identify the Feelings, Fears, and Needs That May Motivate Your Reader.

One of the best-known analyses of needs is Abraham H. Maslow's hierarchy of needs.[13] Physiological needs are the most basic, followed by needs for safety and security, for love and a sense of belonging, for esteem and recognition, and finally for self-actualization or self-fulfillment. All of us go back and forth between higher- and lower-level needs. Whenever lower-level needs make themselves felt, they usually take priority.

Figure 2.3 shows organizational motivations for each of the levels in Maslow's hierarchy. Often a product or idea can meet needs on several levels. Focus on the ones that audience analysis suggests are most relevant for your audience, but remember that even the best analysis may not reveal all of a reader's needs. For example, a well-paid manager may be worried about security needs if her spouse has lost his job.

FIGURE 2.3 Organizational Motivations for Maslow's Hierarchy of Needs

Self-actualization
- Using your talents and abilities.
- Finding solutions to problems.
- Serving humanity.
- Self-respect and pride.
- Being the best you can be.

Esteem, recognition
- Being publicly recognized for achievements.
- Being promoted or gaining authority.
- Having status symbols.
- Having a good personal reputation.
- Having a good corporate reputation.

Love, belonging
- Having friends, working with people you like.
- Cooperating with other people on a project.
- Conforming to a group's norms.
- Feeling needed.
- Being loyal or patriotic.
- Promoting the welfare of a group you identify with or care about.

Safety, security
- Earning enough to afford a comfortable standard of living.
- Having pleasant working conditions.
- Having good medical coverage and pension plan.
- Understanding the reasons for actions by supervisors.
- Being treated fairly.
- Saving time and money.
- Conserving human and environmental resources.

Physical
- Earning enough to pay for basic food, clothing, shelter, and medical care.
- Having safe working conditions.

2. Identify the Features of Your Product or Policy That Could Meet the Needs You've Identified.

Sometimes just listing the reader's needs makes it obvious which feature meets a given need. Sometimes several features together meet the need.

Suppose that you want to persuade people to come to the restaurant you manage. Depending on what features your restaurant offered, you could appeal to one or more of the following subgroups:

Subgroup	Features to meet the subgroup's needs
People who work outside the home	A quick lunch; a relaxing place to take clients or colleagues
Parents with small children	High chairs, child-size portions, and things to keep the kids entertained
People who eat out a lot	Variety both in food and in decor
People on tight budgets	Economical food; a place where they don't need to tip (cafeteria or fast food)
People on special diets	Low-sodium and low-calorie dishes; vegetarian food; kosher food

People to whom eating out is part of an evening's entertainment	Music or a floor show; elegant surroundings; reservations so they can get to a show or event after dinner; late hours so they can come to dinner after a show or game

To develop your benefits, think about the details of each one. If your selling point is your relaxing atmosphere, think about the specific details that make the restaurant relaxing. If your strong point is elegant dining, think about all the details that contribute to that elegance.

3. Show How the Reader Can Meet His or Her Needs With the Features of the Policy or Product.

Features alone rarely motivate readers. Instead, link the feature to the readers' needs—and provide details to make the benefit vivid.

> Weak: We have placemats with riddles.
>
> Better: Answering all the riddles on Monical's special placemats will keep the kids happy till your pizza comes. If they don't have time to finish (and they may not, since your pizza will be ready so quickly), just take the riddles home—or answer them on your next visit.

Reader benefits improve both the attitudes and the behaviour of the people you work with and write to. They make people view you more positively; they make it easier for you to accomplish your goals.

Expectancy theory says most people try to do their best only when they believe they can succeed and when they want the rewards that success brings. Reader benefits tell or remind readers that they can do the job and that success will be rewarded.[14] Thus they help overcome two problems that reduce motivation: people may not think of all the possible benefits, and they may not understand the relationships among efforts, performance, and rewards.[15]

Writing or Speaking to Multiple Audiences with Different Needs

Many business and administrative messages go not to a single person but to a larger audience. When the members of your audience share the same interests and the same level of knowledge, you can use the principles outlined above for individual readers or for members of homogeneous groups. But often different members of the audience have different needs.

Rachel Spilka has shown that talking to readers both inside and outside the organization helped corporate engineers adapt their documents successfully. Talking to readers and reviewers helped writers involve readers in the planning process, understand the social and political relationships among readers, and negotiate conflicts orally rather than depending solely on the document. These writers were then able to think about content as well as about organization and style, appeal to common grounds (such as reducing waste or increasing productivity) that several readers shared, and reduce the number of revisions needed before documents were approved.[16]

When it is not possible to meet everyone's needs, meet the needs of gatekeepers and decision makers first.

Content and choice of details

■   Provide an overview or executive summary for readers who want just the main points.

- In the body of the document, provide enough detail for decision makers and for anyone else who could veto your proposal.
- If the decision makers don't need details that other audiences will want, provide those details in appendices—statistical tabulations, earlier reports, and so forth.

Organizing the document

- Use headings and a table of contents so readers can turn to the portions that interest them.
- Organize your message based on the decision makers' attitudes toward it.

Level of formality

- Avoid personal pronouns. *You* ceases to have a specific meaning when several different audiences use a document.
- If both internal and external audiences will use a document, use a slightly more formal style than you would in an internal document.
- Use a more formal style when you write to international audiences.

Use of technical terms and theory

- In the body of the document, assume the degree of knowledge that decision makers will have.
- Put background information and theory under separate headings. Then readers can use the headings and the table of contents to read or skip these sections, as their knowledge dictates.
- If decision makers will have more knowledge than other audiences, provide a glossary of terms (refer readers to glossary early in the document).

Goodwill

Goodwill smooths the challenges of business and administration. Companies have long been aware that treating customers well pays off in more sales and higher profits. Goodwill is important in internal as well as external documents. More and more organizations are realizing that treating employees well is financially wise as well as ethically sound. Nortel, MCI Communications, and Electronic Data Systems have also found that internal goodwill has a measurable effect on the bottom line.[17] Researcher Jim Collins found that the most financially successful companies put "people first, strategy second." Another study found that companies that "manage people right" outperformed other companies by 30% to 40%.[18]

You-attitude, positive emphasis, and bias-free language are three ways to help build goodwill. Writing that shows you-attitude speaks from the reader's point of view, not selfishly from the writer's. Positive emphasis means focusing on the positive rather than the negative aspects of a situation. Bias-free language is language that does not discriminate against people on the basis of sex, physical condition, race, age, or any other category. All three help you achieve your purposes and make your messages friendlier, more persuasive, more professional, and more humane. They suggest that you care not just about money but also about your readers and their needs and interests.

You-Attitude

You-attitude is a style of writing that looks at things from the reader's point of view, emphasizing what the reader wants to know, respecting the reader's intelligence, and protecting the reader's ego. To apply you-attitude, use the five techniques below. As we look at examples of these techniques, note that many of the you-attitude revisions are *longer* than the sentences lacking you-attitude. You-attitude sentences have *more* information, so they are often longer. They are not wordy, however. **Wordiness** means having more words than the meaning requires. We can add information and still keep the writing tight.

1. Talk about the Reader, Not about Yourself.

Readers want to know how they benefit or are affected. When you provide this information, you make your message more complete and more interesting.

Lacks you-attitude: I have negotiated an agreement with Apex Rent-a-Car that gives you a discount on rental cars.

You-attitude: As a Sunstrand employee, you can now get a 20% discount when you rent a car from Apex.

The first sentence focuses on what the writer does, not on what the reader receives. Any sentence that focuses on the writer's work or generosity lacks you-attitude, even if the sentence contains the word *you*. Instead of focusing on what we are giving the reader, focus on what the reader can now do.

Lacks you-attitude: We are shipping your order of September 21 this afternoon.

You-attitude: The two dozen Corning Ware starter sets you ordered will be shipped this afternoon and should reach you by September 28.

The reader is less interested in when we shipped the order than in when it will arrive. Note that the phrase "should reach you by" leaves room for variations in delivery schedules. Give the reader the name of the carrier, so the reader knows whom to contact if the order doesn't arrive promptly.

2. Refer to the Reader's Request or Order Specifically.

When you write about the reader's request, order, or policy, refer to it specifically, not as a generic *your order* or *your policy*. If your reader is an individual or a small business, it's friendly to specify the content of the order; if you're writing to a company with which you do a great deal of business, give the invoice or purchase order number.

Lacks you-attitude: Your order . . .

You-attitude
(to individual):   The desk chair you ordered . . .

You-attitude
(to a large store):   Your invoice #783329 . . .

3. Don't Talk about Feelings Except to Congratulate or Offer Sympathy.

In most business situations, your feelings are irrelevant and should be omitted.

Lacks you-attitude: We are happy to extend you a credit line of $5,000.

You-attitude: You can now charge up to $5,000 on your Visa card.

The reader doesn't care whether you're happy; the reader cares about the situation from his or her point of view.

It *is* appropriate to talk about your own emotions in a message of congratulations or condolence.

You-attitude: Congratulations on your promotion to district manager! I was really pleased to read about it.

In internal memos, it may be appropriate to comment that a project has been gratifying or frustrating. In the letter of transmittal that accompanies a report, it is permissible to talk about your feelings about doing the work. But even other readers in your own organization are primarily interested in their own concerns, not in your feelings.

Don't talk about the reader's feelings, either. It's distancing to have someone else tell us how we feel—especially if the writer is wrong.

Lacks you-attitude: You'll be happy to hear that Open Grip Walkway Channels meet OHS requirements.

You-attitude: Open Grip Walkway Channels meet OHS requirements.

When you have good news for the reader, simply give the good news.

Lacks you-attitude: You'll be happy to hear that your scholarship has been renewed.

You-attitude: Congratulations! Your scholarship has been renewed.

4. In Positive Situations, Use *you* More Often than *I*. Use *we* When it Includes the Reader.

Whenever possible, focus on the reader, not on you or your company.

Lacks you-attitude: We provide health insurance to all employees.

You-attitude: You receive health insurance as a full-time Procter & Gamble employee.

Most readers are tolerant of the word *I* in e-mail messages, which seem like conversation. Edit paper documents to use *I* rarely if at all. *I* suggests that you're concerned about personal issues, not about the organization's problems, needs, and opportunities. *We* works well when it includes the reader. Avoid *we* if it excludes the reader (as it would in a letter to a customer or supplier or as it might in a memo about what *we* in management want *you* to do).

5. In Negative Situations, Avoid the Word *you*. Use Passive Verbs and Impersonal Expressions to Avoid Assigning Blame.

When you report bad news, use a noun for a group of which the reader is a part instead of *you* so readers don't feel that they're singled out for bad news.

Lacks you-attitude: You must get approval from the director before you publish any articles or memoirs based on your work in the agency.

You-attitude: Agency personnel must get approval from the director to publish any articles or memoirs based on their work at the agency.

Use passive verbs and impersonal expressions to avoid blaming the reader. **Passive verbs** describe the action performed on something, without necessarily saying who did it. (See ➡ Chapter 4 for a full discussion of passive verbs.) **Impersonal expressions** omit people and talk only about things.

In most business writing, active verbs are better. But when your reader is at fault, passive verbs may be useful to avoid assigning blame.

Lacks you-attitude: You made no allowance for inflation in your estimate.

You-attitude (passive):   No allowance for inflation has been made in this estimate.

You-attitude (impersonal):   This estimate makes no allowance for inflation.

Though some might argue that an estimate, for example, is inanimate and can't "make" anything, in the pragmatic world of business writing, impersonal expressions often help you convey criticism tactfully.

You-Attitude with International Audiences

When U.S. businesses communicate with international audiences, they need to adjust their point of view.

The United States is in the middle of most of the maps sold in the United States. It isn't in the middle of maps sold elsewhere in the world.

The United States clings to a measurement system that has been abandoned by most of the world. When writing for international audiences, use the metric system.

Even pronouns and direction words need attention. *We* may not feel inclusive to readers with different assumptions and backgrounds. *Here* won't mean the same thing to a reader in Bonn as it does to one in Baie Comeau.

Good messages apply you-attitude beyond the sentence level by using content and organization as well as style to build goodwill.

To create goodwill with content,

- Be complete. When you have lots of information to give, consider putting some details in an appendix, which may be read later.
- Anticipate and answer questions the reader is likely to have.
- When you include information the reader didn't ask for, show why it is important.
- Show readers how the subject of your message affects them.

To organize information to build goodwill,

- Put information readers are most interested in first.
- Arrange information to meet your reader's needs, not yours.
- Use headings and lists so that the reader can find key points quickly.

Consider the letter in Figure 2.4. As the red marginal notes indicate, many individual sentences in this letter lack you-attitude. Fixing individual sentences could improve the letter. However, it really needs to be totally rewritten.

Figure 2.5 shows a possible revision of this letter. The revision is clearer, easier to read, and friendlier.

FIGURE 2.4   A Letter Lacking You-Attitude

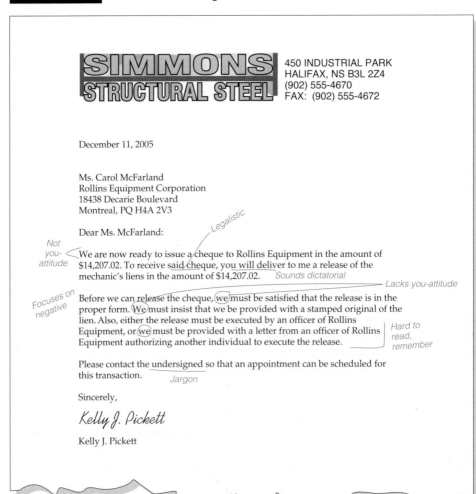

FIGURE 2.5 A Letter Revised to Improve You-Attitude

450 INDUSTRIAL PARK
HALIFAX, NS B3L 2Z4
(902) 555-4670
FAX: (902) 555-4672

December 11, 2005

Ms. Carol McFarland
Rollins Equipment Corporation
18438 Decarie Boulevard
Montreal, PQ H4A 2V3

Dear Ms. McFarland:

Starts with main point from the reader's point of view

Focuses on what reader gets

Let's clear up the lien in the Allen contract.

Rollins will receive a cheque for $14,207.02 when you give us a release for the mechanic's lien of $14,207.02. To assure us that the release is in the proper form,

1. Give us a stamped original of the lien indicating the document's district court number, and

2. Either
   a. Have an officer of Rollins Equipment sign the release
      or
   b. Give us a letter from a Rollins officer authorizing someone else to sign the release.

List makes it easy to see that reader needs to do two things—and that the second can be done in two ways.

Call me to tell me which way is best for you. *Emphasizes reader's choice*

Sincerely,

Kelly J. Pickett

Kelly J. Pickett   *Extension number makes*
Extension 5318   *it easy for reader to phone.*

Positive Emphasis

Some negatives are necessary. As Stephen Hlibok points out, when you have bad news to give the reader—announcements of layoffs, product defects and recalls, price increases—straightforward negatives build credibility. (See ➡ Chapter 6 on how to present bad news.) Sometimes negatives are needed to make people take a problem seriously. And sometimes negatives create a "reverse psychology" that makes people look favourably at your product. Rent-a-Wreck is thriving. (The cars really don't look so bad.)[19]

But in most situations, it's better to be positive. Annette N. Shelby and N. Lamar Reinsch, Jr., found that business people responded more positively to positive than to negative language and were more likely to say they would act on a positively worded request.[20] Martin Seligman's research for Met Life found that optimistic salespeople sold 37% more insurance than pessimistic colleagues. As a result, Met Life began hiring optimists even when they failed to meet the company's other criteria. These "unqualified" optimists outsold pessimists 21% in their first year and 57% in the next.[21]

Create positive emphasis by using the following five techniques.

1. Avoid Negative Words and Words with Negative Connotations.

Figure 2.6 lists some common negative words. If you find one of these words in a draft, try to substitute a more positive word. When you must use a negative, use the *least negative* term that will convey your meaning.

The following examples show how to replace negative words with positive words.

Negative: We have failed to finish taking inventory.

Better: We haven't finished taking inventory.

Still better: We will be finished taking inventory Friday.

Negative: If you can't understand this explanation, feel free to call me.

Better: If you have further questions, just call me.

Still better: Omit the sentence.

If a sentence has two negatives, substitute one positive term.

Negative: Never fail to back up your disks.

Better: Always back up your disks.

When you must use a negative term, use the least negative word that is accurate.

Negative: Your balance of $835 is delinquent.

Better: Your balance of $835 is past due.

Beware of **hidden negatives:** words that are not negative in themselves but become negative in context. *But* and *however* indicate a shift, so, after a positive statement, they are negative. Even positives may backfire if they suggest that in the past the service or product was bad.

FIGURE 2.6   Negative Words to Avoid

afraid	hesitate	trivial	**Some *mis*-words:**
anxious	ignorant	trouble	misfortune
avoid	ignore	wait	mistake
bad	impossible	weakness	missing
careless	injury	worry	
damage	lacking	wrong	**Many *un*- words:**
delay	loss		unclear
delinquent	neglect	**Some *dis*- words:**	unfair
deny	never	disapprove	unfortunate
difficulty	no	dishonest	unfortunately
eliminate	not	dissatisfied	unpleasant
error	objection		unreasonable
except	problem	**Many *in*- words:**	unreliable
fail	reject	inadequate	unsure
fault	sorry	incomplete	
fear	terrible	inconvenient	
		insincere	

Some stores might say, "Put books you don't want here." But Bookseller Joseph Best in Lexington, KY, uses positive emphasis.

Negative: I hope this is the information you wanted.
              [Implication: I'm not sure.]

Better: Enclosed is a brochure about road repairs scheduled for 2006–08.

Still better: The brochure contains a list of all roads and bridges scheduled for repair during 2006–08. Call Gwen Wong at 555-3245 for specific dates when work will start and stop, and for alternate routes.

Negative: Now Crispy Crunch tastes better.
              [Implication: it used to taste terrible.]

Better: Now Crispy Crunch tastes even better.

Removing negatives does not mean being arrogant or pushy.

Negative: I hope that you are satisfied enough to place future orders.

Arrogant: I look forward to receiving all of your future business.

Better: Call Mercury whenever you need computer chips.

When you eliminate negative words, be sure to maintain accuracy. Words that are exact opposites will usually not be accurate. Instead, use specifics to be both positive and accurate.

Negative: Customers under 60 are not eligible for the Prime Time discount.

Not true: You must be over 60 to be eligible for the Prime Time discount.

True: If you're 60 or older, you can save 10% on all your purchases with RightWay's Prime Time discount.

Legal phrases also have negative connotations for most readers and should be avoided whenever possible. The idea will sound more positive if you use normal English.

Side Effects? What Side Effects?*

The U.S. Food and Drug Administration (FDA) requires full-length ads recommending specific drugs for specific medical conditions to list major side effects. Some products attempt to get around the rule by preparing two short ads.

Claritin used the technique in magazine ads picturing celebrity Joan Lunden. A first small ad says in large type, "Joan Clears the Air About Seasonal Allergies." No product is mentioned. The second small ad reads, "Joan Lunden Asks: Curious about Claritin?" Neither ad mentions side effects.

The FDA declared the Claritin ads "misleading" and forced the company to stop using them. The FDA is exploring the issues in TV ads and may end up rewriting its rules.

But whether the rules change or not, it isn't ethical to omit negatives if customers need the information to make decisions.

*Based on Chris Adams, "Xenical Ads Avoid Listing Unpleasant Side Effects," *The Wall Street Journal*, April 3, 2001, B1, B6.

Negative:	If your account is still delinquent, a second legal notice will be sent to you informing you that cancellation of your policy will occur 30 days after the date of the legal notice if we do not receive your cheque.
Better:	Even if your cheque is lost in the mail and never reaches us, you still have a 30-day grace period. If you do get a second notice, you will know that your payment hasn't reached us. To keep your account in good standing, stop payment on the first cheque and send a second one.

2. Focus on What the Reader Can Do Rather than on Limitations.

Eliminate double negatives. When there are limits, or some options are closed, focus on the alternatives that remain.

Negative:	We will not allow you to charge more than $1,500 on your VISA account.
Better:	You can charge $1,500 on your new VISA card.
or:	Your new VISA card gives you $1,500 in credit that you can use at thousands of stores nationwide.

Check for you-attitude. In the last example, "We will allow you to charge $1,500" would be positive, but it lacks you-attitude.

When you have a benefit and a requirement the reader must meet to get the benefit, the sentence is usually more positive if you put the benefit first.

Negative:	You will not qualify for the student membership rate of $25 a year unless you are a full-time student.
Better:	You get all the benefits of membership for only $25 a year if you're a full-time student.

3. Justify Negative Information by Giving a Reason or Linking It to a Reader Benefit.

A reason can help your reader see that the information is necessary; a benefit can suggest that the negative aspect is outweighed by positive factors. Be careful, however, to make the logic clear and to leave no loopholes.

Negative:	We cannot sell computer disks in lots of less than 10.
Loophole:	To keep down packaging costs and to help you save on shipping and handling costs, we sell computer disks in lots of 10 or more.

Suppose the customer says, "I'll pay the extra shipping and handling. Send me seven." If you can't or won't sell in lots of less than 10, you need to write:

Better:	To keep down packaging costs and to help customers save on shipping and handling costs, we sell computer disks only in lots of 10 or more.

If you link the negative element to a benefit, be sure it is a benefit the reader will acknowledge. You may think you're doing customers a favour by limiting their credit so they don't get in over their heads and go bankrupt. They may think they'd be better off with more credit so they could expand in hopes of making more sales and more profits.

4. If the Negative is Truly Unimportant, Omit It.

Omit negatives only when

- The reader does not need the information to make a decision.
- You have already given the reader the information, and he or she has access to the previous communication.
- The information is trivial.

The following examples suggest the kind of negatives you can omit:

Negative: A one-year subscription to *PC Magazine* is $49.97. That rate is not as low as the rates charged for some magazines.

Better: A one-year subscription to *PC Magazine* is $49.97.

Still better: A one-year subscription to *PC Magazine* is $49.97. You save 43% off the newsstand price of $87.78.

5. Put the Negative Information in the Middle and Present It Compactly.

The beginning and end are always positions of emphasis. Use these positions for ideas you want to emphasize. Put negatives in the middle of a paragraph rather than in the first or last sentence and in the middle of the message rather than in the first or last paragraphs.

When a letter or memo runs several pages, remember that the bottom of the first page is also a position of emphasis, even if it is in the middle of a paragraph, because of the extra white space of the bottom margin. (The tops and bottoms of subsequent pages don't get this extra attention.) If possible, avoid placing negative information at the bottom of the first page.

Giving a topic lots of space emphasizes it. Therefore, you can de-emphasize negative information by giving it as little space as possible. Give negative information only once in your message. Don't list negatives vertically on the page since lists take space and emphasize material.

Tone, Power, and Politeness

Tone is the implied attitude of the writer toward the reader. If the words of a document seem condescending or rude, tone is a problem. Tone is tricky because it interacts with power: the words that might seem friendly from a superior to a subordinate may seem snobbish or impertinent if used by the subordinate to the superior. Norms for politeness are cultural and generational. Language that is acceptable within one group may be unacceptable if used by someone outside the group.

The desirable tone for business writing is businesslike but not stiff, friendly but not phony, confident but not arrogant, polite but not grovelling. The following guidelines will help you achieve the tone you want.

■ **Use courtesy titles for people outside your organization whom you don't know well.** Many Canadian organizations use first names for everyone, whatever their age or rank. But some people don't like being called by their first names by people they don't know or by someone much younger. When you talk or write to people outside your organization, use first names only if you've established a personal relationship. If you don't know someone well, use a courtesy title:

Dear Mr. Reynolds:

Dear Ms Lee:

■ **Be aware of the power implications of the words you use.** "Thank you for your co-operation" is generous coming from a superior to a subordinate; it's not appropriate in a message to your superior.

Different ways of asking for action carry different levels of politeness.[22]

Order: Turn in your time card by Monday.
(lowest politeness)

Polite order: Please turn in your time card by Monday.
(mid-level politeness)

A Soft Answer Turneth Away Lawsuits*

Lawyers usually tell individuals and companies not to admit liability lest the admission become evidence in a lawsuit for damages. Maybe that's good advice in major crises where the CEO has a responsibility to stockholders to reduce the company's legal liability.

But one soft drink company found that sincere apologies satisfied people, so they didn't sue.

The company had a spate of complaints about exploding bottles. But instead of giving people a form to fill out and saying, "Contact our risk department," service representatives were told to empathize and apologize.

The company's liability expenses went down $2 million in a year.

*Based on Cynthia Crossen, "The Simple Apology after Poor Service Is in Very Sorry State," *The Wall Street Journal*, November 29, 1990, B8; and Lisa Tyler, "Liability Means Never Being Able to Say You're Sorry: Corporate Guilt, Legal Constraints, and Defensiveness in Corporate Communication," *Management Communication Quarterly* 11, no. 1 (August 1997): 51–73.

R-E-S-P-E-C-T*

Most major airlines and hotel chains provide disability training to employees. . . . I recognize when someone has been trained—to offer me a Braille menu, use my name when addressing me, or take a moment to orient me to a new environment. What I appreciate even more, though, is . . . simple, common courtesy.

I don't care how many pages in an employee manual somewhere are devoted to . . . the dos and don'ts of interacting with someone who is deaf, blind, or mentally retarded. . . .

Ask me where I'd like to sit, whether I need help getting there, and what other kinds of help I need.

Please, assume that I know more about my disability than anyone else ever could. . . .

Too many companies, it seems to me, are busy shaking in their boots over the imagined high cost of accommodating people with disabilities when, in many instances, a good old-fashioned refresher course in manners would cover most bases.

*Quoted from Deborah Kendrick, "Disabled Resent Being Patronized," *Columbus Dispatch*, July 21, 1996, 3B.

| Indirect request:
(higher politeness) | Time cards should be turned in by Monday. |
| Question:
(highest politeness) | Would you be able to turn in your time card by Monday? |

You need more politeness if you're asking for something that will inconvenience the reader and help you more than the person who does the action. Generally, you need less politeness when you're asking for something small, routine, or to the reader's benefit. Some discourse communities, however, prefer that even small requests be made politely.

| Lower politeness: | To start the scheduling process, please describe your availability for meetings during the second week of the month. |
| Higher politeness: | Could you let me know what times you'd be free for a meeting the second week of the month? |

Generally, requests sound friendliest when they use conversational language.

| Poor tone: | Return the draft with any changes by next Tuesday. |
| Better tone: | Let me know by Tuesday whether you'd like any changes in the draft. |

■ **When you must give bad news, consider hedging your statement.** Auditors' suggestion letters rarely say directly that firms are using unacceptable accounting practices. Instead, they use three strategies to be more diplomatic: specifying the time ("currently, the records are quite informal"), limiting statements ("it appears," "it seems"), and using impersonal statements that do not specify who caused a problem or who will perform an action.[23]

Reducing Bias in Business Communication

Everything we do in good business communication attempts to build goodwill. Bias-free language and bias-free visuals help sustain the goodwill we work so hard to create.

Bias-free language is language that does not discriminate against people on the basis of gender, abilities, race, age, or any other category. It includes all readers, helps to sustain goodwill, is fair and friendly, and complies with the law. Since the 1980s in Canada, bias-free language has been at the heart of policies promoting multiculturalism (Canadian Multiculturalism Act, 1988), advancing human rights, reducing barriers to the participation in the workforce of equity groups, advancing their participation in the public service, and extending access of information and access to programs and services for all Canadians. With similar goals in mind, provinces, universities and colleges, non-governmental organizations, and businesses have developed bias-free language policies and guidelines.

Check to be sure that your language is non-sexist, non-racist, and non-agist. When you talk about people with disabilities or diseases, talk about the people, not the condition. When you produce newsletters or other documents with photos and illustrations, choose a sampling of the whole population, not just part of it.

Making Language Non-Sexist

Non-sexist language treats both sexes neutrally. Check to be sure that your writing is free from sexism in four areas: words and phrases, job titles, courtesy titles, and pronouns.

If you find any of the terms in the first column in Figure 2.7 in your writing or your company's documents, replace them with terms from the second column.

FIGURE 2.7 Getting Rid of Sexist Terms and Phrases

Instead of	Use	Because
The girl at the front desk	The woman's name or job title: "Ms. Browning," "Rosa," "the receptionist"	Call female employees *women* just as you call male employees *men*. When you talk about a specific woman, use her name, just as you use a man's name to talk about a specific man.
The ladies on our staff	The women on our staff	Use parallel terms for males and females. Therefore, use *ladies* only if you refer to the males on your staff as *gentlemen*. Few businesses do, since social distinctions are rarely at issue.

Manpower
  Manhours
  Manning
	Personnel
	  Hours or worker hours
	  Staffing
		The power in business today comes from both women and men. If you have to write to Manpower, you are stuck with the term. When you talk about other organizations, however, use non-sexist alternatives.

Managers and their wives	Managers and their guests	Managers may be female; not everyone is married.

Not every word containing *man* is sexist. For example, *manager* is not sexist. The word comes from the Latin *manus* meaning *hand;* it has nothing to do with maleness.

Avoid terms that assume that everyone is married or is heterosexual.

Biased: You and your husband or wife are cordially invited to the dinner.

Better: You and your guest are cordially invited to the dinner.

Use neutral titles that do not imply that a job is held only by men or only by women. Many job titles are already neutral: accountant, banker, doctor, engineer, inspector, manager, nurse, pilot, secretary, technician, to name a few. Other titles reflect gender stereotypes and need to be changed.

Instead of	Use
Businessman	A specific title: executive, accountant, department head, business person
Chairman	Chair, chairperson, moderator
Foreman	Supervisor
Salesman	Salesperson, sales representative
Waitress	Server
Woman lawyer	Lawyer
Workman	Worker, employee. Or use a specific title: crane operator

Memos normally use first and last names without courtesy titles. Letters, however, require courtesy titles in the salutation unless you're on a first-name basis with your reader. (See ➡ Chapter 5 for examples of memo and letter formats.)

■ When you know your reader's name and gender, use courtesy titles that do not indicate marital status: *Mr.* for men and *Ms.* for women. There are, however, two exceptions:

  1. If the woman has a professional title, use that title if you would use it for a man.

Dr. Kristen Sorenson is our new company physician.
The Rev. Elizabeth Townsley gave the invocation.

2. If the woman prefers to be addressed as *Mrs.* or *Miss,* use the title she prefers rather than *Ms.* (You-attitude takes precedence over non-sexist language: address the reader as she—or he—prefers to be addressed.) To find out if a woman prefers a traditional title,

    a. Check the signature block in previous correspondence. Use the title she designates.

    b. Notice the title a woman uses in introducing herself on the phone. If she says, "This is Robin Stine," use *Ms.* when you write to her. If she says, "I'm Mrs. Stine," use the title she specifies.

    c. Check your company directory. In some organizations, women who prefer traditional titles can list them with their names.

    d. When you're writing job letters or crucial correspondence, call the company and ask the receptionist which title your reader prefers.

Ms is particularly useful when you do not know a woman's marital status.

In addition to using parallel courtesy titles, use parallel forms for names.

Not Parallel	Parallel
Members of the committee will be Mr. Jones, Mr. Yacone, and Lisa.	Members of the committee will be Mr. Jones, Mr. Yacone, and Ms. Melton.
	or
	Members of the committee will be Irving, Ted, and Lisa.

- When you know your reader's name but not the gender, either
  1. Call the company and ask the receptionist, or
  2. Use the reader's full name in the salutation:
      Dear Chris Crowell:
      Dear J. C. Meath:
- When you know neither the reader's name nor gender, you have three options:
  1. Use a letter format that omits the salutation. The AMS Simplified letter format (see ➡ Chapter 5) includes the inside address and uses a subject line but omits the salutation and complimentary close.
      SUBJECT: RECOMMENDATION FOR BEN WANDELL
  2. Use the reader's position or job title:
      Dear Loan Officer:
      Dear Registrar:
  3. Use a general group to which your reader belongs:
      Dear Investor:
      Dear Admissions Committee:

Terms that are meant to be positive (Dear Careful Shopper: or Dear Concerned Citizen:) may backfire if readers see them as manipulative flattery.

Although many people claim to dislike Dear Friend: as a salutation in a form letter, research shows that letters using it bring in a higher response than letters with no salutation.

Pronouns

When you write about a specific person, use the appropriate gender pronouns:

In his speech, John Jones said that . . .

In her speech, Judy Jones said that . . .

When you are writing not about a specific person but about anyone who may be in a given job or position, traditional gender pronouns are sexist.

Sexist: a. Each supervisor must certify that the time sheet for his department is correct.

Sexist: b. When the nurse fills out the accident report form, she should send one copy to the Central Division Office.

There are four ways to eliminate sexist generic pronouns: use plurals, use second-person *you*, revise the sentence to omit the pronoun, or use pronoun pairs.

1. Use plural nouns and pronouns.

    Non-sexist: a. Supervisors must certify that the time sheets for their departments are correct.

    Note: When you use plural nouns and pronouns, other words in the sentence may need to be made plural too (*time sheets* and *departments* here). Avoid mixing singular nouns and plural pronouns.

    Non-sexist but lacks agreement: a. Each supervisor must certify that the time sheet for their department is correct.

    The lack of agreement between singular *supervisor* and plural *their* is acceptable orally but is not yet acceptable to many readers in writing.

2. Use *you*.

    Non-sexist: a. You must certify that the time sheet for your department is correct.

    Non-sexist: b. When you fill out an accident report form, send one copy to the Central Division Office.

    You is particularly good for instructions and statements of the responsibilities of someone in a given position. Using *you* may shorten sentences and make your writing more direct.

3. Substitute an article (*a, an,* or *the*) for the pronoun, or revise the sentence so that the pronoun is unnecessary.

    Non-sexist: a. The supervisor must certify that the time sheet for the department is correct.

    Non-sexist: b. The nurse will
       1. Fill out the accident report form.
       2. Send one copy of the form to the Central Division Office.

4. When you must focus on the action of an individual, use pronoun pairs.

    Non-sexist: a. The supervisor must certify that the time sheet for his or her department is correct.

    Non-sexist: b. When the nurse fills out the accident report form, she or he should send one copy to the Central Division Office.

Making Language Non-Racist and Non-Agist

Language is **non-racist** and **non-agist** when it treats all races and ages fairly, avoiding negative stereotypes of any group. Use these guidelines to check for bias in documents you write or edit:

- **Give someone's race or age only if it is relevant to your story.** When you do mention these characteristics, give them for everyone in your story—not just the non-Caucasian, non-young-to-middle-aged adults you mention.

- **Refer to a group by the term it prefers. As preferences change, change your usage.** The naming of Aboriginal peoples in Canada has undergone significant change since the 1970s and 1980s as many First Nations discard the names assigned to them by Europeans and assert their own right to determine their identities—and to use their own languages and spelling systems. Thus, *Anishnabe* is preferred to *Ojibwa(y)*, *Mi'kmaq* to *Micmac*, for instance.

The Government of Canada Terminology and Language Standardization Board (Public Works) recommended that *Aboriginal* and *Native* (and *Indigenous* for international groups) be capitalized in line with other ethnic, geographic, and linguistic designations: *Asian, Hispanic, Nordic*. *Aboriginal* was to be used as an adjective (as in *Aboriginal peoples*) and not *Aboriginals*.

Similarly, it is important not to talk about *Canada's Aboriginal peoples* or *Aboriginal Canadians*, but to respect *Aboriginal peoples* in Canada. *First Nations* is preferred to *Status Indians*; *First Peoples* includes Indians of all statuses.[24]

Fifty years ago, *Negro* was preferred as a more dignified term than *colored* for African Americans. As times changed, *Black* and *African American* replaced it. Surveys in the mid-1990s showed that almost half of blacks aged 40 and older preferred *Black*, but those 18 to 39 preferred *African American*.[25]

Oriental has now been replaced by *Asian*.

Older people and *mature customers* are more generally accepted terms than *senior citizens* or *golden agers*.

■ **Avoid terms that suggest that competent people are unusual.** The statement "She is an intelligent black woman" suggests that the writer expects most black women to be stupid. "He is an asset to his race" suggests that excellence in the race is rare. "He is a spry 70-year-old" suggests that the writer is amazed that anyone that old can still move.

Talking about People with Disabilities and Diseases

A disability is a physical, mental, sensory, or emotional impairment that interferes with the major tasks of daily living. According to a 2001 Canadian survey of the ten provinces (but excluding those living in institutions, in the territories

Technology helps blind people contribute fully as members of the workforce. This Braille keyboard allows a computer engineer to key in commands and data. Computer programs such as JAWS can read computer screens out loud.

or on First Nations reserves), 12.4% of Canadians (or 3.6 million) currently have a disability; the number of people with disabilities will rise as the population ages. Almost one-third of Aboriginal peoples report a disability.[26]

■ *People-first language* **focuses on the person, not the condition. People-first language** names the person first, then adds the condition.

Instead of	Use	Because
The mentally retarded	People with mental retardation	The condition does not define the person or his or her potential.
Cancer patients	People being treated for cancer	

■ **Avoid negative terms, unless the audience prefers them.** You-attitude takes precedence over positive emphasis: use the term a group prefers. People who lost their hearing as infants, children, or young adults often prefer to be called *deaf*, or *Deaf* in recognition of Deafness as a culture. But people who lose their hearing as older adults often prefer to be called *hard of hearing*.

Just as people in a single ethnic group may prefer different labels based on generational or cultural divides, so differences exist within the disability community.

Using the right term requires keeping up with changing preferences. If your target audience is smaller than the whole group, use the term preferred by that audience, even if the group as a whole prefers another term.

Some negative terms, however, are never appropriate. Negative terms such as *afflicted, suffering from,* and *struck down* also suggest an outdated view of any illness as a sign of divine punishment.

Instead of	Use	Because
Confined to a wheelchair	Uses a wheelchair	Wheelchairs enable people to escape confinement.
AIDS victim	Person with AIDS	Someone can have a disease without being victimized by it.
Abnormal	Atypical	People with disabilities are atypical but not necessarily abnormal.

Choosing Bias-Free Photos and Illustrations

When you produce a document, check the visuals for possible bias. Do they show people of both sexes and various ages and races? People using wheelchairs? It's OK to have individual pictures that have just one gender or one race. But the general impression should suggest that diversity is desirable and normal.

Check relationships and authority figures as well as numbers. If all the men appear in business suits and the women in servers' uniforms, the pictures are sexist. If the only First Nations or Métis people pictured are in similarly subordinate roles, the photos support racism even when an equal number of people from each race are shown.

In 1997, as Marilyn Dyrud has shown, only 22% of the images of humans in clip art files were women, and most of those showed women in traditional roles. An even smaller percentage pictured members of minority groups.[27] Don't use biased clip art or stock photos: create your own bias-free illustrations.

Positive Emphasis Is Good for Your Health*

According to a 30-year study by the Mayo Clinic, optimists live almost 20% longer than pessimists. Optimists are better at coping with stress and have more disease-fighting T-cells.

Experts believe we can learn to be optimistic. If you tend to be pessimistic,

■ Set realistic goals so that you can succeed.

■ Look for lessons. When you learn something from a bad experience, you can change the way you respond in the future.

■ Look for silver linings.

■ Think happy thoughts. When something minor goes wrong, focus on a good memory.

■ Smile. Smiling—even when you don't initially feel happy—can improve your mood.

*Based on Donald D. Hensrud, "How to Live Longer (and Love It)," *Fortune*, April 30, 2001, 210; and Judith Newman, "Sailing Through the Blues," *Reader's Digest*, January 2001, 145–148.

Summary of Key Points

- The **primary audience** will make a decision or act on the basis of your message. The **secondary audience** may be asked by the primary audience to comment on your message or to implement your ideas after they've been approved. The **initial audience** routes the message to other audiences and may assign the message. A **gatekeeper** controls whether the message gets to the primary audience. A **watchdog audience** has political, social, or economic power and may base future actions on its evaluation of your message.

- Empathy is crucial to good audience analysis.

- The following questions provide a framework for audience analysis:
    1. What will the audience's initial reaction be to the message?
    2. How much information does the audience need?
    3. What obstacles must you overcome?
    4. What positive aspects can you emphasize?
    5. What are the audience's expectations about the appropriate language, structure, and format for messages?
    6. How will the audience use the document?

- **Reader benefits** are benefits or advantages that the reader gets by using the writer's services, buying the writer's products, following the writer's policies, or adopting the writer's ideas.

- Good reader benefits are adapted to the audience, based on **intrinsic** rather than **extrinsic motivators,** supported by clear logic and explained in adequate detail, and phrased in you-attitude. Extrinsic benefits reduce the satisfaction in doing something for its own sake.

- To create reader benefits,
    1. Identify the feelings, fears, and needs that may motivate your reader.
    2. Identify the features of your product or policy that could meet the needs you've identified.
    3. Show how the reader can meet his or her needs with the features of the policy or product.

- When you write to multiple audiences, use the primary audience to determine level of detail, organization, level of formality, and use of technical terms and theory.

- **You-attitude** is a style of writing that looks at things from the reader's point of view, emphasizing what the reader wants to know, respecting the reader's intelligence, and protecting the reader's ego.
    1. Talk about the reader, not about yourself.
    2. Refer to the reader's request or order specifically.
    3. Don't talk about feelings except to congratulate or offer sympathy.
    4. In positive situations, use *you* more often than *I*. Use *we* when it includes the reader.
    5. In negative situations, avoid the word *you*. Use passive verbs and impersonal expressions to avoid assigning blame.

- Apply you-attitude beyond the sentence level by using organization and content as well as style to build goodwill.

- **Positive emphasis** means focusing on the positive rather than the negative aspects of a situation.
    1. Avoid negative words and words with negative connotations.
    2. Focus on what the reader can do rather than on limitations.
    3. Justify negative information by giving a reason or linking it to a reader benefit.

4. If the negative is truly unimportant, omit it.

5. Put the negative information in the middle and present it compactly.

■ The desirable tone for business writing is businesslike but not stiff, friendly but not phony, confident but not arrogant, polite but not grovelling. The following guidelines will help you achieve the tone you want:

  ■ Use courtesy titles for people outside your organization whom you don't know well.

  ■ Be aware of the power implications of the words you use.

  ■ When you must give bad news, consider hedging your statement.

  ■ Writing should be free from sexism in four areas: words and phrases, job titles, courtesy titles, and pronouns.

  ■ Bias-free language is fair and friendly; it complies with the law. It includes all readers; it helps to sustain goodwill.

  ■ Check to be sure that your language is non-sexist, non-racist, and non-agist. When you talk about people with disabilities or diseases, use the term they prefer. When you produce newsletters or other documents with photos and illustrations, picture a sampling of the whole population, not just part of it.

CHAPTER 2 # Exercises and Problems

Getting Started

2.1 Identifying Audiences

In each of the following situations, label the audiences as initial, gatekeeper, primary, secondary, or watchdog:

1. Russell is seeking venture capital so that he can expand his business of offering soccer camps to youngsters. He's met an investment banker whose clients regularly hear presentations from business people seeking capital. The investment banker decides who will get a slot on the program, based on a comprehensive audit of each company's records and business plan.

2. Maria has created a Web page for her travel agency. She hopes to sell tickets for both leisure and business travel.

3. Paul works for the mayor's office in a big city. As part of a citywide cost-cutting measure, a blue-ribbon panel has recommended requiring employees who work more than 40 hours in a week to take compensatory time off rather than being paid overtime. The only exceptions will be the police and fire departments. The mayor asks Paul to prepare a proposal for the city council, which will vote on whether to implement the change. Before they vote, council members will hear from (1) citizens, who will have an opportunity to read the proposal and communicate their opinions to the city council; (2) mayors' offices in other cities, who may be asked about their experiences; (3) union representatives, who may be concerned about the reduction in income that will occur if the proposal is implemented; (4) department heads, whose ability to schedule work might be limited if the proposal passes; and (5) the blue-ribbon panel and good-government lobbying groups. Council members come up for re-election in six months.

2.2 Identifying and Developing Reader Benefits

Listed here are several things an organization might like its employees to do:

1. Use less paper.

2. Attend a brown-bag lunch to discuss ways to improve products or services.

3. Become more physically fit.

4. Volunteer for community organizations.

5. Ease a new hire's transition into the unit.

As Your Professor Directs,

a. Identify the motives or needs that might be met by each of the activities.

b. Take each need or motive and develop it as a reader benefit in a ~~full paragraph~~ sentence. Use additional paragraphs for the other needs met by the activity. Remember to use you-attitude!

2.3   Sending a Question to a Web Site

Send a question or other message that calls for a response to a Web site. You could

- Ask a question about a product.
- Apply for an internship or a job (assuming you'd really like to work there).
- Ask for information about an internship or a job.
- Ask a question about an organization or a candidate before you donate money or volunteer.
- Offer to volunteer for an organization or a candidate. You can offer to do something small and one-time (e.g., spend an afternoon stuffing envelopes, put up a yard sign), or you can, if you want to, offer to do something more time consuming or even ongoing.

Pick a specific organization you might use and answer the following questions about it:

1. Does the organization ask for questions or offers? Or will yours come out of the blue?
2. How difficult will it be for the organization to supply the information you're asking for or to do what you're asking it to do? If you're applying for an internship or offering to volunteer, what skills can you offer? How much competition do you have?
3. What can you do to build your own credibility so that the organization takes your question or request seriously?

2.4   Persuading Students to Use Credit Cards Responsibly

Many college and university students carry high balances on credit cards, in addition to student and car loans. You want to remind students on your campus to use credit cards responsibly.

Answer the following questions about students on your campus:

1. What socio-economic groups do students on your campus come from?
2. Do students on your campus frequently receive credit card solicitations in the mail? Do groups set up tables or booths inviting students to apply for credit cards?
3. What resources exist on campus or in town for people who need emergency funds? For people who are overextended financially?
4. What channel will best reach students on your campus?
5. What tone will work best to reach the students who are overextended and really need to read the document?

2.5   Evaluating the Ethics of Positive Emphasis

The first term in each line below is negative; the second is a positive term that is sometimes substituted for it. Which of the positive terms seem ethical? Which seem unethical? Briefly explain your choices.

junk bonds	high-yield bonds
second mortgage	home equity loan

tax	user fee
nervousness	adrenaline
problem	challenge
price increase	price change

2.6   Improving You-Attitude and Positive Emphasis

Revise these sentences to improve you-attitude and positive emphasis. Eliminate any awkward phrasing. In some cases, you may need to add information to revise the sentence effectively.

1. We cannot provide vegetarian meals unless you let us know at least three days in advance.
2. We are pleased to provide free e-mail accounts to students.
3. You'll be happy to know that we have installed an ATM for your convenience.
4. We're swamped. We won't be able to get your order out to you until Friday morning.
5. If the above information is unclear, or if further information on this or any other topic is necessary, please do not hesitate to contact me.
6. I have been using e-mail both in my internship and in classes. I realize that almost everyone now does have experience with e-mail, but at least I won't be behind.
7. I am anxious to discuss this problem with you.
8. Medical certification can delay shutoff of electrical service for non-payment of bills. If someone in your home needs electricity to assure health and well-being, signing up for our medical certification will delay disconnection for 30 days.

9. I had a difficult time evaluating the Web page. The sheer size of the site made it difficult to browse. After considerable time, I decided that, although it is huge, the site is thorough and well designed.

10. We cannot process your request for a reservation because some information is missing.

2.7   Eliminating Biased Language

Explain the source of bias in each of the following, and revise to remove the bias.

1. We recommend hiring Jim Ryan and Elizabeth Shuman. Both were very successful summer interns. Jim drafted the report on using rap music in ads, and Elizabeth really improved the looks of the office.

2. All sales associates and their wives are invited to the picnic.

3. Although he is blind, Mr. Morin is an excellent group leader.

4. Unlike many blacks, Yvonne has extensive experience designing Web pages.

5. Chris Renker
   Pacific Perspectives
   Centennial Square
   Victoria, BC
   Gentlemen:

6. Serge Dagenais has very good people skills for a man.

7. *Parenting 2000* shows you how to persuade your husband to do his share of child care chores.

8. Mr. Paez, Mr. O'Connor, and Tonya will represent our office at the convention.

9. Sue Corcoran celebrates her 50th birthday today. Stop by her cubicle at noon to get a piece of cake and to help us sing "The Old Grey Mare Just Ain't What She Used to Be."

10. Because older customers tend to be really picky, we will need to give a lot of details in our ads.

E-Mail Messages

2.8   Responding to a Complaint

You're Director of Corporate Communications; the employee newsletter is produced by your office. Today you get this e-mail message from Caroline Huber:

> Subject: Complaint about Sexist Language
>
> The article about the "Help Desk" says that Martina Luna and I "are the key customer service representatives 'manning' the desk." I don't MAN anything! I WORK.

Respond to Caroline. And send a message to your staff, reminding them to edit newsletter stories as well as external documents to replace biased language.

Communicating at Work

2.9   Evaluating You-Attitude and Positive Emphasis in Documents That Cross Your Desk

Identify three sentences from items that cross your desk that use (or should use) you-attitude and positive emphasis. If the sentences are good, write them down or attach a copy of the document(s) marking the sentence(s) in the margin. If the sentences need work, provide both the original sentence and a possible revision.

As Your Professor Directs,

a. Turn in the sentences and revisions.

b. Share the sentences and revisions with the class in a brief oral presentation.

c. Discuss the sentences and revisions with a group of students. What patterns do you see?

Letter and Memo Assignments

2.10   Analyzing an Organization's Culture

Interview several people about the culture of their organization. Possible organizations include

- Businesses, government agencies, and non-profit organizations.
- Sports teams.
- Departments in a community college, college, or university.

To learn about the corporate culture, use your own experiences, interviews with employees, published sources, or the Web. Interview questions include the following:

- Tell me about someone in this organization you admire. Why is he or she successful?
- Tell me about someone who failed in this organization. What did he or she do wrong?
- What ceremonies and rituals does this organization have? Why are they important?
- Why would someone join this group rather than a competitor?

To research corporate culture on the Web, check

- The company's site (usually under "about XYZ" or "working at XYZ"). In addition to explicit descriptions of corporate culture, check the mission

and values statements and pages about employee benefits and regulations.

- Independent sites, especially job sites. Some job sites give information about corporate cultures. Some post company recruiting videos. (What kind of employees does the company seem to be looking for?)
- Opposition sites put up by unhappy employees and customers. To find these in a search engine, type in the company name and "opinion."
- Articles published about the company on www.inc.com, www.fastcompany.com, www.businessweek.com, www.wsj.com, or other business Web sites.

As Your Professor Directs,

a. Share your results orally with a small group of students.

b. Present your results orally to the class.

c. Present your results in a memo to your professor.

d. Share your results with a small group of students and write a joint memo reporting the similarities and differences you found.

2.11   Evaluating Bias in Visuals

Evaluate the portrayals of people in one of the following:

- Ads in one issue of a business magazine
- A company's annual report
- A company's Web page.

Do the visuals show people of both genders and all races? Is there a sprinkling of people of various ages and physical conditions? What do the visuals suggest about who has power?

2.12   Revising a Form Letter

You've taken a part-time job at a store that sells fine jewellery. In orientation, the manager tells you that the store photographs jewellery it sells or appraises and mails the photo as a goodwill gesture after the transaction. However, when you see the form letter, you know that it doesn't build much goodwill—and you say so. The manager says, "Well, you're in university. Suppose you rewrite it."

Rewrite the letter. Use square brackets for material (like the customer's name) that would have to be inserted in the form letter to vary it for a specific customer. Add information that would help build goodwill.

Dear Customer:

We are most happy to enclose a photo of the jewellery that we recently sold you or appraised for you. We feel that this added service, which we are happy to extend to our fine customers, will be useful should you wish to insure your jewellery or need to identify it should you have the misfortune of suffering a loss.

We trust you will enjoy this additional service. We thank you for the confidence you have shown by coming to our store.

Sincerely,
Your Sales Associate

3 Planning, Composing, and Revising

- The Ways Good Writers Write
- Activities in the Composing Process
- Using Your Time Effectively
- Brainstorming, Planning, and Organizing Business Documents

- Revising, Editing, and Proofreading
- Getting and Using Feedback
- Summary of Key Points

AN INSIDE PERSPECTIVE

Planning, Composing, and Revising

Auditing financial statements is one part of an auditor's responsibility. The task of communicating findings—timely, relevant, clear, concise, and factual—is an onerous one in an environment of public skepticism after Enron and the reduction of the Big Five accounting firms to the Big Four. Public trust and professional integrity are at stake.

Planning is critical and typically takes one-third of the writing time. Analyzing the purpose—informative, persuasive, and so on—and audience before beginning to write is the basis of writing success.

Thinking about audience means considering what information is needed, when and where, so that the audience can easily follow the document and make good use of its contents. When you have multiple audiences (including the media and general public), you face added challenges in finding the language and organization that will satisfy needs.

An outline or overview at the beginning of report or proposal writing helps identify the messages, the parts, and the headings that will orient and guide readers. Developing an overview is as helpful to writers as to readers, simplifying the choices writers have to make and saving valuable time.

Traditional images of number-crunching accountants are being challenged both by ad campaigns to attract and retain new talent to the profession and by new accountants across Canada, who are as concerned with the accuracy of their reports as with the currency of their image. Jean Desrochers, Mélanie Kamel, Emmanuel Dubourg, and Eve Gamache, four chartered accountants, are featured in the ad of the Ordre des comptables agréés du Québec promoting "the Best Education, the Widest Choice of Careers, and an Average Annual Salary of $105,000."

Even the best of planning does not eliminate revising and editing: inviting feedback, checking usability, pruning wordiness, eliminating vagueness, and ensuring fluency and accuracy. Now you are ready for the final check of spellings and names, facts and figures—and the next stage in communicating your findings. Even carefully planned and written audit reports, for instance, need further explaining so that their multiple audiences can make best use of them.

Skilled performances look easy and effortless. In reality, as every dancer, musician, and athlete knows, they're the products of hard work, hours of practice, attention to detail, and intense concentration. Like skilled performances in other arts, writing rests on a base of work.

The Ways Good Writers Write

No single writing process works for all writers all of the time. However, good writers and poor writers seem to use different processes.[1] Good writers are more likely to

- Realize that the first draft will not be perfect.
- Write regularly.
- Break big jobs into small chunks.
- Have clear goals focusing on purpose and audience.
- Have several different strategies to choose from.
- Use rules flexibly.
- Wait to edit until after the draft is complete.

Research shows that experts differ from novices in identifying and analyzing the initial problem more effectively, understanding the task more broadly and deeply, drawing from a wider repertoire of strategies, and seeing patterns more clearly. Experts actually composed more slowly than novices, perhaps because they rarely settled for work that was just "OK." Finally, experts were better at evaluating their own work.[2]

Thinking about the writing process and consciously adopting "expert" processes will help you become a more expert writer.

Activities in the Composing Process

Most researchers would agree that writing processes can include eight activities: planning, gathering, writing, evaluating, getting feedback, revising, editing, and proofreading. The activities do not have to come in this order. Not every writing task demands all eight.

Planning includes all the thinking you do. It includes such activities as analyzing the problem, defining your purposes, and analyzing the audience (◄ Chapter 2); thinking of ideas; and choosing a pattern of organization or making an outline. Planning includes not only devising strategies for the document as a whole but also generating "mini-plans" that govern sentences or paragraphs.

Gathering includes physically getting the data you need. It can mean simply getting a copy of the letter you're responding to; it can also mean conducting informal and formal research—everything from getting a computer printout or checking something on the Web to administering a questionnaire or conducting a focus group (► Chapter 11).

Writing is the act of putting words on paper or on a screen, or of dictating words to a machine or a secretary. Writing can take the form of lists, fragmentary notes, stream-of-consciousness writing, or formal drafts.

Evaluating means rereading your work and measuring it against your goals and the requirements of the situation and audience. The best evaluation results from *re-seeing* your draft as if someone else had written it. Will your audience understand it? Is it complete? Convincing? Friendly?

You can evaluate *every* activity in the process, not just your draft. Is your view of purposes adequate? Do you have enough information to write? Are your sources believable? Do your revisions go far enough?

Getting feedback means asking someone else to evaluate your work. Again, you could get feedback on every activity, not just your draft. Is your pattern of organization appropriate? Does a revision solve an earlier problem? Are there any typos in the final copy?

Revising means making changes in the draft suggested by your own evaluation or by feedback from someone else: adding, deleting, substituting, or rearranging. Revision can be changes in single words, but more often it means major additions, deletions, or substitutions as the writer measures (evaluates) the draft against purpose and audience, and reshapes the document to make it more effective.

Editing means checking the draft to see that it satisfies the requirements of standard English and the principles of business writing. Here you'd correct spelling and mechanical errors, and check word choice and format. Unlike revision, which can produce major changes in meaning, editing focuses on the local aspects of writing.

Proofreading means checking the final copy to see that it's free from typographical errors.

Note the following points about these eight activities:

- **The activities do not have to come in this order.** Some people may gather data *after* writing a draft when they see that they need more specifics to achieve their purposes.

- **You do not have to finish one activity to start another.** Some writers plan a short section and write it, plan the next short section and write it, and so on through the document. Evaluating what is already written may cause a writer to do more planning or to change the original plan.

- **Most writers do not use all eight activities for all the documents they write.** You'll use more activities when you write a certain kind of document, about a subject or to an audience that's new to you.

Research about what writers really do has destroyed some of the stereotypes we used to have about the writing process. Consider planning. Traditional advice stressed the importance of planning and sometimes advised writers to make formal outlines for everything they wrote. But we know now that not all good documents are based on outlines.[3] A study on writer's block found that some ineffective writers spent so much time planning that they left too little time to write the assignment.[4] "Plan!" is too simplistic to be helpful. Instead, we need to talk about how much and what kind of planning for what kind of document.

Using Your Time Effectively

To get the best results from the time you have, spend only one-third of your time actually "writing." Spend at least another one-third of your time analyzing the situation and your audience, gathering information, and organizing what you have to say. Spend the final third evaluating what you've said, revising the draft(s) to meet your purposes and the needs of the audience and the organization, editing a late draft to remove any errors in grammar and mechanics, and proofreading the final typed copy.

When you get an assignment, think about all the steps you'll need to go through so that you can plan your time for that project. Certainly two different writers might need different amounts of time to produce the same quality document. But for any one writer, different projects have different lead times, as Figure 3.1 shows.

One Writer's Process for Memos and Reports*

I was asked to prepare the business's annual marketing plan. This … experience … forced me to think about what I wanted to say, my audiences, and what they wanted and needed to know. From the beginning I recognized that I needed to explain what our industry was, how we were positioned, what our growth objectives were, and how we were going to reach them.

Writing the first draft of the plan was very daunting; I had many false starts and had to rewrite paragraphs and complete sections. Sometimes when I revisited the text, I realized that points were not clearly stated or that insight was lacking. I ended up abandoning my first plan and instead telling a story about what we had done and what we wanted to do. . . .

I begin business plans—and other documents—by outlining the key elements to include. It's useful to jot down ideas and thoughts without attempting to be grammatically correct. . . .

Once I feel basically satisfied with a draft, I go through it page by page for content, flow, and proper grammar. . . . Not surprisingly, one needs to go through more than one iteration to incorporate editorial comments, reorganize the text, and have it proofread by more than one pair of eyes!

*Quoted from Robert A. Brullo to Kitty Locker, March 22, 1999.

FIGURE 3.1   Timelines for Various Documents (Your actual times may vary.)

E-Mail message answering a simple question. Total time: 15 minutes

5 minutes	5 minutes	5 minutes
Read the question. Gather any information necessary for reply. Plan the message.	Draft the message.	Reread the message. Run the message through spell-checker. Make small changes. Send the message.

E-Mail message answering a question that requires simple research. Total time: 2 hours

1 hour	30 minutes	30 minutes
Read the question. Think about what is needed to reply. Do research (on the Web, ask people, etc.) Analyze the information. Plan the message.	Draft the message and any attachments.	Reread the message. Revise the message and attachments. Run the message through spell-checker. Send the message.

Memo explaining a new policy. Total time: 6½ hours

90 minutes	90 minutes	90 minutes	30 minutes	90 minutes
Understand the policy. Answer the questions for analysis. Think about document design. Organize the message.	Draft.	Reread draft. Measure draft against analysis questions and principles of business communication. Revise draft.	Ask for feedback.	Revise draft based on feedback. Run spell-checker. Proof by eye. Initial memo. Duplicate and distribute document.

Report recommending ways to improve customer service. Total time: 30 business days

6 days	1 day	2 days	9 days
Collect information about weaknesses in service. Plan research to gather more information. Get library sources; check the Web; plan survey or interview questions. Write proposal to do research to find solution.	Ask for feedback on proposal, research plan.	Revise proposal.	Conduct research. Analyze data. Create visuals for report. Prepare appendices.

5 days	1 day	5 days	1 day
Draft report. Evaluate draft against proposal and principles of business communication.	Ask for feedback on recommendations, report design, and visuals.	Revise report. Revise visuals. Plan oral presentation. Edit document and visuals. Run spell-checker. Proof by eye. Duplicate document.	Submit report. Present results orally.

Brainstorming, Planning, and Organizing Business Documents

Spend at least one-third of your time planning and organizing before you begin to write. The better your ideas are when you start, the fewer drafts you'll need to produce a good document. Start by asking questions from ◀ Chapter 1 to identify what's at stake and what message and channel are appropriate. Use the strategies described in Chapter 2 to analyze audience (◀ p. 31) and identify reader benefits (◀ p. 38). Gather information you can use for your document.

Sometimes your content will be determined by the situation. Sometimes, even when it's up to you to think of reader benefits or topics to include in a report, you'll find it easy. If ideas won't come, try the following techniques:

- **Brainstorming.** Think of all the ideas you can, without judging them. Consciously try to get at least a dozen different ideas before you stop. The first idea you have may not be the best.

- **Freewriting.**[5] Make yourself write, without stopping, for 10 minutes or so, even if you must write "I will think of something soon." At the end of 10 minutes, read what you've written, identify the best point in the draft, then set it aside, and write for another 10 uninterrupted minutes. Read this draft, marking anything that's good and should be kept, and then write again for another 10 minutes. By the third session, you will probably produce several sections that are worth keeping—maybe even a complete draft that's ready to be revised.

- **Clustering.**[6] Write your topic in the middle of the page and circle it. Write down the ideas the topic suggests, circling them, too. (The circles are designed to tap into the non-linear half of your brain.) When you've filled the page, look for patterns or repeated ideas. Use different coloured pens to group related ideas. Then use these ideas to develop reader benefits in a memo, questions for a survey, or content for the body of a report. Figure 3.2 presents the clusters that one writer created about business communication.

- **Talk to your audiences.** As Rachel Spilka's research shows, talking to internal and external audiences helped writers involve readers in the planning process, understand the social and political relationships among readers, and negotiate conflicts orally rather than depending solely on the document. These writers were then able to think about content as well as about organization and style, appeal to common grounds (such as reducing waste or increasing productivity) that several readers shared, and reduce the number of revisions needed before documents were approved.[7]

Thinking about the content, layout, or structure of your document can also give you ideas. For long documents, write out the headings you'll use. For anything that's under five pages, less formal notes will probably work. You may want to jot down ideas to use as the basis for a draft. For an oral presentation, a meeting, or a document with lots of visuals, try creating a **storyboard,** with a rectangle representing each page or unit. Draw a box with a visual for each main point. Below the box, write a short caption or label.

Letters and memos will go faster if you choose a basic organizational pattern before you start. Chapters 5, 6, and 7 give detailed patterns of organization for the most common kinds of letters and memos. You may want to customize those patterns with a planning guide[8] to help you keep the "big picture" in mind as you write. Figure 3.3 shows planning guides developed for specific kinds of documents.

As you plan your document, pay attention to signals from your boss and the organization's culture (◀ p. 31). For example, if the organization has a style manual that specifies whether *data* is singular or plural, follow its guidelines.

FIGURE 3.2   Clustering Helps Generate Ideas

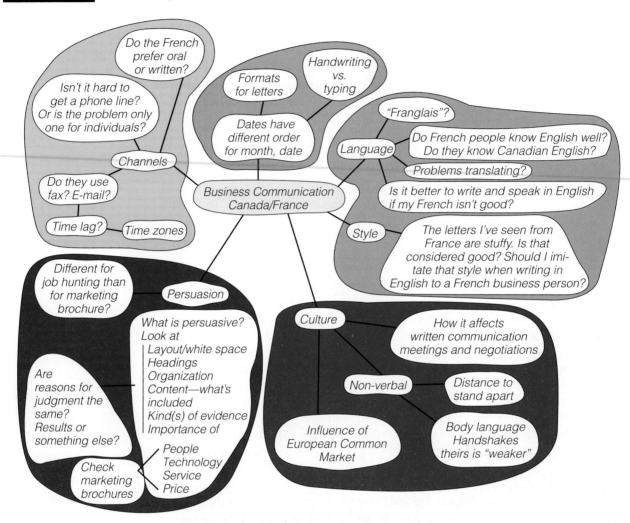

If the organization has an ethics counsellor, think about consulting him or her as you decide what to write in a situation with ethical implications. Talk to people in the organization who will be affected by what you are announcing or proposing, to better understand their concerns. In some organizations, your boss may want to see an early planning draft (see ➡ Figure 3.8 on p. 78) to see that you're on the right track. In other organizations, you may be expected to do a great deal of revising on your own before anyone else sees the document.

Revising, Editing, and Proofreading

Good writers make their drafts better by judicious revising, editing, and proofreading. Good writers also know *when* they should invest time and energy in the careful process of revising, editing, and proofreading. They know that too much concern with correctness in early drafts can block writing.

What to Look for When You Revise

Every chapter in this book suggests questions you should ask as you revise. When you write to an audience you know well, you may be able to check everything at

FIGURE 3.3   Customized Planning Guides for Specific Documents

Planning guide for a trip report
- The Big Picture from the Company's Point of View: We Can Go Forward on the Project.
- Criteria/Goals
- What We Did
- Why We Know Enough to Go Forward
- Next Steps

Planning guide for a proposal
- Customer's Concern #1 Our Proposal/Answer
- Customer's Concern #2 Our Proposal/Answer
- Customer's Concern #3 Our Proposal/Answer
- Customer's Concern #4 Our Proposal/Answer
- Ask for Action

Planning guide for an e-mail message
- My Purpose
- Points I Want to Make
- Document(s) to Attach
- Next Steps

Planning guide for a credit rejection
- Reason
- Refusal
- Alternative (Layaway/ Co-signer/Provide more information)
- Goodwill Ending

Source: E-mail and proposal guides based on Fred Reynolds, "What Adult Work-World Writers Have Taught Me About Adult Work-World Writing," *Professional Writing in Context: Lessons from Teaching and Consulting in Worlds of Work* (Hillsdale, NJ: Lawrence Erlbaum Associates, 1995), 18, 20.

once. When you're writing to a new audience or have to solve a particularly difficult problem, plan to revise the draft at least three times.

The first time, look for content and clarity. Go back to the analysis questions in ◄▥ Chapters 1 and 2 to make sure you've fulfilled all the necessary purposes and have reader benefits for each audience. The second time, check the organization and layout. Finally, check style and tone (▥► Chapter 4).

Use the information in ◄▥ Chapter 2 to check for you-attitude, positive emphasis, and bias-free language. Use the 10 techniques in ▥► Chapter 4 to make sure sentences and paragraphs are tight, smooth, and friendly. Figure 3.4 summarizes the questions you should ask. Check whether design supports a visually inviting, readable document (▥► Appendix A).

Often you'll get the best revision by setting aside your draft, getting a blank page or screen, and redrafting. This strategy takes advantage of the thinking you did on your first draft without locking you into the sentences in it. Use WIRMI (▥► p. 87) to replace awkward phrasing with what you really want to say.

As you revise, be sure to read the document through from start to finish. This is particularly important if you've composed in several sittings or if you've used text from other documents. Researchers have found that such documents tend to be well organized but don't flow well.[9] You may need to add transitions, cut repetitive parts, or change words to create a uniform level of formality throughout the document.

If you're really in a time bind, do a light revision (Figure 3.5). The quality of the final document may not be as high as with a thorough revision, but even a light revision is better than skipping revision altogether.

Using Spell- and Grammar Checkers

If you use a computer to prepare your documents, use a spell-checker to catch typos.

But you still need to proofread by eye.

Spell-checkers work by matching words: they will signal any group of letters not listed in their dictionaries. However, they cannot tell that a word is missing or that the meaning demands *of* rather than *or,* *not* rather than *now,* or *manager* rather than *manger.*

Grammar-checkers can help a writer whose command of grammar and mechanics is weak. However, since grammar-checkers do not catch all errors, it's worth taking the time to master grammar and mechanics so you can edit and proofread yourself.

FIGURE 3.4

✓ **CHECKLIST**   Thorough Revision Checklist

Content and clarity

- [ ] Is your view of purposes complete? Does your document meet the needs of the organization and of the reader—and make you look good?
- [ ] Have you given readers all the information they need to understand and act on your message?
- [ ] Is all the information accurate?
- [ ] Is each sentence clear? Is the message free from apparently contradictory statements?
- [ ] Is the logic clear and convincing? Are generalizations and benefits backed up with adequate supporting detail?

Organization and layout

- [ ] Is the pattern of organization appropriate for your purposes, audience, and situation?
- [ ] Are transitions between ideas smooth? Do ideas within paragraphs flow smoothly?
- [ ] Does the design of the document make it easy for readers to find the information they need? Is the document visually inviting?
- [ ] Are the points emphasized by layout ones that deserve emphasis?
- [ ] Are the first and last paragraphs effective?

Style and tone

- [ ] Is the message easy to read?
- [ ] Is the message friendly and free from sexist language?
- [ ] Does the message build goodwill?

What to Look for When You Edit

Even good writers need to edit, since no one can pay attention to surface correctness while thinking of ideas. Editing should always *follow* revision. There's no point in taking time to fix a grammatical error in a sentence that may be cut when you clarify your meaning or tighten your style. Most writers edit more accurately when they print out a copy of a document and edit the hard copy. But beware: laser printing makes a page look good but does nothing to correct errors.

Check to be sure that the following are accurate:

- Sentence structure
- Subject–verb and noun–pronoun agreement
- Punctuation
- Word usage
- Spelling—including spelling of names
- Numbers

FIGURE 3.5

✓ **CHECKLIST**   Light Revision Checklist

- [ ] Are the first and last paragraphs effective?
- [ ] Does the design of the document make it easy for readers to find the information they need?
- [ ] Have you told the reader what to do?

You need to know the rules of grammar and punctuation to edit. Most writers make a small number of errors over and over. If you know that you have trouble with dangling modifiers or subject–verb agreement, for example, specifically look for them in your draft. Also look for any errors that especially bother your boss and correct them.

A command of standard grammar will help you build the credible, professional image you want to create with everything you write.

How to Correct Grammar

With the possible exception of spelling, grammar is the aspect of writing that writers seem to find most troublesome. Faulty grammar is often what executives are objecting to when they complain that college graduates or MBAs "can't write."

Subjects and verbs *agree* when they are both singular or both plural.

Incorrect: The accountants who conducted the audit was recommended highly.

Correct: The accountants who conducted the audit were recommended highly.

Subject–verb agreement errors often occur when other words come between the subject and the verb. Edit your draft by finding the subject and the verb of each sentence.

Canadian usage treats company names and the words *company* and *government* as singular nouns.

Correct (Canadian)   Uniglobe Carefree Travel Group trains its agents well.

Use a plural verb when two or more singular subjects are joined by *and*.

Correct: Larry McGreevy and I are planning to visit the client.

Use a singular verb when two or more singular subjects are joined by *or, nor,* or *but*.

Correct: Either the shipping clerk or the superintendent has to sign the order.

When the sentence begins with *Here* or *There*, make the verb agree with the subject that follows the verb.

Correct: Here is the booklet you asked for.

Correct: There are the blueprints I wanted.

Errors in **noun–pronoun agreement** occur if a pronoun is of a different number or person than the word it refers to.

Incorrect: All drivers of leased automobiles are billed $100 if damages to his automobile are caused by a collision.

Correct: All drivers of leased automobiles are billed $100 if damages to their automobiles are caused by collisions.

Incorrect: A manager has only yourself to blame if things go wrong.

Correct: As a manager, you have only yourself to blame if things go wrong.

The following words require a singular pronoun:

everybody   neither
each   nobody
either   a person
everyone

Correct: Everyone should bring his or her copy of the manual to the next session on changes in the law.

Why Errors Matter*

Errors in a document can make it harder to figure out what the writer meant. On rare occasions, errors can even change the meaning.

Errors also create a negative image of the writer. Professor Larry Beason found that business people judged the authors of errors to be not only poor writers but also poor business people.

*Based on Larry Beason, "Language Errors in Business Documents: A Study of Business People's Reactions to Error," Southwest Federation of Administrative Disciplines Convention, Dallas, TX, March 4–7, 1998.

Make sure *this* and *it* refer to a specific noun in the previous sentence. If either refers to an idea, add a noun ("this strategy") to make the sentence grammatically correct.

Use *who* and *whom* to refer to people and *which* to refer to objects. *That* can refer to anything: people, animals, organizations, and objects.

Correct: The new Executive Director, who moved here from Burnaby, is already making friends.

Correct: The information that she wants will be available tomorrow.

Correct: This confirms the price that I quoted you this morning.

A **modifier** is a word or phrase that gives more information about the subject, verb, or object in a clause. A **dangling modifier** is not clearly related to the word it limits or modifies. Reword the modifier so that it is grammatically correct and logically modifies the subject.

Incorrect: Confirming our conversation, the truck will leave Monday. [The speaker is doing the confirming. But the speaker isn't in the sentence.]

Incorrect: At the age of eight, I began teaching my children about Canadian business.
[This sentence says that the author was eight when he or she had children who could understand business.]

Correct a dangling modifier in one of these ways:

■   Recast the modifier as a subordinate clause.

Correct: As I told you, the truck will leave Monday.

Correct: When they were eight, I began teaching my children about Canadian business.

■   Revise the main clause so its subject or object can be modified by the now-dangling phrase.

Correct: Confirming our conversation, I have scheduled the truck to leave Monday.

Correct: At the age of eight, my children began learning about Canadian business.

Whenever you use a verb or adjective that ends in *-ing*, ensure it modifies the grammatical subject of your sentence. If it doesn't, reword the sentence.

A **misplaced modifier** appears to modify another element of the sentence than the writer intended.

Incorrect: Customers who complain often alert us to changes we need to make.
[Does the sentence mean that customers must complain frequently to teach us something? Or is the meaning that frequently we learn from complaints?]

Correct a misplaced modifier by moving it closer to the word it modifies or by adding punctuation to clarify your meaning. If a modifier modifies the whole sentence, use it as an introductory phrase or clause; follow it with a comma.

Correct: Often, customers who complain alert us to changes we need to make.

Items in a series or list must have the same grammatical (or **parallel**) structure.

Not parallel: In the second month of your internship, you will
    1. Learn how to resolve customers' complaints.
    2. Supervision of desk staff.
    3. Interns will help plan store displays.

Parallel: In the second month of your internship, you will
    1. Learn how to resolve customers' complaints.

2. Supervise desk staff.
3. Plan store displays.

Also parallel: Duties in the second month of your internship include resolving customers' complaints, supervising desk staff, and planning store displays.

When you have two or three items in a list (whether the list is horizontal or vertical) ensure the items are in the same grammatical form. If possible, put lists vertically to make them easier to see.

How to Correct Punctuation

Punctuation marks are road signs to help readers predict what comes next. (See Figure 3.6.)

When you move from the subject to the verb, no comma is needed. When you end an introductory phrase or clause, the comma tells readers the introduction is over and you're turning to the main clause. When words interrupt the main clause, like this, commas tell the reader when to turn off the main clause for a short side route and when to return.

Some people have been told to put commas where they'd take breaths. That's bad advice. How often you'd take a breath depends on how big your lung capacity is, how fast and how loud you're speaking, and the emphasis you want. Commas aren't breaths. Instead, like other punctuation, they're road signs.

A sentence contains at least one main clause. A **main** or **independent clause** is a complete statement. A **subordinate** or **dependent clause** contains both a subject and verb but is not a complete statement and cannot stand by itself. A phrase is a group of words that does not contain both a subject and a verb.

Main clauses

Your order will arrive Thursday.

He dreaded talking to his supplier.

I plan to enroll for summer school classes.

Subordinate clauses

if you place your order by Monday

because he was afraid the product would be out of stock

since I want to graduate next spring

Phrases

With our current schedule

As a result

After talking to my adviser

FIGURE 3.6 What Punctuation Tells the Reader

Mark	Tells the reader
Period	We're stopping.
Semicolon	What comes next is closely related to what I just said.
Colon	What comes next is an example of what I just said.
Dash	What comes next is a dramatic example of or a shift from what I just said.
Comma	What comes next is a slight turn, but we're going in the same basic direction.

A clause with one of the following words will be subordinate: *after, although, though, because, since, before, until, if, when, whenever, while, as*.

Using the correct punctuation will enable you to avoid three major sentence errors: comma splices, run-on sentences, and sentence fragments.

A **comma splice** or **comma fault** occurs when two main clauses are joined only by a comma (instead of by a comma and a coordinating conjunction).

Incorrect: The contest will start in June, the date has not been set.

Correct a comma splice in one of the following ways:

- If the ideas are closely related, use a semicolon rather than a comma. If they aren't closely related, start a new sentence.

  Correct: The contest will start in June; the exact date has not been set.

- Add a coordinating conjunction.

  Correct: The contest will start in June, but the exact date has not been set.

- Subordinate one of the clauses.

  Correct: Although the contest will start in June, the exact date has not been set.

Remember that you cannot use just a comma with the following transitions: *however, therefore, nevertheless, moreover*.

Instead, either use a semicolon to separate the clauses or start a new sentence.

Incorrect: Computerized grammar checkers do not catch every error, however, they may be useful as a first check before an editor reads the material.

Correct: Computerized grammar checkers do not catch every error. However, they may be useful as a first check before an editor reads the material.

A **run-on sentence** strings together several main clauses using *and, but, or, so,* and *for*. Run-on sentences and comma splices are "mirror faults." A comma splice uses *only* the comma and omits the coordinating conjunction, while a run-on sentence uses *only* the conjunction and omits the comma. Correct a short run-on sentence by adding a comma. Separate a long run-on sentence into two or more sentences. Consider subordinating one or more of the clauses.

Incorrect: We will end up with a much smaller markup but they use a lot of this material so the volume would be high so try to sell them on fast delivery and tell them our quality is very high.

Correct: Although we will end up with a much smaller markup, volume would be high since they use a lot of this material. Try to sell them on fast delivery and high quality.

A **fused sentence** results when two sentences or more are *fused*, or joined with neither punctuation nor conjunctions. To fix the error, add the punctuation, add a conjunction, or subordinate one of the clauses.

Incorrect: The advantages of Intranets are clear the challenge is persuading employees to share information.

Correct: The advantages of Intranets are clear; the challenge is persuading employees to share information.

Also correct: Although the advantages of Intranets are clear, the challenge is persuading employees to share information.

In a **sentence fragment,** a group of words that is not a complete sentence is punctuated as if it were a complete sentence.

Incorrect: Observing these people, I have learned two things about the program. The time it takes. The rewards it brings.

To fix a sentence fragment, either add whatever parts of the sentence are missing or incorporate the fragment into the sentence before it or after it.

Correct: Observing these people, I have learned that the program is time consuming but rewarding.

Use a **colon** to separate a main clause and a list that explains the last element in the clause. The items in the list are specific examples of the word that appears immediately before the colon.

Please order the following supplies:

Printer cartridges

Company letterhead

Company envelopes

When the list is presented vertically, some authorities suggest capitalizing the first letter of each item in the list. When the list is run in with the sentence, don't capitalize the first letter after the colon.

Please order the following supplies: printer cartridges, company letterhead, and company envelopes.

Do not use a colon when the list is grammatically part of the main clause.

Incorrect: The rooms will have coordinated decors in natural colours such as: eggplant, moss, and mushroom.

Correct: The rooms will have coordinated decors in natural colours such as eggplant, moss, and mushroom.

Also Correct: The rooms will have coordinated decors in a variety of natural colours: eggplant, moss, and mushroom.

If the list is presented vertically, some authorities suggest introducing the list with a colon even though the words preceding the colon are not a complete sentence.

Use a colon to join two independent clauses when the second clause explains or restates the first clause.

Selling is simple: give people the service they need, and they'll come back with more orders.

Use **commas** to separate the main clause from an introductory clause, the reader's name, or words that interrupt the main clause. Note that commas both precede and follow the interrupting information.

R. J. Garcia, the new sales manager, comes to us from the Hamilton office.

A **non-essential clause** gives extra information that is not needed to identify the noun it modifies. Because non-essential clauses give extra information, they need extra commas.

Sue Decker, who wants to advance in the organization, has signed up for the company training program in sales techniques.

Do not use commas to set off information that restricts the meaning of a noun or pronoun. **Essential clauses** give essential, not extra, information.

Anyone ☐ who wants to advance in the organization ☐ should take advantage of on-the-job training.

Do not use commas to separate the subject from the verb, even if you would take a breath after a long subject.

Incorrect: Laws require that anyone collecting $5,000 or more on behalf of another person, apply to schools and private individuals as well to charitable groups and professional fundraisers.

Correct: Laws require that anyone collecting $5,000 or more on behalf of another person ☐ apply to schools and private individuals as well to charitable groups and professional fundraisers.

Use a comma after the first clause in a compound sentence if the clauses are long or if they have different subjects.

This policy eliminates all sick-leave credit of the employee at the time of retirement, and payment will be made only once to any individual.

Do not use commas to join independent clauses without a conjunction. Doing so produces comma splices.

Use commas to separate items in a series. Using a comma before the *and* or *or* is not required by some authorities, but using a comma always adds clarity. The comma is essential if any of the items in the series themselves contain the word *and*.

The company pays the full cost of hospitalization insurance for eligible employees, spouses, and unmarried dependent children under age 23.

Use dashes to emphasize an insertion or a break in thought.

All the indicators—from the promising sustainability figures to the improved vulnerability performance—were welcomed by the auditor.

Ryertex comes in 30 grades—each with a special use.

To type a dash, use two hyphens with no space before or after, or insert a dash from the word processor's symbols list.

Use **parentheses** to set off words, phrases, or sentences used to explain or comment on the main idea.

For the thinnest Ryertex (.038 cm) only a single layer of the base material may be used, while the thickest (25.4 cm) may contain over 600 greatly compressed layers of fabric or paper. By varying the fabric used (cotton, asbestos, glass, or nylon) or the type of paper, and by changing the kind of resin (phenolic, melamine, silicone, or epoxy), we can produce 30 different grades.

Any additional punctuation goes outside the second parenthesis when the punctuation applies to the whole sentence. Punctuation goes inside when it applies only to the words in the parentheses.

Please check the invoice to see if credit should be issued. (A copy of the invoice is attached.)

Use **semicolons** to join two independent clauses when they are closely related.

We'll do our best to fill your order promptly; however, we cannot guarantee a delivery date.

Using a semicolon suggests that the two ideas are very closely connected. Using a period and a new sentence is also correct but implies nothing about how closely related the two sentences are. In this case, a semicolon could be replaced by a period and a capital letter. It has a sentence on both sides.

Use semicolons to separate items in a series when the items themselves contain commas.

> The final choices for the new plant are Toronto, Ontario; Halifax, Nova Scotia; Calgary, Alberta; and Burnaby, British Columbia.

How to Catch Typos

Proofread every document both with a spell-checker and by eye to catch the errors a spell-checker can't find.

Proofreading is hard because writers tend to see what they know should be there rather than what really is there. Since it's always easier to proof something you haven't written, you may want to swap papers with a colleague. (Be sure the person looks for typos, not content.)

To proofread,

- Read once quickly for meaning, to see that nothing has been left out.
- Read a second time, slowly. When you find an error, correct it and then *re-read that line*. Readers tend to become less attentive after they find one error and may miss other errors close to the one they've spotted.
- To proofread a document you know well, read the lines backward or the pages out of order.

Always triple-check numbers, headings, the first and last paragraphs, and names.

Use the proofreading symbols in Figure 3.7 to make corrections when you are working on a hard copy.

FIGURE 3.7   Proofreading Symbols

ℯ	delete	⌐	move up
⤬	insert a letter	⌐	move down
¶	start a new paragraph here	#	leave a space
(stet)	stet (leave as it was before the marked change)	⌒	close up
(sp)	spell out	‖	align vertically
(tr)	transpose (reverse)	⌄	insert comma
(lc)	lower case (don't capitalize)	⌄	insert apostrophe
≡	capitalize	⌄⌄	insert quotation marks
(ital)	set in italic type	⊙	insert period
[	move to left	⌃	insert semicolon
]	move to right	⊙	insert colon
][	centre	⫫	insert hyphen

Your Edits May Be Showing*

When SCO Group, a litigious Lindon (Utah) software company, filed a breach of contract suit in Michigan against DaimlerChrysler [, . . . a] CNET News reporter, poking through the Microsoft Word filing, discovered that the case had originally been drawn up as a suit against Bank of America in a California court. . . .

[H]idden in a Word, Excel, or PowerPoint file may [be] the names of the author and anyone who edited the document, reviewers' comments, . . . and deleted text. . . .

A *Wired News* analysis of a Word document circulated by California Attorney General Bill Lockyer urging other attorneys to crack down on file-sharing showed that the text had been edited or reviewed by an official of the Motion Picture Association of America. . . .

Nearly every business exchanges electronic documents with partners, competitors, and customers. . . . [To remove sensitive information,] select "Track Changes" from the tools menu and view the document as "Final Showing Markup." Make sure that all your changes have been either accepted or rejected by the program—a step that removes the tracking information. And make sure all versions but the last have been deleted.

*Quoted from Stephen H. Wildstrom, "Don't Let Word Give Away Your Secrets," *BusinessWeek*, April 19, 2004, 26.

Getting and Using Feedback

Getting feedback almost always improves a document. In many organizations, it's required. All external documents must be read and approved before they go out. The process of drafting, getting feedback, revising, and getting more feedback is called **cycling**. Susan Kleimann studied a 10-page document whose 20 drafts made a total of 31 stops on the desks of nine reviewers on four different levels.[10] Being asked to revise a document is a fact of life in businesses, government agencies, and non-profit organizations.

You can improve the quality of the feedback you get by telling people which aspects you'd especially like comments about. For example, when you give a reader the outline or planning draft,[11] you might want to know whether the general approach is appropriate. After your second draft, you might want to know whether reader benefits are well developed. When you reach the polishing draft, you'll be ready for feedback on style and grammar. Figure 3.8 lists questions to ask.

It's easy to feel defensive when someone criticizes your work. If the feedback stings, put it aside until you can read it without feeling defensive. Even if you think that the reader hasn't understood what you were trying to say, the fact that the reader complained usually means the section could be improved. Rephrasing the statement, giving more information or examples, or documenting the source may clarify.

Reading feedback carefully is a good way to understand the culture of your organization. Are you told to give more details or to shorten messages? Does your boss add headings and bullet points? Look for patterns in the comments, and apply what you learn in your next document.

Remember too that the widespread use of word processors is raising readers' expectations. Readers are now more likely to ask for a revision; they care about the physical appearance of documents. Because word processing makes it easy to correct typos, change spacing and margins, and insert graphics, readers are less tolerant of badly designed documents and of documents with obvious corrections.

FIGURE 3.8

✓ **CHECKLIST**   Questions to Ask Readers

Outline or planning draft
☐ Does the plan seem on the right track?
☐ What topics should be added? Should any be cut?
☐ Do you have any other general suggestions?

Revising draft
☐ Does the message satisfy all its purposes?
☐ Is the message adapted to the audience(s)?
☐ Is the organization effective?
☐ What parts aren't clear?
☐ What ideas need further development?
☐ Do you have any other suggestions?

Polishing draft
☐ Are there any problems with word choice or sentence structure?
☐ Did you find any inconsistencies?
☐ Did you find any typos?
☐ Is the document's design effective?

Summary of Key Points

■ Processes that help writers write well include not expecting the first draft to be perfect, writing regularly, breaking the writing task into manageable parts, having clear goals, focusing on audience, knowing many different strategies, using rules as guidelines rather than as absolutes, and waiting to edit until after the draft is complete.

■ Writing processes can include eight activities: planning, gathering, writing, evaluating, getting feedback, revising, editing, and proofreading. **Revising** means changing the document to make it better satisfy the writer's purposes and the audience. **Editing** means making local changes that make the document grammatically correct. **Proofreading** means checking to be sure the document is free from typographical errors. The activities do not have to come in any set order.

■ To think of ideas, try **brainstorming, freewriting** (writing without stopping for 10 minutes or so), and **clustering** (brainstorming with circled words on a page).

■ You can improve the quality of the feedback you get by telling people which aspects of a draft you'd like comments about. If a reader criticizes something, fix the problem. If you think the reader misunderstood you, try to figure out what caused the misunderstanding and revise the draft so that the reader can see what you meant.

■ If the writing situation is new or difficult, plan to revise the draft at least three times. The first time, look for content and clarity. The second time, check the organization and layout. Finally, check style and tone.

CHAPTER 3 Exercises and Problems

Getting Started

3.1 Interviewing Writers about Their Composing Processes

Interview someone about the composing process(es) he or she uses for on-the-job writing. Questions you could ask include the following:

■ What kind of planning do you do before you write? Do you make lists? Formal or informal outlines?

■ When you need more information, where do you get it?

■ How do you compose your drafts? Do you dictate? Draft with pen and paper? Compose on screen? How do you find uninterrupted time to compose?

■ When you want advice about style, grammar, and spelling, what source(s) do you consult?

■ Does your superior ever read your drafts and make suggestions?

■ Do you ever work with other writers to produce a single document? Describe the process you use.

■ Describe the process of creating a document where you felt the final document reflected your best work. Describe the process of creating a document you found difficult or frustrating. What sorts of things make writing easier or harder for you?

As Your Professor Directs,

a. Share your results orally with a small group of students.

b. Present your results in an oral presentation to the class.

c. Present your results in a memo to your professor.

d. Share your results with a small group of students and write a joint memo reporting the similarities and differences you found.

3.2   Analyzing Your Own Writing Processes

Save your notes and drafts from several assignments so that you can answer the following questions:

- Which practices of good writers do you follow?
- Which of the eight activities discussed in this chapter do you use?
- How much time do you spend on each of the eight activities?
- What kinds of revisions do you make most often?
- Do you use different processes for different documents, or do you have one process that you use most of the time?
- What parts of your process seem most successful? Are there any places in the process that could be improved? How?

- What relation do you see between the process(es) you use and the quality of the final document?

As Your Professor Directs,

a. Discuss your process with a small group of other students.

b. Write a memo to your professor analyzing in detail your process for composing one of the papers for this class.

c. Write a memo to your professor analyzing your process during the term. What parts of your process(es) have stayed the same throughout the term? What parts have changed?

Getting It Right

3.3   Checking Spell- and Grammar-Checkers

Each of the following paragraphs contains errors in grammar, spelling, and punctuation. Which errors does your spell- or grammar-checker catch? Which errors does it miss? Does it flag as errors any words that are correct?

a. Answer to an Inquiry

Enclosed are the tow copies you requested of our pamphlet, "Using the Internet to market Your products. The pamphelt walks you through the steps of planning the Home Page (The first page of the web cite, shows examples of other Web pages we have designed, and provide a questionaire that you can use to analyze audience the audience and purposes.

b. Performance Appraisal

Most staff accountants complete three audits a month. Ellen has completed 21 audits in this past six months she is our most productive staff accountant. Her technical skills our very good however some clients feel that she could be more tactful in suggesting ways that the clients accounting practices courld be improved.

c. Brochure

Are you finding that being your own boss crates it's own problems? Take the hassle out of working at home with a VoiceMail Answering System. Its almost as good as having your own secratery.

d. Presentation Slides

How to Create a Web résumé

- Omit home adress and phone number
- Use other links only if they help an employer evalaute you.
  - ☐ Be Professional.
  - ☐ Carefully craft and proof read the phrase on the index apage.

How to Create a Scannable Résumé

- Create a "plain vanilla" document.
- Use include a "Keywords" section. Include personality trait sas well as accomplishments.
- Be specific and quantifyable.

3.4   Checking Punctuation and Grammar

Identify and correct the errors in the following passages.

a.   Company's are finding it to their advantage to cultivate their suppliers. Partnerships between a company and it's suppliers can yield hefty payoffs for both company and supplier. One example is Bailey Controls, an Ontario headquartered company. Bailey make control systems for big factories. They treat suppliers almost like departments of their own company. When a Bailey employee passes a laser scanner over a bins bar code the supplier is instantly alerted to send more parts.

b.   Entrepreneur Trip Hawkins appears in Japanese ads for the video game system his company designed. "It plugs into the future! he says in one ad, in a cameo spliced into shots of U.S kids playing the games. Hawkins is one of several US celebrieties and business people whom plug products on Japanese TV. Jodie Foster, harrison ford, and Charlie Sheen adverstises canned coffee beer and cigarettes respectively.

3.5   Providing Punctuation

Provide the necessary punctuation in the following sentences. Note that not every box requires punctuation.

1. The system ☐ s ☐ user ☐ friendly design ☐ provides screen displays of work codes ☐ rates ☐ and client information.

2. Many other factors also shape the organization ☐ s ☐ image ☐ advertising ☐ brochures ☐ proposals ☐ stationery ☐ calling cards ☐ etc.

3. Charlotte Ford ☐ author of ☐ Charlotte Ford ☐ s ☐ Book of Modern Manners ☐☐ says ☐☐ Try to mention specifics of the conversation to fix the interview permanently in the interviewer ☐ s ☐ mind and be sure to mail the letter the same day ☐ before the hiring decision is made ☐☐

4. What are your room rates and charges for food service ☐

5. We will need accommodations for 150 people ☐ five meeting rooms ☐ one large room and four small ones ☐ ☐ coffee served during morning and afternoon breaks ☐ and lunches and dinners.

6. The current student page of Georgian College ☐ s Web site has a link to Turnitin ☐ an on ☐ line plagiarism prevention tool ☐ to help students improve their research and writing skills.

7. Most computer packages will calculate three different sets of percentages ☐ row percentages ☐ column percentages ☐ and table percentages ☐

8. In today ☐ s ☐ economy ☐ it ☐ s almost impossible for a firm to extend credit beyond it ☐ s regular terms.

9. The Department of Transportation does not have statutory authority to grant easements ☐ however ☐ we do have authority to lease unused areas of highway right ☐ of ☐ way.

10. The program has two goals ☐ to identify employees with promise ☐ and to see that they get the training they need to advance.

3.6   Creating Agreement

Revise the following sentences to correct errors in noun–pronoun and subject–verb agreement.

1. If there's any tickets left, they'll be $17 at the door.

2. A team of people from marketing, finance, and production are preparing the proposal.

3. Image type and resolution varies among clip art packages.

4. Your health and the health of your family is very important to us.

5. If a group member doesn't complete their assigned work, it slows the whole project down.

6. Baker & Baker was offended by the ad agency's sloppy proposal, and they withdrew their account from the firm.

7. The first step toward getting out of debt is not to add any more to it. This means cutting up your old credit card.

8. Contests are fun for employees and creates sales incentives.

9. The higher the position a person has, the more professional their image should be.

10. A new employee should try to read verbal and non-verbal signals to see which aspects of your job are most important.

3.7   Improving Modifiers

Revise the following sentences to correct dangling and misplaced modifiers.

1. Originally a group of four, one member dropped out after the first meeting due to a death in the family.
2. Examining the data, it is apparent that most of our sales are to people on the northwest side of the city.
3. As a busy professional, we know that you will want to take advantage of this special offer.
4. Often documents end up in files that aren't especially good.
5. By making an early reservation, it will give us more time to coordinate our trucks to better serve you.

3.8   Creating Parallel Structure

Revise the following sentences to create parallel structure.

1. To narrow a Web search,
   - Put quotation marks around a phrase when you want an exact term.
   - Many search engines have wild cards (usually an asterisk) to find plurals and other forms of a word.
   - Reading the instructions on the search engine itself can teach you advanced search techniques.
2. Men drink more alcoholic beverages than women.
3. Each issue of *Hospice Care* has articles from four different perspectives: legislative, health care, hospice administrators, and inspirational authors.
4. The university is one of the largest employers in the community, brings in substantial business, and the cultural impact is also big.
5. These three tools can help competitive people be better negotiators:
   1. Think win–win
   2. It's important to ask enough questions to find out the other person's priorities, rather than jumping on the first advantage you find.
   3. Protect the other person's self-esteem.

   These three questions can help co-operative people be better negotiators:
   1. Can you develop a specific alternative to use if negotiation fails?
   2. Don't focus on the bottom line. Spend time thinking about what you want and why you need it.
   3. Saying "You'll have to do better than that because …" can help you resist the temptation to say "yes" too quickly.

3.9   Correcting Sentence Errors

Revise the following sentences to correct comma splices, run-on-sentences, fused sentences, and sentence fragments.

1. Members of the group are all experienced presenters, most have had little or no experience using PowerPoint.
2. Proofread the letter carefully and check for proper business format because errors undercut your ability to sell yourself so take advantage of your opportunity to make a good first impression.
3. Some documents need just one pass others need multiple revisions.
4. Videoconferencing can be frustrating. Simply because little time is available for casual conversation.
5. Entrepreneurs face two main obstacles. Limited cash. Lack of business experience.
6. The margin on pet supplies is very thin and the company can't make money selling just dog food and the real profit is in extras like neon-coloured leashes, so you put the dog food in the back so people have to walk by everything else to get to it.
7. The company's profits jumped 15%. Although its revenues fell 3%.
8. The new budget will hurt small businesses it imposes extra fees it raises the interest rates small businesses must pay.
9. Our phones are constantly being used. Not just for business calls but also for personal calls.
10. Businesses are trying to cut travel costs, executives are taking fewer trips and flying out of alternate airports to save money.

3.10   Editing for Grammar and Usage

Revise the following sentences to eliminate errors in grammar and usage.

1. The number of students surveyed that worked more than 20 hours a week was 60%.

2. Not everyone is promoted after six months some people might remain in the training program a year before being moved to a permanent assignment.

3. The present solutions that has been suggested are not adequate.

4. At times while typing and editing, the text on your screen may not look correct.

5. All employees are asked to cut back on energy waste by the manager.

6. The benefits of an online catalogue are

    1. We will be able to keep records up-to-date;

    2. Broad access to the catalogue system from any networked terminal on campus;

    3. The consolidation of the main catalogue and the catalogues in the departmental and branch libraries;

    4. Cost savings.

7. You can take advantage of several banking services. Such as automatic withdrawal of a house or car payment and direct deposit of your paycheque.

8. As a first-year, business administration was intriguing to me.

9. Thank you for the help you gave Joanne Jackson and myself.

10. I know from my business experience that good communication among people and departments are essential in running a successful corporation.

AN INSIDE PERSPECTIVE

Writing for Real People

Plain-language writers emphasize audience research because once you know your readers, you can make choices that will make reading easier for them. You make these choices in tone, grammar, vocabulary, and design.

Project manager of Plain Train: Plain Language Online Training, founder of the Plain Language Association International, and owner of plainlanguage.com, Cheryl Stephens is a writer and editor who trains professionals in communication, leadership, and people skills.

www.cherylstephens.com

Conversational Style

- Choose everyday, familiar words.
- Use words that explain rather than mask meaning: *end, stop, finish,* or *close* instead of *terminate. Agree* or *comply* instead of *accede to.* Wouldn't you be upset by a letter from your lawyer saying, "Your will is now ready; please come in for execution"?
- In trying to be conversational, don't veer toward trendy. Remember, slang is an in-language for a certain group.
- Don't use technical words or jargon like *stem turns, gender segmentation, functional parameters,* or *marginal cost-pricing* unless you are talking to experts in those fields.

Brevity and Simplicity

People won't take the time to search a lengthy document for its essential message. Readers scan a long document to decide whether it has relevance to them. If the headings or graphics don't shout READ ME, the document will be dropped. In order to be read, documents must look interesting, relevant, brief, and easy.

Get Real, Be Clear

Today's audience is more diverse, and individuals have less time and patience for unnecessary complexity. You must expect that your audience has different needs and expectations than you. Watch the way you write and seek the common good: clear, easy, readable writing.

Good business and administrative writing should sound like a person talking to another person. Unfortunately, much of the writing produced in organizations today seems to have been written by faceless bureaucrats rather than by real people.

Using an easy-to-read style makes the reader respond more positively to your ideas. You can make your writing easier to read in two ways. First, you can make individual sentences and paragraphs easy to read, so that skimming the first paragraph or reading the whole document takes as little work as possible. Second, you can make the document look visually inviting and structure it with signposts to guide readers through it. This chapter focuses on ways to make words, sentences, and paragraphs easier to read. See ➠ Appendix A, which will discuss ways to make the document as a whole easier to read.

Good Style in Business and Administrative Writing

Good business and administrative writing is closer to conversation and less formal than the style of writing that has traditionally earned high marks in college and university essays and term papers. (See Figure 4.1.) However, many business professors also like term papers that are easy to read and use good visual impact.

Most people have several styles of talking, which they vary instinctively depending on the audience. Good writers have several styles, too. An e-mail to your boss complaining about the delays from a supplier will be informal; a letter to the supplier demanding better service will be more formal.

Reports tend to be more formal than letters and memos, since they may be read many years in the future by audiences the writer can barely imagine. In reports, avoid contractions, spell out acronyms and abbreviations the first time you use them, and avoid personal pronouns. Since so many people read reports, *you* doesn't have much meaning. See ➠ Chapter 12 for more about report style.

Keep the following points in mind as you choose a level of formality for a specific document:

FIGURE 4.1   Different Levels of Style

Feature	Conversational style	Good business style	Traditional term-paper style
Formality	Highly informal	Conversational; sounds like a real person talking	More formal than conversation would be, but retains a human voice
Use of contractions	Many contractions	OK to use occasional contractions	Few contractions, if any
Pronouns	Uses *I*, first- and second-person pronouns	Uses *I*, first- and second-person pronouns	First- and second-person pronouns kept to a minimum
Level of friendliness	Friendly	Friendly	No effort to make style friendly
How personal	Personal; refers to specific circumstances of conversation	Personal; may refer to reader by name; refers to specific circumstances of readers	Impersonal; may generally refer to *readers* but does not name them or refer to their circumstances
Word choice	Short, simple words; slang	Short, simple words but avoids slang	Many abstract words; scholarly, technical terms
Sentence and paragraph length	Incomplete sentences; no paragraphs	Short sentences and paragraphs	Sentences and paragraphs usually long
Grammar	Can be ungrammatical	Uses standard edited English	Uses standard edited English
Visual impact	Not applicable	Attention to visual impact of document	No particular attention to visual impact

- Use a friendly, informal style to someone you've talked with.
- Avoid contractions, clichés, slang, and even minor grammatical lapses in paper documents to people you don't know. Abbreviations are OK in e-mail messages if they're part of the group's culture.
- Pay particular attention to your style when you write to people in positions of power over you or when you must give bad news. Reliance on nouns rather than on verbs and a general deadening of style increase when people are under stress or feel insecure.[1] Confident people are more direct. Edit your writing so that you sound confident, whether you feel that way or not.

Good business style allows for individual variation. The personal style of the opening paragraphs of CEO William J. Doyle's annual report letter (Figure 4.2) suggests energy and drive, engagement and empathy.

Evaluating "Rules" about Writing

Some "rules" are grammatical conventions. For example, standard edited English requires that each sentence have a subject and verb, and that the subject and verb agree. Business writing normally demands standard grammar, but exceptions exist. Promotional materials such as brochures, advertisements, and sales and fundraising letters may use sentence fragments to mimic the effect of speech.

FIGURE 4.2   William J. Doyle's Letter Uses Good Business Style

2003 Business Highlights
· Sold record potash volumes
· Acquired 26 percent interest in Arab Potash Company
· Nitrogen prices increased
· Realized $90 million in natural gas hedges

Financial Highlights

All financial data in this report are stated in US dollars
$ millions except per-share amounts

	2003	2002	2001
Net sales	$2,465.8	$1,928.7	$2,080.8
Net (loss) income	$ (126.3)	$ 53.6	$ 121.2
Adjusted net income *	$ 76.9	$ 53.6	$ 121.2
Net (loss) income per diluted share	$ (2.42)	$ 1.03	$ 2.32
Adjusted net income per diluted share *	$ 1.46	$ 1.03	$ 2.32
Gross margin	$ 380.4	$ 307.3	$ 407.3
EBITDA *	$ 171.8	$ 386.0	$ 455.4
Adjusted EBITDA *	$ 417.7	$ 386.0	$ 455.4
Cash flow prior to working capital changes *	$ 364.5	$ 289.2	$ 345.8
Cash provided by operating activities	$ 381.5	$ 316.4	$ 75.7

See reconciliation and description of certain non-GAAP measures in Financial Performance Indicators on Pages 48-50

To our shareholders:

Why fertilizer? The answers are as diverse as the people who see the value of our products. Farmers, environmentalists and social scientists all appreciate the importance of fertilizer in food production and land conservation.

My answer to the question "Why fertilizer?" was shaped on a year-long trip that followed my college graduation in 1972. I visited countries that were prosperous and others that struggled to provide the basic elements for survival. I saw nations where food was plentiful and places where people faced starvation on a daily basis. I learned that fundamental human needs — water, food, growth, hope — should never be taken for granted.

Kofi Annan, Secretary-General of the United Nations, has consistently championed agricultural development as the foundation for health, economic stability and world peace. The insight of that sentiment is at the heart of why fertilizer is so important—not just for our individual needs, but to world development.

Fertilizer replenishes the strength of the soil, empowering it to supply the nutrient content in the food we eat. It drives agricultural production, which has been the basis for every developed nation around the world. It enables people to feed themselves and trade for things they need. That contributes to economic opportunities, health and happiness.

That's why I believe fertilizer is so important and why the opportunities for PotashCorp remain bountiful.

William J. Doyle, President and Chief Executive Officer

Short sentences, personal pronouns, parallel constructions, and action verbs mark the good business style.

For visual impact, the tables, italicized sidebar, and bolded salutation highlight the values of the corporation and its product.

Source: PotashCorp.

Other "rules" may be conventions adopted by an organization so that its documents will be consistent. For example, a company might decide to capitalize job titles (e.g., *Production Manager*) even though grammar doesn't require the capitals, or always to use a comma before *and* in a series, even though a sentence can be grammatical without the comma.

Still other "rules" are attempts to codify "what sounds good." To evaluate these "rules," you must consider your audience, the community of practice, discourse community, and organizational culture (◀ p. 31), your purposes, and the situation. If you want the effect produced by an impersonal style and polysyllabic words, use them. But use them only when you want the distancing they produce.

Building a Better Style

To improve your style and make it vivid and vigorous,

- Start a clean page or screen, so that you aren't locked into old sentence structures.
- Try WIRMI: *What I Really Mean Is.*[2] Then write the words.
- Try reading your draft out loud to someone sitting about one metre away—about as far away as you'd sit in casual conversation. If the words sound stiff, they'll seem stiff to a reader, too.
- Ask someone else to read your draft out loud. Readers stumble because the words on the page aren't what they expect to see. The places where that person stumbles are places where your writing can be better.
- Read widely and write a *lot*.
- Study revised sentences, like those in Figure 4.3.
- Use the 10 techniques in Figure 4.4 to polish your style.

The home page of the Canadian federal government's Plain Language On-line Training (www.plainlanguagenetwork.org/plaintrain/index.html) practises what it preaches in welcoming people to Plain Train and inviting them to

FIGURE 4.3 Mutual Fund Prospectuses Revised to Meet the SEC's Plain English Guidelines

	Old prospectus	New prospectus
John Hancock Sovereign Balanced Fund	The fund utilizes a strategy of investing in those common stocks which have a record of having increased their shareholder dividend in each of the preceding ten years or more.	The fund's stock investments are exclusively in companies that have increased their dividend payout in each of the last ten years.
State Street Research Equity Income Fund	The applicability of the general information and administrative procedures set forth below accordingly will vary depending on the investor and the record-keeping system established for a shareholder's investment in the Fund. Participants in 401(k) and other plans should first consult with appropriate persons at their employer or refer to the plan materials before following any of the procedures below.	If you are investing through a large retirement plan or other special program, follow the instructions in your program materials.
State Street Research Equity Income Fund	The net asset value of the fund's shares will fluctuate as market conditions change.	The fund's shares will rise and fall in value.

Source: Toddi Gutner, "At Last, the Readable Prospectus," *BusinessWeek*, April 13, 1998, 100E10. Reprinted by special permission. Copyright © 1998 by The McGraw-Hill Companies, Inc.

How Big is Huge?*

When two people use the same word to mean different things, bypassing occurs.

A potential client told Lois Geller that he wanted a "huge" advertising campaign for his company. She spent three weeks preparing a proposal for a $500,000 ad campaign. The client was horrified. It turned out that his budget for the whole previous year had been $10,000. To the client, a $5,000 campaign would have been "huge."

*Based on Alan Horowitz, "Can You Hear What I Hear?" *Selling Power*, July/August 2001, 70.

FIGURE 4.4   Ten Ways to Make Your Writing Easier to Read

As you choose words,

1. Use words that are accurate, appropriate, and familiar.
2. Use technical jargon only when it is essential and known to the reader. Eliminate business jargon.

As you write and revise sentences,

3. Use active verbs most of the time.
4. Use verbs—not nouns—to carry the weight of your sentence.
5. Tighten your writing.
6. Vary sentence length and sentence structure.
7. Use parallel structure. Use the same grammatical form for ideas that have the same logical function.
8. Put your readers in your sentences.

As you write and revise paragraphs,

9. Begin most paragraphs with topic sentences so that readers know what to expect in the paragraph.
10. Use transitions to link ideas.

"Click on the Conductor for the guided tour; click on the Train for the digest." Plain language is about access and equity, respect and responsibility, transparency and accountability. It is less about following rules and substituting simple for more complex language than it is about adopting a new attitude or approach to writing. Plain language helps make our writing clear because it begins with the needs of the reader and matches those with the needs of the writer. The result is both effective and efficient because the reader can understand the message.

Ten Ways to Make Your Writing Easier to Read

Direct, simple writing is easier to read. James Suchan and Robert Colucci tested two versions of a memo report. The "high-impact" version had the "bottom line" (the purpose of the report) in the first paragraph, simple sentences in normal word order, active verbs, concrete language, short paragraphs, headings and lists, and first- and second-person pronouns. The high-impact version took 22% less time to read. Readers said they understood the report better, and tests showed that they really did understand it better.[3] Another study showed that high-impact instructions were more likely to be followed.[4] We'll talk about layout, headings, and lists in ➡ Appendix A.

As You Choose Words

The best word depends on context: the situation, your purposes, your audience, the words you have already used.

Accurate words mean what you want to say. Appropriate words convey the attitudes you want and fit well with the other words in your document. Familiar words are easy to read and understand.

Some meanings have already evolved before we join the conversation. We may learn the meaning of words, of actions, or of office layouts by being alert and observant. We learn some meanings by formal and informal study: the importance of "generally accepted accounting principles," the best strategies for increasing the size of donations in a fundraising letter, or what the garbage can on a computer screen symbolizes. Some meanings are negotiated as we interact one-on-one with another person, attempting to communicate. Some words persist, even though the reality behind them has changed. In nine of the ten largest U.S. cities, so-called "minorities" are already in the majority.[5]

In multicultural Canada, Toronto has fast emerged as one of the world's most diverse cities. In 1931, 81% of a city population of 631,207 was British in origin; by 1996 only 16% of 4.2 million self-identified as exclusively British (Statistics Canada, 1998). In 1998, Toronto adopted its motto, "Diversity, Our Strength."[6]

Accurate denotations.   To be accurate, a word's denotation must match the meaning the writer wishes to convey. Denotation is a word's literal or dictionary meaning. Most common words in English have more than one denotation. The word *pound*, for example, means, or denotes, a unit of weight, a place where stray animals are kept, a unit of money in the British system, and the verb to hit. Coca-Cola spends an estimated $20 million a year to protect its brand names so that Coke will denote only that brand and not just any cola drink.

When two people use the same word to mean, or denote, different things, **bypassing** (◄ p. 88) occurs. For example, *risk* may be an economic term dealing with efficiency; for an environmentalist the word may denote health concerns. Progress is possible only when the writer and readers agree on a meaning.

Problems also arise when writers misuse words. President George W. Bush is a major source: "The law I sign today directs new funds and new focus to the task of collecting vital intelligence on terrorist threats and on weapons of mass production[7]" [*production* for *destruction*].

An example of a misused word in an idiom (when people have forgotten the metaphor on which it depends) is *Tow the line*. To *toe the line* is to conform to a general policy or principle (especially when unwilling or pressured to do so).

Earn a free lunch.[8]

(A lunch one earns isn't free.)

Accurate denotations can make it easier to solve problems. In one production line with a high failure rate, the largest category of defects was *missed operations*. At first, the supervisor wondered if the people on the line were lazy or irresponsible. But some checking showed that several different problems were labelled *missed operations:* parts installed backward, parts that had missing screws or fasteners, parts whose wires weren't connected. Each of these problems had a different solution. Using accurate words redefined the problem and enabled the production line both to improve quality and to cut repair costs.[9]

Using words correctly remains a challenge for many. If you can master the distinctions between commonly confused pairs of words, you will communicate more accurately and effectively. Don't confuse the following:

accept (receive) and *except* (exclude)

adept (skilled) and *adopt* (take as one's own)

affect (verb: to influence) and *effect* (verb: to produce; noun: result)

a lot (many) and *allot* (divide or give to)

between (used with two) and *among* (used with more than two)

compose (make up) and *comprise* (consist of)

discreet (tactful) and *discrete* (distinct)

lie (recline, tell falsehood) and *lay* (put object on something) *principal* (adjective: main; noun: person in charge and money lent at interest) and *principle* (rule, code of conduct)

stationary (not moving) and *stationery* (paper)

Appropriate connotations.   Words are appropriate when their connotations, that is, their emotional associations or colourings, convey the attitude you want. Many words carry connotations of approval or disapproval, disgust or delight.

Positive word	Negative word
assume	guess
curious	nosy
cautious	fearful
firm	obstinate
flexible	wishy-washy

A supervisor can "tell the truth" about a subordinate's performance and yet write either a positive or a negative performance appraisal, based on the connotations of the words in the appraisal. Consider an employee who pays close attention to details. A positive appraisal might read, "Terry is a meticulous team member who takes care of details that others sometimes ignore." But the same behaviour might be described negatively: "Terry is hung up on trivial details."

Advertisers carefully choose words with positive connotations. Expensive cars are never *used;* instead, they're *pre-owned, experienced,* or even *previously adored.*[10]

Words may also connote status. Both *salesperson* and *sales representative* are non-sexist job titles. But the first sounds like a clerk in a store; the second suggests someone selling important items to corporate customers.

Connotations change over time. The word *charity* had acquired such negative connotations by the 19th century that people began to use the term *welfare* instead. Now, *welfare* has acquired negative associations.

Ethical implications of word choice.   How positively can we present something and still be ethical? Pressure-treated lumber sounds acceptable. But naming the material injected under pressure—arsenic-treated lumber—may lead the customer to make a different decision. We have the right to package our ideas attractively, but we have the responsibility to give the public or our superiors all the information they need to make decisions.

Word choices have ethical implications in other contexts as well. For example, as the racial and ethnic makeup of the workforce has changed, more companies have adopted the language of "managing diversity." People tend to view this language as positive, because it presumes employees' differences can be an asset to their employer, not a source of difficulty. However, communication professors Erika Kirby and Lynn Harter point out that referring to employees as resources to be managed places corporate financial interests above employees' human interests. The risk is that managers may forget ethical dimensions of how they treat their diverse employees.[11]

Familiar words.   Use familiar words, words that are in almost everyone's vocabulary. Use the word that most exactly conveys your meaning, and try to use specific, concrete words, which are easier to understand and remember.[12]

The following list gives a few examples of short, simple alternatives:

Formal and stuffy	Short and simple
ameliorate	improve
commence	begin
enumerate	list
finalize	finish, complete
prioritize	rank
utilize	use
viable option	choice

There are four exceptions to the general rule that "shorter is better":

1. Use a long word if it is the only word that expresses your meaning exactly.
2. Use a long word if it is more familiar than a short word. *Send out* is better than *emit* and *a word in another language for a geographic place or area* is better than *exonym* because more people know the first item in each pair.
3. Use a long word if its connotations are more appropriate. *Exfoliate* is better than *scrape off dead skin cells*.
4. Use a long word if the discourse community (◀ p. 32) prefers it.

There are two kinds of **jargon.** The first is the specialized terminology of a technical field. *LIFO* and *FIFO* are technical terms in accounting; *byte* and *baud* are computer jargon. A job application letter is the one occasion when it's desirable to use technical jargon: using the technical terminology of the reader's field suggests that you're a peer who also is competent in that field. In other kinds of messages, use technical jargon only when the term is essential and known to the reader.

If a technical term has a "plain English" equivalent, use the simpler term:

Jargon: Foot the average monthly budget column down to Total Variable Costs, Total Management Fixed Costs, Total Sunk Costs, and Grand Total.

Better: Add the figures in the average monthly budget column for each category to determine the Total Variable Costs, the Total Management Fixed Costs, and the Total Sunk Costs. Then add the totals for each category to arrive at the Grand Total.

The revision here is longer but better because it uses simple words. The original will be meaningless to a reader who does not know what *foot* means.

The second kind of jargon is the **businessese** that some writers still use: *as per your request, enclosed please find, please do not hesitate.* Some writers call these terms *deadwood,* since they are no longer living words. If any of the terms in the first column of Figure 4.5 show up in your writing, replace them with more modern language.

Prune   Dried Plum

Sales of prunes fell 14% from 1993 to 1999. To stop the slide, what had been the California Prune Board decided to change the product's name (and its own). Changing the product's name required approval from the US Food and Drug Administration. Now you don't buy prunes; you buy "dried plums."

FIGURE 4.5 Getting Rid of Business Jargon

Instead of	Use	Because
At your earliest convenience	The date you need a response	If you need it by a deadline, say so. It may never be convenient to respond.
As per your request; 65 kilometres per hour	As you requested; 65 kilometres an hour	*Per* is a Latin word for *by* or *for each*. Use *per* only when the meaning is correct; avoid mixing English and Latin.
Enclosed please find	Enclosed is; Here is	An enclosure isn't a treasure hunt. If you put something in the envelope, the reader will find it.
Forward same to this office.	Return it to this office.	Omit legal jargon.
Hereto, herewith	Omit	Omit legal jargon.
Please be advised; Please be informed	Omit—simply start your response	You don't need a preface. Go ahead and start.
Please do not hesitate	Omit	Omit negative words.
Pursuant to	According to; or omit	*Pursuant* does not mean *after*. Omit legal jargon in any case.
Said order	Your order	Omit legal jargon.
This will acknowledge receipt of your letter.	Omit—start your response	If you answer a letter, the reader knows you got it.
Trusting this is satisfactory, we remain	Omit	Eliminate *-ing* endings. When you are through, stop.

As You Write and Revise Sentences

At the sentence level, you can do many things to make your writing easy to read. "Who does what" sentences with active verbs make your writing more forceful.

Passives are usually made up of a form of the verb *to be* plus a past participle. *Passive* has nothing to do with *past*. Passives can be past, present, or future:

were received	(in the past)
is recommended	(in the present)
will be implemented	(in the future)

To spot a passive, find the verb. If the verb describes something that the grammatical subject is doing, the verb is active. If the verb describes something that is being done to the grammatical subject, the verb is passive.

Active	**Passive**
The customer received 500 widgets.	Five hundred widgets were received by the customer.
I recommend this method.	This method is recommended by me.
The federal agencies will implement the program.	The program will be implemented by the federal agencies.

Verbs can be changed from active to passive by making the direct object (in the oval) the new subject (in the box). To change a passive verb to an active one, you must make the agent ("by _____" in < >) the new subject. If no agent is specified in the sentence, you must supply one to make the sentence active.

Active

The plant manager approved the request.

The committee will decide next month.

[You] Send the customer a letter informing her about the change.

Passive

The request was approved by the <plant manager.>

A decision will be made next month. No agent in sentence.

A letter will be sent informing the customer of the change. No agent in sentence.

Passive verbs have at least three disadvantages:

1. If all the information in the original sentence is retained, passive verbs make the sentence longer. Passives take more time to understand.[13]
2. If the agent is omitted, it's not clear who is responsible for doing the action.
3. Using many passive verbs, especially in material that has a lot of long words, can make the writing boring and pompous.

Passive verbs are desirable in these situations:

1. Use passives to emphasize the object receiving the action, not the agent.

   Your order was shipped November 15.

   The customer's order, not the shipping clerk, is important.

2. Use passives to provide coherence within a paragraph. A sentence is easier to read if "old" information comes at the beginning of a sentence. When you have been discussing a topic, use the word again as your subject even if that requires a passive verb.

   The bank made several risky loans in the late 1990s. These loans were written off as "uncollectible" in 2001.

   Using *loans* as the subject of the second sentence provides a link between the two sentences, making the paragraph as a whole easier to read.

3. Use passives to avoid assigning blame.

   The order was damaged during shipment.

   An active verb would require the writer to specify *who* damaged the order. The passive here is more tactful.

Put the weight of your sentence in the verb to make your sentences more forceful and up to 25% easier to read.[14] When the verb is a form of the verb *to be*, revise the sentence to use a more forceful verb.

Weak: The financial advantage of owning this equipment instead of leasing it is 10% after taxes.

Better: Owning this equipment rather than leasing it will save us 10% after taxes.

Nouns ending in *-ment*, *-ion*, and *-al* often hide verbs.

make an adjustment	adjust
make a payment	pay
make a decision	decide
reach a conclusion	conclude
take into consideration	consider
make a referral	refer
provide assistance	assist

Use verbs to present the information more forcefully.

Weak: We will perform an investigation of the problem.

Better: We will investigate the problem.

Writing for the Web*

Writers preparing content for a Web site should keep in mind the physical demands of reading a computer screen. Reading a screen is more tiring than reading a printed page, so readers tend to scan. Internet users also tend to be in a hurry to find whatever they are looking for. Writing for the Web is therefore most effective when it follows these guidelines:

- Write concisely.
- Put the main point first; then provide details.
- Break up the text with headings that describe the content.
- Choose easy-to-read type fonts.
- Use informal and direct language; don't try to be cute and clever.
- Keep hyperlinks to a minimum.

*Based on Change Sciences Group, "Writing for the Web: Best Practices," Change Sciences Research Brief (Irvington, NY: Change Sciences Group, 2003), downloaded at http://www.changesciences.com.

Weak: Selection of a program should be based on the client's needs.

Better: Select the program that best fits the client's needs.

Writing is wordy if the same idea can be expressed in fewer words. Unnecessary words increase keying and reading time, bore your reader, and make your meaning more difficult to decipher.

Good writing is tight; however, tight writing may be long because it is packed with ideas. In ← Chapter 2, we saw that revisions to create you-attitude and positive emphasis (← pp. 44, 47, respectively) and to develop reader benefits were frequently *longer* than the originals because the revision added information not given in the original.

Sometimes you may be able to look at a draft and see immediately how to tighten it. When the solution isn't obvious, try the following strategies for tightening your writing.

a. Eliminate words that say nothing.   Cut words if the idea is already clear from other words in the sentence. Substitute single words for wordy phrases.

Wordy: Keep this information on file for future reference.

Tighter: Keep this information for reference.

or: File this information.

Wordy: Ideally, it would be best to put the billing ticket just below the CRT screen and above the keyboard.

Tighter: If possible, put the billing ticket between the CRT screen and the keyboard.

Phrases beginning with *of, which,* and *that* can often be shortened.

Wordy: the question of most importance

Tighter: the most important question

Wordy: the estimate that is enclosed

Tighter: the enclosed estimate

Sentences beginning with *There are* or *It is* can often be tighter.

Wordy: There are three reasons for the success of the project.

Tighter: Three reasons explain the project's success.

Wordy: It is the case that university graduates advance more quickly in the company.

Tighter: University graduates advance more quickly in the company.

Check your draft. If you find these phrases, or any of the unnecessary words shown in Figure 4.6, eliminate them.

b. Use gerunds and infinitives to make sentences shorter and smoother.   A gerund (the *-ing* form of a verb) is a verb used as a noun. In the sentence, "Running is my favourite activity," *running* is the subject of the sentence. **An infinitive is the form of the verb that is preceded by *to: to run* is the infinitive.**

In the revision below, a gerund (*purchasing*) and an infinitive (*to transmit*) tighten the revision.

Wordy: A plant suggestion has been made where they would purchase a QWIP machine for the purpose of transmitting test reports between plants.

Tighter: The plant suggests purchasing a QWIP machine to transmit test reports between plants.

Even when gerunds and infinitives do not greatly affect length, they often make sentences smoother and more conversational.

FIGURE 4.6   Words to Cut

Cut the following words	Cut redundant words	Substitute a single word for a wordy phrase	
quite	a period of three months	at the present time	now
really	during the course of the negotiations	due to the fact that	because
very	during the year of 2004	in the event that	if
	maximum possible	in the near future	soon (or give the date)
	past experience	prior to the start of	before
	plan in advance	on a regular basis	regularly
	refer back		
	the colour blue		
	true facts		

c. Combine sentences to eliminate unnecessary words.   In addition to saving words, combining sentences focuses the reader's attention on key points, adds energy, and sharpens the relationship between ideas, thus making your writing more coherent.

Wordy: I conducted this survey by telephone on Sunday, April 21. I questioned two groups of seniors—male and female—who, according to the Student Directory, were still living in the dorms. The purpose of this survey was to find out why some seniors continue to live in the dorms even though they are no longer required by the University to do so. I also wanted to find out if there were any differences between male and female seniors in their reasons for choosing to remain in the dorms.

Tighter: On Sunday, April 21, I phoned seniors living in the dorms to find out (1) why they continue to live in the dorms even though they are no longer required to do so, and (2) whether men and women had the same reasons for staying in the dorms.

d. Put the meaning of your sentence into the subject and verb to cut the number of words.   Put the core of your meaning into the subject and verb of your main clause.

Wordy: The reason we are recommending the computerization of this process is because it will reduce the time required to obtain data and will give us more accurate data.

Better: We are recommending the computerization of this process because it will save time and give us more accurate data.

Tight: Computerizing the process will give us more accurate data more quickly.

Readable prose mixes sentence lengths and varies sentence structure. A really short sentence (under 10 words) can add punch to your prose. Really long sentences (over 30 or 40 words) are danger signs.

You can vary sentence patterns in several ways. First, you can mix simple, compound, and complex sentences. **Simple sentences** have one **main** or **independent clause**:

We will open a new store this month.

A main clause is a complete sentence with subject and verb. A **subordinate** or **dependent clause** contains a subject and verb but is not a complete statement and cannot stand by itself.

Compound sentences have two main clauses joined with *and, but, or,* or another conjunction. Compound sentences work best when the ideas in the two clauses are closely related.

> We have hired staff, and they will complete their training next week.

> We wanted to have a local radio station broadcast from the store during its grand opening, but the DJs were already booked.

Complex sentences have one main and one **subordinate** or **dependent clause**; they are good for showing logical relationships.

> When the stores open, we will have balloons and specials in every department.

> Because we already have a strong customer base in the northwest, we expect the new store to be just as successful as the store in the Granville Mall.

You can also vary sentences by changing the order of elements. Normally the subject comes first.

> We will survey customers later in the year to see whether demand warrants a third store on campus.

To create variety, occasionally begin the sentence with some other part of the sentence.

> Later in the year, we will survey customers to see whether demand warrants a third store on campus.

> To see whether demand warrants a third store on campus, we will survey customers later in the year.

Use these guidelines for sentence length and structure:

- Always edit sentences for tightness. Even a 17-word sentence can be wordy.
- When your subject matter is complicated or full of numbers, make a special effort to keep sentences short.
- Use long sentences
    - To show how ideas are linked to each other.
    - To avoid a series of short, choppy sentences.
    - To reduce repetition.
- Group the words in long and medium-length sentences into chunks that the reader can process quickly.[15]
- When you use a long sentence, keep the subject and verb close together.

Let's see how to apply the last three principles.

a. **Use long sentences to show how ideas are linked to each other; to avoid a series of short, choppy sentences; and to reduce repetition.** The following sentence is hard to read not simply because it is long but because it is shapeless. Just cutting it into a series of short, choppy sentences doesn't help. The best revision uses medium-length sentences to show the relationship between ideas.

> Too long: It should also be noted in the historical patterns presented in the summary, that though there were delays in January and February which we realized were occurring, we are now back where we were about a year ago, and that we are not off line in our collect receivables as compared to last year at this time, but we do show a considerable over-budget figure because of an ultraconservative goal on the receivable investment.

> Choppy: There were delays in January and February. We knew about them at the time. We are now back where we were about a year ago. The summary shows this. Our present collect receivables are in line with last year's.

> However, they exceed the budget. The reason they exceed the budget is that our goal for receivable investment was very conservative.

Better: As the summary shows, although there were delays in January and February (of which we were aware), we have now regained our position of a year ago. Our present collect receivables are in line with last year's, but they exceed the budget because our goal for receivable investment was very conservative.

b. **Group the words in long and medium-length sentences into chunks.** The "better" revision above has seven chunks. Any sentence pattern will get boring if repeated. Use different sentence patterns to keep your prose interesting.

c. **Keep the subject and verb close together.** Often you can move the subject and verb closer together if you put the modifying material in a list at the end of the sentence. For maximum readability, present the list vertically.

Hard to read: Movements resulting from termination, layoffs and leaves, recalls and reinstates, transfers in, transfers out, promotions in, promotions out, and promotions within are presently documented through the Payroll Authorization Form.

Smoother: The following movements are documented on the Payroll Authorization Form: termination, layoffs and leaves, recalls and reinstates, transfers in and out, and promotions in, out, and within.

Still better: The following movements are documented on the Payroll Authorization Form:
- Termination
- Layoffs and leaves
- Recalls and reinstates
- Transfers in and out
- Promotions in, out, and within

Parallel structure puts words, phrases, or clauses in the same grammatical and logical form. In the following faulty example, *by reviewing* is a gerund, while *note* is an imperative verb. Make the sentence parallel by using both gerunds or both imperatives.

Faulty: Errors can be checked by reviewing the daily exception report or note the number of errors you uncover when you match the lading copy with the file copy of the invoice.

Parallel: Errors can be checked by reviewing the daily exception report or by noting the number of errors you uncover when you match the lading copy with the file copy of the invoice.

Also parallel: To check errors, note
1. The number of items on the daily exception report.
2. The number of errors discovered when the lading copy and the file copy are matched.

Note that a list in parallel structure must fit grammatically into the umbrella sentence that introduces the list.

Words must also be logically parallel. In the following faulty example, *juniors, seniors,* and *athletes* are not three separate groups. The revision groups words into non-overlapping categories.

Faulty: I interviewed juniors and seniors and athletes.

Parallel: I interviewed juniors and seniors. In each rank, I interviewed athletes and non-athletes.

When Is a Tax Cut Not a Tax Cut? When It's a Refund.*

[President George W. Bush] is smart enough to have figured one thing out: Words are weapons. …

The unpopular concept of school vouchers has become "opportunity scholarships." … Similarly, Bush has relabeled churches, which many Americans do not think should receive federal support, as "faith-based institutions." Watered-down penalties on Iraq are "smart sanctions." …

The upside of choosing *le mot juste* can be huge, as previous administrations have demonstrated. Reagan scored a coup when he christened the MX missile the Peacekeeper at the height of the Cold War. … More recently, Clinton reshaped the debate over the trade with China when he ditched the elitist-sounding term "Most-Favored Nation" trade status in favor of the more egalitarian handle "Normal Trade Relations." …

Terminology also play[ed] a big role in [cutting] the estate tax—which is now being called the "death tax." ["Estate" is the term for the total amount of assets left by someone who dies. The term sounds like something only rich people have.] But everybody dies.

*Quoted from Richard S. Dunham, "When Is a Tax Cut Not a Tax Cut?" *BusinessWeek,* March 19, 2001, 38–39.

Parallel structure is a powerful device for making your writing tighter, smoother, and more forceful. As Figure 4.7 shows, parallelism often enables you to tighten your writing. To eliminate repetition in parallel lists, see Figure 4.8. Use second-person pronouns (*you*) rather than third-person (*he, she, one*) to give your writing more impact. *You* is both singular and plural; it can refer to a single person or to every member of your organization.

Third-person:	Funds in a participating employee's account at the end of each six months will automatically be used to buy more stock unless a "Notice of Election Not to Exercise Purchase Rights" form is received from the employee.
Second-person:	Once you begin to participate, funds in your account at the end of each six months will automatically be used to buy more stock unless you turn in a "Notice of Election Not to Exercise Purchase Rights" form.

Be careful to use *you* only when it refers to your reader.

Incorrect:	My visit with the outside sales rep showed me that your schedule can change quickly.
Correct:	My visit with the outside sales rep showed me that schedules can change quickly.

As You Write and Revise Paragraphs

Paragraphs are visual and logical units. Use them to chunk your sentences.

A good paragraph has **unity;** that is, it discusses only one idea, or topic. The **topic sentence** states the main idea and provides a scaffold to structure your document. Your writing will be easier to read if you make the topic sentence explicit and put it at the beginning of the paragraph.[16]

FIGURE 4.7   Use Parallelism to Tighten Your Writing

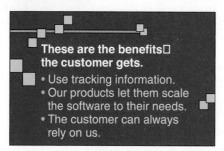

Faulty

Parallel

FIGURE 4.8   Eliminate Repeated Words in Parallel Lists

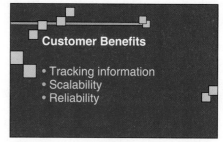

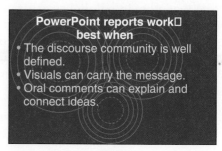

Wordy

Tight

Hard to read
(no topic
sentence):

In fiscal 2005, the company filed claims for refund of federal income taxes of $3,199,000 and interest of $969,000 paid as a result of an examination of the company's federal income tax returns by the Canada Revenue Agency (CRA) for the years 2000 through 2002. It is uncertain what amount, if any, may ultimately be recovered.

Better (paragraph
starts with
topic sentence):

The company and the Canada Revenue Agency (CRA) disagree about whether the company is owed back taxes. In fiscal 2005, the company filed claims for a refund of federal income taxes of $3,199,000 and interest of $969,000 paid as a result of an examination of the company's federal income tax returns by the CRA for the years 2000 through 2002. It is uncertain what amount, if any, may ultimately be recovered.

A good topic sentence forecasts the structure and content of the paragraph.

Plan B also has economic advantages.

(Prepares the reader for a discussion of B's economic advantages.)

We had several personnel changes in June.

(Prepares the reader for a list of the month's terminations and hires.)

When the first sentence of a paragraph is not the topic sentence, readers who skim may miss the main point. Move the topic sentence to the beginning of the paragraph. If the paragraph does not have a topic sentence, you will need to write one. If you can't think of a single sentence that serves as an "umbrella" to cover every sentence, the paragraph lacks unity. To solve the problem, either split the paragraph into two or eliminate the sentence that digresses from the main point.

Transition words and sentences signal the connections between ideas to the reader. **Transitions** tell whether the next sentence continues the previous thought or starts a new idea; transitions can tell whether the idea that comes next is more or less important than the previous thought. Figure 4.9 lists some of the most common transition words and phrases.

Readability Formulas and Good Style

Readability formulas attempt to measure objectively how easy something is to read. However, since they don't take many factors into account, the formulas are at best a very limited guide to good style.

FIGURE 4.9   Transition Words and Phrases

To show addition or continuation of the same idea	To introduce an example	To show that the contrast is more important than the previous idea	To show time
and	for example (e.g.)	but	after
also	for instance (i.e.)	however	as
first, second, third	indeed	nevertheless	before
in addition	to illustrate	on the contrary	in the future
likewise	namely		next
similarly	specifically	**To show cause and effect**	then
To introduce the last or most important item	**To contrast**	as a result	until
finally	in contrast	because	when
furthermore	on the other hand	consequently	while
moreover	or	for this reason	**To summarize or end**
		therefore	in conclusion
			finally

The Boss Won't Let Me Write That Way

When a writing consultant urged them to use *I*, the engineers in R&D at one firm claimed they couldn't: "Our boss won't let us." The consultant checked with their boss, the vice-president for research and development. He said, "I don't care what words they use. I just want to be able to understand what they write."

Moral 1: If you think your boss doesn't want you to use a word, ask. A few bosses do prize formal or flowery language. Most don't.

Moral 2: Even if your boss has the same background you do, he or she won't necessarily understand what you write. Revise your memos and reports so they're clear and easy to read.

Moral 3: What's in the file cabinet isn't necessarily a guide to good writing for your organization.

Computer packages that analyze style may give you a readability score. Some companies require that guarantees and other consumer documents meet certain scores.

The two best-known readability formulas—the Gunning Fog Index and the Flesch Reading Ease Scale—depend heavily on word length and sentence length. But as Janice C. Redish and Jack Selzer have shown,[17] using shorter words and sentences will not necessarily make a passage easy to read. Short words are not always easy to understand, especially if they have technical meanings (e.g., *waive, bear market, liquid*). Short, choppy sentences and sentence fragments are actually harder to understand than well-written medium-length sentences.

No reading formula yet devised takes into account three factors that influence how easy a text is to read: the complexity of the ideas, the organization of the ideas, and the layout and design of the document.

Instead of using readability formulas to measure style, test your draft with the people for whom it is designed. How long does it take them to find the information they need? Do they make mistakes when they try to use the document? Do they think the document is easy to use? Answers to these questions can give us much more accurate information than any readability score.

Organizational Preferences for Style

Different organizations and bosses may legitimately have different ideas about what constitutes good writing. If the style the company prefers seems reasonable, use it. If the style doesn't seem reasonable—if you work for someone who likes flowery language or wordy paragraphs, for example—you have several choices.

- Go ahead and use the techniques in this chapter. Sometimes seeing good writing changes people's minds about the style they prefer.
- Help your boss learn about writing. Show him or her this book or the research cited in the notes to demonstrate how a clear, crisp style makes documents easier to read.
- Recognize that a style may serve other purposes than communication. An abstract, hard-to-read style may help a group forge its own identity. James Suchan and Ronald Dulek have shown that Navy officers preferred a passive, impersonal style because they saw themselves as followers.[18] When big words, jargon, and wordiness are central to a group's self-image, change will be difficult, since changing style will mean changing the corporate culture.
- Ask. Often the documents that end up in files aren't especially good; later, other workers may find these and copy them, thinking they represent a corporate standard. Bosses may in fact prefer better writing.

Building a good style takes energy and effort, but it's well worth the work. Good style can make every document more effective; good style can help make you the good writer so valuable to every organization.

Summary of Key Points

- Good style in business and administrative writing is less formal, more friendly, and more personal than the style usually used for term papers.
- To improve your style,
  1. Start a clean page or screen so that you aren't locked into old sentence structures.
  2. Try WIRMI: *What I Really Mean Is*. Then write the words.

3. Try reading your draft out loud to someone sitting about one metre away. If the words sound stiff, they'll seem stiff to a reader, too.

4. Ask someone else to read your draft out loud. Readers stumble because the words on the page aren't what they expect to see. The places where that person stumbles are places where your writing can be better.

5. Write a *lot.*

■ Use the following techniques to make your writing easier to read:
As you choose words,
1. Use words that are accurate, appropriate, and familiar. Denotation is a word's literal meaning; connotation is the emotional colouring that a word conveys.
2. Use technical jargon only when it is essential and known to the reader. Eliminate business jargon.

As you write and revise sentences,
3. Use active verbs most of the time. Active verbs are better because they are shorter, clearer, and more interesting.
4. Use verbs—not nouns—to carry the weight of your sentence.
5. Tighten your writing. Writing is wordy if the same idea can be expressed in fewer words.
   a. Eliminate words that say nothing.
   b. Use gerunds and infinitives to make sentences shorter and smoother.
   c. Combine sentences to eliminate unnecessary words.
   d. Put the meaning of your sentence into the subject and verb to cut the number of words.
6. Vary sentence length and sentence structure.
7. Use parallel structure. Use the same grammatical form for ideas that have the same logical function.
8. Put your readers in your sentences.

As you write and revise paragraphs,
9. Begin most paragraphs with topic sentences so that readers know what to expect in the paragraph.
10. Use transitions to link ideas.

■ Readability formulas are not a sufficient guide to style. They imply that all short words and all short sentences are equally easy to read; they ignore other factors that make a document easy or hard to read: the complexity of the ideas, the organization of the ideas, and the layout and design of the document.

■ Different organizations and bosses may legitimately have different ideas about what constitutes good writing.

CHAPTER 4 Exercises and Problems

Getting Started

4.1 Identifying Words with Multiple Denotations

a. Each of the following words has several denotations. How many can you list without going to a dictionary? How many additional meanings does a good dictionary list?

browser	log
court	table

b. List five words that have multiple denotations.

4.2   Evaluating the Ethical Implications of Connotations

In each of the following pairs, identify the more favourable term. Is its use justified? Why or why not?

1. wastepaper   recovered fibre
2. feedback   criticism
3. deadline   due date
4. scalper   ticket reseller
5. budget   spending plan

4.3   Choosing Levels of Formality

Identify the more formal word in each pair. Which term is better for most business documents? Why?

1. adapted to   geared to
2. befuddled   confused
3. assistant   helper
4. pilot project   testing the waters
5. cogitate   think

Choosing Your Words

4.4   Eliminating Jargon and Simplifying Language

Revise these sentences to eliminate jargon and to use short, familiar words. In some sentences, you'll need to reword, reorganize, or add information to produce the best revision.

1. Computers can enumerate pages when the appropriate keystroke is implemented.
2. Any alterations must be approved during the 30-day period commencing 60 days prior to the expiration date of the agreement.
3. As per your request, the undersigned has obtained estimates of upgrading our computer system. A copy of the estimated cost is attached hereto.
4. Please be advised that this writer is in considerable need of a new computer.
5. Enclosed please find the proposed schedule for the training session. In the event that you have alterations that you would like to suggest, forward same to my office at your earliest convenience.

4.5   Changing Verbs from Passive to Active

Identify the passive verbs in the following sentences and convert them to active verbs. In some cases, you may need to add information to do so. You may use different words as long as you retain the basic meaning of the sentence. Remember that imperative verbs are active, too.

1. The business plan was written by Tyrone King.
2. The cost of delivering financial services is being slashed by computers, the Internet, and toll-free phone lines.
3. When the vacation schedule is finalized it is recommended that it be routed to all supervisors for final approval.
4. As stated in my résumé, I have designed Web pages for three student organizations.
5. Material must not be left on trucks outside the warehouse. Either the trucks must be parked inside the warehouse or the material must be unloaded at the time of receiving the truck.

4.6   Reducing Wordiness

1. Eliminate words that say nothing. You may use different words.
   a. There are many businesses that are active in community and service work.
   b. The purchase of a new computer will allow us to produce form letters quickly. In addition, return on investment could be calculated for proposed repairs. Another use is that the computer could check databases to make sure that claims are paid only once.
   c. Our decision to enter the South American market has precedence in the past activities of the company.
2. Use gerunds and infinitives to make these sentences shorter and smoother.
   a. The completion of the project requires the collection and analysis of additional data.
   b. The purchase of laser printers will make possible the in-house production of the newsletter.

c. The treasurer has the authority for the investment of assets for the gain of higher returns.

3. Combine sentences to show how ideas are related and to eliminate unnecessary words.

   a. Some customers are profitable for companies. Other customers actually cost the company money.

b. If you are unable to come to the session on dental coverage, please call the human resources office. You will be able to schedule another time to ask questions you may have about the various options.

c. Major Japanese firms often have employees who know English well. Canadian companies negotiating with Japanese companies should bring their own interpreters.

4.7   Improving Parallel Structure

Revise each of the following sentences to create parallelism.

1. The orientation session will cover the following information:

   - Company culture will be discussed.

   - How to use the equipment.

   - You will get an overview of key customers' needs.

2. Five criteria for a good Web page are content that serves the various audiences, attention to details, and originality. It is also important to have effective organization and navigation devices. Finally, provide attention to details such as revision date and the Webmaster's address.

3. When you leave a voice mail message,

   - Summarize your main point in a sentence or two.

   - The name and phone number should be given slowly and distinctly.

   - The speaker should give enough information so that the recipient can act on the message.

   - Tell when you'll be available to receive the recipient's return call.

4.8   Using Topic Sentences

Make each of the following paragraphs more readable by opening each paragraph with a topic sentence. You may be able to find a topic sentence in the paragraph and move it to the beginning. In other cases, you'll need to write a new sentence.

1. At Disney World, a lunch put on an expense account is "on the mouse." McDonald's employees "have ketchup in their veins." Business slang flourishes at companies with rich corporate cultures. Memos at Procter & Gamble are called "reco's" because the model P&G memo begins with a recommendation.

2. The first item on the agenda is the hiring for the coming year. George has also asked that we review the agency goals for the next fiscal year. We should cover this early in the meeting since it may affect our hiring preferences. Finally, we need to announce the deadlines for grant proposals, decide which grants to apply for, and set up a committee to draft each proposal.

3. Separate materials that can be recycled from your regular trash. Pass along old clothing, toys, or appliances to someone else who can use them. When you purchase products, choose those with minimal packaging. If you have a yard, put your yard waste and kitchen scraps (excluding meat and fat) in a compost pile. You can reduce the amount of solid waste your household produces in four ways.

4.9   Revising Paragraphs

Revise each paragraph to make it easier to read. Change, rearrange, or delete words and sentences; add any material necessary.

a. Once a new employee is hired, each one has to be trained for a week by one of our supervisors at a cost of $1,000 each which includes the supervisor's time. This amount also includes half of the new employee's salary, since new hires produce only half the normal production per worker for the week. This summer $24,000 was spent in training 24 new employees. Absenteeism increased in the department on the hottest summer days. For every day each worker is absent we lose $200 in lost production. This past summer there was a total of 56 absentee days taken for a total loss of $11,200 in lost production. Turnover and absenteeism were the causes of an unnecessary expenditure of over $35,000 this summer.

b. One service is investments. General financial news and alerts about companies in the customer's portfolio are available. Quicken also provides assistance in finding the best mortgage rate and in providing assistance in making the decision whether to refinance a mortgage. Another service from Quicken is advice for the start and management of a small business. Banking services, such as paying bills and applying for loans, have long been available to Quicken subscribers. The taxpayer can be walked through the tax preparation process by Quicken. Someone considering retirement can use Quicken to ascertain whether the amount being set aside for this purpose is sufficient. Quicken's Web site provides seven services.

4.10   Writing Paragraphs

Write a paragraph on each of the following topics.

a. Discuss your ideal job.

b. Summarize a recent article from a business magazine or newspaper.

c. Explain how technology is affecting the field you plan to enter.

d. Explain why you have or have not decided to work while you attend university.

e. Write a profile of someone who is successful in the field you hope to enter.

As Your Professor Directs,

a. Label topic sentences, active verbs, and parallel structure.

b. Edit a classmate's paragraphs to make the writing even tighter and smoother.

4.11   Choosing the Right Word

Choose the right word for each sentence.

1. The audit revealed a small (amount, number) of errors.

2. Diet beverages have (fewer, less) calories than regular drinks.

3. In her speech, she (implied, inferred) that the vote would be close.

4. We need to redesign the stand so that the catalogue is eye level instead of (laying, lying) on the desk.

5. (Their, There, They're) is some evidence that (their, there, they're) thinking of changing (their, there, they're) policy.

6. The settlement isn't yet in writing; if one side wanted to back out of the (oral, verbal) agreement, it could.

7. In (affect, effect), we're creating a new department.

8. The firm will be hiring new (personal, personnel) in three departments this year.

9. Several customers have asked that we carry more campus merchandise, (i.e., e.g.,) pillows and mugs with the university seal.

10. We have investigated all of the possible solutions (accept, except) adding a turning lane.

4.12   Tracking Your Own Mechanical Errors

Analyze the mechanical errors (grammar, punctuation, word use, and typos) in each of your papers.

■ How many different errors are marked on each paper?

■ Which three errors do you make most often?

■ Is the number of errors constant in each paper, or does the number increase or decrease during the term?

As Your Professor Directs,

a. Correct each of the mechanical errors in one or more papers.

b. Deliberately write two new sentences in which you make each of your three most common errors. Then write the correct version of each sentence.

c. Write a memo to your professor discussing your increasing mastery of mechanical correctness during the semester.

d. Briefly explain to the class how to avoid one kind of error in grammar, punctuation, or word use.

Letters, Memos, and E-Mail Messages

5 Informative and Positive Messages

AN INSIDE PERSPECTIVE

Informative and Positive Messages

Relationships built on a foundation of powerful and credible communications are key to the success of Canadian Tire Corporation. In an era of intense scrutiny and skepticism, the Canadian Tire communication team maintains a strong relationship with Canadians.

Communicating with 10 million households weekly and with more than 225 million annually, the communication team's presence is felt in decision-making and daily operations. Its ability to communicate with everyone and to mobilize and focus 45,000 team members is as essential to corporate success as any strategy or sales forecast.

Regulatory change, stakeholder demands, mandatory disclosure, and the need for transparency mean that a CEO's ability to communicate effectively with stakeholders is a leadership attribute that is taking on increasing importance. In fact, Wayne Sales often refers to himself as the Chief Communication Officer at Canadian Tire.

He is motivated by the words of aviation pioneer Anne Morrow Lindbergh who said that good communication is as stimulating as black coffee and just as hard to sleep after. If good communication is challenging, it's worth it. It is so powerful precisely because of the commitments of time and energy—and the attention to audience needs.

In the competition for audience attention, it's as well to remember that people forget as much as two-thirds of what they've heard or read in 24 hours. That is why there is a persuasive element in all writing. With nearly universal brand recognition, Canadian Tire clearly is getting its message across to Canadians.

Wayne Sales, President and CEO, Canadian Tire Corporation, and winner of the 2005 Canadian Public Relations Society's Award of Excellence in Public Relations, promotes the value of informative and persuasive messages inside and outside the organization.

www.canadiantire.ca

Source: Wayne Sales, "A Seat at the Table," *Blitz Magazine*, 44, 1–5.

Business messages must meet the needs of the writer (and the writer's organization), be sensitive to the audience, and accurately reflect the topic being addressed. Informative and positive messages are the bread-and-butter correspondence in organizations.

When we need to convey information to which the reader's basic reaction will be neutral, the message is **informative**. If we convey information to which the reader's reaction will be positive, the message is a **positive** or **good news message.** Neither message immediately asks the reader to do anything. You usually do want to build positive attitudes toward the information you are presenting, so in that sense, even an informative message has a persuasive element. ➡ Chapter 6 will discuss messages where the reader will respond negatively; ➡ Chapters 7 and 8 discuss messages where you want the reader to act.

Informative and positive messages include acceptances; positive answers to reader requests; congratulatory notes; responses to complaints; information about procedures, products, services, or options; announcements of policy changes that are neutral or positive; and changes that are to the reader's advantage.

Even a simple informative or good news message usually has several purposes.

Primary purposes:

■ To give information or good news to the reader or to reassure the reader

■ To have the reader read the message, understand it, and view the information positively

■ To de-emphasize any negative elements

Secondary purposes:

■ To build the credibility of the writer

■ To enhance the reputation of the writer's organization

■ To cement a good relationship between the writer and reader

■ To ensure the message doesn't require more messages and create more work for the writer

Informative and positive messages are not necessarily short. Instead, the length of a message depends on your purposes, the audience's needs, and the complexity of the situation. A public health inspector got a lot of teasing from his colleagues because he wrote 10-page inspection reports; the other inspectors rarely wrote more than 4 pages. He got the last laugh, however, when the lawyers complimented him on his reports. For the first time, they were getting enough information to win cases against companies and individuals charged with violating public health legislation. The shorter reports didn't give enough information.

Writing Letters, Memos, and E-Mails

Letters go to someone outside your organization; **memos** go to someone in your own organization; e-mails (with features of letters and memos) go to those inside and outside your organization. In large organizations where each unit is autonomous, however, the organization's culture determines whether people in different units send letters or memos to each other. In some universities and community colleges, for example, faculty send letters if they need to write to faculty in other departments.

Letters and memos have different formats, using and arranging document parts to meet the needs of their different audiences.

The differences in audience and format are the only differences between letters and memos. Both kinds of messages can be long or short, depending

The (Earning) Power of Good Writing*

Communications skills offer the highest return on investment in Canada and the United States, where there is high demand for these skills. A 2001 Canadian study based on a seven-country International Adult Literacy Survey connects labour market success and earning power to literacy skills. Specifically, literacy—the ability to understand and use information in textual form—accounts for one-third of the "return on education," each additional year of education raising earnings by 8.3%.

Similarly, a 2004 study based on the Ontario Immigrant Literacy Survey underlines the impact of communication skills on earnings. A 100-point increase in literacy scores raises earnings by an amount equivalent to that achieved by university graduates as opposed to high school dropouts.

*Based on David A. Green and W. Craig Riddell, *Literacy, Numeracy and Labour Market Outcomes in Canada,* catalogue no. 89-552-MPE (Ottawa: Minister of Industry, 2001) and Ana Ferrer, David A. Green, and W. Craig Riddell, *International Adult Literacy Survey: The Effect of Literacy on Immigrant Earnings,* catalogue no. 89-552-X1E (Ottawa: Minister of Industry, 2004). Retrieved May 4, 2005 from http://www.statcan.ca.

on how much you have to say and how complicated the situation is. Both kinds of messages can be informal when you write to someone you know well, or more formal when you write to someone you don't know, to several audiences, or for the record. Both kinds of messages can be simple responses that you can dash off in 15 minutes; both can take hours of analysis and revision when you've never faced that situation before or when the stakes are high.

If new employers give some grace period before you write paper documents, most will expect you to come to the job electronically literate. E-mails have fast become the number-one choice for internal and external communications.[1]

Although e-mail feels informal and private, it is both public and permanent. Writers welcomed the early informality of e-mail until hasty, careless, or casual words came back to haunt them: lost credibility, lost clients, lost time and opportunities—and even legal liability. The use and overuse of e-mail has led to new business risks and measures:

- Developing e-mail policies and procedures
- Safeguarding access and controls
- Monitoring e-mail use by employees
- Limiting or prohibiting personal use
- Training employees to treat e-mail appropriately

All the principles of good business writing still apply in e-mail: from attending to purpose and audience needs and benefits to checking for grammatical accuracy and completeness of information. Language and tone choices should be made carefully. Once you hit "send," the e-mail becomes public and permanent. Just as some organizations require writers to be concise and limit memos to one page, many insist that there needs to be good reason for anything over one screen in e-mail.

Organizing Informative and Positive Messages

The patterns of organization in this chapter and the chapters that follow will work for 70 to 90% of the writing situations most people in business and government face. Using the appropriate pattern can help you compose more quickly and create a better final product.

- Be sure you understand the reason behind each pattern so that you can change the pattern if necessary. (For example, if you write instructions, any warnings should go up front, not in the middle of the message.)
- Not every message that uses the direct pattern will have all the elements listed. Any elements will go in the order presented in the pattern.
- Sometimes you can present several elements in one paragraph. Sometimes you'll need several paragraphs for just one element.

In real life, writing problems don't come with labels that tell you which pattern to use. ➡ Chapters 5, 6, and 7 offer advice about when to use each pattern.

Figure 5.1 shows how to organize informative and positive messages in a direct pattern.

The letter in Figure 5.2 authorizes a one-year appointment that the reader and writer have already discussed and describes the organization's priorities. Since the writer knows that the reader wants to accept the job, the letter doesn't need to persuade. The opportunity for the professor to study records that aren't available to the public is an implicit reader benefit; the concern for the reader's needs builds goodwill.

FIGURE 5.1   How to Organize Informative and Positive Messages

1. **Give any good news and summarize the main points.** Include the date policies begin and the amount of a discount. If the reader has already raised the issue, make it clear that you're responding.

   Share good news immediately.

2. **Give details, clarification, background.** Don't repeat information you've already given. Do answer all the questions your reader is likely to have; provide all the information necessary to achieve your purposes. Present details in the order of importance to the reader.

3. **Present any negative elements as positively as possible.** A policy may have limits; information may be incomplete; the reader may have to satisfy requirements to get a discount or benefit. Make these negatives clear, but present them as positively as possible.

4. **Explain any reader benefits.** Most informative memos need reader benefits. Show that the policy or procedure helps readers, not just the company. Give enough detail to make the benefits clear and convincing. In letters, you may want to give benefits of dealing with your company as well as benefits of the product or policy.

   In a good news message, it's often possible to combine a short reader benefit with a goodwill ending in the last paragraph.

5. **Use a goodwill ending: positive, personal, and forward looking.** Shifting your emphasis away from the message to the specific reader suggests that serving the reader is your real concern.

Choosing Subject Lines for Informative and Positive Messages

A **subject line** is the title of a document. It aids in filing and retrieving the document, tells readers why they need to read the document, and provides a framework in which to set what you're about to say.

A good subject line meets three criteria: it is specific, concise, and appropriate to the kind of message (positive, negative, persuasive).

The subject line needs to be specific enough to differentiate that message from others on the same subject, but broad enough to cover everything in the message.

Too general:	Training Sessions
Better:	Dates for 2006 Training Sessions
or:	Evaluation of Training Sessions on Conducting Interviews
or:	Should We Schedule a Short Course on Proposal Writing?

Most subject lines are relatively short (not a sentence and with no punctuation at the end)—usually no more than 10 words, often only 3 to 7 words.[2]

Wordy:	Survey of Student Preferences in Regards to Various Pizza Factors
Better:	Students' Pizza Preferences
or:	The Feasibility of a Family Pizza Branch on Campus
or:	What Students Like and Dislike about Giovanni Pizza

If you can't make the subject both specific and short, be specific.

Since your subject line introduces your reader to your message, it must satisfy the psychological demands of the situation; it must be appropriate to your purposes and to the immediate response you expect from your reader. In general, do the same thing in your subject line that you would do in the first paragraph.

When you have good news for the reader, build goodwill by highlighting it in the subject line. When your information is neutral, summarize it concisely for the subject line.

FIGURE 5.2   A Positive Letter

Ifi *INTERNATIONAL FIDELITY INSURANCE COMPANY*	*100 Bloor Street West Toronto, ON M4W 1A5 416-928-5000 Fax: 416-928-5270*

March 7, 2005

Professor Adrienne Prinz
Department of History
McGill University
845 Sherbrooke Street West
Montreal, QC H3A 2T5

Dear Professor Prinz:

Good news — Your appointment as archivist for International Fidelity Insurance has been approved. When you were in Toronto in December, you said that you could begin work June 2. We'd like you to start then if that date is still good for you.   *Tactful*

The Board has outlined the following priorities for your work: *Assumes reader's primary interest is the job*

Negative about lighting and security presented impersonally

1. **Organize and catalogue the archives.** You'll have the basement of the Palmer Building for the archives and can requisition the supplies you need. You'll be able to control heat and humidity; the budget doesn't allow special lighting or security measures.

Details

2. **Prepare materials for a four-hour training session in October** for senior-level managers. We'd like you to cover how to decide what to send to the archives. If your first four months of research uncover any pragmatic uses for our archives (like Royal and SunAlliance Canada's use of archives to teach managers about past pitfalls), include those in the session.

3. **Write an article each month for the employee newsletter** describing the uses of the archives. When we're cutting costs in other departments, it's important to justify committing funds to start an archive program.

These provisions will appeal to the reader

4. **Study the IFI archives to compile** information that (a) can help solve current management problems, (b) could be included in a history of the company, and (c) might be useful to scholars of business history.

Negative that reader will have to reapply presented as normal procedure

5. **Begin work on a corporate history of IFI.** IFI will help you find a publisher and support the book financially. You'll have full control over the content.   *Salary is de-emphasized to avoid implying that reader is "just taking the job for the money"*

Your salary will be $34,000 for six months; your contract can be renewed twice for a total of 18 months. You're authorized to hire a full-time research assistant for $15,000 for six months; you'll need to go through the normal personnel request process to request that that money be continued next year. A file clerk will be assigned full-time to your project. You'll report to me. At least for the rest of this calendar year, the budget for the Archives Project will come from my department.

Subject: Discount on Rental Cars Effective January 2

Starting January 2, as an employee of Amalgamated Industries you can get a 15% discount on cars you rent for business or personal use from Roadway Rent-a-Car.

Subject: Update on Arrangements for Videoconference with France

In the last month, we have chosen the participants and developed a tentative agenda for the videoconference with France scheduled for March 21.

Subject lines in e-mail are even more important than those in letters and memos.[3] Subject lines must be specific, concise, and catchy. Some e-mail users

| **FIGURE 5.2** | A Positive Letter *(continued)* |

Professor Adrienne Prinz
March 7, 2005
Page 2

IFI offices are equipped with Pentium computers with Access, WordPerfect, and Excel. Is there any software that we should buy for cataloguing or research? Are there any office supplies that we need to have on hand June 2 so that you can work efficiently?

In the meantime,

1. Please send your written acceptance right away.

2. Let me know if you need any software or supplies.

3. Send me the name, address, and Social Insurance number of your research assistant by May 1 so that I can process his or her employment papers.

Goodwill ending

4. If you'd like help finding a house or apartment in Toronto, let me know. I can give you the name of a real estate agent.

On June 2, you'll spend the morning in Personnel. Stop by my office at noon. We'll go out for lunch and then I'll take you to the office you'll have while you're at IFI.

Welcome to IFI!

Cordially,

Cynthia Yen

Cynthia Yen
Director of Education and Training

get so many messages that they don't bother reading messages if they don't recognize the sender or if the subject doesn't catch their interest. If you have good news to convey, put it in the subject line. Be as brief as you can. The following subject lines would be acceptable for informative and good news e-mail messages:

- Travel Plans for Sales Meeting
- Your Proposal Accepted
- Reduced Prices During February
- Your Funding Request Approved

Using Reader Benefits in Informative and Positive Messages

Not all informative and positive messages need reader benefits (◄ p. 38). You don't need reader benefits when

- You're presenting factual information only.
- The reader's attitude toward the information doesn't matter.
- Stressing benefits may make the reader sound selfish.
- The benefits are so obvious that to restate them insults the reader's intelligence.

You do need reader benefits when

- You are presenting policies.

Spam Costs*

In 2002, spam accounted for 38% of all e-mail; in 2003, 60%; in January and February 2004, 75%.

- Spam in Canada was exceeded only by that in the United States, China, South Korea, Brazil, and Taiwan.

- One Canadian bank had 30% spam, 20% irrelevant, and only 50% relevant messages.

- Phishing scams (e-mails that appear to come from legitimate sources) collecting data for marketing and ad campaigns reached 35 million a week in the second half of 2004 (up from 9 million in the first half of 2004).

- The Coalition Against Unsolicited Commercial E-Mail in Canada is agitating for Canadian legislation.

*Adapted from Keith Woolhouse, "Reclaim your e-mail," Saskatoon *StarPhoenix* April 10, 2004, E1–2; Simon Avery, "Hacker Alert: Report finds surge in on-line attacks," *The Globe and Mail*, March 21, 2005, B1–5.

■ You want to shape readers' attitudes toward the information or toward your organization.

■ Stressing benefits presents readers' motives positively.

■ Some of the benefits may not be obvious to readers.

Messages to customers or potential customers sometimes include a sales paragraph promoting products or services you offer in addition to the product or service that the reader has asked about. Sales promotion in an informative or positive message should be low-key, not "hard sell."

Reader benefits are hardest to develop when you are announcing policies. The organization probably decided to adopt the policy because it appeared to help the organization. Yet reader benefits are most essential in this kind of message so readers see the reason for the change and support it.

When you present reader benefits, be sure to present advantages *to the reader.* Even if the organization saves money or increases its profits, workers will benefit directly only if they own stock in the company, if they're high up enough to receive bonuses, if the savings enables a failing company to avoid layoffs, or if all of the savings goes directly to employee benefits.

To develop reader benefits for informative and positive messages, use the steps suggested in ◄ Chapter 2. Be sure to think about benefits that come from the activity or policy itself, apart from any financial benefits. Does a policy improve the eight hours people spend at work?

Ending Informative and Positive Messages

Ending a letter, memo, or e-mail gracefully can be a problem in short informative and positive messages. In a one-page memo where you have omitted details and proof, you can tell readers where to get more information. In long messages, you can summarize your basic point. In persuasive messages, as you'll learn in ► Chapter 7, you can tell readers what you want them to do. In a short message containing all the information readers need, either write a goodwill paragraph that refers directly to the reader or the reader's organization, or just stop.

Goodwill endings should focus on the business relationship you share with your reader. When you write to one person or organization, a good last paragraph fits that audience so specifically that it would not work with any other.

Use a paragraph that shows you see your reader as an individual. Possibilities include complimenting the reader for a job well done, describing a reader benefit, or looking forward to something positive that relates to the subject of the message.

In the following examples, a letter answers the question "When a patient leaves the hospital and returns, should we count it as a new stay?" For one company the answer was that if a patient was gone from the hospital overnight or longer, the hospital should start a new claim when the patient was readmitted.

Weak closing paragraph:	Should you have any questions regarding this matter, please feel free to call me.
Goodwill paragraph:	Many employee-patients appreciate the freedom to leave the hospital for a few hours. It's nice working with a hospital that is flexible enough to offer that option.
Also acceptable:	Omit the paragraph; stop after the explanation.

Some writers end every message with a standard invitation:

If you have questions, please do not hesitate to ask.

That sentence lacks positive emphasis. But revising it to say "feel free to call" still leaves the impression of a clichéd (and insincere) ending. It also invites extra work unecessarily. Most of the time, the writer should omit the sentence entirely.

The memo in Figure 5.3 announces a new employee benefit. The first paragraph summarizes the policy. Paragraphs 2 to 3 give details. Negative elements in paragraph 3 are stated as positively as possible. The last section of the memo gives reader benefits and a goodwill ending.

Distinguishing Varieties of Informative and Positive Messages

Messages can be informative, negative, or persuasive depending on what you have to say. A transmittal, for example, can be positive when you're sending glowing sales figures or persuasive when you want the reader to act on the information. A performance appraisal is positive when you evaluate someone who's doing superbly, negative when you want to compile a record to justify firing someone, and persuasive when you want to motivate a satisfactory

FIGURE 5.3 A Positive Memo

To: All Chamber Employees and Members of the Chamber Insurance Group

From: Lee Ann Rabe, Vice-President for Human Resources

Subject: Dental and Vision Care Benefits Added to Health Plan   *LAR*

Date: March 1, 2005

Good news in subject line and first paragraph

Beginning May 1, employees covered by the Chamber Health Plan will be eligible for dental and vision care benefits.

Details Coverage is extended to employees who (1) work at least half-time and (2) have been employed by the Chamber for at least three months. Coverage has been consolidated with our existing carrier:
- To ease administration
- To maximize cost savings
- To simplify submission of claims

Negatives presented as positively as possible

Costs and coverage of ongoing benefits of the Chamber Health Plan remain the same. Dental and vision coverage is available for a fee; limitations apply. For information about the specifics of the extended Chamber Health Plan, pick up a brochure in the Human Resources Department.

The new policy will affect not only Chamber employees but also the small businesses that are a part of the Chamber's Health Plan. New businesses may see the change as a reason to join the Chamber—and the Health Plan. Growth in the Health Plan creates a wider base for insurance premiums and helps keep costs as low as possible. Additional Chamber members give us the funds and resources to plan more conferences for members. These conferences, such as the recent "R&D in Small Businesses," help Chamber members do business successfully.

Reader Benefits

Making the Health Plan more comprehensive and maintaining access and affordability keeps us competitive with other major Canadian cities. As we face increasing competition to recruit and retrain the best employees, businesses are carefully considering possible moves. A policy change like this one shows the Chamber's continued goodwill and investment in our employees' health and happiness and will make convincing businesses to relocate here that much easier.

Selling Barrie as a good place to live and do business has never been easier.

Goodwill ending

worker to continue to improve. A collection letter is persuasive; it becomes negative in the last stage when you threaten legal action.

Writing Transmittals

When you send someone something in an organization, attach a memo or letter of transmittal explaining what you're sending. A transmittal can be as simple as a Post-it™ note with "FYI" ("for your information") written on it, or it can be a separate typed document.

Organize a memo or letter of transmittal in this order:

1. Tell the reader what you're sending.
2. Summarize the main point(s) of the document.
3. Indicate any special circumstances or information that would help the reader understand the document. Is it a draft? Is it a partial document that will be completed later?
4. Tell the reader what will happen next. Will you do something? Do you want a response? If you do want the reader to act, specify exactly what you want the reader to do and give a deadline.

Frequently transmittals have important secondary purposes. Consider the writer's purpose in Figure 5.4, a transmittal from a lawyer to her client. The primary purpose of this transmittal is to give the client a chance to affirm that his story and the lawyer's understanding of it are correct. If there's anything wrong, the lawyer wants to know *before* she files the brief. But an important secondary purpose is to build goodwill: "I'm working on your case; I'm earning my fee." The greatest number of complaints officially lodged against lawyers are for the lawyer's neglect—or what the client perceives as neglect—of the client's case.

Sending Confirmations

Many informative messages record oral conversations. These messages are generally short and give only the information shared orally; they go to the other party in the conversation. Start the message by indicating that it is a confirmation, not a new message:

As we discussed on the phone today, …

As I told you yesterday, …

Here is the meeting schedule we discussed earlier today.

Summarizing

You may be asked to summarize a conversation, document, or an outside meeting for colleagues or superiors. (Minutes of an internal meeting are usually more detailed. See Chapter 10 for advice on writing minutes of meetings.)

In a summary of a conversation for internal use, identify

- People present
- Topic of discussion
- Decisions made
- Actions needed

FIGURE 5.4 A Transmittal

DREW & Associates

100 Eaton Plaza • Hamilton, ON L8P 2Y3 • 905.555.4783 • Fax 905.555.4784

October 8, 2005

Mr. Charles Gibney
Personnel Manager
Roydon Interiors
146 Main Street East
Hamilton, ON L8E 1J5

Dear Mr. Gibney:

Paragraph one tells reader what is enclosed and summarizes main points

Here is a copy of the brief we intend to file with the Ontario Court of Appeal in support of our position that the sex discrimination charge against Roydon Interiors should be dropped.

Will you please examine it carefully to make sure that the facts it contains are correct? If you have changes to suggest, please call my office by October 22nd, so that we can file the brief by October 24th.

Sincerely,

Last paragraph asks for action by a specific date

Diana Drew

Diana Drew

To summarize a document

- Start with the main point.
- Give supporting evidence or details.
- Evaluate the document, if desired. Should others in the company read this book? Should someone in the company write a letter to the editor responding to this newspaper article?

When you visit a client or go to a conference your company needs to know what *it* should do as a result of the meeting.

Summarize a visit with a client or customer in this way:

1. Put the main point from your organization's point of view—the action to be taken, the perceptions to be changed—in the first paragraph.
2. Provide an **umbrella paragraph** to cover and foreshadow the points you will make in the report.
3. Provide necessary detail to support your conclusions and cover each point. Use lists and headings to make the structure of the document clear.

In the following example, the first paragraph summarizes the sales representative's conclusions after a call on a prospective client:

Consolidated Tool Works is an excellent prospect for purchasing a Matrix-Churchill grinding machine. To get the order, we should

1. Set up a visit for CTW personnel to see the Matrix-Churchill machine in Saskatoon.
2. Guarantee 60-day delivery if the order is placed by the end of the quarter.
3. Extend credit terms to CTW.

Writing Thank-You and Congratulatory Notes

Sending a **thank-you note** will make people more willing to help you again in the future. Thank-you letters can be short but must be prompt. They need to be specific to sound sincere.

Congratulating someone can cement good feelings between you and the reader and enhance your own visibility. Again, specifics help.

Avoid language that may seem condescending or patronizing. A journalism professor was offended when a former student wrote to congratulate her for a feature article that appeared in a major newspaper. As the professor pointed out, the letter's language implied that the writer had more status than the person being praised. The praiser was "quite impressed," congratulated the professor on reaching a conclusion that she had already reached, and assumed that the professor would have wanted to discuss matters with the praiser. To the professor, "Keep up the good work!" implied that the one cheering her on had been waiting for ages at the finish line.[4]

Granting Adjustments and Responding to Complaints

A study sponsored by Travelers Insurance showed that when people had gripes but didn't complain, only 9% would buy from the company again. But when people did complain—and their problems were resolved quickly—82% would buy again.[5] (For an e-mail response to a complaint, see Figure 5.12.)

When you grant a customer's request for an adjusted price, discount, replacement, or other benefit to resolve a complaint, do so in the very first sentence.

Thank-you notes can be written on standard business stationery, using standard formats. But one student noticed that his adviser really liked cats and had pictures of them in her office. So he found a cat card for his thank-you note.

Like businesses, post-secondary institutions are increasingly preoccupied with improving the quality of their service and nourishing the loyalty of their employees. In advancing its strategic plan to become Canada's best comprehensive university, Carleton University emphasizes employee training. Employees work to identify needs as well as barriers to good service, changing workplace culture and behaviours in the process.

Your Visa bill for a night's lodging has been adjusted to $63. Next month a credit of $37 will appear on your bill to reimburse you for the extra amount you were originally asked to pay.

Don't talk about your own process in making the decision. Don't say anything that sounds grudging. Give the reason for the original mistake only if it reflects credit on the company. (In most cases, it doesn't, so the reason should be omitted.)

Formatting Letters, Memos, and E-mails

Whatever the message—informative, positive, negative, or persuasive—document format plays its part in getting the message across, in building writer and organization credibility, and in solidifying a good relationship between writer and reader. How a document looks tells the reader how caring, careful, and professional the writer is.

Knowing business community standards (and the standards of your own organization) helps you ensure that your letters, memos, and e-mails will send appropriate messages.

Formatting Letters

Many organizations and writers choose one of three letter formats (Figure 5.5): **block format** (Figure 5.6), **modified block format** (Figure 5.7), or the **Administrative Management Society (AMS) Simplified format** (Figure 5.8). Your organization may make minor changes from the examples in margins or spacing.

Use the same level of formality in the **salutation,** or greeting, as you would in talking to someone on the phone: *Dear Glenn* if you're on a first-name basis, *Dear Mr. Helms* if you don't know the reader well enough to use the first name.

Bad Words*

Ruth King, who coaches building contractors, has advice for employees who handle customer complaints. When a customer complains, King says, avoid using the following words in your reply:

- **We're busy.** These words focus on your organization; you should focus on the customer. State the earliest possible time you can give your attention to the problem.

- **No.** When a customer is angry, the word *no* is like "gasoline on a fire." Instead, offer reasonable alternatives to choose from.

- **We can't.** These words are as infuriating as *no*. Again, specify what you *can* offer.

- **It's our policy.** Writing about the organization's policy takes the focus off the customer and is yet another way to say what you will not do. Customers aren't interested in policies, and they are likely to ask that the policy be changed or waived. Focus on alternatives that are available.

*Based on Ruth King, "Five Things You Should Never Say to Customers," *Journal of Light Construction*, October 2003, downloaded from http://www.jlconline.com.

FIGURE 5.5   Comparing and Contrasting Letter Formats

	Block	Modified block	AMS Simplified
Date and signature block	Lined up at left margin	Lined up ½ or ⅔ of the way over to the right	Lined up at left margin
Paragraph indentation	None	Optional	None
Salutation and complimentary close	Yes	Yes	None
Subject line	Optional	Rare	Yes
Lists, if any	Indented	Indented	At left margin
Writer's signature	Yes	Yes	None
Writer's typed name	Upper- and lowercase	Upper- and lowercase	Full capital letters
Paragraph spacing	Single-spaced, double-space between	Single-spaced, double-space between	Single-spaced, double-space between

Omitting the salutation is particularly good when you do not know the reader's name or do not know which courtesy title (◄ p. 53) to use. However, readers like to see their names—something merge functions in word processing programs allow you to do even in a form letter.

The Simplified letter format is good in business-to-business mail, or in letters where you are writing to anyone who holds a particular position (admissions officer, customer service representative) rather than to a specific person. It is too cold and distancing for cultures that place a premium on relationships.

Sincerely and *Yours truly* are standard **complimentary closes.** When you are writing to people in special groups or to someone who is a friend as well as a business acquaintance, you may want to use a less formal close. Depending on the circumstances, the following informal closes might be acceptable: *Yours for a better environment, Cordially,* or even *Ciao.*

In **mixed punctuation,** a colon follows the salutation and a comma follows the close. In a sales or fundraising letter, it is acceptable to use a comma after the salutation to make the letter look like a personal letter rather than like a business letter. In **open punctuation,** omit all punctuation after the salutation and the close. Mixed punctuation is traditional. Open punctuation is faster to type.

Subject lines are required in memos; they are optional in letters (where they follow the salutation or, in some organizations, the inside address). Good subject lines are specific, concise, and appropriate for your purposes and the response you expect from your reader.

For examples of subject lines in informative, positive, negative, and persuasive messages, see ➡ chapters 5, 6, and 7.

A **reference line** (keyed two lines below the date line) refers the reader to the number used on the previous correspondence this letter replies to, or the order or invoice number this letter is about. Very large organizations, like Canada Revenue Agency, use numbers on every piece of correspondence they send out so that it is possible to find quickly the earlier document to which an incoming letter refers.

Letterhead is preprinted stationery with the organization's name, logo, address, and phone number (see figures 5.6, 5.7, and 5.8). Figure 5.9 shows how to set up modified block format when you do not have letterhead. (It is also acceptable to use block format without letterhead.)

When your letter runs two or more pages, use a heading on the second page to identify it. Using the reader's name helps the writer, who may be printing out many letters at a time, to make sure the correct second page gets in the

FIGURE 5.6 Block Format on Letterhead (mixed punctuation; collection letter)

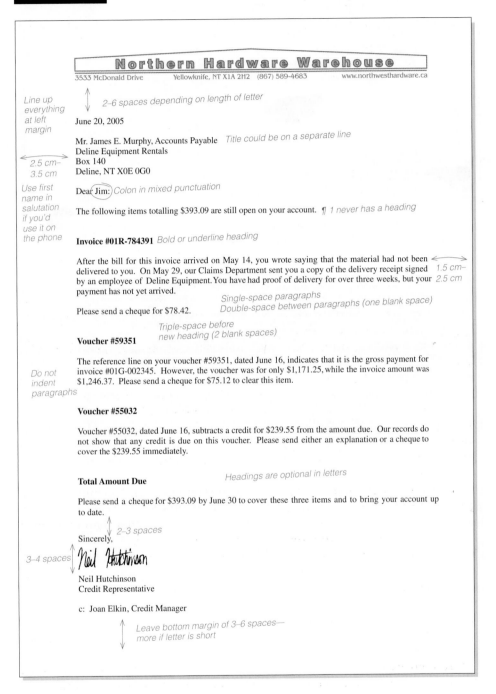

envelope. The two most common formats are shown in figures 5.6 and 5.7. Even when the signature block is on the second page, it is still lined up with the date on the first page.

FIGURE 5.7   Modified Block Format on Letterhead (mixed punctuation; recommendation letter)

Coast Information Systems

151 Hastings Street West • Vancouver, BC V6B 1H4 • (604) 405-7849 • www.coast.ca

2–6 spaces

2–4 spaces

September 15, 2005

Line up date with signature block ½ or ⅔ of the way over to the right

Ms. Mary E. Louie
Personnel Director
Chandler Communication Technologies
1040 Moss Street
Victoria, BC V8V 4P1   *Postal code on same line*

2.5 cm–3.5 cm

Dear Ms. Louie: *Colon in mixed punctuation*

1.5 cm–2.5 cm

Indenting ¶ is optional in modified block

Let me respond to your request for an evaluation of Colleen Woodsworth. Colleen was hired as a clerk-typist by Coast Information Systems on April 4, 2003, and was promoted to Administrative Assistant on August 1, 2004. At her review in June, I recommended that she be promoted again. She is an intelligent young woman with good work habits and a good knowledge of computer software.

Single-space paragraphs

As an Administrative Assistant, Colleen not only handles routine duties such as processing time cards, ordering supplies, and entering data, but also screens calls for two marketing specialists, answers basic questions about Coast Information Systems, compiles the statistics I need for my monthly reports, and investigates special assignments for me. In the past eight months, she has investigated freight charges, inventoried department hardware, and transferred files to CD-ROMs. I need only to give her general directions: she has a knack for tracking down information quickly and summarizing it accurately.

Double-space between paragraphs (one blank line)

Although the department's workload has increased during the year, Colleen manages her time so that everything gets done on schedule. She is consistently poised and friendly under pressure. Her willingness to work overtime on occasion is particularly remarkable considering that she has been going to college part-time ever since she joined our firm.

At Coast Information Systems, Colleen uses Microsoft Word and Access software. She tells me that she has also used WordPerfect and PowerPoint in her university classes.

If Colleen were staying in Vancouver, we would want to keep her. She has the potential either to become an Executive Secretary or to move into line or staff work, especially once she completes her degree. I recommend her highly.

2–3 spaces

Headings are optional in letters

Sincerely,   *Comma in mixed punctuation*

3–4 spaces

Jeanne Cederlind
Jeanne Cederlind
Vice President, Marketing
jeanne_c@coast.ca

Line up signature block with date

2–4 spaces

Encl.: Evaluation Form for Colleen Woodsworth

Leave at least 3–6 spaces at bottom of page—more if letter is short

1.25 cm–2.5 cm

Mary Louie   ← *Reader's name*
January 20, 2005
Page 2

Plain paper for page 2

When a letter runs two or more pages, use letterhead only for page 1. For the remaining pages, use plain paper that matches the letterhead in weight, texture, and colour.

FIGURE 5.8 AMS Simplified Format on Letterhead (request letter)

McFarlane HOSPITAL **Dental**

1680 Richmond Street North, London, ON N6G 3Y9   (519) 655-3113

2–4 spaces

Line up everything at left margin

August 24, 2005

2–4 spaces

2.5 cm– 3.5 cm

Melinda Hamilton
Medical Services Division
Information Management Services, Inc.
1181 Eglinton Avenue East
Toronto, ON M5W 1C2

Triple space (2 blank spaces)   *Subject line in full capital letters*

REQUEST FOR INFORMATION ABOUT COMPUTER SYSTEMS

No salutation

We're interested in upgrading our computer system and would like to talk to one of your marketing representatives to see what would best meet our needs. W e will use the following criteria to choose a system:

1. Ability to use our current software and data files.   *Double-space (one blank space)*

                                                            between items in list if any items

2. Price, prorated on a three-year expected life.   *are more than one line long*

3. Ability to provide auxiliary services, e.g., controlling inventory of supplies, monitoring patients' health profiles, and faster processing of insurance forms.

4. Freedom from downtime.

Triple-space (two blank spaces) between list, next paragraph

Do not indent paragraphs

McFarlane Dental Clinic has six associates and six licensed dental therapists. In the next five years, we expect to add two dentists specializing in orthodontics and surgical procedures.

Could we meet the first or the third week in September? We are eager to have the new system installed by Christmas if possible.

Please call me to schedule an appointment.   *Headings are optional in letters*

No close; no signature

HUGH STARR   *Writer's name in full capital letters*
Controller

2–4 spaces

Encl.:   Specifications of Current System
         Databases Currently in Use

c: Rene Lavasseur

Leave 3–6 spaces at bottom of page—more if letter is short

To eliminate typing the reader's name and address on an envelope, some organizations use envelopes with cut-outs or windows so that the **inside address** (the reader's name and address) on the letter can be used for delivery. If your organization does this, adjust your margins, if necessary, so that the whole inside address is visible.

Many letters are accompanied by other documents called **enclosures,** since they are enclosed in the envelope. The writer should refer to the enclosures in the body of the letter: "As you can see from my résumé, …" The enclosure line reminds the person who seals the letter to include the enclosures.

FIGURE 5.9   Modified Block Format without Letterhead (open punctuation; adjustment request)

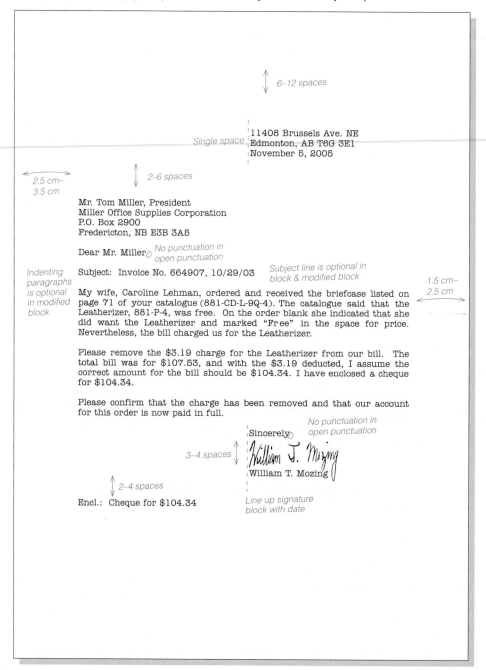

6–12 spaces

Single space   11408 Brussels Ave. NE
Edmonton, AB T6G 3E1
November 5, 2005

2.5 cm–3.5 cm

2–6 spaces

Mr. Tom Miller, President
Miller Office Supplies Corporation
P.O. Box 2900
Fredericton, NB E3B 3A5

Dear Mr. Miller   *No punctuation in open punctuation*

Indenting paragraphs is optional in modified block

Subject: Invoice No. 664907, 10/29/03   *Subject line is optional in block & modified block*

1.5 cm–2.5 cm

My wife, Caroline Lehman, ordered and received the briefcase listed on page 71 of your catalogue (881-CD-L-9Q-4). The catalogue said that the Leatherizer, 881-P-4, was free. On the order blank she indicated that she did want the Leatherizer and marked "Free" in the space for price. Nevertheless, the bill charged us for the Leatherizer.

Please remove the $3.19 charge for the Leatherizer from our bill. The total bill was for $107.53, and with the $3.19 deducted, I assume the correct amount for the bill should be $104.34. I have enclosed a cheque for $104.34.

Please confirm that the charge has been removed and that our account for this order is now paid in full.

Sincerely   *No punctuation in open punctuation*

3–4 spaces

William J. Mozing

William T. Mozing   *Line up signature block with date*

2–4 spaces

Encl.: Cheque for $104.34

Sometimes you write to one person but send copies of your letter to other people. If you want the reader to know that other people are getting copies, list their names on the last page. The abbreviation *cc* originally meant *carbon copy* but now means *computer copy*. Other acceptable abbreviations include *pc* for *photocopy* or simply *c* for *copy*. You can also send copies called **blind copies** to other people without telling the reader. Blind copies are listed only on the copy saved for the file with the abbreviation *bc* preceding the names of people getting these copies.

Formatting Envelopes

Canada Post Corporation requires consistency for efficient handling of business envelopes.[6] Follow these steps:

1. If your business address is not already printed in the upper left-hand corner, enter name, street address, city, province or territory, and postal code.
2. Use punctuation only where it is part of a proper name (St. John's).
3. Enter reader address information.
4. Use these abbreviations for province or territory: Alberta (AB); British Columbia (BC); Manitoba (MB); New Brunswick (NB); Newfoundland and Labrador (NL); Northwest Territories (NT); Nova Scotia (NS); Nunavut (NU); Ontario (ON); Prince Edward Island (PE); Quebec (QC); Saskatchewan (SK); Yukon (YT).
5. Print postal codes in uppercase (one space between the first three and last three characters) two spaces after the two-letter symbol representing the province or territory.
6. Place stamp in upper right-hand corner.
7. For more detailed advice, see the Postal Guide on the Canada Post Web site at www.canadapost.ca

Formatting Memos and E-Mails

Memos—whether electronic or paper—are standard means of communicating. E-mail programs prompt you to supply the various parts of the format in the **guide headings** (*To/From/Subject*); they supply date and time automatically. Memos and e-mails follow similar format and structure, though some writers still treat e-mail messages as informal letters.

Memos and e-mails omit both the salutation and the close entirely. Although e-mails may be treated as memos, many writers still begin with an informal salutation and close with a signature block. Memos never use indented paragraphs. Subject lines are required; headings are optional. Never use a separate heading for the first paragraph.

Figure 5.10 illustrates the standard memo format typed on a plain sheet of paper. Note that the first letters of the reader's name, the writer's name, and the subject phrase are lined up vertically. Note also that memos are usually initialled by the To/From block. Initialling tells the reader that you have proofread the memo and prevents someone sending a memo you did not in fact write.

Some organizations have special letterhead for memos. When *To/From/Date/Subject* are already printed on the form, writer's and reader's names, date, and subject are set at the main margin to save typing time. (See Figure 5.11.)

Some organizations alter the order of items in the To/From/Date/Subject block. Some use word-processing templates. Some organizations ask employees to sign memos rather than simply initialling them. The signature goes below the last line of the memo, starting halfway over on the page, and prevents anyone's adding unauthorized information.

If the memo runs two pages or more, set up the second and subsequent plain pages in one of the following ways.

> Brief Subject Line or Reader's Name
> Date
> Page Number

or

> Brief Subject Line or Reader's Name   Page Number   Date

E-mail Etiquette Checklist*

- Ensure message is necessary.
- Use accurate, concise, and specific subject line.
- Choose appropriate language, tone, and organization.
- Never send angry or emotional messages.
- Limit use of block capitals or other enhanced text or special formatting.
- Use high-priority feature only for urgent messages.
- Keep to one topic or purpose per e-mail.
- Retain only enough of the original message to aid writer to whom you are responding.
- Insert attachments only for long, heavily formatted, or non-text files (Excel, PowerPoint slides).
- Tell your reader what attachment program you have used.
- Open attachments only when you are confident about the source.
- Forward e-mails only when (a) they are not confidential and (b) you are confident about the source.
- Use "reply to all" function cautiously.
- Carefully revise, edit, and proofread before sending.

*Adapted from Keith Woolhouse, "Reclaim your e-mail," Saskatoon *StarPhoenix* April 10, 2004, E1–2; Kitty O. Locker, Stephen Kyo Kaczmarek, and Kathryn Braun, *Business Communication: Building Critical Skills* Toronto: McGraw-Hill Ryerson, 2005, 268–269.

FIGURE 5.10   Memo Format (on plain paper; informative message)

Everything lined up at left   *Plain paper*

2–4 spaces ↕ October 7, 2005

Line up

Double space (one blank space)   To: Annette T. Califero

    From: Kyle B. Abrams *KBA*   *Writer's initials added in ink*

2.5 cm– 3.5 cm   Subject: A Low-Cost Way to Reduce Energy Use   *Capitalize first letter of each major word in subject line*

No heading for ¶ 1   As you requested, I've investigated low-cost ways to reduce our energy use. Reducing the building temperature on weekends is a change that we could make immediately, that would cost nothing, and that would cut our energy use by about 6%.   *1.5 cm– 2.5 cm*

Triple space before each new heading (two blank spaces)

The Energy Savings from a Lower Weekend Temperature   *Bold or underline headings*

Single-space paragraphs; double-space between paragraphs (one blank space)   Lowering the temperature from 20°C to 15.5°C from 8 P.M. Friday evening to 4 A.M. Monday morning could cut our total consumption by 6%. It is not feasible to lower the temperature on weeknights because a great many staff members work late; the cleaning crew also is on duty from 6 P.M. to midnight. Turning the temperature down for only four hours would not result in a significant heat saving.

Turning the heat back up at 4 a.m. will allow the building temperature to be back to 20°C by 9 A.M. Our furnace already has computerized controls that can be set to automatically lower and raise the temperature.

Triple sp (two blank spaces)

How a Lower Temperature Would Affect Employees   *Capitalize first letter of each major word of heading*

Do not indent paragraphs   A survey of employees shows that only seven people use the building every weekend or almost every weekend. Eighteen percent of our staff have worked at least one weekend day in the last two months; 52% say they "occasionally" come in on weekends.

People who come in for an hour or less on weekends could cope with the lower temperature just by wearing warm clothes. However, most people would find 15.5°C too cool for extended work. Employees who work regularly on weekends might want to install space heaters.

Action Needed to Implement the Change

Would you also like me to check into the cost of buying a dozen portable space heaters? Providing them would allow us to choose units that our wiring can handle and would be a nice gesture toward employees who give up their weekends to work. I could have a report to you in two weeks.

We can begin saving energy immediately. Just authorize the lower temperature, and I'll see that the controls are reset for this weekend.

Memos are initialled by To/From/Subject block—no signature   *Headings are optional in memos*

Solving a Sample Problem

Real-life problems are richer and less well defined than textbook problems and cases. But even textbook problems require analysis before you begin to write. Before you tackle the assignments for this chapter, examine the following problem. See how the analysis questions probe the basic points required for a solution. Study the two sample solutions to see what makes one unacceptable and the other one good. Note the recommendations for revision that could make the good solution excellent.[7] The checklist at the end of the chapter (➡ p. 129) can help you evaluate a draft.

FIGURE 5.11 Memo Format (on memo letterhead; good news)

Kimball, Walls, and Morganstern

Line up horizontally with printed To/From/Date/Subject

To: Annette T. Califero   *Capitalize first*
                                                                  letter of each major
From: Kyle B. Abrams *KBA* *Writer's initials added in ink* *word in subject line*

Date: March 15, 2005

Subject: The Effectiveness of Reducing Building Temperatures on Weekends
                Triple space

*Margin lined up
with items in
To/From/Date/
Subject
block to save
typing time*

Reducing the building temperature to 15.5°C on weekends has cut energy use by 4% compared to last year's use from December to February and has saved our firm $22,000.   *1.5 cm–*
                                                                  2.5 cm

This savings is particularly remarkable when you consider that this winter has been colder than last year's, so that more heat would be needed to maintain the same temperature.

Fewer people have worked weekends during the past three months than during the preceding three months, but snow and bad driving conditions may have had more to do with keeping people home than the fear of being cold. Five of the 12 space heaters we bought have been checked out on an average weekend. On one weekend, all 12 were in use and some people shared their offices so that everyone could be in a room with a space heater.

Fully 92% of our employees support the lower temperature. I recommend that we continue turning down the heat on weekends through the remainder of the heating season and that we resume the practice when the heat is turned on next fall.
                                    Headings are optional in memos

Problem

Sentinel Insurance uses computers to handle its payments and billings. There is often a time lag between receiving a payment from a customer and recording it on the computer. Sometimes, while the payment is in line to be processed, the computer sends out additional notices: past-due notices, collection letters, even threats to sue. Customers are frightened or angry and write asking for an explanation. In most cases, if they just waited a little while, the situation would be straightened out. But policyholders are afraid that they'll be without insurance because the company thinks the bill has not been paid.

Sentinel doesn't have the time to check each individual situation to see if the cheque did arrive and has been processed. It wants you to write a letter that will persuade customers to wait. If something is wrong and the payment never reached Sentinel, the company would send a legal notice to that effect saying the policy would be cancelled by a certain date (which the notice would specify) at least 30 days after the date on the original premium bill. Continuing customers always get this legal notice as a third chance (after the original bill and the past-due notice).

Prepare a form letter that can go out to every policyholder who claims to have paid a premium for automobile insurance and resents getting a past-due notice. The letter should reassure readers and build goodwill for Sentinel.

FIGURE 5.12   An E-Mail Reply with Copies (response to a complaint)

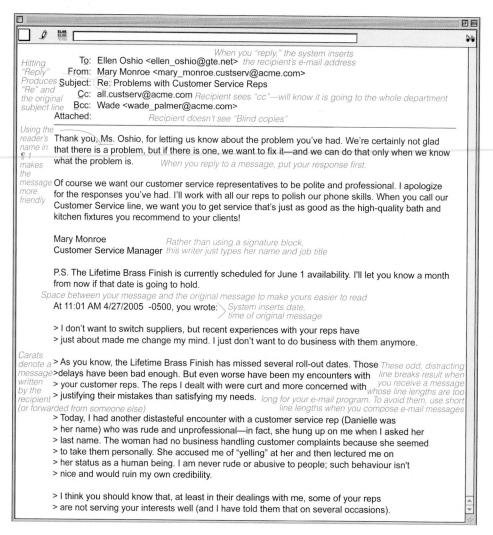

When you "reply," the system inserts

Hitting "Reply" Produces "Re" and the original subject line

To: Ellen Oshio <ellen_oshio@gte.net>   *the recipient's e-mail address*
From: Mary Monroe <mary_monroe.custserv@acme.com>
Subject: Re: Problems with Customer Service Reps
Cc: all.custserv@acme.com   *Recipient sees "cc"—will know it is going to the whole department*
Bcc: Wade <wade_palmer@acme.com>
Attached: *Recipient doesn't see "Blind copies"*

Using the reader's name in ¶ 1 makes the message more friendly

Thank you, Ms. Oshio, for letting us know about the problem you've had. We're certainly not glad that there is a problem, but if there is one, we want to fix it—and we can do that only when we know what the problem is.   *When you reply to a message, put your response first.*

Of course we want our customer service representatives to be polite and professional. I apologize for the responses you've had. I'll work with all our reps to polish our phone skills. When you call our Customer Service line, we want you to get service that's just as good as the high-quality bath and kitchen fixtures you recommend to your clients!

Mary Monroe   *Rather than using a signature block,*
Customer Service Manager   *this writer just types her name and job title*

P.S. The Lifetime Brass Finish is currently scheduled for June 1 availability. I'll let you know a month from now if that date is going to hold.
Space between your message and the original message to make yours easier to read
At 11:01 AM 4/27/2005 -0500, you wrote: *System inserts date, time of original message*

> I don't want to switch suppliers, but recent experiences with your reps have
> just about made me change my mind. I just don't want to do business with them anymore.

Carats denote a message written by the recipient (or forwarded from someone else)

> As you know, the Lifetime Brass Finish has missed several roll-out dates. Those   *These odd, distracting*
>delays have been bad enough. But even worse have been my encounters with   *line breaks result when*
> your customer reps. The reps I dealt with were curt and more concerned with   *you receive a message*
> justifying their mistakes than satisfying my needs.   *long for your e-mail program. To avoid them, use short*   *whose line lengths are too*
> Today, I had another distasteful encounter with a customer service rep (Danielle was   *line lengths when you compose e-mail messages*
> her name) who was rude and unprofessional—in fact, she hung up on me when I asked her
> last name. The woman had no business handling customer complaints because she seemed
> to take them personally. She accused me of "yelling" at her and then lectured me on
> her status as a human being. I am never rude or abusive to people; such behaviour isn't
> nice and would ruin my own credibility.

> I think you should know that, at least in their dealings with me, some of your reps
> are not serving your interests well (and I have told them that on several occasions).

Analysis of the Problem

1.   Who is your audience? What audience characteristics are relevant to this particular message?

     Automobile insurance customers who say they've paid but have still received a past-due notice. They're afraid they're no longer insured. Since it's a form letter, different readers will have different situations: in some cases payments did arrive late, in some cases the company made a mistake, in some the reader never paid (cheque was lost in mail, unsigned, bounced, etc.).

2.   What are your purposes in writing?

     To reassure readers that they're covered for 30 days. To inform them that they can assume everything is OK *unless* they receive a second notice. To avoid further correspondence on this subject. To build goodwill for Sentinel: (a) we don't want to suggest Sentinel is error prone or too cheap to hire enough people to do the necessary work; (b) we don't want readers to switch companies; (c) we do want readers to buy from Sentinel when they're ready for more insurance.

3.   What information must your message include?

Sharing information is crucial to business success. To drive home that point, Siemens deposited 60 managers from around the world on the shores of a lake south of Munich, Germany, and told them to build rafts. They weren't allowed to talk: They had to write messages and diagrams on flip charts. Back in the office, ShareNet lets employees around the world ask questions and share answers.

Readers are still insured. We cannot say whether their cheques have now been processed (company doesn't want to check individual accounts). Their insurance will be cancelled if they do not pay after receiving the second past-due notice (the legal notice).

4. What reasons or reader benefits will your reader find convincing?
    Computers help us provide personal service to policyholders. We offer policies to meet all their needs. Both of these points would need specifics to be interesting and convincing.

5. What objection(s) can you expect your reader(s) to have? What negative elements of your message must you de-emphasize or overcome?
    Computers appear to cause errors. We don't know if the cheques have been processed. We will cancel policies if their cheques don't arrive.

6. How will the context affect reader response? The economy? The time of year? Morale in the organization? The relationship between the reader and writer? Any special circumstances?
    The insurance business is highly competitive—other companies offer similar rates and policies. The customer could get a similar policy for about the same money from someone else. Most people find that money is tight, so they'll want to keep insurance costs low. Yet the fact that prices are steady or rising means that the value of what they own is higher—they need insurance more than ever.

    Many insurance companies are refusing to renew policies (car, liability, malpractice insurance). These refusals to renew have received lots of publicity, and many people have heard horror stories about companies and individuals whose insurance has been cancelled or not renewed after a small number of claims. Readers don't feel very kindly toward insurance companies.

    Drivers have a legitimate worry when laws everywhere in Canada require basic coverage for all vehicles driven on public roads, and the provinces of British Columbia, Saskatchewan, and Manitoba require the purchase of insurance when drivers obtain vehicle registration.

Discussion of the Sample Solutions

The solution in Figure 5.13 is unacceptable. The red marginal comments show problem spots. Since this is a form letter, we cannot tell customers we have their cheques; in some cases, we may not. The letter is far too negative. The explanation in paragraph 2 makes Sentinel look irresponsible and uncaring.

FIGURE 5.13 An Unacceptable Solution to the Sample Problem

> Need date
>
> Dear Customer:
>
> *This explanation makes company look bad*
>
> Relax. We got your cheque.   *Not necessarily true; reread problem*
>
> There is always a time lag between the time payments come in and the time they are processed. While payments are waiting to be processed, the computer with super-human quickness is sending out past-due notices and threats of cancellation.
>
> *Need to present this positively*
>
> Cancellation is not something you should worry about. No policy would be cancelled *Too negative* without a legal notice to that effect giving a specific date for cancellation, which would be at least 30 days after the date on the original premium notice.
>
> If you want to buy more insurance, just contact your local Sentinel agent. We will be happy to help you.
>
> Sincerely,   *This paragraph isn't specific enough to work as a reader benefit. It lacks you-attitude and positive emphasis.*

Paragraph 3 is far too negative. Paragraph 4 is too vague; there are no reader benefits; the ending sounds selfish.

A major weakness with the solution is that it lifts phrases straight out of the problem; the writer does not seem to have thought about the problem or about the words he or she is using. Measuring the draft against the answers to the questions for analysis suggests that this writer should start over.

The solution in Figure 5.14 is much better. The blue marginal comments show the letter's strong points. The message opens with the good news that is

FIGURE 5.14 A Good Solution to the Sample Problem

> Need date
>
> Dear Customer: *Better: use computer to personalize. Put in name and address of a specific reader*
>
> Your auto insurance is still in effect.   *Good ¶ 1. True for all readers*
>
> *Good to treat notice as information, tell reader what to do if it arrives*
>
> Past-due notices are mailed out if the payment has not been processed within three days after the due date. This may happen if a cheque is delayed in the mail or arrives without a signature or account number. When your cheque arrives with all the necessary information, it is promptly credited to your account.   *Good you-attitude*
>
> Even if a cheque is lost in the mail and never reaches us, you still have a 30-day grace period. If you do get a second notice, you'll know that we still have not received your cheque. To keep your insurance in force, just stop payment on the first cheque and send a second one.
>
> *Benefits of using computers*
>
> Computer processing of your account guarantees that you get any discounts you're eligible for: multi-car, accident-free record, good student. If you have a claim, your agent uses computer tracking to find matching parts quickly, whatever car you drive. You get a cheque quickly—usually within three working days—without having to visit dealer after dealer for time-consuming estimates.   *Too negative*   *Better to put in agent's name, phone number*
>
> *Need to add benefits of insuring with Sentinel*
>
> Today, your home and possessions are worth more than ever. You can protect them with Sentinel Insurance's homeowners' and tenants' policies. Let your local agent show you how easy it is to give yourself full protection. If you need a special rider to insure a personal computer, a coin collection, or a fine antique, you can get that from Sentinel, too.   *Good specifics*
>
> Whatever your insurance needs—auto, home, life, or medical—one call to Sentinel can do it all.   *Acceptable ending*
>
> Sincerely,

✓ **CHECKLIST** Checklist for Informative and Positive Messages

☐ In positive messages, does the subject line give the good news? In either message, is the subject line specific enough to differentiate this message from others on the same subject?

☐ Does the first paragraph summarize the information or good news? If the information is too complex to fit into a single paragraph, does the paragraph list the basic parts of the policy or information in the order in which the memo discusses them?

☐ Is all the information given in the message? [The information needed will vary depending on the message, but information about dates, places, times, and anything related to money usually needs to be included. When in doubt, ask!]

☐ In messages announcing policies, is there at least one reader benefit for each segment of the audience? Are all reader benefits ones that seem likely to occur in this organization?

☐ Is each reader benefit developed, showing that the benefit will come from the policy and why the benefit matters to this organization? Do the benefits build on the job duties of people at this organization and the specific circumstances of the organization?

☐ Does the message end with a positive paragraph—preferably one that is specific to the readers, not a general one that could fit any organization or policy?

☐ Does the message use you-attitude and positive emphasis?

☐ Is the style easy to read and friendly?

☐ Is the visual design of the message inviting?

☐ Is the format correct?

☐ Does the message use standard grammar? Is it free from typos?

Originality in a positive or informative message may come from

- Creating good headings, lists, and visual impact
- Developing reader benefits
- Thinking about readers and giving details that answer their questions and make it easier for them to understand and follow the policy

---

true for all readers. (Whenever possible, one should use the good-news pattern of organization.) Paragraph 2 explains Sentinel's policy. It avoids assigning blame and ends on a positive note. The negative information is buried in paragraph 3 and is presented positively: the notice is information, not a threat; the 30-day extension is a "grace period." Telling the reader now what to do if a second notice arrives eliminates the need for a second exchange of letters. Paragraph 4 offers benefits for using computers, since some readers may blame the notice on computers, and offers benefits for being insured by Sentinel. Paragraph 5 promotes other policies the company sells and prepares for the last paragraph.

As the red comments indicate, this good solution could be improved by personalizing the salutation and by including the name and number of the local agent. Computers could make both of those insertions easily. This good letter could be made excellent by revising paragraph 4 so that it doesn't end on a negative note and by using more reader benefits. For instance, do computers help agents advise clients of the best policies for them? Does Sentinel offer good service—quick, friendly, non-pressured—that could be stressed? Are agents well trained? All of these might yield ideas for additional reader benefits.

Summary of Key Points

- Informative and positive messages normally use the following direct pattern of organization:
  1. Give any good news and summarize the main points.
  2. Give details, clarification, background.
  3. Present any negative elements—as positively as possible.
  4. Explain any reader benefits.
  5. Use a goodwill ending: positive, personal, and forward looking.
- **Letters** go to people in other organizations. **Memos** go to people within your own organization.
- Letters and memos use different formats for their different audiences.
- The title of a document, a good subject line meets three criteria: it's specific; it's reasonably short; and it's adapted to the kind of message (positive, negative, persuasive). If you can't make the subject both specific and short, be specific.
- The subject line for an informative or positive message should highlight any good news and summarize the information concisely.
- Use reader benefits in informative and positive messages when
  - You are presenting policies.
  - You want to shape readers' attitudes toward the information or toward your organization.
  - Stressing benefits addresses readers' motives positively.
  - Some of the benefits may not be obvious to readers.
- **Goodwill endings** should focus on the business relationship you share with your reader or the reader's organization. The last paragraph of a message to a group should apply to the whole group.
- Document format tells your reader how caring, careful, and professional the writer is.
- Use the analysis questions listed in ◀▥ Chapter 1 to probe the basic points needed for successful informative and positive messages.

| CHAPTER 5 | Exercises and Problems |

Getting Started

5.1   Memos for Discussion—Introducing a Suggestion System

Your organization has decided to institute a suggestion system. Employees on hourly pay scales will be asked to submit suggestions. (Managers and other employees on salary are not eligible for this program; they are supposed to be continually suggesting ways to improve things as part of their regular jobs.) If the evaluating committee thinks that the suggestion would save money, the employee will receive 10% of the first year's estimated annual savings. If the suggestion won't save money but will improve work conditions, service, or morale, the employee will get a cheque for $50.

The following memos are possible approaches. How well does each message meet the criteria in the checklist for informative and positive messages?

1.   Subject: Suggestions Unlimited (SU)

I want to introduce you to Suggestions Unlimited (SU). This program enables the production worker to offer ideas about improving his job description, working conditions, and general company procedures. The plan can operate as a finely tuned machine, with great ideas as its product.

Operation will begin November 1. Once a week, a designate of SU will collect the ideas and turn them over to the SU Committee. This committee will evaluate and judge the proposed changes.

Only employees listed as factory workers are eligible. This excludes foremen and the rest of supervisory personnel. Awards are as follows:

1. Awards of $50 will be given to those ideas judged operational. These are awarded monthly.

2. There will be grand prizes given for the best suggestions over the six-month span.

Ideas are judged on feasibility, originality, operational simplicity, and degree of benefit to the worker and company. Evaluation made by the SU Committee is final. Your questions should be channelled to my office.

2.   Subject: Establishment of Suggestions Unlimited

We announce the establishment of Suggestions Unlimited. This new program is designed to provide a means for hourly employees to submit suggestions to company management concerning operations and safety. The program will also provide an award system to compensate non-management employees for implemented suggestions.

Here is how the program will work: beginning October 1, suggestions can be submitted by hourly workers to the company on Form 292, which will be furnished to all plants and their departments by October 1. On the form, the submitting employee should include the suggestion, his or her name, and the department number. The form can be deposited in a suggestion drop box, which will be located near the personnel office in each plant.

Any suggestion dealing with the improvement of operations, safety, working conditions, or morale is eligible for consideration. The award structure for the program will be as follows:

1. For an implemented suggestion that improves safety or efficiency with no associated monetary benefits or cost reduction: $50.

2. For an implemented suggestion that makes or saves the company money: 10% of the first year's estimated annual savings or additional revenue.

It is hoped that we will have a good initial and continuous response from all hourly employees. This year, we are out to try to cut production costs, and this program may be the vehicle through which we will realize new savings and increased revenues. New ideas that can truly increase operational efficiency or cut safety problems will make the company a nicer place for all employees. A safer work environment is a better work environment. If department operations can be made more efficient, this will eventually make everyone's job just a little easier, and give that department and its employees a sense of pride.

3.   Subject: New Employee Suggestion System

Beginning October 1, all of you who are hourly employees of Video Adventures will be able to get cash awards when your suggestions for improving the company are implemented.

Ideas about any aspect of Video Adventures are eligible: streamlining behind-the-counter operations, handling schedule problems, increasing the life of videotapes.

- If your idea cuts costs or increases income (e.g., increasing membership sales, increasing the number of movie rentals per customer), you'll receive 10% of the first year's estimated annual savings.

- If the idea doesn't save money but does improve service, work conditions, or morale, you'll receive a cheque for $50.

To submit a suggestion, just pick up a form from your manager. On the form, explain your suggestion, describe briefly how it could be implemented, and show how it will affect Video Adventures. Return the completed form in the new suggestion box behind the back counter. Suggestions will be evaluated at the end of each month. Turn in as many ideas as you like!

Think about ways to solve the problems you face every day. Can we speed up the check-in process? Cut paperwork? Give customers faster service? Increase the percentage of customers who bring back their tapes on time? As you serve people at the counter, ask them what they'd like to see at Video Adventures.

Your ideas will keep Video Adventures competitive. Ten years ago, Video Adventures was the only video store on the west side of town. Now there are six other video stores within a two-mile radius, and even the grocery stores rent videotapes. Efficiency, creativity, and service can keep Video Adventures ahead.

Employees whose ideas are implemented will be recognized in the regional Video Adventures newsletter. The award will also be a nice accomplishment to add to any university or community college application or résumé. By suggesting ways to improve Video Adventures, you'll demonstrate your creativity and problem-solving abilities. And you'll be able to share the credit for keeping Video Adventures' reputation as the best video store in town.

5.2   E-Mails for Discussion—Saying Yes to a Subordinate

Today, you get this request from a subordinate.

Subject: Request for Leave

You know that I've been feeling burned out. I've decided that I want to take a three-month leave of absence this summer to travel abroad. I've got five weeks of vacation time saved up; I would take the rest as unpaid leave. Just guarantee that my job will be waiting when I come back!

You decide to grant the request. The following messages are possible responses. How well does each message meet the criteria in the checklist for informative and positive messages?

1.   Subject: Re: Request for Leave

I highly recommend Italy. Spend a full week in Florence, if you can. Be sure to visit the Brancacci Chapel—it's been restored, and the frescoes are breathtaking. And I can give you the names of some great restaurants. You may never want to come back!

2.   Subject: Your Request for Leave

As you know, we are in a very competitive position right now. Your job is important, and there is no one who can easily replace you. However, because you are a valued employee, I will permit you to take the leave you request, as long as you train a replacement before you leave.

3.   Subject: Your Request for Leave Granted

Yes, you may take a three-month leave of absence next summer using your five weeks of accumulated vacation time and taking the rest as unpaid leave. And yes, your job will be waiting for you when you return!

I'm appointing Garrick to take over your duties while you're gone. Talk with him to determine how much training time he'll need, and let me know when the training is scheduled.

Have a great summer! Let us know every now and then how you're doing!

E-Mail Messages

5.3   Announcing an Electronic Newsletter

Your organization has decided to create an electronic newsletter to build goodwill with its customers. You have created a mailing list of customers' e-mail addresses and plan to send them monthly messages with information related to your industry. The goal is that customers will think of your organization as a valuable source of expertise, so they will prefer to do business with you.

Think about the qualities customers are likely to value in a monthly electronic newsletter. Keep in mind that many people like to review their e-mail quickly and are annoyed by spam.

As marketing manager, write an e-mail to your customers, announcing the electronic newsletter. Include an overview of the benefits and the kinds of information that will be included.

Hints:

- Pick a business, government, or non-profit organization that you know something about.
- Identify who your customers are and what will interest them. What information do you have that might be harder for your customers to learn? Will you provide hyperlinks to other information on the Web?
- Be sure the subject line is clear and appealing.
- What can customers do if they are not interested in receiving your newsletter?

Communicating at Work

5.4   Praising Work Done Well

Write a memo to a co-worker (with a copy to the person's supervisor) thanking him or her for helping you or complimenting him or her on a job well done.

5.5   Giving Good News

Write to a customer, to a vendor, or to your boss announcing good news. Possibilities include a product improvement, a price cut or special, an addition to your management team, or a new contract.

Letter and Memo Assignments

5.6   Reminding Guests about the Time Change

Twice a year most of Canada (Saskatchewan is an exception), switches to daylight saving time and back again. The time change can be disruptive for hotel guests, who may lose track of the date, forget to change the clocks in their rooms, and miss appointments as a result.

Prepare a form letter to leave in each hotel room reminding guests of the impending time change. What should guests do?

Write the letter.

Hints:

■ Use an attention-getting page layout so readers don't ignore the message.

■ Pick a specific hotel or motel chain you know something about.

■ Use the letter to build goodwill for your hotel or motel chain. Use specific references to services or features the hotel offers, focusing not on what the hotel does for the reader, but on what the reader can do at the hotel.

5.7   Answering an International Inquiry

Your business, government, or non-profit organization has received the following inquiries from international correspondents. (You choose the country the inquiry is from.)

1. Please tell us about a new product, service, or trend so that we can decide whether we want to buy, license, or imitate it in our country.

2. We have heard about a problem [technical, social, political, or ethical] that occurred in your organization. Could you please tell us what really happened and estimate how it is likely to affect the long-term success of the organization?

3. Please tell us about college or university programs in this field. We are interested in sending some of our managers to your country to complete a degree.

4. We are considering setting up a plant in your city. We have already received adequate business information. However, we would also like to know how comfortable our nationals will feel. Do people in your city speak our language? How many? What opportunities exist for our nationals to improve their English? Does your town already have people

from a wide mix of nations? Which are the largest groups?

5. Our organization would like to subscribe to an English-language trade journal. Which one would you recommend? Why? How much does it cost? How can we order it?

As Your Professor Directs,

a. Answer one or more of the inquiries. Assume that your reader either reads English or can have your message translated.

b. Write a memo to your professor explaining how you've adapted the message for your audience.

Hints:

■ Even though you can write in English, English may not be your reader's native language. Write a letter that can be translated easily.

■ In some cases, you may need to spell out background information that might not be clear to someone from another country.

5.8   Providing Information to Job Applicants

Your company is in a prime vacation spot, and as personnel manager you get many letters from students asking about summer jobs. Company policy is to send everyone an application for employment, a list of the jobs you expect to have open that summer with the rate of pay for each, a description of benefits for seasonal employees, and an interview schedule. Candidates must come for an interview at their own expense and should call to schedule a time in advance. Competition is keen: only a small percentage of those interviewed will be hired.

Write a form letter to students who have written to you asking about summer jobs. Give them the basic information about the hiring procedure and tell them what to do next. Be realistic about their chances, but maintain their interest in working for you.

5.9 Summarizing *The Globe and Mail Report on Business*

Today, your in-basket contains this message from your boss:

> As you know, I'm leaving tomorrow for a vacation in Egypt. While I'm gone, will you please scan *The Globe and Mail Report on Business* every day and summarize any articles that are relevant to our business? I'd like your summary in hard copy on my desk when I return.

As Your Professor Directs,

a. Scan *The Globe and Mail Report on Business* for one week, two weeks, or until you find three to five relevant articles for the company you have chosen.

b. Summarize the articles in a memo.

c. Compare summaries with a small group of students. Do summaries of the same article for different organizations focus on different points?

d. Present one of your summaries to the class.

Hints:

■ Pick an organization you know something about. If the organization is large, focus on one division or department.

■ Provide an overview to let your boss know whether the articles you've summarized are on a single topic or on several topics.

■ Show how each article relates to the organization.

■ Give the full citation (see ➡ Chapter 11) so that it's easy to track down articles if the boss wants to see the original.

5.10 Summarizing Information

Summarize one or more of the following:

1. Richard B. Chase and Sriram Dasu, "Want to Perfect Your Company's Service? Use Behavioral Science," *Harvard Business Review,* June 2001, 79–84; reprint R0106D.

2. One of Jakob Nielsen's Alertboxes www.useit.com/alertbox.

3. An article or web page published by Adbusters Media Foundation (www.adbusters.com).

4. The criticisms of a company on an "anticorporate activism" Web site (in a search engine, key in the company name and "customer opinion").

5. An article assigned by your professor.

6. An article or Web page of your choice.

As Your Professor Directs,

a. Write a summary of no more than 100 words.

b. Write a 250- to 300-word summary.

c. Write a one-page summary.

d. Compare your summary to those of a small group of students. Did everyone agree on what information to include? How do you account for any differences?

6 Negative Messages

AN INSIDE PERSPECTIVE

Negative Messages

Delivering bad news is one of the most difficult tasks a leader may be asked to perform. To reduce the potential for dysfunctional behaviour, bad news should be communicated openly and honestly, despite how difficult the news may be for the employees to hear.

Preparation is required to effectively communicate bad news to employees so they understand the reasons for a decision and how it affects them. Be able to answer the following key questions:

- What is the big picture? Why is the change needed?

- What is the purpose of the change?

- How does the bad news relate to corporate/business objectives?

- How will the bad news affect employees, customers, and shareholders?

A communications and organizational effectiveness consultant, Rajani Kamath formerly led the leadership effectiveness and communication efforts for the Card Operations business at Amex Canada Inc., a wholly owned subsidiary of American Express Travel Related Services Company.

"In 1998, a decision was made to eliminate the third shift (12 A.M. to 8 A.M.) in one of our departments at Amex due to a reduction in workflow. We needed to communicate these layoffs not only to the nearly 80 employees who would be directly affected but also to people who would be indirectly affected. Otherwise, rumours would run rampant. Everyone needed to hear the bad news at about the same time.

"The department leaders met face to face with the third-shift employees to inform them of the organizational decision. The leaders communicated the bad news openly and honestly, and allowed employees to ask questions and voice their concerns immediately. Whenever possible, third-shift employees were reassigned to positions in other departments.

"Management teams in other departments then sent a memo about the reorganization to all other employees.

"Well-planned, honest communication paid dividends because the employees had a clear understanding for the reasons behind the decision and how the decision would affect them."

In a **negative message,** the basic information we have to convey is bad news; we expect the reader to be disappointed or angry.

Negative messages include

- Rejections and refusals
- Announcements of policy changes that do not benefit customers or consumers
- Requests the reader will see as insulting or intrusive
- Negative performance appraisals
- Disciplinary notices
- Product recalls or notices of defects

A negative message always has several purposes:

Primary purposes:

- To give the reader the bad news
- To have the reader read, understand, and accept the message
- To maintain as much goodwill as possible

Secondary purposes:

- To build a good image of the writer
- To build a good image of the writer's organization
- To reduce or eliminate future correspondence on the same subject so the message doesn't create more work for the writer
- To reduce risk and avoid legal liability

Even when it is not possible to make the reader happy with the news we must convey, we still want readers to feel that

- They have been taken seriously.
- Our decision is fair and reasonable.
- If they were in our shoes, they would make the same decision.

In other words, negative messages always require a level of persuasion (➡ Chapter 7)

Organizing Negative Letters, Memos, and E-Mails

Although negative messages are typically associated with the extremes of discipline, rejections, and refusals, even minor negatives (a small rate increase, for example) and potentially positive messages (even a congratulatory note) can qualify as bad news if writers do not adopt the appropriate tone and tactics.

The direct approach illustrated in ◄▬ Chapter 5 is appropriate for negative messages when

- Announcing bad news to subordinates
- Announcing policy decisions
- Dealing with clients who prefer a direct approach
- Demonstrating firmness is necessary and maintaining goodwill is not (discontinuing clients, sending final collections letter)

The first pattern in Figure 6.1 helps writers maintain goodwill.

Figure 6.2 illustrates how the basic pattern for negative messages can be used. This letter omits the reason, probably because the change benefits the company, not the customer. Putting the bad news first (though pairing it

The Awful News*

Sharing the bad news, all the news, may be the only way to save a company.

After six years of dot-com success, the bubble burst. And suddenly Logical Net, an $8 million Internet service provider based in Albany, New York, couldn't collect its accounts receivable from its customers. In six months, the company went from earning money to losing $130,000 a month. Bankruptcy loomed.

The CEO decided to share all of the company's financial information with his managers. To avoid bankruptcy, he needed help from everyone in the company. He hoped that opening the books would create buy-in.

It worked.

Employees found ways to eliminate waste and save money. Salespeople focused on bringing in recurring revenues and nudged customers to pay their bills. The company was saved. And the corporate culture changed. Now all employees think about the financial implications of everything they do.

*Based on Ilan Mochari, "The Talking Cure," *Inc.*, November 2001, 122–123.

FIGURE 6.1   How to Organize Negative Messages

Negative letters	Negative memos to superiors	Negative memos to peers and subordinates
1. **When you have a reason that readers will understand and accept, give the reason before the refusal.** A good reason prepares the reader to expect the refusal.	1. **Describe the problem.** Tell what's wrong, clearly and unemotionally.	1. **Describe the problem.** Tell what's wrong, clearly and unemotionally.
2. **Give the negative information or refusal just once, clearly.** Inconspicuous refusals can be missed altogether, making it necessary to say *no* a second time.	2. **Tell how it happened.** Provide the background. What underlying factors led to this specific problem?	2. **Present an alternative or compromise, if one is available.** An alternative not only gives readers another way to get what they want but also suggests that you care about readers and helping them meet their needs.
3. **Present an alternative or compromise, if one is available.** An alternative not only gives readers another way to get what they want but also suggests that you care about readers and helping them meet their needs.	3. **Describe the options for fixing it.** If one option is clearly best, you may need to discuss only one. But if the reader will think of other options, or if different people will judge the options differently, describe all the options, giving their advantages and disadvantages.	3. **If possible, ask for input or action.** People in the audience may be able to suggest solutions. And workers who help make a decision are far more likely to accept the consequences.
4. **End with a positive, forward-looking statement.**	4. **Recommend a solution and ask for action.** Ask for approval so that you can go ahead to make the necessary changes to fix the problem.	

immediately with an alternative) makes it more likely that the recipient will read the letter. If this letter seemed to be just a routine renewal, or if it opened with the good news that the premium was lower, few recipients would read the letter carefully, and many would not read it at all. Then, if they had accidents and found that their coverage was reduced, they'd blame the company for not communicating clearly. Emphasizing the negative here is both good ethics and good business.

The best way to organize a negative memo depends on whether you're writing to a superior, peer, or subordinate, and on the severity of the negative information.

Your superior expects you to solve minor problems by yourself. But sometimes, solving a problem requires more authority or resources than you have. When you give bad news to a superior, also recommend a way to deal with the problem. Turn the negative message into a persuasive one (➡ Chapter 7). See the middle column in Figure 6.1.

When you must pass along serious bad news to peers and subordinates, use the variation in the last column in Figure 6.1.

No serious negative (such as being downsized or laid off) should come as a complete surprise. Managers can prepare for possible negatives by giving full information as it becomes available. It is also possible to let the people who will be affected by a decision participate in setting the criteria. Someone who has bought into the criteria for awarding cash for suggestions or retaining workers is more likely to accept decisions using such criteria.

Montreal-based Jetsgo's founder Michel Leblanc faced widespread criticism when he abruptly announced in the middle of winter holidays (March 2005) the grounding of the airline. Neither the 17,000 travellers left in limbo nor the 1,200

FIGURE 6.2   A Negative Letter

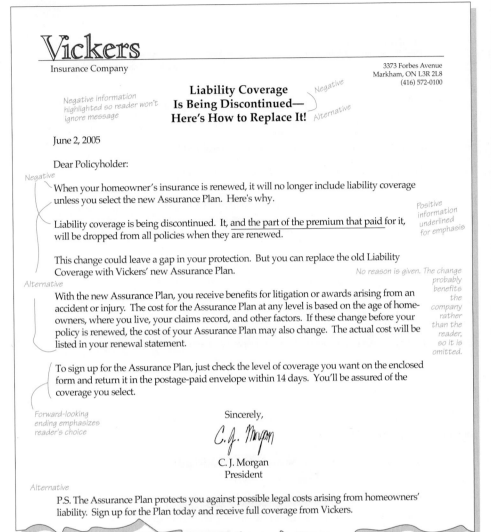

Vickers
Insurance Company

3373 Forbes Avenue
Markham, ON L3R 2L8
(416) 572-0100

Negative information highlighted so reader won't ignore message

Liability Coverage Is Being Discontinued— Here's How to Replace It!

Negative

Alternative

June 2, 2005

Dear Policyholder:

Negative

When your homeowner's insurance is renewed, it will no longer include liability coverage unless you select the new Assurance Plan. Here's why.

Liability coverage is being discontinued. It, and the part of the premium that paid for it, will be dropped from all policies when they are renewed.

Positive information underlined for emphasis

This change could leave a gap in your protection. But you can replace the old Liability Coverage with Vickers' new Assurance Plan.

Alternative

No reason is given. The change probably benefits the company rather than the reader, so it is omitted.

With the new Assurance Plan, you receive benefits for litigation or awards arising from an accident or injury. The cost for the Assurance Plan at any level is based on the age of home-owners, where you live, your claims record, and other factors. If these change before your policy is renewed, the cost of your Assurance Plan may also change. The actual cost will be listed in your renewal statement.

To sign up for the Assurance Plan, just check the level of coverage you want on the enclosed form and return it in the postage-paid envelope within 14 days. You'll be assured of the coverage you select.

Forward-looking ending emphasizes reader's choice

Sincerely,

C. J. Morgan

C. J. Morgan
President

Alternative

P.S. The Assurance Plan protects you against possible legal costs arising from homeowners' liability. Sign up for the Plan today and receive full coverage from Vickers.

employees who discovered themselves unemployed overnight had been prepared for the announcement.

Employees learned the news via 1:00 A.M. telephone calls and via an e-mail in which Leblanc blamed an unnamed creditor for the situation. Employees had been kept in the dark when Jetsgo instructed pilots to fly aircraft to Quebec "for air worthiness checks" that were not in fact ordered. The Jetsgo fleet was, however, safe from creditors in Quebec. Although Leblanc apologized to travellers, he remained unapologetic about his little "white lie" to employees. "You can't tell them, or the job won't get done," Leblanc argued. Conceding that "the name Jetsgo has been blemished badly," Leblanc acknowledged a name change was a possibility.[1]

When the bad news is less serious, as in Figure 6.3, use the pattern for negative letters unless your knowledge of the reader(s) suggests that another pattern will be more effective. When sending a negative message to a "feeling type," you might want to delay the negative by using a buffer (a neutral or positive sentence) even though the organization's discourse community (◀ p. 32) as a whole favours directness.

FIGURE 6.3	A Negative Memo to Subordinates

Memo

Markham Consulting Services

Date:	January 10, 2005
To:	All Employees
From:	Floyd E. Loer, Dorothy A. Walters, and Stewart Mattson
Subject	Accounting for Work Missed Due to Bad Weather

Reason — As you know, Markham Consulting Services is always open for our customers, whatever the weather. Employees who missed work during the snowstorm last week may count the absence as vacation, sick day(s), or personal day(s).

Refusal, stated as positively as possible — Hourly workers who missed less than a day have the option of taking the missed time as vacation, sick, or personal hours or of being paid for the hours they worked.

One small positive — Approval of vacation or personal days will be automatic; the normal requirement of giving at least 24 hours' notice is waived.

Goodwill ending — Thanks for all the efforts you have made to continue giving our customers the best possible service during one of the snowiest winters on record.

For memos, the context of communication is crucial. The reader's reaction is influenced by the following factors:

- Do you and the reader have a good relationship?
- Does the organization treat people well?
- Have readers been warned of possible negatives?
- Have readers bought into the criteria for the decision?
- Do communications after the negative build goodwill?

Tiburon, a company that provides public safety systems and services, used "open book management"—sharing all its financial information with employees. When the company had to lay off 80 of its 320 employees, the layoffs weren't a surprise, and people understood that the layoffs were necessary. Says founder and CEO Bruce Kelling, "I even received calls and in one case a letter from terminated employees, offering condolences, knowing how difficult it was for the company and that we did the right thing." Cuts to the rank-and-file hurt less when it's clear that senior managers are also taking cuts.[2]

Choosing Subject Lines for Negative Messages

When you write to superiors, use a subject line (◄— p. 109) that focuses on solving the problem.

Subject: Improving Our Subscription Letter

When you write to peers and subordinates, put the topic (but not your action on it) in the subject line.

> Subject: Status of Conversion Table Program
>
> Owing to heavy demands on our time, we have not yet been able to write programs for the conversion tables you asked for.

Use a negative subject line in e-mail messages.

> Subject: Delay in Converting Tables

Use a negative subject line in letters and memos when you think readers may ignore what they think is a routine message. Major negatives, like firing someone, should be delivered in person, not by e-mail.

The best subject line for negative e-mail messages depends on whether you're refusing a request or initiating the negative. When you say *no* to an e-mail request, just hit "reply" and use "Re:" plus whatever the original subject line was for your response. When you write a new message, you will have to decide whether to use the negative in the subject line. The subject line should contain the negative when

- **The negative is serious.** Many people do not read all their e-mail messages. A neutral subject line may lead the reader to ignore the message.
- **The reader needs the information to make a decision or act.**
- **You report your own errors** (as opposed to the reader's).

Thus the following would be acceptable subject lines in e-mail messages:

> Subject: We Lost The Bay's Account
>
> Subject: Power to Be Out Sunday, March 8
>
> Subject: Error in Survey Data Summary

When you write to people whom you know well, exaggerated subject lines are acceptable:

> Subject: Gloom, Despair, and Agony

In other situations, a neutral subject line is acceptable.

> Subject: Results of 360° Performance Appraisals

Wording the Parts of a Negative Message

This section provides more information about wording each part of a negative message.

Buffers

Traditionally, textbooks recommended that negative messages open with buffers. A **buffer** is a neutral or positive statement that allows you to delay the negative and prepare the reader. Recent research in the United States suggests that buffers do not make readers respond more positively,[3] and good buffers are very hard to write.

Even though buffers are hard to write, they remain important signals of tact and diplomacy for many audiences. That includes Canadians who value their history of treaty making with First Nations, their experience with negotiation, and association with diplomacy and peacekeeping under the auspices of the United Nations. Compromise has even been described as "the Canadian way."[4] A direct

Straight Talk with Employees*

Employees say they want organizations to be honest and open about bad news. In a survey by human resource specialists Towers Perrin, more than 90 percent of employees said they want the plain facts about their organization's performance and their jobs. They respect organizations for communicating honestly. However, half said they think their employer tends to overdo putting a positive spin on the facts.

*Based on Institute of Management and Administration (IMA), "The Best Policy Now: Less 'Spin' and More Honesty," *HR Focus*, April 2004; and IMA, "Need to Deliver Bad News? How and Why to Tell It Like It Is," *HR Focus*, November 2003, both downloaded from http://www.findarticles.com.

InSite

www.dare.com/home/default.asp

Being able to say *no* is a necessary skill in life as well as in business. Some of the techniques offered by Drug Abuse Resistance Education (D.A.R.E.) may be more appropriate for saying no to friends than to co-workers or customers. However, even in business, simply not answering—similar to walking away—is one of the most common ways to refuse a request.

no-nonsense style may be preferred in the United States, but many Canadians appreciate indirection and the art of tactful, careful preparation for negative messages.

To be effective, a buffer must put the reader in a good frame of mind, without implying a positive answer, and provide a natural transition to the body of the letter. The kinds of statements most often used as buffers are good news, facts and chronologies of events, references to enclosures, thanks, and statements of principle.

1. Start with any good news or positive elements the letter contains.

> Starting Thursday, June 26, you'll have access to your money 24 hours a day at First Nations Bank of Canada.

Letter announcing that the drive-up windows will be closed for two days while automatic teller machines are installed

2. State a fact or provide a chronology of events.

> As a result of the new graduated dues schedule—determined by vote of the Delegate Assembly last December and subsequently endorsed by the Executive Council—members are now asked to establish their own dues rate and to calculate the total amount of their remittance.

Announcement of a new dues structure that will raise most members' dues

3. Refer to enclosures in the letter.

> Enclosed is a new sticker for your car. You may pick up additional ones in the office if needed. Please *destroy* old stickers bearing the signature of "L.S. LaVoie."

Letter announcing increase in parking rental rates

4. Thank (or compliment) the reader for something he or she has done.

> Thank you for scheduling appointments for me with so many senior people at First Nations Bank of Canada. My visit there March 14 was very informative.

Letter refusing a job offer

5. State a general principle.

> Good drivers should pay substantially less for their auto insurance. The Good Driver Plan was created to reward good drivers (those with five-year accident-free records) with our lowest available rates. A change in the plan, effective January 1, will help keep those rates low.

Letter announcing that the company will now count traffic tickets, not just accidents, in calculating insurance rates—a change that will raise many people's premiums

Some readers will feel betrayed by messages whose positive openers delay the central negative point. Therefore, use a buffer only when the reader (individually or culturally) values harmony or when the buffer serves another purpose (e.g., "thank you" for a letter).

Reasons

Research in the United States shows that readers who described themselves as "totally surprised" had much more negative feelings than did those who expected the refusal.[5] A clear and convincing reason prepares the reader to accept the negative.

The following reason is inadequate.

Weak reason: The goal of the Lennoxville CHARGE-ALL Centre is to provide our customers faster, more personalized service. Since you now live outside the Lennoxville CHARGE-ALL service area, we can no longer offer you the advantages of a local CHARGE-ALL Centre.

If the reader says, "I don't care if my bills are slow and impersonal," will the company let the reader keep the card? No. The real reason for the negative is that the bank's franchise allows it to have cardholders only in a given geographical region.

Real reason: Each local CHARGE-ALL centre is permitted to offer accounts to customers within our region. The Lennoxville CHARGE-ALL centre serves customers east of Montreal. You can continue to use your current card until it expires. When that happens, you'll need to open an account with a CHARGE-ALL centre that serves the province of Quebec.

Don't hide behind "company policy": readers will assume the policy is designed to benefit you at their expense. If possible, show how readers benefit from the policy. If they do not benefit, don't mention policy at all.

Weak reason: I cannot write an insurance policy for you because company policy does not allow me to do so.

Better reason: Gorham insures cars only when they are normally garaged at night. Standard insurance policies cover a wider variety of risks and charge higher fees. Limiting the policies we write gives Gorham customers the lowest possible rates for auto insurance.

Avoid saying that you *cannot* do something. Most negative messages exist because the writer or company has chosen certain policies or cutoff points. In the example above, the company could choose to insure a wider variety of customers if it wanted to do so.

If you have several reasons for saying *no*, use only those that are strong and watertight. If you give five reasons and readers dismiss two of them, readers may feel that they've won and should get the request.

Weak reason: You cannot store large bulky items in the dormitory over the summer because moving them into and out of storage would tie up the stairs and the elevators just at the busiest times when people are moving in and out.

Way to dismiss the reason: We'll move large items before or after the two days when most people are moving in or out.

If you do not have a good reason, omit the reason rather than use a weak one. Even if you have a strong reason, omit it if it makes the company look bad.

Reason that hurts company: Our company is not hiring at the present time because profits are down. In fact, the downturn has prompted top management to reduce the salaried staff by 5% just this month, with perhaps more reductions to come.

Better: Our company does not have any openings now.

Negatives

De-emphasize the negative (in this case a refusal) by putting it in the same paragraph as the reason, rather than in a paragraph by itself.

Sometimes you may be able to imply the refusal rather than stating it directly.

Direct refusal: You cannot get insurance for just one month.

Implied refusal: The shortest term for an insurance policy is six months.

Be sure the implication is crystal clear. Any message can be misunderstood, but an optimistic or desperate reader is particularly unlikely to understand a negative message. One of your purposes in a negative message is to close the door on the subject. You do not want to have to write a second letter saying that the real answer is *no.* You want to maintain company credibility while incurring no legal liability.

Alternatives

Giving the reader an alternative or a compromise, if one is available, is a good idea for several reasons:

- It offers the reader another way to get what he or she wants.
- It suggests that you really care about the reader and about helping to meet his or her needs.
- It enables the reader to re-establish the psychological freedom you limited when you said *no.*
- It allows you to end on a positive note and to present yourself and your organization as positive, friendly, and helpful.

When you give an alternative, give readers all the information they need to act on it, but don't take the necessary steps. Let readers decide whether to try the alternative.

Negative messages limit the reader's freedom. People may respond to a limitation of freedom by asserting their freedom in some other arena. Jack W. Brehm calls this phenomenon **psychological reactance.**[6] Psychological reactance is at work when a customer who has been denied credit no longer buys even on a cash basis, or a subordinate who has been passed over for a promotion gets back at the company by deliberately doing a poor job.

An alternative allows the reader to react in a way that doesn't hurt you. By letting readers decide for themselves whether they want the alternative, you allow them to re-establish their sense of psychological freedom.

The specific alternative will vary depending on the circumstances. In Figure 6.4, the company is unwilling to quote a price on an item on which it cannot be competitive. In different circumstances, the writer might offer different alternatives.

Endings

If you have a good alternative, refer to it in your ending: "Let me know if you can use A515 grade 70."

The best endings look to the future.

> Wherever you have your account, you'll continue to get all the service you've learned to expect from CHARGE-ALL, and the convenience of charging items at over a million stores, restaurants, and hotels in Canada—and in Lennoxville, too, whenever you come back to visit!

Letter refusing to continue charge account for a customer who has moved

Avoid endings that seem insincere.

> We are happy to have been of service, and should we be able to assist you in the future, please contact us.

FIGURE 6.4 A Refusal with an Alternative

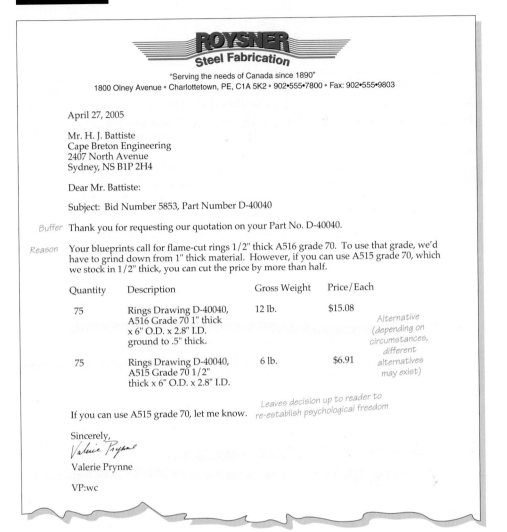

This ending lacks you-attitude and would not be good even in a positive message. In a situation where the company has just refused to help, it's likely to sound sarcastic or sadistic.

Checking Tone in Negative Messages

Tone—the implied attitude of the author toward the reader and the subject—is particularly important when you want readers to feel that you have taken their requests seriously. Check your draft carefully for positive emphasis (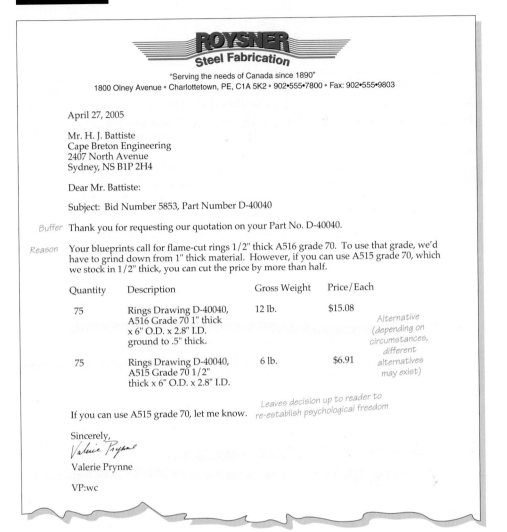 p. 47) and you-attitude (p. 43), both at the level of individual words and at the level of ideas.

If language and tone problems can mean that a congratulatory letter may end up insulting (p. 116), an apology for lateness at an interview that suggests the interviewer's directions were unclear is also likely to be heard as a negative message.

Similarly, when Tim Hortons promoted its 2005 "Get Mugged with Tim Hortons" campaign (punning on its famous mugs), the company was forced to withdraw and apologize to the family of Erin Sperrey who had been murdered while working the night shift at Tim Hortons in Caribou, Maine.[7]

Writing in electronic formats has added to some writers' difficulties in communicating negative messages. Whether they are high school students chatting on MSN, employees responding too hastily or too angrily to colleagues, or business leaders musing in e-mail, many are finding that their "private" messages are creating serious conflict as well as public liabilities. Flaming among employees, for example, can lead to dismissal.

Dr. Liss Jeffrey, director of the McLuhan Global Research Network, University of Toronto, warns, "There is no childhood in cyberspace. Young people are getting into trouble, trouble that will follow them around for good and forever." Some face suspension or expulsion from school, while others face humiliating exposure on Web sites or in chat rooms.

Others share the fate of business leaders whose e-mail musings have become evidence in legal cases. Their e-mails like "archaeological artifacts" leave "a permanent record of what went on behind closed doors" and capture "the deep cynicism that executives can have toward investors," says Michael Useem, ethics and leadership professor, Wharton School of Business.

Conrad Black for one was "not prepared to re-enact the French Revolutionary renunciation of the rights of nobility. We are proprietors after all, beleaguered though we may be." As in the case of Enron, his words are returning to haunt him.[8]

Figure 6.5 lists some of the phrases to avoid in negative messages.

Even the physical appearance and timing of a letter can convey tone. An obvious form rejection letter suggests that the writer has not given much consideration to the reader's application. An immediate negative suggests that the rejection didn't need any thought. A negative delivered just before a major holiday seems especially unfeeling.

Handling Apologies

Not all negative messages need to include apologies.

- **No explicit apology is necessary if the error is small and if you are correcting the mistake.**

    Negative: I'm sorry the clerk did not credit your account properly.

    Better: Your statement has been corrected to include your payment of $263.75.

- **Do not apologize when you are not at fault.** When you have done everything you can and when a delay or problem is due to circumstances beyond your control, you aren't at fault and don't need to apologize. It may be appropriate to include an explanation so the reader knows you weren't

| FIGURE 6.5 | Avoid These Phrases in Negative Messages |

Phrase	Because
I am afraid that we cannot	You aren't fearful. Don't hide behind empty phrases.
I am sorry that we are unable	You probably are *able* to grant the request; you simply choose not to. If you are so sorry about saying *no*, why don't you change your policy and say *yes*?
I am sure you will agree that	Don't assume that you can read the reader's mind.
Unfortunately	*Unfortunately* is negative in itself. It also signals that a refusal is coming.

negligent. If the news is bad, put the explanation first. If you have good news for the reader, put it before your explanation.

Negative:	I'm sorry that I could not answer your question sooner. I had to wait until the sales figures for the second quarter were in.
Better (neutral or bad news):	We needed the sales figures for the second quarter to answer your question. Now that they're in, I can tell you that …
Better (good news):	The new advertising campaign is a success. The sales figures for the second quarter are in, and they show that …

■ **When you apologize, do it early, briefly, and sincerely.** Apologize only once, early in the message. Let the reader move on to other, more positive information. Focus, for example, on what you have done to correct the situation.

If you don't know whether or not any inconvenience has resulted, don't raise the issue at all.

Negative:	I'm sorry I didn't answer your letter sooner. I hope that my delay hasn't inconvenienced you.
Better:	I'm sorry I didn't answer your letter sooner.

In business documents, apologize only when you are at fault. According to linguist Deborah Tannen, U.S. women use "I'm sorry" both to mean "I'm responsible for the error or problem" and "It's too bad that this situation happened." She claims that U.S. men interpret "I'm sorry" as admitting guilt and avoid using the words to avoid being put down in a conversation.[9] Certainly not all women or all men fit these generalizations. Nevertheless, be aware that "I'm sorry" may be interpreted as an admission of error, and avoid overusing the phrase.

Considering Alternative Strategies for Negative Situations

Whenever you face a negative situation, consider recasting it as a positive or persuasive message.

If the negative information will directly lead to a benefit that you know readers want, use the pattern of organization for informative and positive messages:

Situation:	You're raising parking rates to pay for lot maintenance, ice and snow removal, and signs so tenants can have cars that park in their spots towed away—all services tenants have asked for.
Negative:	Effective May 1, parking rentals will go up $5 a month.
Positive emphasis:	Effective May 1, if someone parks in your spot, you can have the car towed away. Signs are being put up announcing that all spaces in the lot are rented. Lot maintenance is also being improved. The lot will be resurfaced this summer, and arrangements have been made for ice and snow removal next winter.

Often a negative situation can be recast as a persuasive message (➡ see Chapter 7). If your organization has a problem, ask readers to help solve it. A solution that workers have created will be much easier to implement.

When the Association for Business Communication raised dues in 1987, the executive director wrote a persuasive letter urging members to send in renewals early so they could beat the increase. The letter shared some of the qualities of any persuasive letter: using an attention-getting opener, offsetting the negative by setting it against the benefits of membership, telling the reader what to do, and ending with a picture of the benefit the reader received by acting. More recent increases, however, have been announced directly.

Humour can defuse negative messages.

Kathryn McGrath, head of the Securities and Exchange Commission's division of investment management, needed to tell an investment firm that its ad was illegal. The ad showed an index finger pointing up and large bold letters saying that performance was "up," too. Tiny print at the bottom of the page admitted that performance figures hadn't been adjusted to include front-end sales charges. Rather than writing a heavy-handed letter, McGrath sent the firm a photocopy of a thumb pointing down. The ad never ran again.[10]

Humour works best when it's closely related to the specific situation and the message. Humour that seems tacked on is less likely to work. Never use humour that belittles readers.

Distinguishing Varieties of Negative Messages

Among the most difficult kinds of negative messages to write are rejections and refusals, and layoffs and firings.

Rejections and Refusals

When you refuse requests from people outside your organization, try to use a buffer. Give an alternative if one is available. For example, if you are denying credit, it may still be possible for the reader to put an expensive item on layaway.

Politeness and length help. In two studies, job applicants preferred rejection letters that addressed them as *Mr./Ms.* rather than calling them by their first names, that said something specific about their good qualities, that phrased the refusal itself indirectly, that offered alternatives (such as another position the applicant might be qualified for), and that were longer.[11]

Double-check the words in the draft to be sure the reason can't backfire if it is applied to other contexts. The statement that a plant is "too noisy and dangerous" for a group tour could be used as evidence against the company in a worker's compensation claim.[12]

Schwinn needed a new product line to attract sophisticated cyclists. This apology for its old, boring line moves quickly to a discussion of its new technology. By evoking an experience every cyclist has had, the headline also suggests that falling is a minor event.

When you refuse requests within your organization, use your knowledge of the organization's culture and of the specific individual to craft your message. In some organizations, it may be appropriate to use company slogans, offer whatever help already-established departments can give, and refer to the individual's good work (if you indeed know that it is good). In other, less personal organizations, a simple negative without embellishment may be more appropriate.

Layoffs and Firings

Information about layoffs and firings is normally delivered orally but accompanied by a written statement explaining severance pay or unemployment benefits that may be available.

If a company is in financial trouble, management needs to communicate the problem clearly. Sharing information and enlisting everyone's help in finding solutions may make it possible to save jobs. Sharing information also means that layoff notices, if they become necessary, will be a formality; they should not be new information to employees.

Give the employee the real reason for the firing. Offering a face-saving reason unrelated to poor performance can create legal liabilities. But avoid broadcasting the reason: to do so can leave the company liable to a defamation suit.[13]

Solving a Sample Problem

Solving negative problems requires careful analysis. The checklist at the end of the chapter on ➡ p. 152 can help you evaluate your draft.

Problem

You're director of employee benefits for a Fortune 500 company. Today, you received the following memo:

| From: | Michelle Jagtiani |
| Subject: | Getting My Retirement Benefits |

Next Friday will be my last day here. I am leaving [name of company] to take a position at another firm.

Please process a cheque for my retirement benefits, including both the deductions from my salary and the company's contributions for the last six and a half years. I would like to receive the cheque by next Friday if possible.

You have bad news for Michelle. Although the company does contribute an amount to the retirement fund equal to the amount deducted for retirement from the employee's paycheque, employees who leave with less than seven years of employment get only their own contributions. Michelle will get back only the money that has been deducted from her own pay, plus 4% interest compounded quarterly. Her payments and interest come to just over $17,200; the amount could be higher depending on the amount of her last paycheque, which will include compensation for any unused vacation days and sick leave. Furthermore, since the amounts deducted were not considered taxable income, she will have to pay income tax on the money she will receive.

You cannot process the cheque until after her resignation is effective, so you will mail it to her. You have her home address on file; if she's moving, she needs to let you know where to send the cheque. Processing the cheque may take two to three weeks.

Write a memo to Michelle.

The Reluctant Messenger*

Richard Schifreen, now a business unit manager for Promega, says,

"I once worked in a company that initiated three rounds of layoffs despite record sales and earnings. I was responsible for terminating people I respected and believed were assets to the company. After a very difficult period of reflection, I realized the following, which helped me:

- "The decision [to lay people off] was made, and there was nothing I could do to change it. . . .

- "Someone was going to give the message to those on the 'hit list,' under conditions decided by the company. . . .

- "However, there was an opportunity to deliver the bad news with respect and compassion; to listen and let those affected know that I cared. . . ."

"Some of the meetings went reasonably well, others didn't. But years later, I believe that I did make a difference. It is possible to make a bad situation just a little bit better, and there is satisfaction in doing so."

*Quoted from Anne Fisher, "The Axman's Anxiety: Readers Share the Pain," *Fortune*, August 13, 2001, 192.

**Effective
Negative
Letters***

Researcher Catherine Schryer asked writers at an insurance company to evaluate the firm's letters denying claims. She found four differences between the letters judged effective and the letters judged ineffective:

■ Good letters were easier to read. Poor letters contained more jargon; longer words and sentences; and stiff, awkward phrasing.

■ Good letters gave fuller reasons for the rejection. Poor letters often used cut and paste text and did not explain terms.

■ Good letters were less likely to talk about the reader's emotions ("angry," "disappointed").

■ Good letters were more likely to portray the writer and reader as active agents.

*Based on Catherine Schryer, "Walking a Fine Line: Writing Negative Letters in an Insurance Company," *Journal of Business and Technical Communication* 14 (October 2000): 445–497.

Analysis of the Problem

1. Who is your audience? What characteristics are relevant to this particular message? If you are writing to more than one reader, how do the readers differ?

    Michelle Jagtiani is your audience. Unless she's a personal friend, you probably wouldn't know why she's leaving and where she's going.

    There's a lot you don't know. She may or may not know much about taxes; she may or may not be able to take advantage of tax-reduction strategies. you can't assume the answers because you wouldn't have them in real life.

2. What are your purposes in writing?

    ■ To tell her that she will get only her own contributions, plus 4% interest compounded quarterly; that the cheque will be mailed to her home address two to three weeks after her last day on the job; and that the money will be taxable as income

    ■ To build goodwill so that she feels that she has been treated fairly and consistently

    ■ To minimize negative feelings she may have

    ■ To close the door on this subject

3. What information must your message include?

    Your message must tell her when the cheque will come; the facts that her cheque will be based on her contributions, not the employer's; that the money will be taxable income; how lump-sum retirement benefits are calculated; the fact that you have her current address on file but need a new address if she's moving.

4. How can you build support for your position? What reasons or reader benefits will your reader find convincing?

    Giving the amount currently in her account may make her feel that she is getting a significant sum of money. Suggesting someone who can give free tax advice (if the company offers this as a fringe benefit) reminds her of the benefits of working with the company. Wishing her luck with her new job is a nice touch.

5. What objection(s) can you expect your reader(s) to have? What negative elements of your message must you de-emphasize or overcome?

    She is getting about half the amount she expected, since she gets no matching funds. She might have been able to earn more than 4 % interest if she had invested the money in the stock market. Depending on her personal tax situation she may pay more tax on the money as a lump sum than would have been due had she paid it each year as she earned the money.

Discussion of the Sample Solutions

The solution in Figure 6.6 is not acceptable. The subject line gives a bald negative with no reason or alternative. The first sentence has a condescending tone that is particularly offensive in negative messages. The last sentence focuses on what is being taken away rather than what remains. Paragraph 2 lacks you-attitude and is vague. The memo ends with a negative. There is nothing anywhere in the memo to build goodwill.

The solution in Figure 6.7, in contrast, is very good. The policy serves as a buffer and explanation. The negative is stated clearly but is buried in the paragraph to avoid overemphasizing it. The second paragraph begins on a positive note by specifying the amount in the account and the fact that the sum might be even higher.

FIGURE 6.6 An Unacceptable Solution to the Sample Problem

To: Michelle Jagtiani

From: Lisa Niaz *LN*

Date: April 21, 2005

Subject: Denial of Matching Funds

Give reason before refusal — You cannot receive a cheque the last day of work and you will get only your own contributions, not a matching sum from the company, because you have not worked for the company for at least seven full years.   *Better to be specific*

This is lifted straight from the problem. The language in problems is often negative and stuffy; information is disorganized. — Your payments and interest come to just over $17,200; the amount could be higher depending on the amount of your last paycheque, which will include compensation for any unused vacation days and sick leave. Furthermore, since the amounts deducted were not considered taxable income, you will have to pay income tax on the money you receive.

The cheque will be sent to your home address. If the address we have on file is incorrect, please correct it so that your cheque is not delayed.   *Negative*

How will reader know what you have on file? Better to give current address as you have it.

Think about the situation and use your own words to create a satisfactory message.

FIGURE 6.7 A Good Solution to the Sample Problem

To: Michelle Jagtiani

From: Lisa Niaz *LN*

Date: April 21, 2005

Subject: Receiving Employee Contributions from Retirement Accounts

Good to state reason in third-person to de-emphasize negative — Employees who leave the company with at least seven full years of employment are entitled both to the company contributions and the retirement benefit paycheque deductions contributed to retirement accounts. Those employees who leave the company with fewer than seven years of employment will receive the employee paycheque contributions made to their retirement accounts.

Good to be specific — You now have $17,240.62 in your account, which includes 4% interest compounded quarterly. The amount you receive could be even higher since you will also receive payment for any unused sick leave and vacation days.

Good to show how company can help — Because you now have access to the account, the amount you receive will be considered taxable income. Beth Jordan in Employee Financial Services can give you information about possible tax deductions and financial investments that can reduce your income taxes.

Good to be specific — The cheque will be sent to your home address on May 16. The address we have on file is 2724 Merriman Road, Toronto, ON, M1M 3P1. If your address changes, please let us know so you can receive your cheque promptly.   *Positive emphasis*

Good luck with your new job!   *Forward looking*

Paragraph 3 contains the additional negative information that the amount will be taxable but offers the alternative that it may be possible to reduce taxes. The writer builds goodwill by suggesting a specific person the reader could contact.

Paragraph 4 tells the reader what address is in the company files (Michelle may not know whether the files are up to date), asks that she update it if necessary, and ends with the reader's concern: getting her cheque promptly.

The final paragraph ends on a positive note. This generalized goodwill is appropriate when the writer does not know the reader well.

Summary of Key Points

- In a negative message, the basic information is bad news; we expect the reader to be disappointed or angry.

- A good negative message conveys the negative information clearly while maintaining as much goodwill as possible. The goal is to make readers feel that they have been taken seriously, that the decision is fair and reasonable, and that they would have made the same decision. Secondary purposes include reducing or eliminating future correspondence, avoiding more work for the writer, maintaining company credibility, and incurring no legal liability.

- Organize negative letters in this way:
    1. Give the reason for the refusal before the negative or refusal itself when you have a reason that readers will understand and accept.
    2. Give the negative just once, clearly.

✓ **CHECKLIST**   Negative Messages

- ☐ Is the subject line appropriate?
- ☐ If a buffer is used, does it avoid suggesting either a positive or a negative response?
- ☐ Is the reason, if it is given, presented before the refusal? Is the reason watertight, with no loopholes?
- ☐ Is the negative information clear?
- ☐ Is an alternative given if a good one is available? Does the message provide all the information needed to act on the alternative but leave the choice up to the reader?
- ☐ Does the last paragraph avoid repeating the negative information?
- ☐ Is tone acceptable—not defensive, but not cold, preachy, or arrogant either?

And, for all messages, not just negative ones,
- ☐ Does the message use you-attitude and positive emphasis?
- ☐ Is the style easy to read and friendly?
- ☐ Is the visual design of the message inviting?
- ☐ Is the format correct?
- ☐ Does the message use standard grammar? Is it free from typos?

Originality in a negative message may come from
- ☐ An effective buffer, if one is appropriate.
- ☐ A clear, complete statement of the reason for the refusal.
- ☐ A good alternative, clearly presented, which shows that you're thinking about what the reader really needs.
- ☐ Adding details that show you're thinking about a specific organization and the specific people in that organization.

3. Present an alternative or compromise, if one is available.

4. End with a positive, forward-looking statement.

- Organize negative memos to superiors in this way:
  1. Describe the problem.
  2. Tell how it happened.
  3. Describe the options for fixing it.
  4. Recommend a solution and ask for action.

- When you must pass along serious bad news to peers and subordinates, use a variation of the pattern to superiors:
  1. Describe the problem.
  2. Present an alternative or compromise, if one is available.
  3. If possible, ask for input or action.

- A **buffer** is a neutral or positive statement that allows you to bury the negative message. Buffers must put the reader in a good frame of mind, without implying a positive answer, and provide a natural transition to the body of the letter. Use a buffer only when the reader values harmony or when the buffer serves a purpose in addition to simply delaying the negative.

- The kinds of statements most often used as buffers are (1) good news, (2) facts and chronologies of events, (3) references to enclosures, (4) thanks or compliments, and (5) statements of principle.

- Make the negative or refusal crystal clear.

- Giving the reader an alternative or a compromise
  - Offers the reader another way to get what he or she wants
  - Suggests that you really care about the reader and about helping to meet his or her needs
  - Enables the reader to re-establish the psychological freedom you limited when you said *no*
  - Allows you to end on a positive note and to present yourself and your organization as positive, friendly, and helpful

- People may respond to limits by striking out in ways that are unacceptable. This effort to re-establish freedom is called **psychological reactance.**

- Many negative situations can be redefined to use the patterns of organization for informative and positive or for persuasive messages. Humour sometimes works to defuse negative situations.

- Use the analysis questions in ◀▥ Chapter 1 to solve negative problems.

CHAPTER 6 Exercises and Problems

Getting Started

6.1 Letters for Discussion—Credit Refusal

As director of customer service at C'est Bon, an upscale furniture store, you manage the store's credit. Today you will reject an application from Francine Devereux. Although her income is fairly high, her last two payments on her student loans were late, and she has three bank credit cards, all charged to the upper limit, on which she's made just the minimum payment for the last three months.

The following letters are possible approaches to giving her the news. How well does each message meet the criteria in the checklist for negative messages?

1.   Dear Ms. Devereux:

Your request to have a C'est Bon charge account shows that you are a discriminating shopper. C'est Bon sells the finest merchandise available.

Although your income is acceptable, records indicate that you carry the maximum allowable balances on three bank credit cards. Moreover, two recent payments on your student loans have not been made in a timely fashion. If you were given a C'est Bon charge account, and if you charged a large amount on it, you might have difficulty paying the bill, particularly if you had other unforeseen expenses (car repair, moving, medical emergency) or if your income dropped suddenly. If you were unable to repay, with your other debt you would be in serious difficulty. We would not want you to be in such a situation, nor would you yourself desire it.

Please reapply in six months.

Sincerely,

2.   Dear Francine:

No, you can't have a C'est Bon credit card—at least not right now. Get your financial house in order and try again.

Fortunately for you, there's an alternative. Put what you want on layaway. The furniture you want will be held for you, and paying a bit each week or month will be good self-discipline.

Enjoy your C'est Bon furniture!

Sincerely,

3.   Dear Ms. Devereux:

Over the years, we've found that the best credit risks are people who pay their bills promptly. Since two of your student loan payments have been late, we won't extend store credit to you right now. Come back with a record of six months of on-time payments of all bills, and you'll get a different answer.

You might like to put the furniture you want on layaway. A $50 deposit holds any item you want. You have six months to pay, and you save interest charges.

You might also want to take advantage of one of our Saturday Seminars. On the first Saturday of each month at 11 A.M., our associates explain one topic related to furniture and interior decorating. Upcoming topics are

How to Wallpaper a Room	February 5
Drapery Options	March 6
Persian Carpets	April 1

Sincerely,

6.2 E-Mails for Discussion—Saying *No* to a Colleague

A colleague in another provincial agency has e-mailed you asking if you would like to use the payroll software her agency developed. You wouldn't. Switching to a new program would take a lot of time, and what you have works well for you.

The following messages are possible approaches to giving her the news. How well does each message meet the criteria in the checklist for negative messages?

1. Subject: Re: Use Our Software?

   No.

2. Subject: Re: Use Our Software?

   Thanks for telling me about the payroll software your team developed. What we have works well for us. Like every other agency, we're operating on a bare-bones budget, and no one here wants to put time (that we really don't have) into learning a new program. So we'll say, no, thanks!

3. Subject: Re: Use Our Software?

   The payroll software your team developed sounds very good.

   I might like to use it, but the people here are computer phobic. They HATE learning new programs. So, being a good little computer support person, I soldier on with the current stuff. (And people wonder why the provincial government is SO INEFFICIENT! Boy, the stories I could tell!)

   Anyway, thanks for the offer. Keep me posted on the next development—maybe it will be something so obviously superior that even the Neanderthals here can see its advantages!

6.3 Revising a Negative Message

Rewrite and reorganize the following negative message to make it more positive. Eliminate any sentences that are not needed.

Dear Tenant:

Effective March 1, the rent for your parking space will go up $10 a month. However, our parking lot is still not the most expensive in town.

Many of you have asked us to provide better snow and ice removal and to post signs saying that all spaces are rented so that a car can be towed if it parks in your space. Signs will be posted by March 1, and, if we get any more snow, Acme Company will have the lot cleared by 7 A.M.

Enclosed is a new parking sticker. Please hang it on your rearview mirror.

Sincerely,

A. E. Jackson

E-Mail Messages

6.4 Notifying Students That They May Not Graduate

The University of Regina asks students to file an application to graduate one term before they plan to graduate. The application lists the courses the student has already had and those he or she will take in the last two terms. Your office reviews the lists to see that the student will meet the requirements for total number of hours, hours in the major, and general education requirements. Some students have forgotten a requirement or not taken enough courses and cannot graduate unless they take more courses than those they have listed.

As Your Professor Directs,

Write form e-mail messages to the following audiences. Leave blanks for the proposed date of graduation and specific information that must be merged into the message:

a. Students who have not taken enough total hours.

b. Students who have not fulfilled all the requirements for their majors.

c. Students who are missing one or more general education courses.

d. Advisers of students who do not meet the requirements for graduation.

6.5 Correcting a Mistake

Today, as you reviewed some cost figures, you realized they didn't fit with the last monthly report you filed. You had pulled the numbers together from several sources, and you're not sure what happened. Maybe you miscopied, or didn't save the final version after you'd checked all the numbers. But whatever the cause, you've found errors in three categories. You gave your boss the following totals:

Personnel	$2,843,490
Office supplies	$43,500
Telephone	$186,240

E-mail your boss to correct the information.

As Your Professor Directs,

Write e-mail messages for the following situations:

a. The correct numbers are

Personnel	$2,845,490
Office supplies	$34,500
Telephone	$186,420

b. The correct numbers are

Personnel	$2,845,490
Office supplies	$84,500
Telephone	$468,240

Variations for each situation:

i. Your boss has been out of the office; you know she hasn't seen the data yet.

ii. Your boss gave a report to the executive committee this morning using your data.

Hints:

- How serious is the mistake in each situation?
- In which situations, if any, should you apologize?
- Should you give the reason for the mistake? Why or why not?
- How do your options vary depending on whether your job title gives you responsibility for numbers and accounting?

6.6 Refusing to Post E-Mail Addresses

You're the Web Weaver for a major organization. Today, you get this e-mail:

Subject: Want E-Mail Addresses

Your "contact us" page does not give the e-mail addresses of your executives and managers. Could you please list them?

You could, but the company isn't willing to. Some time ago, you *did* list them, and some slightly twisted individual from outside the company flooded the addresses with spam, viruses, and hate mail. To protect your employees and your system, you removed them.

Answer the e-mail message.

6.7 Telling Employees to Remove Personal Web Pages

You're director of management and information systems (MIS) in your organization. At your monthly briefing for management, a vice-president complained that some employees have posted personal Web pages on the company's Web server.

"It looks really unprofessional to have stuff about cats and children and musical instruments. How can people do this?"

You took the question literally. "Well, some people have authorization to post material—price changes, job listings, marketing information. Someone who has authorization could put up anything."

Another manager said, "I don't think it's so terrible—after all, there aren't any links from our official pages to these personal pages."

A third person said, "But we're paying for what's posted—so we pay for server space and connect time. Maybe it's not much right now, but as more and more people become Web-literate, the number of people putting up unauthorized pages could spread. We should put a stop to this now."

The vice-president agreed. "The Web site is carefully designed to present an image of our organization. Personal pages are dangerous. Can you imagine the flak we'd get if someone posted links to pornography?"

You said, "I don't think that's very likely. If it did happen, as system administrator, I could remove the page."

The third speaker said, "I think we should remove all the pages. Having any at all suggests that our people have so much extra time that they're playing on the Web. That suggests that our prices are too high and may make some people worry about quality. In fact, I think that we need a new policy prohibiting personal pages on the company's Web server. And any pages that are already up should be removed."

A majority of the managers agreed and told you to write a message to all employees. Create an e-mail message to tell employees that you will remove the personal pages already posted and that no more will be allowed.

Hint:

- Suggest other ways that people can post personal Web pages. Commercial services are possibilities. (Check to be sure that the groups you recommend are still offering Web sites. If possible, get current prices.)
- Give only reasons that are watertight and make the company look good.

Communicating at Work

As Your Professor Directs in 6.8 and 6.9,

a. Prepare notes for a meeting with or phone call to the person to whom you must give the bad news.

b. Write a paper or e-mail document to achieve the goal.

c. Write a memo to your professor describing the situation and culture at your workplace and explaining your rhetorical choices (medium, strategy, tone, wording, graphics or document design, and so forth).

d. Examine your organization's files for messages responding to similar situations in the past. Are the messages effective? Why or why not? Write a memo to your professor analyzing the messages, including copies of them, or make a presentation to the class, using the messages as handouts, transparencies, or slides.

6.8 Telling the Boss about a Problem

In any organization, things sometimes go wrong. Tell your supervisor about a problem in your unit and recommend what should be done.

6.9 Refusing a Customer Request

The customer isn't always right. Sometimes customers ask for things you're truly unable to provide. Even more frequently, you say *no* because the refusal serves your organization's needs. Think of a situation where a customer asked for something your organization could not provide or felt was unreasonable. Write a response refusing the request.

Letter and Memo Assignments

6.10   Correcting Misinformation

You're the director of the city's Water Department. Your mail today contains this letter:

> When we bought our pool, the salesman told us that you would give us a discount on the water bill when we fill the pool. Please start the discount immediately. I tried to call you three times and got nothing but busy signals.
>
> Sincerely,
>
> *Larry Shadburn-Butler*
>
> Larry Shadburn-Butler

The salesperson was wrong. You don't provide discounts for pools (or anything else). At current rates, filling a pool with a garden hose costs from $8.83 (for a 1,800-gallon pool) to $124.67 (for 26,000 gallons) in the city. Filling a pool from any other water source would cost more. Rates are 30% higher in the suburbs and 50% higher in unincorporated rural areas. And you don't have enough people to answer phones. You tried a voice-mail system but eliminated it when you found people didn't have time to process all the messages that were left. But the city budget doesn't allow you to hire more people.

As Your Professor Directs,

a.   Write a letter to Mr. Shadburn-Butler.

b.   Write a letter to all the stores that sell swimming pools, urging them to stop giving customers misinformation.

c.   Write a notice for the one-page newsletter that you include with quarterly water bills. Assume that you can have half a page for your information.

6.11   Dropping Clients

Your bank's software allows you to calculate how profitable each client is. You've discovered that you lose money on corporate loans when the company has no other banking relationship with you. The bank's Lending Committee has decided to notify the corporate customers in this category—nearly 20% of your corporate customers—that it will drop them or extend less credit. If a customer's loan is due, you won't renew it. If the due date is some time away, you are asking companies to find other lenders in the next six months. Of course, you will continue to fund the loan if a company makes significant use of your other services, such as chequing, cash management, asset management, investment banking, and securities underwriting.

Prepare a form letter to go to the customers whom you plan to drop.

6.12   Rejecting a Member's Request

All non-supervisory workers employed by your provincial government are union members. As a paid staff person for the union, you spend about a third of your time writing and editing the monthly magazine, *Public [Your Province] Employee*. You receive this letter:

Dear Editor:

Every month, we get two copies of the union magazine—one addressed to me, one to my husband. We have different last names, so your computer may not realize that we're connected, but we are, and we don't need two copies. Sending just one copy will save printing and postage costs and reduce environmental waste. My name is Dorothy Livingston; my husband is Eric Beamer. Please combine our listings to send just one copy.

Sincerely,

Dorothy Livingston

Dorothy Livingston

As it happens, a couple of years ago you investigated possible savings of sending just one mailing to couples who both work for the province. Sophisticated computerized merge/purge programs to eliminate duplicates are far too expensive for the union's tight budget. And going through the mailing list manually to locate and change duplications would cost more than would be saved in postage. Printing costs wouldn't necessarily drop either, since it actually costs less for each copy to print big runs.

But you want to build goodwill—both to this writer, and for the union in general. Extra copies of the magazine (whether a double mailing or simply a copy someone is finished with) could be given to a non-member or taken to a doctor's or dentist's waiting room. Such sharing would help spread public support for the union and state workers.

Write a letter to Ms. Livingston, explaining why you can't combine mailings.

7 Persuasive Messages

AN INSIDE PERSPECTIVE

Persuasive Messages

To achieve her dream of creating economic development opportunities for her people, Chief Sophie Pierre had to build a powerful case based on compelling logic and powerful emotional appeals. Chief Sophie Pierre called on statistics and stories, testimonials, and expert advice, underlining direct and indirect benefits, to overcome resistance, build support, motivate action, and realize her vision for the St. Eugene Mission, site of a residential school until 1970.

A celebrated leader of Ktunaxa Kinbasket Tribal Council and chief of the St. Mary's Indian Band in the East Kootenay, British Columbia, Chief Sophie could count on her credibility in promoting her vision of converting a painful past of residential school abuse into a productive future of economic development.

Chief Sophie Pierre's creativity, credibility, and capacity to influence have earned her many awards—National Aboriginal Achievement Award, Council for the Advancement of Native Development Officers (CANDO) Economic Developer of the Year, and Queen's Golden Jubilee Medal, for instance—but she gives credit to the Ktunaxa Nation Bands.

First, she had to secure the support of the five bands of the Ktunaxa Nation for her plan to convert the mission on First Nations land into a $45 million resort—complete with hotel, casino, golf course, aquatic and fitness complex, teepee camp, arts and crafts co-operative, and a Ktunaxa interpretive centre. Next, she had to overcome bureaucratic and other resistances, persuade decision makers, secure investment partners, and build business relationships.

In achieving her vision and creating over 250 jobs, the 20-year chief and former residential school member found inspiration in the words of Elder Mary Paul: "Since it was within the St. Eugene Mission that the culture of the Kootenay Indian was taken away, it should be within that building that it is returned."

Whether you're selling safety equipment or ideas, effective persuasion is based on accurate logic (◄▥ Chapter 1), effective emotional appeal, and credibility or trust. Reasons have to be reasons the audience finds important; emotional appeal is based on values the audience cares about; credibility is in the eye of the beholder.

In Classical Greece, Aristotle's *Rhetoric* promoted these same elements in elaborating the art of rhetoric or persuasion:

- *Pathos*: appeal to values, needs, and beliefs shared with audience
- *Logos*: appeal to sound reasoning or logic
- *Ethos*: audience perception of speaker's/writer's good character or credibility

In the 21st century, businesses and other administrative agencies depend more and more on persuasion and buy-in to get quality work done. You can command people to make widgets, but you can't command people to be creative. And even if you're making widgets, just going through the motions isn't enough. You want people to make high-quality widgets, while reducing scrap and other costs. Internal commitment is needed to make that happen.

External motivation doesn't last. Some people will buy a certain brand of pizza if they have a "2 for 1" coupon. But if the coupon expires, or if another company offers the same deal, customers may leave. In contrast, if customers like your pizza better, if they are motivated internally to choose it, then you may keep your customers even if another company comes in with a lower price.

Persuasive messages include

- Orders and requests
- Proposals and recommendations
- Reports recommending action
- Job application letters
- Efforts to change people's behaviour, such as collection letters, criticisms, or performance appraisals
- Public-service ads designed to reduce drunk driving
- Sales and fundraising letters (see ▥➡ Chapter 8)

All persuasive messages have several purposes:

Primary purposes:

- To have the reader act
- To provide enough information so that the reader knows exactly what to do
- To overcome any objections that might prevent or delay action

Secondary purposes:

- To build a good image of the writer
- To enhance the reputation of the writer's organization
- To cement a good relationship between the writer and reader
- To reduce or eliminate future correspondence on the same subject so the message doesn't create more work for the writer

Analyzing a Persuasive Situation

Choose a persuasive strategy based on your answers to four questions.

1. What Do You Want People to Do?

Identify the specific action you want and the person who has the power to do it. If your goal requires several steps, specify what you want your audience to

Persuasion and Emotional Intelligence*

Emotional intelligence is the buzzword for what enables people to succeed in the workplace. Psychologist Daniel Goleman studied 181 jobs in 121 companies worldwide. He separated technical skills from emotional competencies. The latter were twice as important: "The abilities considered vital for success were emotional competencies like trustworthiness, adaptability, and a talent for collaboration."

For high-level executive jobs, says Goleman, perhaps the most important characteristic is "How persuasive are you? Can you get 'buy-in' for your ideas from the people around you? … [Can you] articulat[e] a mission or a goal and … bring everyone on board to get it accomplished [?] Can you take the pulse of a group, understand its unspoken currents of thought and concerns, and communicate with people in terms they can understand and embrace? That is great leadership. And it takes huge social intelligence, including a strongly developed sense of empathy."

*Based on and quotations taken from Anne Fisher, "Success Secret: A High Emotional IQ," *Fortune*, October 26, 1998, 293–294.

do *now.* For instance, your immediate goal may be to have people come to a meeting or let you make a presentation, even though your long-term goal is a major sale or a change in policy.

2. What Objections, If Any, Will the Audience Have?

If you're asking for something that requires little time, money, or physical effort and for an action that's part of the person's regular duties, the audience is likely to have few objections. For example, when you order a product, the firm is happy to supply it.

Often, however, you'll encounter some resistance. People may be busy and may have other uses for their time and money. To be persuasive, you need to show your audience that your proposal meets their needs; you need to overcome any objections.

People are likely to be most aware of and willing to share objective concerns such as time and money. They will be less willing to tell you that their real objection is emotional. Readers have a **vested interest** in something if they benefit directly from keeping things as they are. People who are in power have a vested interest in retaining the system that gives them their power. For example, someone who designed a system has a vested interest in protecting that system from criticism.

Both individuals and organizations have self-images. It's easier for readers to say *yes* when you ask for something that is consistent with that self-image. For example, Aramis persuaded men to buy its over-the-counter skin peel, Lift Off, by linking it to shaving: men who exfoliated with the product could reduce their shaving time by one-third.[1]

3. How Strong Is Your Case?

The strength of your case is based on three aspects of persuasion: argument, credibility, and emotional appeal.

Argument refers to the reasons or logic you offer. Sometimes you may be able to prove conclusively that your solution is best. Sometimes your reasons may not be as strong, the benefits may not be as certain, and obstacles may be difficult or impossible to overcome. For example, suppose that you wanted to persuade your organization to offer a tuition reimbursement plan for employees. You'd have a strong argument if you could show that tuition reimbursement would improve the performance of marginal workers or that reimbursement would be an attractive recruiting tool in a tight job market. However, if dozens of fully qualified workers apply for every opening you have, your argument would be weaker. The program might be nice for workers, but you'd have a hard job proving that it would help the company.

Credibility is the audience's response to you as the source of the message. Credibility in the workplace has three sources: knowledge, image, and relationships.[2] Citing experts can make your argument more credible. In some organizations, workers build credibility by getting assigned to high-profile teams. You build credibility by your track record. The more reliable you've been in the past, the more likely people are to trust you now.

Building a relationship with someone—even if the relationship is based on an outside interest, like sports or children—makes it easier for that person to see you as an individual and to trust you.

When you don't yet have the credibility that comes from being an expert or being powerful, build credibility by the language and strategy you use:

■ **Be factual.** Don't exaggerate. Use concrete language and reliable statistics.

Stare at own risk.

CRESCENDO
RISING CRUST PIZZA
McCain

The Teen Factor. The sensory, emotional, and motivational appeals of McCain Foods Ltd. have worked with teens without turning off their parents.

- **Be specific.** If you say "X is better," show in detail *how* it is better. Show the reader exactly where the savings or other benefits come from.
- **Be reliable.** If you suspect that a project will take longer to complete, cost more money, or be less effective than you originally thought, tell your audience *immediately*. Negotiate a new schedule that you can meet.

Emotional appeal means making the reader *want* to do what you ask. People don't make decisions—even business decisions—based on logic alone. Consumers, for instance, don't make purchasing decisions on logical grounds. They care about relationships with the products and services, according to marketer Marie Germain. The Four Ps of marketing—product, place, price, and promotion—are simple "left-brain" models, she says. Conscious memory explains only about 5% of the reasons people buy. And they have a habit of focusing attention on the competition, so that everyone ends up emulating the competition or working too hard to be different. "It's better to be better than to be different," says Germain.

She is supported by the findings of Joe Calloway, author of *Becoming a Category of One*, who claims, "The place to differentiate is in that very personal sensory-emotional realm of what the customer feels." Consider Krispy Kreme's ability to sell fatty food because it frees us from those who would tell us what not to eat.

Or consider McCain Foods' success after trying to persuade parents that their product was as good as delivery and better than Kraft's Delissio. Although first to market in Canada, McCain's lost market share. Then the company targeted teens in a campaign that has seen sales up 25% in January 2005.[3]

4. What Kind of Persuasion Is Best for the Organization and the Culture?

A strategy that works in one organization may not work somewhere else. James Suchan and Ron Dulek point out that DEC's corporate culture values no-holds-barred aggressiveness. "Even if opposition is expected, a subordinate should write a proposal in a forceful, direct manner."[4] In another organization with different cultural values, an employee who used a hard-sell strategy for a request antagonized the boss.[5]

Responding to Criticism*

By definition, your boss criticizes you during a performance appraisal. Criticism often feels like an attack, and when we are attacked, most of us try to defend ourselves. But doing that in a performance appraisal just makes us look like we can't take criticism.

Fernando Flores, former Chilean minister of finance and current consultant, recommends the following script to respond to criticism: "[Name,] thank you for your assessment. I appreciate your sincerity. I would like to have further conversations with you about the topic."

This script does three things. First it is non-defensive and avoids escalating the conflict. Second, it recognizes that the boss means what he or she says (whether or not the criticism is on target). Third, it asks for further discussion. This discussion might involve probing the meaning of the criticism more fully or discussing ways to improve or even discussing competing agendas that create a double bind for you.

*Based on Harriet Rubin, "The Power of Words," *Fast Company*, January 1999, 144.

Using Your Analysis to Choose a Persuasive Strategy

If your organization prefers a specific approach, use it. If your organization has no preference, or if you do not know your readers' preference, use the following guidelines to choose a strategy:

- Use the **direct request (good news) pattern** when
  - The audience will do as you ask without any resistance.
  - You need responses only from people who will find it easy to do as you ask.
  - Busy readers may not read all the messages they receive.
- Use the **indirect problem-solving (bad news) pattern** when the audience may resist doing as you ask and you expect logic to be more important than emotion in the decision.
- Use the **sales** or **star-chain-knot pattern** presented in ➡ Chapter 8 when the audience may resist doing as you ask and you expect emotion to be more important than logic in the decision.

Writing Persuasive Direct Requests

When you expect quick agreement, save the reader's time by presenting the request directly (see Figure 7.1).

The direct request does not contain reader benefits and does not need to overcome objections: it simply asks for what is needed (see Figure 7.2).

Direct requests should be direct. Don't make the reader guess what you want.

Indirect request: Is there a newer version of the 2001 *Accounting Reference Manual?*

Direct request: If there is a newer version of the 2001 *Accounting Reference Manual*, please send it to me.

In a direct request, put the request, the topic of the request, or a question in the subject line (Request for Updated Software).

In some direct requests, your combination of purposes may suggest a different pattern of organization. For example, in a letter asking an employer to reimburse you for expenses after a job interview, you'd want to thank your hosts for their hospitality and cement the good impression you made at the interview. To do that, you'd spend the first several paragraphs talking about the trip and the interview. Only in the last third of the letter (or even in the P.S.) would you put your request for reimbursement.

FIGURE 7.1   How to Organize a Persuasive Direct Request

1. **Consider asking immediately for the information or service you want.** Delay the request if it seems too abrupt or if you have several purposes in the message.

2. **Give readers all the information they will need to act on your request.** Number your questions or set them off with bullets so the reader can check to see that all of them have been answered.

   In a claim (where a product is under guarantee or a shipment was defective), explain the circumstances so that the reader knows what happened. Be sure to include all the relevant details: date of purchase, model or invoice number, and so on.

   In more complicated direct requests, anticipate possible responses. Suppose you're asking for information about equipment meeting certain specifications. Explain which criteria are most important so that the reader can recommend an alternative if no single product meets all your needs. You may also want to tell the reader what your price constraints are and ask whether the item is in stock or must be special-ordered.

3. **Ask for the action you want.** Do you want a cheque? A replacement? A catalogue? Answers to your questions? If you need an answer by a certain time, say so. If possible, show the reader why the time limit is necessary.

FIGURE 7.2 A Direct Request

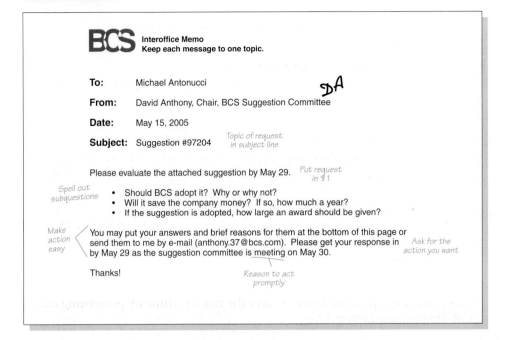

BCS Interoffice Memo
Keep each message to one topic.

To: Michael Antonucci

From: David Anthony, Chair, BCS Suggestion Committee

Date: May 15, 2005

Subject: Suggestion #97204 *Topic of request in subject line*

Please evaluate the attached suggestion by May 29. *Put request in ¶ 1*

Spell out subquestions
- Should BCS adopt it? Why or why not?
- Will it save the company money? If so, how much a year?
- If the suggestion is adopted, how large an award should be given?

Make action easy You may put your answers and brief reasons for them at the bottom of this page or send them to me by e-mail (anthony.37@bcs.com). Please get your response in by May 29 as the suggestion committee is meeting on May 30. *Ask for the action you want*

Thanks! *Reason to act promptly*

Writing Persuasive Problem-Solving Messages

Use an **indirect** approach and the problem-solving pattern of organization when you expect resistance from your reader but can show that doing what you want will solve a problem you and your reader share. The pattern in Figure 7.3 allows you to disarm opposition by showing all the reasons in favour of your position before you give your readers a chance to say *no*.

Figure 7.4 uses the problem-solving pattern of organization. Reader benefits can be brief in this kind of message since the biggest benefit comes from solving the problem.

When you have a reluctant reader, putting the request in the subject line just gets a quick *no* before you've had a chance to give all your arguments. One option is to use a **directed subject line** that makes your stance on the issue clear.[6] In the following examples, the first is the most neutral. The remaining two increasingly reveal the writer's preference.

> Subject: A Proposal to Change the Formula for Calculating Retirees' Benefits

> Subject: Arguments for Expanding the Wolfville Plant

> Subject: Why Cassano's Should Close Its West Side Store

Catching Attention and Developing a Common Ground

In order to persuade, you need first to catch attention by beginning with a startling fact or statistic, engaging question, thoughtful compliment, striking headline, or quotation. For example, instead of making a general claim about the costs of poverty, mention that "every single day 30,000 children are dying as a result of extreme poverty."

A common ground avoids the me-against-you of some persuasive situations and suggests that both you and your audience have a mutual interest in solving the problems you face.

FIGURE 7.3   How to Organize a Persuasive Problem-Solving Message

1. **Catch the reader's interest by mentioning a common ground.** Show that your message will be interesting or beneficial. You may want to catch attention with a negative (which you will go on to show can be solved).

2. **Define the problem you both share (which your request will solve).** Present the problem objectively: don't assign blame or mention personalities. Be specific about the cost in money, time, lost goodwill, and so on. You have to convince readers that *something* has to be done before you can convince them that your solution is the best one.

3. **Explain the solution to the problem.** If you know that the reader will favour another solution, start with that solution and show why it won't work before you present your solution.

     Present your solution without using the words *I* or *my.* Don't let personalities enter the picture; don't let the reader think he or she should say *no* just because you've had other requests accepted recently.

4. **Show that positives outweigh any negative elements (cost, time, etc.).**

5. **Summarize any additional benefits of the solution.** The main benefit—solving the problem—can be presented briefly since you described the problem in detail. However, if there are any additional benefits, mention them.

6. **Ask for and motivate the action you want.** Often your reader will authorize or approve something; other people will implement the action. Give your reader a reason to act promptly, perhaps offering a new reader benefit. ("By buying now, we can avoid the next quarter's price hikes.")

Read This*

Busy executives get so many messages a day that they can't pay attention to all of them. One study found that executives were most likely to pay attention to messages that

- Were personalized
- Evoked an emotional response
- Came from a credible sender
- Were concise

*Based on Thomas H. Davenport and John C. Beck, "Getting the Attention You Need," *Harvard Business Review*, September–October 2000, 124.

The best common grounds are specific. Often a negative—a problem the reader will want to solve—makes a good common ground.

Weak common ground:	This program has had some difficulty finding enough individuals to volunteer their services for the children. As a result, we are sometimes unable to provide the one-on-one mentoring that is our goal.
Improved common ground:	On five Sundays in the last three months, we've had too few volunteers to provide one-on-one mentoring. Last Sunday, we had just two students to take eight children to the Museum of Science and Industry.

Defining the Problem

Include a problem description that is concise, concrete, and carefully targeted to your audience. In recommending a new wellness program, the following might arouse management interest: With job stress creating 60% of absenteeism, reducing productivity, and sucking the profits out of the business, a wellness program is an investment that returns $3 in cost benefits for every $1 spent.

Explaining the Solution to the Problem

Avoiding judgmental language or personal references (*I, me*), present your solution in factual, reliable, impersonal terms. For example, supply figures to support your claim about profits being sucked out of the business: Absenteeism costs in Canada are estimated at $8.6 billion annually; Vancouver Airport Authority experienced a drop in absenteeism among participants in its Workplace Wellness Program from 4.07% to 2.56%.[7] At a time when employee retention is becoming an issue, survey results on employee satisfaction would add to the logical appeals.

If you know that your readers will hear other points of view, or if your audience's initial position is negative, you have to deal with their objections to persuade them. The stronger the objection is, the earlier in your message you should deal with it.

FIGURE 7.4   A Problem-Solving Persuasive Message

Persuading the Boss*

Memorandum

To: All Staff Members

From: Melissa J. Gutridge   *MJG*

Date: February 16, 2005

Subject: Why We Are Implementing a New Sign-Out System   *Directed subject line indicates writer's position*

Common ground

Problem

Successfully mainstreaming our clients into the community is very important and daily interaction with the public is necessary. Our clients enjoy the times they get to go to the mall or out to lunch instead of remaining here all day. Recently, however, clients have been taken out on activities without a staff member's knowing where the client is or with whom.

Specific example of problem

We need to know where all clients are at all times because social workers, psychologists, and relatives constantly stop by unannounced. Last week Janet's father stopped by to pick her up for a doctor's appointment and she was not here. No one knew where she was. Naturally her father was very upset and wanted to know what kind of program we were running. Such situations are damaging to the good reputation of our staff and program.

Solution presented impersonally

Additional reader benefit

Starting Monday, February 23, a sign-out board will be located by Betty's desk. Please write down where you and the client are going and when you expect to be back. When signing out, help clients sign themselves out. We can turn this into a learning experience for our clients. Then when a social worker stops by to see someone who isn't here, we can simply look at the sign-out board to tell where the client is and when he or she will return.

Please help keep up the superb reputation you have helped Community LIving earn as a quality centre for adults with disabilities. Sign out yourself and clients at all times.

Ask for action

When a close friend confided his HIV-positive status to her, [Lynn Kutner decided to become] a Spokebuster—someone who does all five [bicycle] rides [to raise funds for AIDS] in a year. …

Although Kutner, … who supervises a team of four people, was entitled to some vacation time, she knew that requesting 20 days off was unusual. So she submitted a formal request nine months in advance and talked at length with her boss about why doing all five rides was so important to her. She also explained that at the most she'd be out of the office for a week and a half at a time.

"I was able to demonstrate that I was going to be in the office enough to follow through with my commitments," she says. … "Initially people were concerned, but it was clearly something that I thought through. And it meant a lot to me; my level of commitment carried a lot of weight."

Kutner's participation had a clear work benefit: She says she's now less intimidated by new tasks and [is] more efficient. … Nobody was surprised when she asked to go this year, she says, and nobody objected.

*Quoted from Erica Rasmusson, "Doing Well, Doing Good," *Working Woman*, December/January 2001, 42.

The best way to deal with an objection is to eliminate it. James Davis keeps frequently ordered items in stock to eliminate the objection "I don't want to wait." To sell Jeep Cherokees in Japan, Mitsuru Sato convinced Chrysler to put the driver's seat on the right side, to make an extra preshipment quality check, and to rewrite the instruction booklet in Japanese style, with big diagrams and cartoons.[8]

If an objection is false and is based on misinformation, give the response to the objection without naming the objection. In a brochure, you can present responses with a "question/answer" format.

Showing that Positives Outweigh Negatives

If real objections remain, try one or more of the following strategies to counter objections:

1. Specify how much time and/or money is required—it may not be as much as the reader fears.

Distributing flyers to each house or apartment in your neighbourhood will probably take two afternoons.

2.   Put the time and/or money in the context of the benefits they bring.

> The additional $152,500 will (1) allow the Open Shelter to remain open 24 rather than 16 hours a day, (2) pay for three social workers to help men find work and homes, and (3) keep the neighbourhood bank open, so that men don't have to cash cheques in bars and so that they can save up the $800 they need to have upfront to rent an apartment.

3.   Show that money spent now will save money in the long run.

> By buying a $100 safety product, you can avoid $500 in Occupational Health and Safety fines.

4.   Show that doing as you ask will benefit some group or cause the reader supports, even though the action may not help the reader directly. This is the strategy used in fundraising letters, discussed in detail in ➡ Chapter 8.

> By being a Big Brother or a Big Sister, you'll give a child the adult attention he or she needs to become a well-adjusted, productive adult.

5.   Show the reader that the sacrifice is necessary to achieve a larger, more important goal to which he or she is committed.

> These changes will mean more work for all of us. But we've got to cut our costs 25% to keep the plant open and to keep our jobs.

6.   Show that the advantages as a group outnumber or outweigh the disadvantages as a group.

> None of the locations is perfect. But the Burnaby location gives us the most advantages and the fewest disadvantages.

7.   Turn a disadvantage into an opportunity.

> With the hiring freeze, every department will need more lead time to complete its own work. By hiring another person, the Planning Department could provide that lead time.

The draft in Figure 7.5 makes the mistake of attacking readers in a negative message. Making the memo less accusatory would help, but the message doesn't need to be negative at all. Instead, the writer can take the information in paragraph 3 and use it as the attention-getter and common ground for a problem-solving persuasive message. Figure 7.6 shows a possible revision.

Sense impressions—what the reader sees, hears, smells, tastes, feels—evoke a strong emotional response. **Psychological description** (Figure 7.7) means creating a scenario rich with sense impressions so readers can picture themselves using your product or service and enjoying its benefits. You can also use psychological description to describe the problem your product will solve. Psychological description works best early in the message to catch readers' attention.

Summarizing Benefits and Building Emotional Appeal

Stories and psychological description are effective ways of building emotional appeal and underlining benefits. Emotional appeal works best when people want to be persuaded.

FIGURE 7.5 Original Unprofessional Memo Attacking Readers

Inter-office Memorandum

To: Todd Neumann

From: Heather Johnson *HJ*

Date: October 24, 2005

Subject: Problems with Instrument Lab Results

Accusatory tone makes this writer look unprofessional

Negative

Makes reader feel incompetent

Accusatory tone

The Instrument Technicians Lab again seems to believe that if a result is printed out, it is the correct answer. It doesn't seem to matter that the chromatogram is terribly noisy, the calibration standards are over a month old, or the area of the internal standards is about half what it should be. What does it matter if the correction factor is 1286 and at the very minimum it should be 1300? That's an average of two results—so what if the calibration standard is six weeks old? I'm aware that the *Lacks you-attitude (YA)* conditions in the lab have contributed to the discouraged atmosphere, but I don't feel it's an excuse for the shape of the lab and the equipment. The G.C. columns are in bad shape just from abuse. I've lost count of the number of 10 ml syringes the lab has buried (at least $20 each) mainly because they were not properly rinsed and the plungers were lost trying to push through dried protein material. When was the last time the glass insert in the B column was changed or even looked at? Has anyone checked the filter on the Autolab I?

Attacks reader

Insults and attacks reader

Lacks YA

During the last six months, I have either reminded the technician of such things or written reminders in the log book. Isn't it time for our responsible lab technicians to take on this responsibility? Shouldn't they have fresh standards made up, especially when they know a run is coming? Granted, we've had many false starts, but I am still uncomfortable that the technicians will be ready when the time comes.

Lacks YA

Problem presented as reader's fault, not a common problem that both share

I don't feel that I should have to go over the chromatograms, printouts, and G.C. book every time we submit samples for analysis. However, just two weeks ago I sent out results without doing this and immediately received a call that the results were impossible—and they were because unacceptable KF was used, the result of an old calibration standard.

Lacks YA

One other item bothers me. I don't know how to get the technicians interested in the way the Autolab integrates each peak when they don't seem to look at anything other than the answer. I feel it's very important they learn this so they will know when a peak has been incorrectly integrated.

Attacks and insults reader

I think it's time they either take hold and run the lab themselves or they be treated as if they were children and told what to do, which means they'll need a baby-sitter. I also would like to see them *Whole ¶ lacks YA* read the Autolab I Instruction Manual and take the tape courses on the gas chromatograph and the Autolab I. I really think the above should be a mandatory part of their training.

The overall attitude and morale of the lab must be raised and a step in that direction is to give them the responsibility that they were supposed to have in the first place and expect them to accept it. These people are being called technicians but they are actually classed as chemists and should be assuming more initative and responsibility.

Attacks reader

Even when you need to provide statistics or numbers to convince the careful reader that your anecdote is a representative example, telling a story first makes your message more persuasive. Stories alone are more effective than a combination of stories and statistics; the combination was more effective than statistics alone. Recent research suggests that stories are more persuasive because people remember them.[9]

Asking for and Motivating Action

The longer people delay, the less likely they are to carry through with the action they had decided to take. In addition, you want a fast response so you can go ahead with your own plans.

Request action by a specific date. Try to give people at least a week or two: they have other things to do besides respond to your requests. Set deadlines in the middle of the month, if possible. If you say, "Please return this by March 1,"

FIGURE 7.6   Revised Memo Creating a Common Ground and a Professional Image

BIERNAT LABORATORIES

Straightforward problem-solving approach is the mark of a professional manager

Inter-office Memorandum

To: Todd Neumann

From: Heather Johnson

Date: October 24, 2005

Subject: Cutting Requests for Rework   *Positive subject line*

Common ground:

Problem writer and reader share

Two weeks ago a customer called to tell me that the results we'd sent out were impossible. I checked, and the results were wrong because we'd used an old calibration standard.

Redoing work for outside customers and for in-house projects doubles our workload. Yet because people don't trust our results, we're getting an increasing number of requests for rework.

Writer shows understanding of reader's problems

Part of the problem is that we've had so many false starts. Customers and especially in-house engineers say they'll need a run but then don't have the materials for another day or even a week. Paul Liu has told me that these schedule glitches are inevitable. We'll just have to prepare fresh calibration standards every time a run is scheduled—and prepare them again when the run actually is ready.

You've told me that the equipment in the lab is unreliable. The Capital Expenditures Request includes a line item for G.C. columns and a new gas chromatograph. We'll be able to be more persuasive at the Board meeting if we can show that we're taking good care of the equipment we have. Please remind your staff to

- Rinse the 10-ml syringes every day.

- Check the glass insert in the B column every week.

- Check the filter on the Autolab I every week.

List emphasizes what reader needs to do

Treats reader as an equal who can help solve the problem

Do workers find the Autolab I instruction manual and the tape courses on the gas chromatograph and the Autolab I helpful? If the manual is hard to use or the tape course is boring, perhaps we should ask the manufacturer to redo them and, in the meantime, to send a service worker to offer a short course for our workers. What do you think would be the best way to increase the technical expertise of our staff?

By getting our results right the first time, we can eliminate the rework and give both customers and in-house clients better service.

Links desired action to benefit and picture of the problem being solved

people will think, "I don't need to do this till March." Ask for the response by February 28 instead. If you can use a response even after the deadline, say so. Otherwise, people who can't make the deadline may not respond at all.

Show why you need a quick response:

- **Show that the time limit is real.** Perhaps you need information quickly to use it in a report that has a due date.
- **Show that acting now will save time or money.** If business is slow and your industry isn't doing well, then your company needs to act now (to economize, to better serve customers) in order to be competitive. If business is booming and everyone is making a profit, then your company needs to act now to get its fair share of the available profits.

<table>
<tr><td>FIGURE 7.7</td><td>Using Psychological Description to Develop Reader Benefits</td></tr>
</table>

You–attitude psychological description

The Colonial Room

Visual details

When you dine in the Union Colonial Room, it's easy to imagine yourself a guest in a fine mansion. Light from the gleaming chandeliers reflects from a hand-carved mirror hanging over the dark, polished buffet. Here you can dine in quiet elegance amid furnishings adapted from 18th-century Georgian homes.

Perhaps you'd like a dinner of stuffed rainbow trout. Or the pork fricassee. The menu features a variety of complete meals that are changed daily, as well as the regular a la carte service. Whatever your choice, you'll enjoy an evening of fine dining at very reasonable prices.

The Union Colonial Room is located on the northeast corner of the first floor. Dinners are served Monday through Friday from 5:30 to 7:30 P.M. Please call 333-0690 for reservations, and enjoy the flavour of the Colonies tonight.

Details appeal to sight, taste, smell

Emphasis on reader's choice— Not every reader will want the same thing

The Cafeteria

In the Illini Union Cafeteria, you start out with an empty tray and silverware. Then comes the food, several yards of it, all yours for the choosing. By the time you've finished, your empty tray has become a delicious meal.

In the morning, the inviting aroma of breakfast fills the air. Feast your eyes and then your appetite on the array of eggs, bacon, pancakes, toast, sausage, rolls, juices, and coffee … They're all waiting to wake you up with good taste. Have a hearty breakfast or make it quick and tasty. The warm, freshly baked rolls and coffee cakes practically beg to be smothered in butter and savoured with a cup of hot coffee.

By 11 A.M. the breakfast menu has made way for lunch. Here come the hot Reuben sandwiches and the toasty grilled cheese. Soups and salads make their appearance. A variety of vegetables are dressed up to entice you, and several main dishes lead the luncheon parade. Any number of complete meals can take shape as you move along.

What? Back for dinner? Well, no wonder! The Cafeteria sets out a wide selection of entrees and side dishes. Veal parmigiana sizzles for your attention but the roast beef right next to it is tough competition. Tomorrow the fried chicken might be up for selection. Choose the dinner combination that best fits your appetite.

The newly remodelled Cafeteria is on the ground floor and is open for breakfast from 7 to 11 A.M. Monday through Saturday and 8 to 11 A.M. on Sunday. Lunch is served from 11 A.M. to 1:15 P.M. Monday through Saturday and 11 A.M. to 2 P.M. on Sunday. Dinner is served from 4:45 to 7 P.M. Monday through Friday.

A meal in a restaurant is expensive. A meal at home is a chore. But a meal at the Cafeteria combines good food and reasonable prices to make dining a pleasure.

■ **Show the cost of delaying action.** Will labour or material costs be higher in the future? Will delay mean more money spent on repairing something that will still need to be replaced?

Checking Tone in Persuasive Messages

The best phrasing depends on your relationship to the reader. When you ask for action from people who report directly to you, orders ("Get me the Ervin file") and questions ("Do we have the third-quarter numbers yet?") will work. When you need action from co-workers, superiors, or people outside the organization, you need to be more forceful but also more polite.

Avoiding messages that sound parental or preachy is often a matter of tone. Saying "Please" is essential, especially to people on your level or outside the organization. Tone will also be better when you give reasons for your request or reasons to act promptly.

Parental: Everyone is expected to comply with these regulations. I'm sure you can see that they are common-sense rules needed for our business.

Better: Even on casual days, visitors expect us to be professional. So leave the gym clothes at home!

Writing to superiors is trickier. You may want to tone down your request by using subjunctive verbs and explicit disclaimers that show you aren't taking a *yes* for granted.

Arrogant: Based on this evidence, I expect you to give me a new computer.

Better: If department funds permit, I would like a new computer.

It can be particularly tricky to control tone in e-mail messages, which tend to sound less friendly than paper documents or conversations. For important requests, compose your message off-line and revise it carefully before you send it.

The subject line of a persuasive e-mail message should make it clear that you're asking for something. To be sure that the reader will read the message, be specific.

Subject: Move Meeting to Tuesday?

Subject: Provide Story for Newsletter?

Subject: Want You for United Way Campaign

Major requests that require changes in values, culture, or lifestyles should not be made in e-mail messages.

Distinguishing Varieties of Persuasive Messages

Collection letters, performance appraisals, and letters of recommendation are among the most common varieties of persuasive messages (see also ➠ Chapter 8).

Collection Letters

Most businesses find that phoning rather than writing results in faster payment. But as more and more companies install voice-mail systems, you will need to write letters when leaving messages doesn't work (see ◄━ Figure 5.6 in Chapter 5).

Collection letters ask customers to pay (as they have already agreed to do) for the goods and services they have already received. Good credit departments send a series of letters a week apart.

Early letters are gentle, assuming that the reader intends to pay but has forgotten or has met with temporary reverses. Early letters can be obvious form letters or even just a second copy of the bill with the words "Second Notice" or "Past Due" stamped on it.

A student who had not yet been reimbursed by a company for a visit to the company's office put the second request in the P.S. of a letter refusing a job offer:

P.S. The cheque to cover my expenses when I visited your office in March hasn't come yet. Could you check to see whether you can find a record of it? The amount was $490 (airfare $290, hotel room $185, taxi $15).

If one or two early letters don't result in payment, call the customer to ask if your company has created a problem. It's possible that the invoice arrived before the product and was filed and forgotten. If any of these situations apply, you'll build goodwill by solving the problem rather than arrogantly asking for payment.[10]

Middle letters are more assertive in asking for payment. Figure 7.8 gives an example of a middle letter. This form letter is merged with database information about the customer's name, the amount due, and the magazine the customer is receiving. Other middle letters offer to negotiate a schedule for repayment if

FIGURE 7.8 A Middle Collection Letter

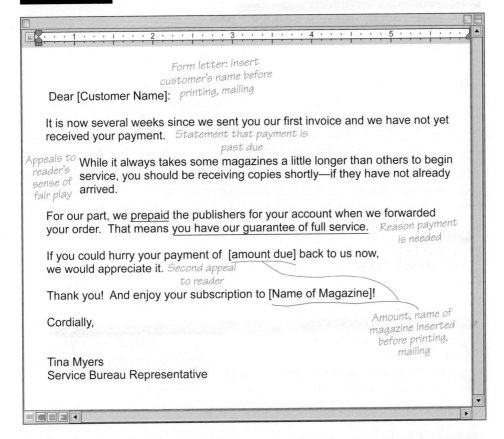

Dear [Customer Name]: *Form letter: Insert customer's name before printing, mailing*

It is now several weeks since we sent you our first invoice and we have not yet received your payment. *Statement that payment is past due*

Appeals to reader's sense of fair play While it always takes some magazines a little longer than others to begin service, you should be receiving copies shortly—if they have not already arrived.

For our part, we <u>prepaid</u> the publishers for your account when we forwarded your order. That means <u>you have our guarantee of full service.</u> *Reason payment is needed*

If you could hurry your payment of [amount due] back to us now, we would appreciate it. *Second appeal to reader*

Thank you! And enjoy your subscription to [Name of Magazine]! *Amount, name of magazine inserted before printing, mailing*

Cordially,

Tina Myers
Service Bureau Representative

the reader is not able to pay the whole bill immediately, may remind the reader of the importance of a good credit rating, educate the reader about credit, and explain why the creditor must have prompt payment.

Late letters threaten legal action if the bill is not paid. At this point, you must assume that only serious consequences will change the behaviour. Short of legal action, you may threaten turning the account over to a collection agency.

Still, expressions of reluctance are in order—combined with a promise to act if the customer does not pay the amount due within a specified time limit (say, 10 days).

Many small businesses find that establishing personal relationships with customers is the best way to speed payment.

Performance Appraisals

At regular intervals, supervisors evaluate, or appraise, the performance of their subordinates. In most organizations, employees have access to their files; sometimes they must sign the appraisal to show that they've read it. The superior normally meets with the subordinate to discuss the appraisal.

Appraisals both protect the organization and motivate the employee. These two purposes may conflict. Most of us will see a candid appraisal as negative; we need praise and reassurance to believe that we're valued and can do better. But the praise that motivates someone to improve can come back to haunt the company if the person does not eventually do acceptable work. An organization is in trouble if it tries to fire someone whose evaluations never mention mistakes.

Negotiating a Raise*

■ Seek assignments where you can implement ideas and be accountable for results. Tangible accomplishments increase your worth.

■ Be able to show how your work helps the whole organization, not just your own unit.

■ Know what your job is worth. See www.labourmarketinformation.ca, www.salaryexpert.com, www.wageweb.com, www.execunet.com.

■ Prepare your boss for the discussion. Perhaps even write out a proposal explaining what comparable jobs pay, what you want, and why you think you deserve a raise. Base your argument not on what you need the money for, but on your contribution to the organization's bottom line.

■ Consider alternatives. If a raise isn't possible, what about an extra week of vacation?

*Adapted from Michael O'Malley, "How to Get the Raise You Deserve," *Fortune*, September 7, 1998, 169–170; Hal Lancaster, "Managing Your Career," *The Wall Street Journal*, September 1, 1998, B1; and *American Demographics*, "For the Bookmark," November 1998, 21.

Avoid labels (*wrong, bad*) and inferences (see ◀▥ Chapter 1). Instead, cite specific observations that describe behaviour.

Inference:	Sam is an alcoholic.
Vague observation:	Sam calls in sick a lot. Subordinates complain about his behaviour.
Specific observation:	Sam called in sick a total of 12 days in the last two months. After a business lunch with a customer last week, Sam was walking unsteadily. Two of his subordinates have said that they would prefer not to make sales trips with him because they find his behaviour embarrassing.

Sam might be having a reaction to a physician-prescribed drug; he might have a mental illness. A supervisor who jumps to conclusions creates ill will, closes the door to solving the problem, and may provide grounds for legal action against the organization.

Be specific in an appraisal.

Too vague:	Sue does not manage her time as well as she could.
Specific:	Sue's first three weekly sales reports have been three, two, and four days late, respectively; the last weekly sales report for the month is not yet in.

Without specifics, Sue won't know that her boss objects to late reports. She may think that she is being criticized for spending too much time on sales calls or for not working 80 hours a week. Without specifics, she might change the wrong things in a futile effort to please her boss.

Figure 7.9 shows a performance appraisal for a member of a collaborative business communication group who is doing good work.

Letters of Recommendation

In an effort to protect themselves against lawsuits, some companies state only how long they employed someone and the position that person held. Such bare-bones letters have themselves been the target of lawsuits when employers did not reveal relevant negatives. Whatever the legal climate, there may be times when you want to recommend someone for an award or for a job.

Letters of recommendation must be specific. General positives that are not backed up with specific examples and evidence are seen as weak recommendations. Letters of recommendation that focus on minor points also suggest that the person is weak.

Either in the first or the last paragraph, summarize your overall evaluation of the person. Early in the letter, perhaps in the first paragraph, show how well and how long you've known the person. In the middle of the letter, offer specific details about the person's performance. At the end of the letter, indicate whether you would be willing to rehire the person and repeat your overall evaluation. See ◀▥ Figure 5.7 in Chapter 5 for a sample letter of recommendation.

Solving a Sample Problem[11]

Problem

In one room in the production department of Martin Electronics Company, employees work on TV picture tubes under conditions that are scarcely bearable due to the heat. Even when the temperature outside is only 23°C, it is over 30°C in the "monitor room." In June, July, and August, 24 out of 36 workers quit because they couldn't stand the heat. This turnover happens every summer.

FIGURE 7.9 A Performance Appraisal

To: Barbara Buchanan

From: Brittany Papper *BAP*

Date: February 13, 2005

Subject line indicates that memo is a performance appraisal

Subject: Your Performance Thus Far in Our Collaborative Group

Overall evaluation You have been a big asset to our group. Overall, our business communication group has been one of the best groups I have ever worked with, and I think that only minor improvements are needed to make our group even better.

These headings would need to be changed in a negative performance appraisal

What You're Doing Well

Specific observations provide dates, details of performance You demonstrated flexibility and compatibility at our last meeting before we turned in our proposal on February 12 by offering to type the proposal since I had to study for an exam in one of my other classes. I really appreciated this because I really did not have the time to do it. I will definitely remember this if you are ever too busy with your other classes and cannot type the final report.

Another positive critical incident occurred February 5. We had discussed researching the topic of sexual discrimination in hiring and promotion at MacLennan Insurance. As we read more about what we had to do, we became uneasy about reporting the information from our source who works at MacLennan. I called you later that evening to talk about changing our topic to a less personal one. You were very understanding and said that you agreed that the original topic was a touchy one. You offered suggestions for other topics and had a positive attitude about the adjustment. Your suggestions ended my worries and made me realize that you are a positive and supportive person.

Other strengths Your ideas are a strength that you definitely contribute to our group. You're good at brainstorming ideas, yet you're willing to go with whatever the group decides. That's a nice combination of creativity and flexibility.

Areas for Improvement

Two minor improvements could make you an even better member.

Specific recommendations for improvement The first improvement is to be more punctual to meetings. On February 5 and February 8 you were about 10 minutes late. This makes the meetings last longer. Your ideas are valuable to the group, and the sooner you arrive the sooner we can share in your suggestions.

Specific behaviour to be changed The second suggestion is one we all need to work on. We need to keep our meetings positive and productive. I think that our negative attitudes were worst at our first group meeting February 5. We spent about half an hour complaining about all the work we had to do and about our busy schedules in other classes. In the future if this happens, maybe you could offer some positive things about the assignment to get the group motivated again.

Overall Compatibility

Positive, forward-looking ending I feel that this group has gotten along very well together. You have been very flexible in finding times to meet and have always been willing to do your share of the work. I have never had this kind of luck with a group in the past and you have been a welcome breath of fresh air. I don't hate doing group projects any more!

In a far corner of the room sits a quality control inspector in front of a small fan (the only one in the room). The production workers, in contrast, are carrying 10 kg monitors. As production supervisor, you tried to get air conditioning two years ago, before Martin acquired the company, but management was horrified at the idea of spending $300,000 to insulate and air condition the warehouse (it is impractical to air condition the monitor room alone).

Inflation has pushed the price of insulation and air conditioning up to $500,000, but with such high turnover, you're losing money every summer. Write a memo to Jennifer M. Kirkland, operations vice-president, renewing your request.

Analysis of the Problem

1. Who is your audience? What characteristics are relevant to this particular message? If you are writing to more than one reader, how do the readers differ?

    The operations vice-president will be concerned about keeping costs low and keeping production running smoothly. Kirkland may know that the request was denied two years ago, but another person was vice-president then; Kirkland wasn't the one who said *no*.

2. What are your purposes in writing?

    To persuade Kirkland to authorize insulation and air conditioning. To build a good image of myself.

3. What information must your message include?

    The cost of the proposal. The effects of the present situation.

4. How can you build support for your position? What reasons or reader benefits will your reader find convincing?

    Cutting turnover may save money and keep the assembly line running smoothly. Experienced employees may produce higher-quality parts. Putting in air conditioning would relieve one of the workers' main complaints; it might make the union happier.

5. What objection(s) can you expect your reader(s) to have? What negative elements of your message must you de-emphasize or overcome?

    The cost. The time operations will be shut down while installation is taking place.

6. What aspects of the total situation may affect reader response? The economy? The time of year? Morale in the organization? The relationship between the reader and writer? Any special circumstances?

    The electronics industry is having a shakeout; money is tight; the company will be reluctant to make a major expenditure. Filling vacancies in the monitor room is hard—we are getting a reputation as a bad place to work. Summer is over, and the problem is over until next year.

Discussion of the Sample Solutions

Solution 1, shown in Figure 7.10, is unacceptable. By making the request in the subject line and the first paragraph, the writer invites a *no* before giving all the arguments. The writer does nothing to counter the objections that any manager will have to spending a great deal of money. By presenting the issue in terms of fairness, the writer produces defensiveness rather than creating a common ground. The writer doesn't use details or emotional appeal to show that the problem is indeed serious. The writer asks for fast action but doesn't show why the reader should act now to solve a problem that won't occur again for eight months.

Solution 2, shown in Figure 7.11, is an effective persuasive message. The writer chooses a positive subject line. The opening sentence is negative, catching the reader's attention. However, the paragraph makes it clear that the memo offers a solution to the problem. The problem is spelled out in detail. Emotional impact is created by taking the reader through the day as the temperature rises. The solution is presented impersonally. There are no *I*'s in the memo.

The memo stresses reader benefits: the savings that will result once the investment is recovered. The last paragraph tells the reader exactly what to do and links prompt action to a reader benefit. The memo ends with a positive picture of the problem solved.

FIGURE 7.10 An Unacceptable Solution to the Sample Problem

To: Jennifer M. Kirkland, Operations Vice President

From: Arnold M. Morgan, Production Supervisor *AMM*

Date: October 10, 2005

Subject: Request for Air Conditioning in the Monitor Room   *Request in subject line stiffens resistance when reader is reluctant*

Please put air conditioning in the monitor room. This past summer, two-thirds of our employees quit because it was so hot. It's not fair that they should work in unbearable temperatures when management sits in air conditioned comfort.   *attacks reader*

Inappropriate emphasis on writer I propose that we solve this problem by air conditioning the monitor room to bring down the temperature to 26°C.

Insulating and air conditioning the tube room would cost $500,000.   *Cost sounds enormous without a context*

Please approve this request promptly.

Memo sounds arrogant.
Logic isn't developed.
This attacks reader instead of enlisting reader's support.

✓ **CHECKLIST**   Checklist for Direct Requests

☐ If the message is a memo, does the subject line indicate the request? Is the subject line specific enough to differentiate this message from others on the same subject?

☐ Does the first paragraph summarize the request or the specific topic of the message?

☐ Does the message give all of the relevant information? Is there enough detail?

☐ Does the message answer questions or overcome objections that readers may have without introducing unnecessary negatives?

☐ Does the last paragraph tell the reader exactly what to do? Does it give a deadline if one exists and a reason for acting promptly?

And, for all messages, not just direct requests,

☐ Does the message use you-attitude and positive emphasis?

☐ Is the style easy to read and friendly?

☐ Is the visual design of the message inviting?

☐ Is the format correct?

☐ Does the message use standard grammar? Is it free from typos?

Originality in a direct request may come from

☐ Good lists and visual impact.

☐ Thinking about readers and giving details that answer their questions, overcome any objections, and make it easier for them to do as you ask.

☐ Adding details that show you're thinking about a specific organization and the specific people in that organization.

FIGURE 7.11   A Good Solution to the Sample Problem

To: Jennifer M. Kirkland, Operations Vice-President

From: Arnold M. Morgan, Production Supervisor *AMM*

Date: October 10, 2005

Subject: Improving Summer Productivity

Reader benefit in subject line

Problem creates a common ground

Martin forfeited a possible $186,000 in profits last summer because of a 17% drop in productivity. That's not unusual: Martin has a history of low summer productivity. But we can reverse the trend and bring summer productivity in line with the rest of the year's.

Good to show problem can be resolved

Cause of problem

The problem starts in the monitor room. Because of high turnover and reduced efficiency from workers who are on the job, we just don't make as many monitors as we do during the rest of the year.

Additional reason to solve problem

Both the high turnover and reduced efficiency are due to the unbearable heat in the monitor room. Temperatures in the monitor room average 4°C over the outside temperature. During the summer, when work starts at 8:00 A.M., it's already 29°C in the monitor room. By 11:30 A.M., it's at least 35°C. On six days last summer, it hit 35°C. When the temperatures are that high, we may be violating Occupational Health and Safety regulations.

Production workers are always standing, moving, or carrying 10 kg monitors. When temperatures hit 30°C, they slow down. When no relief is in sight, many of them quit.

We replaced 24 of the 36 employees in the monitor room this summer. When someone quits, it takes an average of five days to find and train a replacement; during that time, the trainee produces nothing. For another five days, the new person can work at only half speed. And even "full speed" in the summer is only 90% of what we expect the rest of the year.

More details about problem

Here's where our losses come from:

Normal production = 50 units a person each day (upd)

Loss due to turnover:
loss of 24 workers for 5 days =	6,000 units
24 at ½ pace for 5 days =	3,000 units
Total loss due to turnover =	9,000 units

Shows detail— Set up like an arithmetic problem

Loss due to reduced efficiency:
loss of 5 upd × 12 workers × 10 days =	600 units
loss of 5 upd × 36 × 50 days =	9,000 units
Total loss due to reduced efficiency =	9,600 units

Total Loss =	18,600 units

Jennifer M. Kirkland   2   October 10, 2005

According to the accounting department, Martin makes a net profit of $10 on every monitor we sell. And, as you know, with the boom in computer sales, we sell every monitor we make. Those 18,600 units we don't produce are costing us $186,000 a year.

Shows where numbers in paragraph 1 come from

Additional benefit

Bringing down the temperature to 25°C (the minimum allowed under federal guidelines) from the present summer average of 35°C will require an investment of $500,000 to insulate and air condition the monitor room. Extra energy costs for the air conditioning will run about $30,000 a year. We'll get our investment back in less than three years. Once the investment is recouped, we'll be making an additional $150,000 a year—all without buying additional equipment or hiring additional workers.

Tells reader what to do

By installing the insulation and air conditioning this fall, we can take advantage of lower off-season rates. Please authorize the Purchasing Department to request bids for the system. Then, next summer, our productivity can be at an all-time high.

Reason to act promptly

Ends on positive note of problem solved, reader enjoying benefit

✓ CHECKLIST   Checklist for Problem-Solving Persuasive Messages

- ☐ If the message is a memo or e-mail, does the subject line indicate the writer's purpose or offer a reader benefit? Does the subject line avoid making the request?
- ☐ Does the first sentence interest the reader?
- ☐ Is the problem presented as a joint problem both writer and reader have an interest in solving, rather than as something the reader is being asked to do for the writer?
- ☐ Does the message give all of the relevant information? Is there enough detail?
- ☐ Does the message overcome objections that readers may have?
- ☐ Does the message avoid phrases that sound dictatorial, condescending, or arrogant?
- ☐ Does the last paragraph tell the reader exactly what to do? Does it give a deadline if one exists and a reason for acting promptly?

And, for all messages, not just persuasive ones,

- ☐ Does the message use you-attitude and positive emphasis?
- ☐ Is the style easy to read and friendly?
- ☐ Is the visual design of the message inviting?
- ☐ Is the format correct?
- ☐ Does the message use standard grammar? Is it free from typos?

Originality in a problem-solving persuasive message may come from

- ☐ A good subject line and common ground.
- ☐ A clear and convincing description of the problem.
- ☐ Thinking about readers and giving details that answer their questions, overcome objections, and make it easier for them to do as you ask.
- ☐ Adding details that show you're thinking about a specific organization and the specific people in that organization.

Summary of Key Points

- The primary purposes in a persuasive message are to have the reader act, to provide enough information so that the reader knows exactly what to do, and to overcome any objections that might prevent or delay action. Secondary purposes are to build a good image of the writer and the writer's organization, to cement a good relationship between the writer and reader, and to reduce or eliminate future correspondence on the same subject.
- Readers have a vested interest in something if they benefit directly from keeping things as they are.
- **Credibility** is the audience's response to you as the source of the message. You can build credibility by being factual, specific, and reliable.
- Use the persuasive strategy your organization prefers.
- Use the **direct request pattern** when the audience will do as you ask without any resistance. Also use the direct request pattern for busy readers in your own organization who do not read all the messages they receive.
- Use the **problem-solving pattern** when the audience may resist doing what you ask and you expect logic to be more important than emotion in the decision.
- When you want people to change their behaviour, don't criticize them. Instead, show that you're on their side, that you and they have a mutual interest in solving a problem.
- Build emotional appeal with stories and psychological description.
- To encourage readers to act promptly, set a deadline. Show that the time limit is real, that acting now will save time or money, or that delaying action will cost more.

- Early in a collection series, remind the reader about the debt matter-of-factly. In middle letters, be more assertive. Try to negotiate for partial payment if the reader is not able to pay the full amount.

- Performance appraisals should cite specific observations, not inferences. They should contain specific suggestions for improvement and identify the two or three areas that the worker should emphasize in the next month or quarter.

- Letters of recommendation must be specific and tell how well and how long you've known the person.

- Use the analysis questions from ⬅ Chapter 1 to analyze persuasive situations.

CHAPTER 7   Exercises and Problems

Getting Started

7.1   Writing Psychological Description

For one or more of the following groups, write two or three paragraphs of psychological description that could be used in a brochure, news release, or direct mail letter directed to members of that group.

1. Having a personal trainer.
    Audiences: Professional athletes.
    Busy managers.
    Someone trying to lose weight.
    Someone making a major lifestyle change after a heart attack.

2. Buying a cell phone.
    Audiences: People who do a lot of big-city driving.
    People who do a lot of driving in rural areas.
    People who do a lot of flying.

3. Buying a laptop computer.
    Audiences: University and community college students.
    Financial planners who visit clients at home.
    Sales representatives who travel constantly.
    People who make PowerPoint presentations.

4. Attending a fantasy sports camp (you pick the sport), playing with and against retired players who provide coaching and advice.

5. Attending a health spa where clients get low-fat and low-calorie meals, massages, beauty treatments, and guidance in nutrition and exercise.

Hints:

- For this assignment, you can combine benefits or programs as if a single source offered them all.

- Add specific details about particular sports, activities, and so on, as material for your description.

- Be sure to move beyond reader benefits to vivid details and sense impressions.

- Put your benefits in you-attitude.

7.2   Evaluating Subject Lines

Evaluate the following subject lines. Is one subject line in each group clearly best? Or does the "best" line depend on company culture, whether the message is a paper memo or an e-mail message, or on some other factor?

1. Subject: Request
    Subject: Why I Need a New Computer
    Subject: Increasing My Productivity

2. Subject: Who Wants Extra Hours?
    Subject: Holiday Work Schedule
    Subject: Working Extra Hours During the Holiday Season

3. Subject: Student Mentors
    Subject: Can You Be an E-Mail Mentor?
    Subject: Volunteers Needed

4. Subject: More Wine and Cheese
    Subject: Today's Reception for Japanese Visitors
    Subject: Reminder

5. Subject: Reducing Absenteeism
    Subject: Opening a Day Care Centre for Sick Children of Employees
    Subject: Why We Need Expanded Day Care Facilities

7.3   Identifying Observations

Susan has taken the following notes about her group's meetings. Which of the following are specific observations that she could use in a performance appraisal of group members? If she had it to do over again, what kinds of details would turn the inferences into observations?

1. Feb. 22: Today was very frustrating. Sam was totally out of it—I wonder if he's on something. Jim was dictatorial. I argued, but nobody backed me up. Masayo might just as well have stayed home. We didn't get anything done. Two hours, totally wasted.

2. February 24: Jim seems to be making a real effort to be less domineering. Today he asked Sam and me for our opinions before proposing his own. And he noticed that Masayo wasn't talking much and brought her into the conversation. She suggested some good ideas.

3. February 28: Today's meeting was OK. I thought Masayo wasn't really focusing on the work at hand. She needs to work on communicating her ideas to others. Sam was doing some active listening, but he needs to work at being on time. Jim was involved in the project. He has strong leadership skills. There were some tense moments, but we got a lot done,
and we all contributed. I got to say what I wanted to say, and the group decided to use my idea for the report.

4. March 5: This week most of us had midterms, and Masayo had an out-of-town gymnastics trip. We couldn't find a time to meet. So we did stuff by e-mail. Sam and Jim found some great stuff at the library and on the Internet. Jim created a tentative schedule that he sent to all of us and then revised. I wrote up a draft of the description of the problem. Then Masayo and I put everything together. I sent my draft to her; she suggested revisions (in full caps so I could find them in the e-mail message). Then I sent the message to everyone. Masayo and Jim both suggested changes, which I made before we handed the draft in.

5. March 15: We were revising the proposal, using Prof. Gertler's comments. When we thought we were basically done, Masayo noticed that we had not responded to all of the specific comments about our introductory paragraph. We then went back and thought of some examples to use. This made our proposal better and more complete.

7.4   Revising a Form Memo

You've been hired as a staff accountant; one of your major duties will be processing expense reimbursements. Going through the files, you find this form memo:

> Subject: Reimbursements
>
> Enclosed are either receipts that we could not match with the items in your request for reimbursement or a list of items for which we found no receipts or both. Please be advised that the Accounting Department issues reimbursement cheques only with full documentation. You cannot be reimbursed until you give us a receipt for each item for which you desire reimbursement. We must ask that you provide this information. This process may be easier if you use the Expense Report Form, which is available in your department.
>
> Thank you for your attention to this matter. Please do not hesitate to contact us with questions.

You know this memo is horrible. In addition to wordiness, a total lack of positive emphasis and you-attitude, and a vague subject line, the document design and organization of information bury the request.

Create a new memo that could be sent to people who do not provide all the documentation they need in order to be reimbursed.

E-Mail Messages

7.5   Asking for More Time and/or Resources

Today, this message shows up in your e-mail inbox from your boss:

> Subject: Want Climate Report
>
> This request has come down from the CEO. I'm delegating it to you. See me a couple of days before the board meeting—the 4th of next month—so we can go over your presentation.
>
> I want a report on the climate for underrepresented groups in our organization. A presentation at the last board of directors' meeting showed that while we do a good job of hiring women and visible minorities, few of them rise to the top. The directors suspect that our climate may not be supportive and want information on it. Please prepare a presentation for the next meeting. You'll have 15 minutes.

Making a presentation to the company's board of directors can really help your career. But preparing a good presentation and report will take time. You can look at exit reports filed by Human Resources when people leave the company, but you'll also need to interview people—lots of people. And you're already working 60 hours a week on three major projects, one of which is behind schedule. Can one of the projects wait? Can someone else take one of the projects? Can you get some help? Should you do just enough to get by? Ask your boss for advice—in a way that makes you look like a committed employee, not a shirker.

7.6   Persuading People to Use Better Passwords

Your computer system requires each employee to change his or her password every three months. But many people choose passwords that are easy to guess. According to Deloitte & Touche's fraud unit, the 10 most commonly used passwords are (1) the employee's name or child's name, (2) "secret," (3) stress-related words ("deadline," "work"), (4) sports teams or terms, (5) "payday," (6) "bonkers," (7) the current season ("autumn," "spring"), (8) the employee's ethnic group, (9) repeated characters ("AAAAA"), (10) obscenities and sexual terms ("Hackers' Delight," *BusinessWeek,* February 10, 1997, 4).

As Director of Management Information Systems (MIS), you want employees to choose passwords that hackers can't guess based on knowing an employee's background. The best passwords contain numbers as well as letters, use more characters (at least five; preferably eight), and aren't real words.

Write an e-mail message to all employees, urging them to choose better passwords.

7.7   Asking for Volunteers

You have an executive position with one of the major employers in town. (Pick a business, non-profit organization, or government office you know something about.) Two years ago, your company "adopted" a local school. You've provided computers and paid for Internet access; a small number of workers have signed up to be mentors. Today you get a call from the school's principal, a friend of yours.

Principal: I'd like to talk to you about the mentoring program. You're providing some mentors, and we're grateful for them, but we need ten times that number.

You: [You wince. This program has not been one of your successes.] I know that part of the program hasn't worked out as well as we hoped it would. But people are really busy here. Not all that many people have two or three hours a week to spend with a kid.

Principal: So you think the time it takes is really the problem.

You: [Maybe your friend will appreciate that you can't force people to do this.] Pretty much.

Principal:	Do you think people would be willing to be mentors if we could find a way for it to take less time?
You:	Maybe. [You sense that a hook is coming, and you're wary.]
Principal:	Your people spend a lot of time on e-mail, don't they?
You:	Yes. Two to three hours a day, for most of them.
Principal:	What if we created a new mentoring structure, where people just e-mailed their mentees instead of meeting with them? That way they could still provide advice and support, but they could do it at any time of the day. And it wouldn't have to take long.
You:	[This sounds interesting.] So people would just have e-mail conversations. That would be a lot easier, and we'd get more people. But can they really have a relationship if they don't meet the kids?

Principal:	Maybe we could have a picnic or go to a game a couple of times a year so people could meet face to face.
You:	And all the kids have computers?
Principal:	Not necessarily at home. But they all have access to e-mail at school. Writing e-mail to professionals will also give them more practice and more confidence. People like to get e-mail.
You:	Not when they get 200 messages a day, they don't.
Principal:	Well, our kids aren't in that category. What do you say?
You:	I think it will work. Let's try it.
Principal:	Great. Just send me a list of the people who are willing to do this, and we'll match them up with the kids. We'd like to get this started as soon as possible.

Write an e-mail message to all employees asking them to volunteer, while you're thinking about it right now.

Memo and Letter Assignments

7.8 Writing Collection Letters

You have a small desktop publishing firm. Unfortunately, not all your clients pay promptly.

As Your Professor Directs,

Write letters for one or more of the following situations:

a. A $450 bill for designing and printing a brochure for Juggles, Inc., a company that provides clowns and jugglers for parties, is now five weeks overdue. You've phoned twice, and each time the person who answered the phone promised to send you a cheque, but nothing has happened.

b. A $2,000 bill for creating a series of handouts for a veterinarian to distribute to clients. This one is really embarrassing: somehow you lost track of the invoice, so you never followed up on the original (and only) bill. The bill is now 72 days overdue.

c. A $3,750 bill for designing and printing a series of 10 brochures for Creative Interiors, a local interior decorating shop, is three weeks past due. When you billed Creative Interiors, you got a note saying that

the design was not acceptable and that you would not be paid until you redesigned it (at no extra charge) to the owner's satisfaction. The owner had approved the preliminary design on which the brochures were based; she did not explain in the note what was wrong with the final product. She's never free when you are; indeed, when you call to try to schedule an appointment, you're told the owner will call you back—but she never does. At this point, the delay is not your fault; you want to be paid.

d. A $100 bill for designing (but not actually creating) a brochure for a cleaning company that, according to its owner, planned to expand into your city. You got the order and instructions by mail and talked to the person on the phone but never met him. You tried to call once since then (as much to try to talk him into having the brochures printed as to collect the $100); the number was no longer in service. You suspect the owner may no longer be in business, but you'd like to get your money if possible.

7.9 Persuading Guests to Allow Extra Time for Checkout

Your hotel has been the headquarters for a convention, and on Sunday morning you're expecting 5,000 people to check out before noon. You're staffing the checkout desk to capacity, but if everyone waits till 11:30 A.M. to check out, things will be a disaster.

So you want to encourage people to allow extra time. And they don't have to stand in line at all: by 4:00 A.M., you'll put a statement of current charges under each

guest's door. If that statement is correct and the guest is leaving the bill on the credit card used at check-in, the guest can just leave the key in the room and leave. You'll mail a copy of the final bill together with any morning charges by the end of the week.

Write a one-page message that can be put on pillows when the rooms are made up Friday and Saturday night.

7.10   Requesting More Funds for the Writing Centre

Your university is facing major budget cuts. A popular idea is to reduce or eliminate funding for the Writing Centre. As the Centre's director, you're horrified by these ideas.

The Writing Centre offers free tutoring in writing to any student or faculty member on campus. Your emphasis is not on fixing an individual paper, but on helping the writer develop strategies that he or she can use not only in this paper but in everything he or she writes.

The services you offer help students do better in classes. Your help is particularly important when budget cuts are leading to larger classes, so that faculty spend less time with each student. Furthermore, your operation is really quite efficient. You have only one paid regular faculty member on your staff; the rest are graduate teaching assistants (who are paid much less than faculty receive) or undergraduate peer tutors. Finally, the dollars involved aren't that great. Cutting the Centre's budget in half would mean you would have to turn away most students. Yet the dollars are small in comparison with the budgets of large departments.

As Your Professor Directs,

a. Write a memo to all faculty urging them to support full funding for the Writing Centre.

b. Write a news release for the campus newspaper about the problem.

c. Identify the person or group on your campus with the power to make budget decisions, and write to that group urging that it support a Writing Centre on your campus. Use information about the centre and the fiscal situation that fits your community college or university.

Hints:

- Visit the Writing Centre on campus to get information about its hours and policies. Sign up for an appointment. What happens in a session? What parts are especially helpful?
- Be sure to prove and limit your claims. Even if the Centre is fully funded, some students will be turned away. Even if its funding is increased, not everyone will write well.
- Be sure to use you-attitude and to make sure that the writing in your message is a good advertisement for your own writing skills.

7.11   Asking a Professor for a Letter of Recommendation

You're ready for the job market and you need letters of recommendation.

As Your Professor Directs,

a. Assume that you've orally asked a professor for a recommendation, and he or she has agreed to write one. "Why don't you write up something to remind me of what you've done in the class? Tell me what else you've done, too. And tell me what they're looking for. Be sure to tell me when the letter needs to be in and whom it goes to."

b. Assume that you've been unable to talk with the professor whose recommendation you want. When you call, no one answers the phone; you stopped by once and no one was in. Write asking for a letter of recommendation.

c. Assume that the professor is no longer on campus. Write him or her a letter asking for a recommendation.

Hints:

- Be detailed about the points you'd like the professor to mention.
- How well will this professor remember you? How much detail about your performance in his or her class do you need to provide?
- Specify the name and address of the person to whom the letter should be written; specify when the letter is due. If there's an intermediate due date (for example, if you must sign the outside of the envelope to submit the recommendation to law school), say so.

7.12   Writing a Performance Appraisal for a Member of a Collaborative Group

During your collaborative writing group meetings, keep a log of events. Record specific observations of both effective and ineffective things that group members do. Then evaluate the performance of the other members of your group. (If there are two or more other people, write a separate appraisal for each of them.)

In your first paragraph, summarize your evaluation. Then in the body of your memo, give the specific details

that led to your evaluation by answering the following questions:

- What specifically did the person do in terms of the task? Brainstorm ideas? Analyze the information? Draft the text? Suggest revisions in parts drafted by others? Format the document or create visuals? Revise? Edit? Proofread? (In most cases, several people will have done each of these activities together. Don't overstate what any one person did.) What was the quality of the person's work?

■ What did the person contribute to the group process? Did he or she help schedule the work? Raise or resolve conflicts? Make other group members feel valued and included? Promote group cohesion? What roles did the person play in the group?

Support your generalizations with specific observations. The more observations you have and the more detailed they are, the better your appraisal will be.

As Your Professor Directs,

a. Write a mid-term performance appraisal for one or more members of your collaborative group. In each appraisal, identify the two or three things the person should try to improve during the second half of the term.

b. Write a performance appraisal for one or more members of your collaborative group at the end of the term. Identify and justify the grade you think each person should receive for the portion of the grade based on group process.

c. Give a copy of your appraisal to the person about whom it is written.

8 Sales, Fundraising, and Promotional Messages

AN INSIDE PERSPECTIVE

Sales, Fundraising, and Promotional Messages

Delivering a persuasive message means knowing your audience, and their motivation and needs. Web publishing has added to the opportunities as well as the challenges of business and administrative communications. Faced with hundreds of millions of pages, Web readers pick and choose, grab and run.

Internet commentator Jakob Nielsen's studies show that readers are more concerned with good writing and content than with navigation or user interface issues. He recommends "flytrap" content that directs readers, uses keywords, provides analysis and personal insight, and ensures quality links.

Marie Germain, CEO of Germain Strengthening Brands of Brighton, Ontario, is a leading communications professional committed to brand development and rethinking traditional paradigms.

www.germaincommunications.com

Whether you are selling ideas, services, or products, the **AIDA** (or **AIRA**) persuasive plan, a variation on the star-chain-knot pattern, can help you attract and retain your audience and underline what is in it for them:

- Gain **A**ttention
- Create **I**nterest
- Build **D**esire (and Reduce **R**esistance)
- Motivate **A**ction

Whether you are encouraging action and orders through a sales letter (adoption), promoting ongoing support or subscriptions (continuance), stopping current practices, such as delaying bill payment (discontinuance), or preventing actions, such as account transfer (deterrence), the four-part AIDA indirect persuasive pattern can support your goals.

Gaining **A**ttention means opening with a provocative headline, startling fact, problem statement, audience benefit, compliment, quotation, summary of problem/action, or point of agreement.

Creating **I**nterest means supporting argument in concrete and specific terms (facts, figures, examples, experts), underlining benefits, and appealing to fairness.

Building **D**esire while reducing **R**esistance means imagining and anticipating scenarios, underlining credibility, and citing testimonials and test results.

Motivating **A**ction means reinforcing benefits, asking for specific response, and giving deadlines linked to incentives.

For tips to help attract and retain readers, see ➡ the end-of-chapter checklist (p. 204).

Douglas & McIntyre Publishing Group, Chrysler Canada, and FedEx are only a few of the companies that use letters to persuade customers to buy their products, visit their showrooms, or use their services. The Canadian Cancer Society, McGill University, and George Brown College are only a few of the organizations that use letters to persuade people to donate time or money to their causes.

Sales and fundraising letters are a special category of persuasive messages. They are known as **direct mail** because they ask for an order, inquiry, or contribution directly from the reader.

In 2002, direct mail accounted for $1.51 billion or 13.8% of yearly Canadian advertising. A Decima Research national poll in September 2003 found that in the previous 12 months 8.5 million Canadians made at least one charitable donation as a result of direct mail; the estimated value of direct mail fundraising is $1.1 billion yearly.[1]

Organizations also use a variety of promotional materials. This chapter discusses two of the most common types: contact letters and brochures.

Fortune 500 companies and well-endowed charitable or political organizations hire professionals to write their direct mail. Professionals charge $5,000 to $25,000 to create a package. And that's just the creative cost: you still have to pay for printing and postage. If you own your own business, you can save money by doing your firm's own direct mail. If you are active in a local group that needs to raise money, writing the letter yourself is likely to be the only way your group can afford to use direct mail. If you can write an equally effective e-mail message, you can cut your costs to about one-fifth of a print mailing![2] The principles in this chapter will help you write solid, serviceable letters and brochures that will build your business and help fund your group.

Sales, fundraising, and promotional messages have several purposes.

Primary purposes:

- To motivate the reader to read the message
- To have the reader act (order the product, schedule a demonstration, send a donation)
- To provide enough information so that the reader knows exactly what to do (even if he or she keeps only the reply coupon)
- To overcome any objections that might prevent or delay action

Secondary purpose:

- To build a good image of the writer's organization (to strengthen the commitment of readers who act, and make readers who do not act more likely to respond positively next time)

Components of Good Direct Mail

Good direct mail has three components: a good product, service, or cause; a good mailing list; and a good appeal. A **good product** appeals to a specific segment of people, can be mailed, and provides an adequate profit margin. A **good service or cause** fills an identifiable need.

A **good mailing list** has accurate addresses and is a good match to the product. Most professional direct mailers rent their lists from companies that specialize in compiling and maintaining lists. Small businesses and charities can use in-house lists of their customers or members and can compile lists of

Selling on Your Cell Phone*

A decade ago, marketers began discovering the advantages of sending sales letters electronically, as e-mail. Now they are getting involved in mobile commerce, sending messages to cell phones via text messaging.

Coca-Cola Company sent messages to several thousand cell phones in Japan, inviting consumers to buy a drink from one of its high-tech Cmode vending machines. For two days, the company enabled consumers using the Cmode vending machines to download an ad jingle as a ring tone when they bought a beverage.

The obvious challenge in writing messages to send to cell phones is to be concise and on target. Text message screens are small. There's no room for flowery adjectives or long anecdotes. A few words have to make the case.

*Based on Chad Terhune and Gabriel Kahn, "Coke Lures Japanese Customers with Cellphone Come-Ons," *The Wall Street Journal*, September 8, 2003, B1, B4.

Lists, Lists, and More Lists*

A huge variety of mailing lists is available commercially, and computer technology enables companies to customize those lists. For instance, infoUSA offers databases of 14 million businesses, 2.5 million start-up businesses, and 200 million residences. Customers can specify location by zip code, type or size of business, estimated household income, age of householder, and other variables. Best Mailing Lists offers 10 million businesses and over 4 million business contacts and professionals, including the following subcategories:

- 6,000 immigration attorneys

- 26,000 pediatricians

- 257,000 yacht owners

- 309,000 corporate owners of manufacturing firms

*infoUSA, "About Our Data—the Finest in the Country," downloaded from http://list.infousa.com on July 8, 2004; and Best Mailing Lists, Inc., home page and "Featured Lists," downloaded from http://www.bestmailing.com on July 9, 2004. Canadian lists are available at http://www.scottsinfo.com and http://www.rsalistservices.com/canadiandatabases.html.

prospects from city directories or other local sources. They may also exchange lists with similar organizations.

A **good appeal** offers a believable description of benefits, links the benefits of the product or service to a need or desire that motivates the reader, makes the reader want to read the letter, and motivates the reader to act. The appeal is made up of the words in the letter, the pictures in the brochure, and all the parts of the package, from outer envelope to reply card.

All three elements are crucial: the best letter in the world won't persuade someone who doesn't have room for a garden to buy a Rototiller. However, this chapter will examine only the elements of a good appeal: how to create a message that will motivate a reader to act, assuming that you already have a good product to sell or a worthy cause to raise funds for, and that you already have a good list of people who might be interested in that product or organization.

Industry wisdom is that a **cold list**—a list of people with no prior connection to your group—will have a 2% response rate. Good timing, a good list, and a good appeal can double or even triple that percentage.

For people who open some of their mail, the three most important factors in deciding whether to open a specific envelope were timing, personalization, and an attractive appearance.[3]

Companies that want people to continue opening direct mail have to be careful that what they send is *not* junk. People today receive so many marketing messages that they are impatient when the messages seem irrelevant.

Basic Direct Mail Strategy

Direct mail strategies start with three basic steps: (1) learn about the product, service, or organization; (2) choose and analyze the target audience; and (3) choose a central selling point. These steps interact; an understanding of your target audience may suggest questions to ask about your product. Information you find in researching the product may suggest an idea for a possible central selling point.

1. Understand Your Product, Service, or Organization.

Try to use the product or service. Talk to volunteers who work for your charitable organization; if possible, visit the site where the good work is done.

To sell a product, ask

- What needs does it meet? What benefits does it provide? What problems does it remove?

- What are the product's objective features? Size? Colour? Materials? How does it work? What options are available?

- How much does it cost? What does the buyer get for the money?

- How is it different from or better than competing products? (If the *details* of differences or superiority are interesting, they may work well in a letter.)

- How easy is it to install? To use? To maintain?

To raise money, ask

- What is the problem your group is helping to solve? (If possible, collect examples to illustrate the need.)

- How, specifically, is your group helping? (Collect stories about specific people, specific gains , and overall figures.)

- What support does your group already get from tax dollars, user fees, ticket sales, and so on? Why are private funds necessary?

■ What are the group's immediate goals? How much will it cost to achieve them?

2. Identify and Analyze Your Target Audience.

The **target audience** is the people who are likely to be interested in buying the product, using the service, or contributing to the cause. In direct mail, you do not try to sell a subscription to *Sports Illustrated* to someone who loathes sports. In addition to those already interested in your product or committed to your cause, the audience always includes people who could be persuaded if you gave them enough evidence.

As ← Chapter 2 explains, you can analyze your audience in terms of demographics (← p. 33)—objective, measurable features: "This letter is going to homeowners who have children between the ages of 4 and 10." You can also use psychographic characteristics (← p. 33)—values, beliefs, goals, and lifestyles: "I'm writing to people who care about protecting the environment." Often a combination of demographic and psychographic characteristics works best: 21-year-old university or community college students may have different reasons for using a health club than do 45-year-old executives, even though both groups want to look good and deal with stress.

3. Choose a Central Selling Point.

Since even a well-defined audience will have people with different motivations and different objections to buying or giving, a direct mail letter needs several selling points. To unify the letter, use a central selling point. A **central selling point** is a reader benefit that by itself could motivate your readers to act and that can serve as an umbrella under which all the other benefits can fit.

Suppose you want to sell copies of a book that explains how to grow vegetables in home gardens. Any of the following statements could be used as central selling points:

■ Fresh vegetables from your own garden taste better than store-bought vegetables that are ripened with chemicals.

■ Vegetables from your own garden are healthier. You control the chemicals you put on them; you can avoid any insecticides and wax that you don't want.

■ It's cheaper to grow your own vegetables than to buy them in a grocery store.

■ Growing vegetables is fun for the whole family. Children will be fascinated by growing plants.

■ Growing your own vegetables is a way to get back to nature, to have a simpler, more natural lifestyle.

A professional direct mailer might test two or more different approaches with samples of the target market, then send the best letter to the whole list. When you can't run a test, how do you choose? First, eliminate any central selling points that don't fit your target audience. Next, use your own understanding of people to decide whether to stress taste, health, economy, fun, or working with nature. If two or more appeals seem equally effective, try writing each of them. In your assignment, use the one that you can develop most effectively.

In a fundraising letter, you must also choose the appeal that will be most powerful for the target audience. A fundraising letter to alumni could use nostalgia, the obligation to repay the university or community college, the feeling of making an investment in young people, or a sense of social responsibility. To create a sense of nostalgia, refer to events that happened when readers were in school. (Check back issues of the community college or university newspaper.)

FIGURE 8.1   How to Organize a Sales or Fundraising Letter

1. Open your letter with a *star* designed to catch the reader's attention.
2. In the body, provide a *chain* of reasons and logic.
3. End by telling the reader what to do and providing a reason to act promptly. Tie up *(knot)* the motivation you have created and turn it into action.

How to Organize a Sales or Fundraising Letter

Use the star-chain-knot pattern[4] to organize your letter (see Figure 8.1).

Opener (Star)

The opener, or **star,** of your letter gives you 30 to 60 seconds to motivate readers to read the rest of the letter.

A good star opener will make readers want to read the letter and provide a reasonable transition to the body of the letter (see Figure 8.2). A very successful subscription letter for *Psychology Today* started out,

> Do you still close the bathroom door when there's no one in the house?

The question is both intriguing in itself and a good transition into the content of *Psychology Today:* practical psychology applied to the quirks and questions we come across in everyday life.

It's essential that the opener not only get the reader's attention but also be something that can be linked logically to the body of the letter. A sales letter started,

> Can You Use $50 This Week?

Certainly that gets attention. But the letter offered the reader only the chance to save $50 on a product. Readers may feel disappointed or even cheated when they learn that instead of getting $50, they have to spend money to save $50.

It's hard to write a brilliant opener the minute you sit down. To brainstorm possible openers, use the four basic modes: questions, narration, startling statements, and quotations.

1. Questions

> Dear Writer:
>
>   What is the best way to start writing?

This letter selling subscriptions to *Writer's Digest* goes on to discuss Hemingway's strategy for getting started on his novels and short stories. *Writer's Digest* offers practical advice to writers who want to be published so the recipient keeps reading.

2. Narration, stories, anecdotes

> Dear Reader:
>
>   She hoisted herself up noiselessly so as not to disturb the rattlesnakes snoozing there in the sun.

FIGURE 8.2 A Form Letter Whose Attention-Getter Mimics an Inside Address

COMPUTER SUPPORT COMPANY
304-8 Ave SW, Calgary, AB T2P 1C2
(403) 661-8960 • Fax: (403) 661-1096

"Johnson Box" highlighting the
offer used for emphasis
visual variety

```
* * * * * * * * * * *
* Five FREE Libraries *
* Worth Up to $615!   *
* * * * * * * * * * * *
```

*Date omitted so letter can be sent
out unchanged
Johnson Box visually substitutes
for date*

*Attention-getter
visually
substitutes
for inside
address,
salutation*

No Other Business
Graphics Software Can
Match the Versatility &
Flexibility of Diagraph!

Let us prove to you that Diagraph is a breakthrough in business
graphics software.

Use Diagraph to turn your ideas, concepts, plans, and data into
organization charts, signs, flow charts, diagrams, forms, and maps.
Diagraph comes with a money-back guarantee. Use it for 30 days and
we're certain that you will have discovered so many uses for
Diagraph that you won't want to part with it.

And now you have two choices: Diagraph/500 for only $99 or
Diagraph/2000 for $395.

Diagraph/500 files are fully compatible with Diagraph/2000 so you
can upgrade to Diagraph/2000 at any time. What's more, the cost of
Diagraph/500 is credited toward your purchase of Diagraph/2000.

See the enclosed data sheet for additional information or call us
today to see how the power of Diagraph can enhance everything you
write!

Sincerely,

Gail McCannon

Gail McCannon
Director, Customer Services

*Signature block lined up with
Johnson Box*

GM:ec

Encl.

P.S. As an added incentive, if you purchase Diagraph/2000 before
November 30, you can select five Diagraph libraries, worth up to
$615, absolutely free. Call for more details.

*Reader benefit saved for a P.S.
People's eyes go to P.S., which they may
read before returning to rest of letter*

To her left, the high desert of New Mexico. Indian country. To her right, the rock carvings she had photographed the day before. Stick people. Primitive animals.

Up ahead, three sandstone slabs stood stacked against the face of the cliff. In their shadow, another carving. A spiral consisting of rings. Curious, the young woman drew closer. Instinctively, she glanced at her watch. It was almost noon. Then just at that moment, a most unusual thing happened.

Suddenly, as if out of nowhere, an eerie dagger of light appeared to stab at the topmost ring of the spiral. It next began to plunge downwards—shimmering, laser-like.

Long, Longer, Longest

Some tests show that six- or even eight-page letters outpull shorter letters. Many political fundraising letters are six pages (particularly during the U.S. primary seasons when candidates are not yet well known).

Long letters are especially good for publications, high-involvement categories like health and investing, or expensive items. Liberty Mint used an eight-page letter to sell 100 castings of Remington's "The Bronco Buster" made of pure silver for $25,000 each.

Even long letters should look easy to read. Many long letters use short paragraphs (just a sentence or two), headings, and highlighted or underlined sections to help skimming.

The Internet is an effective direct marketing channel. The Italian motorcycle company Ducati launched its 2000 and 2001 models on the Internet—and sold out the whole production planned for each year. One $15,000 limited-production vehicle sold out in 31 minutes.

> It pierced the eighth ring. The seventh. The sixth. It punctured the innermost and last. Then just as suddenly as it had appeared, the dagger of light was gone. The young woman glanced at her watch again. Exactly twelve minutes had elapsed.
>
> Coincidence? Accident? Fluke? No. What she may have stumbled across that midsummer morning three years ago is an ancient solar calendar. . . .

The opener of this *Science84* subscription letter both builds suspense so that the reader reads the subscription letter and suggests that the magazine will be as interesting as the letter and as easy to read.

3. Startling statements

> Dear Membership Candidate:
>
> I'm writing to offer you a job.
> It's not a permanent job, understand. You'll be working for only as much time as you find it rewarding and fun.
> It's not even a paying job. On the contrary, it will cost *you* money.

This fundraising letter from Earthwatch invites readers to participate in its expeditions, subscribe to its journal, and donate to its programs. Earthwatch's volunteers help scientists and scholars dig for ruins, count bighorns, and monitor changes in water; they can work as long as they like; they pay their own (tax-deductible) expenses.

4. Quotations

> "I never tell my partner that my ankle is sore or my back hurts. You can't give in to pain and still perform."
>
> —Jill Murphy
> Soloist

Quotations sell season tickets to the Royal Winnipeg Ballet by focusing on the people who work to create the season. The letters encourage readers to see the artists as individuals, to appreciate their hard work, and to share their excitement about each performance.

Body (Chain)

The **chain** is the body of the letter. It provides the logical and emotional links that move readers from their first flicker of interest to the action that is wanted. A good chain answers readers' questions, overcomes their objections, and involves them emotionally.

All this takes space. One of the industry truisms is "The more you tell, the more you sell." Tests show that longer letters bring in more new customers or new donors than do shorter letters. A four-page letter is considered ideal for mailings to new customers or donors.

Can short letters work? Yes, when you're writing to old customers or when the mailing is supported by other media (See Figure 8.4). One study showed that a one-page letter was just as effective as a two-page letter in persuading recent purchasers of a product to buy a service contract.[5] E-mail direct mail is also short—generally just one screen. The shortest letter on record may be the two-word postcard that a fishing lake resort sent its customers: "They're biting!"

Content for the body of the letter can include

- Information readers will find useful even if they do not buy or give
- Stories about how the product was developed or what the organization has done
- Stories about people who have used the product or who need the organization's help
- Word pictures of readers using the product and enjoying its benefits

Action Close (Knot)

The action close, or **knot,** in the letter must do four things:

1. **Tell the reader what to do:** Respond. Avoid *if* ("If you'd like to try …") and *why not* ("Why not send in a cheque?"). They lack positive emphasis and encourage your reader to say *no.*

2. **Make the action sound easy:** Fill in the information on the reply card, sign the card (for credit sales), put the card and cheque (if payment is to accompany the order) in the envelope, and mail the envelope. If you provide an envelope and pay postage, stress those facts.

3. **Offer a reason for acting promptly.** Readers who wait to act are less likely to buy or contribute. Reasons for acting promptly are easy to identify when a product is seasonal or there is a genuine limit on the offer—time limit, price rise scheduled, limited supply, and so on. Sometimes you can offer a premium or a discount if the reader acts quickly. Otherwise, remind readers that the sooner they get the product, the sooner they can benefit from it; the sooner they contribute funds, the sooner their dollars can go to work to solve the problem.

4. **End with a positive picture** of the reader enjoying the product (in a sales letter) or of the reader's money working to solve the problem (in a fundraising letter). The last sentence should never be a selfish request for money.

FIGURE 8.3   A Magazine Subscription Letter

BlackFlash
LENS SITE SCENE

p.o. box 7381, stn. main   (p) 306.374.5115
saskatoon, sk s7k 4j3   editor@blackflash.ca

Dear Reader,

Have you ever seen a perforated photographic diary
running throughout a magazine … or a really cool
Encyclopedia of Underwater Investigations as a removable
bookwork?

You see, **BlackFlash** magazine isn't just about
contemporary art; it's about producing it. By challenging
traditional magazine design, **BlackFlash** pushes the
envelope, pulls some punches, and makes you wish you'd
thought of that first.

BlackFlash: Lens, Site, Scene is the Canadian
magazine of photo-based, electronic and digital art
production with an edge. With each new issue, you'll be
"in the know" on the latest trends, the hottest artists,
and the really neat exhibitions across Canada.

You'll read about exciting new initiatives of innovative
independent curators, specially commissioned features by
Andrew Hunter and Corinna Ghaznavi and new media art
production by the likes of Anthony Kiendl of the wild,
wild web.

                    Controversial and Conversational

Giving equal space to established and emerging writers,
BlackFlash will introduce you to new Canadian voices,
such as Garnet Hertz interviewing Steve Dietz, the
leading web art curator in the United States. And we'll
connect you with writers well known within Canadian
Conversations, such as Edward Morose, Vid Ingelevics, and
Keith Bell. Their ideas about art and art production are
written from a larger context of social concerns,
creating a truly national dialogue.

                                        (over, please…)

(continued)

The action close can also remind readers of the central selling point, stress the guarantee, and mention when the customer will get the product.

Using a P.S.

Studies of eye movement show that people often look to see who a letter is from before they read the letter. Ray Jutkins cites a study showing that 79% of the people who open direct mail read the P.S. first.[6] Therefore, direct mail often uses a deliberate P.S. after the signature block. It may restate the central selling point, preferably in different words so that it won't sound repetitive.

Here are two of the many kinds of effective P.S.'s.

■   Reason to act promptly:

FIGURE 8.3   A Magazine Subscription Letter *(concluded)*

You'll see provocative art and ideas that concern producer and viewer alike … profiles and interviews with emerging and established artists who are making an impact today. **BlackFlash** will show you artists' projects and images that will either inspire or enrage, giving a truly unique perspective, from the centre of the contemporary art debate.

Send for your issue of BlackFlash today!

Don't take our word for it. Read for yourself. You can subscribe now at the introductory rate of only $18 for three issues a year. Just send the enclosed order form with a cheque or money order for $18 in the postage-paid envelope we've provided!

Send for your free issue today!

Sincerely,

Diana Savage   *Lissa Robinson*

Diana Savage   Lissa Robinson
Managing Editor   Managing Editor

P.S. As a special thank-you for your subscription, we'll send you a **free issue** of **BlackFlash** to enjoy right away.

P.S. Once I finish the limited harvest, that's it! I do not store any SpringSweet Onions for late orders. I will ship all orders on a first-come, first-served basis and when they are gone they are gone. Drop your order in the mail today … or give me a call toll free at 800-531-7470!

■ Restatement of central selling point:

P.S. It is not easy to be a hungry child in the Third World. If your parents' crops fail or if your parents cannot find work, there [is] … no free government-provided cafeteria lunches.

Millions of hungry schoolchildren will be depending on CARE Canada this fall. Your gift today will ensure that we will be there—that CARE Canada won't let them down.

Strategy in Sales Letters

The basic strategy in sales letters is satisfying a need. Your letter must remind people of the need your product meets, prove that the product will satisfy that need, show why your product is better than similar products, and make readers *want* to have the product. Use psychological description (p. 168) to show readers how the product will help them. Testimonials from other buyers can help persuade them that the product works; details about how the product is made can carry the message of quality.

Many sales letters make the offer early in the letter—even on the envelope. The exact price, however, is not mentioned until the last quarter of the letter, after the copy makes the reader *want* the product (see Figure 8.3). The only

Canadian Culture and Direct Mail*

In the United States, direct mail letters to total strangers often begin "Dear Friend." Canadian letters, in contrast, are more formal and less likely to imply any relationship other than business to be transacted.

U.S. letters often offer some external reward for responding: a cash rebate, a credit on a bank card, a tote bag. Canadian letters avoid such rewards, perhaps because they suggest that if the product itself is not worth purchasing, the cause is not worth supporting.

*Based on Roger Graves, "'Dear Friend' (?): Culture and Genre in American and Canadian Direct Marketing Letters," *The Journal of Business Communication* 34, no. 3 (July 1997), 235–252.

exception is when you're selling something that has a reputation for being expensive (a luxury car, *Encyclopaedia Britannica*). Then you may want to deal with the price issue early in the letter.

You can make the price more palatable with the following techniques:

1. **Link the price to the benefit the product provides.** "Your piece of history is just $39.95."

2. **Show how much the product costs each day, each week, or each month.** "You can have all this for less than the cost of a cup of coffee a day."

3. **Allow customers to charge sales or pay in instalments.** Your bookkeeping costs will rise, and some sales may be uncollectible, but the total number of sales will increase.

Always offer a guarantee, usually right after the price. The best guarantees are short, convincing, and positive.

Negative: If the magazine fails to meet your expectations, you can cancel at any time and receive a refund on any unmailed copies.

Better: You'll be satisfied or we'll refund your money. I guarantee that.

Strategy in Fundraising Appeals

In a fundraising letter, the basic emotional strategy is **vicarious participation.** By donating money, readers participate vicariously in work they are not able to do personally. This strategy affects the pronouns you use. Throughout the letter, use *we* to talk about your group. However, at the end, talk about what *you* the reader will be doing. End positively, with a picture of the reader's dollars helping to solve the problem.

To achieve both your primary and secondary purposes in fundraising letters, you must give a great deal of information. This information (1) helps to persuade readers; (2) gives supporters evidence to use in conversations with others; and (3) gives readers who are not yet supporters evidence that may make them see the group as worthwhile, even if they do not give money now.

In your close, in addition to asking for money, suggest other ways the reader can help: doing volunteer work, scheduling a meeting on the subject, writing letters to Parliament, the provincial legislature, or the leaders of other countries, and so on. By suggesting other ways to participate, you not only involve readers but also avoid one of the traps of fundraising letters: sounding as though you are selfish, interested in readers only for the money they can give.

Deciding How Much to Ask For

Most letters to new donors suggest a range of amounts, from $25 or $50 (for employed people) up to perhaps double what you *really* expect to get from a single donor. A second strategy is to ask for a small, set amount that nearly everyone can afford ($10 or $15).

One of the several reasons people give for not contributing is that a gift of $25 or $100 seems too small to matter. It's not. Small gifts are important both in themselves and to establish a habit of giving. Some of the people who can give only $25 or even $5 today will someday have more money.[7]

Annual letters to past donors often use the amount of the last donation as the lowest suggested gift, with other gifts 25%, 50%, or even 100% higher.

Always send a thank-you letter to people who respond to your letter, whatever the size of their gifts. By telling about the group's recent work, a thank-you letter can help reinforce donors' commitment to your cause.

Logical Proof in Fundraising Letters

The body of a fundraising letter must prove that (1) the problem deserves the reader's attention, (2) the problem can be solved or at least alleviated, (3) your organization is helping to solve it, (4) private funds are needed, and (5) your organization will use the funds wisely. (See Figure 8.4).

InSite

www.habitat.org

Habitat for Humanity's Web page provides information for potential and current donors, volunteers, and clients.

1. The problem deserves the reader's attention.

No reader can support every cause. Show why the reader should care about solving this problem.

If your problem is life threatening, give some statistics: Tell how many people are killed in Canada every year by drunk drivers. Also tell about one individual who is affected.

2. The problem can be solved or alleviated.

People will not give money if they see the problem as hopeless—why throw money away? Sometimes you can reason by analogy. Cures have been found for other deadly diseases, so it's reasonable to hope that research can find a cure for cancer and AIDS. Sometimes you can show that short-term or partial solutions exist. For example, a UNICEF letter showed that four simple changes could save the lives of millions of children: oral rehydration, immunization, promoting breast feeding, and giving mothers cardboard growth charts so they'll know if their children are malnourished. Those solutions don't affect the underlying causes of poverty, but they do keep children alive while we work on long-term solutions.

3. Your organization is helping to solve or alleviate the problem.

Prove that your organization is effective. Be specific. Talking about your successes in the past helps readers believe that you can accomplish your goals.

4. Private funds are needed to accomplish your group's goals.

If your group does get some tax or foundation money, show why more money is needed. If the organization helps people who might be expected to pay for the service, show why they cannot pay, or why they cannot pay enough to cover the full cost. If some of the funds have been raised by the people who will benefit, make that clear.

5. Your organization will use the funds wisely.

Prove that the money goes to the cause, not just to the cost of fundraising.

Emotional Appeal in Fundraising Letters

Emotional appeal is needed to make people pull out their chequebooks. How strong should emotional appeal be? A mild appeal is unlikely to sway any reader who is not already committed, but readers will feel manipulated by appeals they find too strong and reject them. If you don't know your audience well, use the strongest emotional appeal *you* feel comfortable with.

Emotional appeal is created by specifics. It is hard to care about, or even to imagine, a million people; it is easier to care about one specific person. Details and quotes help us see that person as real and yield greater responses.

Enclosures In Fundraising Letters

Fundraising letters sometimes use inexpensive enclosures to add interest and help carry the message.

Brochures are inexpensive, particularly if you photocopy them. Mailings to alumni have included "Why I Teach at Earlham" (featuring three professors) and letters from students who have received scholarships.

Seeds don't cost much. Mailings from both CARE and the New Forests Fund include four or five seeds of the leucaena, a subtropical tree that can grow 20 feet in a year. Its leaves feed cattle; its wood provides firewood or building materials; its roots reduce soil erosion. (Indeed, the enclosure easily becomes the theme for the letter.)

Reprints of newspaper or magazine articles about the organization or the problem it is working to solve add interest and credibility. Pictures of people the organization is helping build emotional appeal.

Major campaigns may budget for enclosures: pictures of buildings, tapes of oral history interviews, even sea shells and Mason jars.

   A Fundraising Letter

MS Multiple Sclerosis Society of Canada | Société canadienne de la sclérose en plaques SP

William J. McIlroy, M.D., F.R.C.P.(C)
National Medical Advisor

Dear Supporter,

Attention-getter

This month alone we expect that 90 Canadians will be diagnosed with multiple sclerosis. That's why we are working so hard to find a cure before more of us are stricken by this debilitating disease.

Logic and emotional links in body

For reasons that we do not yet fully understand, multiple sclerosis strikes many more people in colder climates, like ours here in Canada, than in warmer ones.

None of our work would be possible, however, if it wasn't for the generosity of people like you, who want to do what they can to help us fight MS.

As fall approaches and the cold weather begins to settle in, I hope you will find it in your heart to make a gift to the Multiple Sclerosis Society of Canada. We are currently supporting 40 critically important research projects that hold great promise in our fight to conquer multiple sclerosis once and for all.

Reason to act

Only research will lead us to the MS cure that we all dream of. And only friends like you can ensure that more promising research receives the funding it deserves.

Positive picture

I hope you will make another generous gift to the MS Society today.

Sincerely,

W. J. McIlroy

William J. McIlroy, M.D., F.R.C.P.(C)
National Medical Advisor
Multiple Sclerosis Society of Canada

P.S. To thank you in advance for your generous support, I'm pleased to send you a notepad with personalized address labels. Enjoy your gift—and let it remind you of all the Canadians who are counting on your help.

Reader benefits highlighted in P.S.

Courtesy of Multiple Sclerosis Society of Canada.

Strategy in Contact Letters

Contact letters do not ask directly for action; instead, they keep in touch with customers or donors.

Contact letters are low key and short—often less than a page. They take as their theme the seasons or a recent event. The end of the letter refers to the relationship between reader and writer and looks to the future.

Some organizations routinely send contact letters to keep their names before clients and customers, particularly for items that are purchased infrequently.

After the September 11, 2001, terrorist attacks, many organizations sent contact letters to customers and donors; the event seemed to cry out for comment. One of the best letters came from Amnesty International (see Figure 8.5).

Strategy in Brochures

Brochures can serve several purposes: they can build general support for an organization or candidate, give specific information ("How to Cope with Chemotherapy"), or even have a reply coupon that readers can return to buy a book, register for a conference, or donate to a cause.

To create a brochure, determine your purpose(s) and your audience(s). Think about where and how your brochure will be distributed. Think about visual constraints and clutter that your brochure needs to overcome: other brochures, a holder that will block the bottom portion of the cover, and so forth. Plan photos and other visual elements.

Draft the text you want to include to get a sense of how much space you need. To keep a brochure size manageable, you may want to focus on just one of the programs or products you offer. For example, the Heifer Project brochure (Figure 8.6) focuses on the Kids 2 Kids program and doesn't mention any of its other programs. Choose a central selling point or theme.

See ➡ Appendix A for information on designing brochures.

Writing Style

Direct mail is the one kind of business writing where elegance and beauty of language matter; in every other kind, elegance is welcome but efficiency is all that finally counts. Direct mail imitates the word choice and rhythm of conversation. The best sales, fundraising, and promotional writing is closer to the language of poetry than to that of academia: it shimmers with images, it echoes with sound, it vibrates with energy.

Many of the things that make writing vivid and entertaining *add* words because they add specifics or evoke an emotional response. Individual sentences should flow smoothly. The passage as a whole may be fun to read precisely because of the details and images that "could have been left out."

For useful tips, visit Dan Kennedy's Web site at www.dankennedy.com or John Carlton's at www.marketingrebel.com. For Web writing, see ➡ end-of-chapter checklist on p. 204.

1. Make Your Writing Interesting.

If the style is long-winded and boring, the reader will stop reading. Eliminating wordiness (⬅ p. 94) is crucial. You've already seen ways to tighten your writing in ⬅ Chapter 4. Direct mail goes further, breaking some of the rules of grammar. In the following examples, note how sentence fragments are used in parallel structure to move the reader along:

> So tiny, it fits virtually unnoticed in your pocket. So meticulously hand-assembled by unhurried craftsmen in Switzerland, that production may never exceed demand. So everyday useful, that you'll wonder how you ever got along without it.

Letter asking for inquiries about Dictaphone

2. Use Sound Patterns to Emphasize Words

When you repeat sounds, you create patterns that catch the reader's attention, please the ear, and emphasize the words they occur in. **Alliteration** occurs

Canadian Giving: Facts and Figures*

Canada is home to the second largest non-profit sector in the world; the Netherlands is top; the U.S. is fifth. The Canadian non-profit sector represents

- 8.6% of the Canadian economy
- More than 50% the size of the entire retail trade sector
- 13% of the Canadian labour force
- Over 2 million full-time-equivalent workers
- $112 billion in revenues and 161,000 organizations
- 87,000 organizations run exclusively by volunteer staff
- 2 billion volunteer hours per year
- 19 million volunteer positions or 1 million full-time jobs
- 11 times as many staff as Canada's largest private-sector employer

*Adapted from "Canada Has World's Second Largest Nonprofit Sector," Association of Fundraising Professionals, http://www.afpnet.org/tier3_cd.cfm?folder_id=2345&content_item_i, retrieved May 8, 2005; Georgina Steinsky-Schwartz, Canadian Centre for Philanthropy and Coalition of National Voluntary Organizations, Speech to the Empire Club of Canada, Toronto, November 16, 2004, Imagine Canada site, http://www.imagine.ca, retrieved February 2, 2005.

FIGURE 8.5   A Contact Letter

WILLIAM F. SCHULZ
EXECUTIVE DIRECTOR

September 21, 2001

Repetition of "Sometimes death comes … But not this time" creates powerful opener.

Dear Amnesty Member,

alliteration

Sometimes death comes in the dark, in the dead of night. But not this time. This time the day could not have been brighter or more beautiful.

Sometimes death comes when we are by ourselves. But not this time. This time it came to those who were surrounded by friends and colleagues.

Sometimes death comes on a battlefield or in a prison cell. But not this time. This time it came in commercial airplanes and pleasant office buildings.

Transition from the event to the organization sending the letter

And sometimes death comes after a long struggle and much anticipation. But not this time. This time it came in an instant. And it appears to have swept in its wake family members of our staff and volunteers, friends of members of our Board and doubtless a good many Amnesty International members themselves.

In keeping with the organization's philosophy, the letter calls for a thoughtful, measured response

Now that it has, you and I have work to do. Not the kind of work that sorts through rubble or loads up body bags, thank God. Those who do *that* work deserve a thousand tears of gratitude. Our work is of a different order but just as important nonetheless. The work of anger, to be sure, but an anger tempered by wisdom. The work of grieving, absolutely, but a grieving that pays homage to suffering. And the work of justice, no question about it, but a justice of which every one of us can be proud.

Rule of 3 with internal contrasts in each line

alliteration

To get to grieving, we must go through anger. And to get to justice, we must go through grieving. Because, as the theologian Sam Keen so eloquently put it, "Every day we are not mourning is a day we will be taking vengeance" and vengeance is different from justice.

Repetition

Those who died on September 11 represent the best that is in us as human beings, as citizens and people. The best that is in us knows that individuals are responsible for this crime — not anonymous masses of people. The best that is in us knows that the guilty deserve to be punished — not those who share their names or their language, their skin color or their religion. It knows that blind hatred corrupts the hater. It knows that the greatest power evil has is to entice the innocent to mimic its practices. It knows that every action has unintended consequences. It knows that the truly strong never forget that in the heart of every stranger lurks a reflection of our own.

Rule of 3

Those who died on September 11 represent the best that is in us, the calling of our highest selves. We owe them anger; we owe them grieving; we owe them justice. But everything that we do now must reflect the best, not the lowest, of our humanity. We pay those precious souls their rightful tribute only by leveling a wise justice, only by exhibiting a tender righteousness. We pay them tribute only by understanding what brought about their deaths and hewing to those principles that call us to a more abundant life.

AMNESTY INTERNATIONAL USA • 322 EIGHTH AVENUE • NEW YORK, NY 10001
(212) 807-8400 • www.amnestyusa.org

(continued)

when several syllables begin with the same sound (See *Science84* opener on p. 190). **Rhyme** is the repetition of the final vowel sounds and, if the words end with consonants, the final consonant sounds. **Rhythm** is the repetition of a pattern of accented and unaccented syllables. The **rule of three** explains that when you have a series of three items that are logically parallel, the last receives the most emphasis.

Rhythm, rhyme, and the rule of three emphasize words in the following example:

FIGURE 8.5 A Contact Letter *(concluded)*

Parallelism Toward those ends, Amnesty International will mourn the victims; we will speak out against impunity for the perpetrators; we will demand that those innocent of crimes be protected and respected; and we will insist that justice is not justice if it fails to adhere to international human rights norms. Both the International Secretariat of Amnesty International and we in AIUSA have appointed Crisis Response Teams to work together in a coordinated, unified response to this tragedy and its aftermath. We will be determining as soon as possible how best our membership can help advance our common goals.

Short sentences ending in consonants bring a sense of closure

Repetition of sentence in ¶ 4 For death has come in an instant. And now there is work to be done.

William F. Schulz
Executive Director

① ② ③ ① ②
Nightcalls, pratfalls, and jungle shrieks ... a scattering of wings, a chattering of monkeys and big, yellow eyes in my headlights! ③

Headline, sales letter for Tom Timmins cigars

3. Use Psychological Description

In a sales letter, you can use psychological description (◀ p. 168) to create a scenario so the reader can picture himself or herself using your product or service and enjoying its benefits. You can also use psychological description to describe the problem your product will solve.

A *Bon Appétit* subscription letter uses psychological description in its opener and in the P.S., creating a frame for the sales letter:

Dear Reader:

First, fill a pitcher with ice.

Now pour in a bottle of ordinary red wine, a quarter cup of brandy, and a small bottle of club soda.

Sweeten to taste with a quarter to half cup of sugar, garnish with slices of apple, lemon, and orange. ...

... then *move your chair to a warm, sunny spot.* You've just made yourself Sangria—one of the great glories of Spain, and the perfect thing to sit back with and sip while you consider this invitation. ...

P.S. One more thing before you finish your Sangria. ...

Leave 'Em Laughing?*

Not too many sales brochures and letters leave you holding your sides with laughter. There may be a good reason. A good joke may put you in a good mood, but it rarely gives the motivation to buy a product or make a donation.

The lack of jokes in sales letters and brochures may seem odd in contrast to the frequency of humour in advertising. The two kinds of writing generally serve different purposes, though. A great deal of advertising is designed to give the audience a positive image of a product or brand. Sales letters and brochures are focused on a more direct response—say, subscribing to a magazine or contributing to a cause. Humour can actually distract the audience from that purpose.

Still, some products use humour in their direct mail, perhaps because humour is part of what they are known for providing. One of the most successful mailings by *The Nation* magazine featured a caricature of President George W. Bush wearing a crown, along with the words "Don't you just love this guy? If your answer is yes, don't open this envelope."

*Based on Beth Negus Viveiros, "No Laughing Matter: Use of Humour in Direct Mail Marketing," *Direct*, January 2003, downloaded from LookSmart's FindArticles, www.findarticles.com.

Volunteering Benefits the Bottom Line*

A survey of 700 corporations by Business in the Community, UK, found 40% believe volunteerism benefits the bottom line.

- One-third of British companies have formal volunteer-time policies.

- One-third of U.S. companies have volunteer-time policies.

- 64% of surveyed Canadian companies have annual volunteer program budgets.

- 44% of Canadian companies used volunteer programs to maintain morale during mergers or downsizing.

- A Volunteer Canada report indicated 14 to 17% competency gains in volunteers.

- Workplace volunteerism reduces employee turnover.

- 80% of Canadians hold companies accountable for employee volunteerism.

- Jantzi Social Index showed helping companies had a 5% better return on investment than the TSE 300.

*Adapted from Julie Travis, "What Goes Around … Corporate Volunteering Boosts the Bottom Line," *Canadian Business*, January 31–February 13, 2005, 67.

FIGURE 8.6   Inside Panels of a Brochure

Inside Panels

"Foster Mother to the Human Race"

Quotation

In a world in which hunger seems to defy large-scale solutions, the answer may well lie with a much smaller one, the goat.

Startling statement

For most of the world's people, goat's milk is the only milk they have ever known. However, in many countries even goat's milk is in short supply. When children — at the most nutritionally vulnerable point in their lives — are deprived of milk, the consequences are disastrous. An absence of milk in their diet makes children easy targets for malnutrition and disease.

Goats offer an ideal solution to this grave situation. Goat's milk is as highly nutritious as that of any dairy animal. In fact, if children drink only one liter of goat's milk per day, they will be consuming all of the protein required for the first six years of life, and more than half of what they need to become teenagers and grow into adulthood. Even more impressive is the fact that this same single liter provides all the calcium required at almost every stage of life.

Just as important, goats require an extremely low investment and are very easy to keep. They will eat almost any kind of forage, need very little space, and are comfortable in a wide range of climates. They can also go longer without water than most other farm animals and reproduce quickly, allowing families to build their herds while producing extra milk to sell for income. Moreover, goat manure makes excellent fertilizer.

Details explain, "Why goats?"

Banners unify panels

Finally, goats and children appear to have a natural affinity for one another. Even young children are able to raise and take care of their family's goats. Such responsibility helps children gain the self-esteem that comes from playing a significant role in their family's economic life.

What money buys

At a cost of only $120 for a goat and the training in its care — or $10 for a share of a goat — Heifer Project's **Kids-2-Kids Campaign** makes it possible for us to send this four-footed economic miracle to needy children and their families all over the world. We invite you to take a glimpse into just some of the places where this miracle is taking place.

Logo banner separates stories

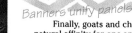

In Nepal

Most paragraphs should be 7 lines or less

Ten years ago, when she got the idea that would change her life, Gyandhari Basel could not even write her own name. Forced as a young girl to migrate from her native hill country to Nepal's southern plains, Gyandhari helped her family eke out a bare living as subsistence farmers. She was typical of many women in her situation, impoverished and soon married with four children of her own.

Gyandhari and several of her friends made the decision to band together to do what had previously been considered impossible. In a land

---

It's hard to imagine any reader really stopping to follow the recipe before finishing the letter, but the scenario is so vivid that one can imagine the sunshine even on a cold, grey day.

4. Make Your Letter Sound Like a Letter, Not an Ad.

Maintain the image of one person writing to one other person that is the foundation of all letters. Use an informal style with short words and sentences, and even slang.

You can also create a **persona**—the character who allegedly writes the letter—to make the letter interesting and keep us reading. Use the rhythms of speech, vivid images, and conversational words to create the effect that the author is a "character."

The following opening creates a persona who fits the product:

Dear Friend:

There's no use trying. I've tried and tried to tell people about my fish. But I wasn't rigged out to be a letter writer, and I can't do it. I can close-haul a sail with the best of them. I know how to pick out the best fish of the catch, I know just which fish will make the tastiest mouthfuls, but I'll never learn the knack of writing a letter that will tell people why my kind of fish—fresh-caught prime-grades, right off the fishing boats with the deep-sea tang still in it—is lots better than the ordinary store kind.

Sales letter, Frank Davis Fish Company.

This letter, with its "Aw, shucks, I can't sell" persona, with language designed to make you see an unassuming fisherman ("rigged out," "close-haul"), was written by a professional advertiser.[8]

InSite

www.networkforgood.org

The Network for Good provides information about charities. Links let you donate online or find volunteer opportunities in your area.

Summary of Key Points

■ The first three steps in writing a sales or fundraising letter are to (1) learn about the product or service, (2) choose and analyze the target audience, and (3) choose a central selling point. The **target audience** is the group of people one expects to be interested in the product, service, or cause. A **central selling point** is a reader benefit that by itself motivates your readers to act and covers all the other benefits.

■ A good **star** (opener) makes readers want to read the letter and provides a reasonable transition to the body of the letter. A good **chain** (body) answers readers' questions, overcomes their objections, and involves them emotionally. A good **knot** (action close) tells readers what to do, makes the action sound easy, gives them a reason for acting promptly, and ends with a reader benefit or a picture of the reader's money helping to solve the problem.

■ In a fundraising letter, the basic strategy is vicarious participation. By donating money, readers participate vicariously in work they are not able to do personally.

■ The primary purpose in a fundraising letter is to get money. An important secondary purpose is to build support for the cause.

■ The body of a fundraising letter must prove that (1) the problem deserves the reader's attention, (2) the problem can be solved or at least alleviated, (3) your organization is helping to solve it, (4) private funds are needed, and (5) your organization will use the funds wisely.

■ **Contact letters** keep in touch with customers or donors.

■ Brochures can build general support for an organization or candidate, give specific information, or even have a reply coupon that readers can return.

■ Good writing in direct mail is interesting. It uses sound patterns to emphasize words, uses psychological description, and is specific and conversational.

✔ **CHECKLIST**   Checklist for Writing on the Web *

Consider user needs and expectations

☐ Users surfing for information are often impatient and in a hurry.
☐ Users spend on average less than 55 seconds on a single site.
☐ Reading on-screen is harder and 25% slower than print reading.
☐ 90% of users do not scroll beyond the first screen.
☐ Only 16% read word by word.

Tailor your message to meet user needs

☐ Plan navigation with reader information needs in mind.
☐ Highlight keywords.
☐ Include search engine.
☐ Ensure one topic per paragraph.
☐ Use headings, subheadings, and bulleted lists.
☐ Use inverted pyramid style (conclusions first).
☐ Use half the words for conventional printed text.
☐ Insert summaries and downloadable, printable versions.
☐ Offer scannable layout.

Add credibility

☐ Revise and edit for good, clear, concise, accurate, and objective writing.
☐ Maintain informality.
☐ Monitor assumptions with global readers in mind.
☐ Use accurate, objective, current, and reliable sources and statistics.
☐ Include high-quality graphics.
☐ Promote hypertext links to reliable sites.
☐ Establish your name and that of your sponsoring organization.
☐ Include contact information and revision dates.

*Based on Harvey Schachter, "How to turn your website into a 'flytrap'," *The Globe and Mail*, September 3, 2004, B18; Jakob Nielsen's Web site http://www.useit.com/papers/webwriting, retrieved May 8, 2005.

CHAPTER 8   # Exercises and Problems

Getting Started

8.1   Evaluating Envelope Teasers

In the following examples, the words in square brackets describe the appearance of the envelope or lettering. The name in parentheses is from the return address. If no name is listed, either the return address is a street address only or there is no return address. Unless otherwise noted, the teaser copy appeared on the front (address side) of the envelope.

Would you open the envelope? Why or why not? Do others in the class agree?

1. (National Glaucoma Research) [In blue handwriting above the address window]

    I didn't want to bother you over the phone.

    I hope I made the right decision.

2. (UNICEF) [Oversize 15.25-by-23 cm envelope. To the right of the address window, a child's colour picture of three children. Below the address window, in blue type]

    How good would it feel to know that a piece of your monthly phone bill can now go to children who need it most?

3. [Plain kraft envelope. In a window in the top right-hand corner, three real pennies show through.]

4. (Doctors without Borders. Médecins sans Frontieres) [In large red type to the right of the address window]

    The Enclosed Bracelet

    Is Not a Toy …

8.2   Evaluating P.S.'s

Evaluate the following P.S.'s. Will they motivate readers to read the whole letter if readers turn to them first? Do they create a strong ending for those who have already read the letter?

1. P.S. It only takes <u>one</u> night's stay in a hotel you read about here, <u>one</u> discounted flight, <u>one</u> budget-priced cruise, or <u>one</u> low-cost car rental to make mailing back your Subscription Certificate well worth it.

   P.P.S.   About your free gift! Your risk-free subscription to CONSUMER REPORTS TRAVEL LETTER comes with a remarkable 314-page book as a FREE GIFT.

2. P.S. Help spread the tolerance message by using your personalized address labels on all your correspondence. And remember, you will receive a free *Teaching Tolerance* magazine right after your tax-deductible contribution arrives.

3. P.S. Every day brings more requests like that of Mr. Agyrey-Kwakey—for our "miracle seeds."

   And it's urgent that we respond to the emergency in Malaysia and Indonesia by replanting those forests destroyed by fire. Please send <u>your gift today</u> and become a partner with us in these innovative projects around the world.

4. P.S. Your FREE GIFT, <u>Editor's Choice Video Clips</u>, is a CD-ROM collection of 250 high-quality AVI videos with sound. You can put these clips on your site with Emblaze VideoPro … or just have fun with them. You get action footage of people at work and at play … beautiful nature scenes … famous places around the world … and many other subjects. <u>Editor's Choice Video Clips</u> is worth $99, but it's yours to keep FREE—even if you decide to return Emblaze VideoPro.

5. P.S. Even as you read this letter, a donated load of food waits for the ticket that will move it to Canada's hungry. Please give today!

8.3   Evaluating Sales and Fundraising Letters

Collect the sales and fundraising letters that come to you, your co-workers, landlord, neighbours, or family. Use the following questions to evaluate each package:

- What mode does the opener use? Is it related to the teaser, if any? Is it related to the rest of the letter? How good is the opener?
- What central selling point or common ground does the letter use?
- What kinds of proof does the letter use? Is the logic valid? What questions or objections are not answered?
- How does the letter create emotional appeal?
- Is the style effective? Where does the letter use sound to emphasize points?
- Does the close tell readers what to do, make action easy, give a reason for acting promptly, and end with a positive picture?
- Does the letter use a P.S.? How good is it?

- Is the letter visually attractive? Why or why not?
- What other items besides the letter are in the package?

As Your Professor Directs,

a. Share your analysis of one or more letters with a small group of your classmates.

b. Analyze one letter in a presentation to the class. Make overhead transparencies or photocopies of the letter to use as a visual aid in your presentation.

c. Analyze one letter in a memo to your professor. Provide a copy or photocopy of the letter along with your memo.

d. With several other students, write a group memo or report analyzing one part of the letter (e.g., openers) or one kind of letter (e.g., political letters, organizations fighting hunger, etc.). Use at least 10 letters for your analysis if you look at only one part; use at least 6 letters if you analyze one kind of letter. Provide copies or photocopies as an appendix to your report.

8.4   Brainstorming Openers for a Magazine Subscription Letter

a. Using at least **two** of the four different modes—question, narration, startling statement, and quotation—write **three** possible openers for a letter urging readers to subscribe to a magazine (you pick the magazine).

b. For each opener indicate (1) what mode it uses and (2) how you would make a transition to the body of

the letter. (You may write out the transition or just describe it, whichever is easier.)

c. Rate the three openers in terms of their effectiveness, and briefly explain the reason for your ratings.

8.5   Evaluating Opener Drafts

The following are the results of a session brainstorming openers for a letter raising funds for a community college that has suffered budget cuts. Suggest ways to improve each opener. Which seems the most promising? Why?

1.   Do you realize that there are students who are getting a poorer education than you got from the same program you attended?

2.   We are in danger of losing our accreditation.

3.   Engineering students using dial calipers of only ⅒ the accuracy needed … cancelled library subscriptions … bigger classes … closed courses … obsolete equipment. … Budget cuts have made it harder for XYZ students to get a good education.

E-Mail Messages

8.6   The Ethics of "Up To"*

As companies struggle to be noticed in direct mail and on the Internet, many are tempted to exaggerate. A phrase that is easy to misuse is *up to*. This phrase suggests the offer approaches the upper limit, but it does not really promise anything. Consumers learn to distrust such unethical appeals—and the companies that make them.

The following e-mail offers contain "up to" promises. Rewrite each offer so that it is both ethical and appealing.

1.   Save up to $22,000 on latest SUV models! Visit dealer for details.

2.   You're pre-approved for up to 10,000 bonus miles! We've reserved up to 10,000 bonus miles. You get 1,000 miles each time you rent a car from selected merchants. You get 200 bonus miles for phone services from selected providers. See reverse for credit card disclosures regarding rates and fees.

3.   Get up to $100 cash back on your telephone service. Eligible customers will receive a $25 coupon for each qualifying service: Long Distance, Privacy Features, DSL Connection, and Wireless Deluxe.

*This exercise based on Herschell Gordon Lewis, "Up to No Good," *Direct*, January 2004.

8.7   Answering an Ethics Question

You're a senior staffer in a charitable organization. Today, you get this message from your boss:

> Subject: Using "Handwritten" Messages
>
> I'd like your feedback on the suggestion from our direct mail consultant to use a mailing with handwritten notes. I understand the argument that this will increase response. But the idea of hiring people who don't have any relation to us to write notes—and implying that the notes are by loyal donors—seems unethical. And frankly, I worry about the image we'd create if our real donors learned that we'd done this.
>
> What do you think?

As Your Professor Directs,

a.   Answer the question, using a charitable organization that you know something about.

b.   Answer the question, assuming that it comes from a federal candidate.

c.   Answer the question, assuming that the strategy has been recommended for a sales rather than for a fundraising letter.

d.   Write an e-mail message to your professor, justifying your answer.

Letter and Brochure Assignments

8.8   Writing a Magazine Subscription Letter

Write a two-page letter persuading new subscribers to subscribe to a magazine of your choice. Assume that your letter would have a reply card and postage-paid envelope. You do NOT have to write these, but DO refer to them in your letter.

Choose a magazine you read or one that deals with a subject or sport you know something about. You may choose a narrower target audience for this letter than the magazine uses. For example, if the magazine is designed to appeal to women ages 18–35, for this assignment you could write to college women, ages 18–35. If you narrow the target audience, be sure to tell your professor.

Hints:

■   Read several issues of the magazine, looking both at editorial content and at ads, to identify the magazine's target audience. Choose a central selling point that will appeal to that audience.

■   Pay special attention to language. To keep your letter moving quickly, consider occasionally using sentence fragments or ellipses. Try to choose vivid, evocative language; try your hand at alliteration or other repetitive patterns.

■   Everyone has had the experience of seeing interesting headlines on a magazine cover but then being disappointed by the stories inside. Be sure to prove your claims by giving examples and specifics. You may use material from previous issues of the magazine; you may need to edit or rewrite it for maximum effect. Choose details that will interest your reader.

■   Get current figures about subscription rates from the magazine itself. It's OK to offer a free issue, a premium, or a discount, but do not depend on the offer alone to motivate people. Your letter must be fully persuasive even without the special premium.

8.9   Writing a Contact Letter

Write a contact letter to go to customers, clients, or donors.

8.10   Creating a Brochure

Create a brochure for a campus group or a non-profit organization. Turn in two copies of your brochure and a memo to your professor explaining your choices for strategy, content, and design. Would this brochure be part of a series? What are the purposes of the brochure? Who are the audiences? Where will the brochure be physically available? Why did you choose your central selling point? Why did you choose to be more or less formal, more or less complete, and so forth? Explain your choices for strategy, content, wording, layout, visuals (if any), and colour (if any).

8.11   Writing a Fundraising Letter

Write a 2½-page letter to raise money from new donors for an organization you support. You must use a real organization, but it does not have to be conducting a fundraising drive now. Assume that your letter would have a reply card and postage-paid envelope. You do NOT have to write these, but DO refer to them in your letter.

Options for organizations include

■   Tax-deductible charitable organizations—churches; synagogues; hospitals; groups working to feed, clothe, and house poor people.

■   Lobbying groups—Mothers Against Drunk Driving, groups working against nuclear weapons, etc.

■   Groups raising money to fight a disease or fund research.

■   Universities trying to raise money for endowments, buildings, scholarships, faculty salaries.

■   Athletic associations raising money for scholarships, equipment, buildings, facilities.

For this assignment, you may also use groups that do not regularly have fundraising drives but that may have special needs. Perhaps a school needs new uniforms for its band or an automatic timing device for its swimming pool.

8.12   Writing a Sales Letter

Write a sales letter to promote a product that you have created/imagined.

Interpersonal Communication

9 Communicating across Cultures

AN INSIDE PERSPECTIVE

Communicating across Cultures

In a global knowledge economy, cultural competence—the skill to bridge the cultural dimensions of human behaviour—is an invaluable asset. If there are models of cultural competence in international settings, we can also find them closer to home. Chief Lawrence Paul of Nova Scotia's Millbrook First Nation is a powerful model of how to communicate across differences and how to do business in Canada today.

Chief Paul has seen enormous change in Nova Scotia. He remembers a time when the reserve was an impoverished ghetto shunned by the local townspeople. It was a time when doctors kept "Indian time"—a one-hour window of opportunity to see the doctor.

All that changed with Chief Paul's vision that his First Nation could create sustainable economic development with positive impacts on the whole region. A powerful storyteller, he is a leader able to communicate his vision and motivate those inside and outside his community to break new business ground. He not only produced a historic deal with three levels of government but also signed partnerships with the private sector. The result is the Truro Power Centre, a thriving multiuse retail and industrial complex that includes big-name retail stores.

People associated with the Truro Power Centre work so effectively together that Ray Merriam, business development and marketing director, marvels at the resilience of Aboriginal culture and business. While few businesses last 50 years and even nations disappear after a few centuries, Aboriginal culture has survived for many thousands of years. "They must have important lessons to teach us."

Chief Lawrence Paul, leader of Nova Scotia's Millbrook First Nation, has brought economic prosperity and opportunity not only to his own First Nation but also to people of the region. Chief Paul is at the heart of cross-cultural communication that is helping rebuild community in Atlantic Canada.

Source: Adapted from Tom Mason, "Tribal Counsel," *Canadian Business*, November 12, 2005, 41–45.

Our values, priorities, and practices are shaped by the culture in which we grow up. Understanding other cultures is crucial if you want to sell your products in other countries, manage an international plant or office, or work in this country for a multinational company headquartered in another country.

The successful international communicator is

■ Aware that his or her preferred values and behaviours are influenced by culture and are not necessarily "right"

■ Flexible and open to change

■ Sensitive to verbal and non-verbal behaviour

■ Aware of the values, beliefs, and practices in other cultures

■ Sensitive to differences among individuals within a culture[1]

The first step in understanding another culture is to realize that it may do things very differently, and that the difference is not bad or inferior. People inhabit several cultures (national, ethnic, religious, professional, and so on) simultaneously. Even within a single culture people differ. The kinds of differences summarized in this chapter can turn into stereotypes, which can be just as damaging as ignorance. Don't try to memorize the material here as a rigid set of rules. Instead, use the examples to get a sense for the kinds of things that differ from one culture to another. Test these generalizations against your experience. When in doubt, ask.

The Importance of Global Business

As we saw in ◀ Chapter 1, exports are essential both to the success of individual businesses and to a country's economy as a whole. *BusinessWeek* reports that two-thirds of all industries either already operate globally or are in the process of doing so.

An increasing share of profits comes from outside the headquarters country. Canadian entrepreneur John H. McCall MacBain has built his business Trader-Classified Media NV into an international success story. Based in the Netherlands and traded in Paris, his company generates 25% of its revenue in Canada with publications like *Trader Classified* and *Bargain Finder*.[2] Michelin earns 35% of its profits in the United States. McDonald's earns more than 62% of its income outside the United States, and almost 98% of Nokia's sales are outside its home country, Finland.[3]

The web of international business is not confined to exports and imports. Many companies—even service businesses—depend on vendors or operations in other countries. More software is written in Ireland than anywhere else in the world. General Electric Capital's customer service calls are answered by 1,000 English-speaking Indian employees in New Delhi 24 hours a day, seven days a week.[4]

For executives in global companies, international experience is often essential for career advancement. Patricia Arnold (currently vice-president, Credit Suisse First Boston, Zurich) started out in financial services in Montreal and Calgary before advancing her career in Albania, Hungary, Switzerland, and Sudan. She gives a lot of credit to bilingual, multicultural Canada (and especially Quebec) for her capacity to make the most of her international experience—something she shares with Howard Davine, a McGill graduate now executive vice-president, Touchstone Television (a division of Disney). Arnold learns as much as she can about the history of her locale and adopts local practices and dress, refusing to be isolated in expatriate communities.[5]

Diversity in Canada

Even if you stay in Canada, you'll work with people whose backgrounds differ from yours. Residents of small towns and rural areas have different notions

Beyond Stereotypes*

Learning about different cultures is important for understanding the different kinds of people we work with. However, leadership coaches Keith Caver and Ancella Livers caution that people are individuals, not just representatives of a cultural group. Caver and Livers have found that co-workers sometimes treat black individuals first as representatives of black culture, and only second as talented and experienced managers.

As an example, Caver and Livers cite the all-too-common situation of a newly hired black manager who participates in a management development activity. The new manager is prepared to answer questions about her area of business expertise, but the only questions directed toward her are about "diversity." African American clients of Caver and Livers have complained that they are often called upon to interpret the behaviour of famous black Americans such as Clarence Thomas or Jesse Jackson, and they wonder whether their white colleagues would feel their race qualifies them to interpret the deeds of famous white Americans.

In this example, stereotypes make well-intentioned efforts at communication offensive.

*Based on Keith A. Caver and Ancella B. Livers, "Dear White Boss," *Harvard Business Review*, November 2002, 76–81.

of friendliness than do people from big cities. British Columbians may talk differently than people in the Maritimes. The cultural icons that resonate for baby boomers may mean little to members of Generation X or Y.

Generation X (born between 1961 and 1982)—popularized by Douglas Coupland and pilloried by the media as "alienated, overeducated, underachieving slackers"—or Generation Y—born to boomers since the 1980s—have been represented as "the generation that won't grow up."[6] But what does it mean to label people as if their ages told you all you need to know or to think that age has more explanatory power than geography, gender, abilities, ethnicity, and so on? Does labelling produce the identities it presumes to discover, encouraging the very alienation it deplores?

The last 15 years have seen a growing emphasis on diversity in the workforce. But people outside the power structure have always worked. In the past, such people (including non-elite white males) may have been relegated to low-status and low-paying jobs, to agricultural or domestic work, or to staff rather than line work and management.

"Diversity" in the workplace comes from many sources: gender, race and ethnicity, regional and national origin, social class, religion, age, sexual orientation, abilities.

Many Americans are already multicultural. According to July 2004 U.S. census figures, a third of Americans are African American, Hispanic, Asian, or Native American.[7] U.S. Census figures released in 2001 show that 17.6% of the population nationally and 39.5% in California speak a language other than English at home.[8]

Bilingual Canada has long compared the diversity of its people to a mosaic. But now immigrants from Italy, Greece, and Hong Kong add their voices to the medley of French, English, and Aboriginal languages. Radio station CHIN in Toronto broadcasts in 32 languages.[9]

Widely recognized for its multilateralism, peacekeeping, social programs, official bilingualism, and multiculturalism, Canada is arguably the most culturally diverse country and Toronto one of the world's most diverse cities. By 2017, Statistics Canada predicts that the so-called invisible minorities will be the visible majority in Toronto and Vancouver. Meantime, the increasing trend of intermarriage is rendering the concept of race less and less important.[10]

By at least one account, Canada's global success is due in large measure to its multiculturalism that teaches empathy and to the fact that it is not a dominant power that thinks only of its own stakeholders.[11]

When Canada came of age with the signing of the *Constitution Act*, 1982, it recognized the Aboriginal and treaty rights of Aboriginal peoples. In recognizing and naming Aboriginal peoples, however, Canada simultaneously obscured the great diversity of those peoples: Mi'kmaq, Cree, Dene, Anishnabe, Algonquin, Nisga'a, Inuit, and Métis, to name but a few.

Ways to Look at Culture

Each of us grows up in a **culture** that provides patterns of acceptable behaviour and belief. We learn our culture at home and at school, at work and at play, and may internalize it to the point that we do not even recognize its power to shape our thoughts, feelings, and behaviours. It becomes so natural and logical as to be invisible. We may not be aware of the most basic features of our own culture until we come into contact with people who do things differently. If we come from a culture where dogs are pets, that interpretation may seem "natural" until we learn that in other cultures, dogs, like chickens, are raised for food.

It has been said that "culture" is "one of the two or three most complex words in the English language." Indeed, Western uses of the word *culture* trace the historical shift from rural to urban living, from tilling the soil ("coulter" means the blade of a ploughshare) to cultivating the mind.[12]

Our cultures are systems within which we see the world, understand our identity, and find meaning. Our culture is not simply decorative (dress, dance, or diet, powwows or tea ceremonies) but dynamic, changing in response to travel and trauma, economic, political, and environmental change.

Our cultures are also complex, contested, and contradictory. What does it mean to be a Canadian, for example? To a Quebecker? To a Newfoundlander? To someone on the Prairies or in the Northwest Territories? To a new Canadian who has just taken the oath of loyalty?

Generalizing about different groups is at the heart of **stereotyping**, which means imposing unfair generalizations and labelling people with unjust images. Stereotyping remains a major barrier to effective cross-cultural communication and to recognizing the true value of those we misrepresent. The result is a loss to businesses, groups, and nations that do not see or use the talents and human capital available to them. The irony is that visible minorities who have the languages and knowledge companies need often feel invisible.[13]

Stereotypes are especially hard to dislodge because of ethnocentrism and confirmation bias. **Ethnocentrism** involves the judgment of others by norms specific to one's own culture. Though the unfair generalizations are often made without awareness of the yardstick of cultural norms, they have the effect of causing hasty judgments that reinforce the belief that one's own group is superior to others. **Confirmation bias** is the process whereby the bias is confirmed when people see what they expect to see; they are blinded to the positive attributes of others.

Another response to diversity is to try and manage it by classifying and categorizing. One such attempt to represent and respect cultural difference is anthropologist Edward T. Hall's distinction between high-context and low-context cultures.[14] The information, environment, and stimuli that surround an event constitute the context within which we communicate.

Canadians may be troubled by the classification "North American" in Figure 9.1 obscuring Canadian differences and by the implication that high-context cultures value the social aspects of communication, while low-context ones see communication's value only in terms of information.

If low-context cultures seem more logical, detailed, action oriented and more individualistic than the collectivist high-context cultures to an American anthropologist, then it may be that his cultural conditioning leads him to see

| **FIGURE 9.1** | Views of Communication in High- and Low-Context Cultures |

	High-context (Examples: Japan, United Arab Emirates)	Low-context (Examples: Germany, North America)
Preferred communication strategy	Indirectness, politeness, ambiguity	Directness, confrontation, clarity
Reliance on words to communicate	Low	High
Reliance on non-verbal signs to communicate	High	Low
Importance of written word	Low	High
Agreements made in writing	Not binding	Binding
Agreements made orally	Binding	Not binding
Attention to detail	Low	High

Source: Adapted from David A. Victor, *International Business Communication* (New York: HarperCollins, 1992), 148, 153, 160.

what he expects to see. Perhaps it blinds him to the elaborate social rituals of his own culture.

What, for example, is the meaning of golf in the business world? Are there no rituals attached to the subtle negotiations of order of play? How many holes before business can be discussed? It's easier to be patient with one's own rituals that seem so logical than with the strange practices of others.

This is why it is so important to be sensitive to our own cultural assumptions as well as those of other groups—and why we need to read Hall's classifications with great caution. If there is some truth to the distinctions he makes among cultural groups, it can be dangerous to exaggerate our differences and ignore what we share.

As Figure 9.1 shows, low-context cultures favour direct approaches and may see indirectness as dishonest or manipulative. The written word is seen as more important than oral statements, so contracts are binding but promises may be broken. Details matter. Business communication practices in North America reflect these low-context preferences.

The discussion that follows focuses on national and regional cultures. But business communication is also influenced by the organizational culture and by personal culture (or social categories of identity), such as gender, race and ethnicity, social class, and so forth. As Figure 9.2 suggests, all of these intersect to determine what kind of communication is needed in a given situation.

Sometimes one kind of culture may be more important than another.

Values, Beliefs, and Practices

Values and beliefs, often unconscious, affect our response to people and situations. Most Canadians, for example, value "fairness." "You're not playing fair" is a sharp criticism calling for changed behaviour. In some countries, however, people expect certain groups to receive preferential treatment. Many Canadians accept competition and believe that it produces better performance. Others believe in the co-operation that has given us social programs, or in the co-operation and consensus building of Aboriginal peoples. The Japanese, however, believe that competition leads to disharmony.

Many Canadians, like U.S. business people, believe that success is based on individual achievement and is open to anyone who excels. In England and in France, success is more obviously linked to social class. And in some countries, people of some castes or races are prohibited by law from full participation in society.

FIGURE 9.2   National Culture, Organizational Culture, and
Personal Culture Overlap

Japan's traditional culture emphasized the group, but there is evidence that this cultural value is changing in new historical conditions. According to research and analysis by David Matsumoto, Japanese cultural norms such as the sacrifice of one's personal time for the company, avoidance of disagreements with one's boss, and the favouring of compliance over individual initiative have become part of Japan's business past. Modern business values in Japan place more emphasis on the individual person's goals and accomplishments.[15]

Values and beliefs are often influenced by religion. Christianity coexists with a view of the individual as proactive. In some Muslim and Asian countries, however, it is seen as presumptuous to predict the future by promising action by a certain date. The Protestant work ethic legitimizes wealth by seeing it as a sign of divine favour. In other Christian cultures, a simpler lifestyle is considered to be closer to God.

Religion affects what foods may be eaten and on what days businesses are open. For example, Hindus do not eat beef; Muslims consider pork unclean; Orthodox Jews eat only kosher meats. In many Muslim countries, Friday, a day of prayer, is an official holiday. During the ninth month of the Muslim lunar calendar, a devout Muslim may be on a pilgrimage to Mecca. An ordinary business day may be a holiday in the country you're visiting.

Even everyday practices differ from culture to culture. North Americans and Europeans put the family name last; Asians put it first. North American and European printing moves from top to bottom and from left to right; Arabic reads from right to left, but still from top to bottom. An American carpenter pushes a saw; a Japanese pulls it. Light switches and door knobs turn opposite ways in Japan and in the United States.[16]

Non-verbal Communication

Non-verbal communication—communication that doesn't use words—takes place all the time. Smiles, frowns, who sits where at a meeting, the size of an office, how long someone keeps a visitor waiting—all these communicate pleasure or anger, friendliness or distance, power and status. Most of the time we are no more conscious of interpreting non-verbal signals than we are conscious of breathing.

When Communication Styles Conflict*

Some cultures differ in their ideas about how business people should communicate. What if you want to close a deal with someone who expects business communications to be flowery or argumentative? If you rarely compose elegant prose, or if you dislike arguments, you may lose the business opportunity unless one of you adapts.

About two-thirds of attempts at Israeli-Indian deals fail, for example, even though the countries share a common business language (English).

Israeli business people generally prefer communication to be simple and direct, even forceful. Israelis also value treating others as equals. Indian English emphasizes politeness, as shown through long, indirect, and poetic sentences. Another sign of politeness is humility.

Indian business people often interpreted correspondence from Israelis to be rude, signalling inability to collaborate appropriately. The Israelis were confused by the indirect wording of Indian messages. They felt unsure about what to expect. However, a study by Nurit Zaidman also found examples of Israeli business people trying to choose polite and elegant language, and of Indian business people simplifying their style.

*Based on Nurit Zaidman, "Cultural Codes and Language Strategies in Business Communication," *Management Communication Quarterly* 14, no. 3 (February 2001): 408–441.

Source: Carol Simpson Cartoons.

"I find cultural diversity in the workplace quite exhilarating. I've learned to say 'NO' in thirty languages."

Yet non-verbal signals can be misinterpreted just as easily as can verbal symbols (words). And the misunderstandings can be harder to clear up because people may not be aware of the non-verbal cues that led them to assume that they aren't liked, respected, or approved. An Arab student assumed that his U.S. roommate disliked him intensely because the U.S. student sat around the room with his feet up on the furniture, soles toward the Arab roommate. Arab culture sees the foot in general and the sole in particular as unclean; showing the sole of the foot is an insult.[17]

Learning about non-verbal language can help us project the image we want to present and make us more aware of the signals we are interpreting.

However, even within a single culture, a non-verbal symbol is such a powerful source of meaning that experts claim that 93% of communication is based on non-verbal signals.[18]

Body Language

Posture and body movements connote energy and openness. North American **open body positions** include leaning forward with uncrossed arms and legs, with the arms away from the body. **Closed** or **defensive body positions** include leaning back, sometimes with both hands behind the head, arms and legs crossed or close together, or hands in pockets. As the labels imply, open positions suggest that people are accepting and open to new ideas. Closed positions suggest that people are physically or psychologically uncomfortable, that they are defending themselves and shutting other people out.

People who cross their arms or legs often claim that they do so only because the position is more comfortable. But notice your own body the next time you're in a perfectly comfortable discussion with a good friend. You'll probably find that you naturally assume open body positions. The fact that so many people in organizational settings adopt closed positions may indicate that many people feel at least slightly uncomfortable in school and on the job.

Knowing something about other cultures may help you realize that a subordinate who doesn't meet your eye may be showing respect rather than dishonesty. But it's impossible to memorize every meaning that every non-verbal sign has in every culture. And in a multicultural workforce, you can't know whether someone retains the meanings of his or her ancestors or has adopted mainstream Canadian meanings. The best solution is to state an observation: "I see you're wearing black." The other person's response will let you know whether the colour is a fashion statement or a sign of mourning.

The Japanese value the ability to sit quietly. They may see the tendency to fidget and shift as an indication of lack of mental or spiritual balance. Even in Canada, interviewers and audiences usually respond negatively to nervous gestures such as fidgeting with a tie or hair or jewellery, tapping a pencil, or swinging a foot.

People from different cultures learn to walk differently. Carmen Judith Nine-Curt observes that Caribbean people move the torso as though it was made up of separable parts, while North American Anglos and Northern Spaniards carry the torso as if it were one piece.[19] People from one culture often react negatively to another culture's walk. The French see the American walk as "uncivilized."[20]

Eye contact

Many Canadians see **eye contact** as a sign of honesty. But in many cultures, dropped eyes are a sign of appropriate deference to a superior. Puerto Rican children are taught not to meet the eyes of adults.[21] The Japanese are taught to look at the neck.[22] In Korea, prolonged eye contact is considered rude. The lower-ranking person is expected to look down first.[23]

Arab men in laboratory experiments looked at each other more than did two American men or two Englishmen.[24] Eye contact is so important that Arabs dislike talking to someone wearing dark glasses or while walking side by side. It is considered impolite not to face someone directly. In Muslim countries, women and men are not supposed to have eye contact.

These differences can lead to miscommunication in the multicultural workplace. Superiors may feel that subordinates are being disrespectful when the subordinate is being fully respectful—according to the norms of his or her culture.

Gestures

Canadians sometimes assume that they can depend on gestures to communicate if language fails. But Birdwhistell reported that "although we have been searching for 15 years [1950–65], we have found no gesture or body motion which has the same meaning in all societies."[25] In Bulgaria, for example, people may nod their heads to signify *no* and shake their heads to signify *yes.*[26]

Gestures that mean approval in Canada may have very different meanings in other countries. The "thumbs up" sign, which means "good work" or "go ahead" in Canada, the United States and most of Western Europe, is a vulgar insult in Greece. The circle formed with the thumb and first finger that means *OK* in Canada is obscene in Southern Italy and can mean "you're worth nothing" in France and Belgium.[27]

Space

Personal space is the distance someone wants between him- or herself and other people in ordinary, non-intimate interchanges. Observation and limited experimentation show that most North Americans, North Europeans, and Asians want a bigger personal space than do Latin Americans, French, Italians, and Arabs. People who prefer lots of personal space are often forced to accept close contact on a crowded elevator or subway.

Even within a culture, some people like more personal space than do others. One study found that men took more personal space than women did.[28] In many cultures, people who are of the same age and sex take less personal space than do mixed-age or mixed-sex groups. Latin Americans will stand closer to people of the same sex than North Americans would, but North Americans stand closer to people of the opposite sex.[29]

Touch

Repeated studies have shown that babies need to be touched to grow and thrive and that older people are healthier both mentally and physically if they are touched. But some people are more comfortable with touch than others. Each kind of person may misinterpret the other. A person who dislikes touch may seem unfriendly to someone who's used to touching. A toucher may seem overly familiar to someone who dislikes touch.

Studies in the United States have shown that touch is interpreted as power: more-powerful people touch less-powerful people. When the toucher had higher status than the recipient, both men and women liked being touched.[30]

Most parts of North America allow opposite-sex couples to hold hands or walk arm-in-arm in public but frown on the same behaviour in same-sex couples. People in Asia, the Middle East, South America, and parts of Africa have the opposite expectation: male friends or female friends can hold hands or

Global Communication Online*

The Internet makes global communication easier via e-mail, text messaging, intranets, chat rooms, and similar applications. But this technology is a true aid to communication only if its users also learn to navigate around cultural and language barriers.

Preferences vary for media choices. Canadians and Americans give high priority to reading and responding to e-mail. Japanese and Italians tend to prefer text messaging and cell phones. In Ukraine, business people expect many matters to be handled face to face, so Ukrainians might delay acting on e-mail.

Differences in business hours can interfere with the rapid feedback that Canadians and Americans expect to receive online Monday through Friday. But in Islamic countries, businesses may be closed on Fridays and open on Sundays. The standard workweek is shorter in France than in Canada and the United States. In southern Europe, many businesses close for a two-hour lunch. As with the choice of medium, the solution is to discuss and plan for such differences.

*Based on Kirk St. Amant, "Communication in International Virtual Offices," *Intercom*, April 2003, 27–28.

walk arm-in-arm, but it is slightly shocking for an opposite-sex couple to touch in public.[31]

In North America, a person sitting at the head of a table is generally assumed to be the group's leader. However, one experiment showed that when a woman sat at the head of a mixed-sex group, observers assumed that one of the men in the group was the leader.[32]

Spatial arrangements

In Canada and the United States, the size, placement, and privacy of one's office connotes status. Large corner offices have the highest status. An individual office with a door that closes connotes more status than a desk in a common area. Japanese firms, however, see private offices as "inappropriate and inefficient," reports Robert Christopher. Only the very highest executives and directors have private offices in the traditional Japanese company, and even they will also have desks in the common areas.[33]

Time

Differences in time zones complicate international phone calls. But even more important are different views of time and attitudes toward time.

Mainstream organizations in Canada—businesses, government, and schools—keep time by the calendar and the clock. Being "on time" is seen as a sign of dependability. Other cultures may keep time by the seasons and the moon, the sun, internal "body clocks," or a personal feeling that "the time is right."

Canadians who believe that "time is money" are often frustrated in negotiations with people who take a much more leisurely approach. Part of the problem is that people in many other cultures want to establish a personal relationship before they decide whether to do business with each other.

Edward T. Hall distinguishes between **monochronic cultures,** which focus on clock time, and **polychronic cultures,** which focus on relationships. When U.S. managers feel offended because a Latin American manager also sees other people during "their" appointments, the two kinds of time are in conflict.[34]

According to some scholars, Europeans schedule fewer events in a comparable period of time than do North Americans. Perhaps as a result, Germans and German Swiss see North Americans as too time conscious.[35]

Other Non-verbal Symbols

Many other symbols can carry non-verbal meanings: clothing, colours, age, and height, to name a few.

In Canada, certain styles and colours of clothing are considered more "professional" and more "credible." In Japan, clothing denotes not only status but also occupational group. Students wear uniforms. Company badges indicate rank within the organization. Workers wear different clothes when they are on strike than they do when they are working.[36]

Colours can also carry meanings in a culture. In Canada, mourners wear black to funerals, while brides wear white. In Japan, white is the colour of death. Purple flowers are given to the dead in Mexico. In Korea, red ink is used to record deaths but never to write about living people.[37] In the United States, the first-place winner gets a blue ribbon. In the United Kingdom, the first-place ribbon is usually red.

Height connotes status in many parts of the world. Executive offices are usually on the top floors; the underlings work below. Even being tall can help a person succeed. Studies have shown that employers are more willing to hire men over 6 feet tall than shorter men with the same credentials. In one study, every extra inch of height brought in an extra \$1,300 a year.[38] But being too big can be a disadvantage. One football player complained that people found him intimidating off the field and assumed that he had no brains.

Oral Communication

Effective oral communication requires cultural understanding. Learning at least a little of the language of the country where you hope to do business will help you in several ways. It will

- Give you a glimpse into the culture
- Help you manage the daily necessities of finding food and getting where you need to go
- Give you more time to think in business negotiations

If at all possible, take your own translator when you travel abroad on business. Brief him or her with the technical terms you'll be using; explain as much of the context of your negotiations as possible. A good translator can also help you interpret non-verbal behaviour and negotiating strategies.

Conversational Style

Deborah Tannen uses the term **conversational style** to denote our conversational patterns and the meaning we give to them: the way we show interest, politeness, appropriateness.[39] Your answers to the following questions reveal your own conversational style:

- How long a pause tells you that it's your turn to speak?
- Do you see interruption as rude? Or do you say things while other people are still talking to show that you're interested and to encourage them to say more?
- Do you show interest by asking lots of questions? Or do you see questions as intrusive and wait for people to volunteer whatever they have to say?

One conversational style is not better or worse than another, but people with different conversational styles may feel uncomfortable without knowing why. A subordinate who talks quickly may be frustrated by a boss who speaks slowly. People who talk more slowly may feel shut out of a conversation with people who talk more quickly. Someone who has learned to make requests directly ("Please pass the salt") may be annoyed by someone who uses indirect requests ("This casserole needs some salt").

Daniel N. Maltz and Ruth A. Borker believe that differences in conversational style (Figure 9.3) may be responsible for the miscommunication that often occurs in male–female conversations. For example, researchers have found that women are much more likely to nod and to say "yes" or "mm hmm" than men are. Maltz and Borker hypothesize that to women, these symbols mean simply "I'm listening; go on." Men, on the other hand, may decode these symbols as "I agree" or at least "I follow what you're saying so far." A man who receives nods and *mm*s from a woman may feel that she is inconsistent and unpredictable if she then disagrees with him. A woman may feel that a man who doesn't provide any feedback isn't listening to her.[40]

Those miscommunications in male-female communications impact women's careers. A survey completed by 250 business women at different career levels (ages 24 to 67) found that they are still waiting for a female-friendly workplace. Most organizations, they feel, are still designed by and for men. Survey respondents believe that men still live by the numbers, while women value relationships. Most are still "Darwinian" in their competitive culture. Most still

Thinking Outside the Timeline*

To organize a convincing argument, the typical European or North American will develop several points and present a case for them one by one. Negotiating a contract, this person might present a list of terms, such as price, quantity, and delivery date, expecting to discuss each one in turn, moving down the list.

The typical Chinese negotiator, in contrast, rarely thinks in terms of a sequence or timeline. Rather, the Chinese are more likely to engage in holistic thinking, considering all the details as part of a whole. They want to see a proposal in its full context and are likely to reconsider individual details repeatedly, as part of studying the entire proposal from various angles.

As a result of this difference, Americans negotiating with Chinese may make costly concessions. In a negotiation between Tandem Computers and China Telecom, the Tandem sales manager offered to reduce the price by 5 per cent in exchange for China Telecom's commitment to sign an order for delivery within one month. The purchasing manager responded that there was no need to rush, but since the price was flexible, the price reduction would be acceptable.

*Based on John L. Graham and N. Mark Lam, "The Chinese Negotiation," *Harvard Business Review*, October 2003, 82–91.

FIGURE 9.3   Different Conversational Styles

	Debating	Relating
Interpretation of questions	See questions as requests for information.	See questions as way to keep a conversation flowing.
Relation of new comment to what last speaker said	Do not require new comment to relate explicitly to last speaker's comment. Ignoring previous comment is one strategy for taking control.	Expect new comments to acknowledge the last speaker's comment and relate directly to it.
View of aggressiveness	See aggressiveness as one way to organize the flow of conversation.	See aggressiveness as directed at audience personally, as negative, and as disruptive to a conversation.
How topics are defined and changed	Tend to define topics narrowly and shift topics abruptly. Interpret statements about side issues as effort to change the topic.	Tend to define topics gradually, progressively. Interpret statements about side issues as effort to shape, expand, or limit the topic.
Response to someone who shares a problem	Offer advice, solutions.	Offer solidarity, reassurance. Share troubles to establish sense of community.

Sources: Based on Daniel N. Maltz and Ruth A. Borker, "A Cultural Approach to Male-Female Miscommunication," *Language and Social Identity*, ed. John J. Gumperz (Cambridge, U.K.: Cambridge University Press, 1982), 213; and Deborah Tannen, *Talking from 9 to 5: Women and Men in the Workplace: Language, Sex and Power* (New York: William Morrow, 1995).

make women feel they have to deny their femininity to fit in. Most women find a huge gap between theory and practice, and many are looking to self-employment as the answer.[41]

Silence

Silence also has different meanings in different cultures and subcultures. During a period of military tension, Greek traffic controllers responded with silence when Egyptian planes requested permission to land. The Greeks intended silence as a refusal; the Egyptians interpreted silence as consent. Several people were killed when the Greeks fired on the planes as they approached the runway.[42] Similarly, men may misunderstand women who respond to offensive remarks with silence.

Voice Qualities

Tone of voice refers to the rising or falling inflection that tells you whether a group of words is a question or a statement, whether the speaker is uncertain or confident, whether a statement is sincere or sarcastic. Anyone who has written dialogue with adverbs ("he said thoughtfully") has tried to indicate tone of voice.

When tone of voice and the meaning of words conflict, people "believe" the tone of voice. One person responded to friends' "How are you?" with the words "Dying, and you?" Most of the friends responded "Fine." Because the tone of voice was cheerful, they didn't hear the content of the words.[43]

Pitch measures whether a voice uses sounds that are low (like the bass notes on a piano) or high. Low-pitched voices are usually perceived as being more authoritative, sexier, and more pleasant to listen to than are high-pitched voices. Most voices go up in pitch when the speaker is angry or excited; some people raise pitch when they increase volume. Women whose normal speaking voices are high may need to practise projecting their voices to avoid becoming shrill when they speak to large groups.

Stress is the emphasis given to one or more words in a sentence. As the following example shows, emphasizing different words can change the meaning.

I'll give you a raise.

> [Implication, depending on pitch and speed: "Another supervisor wouldn't" or "I have the power to determine your salary."]

I'll **give** you a raise.

> [Implication, depending on pitch and speed: "You haven't **earned** it" or "OK, all right, you win. I'm saying 'yes' to get rid of you, but I don't really agree," or "I've just this instant decided that you deserve a raise."]

I'll give **you** a raise.

> [Implication: "But nobody else in this department is getting one."]

I'll give you **a** raise.

> [Implication: "But just one."]

Speakers who use many changes in tone, pitch, and stress as they speak usually seem more enthusiastic, more energetic, and more intelligent. Someone who speaks in a monotone may seem apathetic or unintelligent. Non-native speakers whose first language does not use tone, pitch, and stress to convey meaning and attitude may be misunderstood.

Volume is a measure of loudness or softness. Very soft voices, especially if they are also breathy and high pitched, give the impression of youth and inexperience. People who do a lot of speaking to large groups need to practise projecting their voices so they can increase their volume without shouting.

In some cultures, it is considered rude to shout; loud voices connote anger and imminent violence. In others, everyday conversations are loud.

Writing to International Audiences

Most cultures are more formal than Canada. When you write to international audiences, use titles, not first names; avoid contractions, slang (*goofed*), and sports metaphors (*dropped the ball, out in left field*). Do write in English unless you're extremely fluent in your reader's language. Use familiar items (*agree,* not *concur*) and specific action ones (*buy,* not *get*).

The patterns of organization that work for Canadian audiences may need to be modified in international correspondence. For most cultures, buffer negative messages and make requests more indirect. Make a special effort to avoid phrases that could seem cold and uncaring. Cultural mistakes made orally may be forgotten; those made in writing are permanently recorded.

Business people from Europe and Japan who correspond frequently with North America are beginning to adopt North American directness and patterns of organization. If you don't know your reader well, it may be safer to make your message less direct.

In international business correspondence, list the day before the month:

Not: April 8, 2000

But: 8 April 2000

In addition to attending to bias-free language (◀▥ Chapter 2), it is equally important to check for bias in the visuals that complement your text. Do the visuals represent the diversity of the organization? Of city, region, or country? Is there more than token representation of women, Aboriginal peoples, visible minorities, and people with disabilities? Is there fair representation of people of different ages? Are men in visually prominent positions and women in the background? Do the dress codes send signals about power and hierarchy?

Playing by the Rules?*

- Linda Dunkin writing on the CEO Refresher Web site (www.refresher.com) advises women to change the game and leverage the strengths of their gender: recognize leaders don't need to be heroic, understand that information is stored in databases but knowledge resides in people, build on what is there rather than focusing on what is not there, and "make character the currency of your leadership" (Schachter).

- Forty-five percent of Canada's largest companies do not have a single female director. Most boards have a single female director or have two or three women who represent fewer than one-third of the directors. "Part of the problem for women is that it is all those old guys who are the gatekeepers," says Elizabeth Watson, who has the job of finding directors for public corporations in British Columbia (Church).

*Based on Harvey Schachter, "In a man's game, women must play by own rules," *Globe Careers*, January 18, 2005, C1; Elizabeth Church, "Women still missing at the table," *The Globe and Mail*, September 26, 2003, B1–4.

Overseas, U.S. Business Women May Have the Edge*

[A] growing body of research suggest[s] that American business women abroad may actually enjoy a significant edge over their male counterparts. A study conducted last year by international staffing consultants Cornelius Grove & Associates (www.grovewell.com) concluded that women are often more "nurturing" than men, tend to form close personal connections with colleagues and clients, and are highly respected for it. In China, for example, Cornelius Grove found that a quality called *ren*—which translates loosely as warm-heartedness, benevolence, and a readiness to look out for other people's welfare—is considered essential in business leaders. . . .

"In our interviews with Japanese executives, we find that many of them would much rather work with a woman than a man," [Professor John] Graham writes. Why? "Many American men's conversational style tends toward competitiveness, even aggressiveness, and can get in the way of a free-flowing exchange of information." By contrast, the negotiating style of their female counterparts, emphasizing interpersonal warmth and willingness to listen, [is] much less disconcerting.

*Quoted from Anne Fisher, "Ask Annie: Overseas, U.S. Businesswomen May Have the Edge," *Fortune*, September 28, 1998, 304.

Check your clip art too. Watch for bias built into the representations. One study has shown that 22% of clip art files involving humans pictured women, and the majority portrayed women in traditional roles.[44] How, for example, is culture imaged in clip art? Is it reduced to the arts, to material culture, to exotic others, or what?

Learning More about Intercultural and International Business Communication

Learning to communicate with people from different backgrounds shouldn't be a matter of learning rules. Instead, use the examples in this chapter to get a sense for the kinds of factors that differ from one culture to another. Test these generalizations against your experience. And when in doubt, ask.

If we need to be sensitive to gender differences within and across cultures, the same is true of communicating with or about people with disabilities. Disabilities are mental, physical, sensory, or emotional impairments, only 20% of which are congenital in origin (nutrition, hygiene, violence, limited access to health care, and aging are other factors). Among those of working age in Canada, 14.5% have a disability.

Just as we respect the self-naming of Aboriginal peoples in Canada, so we now adopt the names people with disabilities apply to themselves. The emphasis is on the person and not the disability: on appropriate, positive, and sensitive terms that respect people's abilities. Instead of *blind person*, refer to *a person with a vision impairment*; instead of *confined to a wheelchair*, *a person who uses a wheelchair*; instead of *a victim of an accident*, *a person who sustained an accident*. In some cases a group may prefer to identify themselves as a culture (deaf culture, for example). In such cases, use the preferred term.[45]

Summary of Key Points

- **Culture** provides patterns of acceptable behaviour and beliefs.
- Cultures are logical and learned, complex and contradictory.
- The successful intercultural communicator is
    - Aware that his or her preferred values and behaviours are influenced by culture and are not necessarily "right"
    - Flexible and open to change
    - Sensitive to verbal and non-verbal behaviour
    - Aware of the values, beliefs, and practices in other cultures
    - Sensitive to differences among individuals within a culture
- In **high-context cultures,** most of the information is inferred from the context of a message; little is explicitly conveyed. In **low-context cultures,** context is less important; most information is explicitly spelled out.
- **Non-verbal communication** is communication that doesn't use words.
- Non-verbal signals can be misinterpreted just as easily as can verbal symbols (words).
- **Personal space** is the distance someone wants between him- or herself and other people in ordinary, non-intimate interchanges.
- In **monochronic** cultures, people focus on clock time. In **polychronic** cultures, people focus on relationships.
- **Conversational style** denotes our conversational patterns and the meaning we give to them: the way we show interest, politeness, and appropriateness.
- The patterns of organization that work for Canadian audiences may need to be modified in international correspondence.

CHAPTER 9   Exercises and Problems

Getting Started

9.1   Identifying Sources of Miscommunication

In each of the following situations, identify one or more ways that cultural differences may be leading to miscommunication.

1. Alan is a Canadian sales representative in Mexico. He makes appointments and is careful to be on time. But the person he's calling on is frequently late. To save time, Alan tries to get right to business. But his hosts want to talk about sightseeing and his family. Even worse, his appointments are interrupted constantly, not only by business phone calls but also by long conversations with other people and even the customers' children who come into the office. Alan's first progress report is very negative. He hasn't yet made a sale. Perhaps Mexico just isn't the right place to sell his company's products.

2. To help her company establish a presence in Japan, Susan wants to hire a local interpreter who can advise her on business customs. Kana Tomari has superb qualifications on paper. But when Susan tries to probe about her experience, Kana just says, "I will do my best. I will try very hard." She never gives details about any of the previous positions

she's held. Susan begins to wonder if the résumé is inflated, padded, or even deceptive.

3. Stan wants to negotiate a joint venture with a Chinese company. He asks Tung-Sen Lee if the Chinese people have enough discretionary income to afford his product. Mr. Lee is silent for a time, and then says, "Your product is good. People in the West must like it." Stan smiles, pleased that Mr. Lee recognizes the quality of his product, and he gives Mr. Lee a contract to sign. Weeks later, Stan still hasn't heard anything. If China is going to be so inefficient, he wonders if he really should try to do business there.

4. Elspeth is very proud of her participatory management style. On assignment in India, she is careful not to give orders but to ask for suggestions. But people rarely suggest anything. Even a formal suggestion system doesn't work. And to make matters worse, she doesn't sense the respect and camaraderie of the plant she managed in Canada. Perhaps, she decides gloomily, people in India just aren't ready for a woman boss.

E-Mail Messages

9.2   Sending a Draft to Japan

You've drafted instructions for a consumer product that will be sold in Japan. Before the text is translated, you want to find out if the pictures will be clear. So you send an e-mail to your Japanese counterpart, Takashi Haneda, asking for a response within a week.

Write an e-mail message; assume that you will send the pictures as an attachment.

9.3   Asking about Travel Arrangements

The CEO is planning a trip to visit colleagues in another country (you pick the country). As executive assistant to the CEO of your organization, it's your job to make travel plans. At this stage, you don't know anything except dates and flights. (The CEO will arrive in the country at 7 AM local time on the 28th of next month and stay for three days.) It's your job to find out what the plans are and communicate any of the CEO's requirements.

Write an e-mail message to your contact.

Hints:

- Pick a business, non-profit organization, or government agency you know something about, making assumptions about the kinds of things its executive would want to do during an international visit.

- How much international travelling does your CEO do? Has he or she ever been to this country before? What questions will he or she want answered?

Communicating at Work

9.4   Studying International Communication at Your Workplace

Does your employer buy from suppliers or sell to customers outside the country? Get a sampling of international messages, or interview managers about the problems they've encountered.

As Your Professor Directs,

a. Share your results orally with a small group of students.

b. Present your findings orally to the class.

c. Summarize your findings in a memo to your professor.

d. Join with other students in your class to write a group report.

Web Pages

9.5   Comparing Company Web Pages for Various Countries

Many multinationals have separate Web pages for their operations in various countries.

Analyze three of the country pages of a company of your choice.

■ Is a single template used for pages in different countries, or do the basic designs differ?

■ Are different images used in different countries? What do the images suggest?

■ If you can read the language, analyze the links. What information is emphasized?

■ To what extent are the pages similar? To what extent do they reveal national and cultural differences?

As Your Professor Directs,

a. Write a memo analyzing the similarities and differences you find. Attach printouts of the pages to your memo.

b. Post a message to the class analyzing the pages. Include the URLs as hotlinks.

c. Make an oral presentation to the class. Paste the Web pages into PowerPoint slides.

d. Join with a small group of students to create a group report comparing several companies' Web pages in three specific countries. Attach printouts of the pages.

e. Make a group oral presentation to the class.

Memo, Brochure, and Report Assignments

9.6   Planning a Business Trip

Assume that you're going to Iqaluit, NU, or the capital city of another country on business two months from now. (You pick the country.) Use a search engine to find out

■ What holidays will be celebrated in that month.

■ What the climate will be.

■ What current events are in the news.

■ What key features of business etiquette you should know.

■ What kinds of gifts you should bring to your hosts.

■ What sight-seeing you should try to include.

As Your Professor Directs,

a. Write a memo to your professor reporting the information you found.

b. Post a message to the class analyzing the pages. Include the URLs as hotlinks.

c. Make an oral presentation to the class.

d. Join with a small group of students to create a group report on several countries in a region.

e. Make a group oral presentation to the class.

9.7   Recommending a Candidate for an Overseas Position

Your company sells customized computer systems to large and small businesses around the world. The Executive Committee needs to recommend someone to begin a three-year term as manager of Eastern European Marketing.

As Your Professor Directs,

a. Write a memo to each of the candidates, specifying the questions you would like each to answer in a final interview.

b. Assume that it is not possible to interview the candidates. Use the information here to write a memo to the CEO recommending a candidate.

c. Write a memo to the CEO recommending the best way to prepare the person chosen for his or her assignment.

d. Write a memo to the CEO recommending a better way to choose candidates for international assignments.

e. Write a memo to your professor explaining the assumptions you made about the company and the candidates that influenced your recommendation(s).

Information about the Candidates:

All the candidates have applied for the position and say they are highly interested in it.

1. **Deborah Gere,** 39, Euro-Canadian, single. Employed by the company for eight years in the Toronto and Calgary offices. Currently in the Calgary office as assistant marketing manager; successful. University of Toronto MBA. Speaks Russian fluently; has translated for business negotiations that led to the setting up of the Moscow office. Good technical knowledge, acceptable managerial skills, excellent communication skills, good interpersonal skills. Excellent health; excellent emotional stability. Swims. One child, age 12. Lived in the then–Soviet Union for one year as an exchange student in university; business and personal travel in Europe.

2. **Claude Chabot,** 36, French, single. Employed by the company for 11 years in the Paris and London offices. Currently in the Paris office as assistant sales manager for the European Economic Community; successful. No MBA, but degrees from MIT in the United States and l'Ecole Supérieure de Commerce de Paris. Speaks native French; speaks English and

Italian fluently; speaks some German. Good technical knowledge, excellent managerial skills, acceptable communication skills, excellent interpersonal skills. Excellent health, good emotional stability. Plays tennis. No children. French citizen; lived in the United States for two years, in London for five years (one year in university, four years in the London office). Extensive business and personal travel in Europe.

3. **Linda Moss,** 35, Jamaican Canadian, married. Employed by the company for 10 years in the Atlanta and Toronto offices. Currently assistant manager of Canadian Marketing; very successful. York University MBA. Speaks some French. Good technical knowledge, excellent managerial skills, excellent communication skills, excellent interpersonal skills. Excellent health; excellent emotional stability. Does Jazzercise classes. Husband is an executive at a U.S. company in Detroit; he plans to stay in the States with their children, ages 11 and 9. The couple plans to commute every two to six weeks. Has lived in Toronto for five years; business travel in North America; personal travel in Europe and Latin America.

4. **Steven Hsu,** 42, of Asian Canadian descent, married. Employed by the company for 18 years in the Vancouver office. Currently marketing manager, Western Canada; very successful. UBC MBA. Speaks some Korean. Excellent technical knowledge, excellent managerial skills, good communication skills, excellent interpersonal skills. Good health, excellent emotional stability. Plays golf. Wife is an engineer who plans to do consulting work in eastern Europe. Children ages 8, 5, and 2. Has not lived outside Canada; personal travel in Europe and Asia.

Your committee has received this memo from the CEO.

To:	Executive Committee
From:	Ed Conzachi *ERC*
Subject:	Choosing a Manager for the New Eastern European Office

Please write me a memo recommending the best candidate for manager of East European Marketing. In your memo, tell me whom you're choosing and why; also explain why you have rejected the unsuccessful candidates.

This person will be assuming a three-year appointment, with the possibility of re-appointment. The company will pay moving and relocation expenses for the manager and his or her family.

The Eastern European division currently is the smallest of the company's international divisions. However, this area is poised for growth. The new manager will supervise the Moscow office and establish branch offices as needed.

The committee has invited comments from everyone in the company. You've received these memos.

To: Executive Committee

From: Robert Osborne, Canadian Marketing Manager   *RO*

Subject: Recommendation for Steve Hsu

Steve Hsu would be a great choice to head up the new Moscow office. In the past seven years, Steve has increased sales in the Western Region by 15%—in spite of recessions, floods, and fires. He has a low-key, participative style that brings out the best in subordinates. Moreover, Steve is a brilliant computer programmer. He probably understands our products better than any other marketing or salesperson in the company.

Steve is clearly destined for success in headquarters. This assignment will give him the international experience he needs to move up to the next level of executive success.

To: Executive Committee

From: Becky Exter, Equity Officer   *RRE*

Subject: Hiring the New Manager for East European Marketing

Please be sensitive to equity concerns. The company has a very good record of appointing women and minorities to key positions in the United States and Canada; so far our record in our overseas divisions has been less effective.

In part, perhaps, that may stem from a perception that women and minorities will not be accepted in countries less open than our own. But the experience of several multi-national firms has been that even exclusionary countries will accept people who have the full backing of their countries. Another concern may be that it will be harder for women to establish a social support system abroad. However, different individuals have different ways of establishing support. To assume that the best candidate for an international assignment is a male with a stay-at-home wife is discriminatory and may deprive our company of the skills of some of its best people.

We have several qualified women and minority candidates. I urge you to consider their credentials carefully.

To: Executive Committee   *WED*

From: William E. Dortch, Marketing Manager, European Economic Community

Subject: Recommendation for Debbie Gere

Debbie Gere would be my choice to head the new Moscow office. As you know, I recommended that Europe be divided and that we establish an Eastern European division. Of all the people who have worked on the creation of the new division, Debbie is the best. The negotiations were often complex. Debbie's knowledge of the language and culture was invaluable. She's done a good job in the Calgary office and is ready for wider responsibilities. Eastern Europe is a challenging place, but Debbie can handle the pressure and help us gain the foothold we need.

> To: Ed Conzachi, President
>
> From: Pierre Garamond, Sales Representative,
>   European Economic Community   *PG*
>
> Subject: Recommendation for Claude Chabot
>
> Claude Chabot would be the best choice for Manager of Eastern European Marketing. He is a superb supervisor, motivating us to the highest level of achievement. He understands the complex legal and cultural nuances of selling our products in Europe as only a native can. He also has the budgeting and managerial skills to oversee the entire marketing effort.
>
> You are aware that the company's record of sending Canadian citizens to head international divisions is not particularly good. European Marketing is an exception, but our records in the Middle East and Japan have been poor. The company would gain stability by appointing Europeans to head European offices, Asians to head Asian offices, and so forth. Such people would do a better job of managing and motivating staffs that will comprise primarily nationals in the country where the office is located. Ending the practice of reserving the top jobs for Canadian citizens would also send a message to international employees that they are valued and that they have a future with this company.

> To: Executive Committee
>
> From: Elaine Crispell, Manager, Canadian Marketing   *EC*
>
> Subject: Recommendation for Linda Moss
>
> Linda Moss has done well as assistant manager for the last two and a half years. She is a creative, flexible problem solver. Her productivity is the highest in the office. Though she could be called a "workaholic," she is a warm, caring human being.
>
> As you know, the Canadian division includes French-Speaking Montreal and a large Aboriginal population; furthermore, Toronto is an international and intercultural city. Linda has gained intercultural competence both on a personal and professional level.
>
> Linda has the potential to be our first woman CEO 15 years down the road. She needs more international experience to be competitive at that level. This would be a good opportunity for her, and she would do well for the company.

9.8   Answering an Inquiry about Photos

You've just been named vice-president for diversity, the first person in your organization to hold this position. Today, you receive this memo from Sheila Lathan, who edits the employee newsletter.

Subject: Photos in the Employee Newsletter

Please tell me what to do about photos in the monthly employee newsletter. I'm concerned that almost no single issue represents the diversity of employees we have here.

As you know, our layout allows two visuals each month. One of those is always the employee of the month (EM). In the last year, most of those have been male and all but two have been white. What makes it worse is that people want photos that make them look good. In the photo EM Ron Almos wanted me to use, you can't tell that he's in a wheelchair. Often the EM is the only photo; the other visual is often a graph of sales or something relating to quality.

Even if the second visual is another photo, it may not look balanced in terms of gender and race. After all, 62% of our employees are men, and 78% are white. Should the pictures try to represent those percentages? The leadership positions (both in management and in the union) are even more heavily male and white. Should we run pictures of people doing important things, and risk continuing the imbalance?

I guess I could use more visuals, but then there wouldn't be room for as many stories—and people really like to see their names in print. Plus, giving people information about company activities and sales is important to maintaining goodwill. A bigger newsletter would be one way to have more visuals and keep the content, but with the cost-cutting measures we're under, that doesn't look likely.

What should I do?

As Your Professor Directs,

a.   Work in a small group with other students to come up with a recommendation for Sheila.

b.   Write a memo responding to her.

c.   Write an article for the employee newsletter about the photo policy you recommend and how it relates to the company's concern for diversity.

10 Working and Writing in Groups

- ■ Listening
- ■ Group Interactions
- ■ Conflict Resolution
- ■ Effective Meetings

- ■ Collaborative Writing
- ■ Making the Group Process Work
- ■ Summary of Key Points

AN INSIDE PERSPECTIVE

Working and Writing in Groups

Current trends in business (see ◄▦ Chapter 1) from technology and globalization to outsourcing have made even more important another trend: team or group work. If globalization has made teamwork more necessary, technology has enabled the trend. More and more routine projects from planning and research to proposal and report writing are accomplished by teams.

Businesses and organizations invest in teams because they see in them the potential for these outcomes:

- ■ Improved information sharing and creativity
- ■ Better decision making
- ■ Efficient preparation of documents
- ■ Buy-in
- ■ Increased appreciation of others
- ■ Enhanced morale

From sports to software, former University of Saskatchewan Huskie athletes Dan and Garnette Weber have proven as successful in entrepreneurship as in athletics. Owners of Itracks, they have made an international name for themselves in online market research. Their online data collections solutions are supported by a team of experts in Canada and elsewhere.

www.itracks.com

Teams that work effectively together are therefore a valuable resource in businesses today.

While teams bring many strengths, different perspectives, and complementary skills and talents to the task, they can also bring tensions and conflict. Building the trust needed to succeed in teamwork—whether working in close physical proximity or at the opposite ends of the globe—takes careful preparation and planning, well-defined goals, clear lines of authority, cultural competence, and strong interpersonal and constructive communication skills.

Technology and teamwork support the sort of custom research, online data collection, focus groups, bulletin boards, and surveys that Itracks provides for professional marketing researchers. Whether they are producing quantitative research reaching thousands of participants to support polling organizations or qualitative research involving small focus groups, the Internet and a well-coordinated team are key to Itracks success.

Leading by Listening*

According to business psychologist Debra Condren, the best way to help employees develop their skills is not to give them advice. Rather, managers should coach employees by listening to them.

Condren says that in meetings aimed at mentoring employees, the manager's role should primarily involve listening actively. The manager should talk only about one-quarter of the time.

Managers can help employees think through problems by asking questions that lead them through a decision-making process. For example, the manager can ask, "What would be the advantages and disadvantages of telling the customer what you're telling me? How do you think the customer would respond?" and "Would those benefits outweigh the risks?"

Listening and asking occasional questions helps employees learn to think through problems. In the end, that decision-making skill is more significant than a supply of easy answers from the manager.

*Based on "Better Feedback," *Sales & Marketing Management*, December 2003.

Teamwork is crucial to success in an organization. Some teams produce products, provide services, or recommend solutions to problems. Other teams—perhaps in addition to providing a service or recommending a solution—also produce documents.

Interpersonal communication is communication between people. Interpersonal skills such as listening and dealing with conflict are used in one-to-one interchanges, in problem-solving groups, and in writing groups. These skills will make you more successful on the job, in social groups, and in community service and volunteer work. A focus on quality and customer needs (◀ Chapter 1) explains some of their importance to the Conference Board of Canada (◀ p. 25). In writing groups, giving careful attention to both group process and writing process (◀ p. 64) improves both the final product and members' satisfaction with the group.

Listening

Listening, crucial to building trust, is a learned skill that takes time and energy. However, listening on the job may be more difficult than listening in classes. Many classroom lectures are well organized, with signposts and repetition of key points to help hearers follow. But conversations usually wander. In interchanges with friends and co-workers, you need to listen for feelings, too. Feelings of being rejected or overworked need to be dealt with as they arise. But you can't deal with a feeling unless you are aware of it.

As ◀ Chapter 1 explains, to receive a message, the receiver must first perceive the message, then decode it (that is, translate the symbols into meaning), and then interpret it. In interpersonal communication, **hearing** denotes perceiving sounds. **Listening** means decoding and interpreting them correctly.

In other words, hearing and listening are not the same. Whereas hearing can be involuntary (overhearing a conversation among colleagues), listening requires

- A conscious choice
- A positive attitude and openness
- Attention to verbal and non-verbal cues and context

Although many associate listening with passivity and inaction, listening requires mental activity and physical energy. We learn about our culture, about our selves, and about thinking by listening. Workers typically spend 30–45% of their communication time listening; executives spend 60–70% of theirs.[1]

People in low-context cultures (◀ Chapter 9) may find themselves wanting to get down to business and therefore impatient of the demands of listening, especially when we can process what we hear (1,000–3,000 words per minute) far more quickly than people can typically speak (125–250 words per minute). These listening facts go a long way to explaining why we are not very good listeners, forgetting as much as 50% of what we hear immediately after listening.[2]

Take notes when you can. In addition, to avoid **polite listening** that is mechanical and inattentive, try these strategies:

- Make a list of the questions you have. When is the project due? What resources do you have? What is the most important aspect of this project, from the other person's point of view? During a conversation, listen for answers to your questions.
- At the end of the conversation, check your understanding with the other person. Especially check who does what next.
- After the conversation, write down key points that affect deadlines or how work will be evaluated.

Many listening errors are errors in interpretation. In 1977 when two Boeing 747 jumbo jets ran into each other on the ground in Tenerife, the pilots seemed to have heard the control tower's instructions. The KLM pilot was told to taxi to the end of the runway, turn around, and wait for clearance. But the KLM pilot didn't interpret the order to wait as an order he needed to follow. The Pan Am pilot interpreted *his* order to turn off at the "third intersection" to mean the third *unblocked* intersection. He didn't count the first blocked ramp, so he was still on the main runway when the KLM pilot ran into his plane. The planes exploded in flames; 576 people died.[3]

Listening to people is an indication that you're taking them seriously. **Acknowledgment responses**—nods, *uh huhs,* smiles, frowns—help carry the message that you're listening.

In **active listening,** receivers actively demonstrate that they've heard and understood a speaker by feeding back either the literal meaning or the emotional content or both. Five strategies create active responses:

- Paraphrase the content. Feed back the meaning in your own words.
- Mirror the speaker's feelings. Identify the feelings you think you hear.
- State your own feelings. This strategy works especially well when you are angry.
- Ask for information or clarification.
- Offer to help solve the problem.

Instead of simply mirroring what the other person says, many of us immediately respond in a way that analyzes or attempts to solve or dismiss the problem. People with problems need first of all to know that we hear that they're having a rough time. Figure 10.1 lists some of the responses that block communication.

Active listening takes time and energy. Even people who are skilled active listeners can't do it all the time. Furthermore, active listening works only if you genuinely accept the other person's ideas and feelings. Active listening can reduce the conflict that results from miscommunication, but it alone cannot reduce the

InSite

www.listencoach.com/
LH Profile.html

Test your listening habits.

FIGURE 10.1 Blocking Responses versus Active Listening

Blocking response	**Possible active response**
Ordering, threatening	**Paraphrasing content**
"I don't care how you do it. Just get that report on my desk by Friday."	"You're saying that you don't have time to finish the report by Friday."
Preaching, criticizing	**Mirroring feelings**
"You should know better than to air the department's problems in a general meeting."	"It sounds like the department's problems really bother you."
Interrogating	**Stating one's own feelings**
"Why didn't you *tell* me that you didn't understand the instructions?"	"I'm frustrated that the job isn't completed yet, and I'm worried about getting it done on time."
Minimizing the problem	**Asking for information or clarification**
"You think *that's* bad. You should see what *I* have to do this week."	"What parts of the problem seem most difficult to solve?"
Advising	**Offering to help solve the problem together**
"Well, why don't you try listing everything you have to do and seeing which items are most important?"	"Is there anything I could do that would help?"

Source: The 5 responses that block communication are based on a list of 12 in Thomas Gordon and Judith Gordon Sands, *P.E.T. in Action* (New York: Wyden, 1976), 117–18.

conflict that comes when two people want apparently inconsistent things or when one person wants to change someone else.[4]

Group Interactions

Groups can focus on three different dimensions.

1. **Informational messages** focus on content: the problem, data, and possible solutions.
2. **Procedural messages** focus on method and process. How will the group make decisions? Who will do what? When will assignments be due?
3. **Interpersonal messages** focus on people, promoting friendliness, co-operation, and group loyalty.

Different kinds of communication dominate during the four stages of the life of a task group: orientation, formation, coordination, and formalization.[5]

During **orientation,** when members meet and begin to define their task, groups need to develop some sort of social cohesiveness and to develop procedures for meeting and acting. Interpersonal and procedural comments reduce the tension that always exists in a new group. Insistence on information in this first stage can hurt the group's long-term productivity.

Groups are often most effective when they explicitly adopt ground rules. Figure 10.2 lists some of the most common ground rules used by workplace teams.

During **formation,** conflicts almost always arise when the group chooses a leader and defines the problem. Successful leaders make the procedure clear so that each member knows what he or she is supposed to do. Interpersonal communication is needed to resolve the conflict that surfaces during this phase. Successful groups analyze the problem carefully before they begin to search for solutions.

Coordination is the longest phase and the phase during which most of the group's work is done. While procedural and interpersonal comments help maintain direction and friendliness, most of the comments need to deal with

FIGURE 10.2	Possible Group Ground Rules

- Start on time; end on time.
- Come to the meeting prepared.
- Focus comments on the issues.
- Avoid personal attacks.
- Listen to and respect members' opinions.
- Practise NOSTUESO (No One Speaks Twice Until Everybody Speaks Once)
- If you have a problem with another person, tell that person, not everyone else.
- Ensure that everyone is 70% comfortable with the decision and 100% committed to implementing it.
- If you agree to do something, do it.
- Communicate immediately if you think you may not be able to fulfill an agreement.

Sources: Nancy Schullery and Beth Hoger, "Business Advocacy for Students in Small Groups," Association for Business Communication Annual Convention, San Antonio, November 9–11, 1998; "An Antidote to Chronic Cantankerousness," *Fast Company,* February/March 1998, 176; John Grossmann, "We've Got to Start Meeting Like This," *Inc.,* April 1998, 70; Gary Dessler, *Winning Commitment,* quoted in *Team Management Briefings,* preview issue (September 1998), 5; and 3M Meeting Network, "Groundrules and Agreements," www.3M.com/ meetingnetwork/readingroom/meetingguide_grndrules.html (September 25, 2001).

information. Good information is essential to a good decision. Conflict occurs as the group debates alternate solutions.

In **formalization,** the group seeks consensus. The success of this phase determines how well the group's decision will be implemented. In this stage, the group seeks to forget earlier conflicts.

Roles in Groups

Individual members can play several roles in groups. These roles can be positive or negative.

Positive roles and actions that help the group achieve its task goals include the following:[6]

- **Seeking information and opinions**—asking questions, identifying gaps in the group's knowledge.
- **Giving information and opinions**—answering questions, providing relevant information.
- **Summarizing**—restating major points, pulling ideas together, summarizing decisions.
- **Evaluating**—comparing group processes and products to standards and goals.
- **Coordinating**—planning work, giving directions, and fitting together contributions of group members.

Positive roles and actions that help the group build loyalty, resolve conflicts, and function smoothly include the following:

- **Encouraging participation**—demonstrating openness and acceptance, recognizing the contributions of members, calling on quieter group members.
- **Relieving tensions**—joking and suggesting breaks and fun activities.
- **Checking feelings**—asking members how they feel about group activities and sharing one's own feelings with others.
- **Solving interpersonal problems**—opening discussion of interpersonal problems in the group and suggesting ways to solve them.
- **Listening actively**—showing group members that they have been heard and that their ideas are being taken seriously.

Negative roles and actions that hurt the group's product and process include the following:

- **Blocking**—disagreeing with everything that is proposed.
- **Dominating**—trying to run the group by ordering, shutting out others, and insisting on one's own way.
- **Clowning**—making unproductive jokes and diverting the group from the task.
- **Withdrawing**—being silent in meetings, not contributing, not helping with the work, not attending meetings.

Some actions can be positive or negative depending on how they are used. Criticizing ideas is necessary if the group is to produce the best solution, but criticizing every idea raised without ever suggesting possible solutions blocks a group. Jokes in moderation can defuse tension and make the group more fun; too many can make the work more difficult.

Leadership in Groups

You may have noted that "leader" was not one of the roles listed above. Being a leader does *not* mean doing all the work yourself. Indeed, someone who

Conducting a Meeting*

The example of an orchestra shows that successful meetings require thorough planning and full participation:

"You enter the orchestra hall and pick up the program. It is blank—there is no set of pieces for the evening on the program. The orchestra is about to begin when the maestro strides out. He says, 'Ladies and gentlemen, you'll notice there are no pieces on the program. The reason for that is that we didn't know what you'd want to hear until you got here, and we wanted to leave room for openness and audience participation. Therefore, if you'll shout out the pieces you want to hear we'll do our best to play them.'

"Someone shouts out, 'Beethoven's Ninth is my favourite.'

"The maestro replies, 'That's really too bad. We don't happen to have a chorus handy. Gosh, if we'd known you wanted Beethoven's Ninth, we would have brought our chorus along. . . .'

"More pieces are shouted out, until finally, after about an hour and a half of chaotic activity the maestro announces, 'Ladies and gentlemen, thank you. We have the pieces that you want to hear that we can play. However, . . . I've been informed that the oboist needs to leave to catch a plane to get to her next performance. Therefore, we've asked the oboist to play all the oboe notes right now. Then, as you hear the piece, you yourself can insert them back in where they belong. Thanks for your cooperation.'"

*Quoted from John E. Tropman, *Making Meetings Work: Achieving High Quality Group Decisions*, 2nd ed. (Thousand Oaks, CA: Sage, 2003), 14.

**Evaluating
Teams***

　　[A]t Con-Way
Transportation Services, . . .
teams evaluate *themselves*
through a process called the
Team Improvement Review
(TIR). . . .

　The groups often bring in a
neutral facilitator who leads the
discussions.

　The reviews happen about
every three months. A week
before the TIR meeting,
participants rate team
performance on a 1-to-5 scale
for 31 criteria.

　During the meeting, people
discuss the team's
performance as well as
individual performance in the
context of the team. . . .

　[T]o keep the discussions
focused on performance rather
than on personality [, . . . the
team uses techniques such as]
the Round Robin. Each person
creates two columns on a sheet
of paper, one labelled
"Strengths" and the other
"Something to Work On." Then
each person lists all the
strengths that he or she brings
to the team as well as one thing
to work on. The papers get
passed around the room, and
each team member comments
on everyone else's forms.

*Quoted from "How Con-Way
Reviews Teams," *Fast Company*,
September 1998, 152.

implies that he or she has the best ideas and can do the best work is likely playing the negative roles of blocking and dominating.

Effective groups balance three kinds of leadership:

- Informational leaders generate and evaluate ideas and text.

- Interpersonal leaders monitor the group's process, check people's feelings, and resolve conflicts.

- Procedural leaders set the agenda, make sure that everyone knows what's due for the next meeting, communicate with absent group members, and check to be sure that assignments are carried out.

While it's possible for one person to perform all of these responsibilities, some groups formally or informally rotate or share these responsibilities, so that everyone—and no one—is a leader.

Several studies have shown people who talk a lot, listen effectively, and respond non-verbally to other members in the group are considered to be leaders.[7]

Decision-making Strategies

Probably the least effective decision-making strategy is to let the person who talks first, last, loudest, or most determine the decision.

Voting is quick but may leave people in the minority unhappy with and uncommitted to the majority's plan.

Coming to consensus takes time but results in speedier implementation of ideas as well as greater satisfaction and agreement. Allowing the majority view to prevail means that more people take ownership of the decision, and people are not left feeling like losers.

Two useful strategies are the standard agenda and dot planning.

The **standard agenda** is a seven-step process for solving problems:

1. Understand what the group has to deliver, in what form, by what due date. Identify available resources.
2. Identify the problem. What exactly is wrong? What question(s) is the group trying to answer?
3. Gather information, share it with all group members, and examine it critically.
4. Establish criteria. What would the ideal solution include? What would be a less-than-ideal but still acceptable solution? What legal, financial, moral, or other limitations might keep a solution from being implemented?
5. Generate alternate solutions. Brainstorm and record ideas for the next step.
6. Measure the alternatives against the criteria.
7. Choose the best solution.[8]

Dot planning offers a way for large groups to choose priorities quickly. First, the group brainstorms ideas, recording each on pages that are put on the wall. Then each individual gets two strips of three to five adhesive dots in different colours. One colour represents high priority, the other lower priority. People then walk up to the pages and affix dots by the points they care most about. Some groups allow only one dot from one person on any one item; others allow someone who is really passionate about an idea to put all of his or her dots on it.

Successful Student Groups

A case study of six student groups completing class projects found that students in successful and less successful groups communicated differently in three ways.[9]

First, in the successful groups, the leader set clear deadlines, scheduled frequent meetings, and dealt directly with conflict that emerged in the group.

Second, the successful groups listened to criticism and made important decisions together. Perhaps as a result, everyone in the group could articulate the group's goals. In the less successful groups, a subgroup made decisions and told other members what had been decided.

Third, the successful groups had a higher proportion of members who worked actively on the project. The less successful groups had a much smaller percentage of active members and each had some members who did very little on the final project.

Student groups produce better documents when they disagree over substantive issues of content and document design. The disagreement does not need to be angry: a group member can simply say, "Yes, and here's another way we could do it." Deciding among two (or more) alternatives forces the proposer to explain the rationale for an idea. Even when the group adopts the original idea, considering alternatives rather than quickly accepting the first idea produces better writing.[10]

The students who spent the most time meeting with their groups had the highest grades—on their individual as well as on group assignments.[11]

Peer Pressure and Groupthink

Groups that never express conflict may be experiencing groupthink. **Groupthink** is the tendency for groups to put such a high premium on agreement that they directly or indirectly punish dissent.

Many people feel so much reluctance to express open disagreement that they will say they agree even when objective circumstances would suggest the first speaker cannot be right.

Groups that "go along with the crowd" and suppress conflict ignore the full range of alternatives, seek only information that supports the positions they already favour, and fail to prepare contingency plans to cope with foreseeable setbacks. A business suffering from groupthink may launch a new product that senior executives support but for which there is no demand. Student groups suffering from groupthink turn in inferior documents because they miss opportunities to rethink and revise.

The best correctives to groupthink are to consciously search for additional alternatives, to test one's assumptions against those of a range of other people, and to protect the right of people in a group to disagree.

Working in Diverse Groups

Even people who come from the same part of the country and who have the same jobs may differ in personality type. Savvy group members play to each other's strengths and devise strategies for dealing with differences.

In addition, differences arise from gender, class, race and ethnicity, religion, age, sexual orientation, and physical ability. A growing body of literature shows that ethnically diverse teams produce more and higher-quality ideas.[12]

One problem with our awareness of difference, however, is that when someone feels shut out, he or she can attribute the negative interaction to prejudice, when other factors may be responsible. Conversational style and non-verbal communication are two of the areas that may cause miscommunication (see pp. 215–221).

Conflict Resolution

Conflicts will arise in any group of people who care about the task. Yet many of us feel so uncomfortable with conflict that we pretend it doesn't exist. However,

Power Talk*

A person who feels confident and in control will speak at length, set the agenda for a conversation, stave off interruptions, argue openly, make jokes, and laugh. Such a person is more inclined to make statements, less inclined to ask questions. They are more likely to offer solutions or a program or a plan. . . .

The power deficient drop into conversations, encourage other speakers, ask numerous questions, avoid argument, and rely on gestures such as smiling and nodding that suggest agreement. They tend to offer empathy rather than solutions. They often use unfinished sentences. . . .

The key is figuring out who gets listened to within your corporate culture. That can make you a more savvy user of language. Try to sit in on a meeting as a kind of researcher, observing conversational patterns. . . . Then try to determine who gets noticed and why.

*Quoted from Sarah McGinty, "How You Speak Shows Where You Rank," *Fortune*, February 2, 1998, 156.

Who Does
What

Working successfully in a group depends on being open about preferences, constraints, and skills and then using creative problem-solving techniques.

A person who prefers to outline the whole project in advance may be in a group with someone who expects to do the project at the last minute. Someone who likes to talk out ideas before writing may be in a group with someone who wants to work on a draft in silence and revise it before showing it to anyone. By being honest about your preferences, you make it possible for the group to find a creative solution that builds on what each person can offer.

In one group, Rob wanted to wait to start the project because he was busy with other class work. Mohammed and Natalia, however, wanted to go ahead now because their schedules would get busier later in the term. A creative solution would be for Mohammed and Natalia to do most of the work on parts of the project that had to be completed first (such as collecting data and writing the proposal) and for Rob to do work that had to be done later (such as revising, editing, and proofreading).

unacknowledged conflicts rarely go away: they fester, making the next interchange more difficult.

To reduce the number of conflicts in a group,

- Make responsibilities and ground rules clear at the beginning.
- Discuss problems as they arise, rather than letting them fester till people explode.
- Realize that group members are not responsible for each others' happiness.

Once a conflict arises, groups may need to reopen discussions about responsibilities and confront a troublesome group member.[13]

Figure 10.3 suggests several possible solutions to conflicts that student groups often experience. Often the symptom arises from a feeling of not being respected or appreciated by the group. Therefore, many problems can be averted if people advocate for their ideas in a positive way. A tactful way to advocate for the position you favour is to recognize the contributions others have made, to summarize, and then to hypothesize: "What if . . . ?" "Let's look six months down the road." "Let's think about *x*."[14]

Just as resolving conflict depends on identifying the needs each person is trying to meet, so dealing with criticism depends on understanding the real concern of the critic. Constructive ways to respond to criticism and get closer to the real concern include paraphrasing, checking for feelings, checking inferences, and including good you-attitude.

Paraphrasing

To **paraphrase,** repeat in your own words the verbal content of the critic's message. The purposes of paraphrasing are (1) to be sure that you have heard the critic accurately, (2) to let the critic know what his or her statement means to you, and (3) to communicate the feeling that you are taking the critic and his or her feelings seriously.

Criticism: You guys are stonewalling my requests for information.

Paraphrase: You think that we don't give you the information you need quickly enough.

Checking for feelings

The purposes of checking feelings are to try to understand (1) the critic's emotions, (2) the importance of the criticism for the critic, and (3) the unspoken ideas and feelings that may actually be more important than the voiced criticism.

Criticism: You guys are stonewalling my requests for information.

Feeling check: You sound pretty angry.

Always *ask* the other person if you are right in your perception. Even the best reader of non-verbal cues is sometimes wrong.

Checking for inferences

When you check the inferences you draw from criticism, you identify the implied meaning of the verbal and non-verbal content of the criticism and try to understand *why* the critic is bothered. The purposes of checking inferences are (1) to identify the real (as opposed to the presenting) problem and (2) to communicate the feeling that you care about resolving the conflict.

Criticism: You guys are stonewalling my requests for information.

Inference: Are you saying that you need more information from our group?

FIGURE 10.3   Troubleshooting Group Problems

Symptom	Possible solutions
We can't find a time to meet that works for all of us.	a. Find out why people can't meet at certain times. Some reasons suggest their own solutions. For example, if someone has to stay home with small children, perhaps the group could meet at that person's home. b. Assign out-of-class work to "committees" to work on parts of the project. c. Use e-mail to share, discuss, and revise drafts.
One person isn't doing his or her fair share.	a. Find out what is going on. Is the person overcommitted? Does he or she feel unappreciated? Those are different problems you'd solve in different ways. b. Early on, do things to build group loyalty. Get to know each other as writers and as people. Sometimes, do something fun together. c. Encourage the person to contribute. "Athina, what do you think?" "Kyle, which part of this would you like to draft?" Then find something to praise in the work. "Thanks for getting us started." d. If someone misses a meeting, assign someone else to bring the person up to speed. People who miss meetings for legitimate reasons (job interviews, illness) but don't find out what happened may become less committed to the group. e. Consider whether strict equality is the most important criterion. On a given project, some people may have more knowledge or time than others. Sometimes the best group product results from letting people do different amounts of "work." f. Even if you divide up the work, make all decisions as a group: what to write about, which evidence to include, what graphs to use, what revisions to make. People excluded from decisions become less committed to the group.
I seem to be the only one in the group who cares about quality.	a. Find out why other members "don't care." If they received low grades on early assignments, stress that good ideas and attention to detail can raise grades. Perhaps the group should meet with the professor to discuss what kinds of work will pay the highest dividends. b. Volunteer to do extra work. Sometimes people settle for something that's just OK because they don't have the time or resources to do excellent work. They might be happy for the work to be done—if they didn't have to do it. c. Be sure that you're respecting what each person can contribute. Group members sometimes withdraw when one person dominates and suggests that he or she is "better" than other members.
People in the group don't seem willing to disagree. We end up going with the first idea suggested.	a. Appoint someone to be a devil's advocate. b. Brainstorm so you have several possibilities to consider. c. After an idea is suggested, have each person in the group suggest a way it could be improved. d. Have each person in the group write a draft. It's likely the drafts will be different, and you'll have several options to mix and match. e. Talk about good ways to offer criticism. Sometimes people don't disagree because they're afraid that other group members won't tolerate disagreement.
One person criticizes everything.	a. Ask the person to follow up the criticism with a suggestion for improvement. b. Talk about ways to express criticism tactfully. "I think we need to think about x" is more tactful than "You're wrong." c. If the criticism is about ideas and writing (not about people), value it. Ideas and documents need criticism if we are to improve them.

Inferences can be faulty. In the above interchange, the critic might respond, "I don't need *more* information. I just think you should give it to me without my having to file three forms in triplicate every time I want some data."

Including you-attitude

You-attitude means looking at things from the audience's point of view, respecting the audience, and protecting the audience's ego. The *you* statements that many people use when they're angry attack the audience; they do not illustrate you-attitude. Instead, substitute statements about your own feelings. In conflict, *I* statements show good you-attitude!

Lacks you-attitude:	You never do your share of the work.
You-attitude:	I feel that I'm doing more than my share of the work on this project.
Lacks you-attitude:	Even you should be able to run the report through a spell-checker.
You-attitude:	I'm not willing to have my name on a report with so many spelling errors. I did lots of the writing, and I don't think I should have to do the proofreading and spell checking, too.

Effective Meetings

Meetings have always taken a large part of the average manager's week. Although e-mail has eliminated some meetings, the increased number of teams means that meetings are even more frequent.

Although managers can spend as much as one-quarter of their time in meetings, studies suggest that at least half of meeting time is wasted. A 2005 Microsoft online office survey of 38,000 people in 200 countries found "unclear objectives, lack of team communication and ineffective meetings" topped the list of time-wasters.[15] Indeed, according to management consultant Frank Buchar, "Meeting management is the single most underdeveloped skill in North America." Buchar recommends matching meeting format and size to meeting purpose, bold leadership and member engagement, and facilitation tools (labelling, categorizing, and organizing) involving and equalizing participation.[16]

Meetings can have any of at least six purposes:

- To share information
- To brainstorm ideas
- To evaluate ideas
- To make decisions
- To create a document
- To motivate members

When meetings combine two or more purposes, it's useful to make the purposes explicit. For example, in the meeting of a university senate or a company's board of directors, some items are presented for information. Discussion is possible, but the group will not be asked to make a decision. Other items are presented for action; the group will be asked to vote. A business meeting might specify that the first half hour will be time for brainstorming, with the second half hour devoted to evaluation.

Formal meetings are run under strict rules, like the rules of parliamentary procedure summarized in *Robert's Rules of Order*. Motions must be made formally before a topic can be debated. Each point is settled by a vote. **Minutes**

record each motion and the vote on it. Formal rules help the meeting run smoothly if the group is very large or if the agenda is very long. **Informal meetings,** which are much more common in the workplace, are run more loosely. Votes may not be taken if most people seem to agree. Minutes may not be kept. Informal meetings are better for team building and problem solving.

Planning the agenda (Figure 10.4) is the foundation of a good meeting. A good agenda indicates

- Whether each item is presented for information, for discussion, or for a decision
- Who is sponsoring or introducing each item
- How much time is allotted for each item

Many groups put first routine items on which agreement will be easy. If there's a long list of routine items, save them till the end or dispense with them in an omnibus motion. An **omnibus motion** allows a group to approve many items together rather than voting on each separately.

If the group doesn't formally vote, the leader should summarize the group's consensus after each point. At the end of the meeting, the leader must summarize all decisions and remind the group who is responsible for implementing or following up on each item. If no other notes are taken, someone should record the decisions and assignments. Long minutes will be most helpful if assignments are set off visually from the narrative.

If you're planning a long meeting, for example, a training session or a conference, recognize that networking is part of the value of the meeting. Allow short breaks at least every two hours and generous breaks twice a day so participants can talk informally to each other. If participants will be strangers, include some social functions so they can get to know each other. If they will have different interests or different levels of knowledge, plan concurrent sessions on different topics or for people with different levels of expertise.

Collaborative Writing

Whatever your career, it is likely that some of the documents you produce will be written with a group. Lisa Ede and Andrea Lunsford found that 87% of the

Being Taken Seriously*

It's frustrating to speak in a meeting and have people ignore what you say. Here are some tips for being taken seriously:

- Link your comment to the comment of a powerful person, even if logic suffers a bit. For example, say, "John is saying that we should focus on excellence, AND I think we can become stronger by encouraging diversity."

- Show that you've done your homework. Laura Sloate, who is blind, establishes authority by making sure her first question is highly technical: "In footnote three of the 10K, you indicate. . . ."

- Find an ally in the organization and agree ahead of time to acknowledge each other's contributions to the meeting, whether you agree or disagree with the point being made. Explicit disagreement signals that the comment is worth taking seriously: "Duane has pointed out . . . , but I think that. . . ."

- Use the style of language that powerful people in your organization use.

- Repeat your ideas. Put important ideas in a memo before the meeting.

*Based on Joan E. Rigdon, "Managing Your Career," *The Wall Street Journal*, December 1, 1993, B1; Cynthia Crossen, "Spotting Value Takes Smarts, Not Sight, Laura Sloate Shows," *The Wall Street Journal*, December 10, 1987, A1, A14; and Anne Fisher, "Ask Annie: Putting Your Money Where Your Mouth Is," *Fortune*, September 3, 2001, 238.

FIGURE 10.4 Typical Meeting Agenda

AGENDA

Non-Profit Board Meeting, Monday, September 26, 2005
3:30–5:00 p.m.
Conference room, business office

1. Call to Order; attendance
2. Approval of Agenda
3. Minutes of Meeting of August 22, 2005
4. Report of Chair (decision)
5. Report of Hiring Committee (decision)
6. Report of Fundraising Committee (information)
7. Report of Grants Committee (information)
8. Other Business
9. Date of next board meeting
10. Adjournment

Collaborating on "Remote" Teams*

Technology can link team members who are located far apart. Members of these remote—or virtual—teams share work electronically and communicate via phone calls, e-mail, and instant messaging. Without the advantages of face-to-face communication, how do they keep working relationships strong and projects on track?

Writers Nancy Larbi and Susan Springfield advise that especially on remote teams, team members

- Learn about each other, the client, and the type of project before the project begins.

- Are precise about the project's plan. Someone must be responsible for each element of the plan, and deadlines must be established.

- Monitor assumptions on a remote team, because it is harder for teams to notice when something is not getting done according to expectations.

- Number each version of a document.

- Use word-processing software to track what is changing and who made the change.

- Set up face-to-face meetings if problems arise.

*Based on Nancy E. Larbi and Susan Springfield, "When No One's Home: Being a Writer on Remote Project Teams," *Technical Communication* 51.1, February 2004, 101–108.

700 professionals in seven fields who responded to their survey sometimes wrote as members of a team or a group.[17] Collaboration is often prompted by one of the following situations:

1. The task is too big or the time is too short for one person to do all the work.
2. No one person has all the knowledge required to do the task.
3. A group representing different perspectives must reach a consensus.
4. The stakes for the task are so high that the organization wants the best efforts of as many people as possible; no one person wants the sole responsibility for the success or failure of the document.

Collaborative writing can be done by two people or by a much larger group. The group can be democratic or run by a leader who makes decisions alone. The group may share or divide responsibility for each of the eight stages in the writing process.

There are several ways groups commonly divide the work. One person might do the main writing, with others providing feedback. Another approach is to divide the whole project into smaller tasks and to assign each task (research, drafting, designing, and editing) to a different group member according to skills. This approach shares the workload more evenly but is harder to coordinate. Sometimes group members do not take turns but work together simultaneously, discussing and responding to each other's ideas.[18]

Research in collaborative writing indicates the strategies that produce the best writing. Rebecca Burnett found that student groups that voiced disagreements as they analyzed, planned, and wrote a document produced significantly better documents than those that suppressed disagreement, going along with whatever was first proposed.[19] A case study of two collaborative writing teams found that the successful group distributed power in an egalitarian way, worked to soothe hurt feelings, and was careful to involve all group members. In terms of writing process, the successful group understood the task as a response to a rhetorical situation, planned revisions as a group, saw supervisors' comments as legitimate, and had a positive attitude toward revision.[20] Ede and Lunsford's detailed case studies of collaborative teams in business, government, and science create an "emerging profile of effective collaborative writers": "They are flexible; respectful of others; attentive and analytical listeners; able to speak and write clearly and articulately; dependable and able to meet deadlines; able to designate and share responsibility, to lead and to follow; open to criticism but confident in their own abilities; ready to engage in creative conflict."[21]

Collaborative writing is most successful when the group explicitly discusses the best way to achieve the rhetorical goals. Businesses schedule formal planning sessions for large projects to set up a timeline specifying intermediate and final due dates (from initiation meeting to primary and secondary research to analysis, conclusions, and recommendations, to draft and final report), meeting dates, who will attend each meeting, and who will do what. Putting the plan in writing reduces misunderstandings during the project.

When you plan a collaborative writing project,

- Make your analysis of the problem, the audience, and your purposes explicit so you know where you agree and where you disagree.
- Plan the organization, format, and style of the document before anyone begins to write to make it easier to blend sections written by different authors.
- Consider your work styles and other commitments.
- Build some leeway into your deadlines to allow for scheduling difficulties.

Most writers find that composing alone is faster than composing in a group. However, composing together may reduce revision time later, since the group

A Comfortable Fit?*

Meeting rooms equipped with laptops, pagers, and cell phones help Intel employees collaborate on group projects with colleagues around the world.

examines every choice as it is made. Have the best writer(s) draft the document after everyone has gathered the necessary information. On the evaluation and documentation of online and print sources, see ➟ Chapter 11.

Revising a collaborative document requires attention to content, organization, and style. The following guidelines can make the revision process more effective:

■ Evaluate the content and discuss possible revisions as a group. Brainstorm ways to improve each section so the person doing the revisions has some guidance.

■ Recognize that different people favour different writing styles. If the style satisfies the demands of standard English and the conventions of business writing, accept it even if you wouldn't say it that way.

■ When the group is satisfied with the content of the document, one person—probably the best writer—should make any changes necessary to make the writing style consistent throughout.

A group report needs careful editing and proofreading (➟ Chapter 3).

■ Have at least one person check the whole document for correctness in grammar, mechanics, and spelling and for consistency in the way that format elements, names, and numbers are handled.

■ Run the document through a spell-checker if possible.

■ Even if you use a computerized spell-checker, at least one human being should proofread the document too.

Like any member of the writing team, those handling the editing tasks need to consider how they express their ideas. In many situations, the editor plays the role of diplomat, careful to suggest changes in ways that do not seem to call the writer's abilities into question. Describing the reason for a change is typically more helpful than stating an opinion. Words like *could* and *should* to modify a direction can add a tone of politeness.[22]

Making the Group Process Work

All of the information in this chapter can help your collaborative writing group listen effectively, run meetings efficiently, and deal with conflict constructively. The following suggestions apply specifically to writing groups:

■ "A company's culture is like the clothes you wear. If it's not a good fit for you, you'll never be comfortable" (Trudell).

■ Some businesses are addressing "the perception that the voices of minority groups and women aren't heard in many spheres . . . by making it their mission to support diversity." Lally Rementilla is "an example of how such a culture can create industry leaders." Within 12 years of moving to Canada from the Philippines at age 21, Rementilla had become vice-president for Lucent Technologies Canada. Now director of Business Planning and Analysis at Lavalife Inc, she found in each case companies that "really value diversity" and "take the time to help develop individuals (Coleman)"

■ Diversity is proving good for the bottom line, the payoff coming in "better workers, better results, better business" (Dib).

* Based on Cynthia Trudell, cited in Zena Olijnyk et al, "Canada's Global Leaders," *Canadian Business*, March 28–April 10, 2005, 46; Robert Coleman, "A Drive for Diversity," retrieved August 24, 2004, from http://www.managementmag.com/index.cfm/ci_id/1943/la_id/1/print/true.htm; Kamal Dib, "Diversity Works," *Canadian Business*, March 29–April 11, 2004, 53–54; Pamela K. Henry, *Diversity and the Bottom Line: Prospering in the Global Economy* (Turnkey Press, 2003).

Using Informal Meetings to Advance Your Career

You'll see your supervisor several times a week. Some of these meetings will be accidental: you'll meet by the coffee pot or ride up in the elevator together. Some of them will be deliberately initiated: your boss will stop by your work station, or you'll go to your boss's office to ask for something.

Take advantage of these meetings by planning for them. These informal meetings are often short. An elevator ride, for example, may last about three minutes. So plan 90-second scripts that you can use to give your boss a brief report on what you're doing, ask for something you need, or lay the groundwork for an important issue.

Planning scripts is especially important if your boss doesn't give you much feedback or mentoring. In this case, your boss probably doesn't see you as promotable. You need to take the initiative. Make statements that show the boss you're thinking about ways to work smarter. Show that you're interested in learning more so that you can be more valuable to the organization.

■ Give yourselves plenty of time to discuss problems and find solutions. Purdue students who are writing group reports spend six to seven hours a week outside class in group meetings—not counting the time they spend gathering information and writing their drafts.[23]

■ Take the time to get to know group members and to build group loyalty. Group members will work harder and the final document will be better if the group is important to members.

■ Be a responsible group member. Attend all the meetings; carry out your responsibilities.

■ Be aware that people have different ways of experiencing reality and of expressing themselves. Use the principles of semantics discussed in ◄▮ Chapter 1 to reduce miscommunication.

■ Because talking is "looser" than writing, people in a group can think they agree when they don't. Don't assume that because the discussion went smoothly, a draft written by one person will necessarily be acceptable.

Summary of Key Points

■ **Interpersonal communication** is communication between people.

■ In interpersonal communication, **hearing** denotes perceiving sounds. **Listening** means decoding and interpreting them correctly.

■ To avoid listening errors caused by inattention,
  ■ Be conscious of the points you need to know and listen for them.
  ■ At the end of the conversation, check your understanding with the other person.
  ■ After the conversation, write down key points that affect deadlines or how work will be evaluated.

■ In **active listening,** receivers actively demonstrate that they've heard and understood a speaker by feeding back either the literal meaning or the emotional content or both.

■ Effective groups balance information leadership, interpersonal leadership, and procedural group management.

■ The **standard agenda** is a seven-step process for solving problems. In **dot planning** the group brainstorms ideas. Then each individual affixes adhesive dots by the points or proposals he or she cares most about.

■ Student groups that set clear deadlines, have inclusive decision making, and comprise a high proportion of active members succeed. Students who spent the most time meeting with their groups got the highest grades.

■ **Groupthink** is the tendency for groups to put such a high premium on agreement that they directly or indirectly punish dissent. The best correctives to groupthink are to consciously search for additional alternatives, to test one's assumptions against those of a range of other people, and to protect the right of each person in the group to disagree.

■ Constructive ways to respond to criticism include paraphrasing, checking for feelings, checking inferences and good you-attitude.

■ To make meetings more effective,
  ■ State the purpose of the meeting at the beginning.

- Distribute an agenda that indicates whether each item is for information, for discussion, or for action, and how long each is expected to take.
- If you don't take formal votes, summarize all decisions and remind the group who is responsible for implementing or following up on each item.

- **Collaborative writing** means working with other writers to produce a single document. Writers producing a joint document need to pay attention not only to the basic steps in the writing process but also to the processes of group formation and conflict resolution.

CHAPTER 10 Exercises and Problems

Getting Started

10.1 Identifying Responses That Show Active Listening

Which of the following responses show active listening? Which responses block communication?

1. Comment: Whenever I say something, the group just ignores me.

   Responses:
   - a. That's because your ideas aren't very good. Do more planning before group meetings.
   - b. Nobody listens to me, either.
   - c. You're saying that nobody builds on your ideas.

2. Comment: I've done more than my share of work on this project. But the people who have been freeloading are going to get the same grade I've worked so hard to earn.

   Responses:
   - a. Yes, we're all going to get the same grade.
   - b. Are you afraid we won't do well on the assignment?
   - c. It sounds like you feel resentful.

3. Comment: My parents are going to kill me if I don't have a job lined up when I graduate.

   Responses:
   - a. You know they're exaggerating. They won't *really* kill you.
   - b. Can you blame them? I mean, it's taken you six years to get a degree. Surely you've learned something to make you employable!
   - c. If you act the way in interviews that you do in our class, I'm not surprised. Companies want people with good attitudes and good work ethics.

10.2 Practising Active Listening

Go around the room for this exercise. In turn, let each student complain about something (large or small) that really bothers him or her. Then the next student(s) will

a. Offer a statement of limited agreement that would buy time.

b. Paraphrase the statement.

c. Check for feelings that might lie behind the statement.

d. Offer inferences that might motivate the statement.

10.3   Taking Minutes

As Your Professor Directs,

Have two or more people take minutes of each class or collaborative group meeting for a week. Compare the accounts of the same meeting.

- To what extent do they agree on what happened?

- Does one contain information missing in other accounts?
- Do any accounts disagree on a specific fact?
- How do you account for the differences you find?

10.4   Keeping a Journal about a Group

As you work in a collaborative writing group, keep a journal after each group meeting.

- What happened?
- What roles did you play in the meeting?

- What conflicts arose? How were they handled?
- What strategies could you use to make the next meeting go smoothly?
- Record one observation about each group member.

E-Mail Messages

In Problems 10.5 through 10.7, assume that your group has been asked to recommend a solution.

As Your Professor Directs,

- Send e-mail messages to group members laying out your initial point of view on the issue and discussing the various options.

- As a group, answer the message.
- Write a memo to your professor telling how satisfied you are with
  a. The decision your group reached.
  b. The process you used to reach it.

10.5   Recommending a Policy on Student Entrepreneurs

Assume that your small group comprises the officers in student government on your campus. You receive this e-mail from the vice-president of student services:

> As you know, campus policy says that no student may use campus resources to conduct business-related activities. Students can't conduct business out of dorm rooms or use university e-mail addresses for business. They can't post business Web pages on the university server.
>
> On the other hand, a survey conducted by the Kauffman Centre for Entrepreneurial Leadership showed that 7 out of 10 teens want to become entrepreneurs.
>
> Should campus policy be changed to allow students to use dorm rooms and university e-mail addresses for business? (And then what happens when roommates complain and our network can't carry the increased e-mail traffic?) Please recommend what support (if any) should be given to student entrepreneurs.

Write a group report recommending what (if anything) your campus should do for student entrepreneurs and supporting your recommendation.

Hints:

- Does your campus offer other support for entrepreneurs (courses, a business plan competition,

a start-up incubator)? What should be added or expanded?

- Is it realistic to ask alumni for money to fund student start-ups?

10.6   Recommending a Dress Policy

Assume that your small group comprises your organization's Labour-Management Committee

This e-mail arrives from the CEO:

> In the last 10 years, we became increasingly casual. But changed circumstances seem to call for more formality. Is it time to reinstate a dress policy? If so, what should it be?

Write a group response recommending the appropriate dress for employees and supporting your recommendation.

Hint:

Agree on an office, factory, store, or other workplace to use for this problem.

10.7   Responding to an Employee Grievance

Assume that your small group comprises the Labour-Management committee at the headquarters of a chain of grocery stores. This e-mail arrives from the vice-president for human resources:

> As you know, company policy requires that employees smile at customers and make eye contact with them. In the past 9 months, 12 employees have filed grievances over this rule. They say they are being harassed by customers who think they are flirting with them. A produce clerk claims customers have propositioned her and followed her to her car. Another says "Let *me* decide who I am going to say hello to with a big smile." The union wants us to change the policy to let workers *not* make eye contact with customers, and to allow workers to refuse to carry groceries to a customer's car at night. My own feeling is that we want to maintain our image as a friendly store that cares about customers, but that we also don't want to require behaviour that leads to harassment. Let's find a creative solution.

Write a group response recommending whether to change the policy and supporting your recommendation.

Memo, Manual, and Presentation Assignments

10.8   Answering an Ethics Question

Assume that your small group comprises your organization's Ethics Committee. You receive the following anonymous note:

> People are routinely using the company letterhead to write letters to members of Parliament, senators, and even the prime minister stating their positions on various issues. Making their opinions known is of course their right, but doing so on letterhead stationery implies that they are speaking for the company, which they are not.
>
> I think that the use of letterhead for anything other than official company business should be prohibited.

Determine the best solution to the problem. Then write a message to all employees stating your decision and building support for it.

10.9   Writing a Meeting Manual

Create a manual for students next term telling them how to have effective meetings as they work on collaborative projects.

Source: Adapted from Miles McCall, Beth Stewart, and Timothy Clipson, "Teaching Communication Skills for Meeting Management," *1998 Refereed Proceedings*, Association for Business Communication Southwestern United States, ed. Marsha L. Bayless (Nacogdoches, TX), 68.

10.10   Planning a Game

Many companies are using games and contests to solve problems in an enjoyable way. One company promised to give everyone $30 a month extra if they got the error rate below 0.5%. The rate improved immediately. After several successful months, the incentive went to $40 a month for getting it under 0.3% and finally to $50 a month for getting it under 0.2%. Another company offered workers two "well hours" if they got in by 7 AM every day for a month. An accounting and financial services company divided its employees into two teams. The one that got the most referrals and new accounts received a meal prepared and served by the losing team (the firm paid for the food). Games are best when the people who will play them create them. Games need to make business sense and give rewards to many people, not just a few. Rewards should be small.

Think of a game or contest that could improve productivity or quality in your classroom, on campus, or in a workplace you know well.

As Your Professor Directs,

a.   Write a message to persuade your professor, boss, or other decision maker to authorize the game or contest.

b.   Write a message announcing the game and persuading people to participate in it.

Source: Based on John Case, *The Open-Book Experience: Lessons from Over 100 Companies Who Successfully Transformed Themselves* (Reading, MA: Addison-Wesley, 1998), 129–201.

10.11   Interviewing Workers about Listening

Interview someone who works in an organization about his or her on-the-job listening. Possible questions to ask include the following:

- Whom do you listen to as part of your job? Your superior? Subordinates? (How many levels down?) Customers or clients? Who else?
- How much time a day do you spend listening?
- What people do you talk to as part of your job? Do you feel they hear what you say? How do you tell whether or not they're listening?
- Do you know of any problems that came up because someone didn't listen? What happened?

- What do you think prevents people from listening effectively? What advice would you have for someone on how to listen more accurately?

As Your Professor Directs,

a.   Share your information with a small group of students in your class.

b.   Present your findings orally to the class.

c.   Present your findings in a memo to your professor.

d.   Join with other students to present your findings in a group report.

10.12   Analyzing the Dynamics of a Group

Analyze the dynamics of a task group of which you are a member. Answer the following questions:

1.   Who was the group's leader? How did the leader emerge? Were there any changes in or challenges to the original leader?

2.   Describe the contribution each member made to the group and the roles each person played.

3.   Did any members of the group officially or unofficially drop out? Did anyone join after the group had begun working? How did you deal with

the loss or addition of a group member, both in terms of getting the work done and in terms of helping people work together?

4.   What planning did your group do at the start of the project? Did you stick to the plan or revise it? How did the group decide that revision was necessary?

5.   How did your group make decisions? Did you vote? Reach decisions by consensus?

6. What problems or conflicts arose? Did the group deal with them openly? To what extent did the problems interfere with the group's task?

7. Evaluate your group both in terms of its task and in terms of the satisfaction members felt. How did this group compare with other task groups you've been part of? What made it better or worse?

As you answer the questions,

■ Be honest. You won't lose points for reporting that your group had problems or did something "wrong."

■ Show your knowledge of good group dynamics. That is, if your group did something wrong, show that you know what *should* have been done.

Similarly, if your group worked well, show that you know *why* it worked well.

■ Be specific. Give examples or anecdotes to support your claims.

As Your Professor Directs,

a. Discuss these questions with the other group members.

b. Present your findings orally to the class.

c. Present your findings in an individual memo to your professor.

d. Join with the other group members to write a collaborative memo to your professor.

Reports

11 Planning, Proposing, and Researching Reports

AN INSIDE PERSPECTIVE

Planning, Proposing, and Researching Reports

Strong research and writing is at the heart of many a business or organizational initiative. In problem solving, policy development, and strategic planning, well-written proposals and reports are invaluable. Produced for internal or external audiences, successful proposals and reports depend on effective planning and research as well as careful revising, editing, and proofreading.

Planning and Research

Planning, the first stage of the writing process, importantly clarifies

- Document purpose
- Audience knowledge, needs, possible responses
- Action and outline to meet objectives

Listening to your audience, and attending to explicit and implicit messages, is as critical as the next stage: the formal research. Gathering data and information will strengthen the reliability and cogency of the proposal or report and add to your credibility, while testing your core idea and identifying where revision is required to incorporate new information.

President and Executive Director of the Québec Chantier de l'économie sociale, a non-profit organization including co-operative, non-profit, and social movement representatives, Nancy Neamtan promotes an economy working both outside and with the private sector. Carefully planned proposals and reports are key parts of promoting a social economy that is a powerful economic engine and creator of new opportunities.

www.chantier.qc.ca/

Revising, Editing, and Proofreading

Since effective writing is effective revision, these final stages change organization, argument, and wording to meet purposes and audience needs, while ensuring proposal and report accuracy, clarity, and credibility. Such careful revision clarifies the key messages as well as the headings and other design elements that will make your document reader friendly and action oriented. As Bertolt Brecht has argued, "You cannot just 'write the truth; you have to write it *for* and *to* somebody, somebody who can do something with it."

In sum, investment in planning yields significant returns, and helps proposals and reports highlight profitable initiatives and shape business futures. In addition to strengthening business relationships, careful planning, research, and revising increases productivity and reduces costs.

Proposals and reports depend on research. The research may be as simple as pulling up data with a computer program or as complicated as calling many different people, conducting focus groups and surveys, or even planning and conducting experiments. Care in planning, proposing, and researching reports is needed to produce reliable data.

In writing any report, there are five basic steps:

1. Define the problem.
2. Gather the necessary data and information.
3. Analyze the data and information.
4. Organize the information.
5. Write the report.

After reviewing the varieties of reports, this chapter focuses on the first two steps. ➠ Chapter 12 discusses the last three steps.

Varieties of Reports

Many kinds of documents are called *reports.* In some organizations, a report is a long document or a document that contains numerical data. In others, one- and two-page memos are called *reports.* A short report to a client may use letter format; a report to your manager may use memo format. **Formal reports** contain formal elements such as a title page, a transmittal, a table of contents, and a list of illustrations. **Informal reports** may be letters and memos, fill-in-the-blank forms for regular routine reports (trip or progress, for instance), or even computer printouts of production or sales figures. But all reports, whatever their length or degree of formality, provide the information that people in organizations need to make plans and solve problems.

Reports can provide information, provide information and analyze it, or provide information and analysis to support a recommendation (see Figure 11.1).

FIGURE 11.1 Three Levels of Reports

Reports can provide

Information only

- **Sales reports** (sales figures for the week or month).
- **Quarterly reports** (figures showing a plant's productivity and profits for the quarter).

Information plus analysis

- **Annual reports** (financial data and an organization's accomplishments during the past year).
- **Audit reports** (interpretations of the facts revealed during an audit).
- **Make-good or pay-back reports** (calculations of the point at which a new capital investment will pay for itself).

Information plus analysis plus a recommendation

- **Feasibility reports** evaluate two or more alternatives and recommend which alternative the organization should choose.
- **Justification reports** justify the need for a purchase, an investment, a new personnel line, or a change in procedure.
- **Problem-solving reports** identify the causes of an organizational problem and recommend a solution.

Reports can be called **information reports** if they collect data for the reader, **analytical reports** if they interpret data but do not recommend action, and **recommendation reports** if they recommend action or a solution.

The following reports can be information, analytical, or recommendation reports, depending on what they provide:

- *Progress* and *interim reports* can simply record the work done so far and the work remaining on a project. These reports can also recommend that a project be stopped, continued, or restructured.
- *Trip reports* can simply share what the author learned at a conference or during a visit to a customer or supplier. These reports can also recommend action based on that information.

A Timeline for Writing Reports

When you write a report, plan to spend half your time analyzing your data, writing and revising the draft, and preparing visuals and slides. See Figure 3.1 (⬅ p. 66). When you write a report for a class project:

- Plan to complete at least one-quarter of your research before you write the proposal.
- Begin analyzing your data as you collect it.
- Prepare your list of sources and drafts of visuals as you go along.
- Save at least one-quarter of your time to think and write after all your data are collected. For a collaborative report, you'll need even more time to write and revise.

Upfront planning helps you use your time efficiently.

- Read the sample reports in ➡ Chapter 12 even before you write your proposal.
- Talk to your readers to understand how much detail and formality they want.
- In a company, review earlier reports.
- List all the parts of the report you'll need to prepare.
- Articulate the purposes, audiences, and generic constraints for each part. The fuller idea you have of the final product when you start, the fewer drafts you'll need to write and the better your final product will be.

Defining Problems to be Solved

When you write a report as part of your job, the organization may define the topic. To think of problems for class reports, think about problems that face your college or university; campus housing units; social, religious, and professional groups; local businesses; and municipal, provincial, and federal governments and their agencies. Read your campus and local papers and newsmagazines; watch the news on TV, or listen to it on CBC or a local radio station.

A well-defined report problem in business or administration meets the following criteria:

1. The problem is
   - Real
   - Important enough to be worth solving
   - Narrow but challenging
2. The audience for the report is
   - Real
   - Interested in the problem
   - Able to implement the recommended action

Alissa Kozuh analyzes the words customers type in on the search feature at www.nordstrom.com. She's found five patterns: customers key in particular items ("shoes"), trends ("leopard prints"), departments from the bricks-and-mortar stores ("Brass Plum," the juniors department), designer names, and special occasions ("prom"). The changes she suggested for the site based on her research increased Web sales 32%.

3. The data, evidence, and facts are
   - Sufficient to document the severity of the problem
   - Sufficient to prove that the recommendation will solve the problem
   - Available to *you*
   - Comprehensible to *you*

Often you need to narrow the problem statement. For example, "improving the post-secondary experiences of international students studying in Canada" is far too broad. First, choose one college or university. Second, identify the specific problem. Do you want to increase the social interaction between Canadian and international students? Help international students find housing? Increase the number of ethnic grocery stores and restaurants? Third, identify the specific audience that would have the power to implement your recommendations. Depending on the specific topic, the audience might be the Office of International Studies, the residence counsellors, a service organization on campus or in town, a store, or a group of investors.

Pick a problem you can solve in the time available. Six months of full-time (and overtime) work and a team of colleagues might allow you to look at all the ways to make a store more profitable. If you're doing a report in 6 to 12 weeks for a class that is only one of your responsibilities, limit the topic. You could choose to examine the store's prices and product, its inventory procedures, its overhead costs, its layout and decor, or its advertising budget.

How you define the problem shapes the solutions you find. For example, suppose that a manufacturer of frozen foods isn't making money. If you define the problem as a marketing problem, you may analyze the product's price, image, advertising, and position in the market. But perhaps the problem is really

Defining an Information Problem*

Problem: It took too long for managers to get updates on sales and operations. "When the CEO asked how the quarter was looking," GE Plastics chief information officer John Seral explains, "he got a different answer depending on whom he asked. . . . It could take hours or days."

Solution: GE vice chairman Gary Rogers hatched the idea for a digital dashboard—the continuously updated online display of a company's vital stats. But it fell to Seral to build the system. . . . GE's new "digital cockpits" now give 300 managers access to the company's essential data—on desktop PCs and Blackberry PDAs. The old system required dozens of analysts to compile information and send it up the line; Seral's dashboards have slimmed down those ranks to six. To get the project launched, Seral first asked several senior managers—from quality assurance, manufacturing, and IT [information technology]—to decide what numbers each division would contribute. Then he hired an IT crew to enforce data input. The numbers he could get would be a day old, but that was a fair compromise. . . . "This wasn't just an IT feat," Seral says. "It was about changing the culture so everyone has a common way to look at the business."

*Quoted from Bob Tedeschi, "End of the Paper Chase," *Business 2.0*, March 2003, 64.

that poor inventory management makes overhead costs too high. Defining the problem accurately is essential to finding an effective solution.

Once you've defined your problem, you're ready to write at least a tentative purpose statement. The purpose statement goes both in your proposal and in your final report. A good **purpose statement** makes three things clear:

- The organizational problem or conflict
- The specific technical questions that must be answered to solve the problem
- The rhetorical purpose (to explain, to recommend, to request, to propose) in terms of audience benefits

The following purpose statement has all three elements:

> When banner ads on Web pages first appeared in 1994, the initial reponse, or "click-through" rate was about 10%. However, as ads have proliferated on Web pages, the click-through rate has dropped sharply. Rather than assuming that any banner ad will be successful, we need to ask, What characteristics do successful banner ads share? Are ads for certain kinds of products and services or for certain kinds of audiences more likely to be successful on the Web? The purpose of this report is to summarize the available research and anecdotal evidence and to recommend what Rethink Advertising Agency should tell its clients about whether and how to use banner ads.

Writing Proposals

Proposals suggest a method for finding information or solving a problem[1] and help an organization decide whether to change, decide how to change, or implement a change that is agreed on. (See Figure 11.2.)

Proposals have two goals: to get the project accepted and to get you accepted to do the job. Proposals must stress reader benefits and provide specific supporting details. Attention to details—including good visual impact and proofreading—helps establish your professional image and suggests that you'd give the same care to the project if your proposal is accepted.

To write a good proposal, you need to have a clear view of the problem you hope to solve and the kind of research or other action needed to solve it. A proposal must answer the following questions convincingly:

- **What problem will you solve?** Define the problem as the audience sees it, even if you believe that the presenting problem is part of a larger problem that must first be solved.

FIGURE 11.2   Relationship among Situation, Proposal, and Final Report

Company's current situation	The proposal offers to	The final report will provide
We don't know whether we should change.	Assess whether change is a good idea.	Insight, recommending whether change is desirable.
We need to/want to change, but we don't know exactly what we need to do.	Develop a plan to achieve the desired goal.	A plan for achieving the desired change.
We need to/want to change, and we know what to do, but we need help doing it.	Implement the plan, increase (or decrease) measurable outcomes.	A record of the implementation and evaluation process.

Source: Adapted from Richard C. Freed, Shervin Freed, and Joseph D. Romano, *Writing Winning Proposals: Your Guide to Landing the Client, Making the Sale, Persuading the Boss* (New York: McGraw-Hill, 1995), 21.

■ **How will you solve it?** Prove that your methods and timelines are feasible and that your solution is economic and efficient. Specify the topics you'll investigate. Explain how you'll gather data.

■ **What exactly will you provide for us?** Specify the tangible products you'll produce; explain how you'll evaluate them.

■ **Can you deliver what you promise?** Show that you have the knowledge, the staff, and the facilities to do what you say you will. Describe your previous work in this area, your other qualifications, and the qualifications of any people who will be helping you.

■ **What benefits can you offer?** Show why the company should hire you. Discuss the benefits—direct and indirect—that your firm can provide.

■ **When will you complete the work?** Provide a detailed schedule showing when each phase of the work will be completed.

■ **How much will you charge?** Provide a detailed budget that includes costs for materials, salaries, and overhead.

Government agencies and companies often issue **requests for proposals,** known as **RFPs.** Follow the RFP exactly when you respond to a proposal. Evaluators look only under the heads specified in the RFP. If information isn't there, the proposal gets no points in that category.

Proposals for Class Research Projects

A proposal for a student report usually has the following sections:

1. In your first paragraph (no heading), summarize in a sentence or two the topic and purposes of your report.

2. **Problem.** What organizational problem exists? What is wrong? Why does it need to be solved? Is there a history or background that is relevant?

3. **Feasibility.** Can a solution be found in the time available? How do you know?

4. **Audience.** Who in the organization would have the power to implement your recommendation? What secondary audiences might be asked to evaluate your report? What audiences would be affected by your recommendation? Will anyone in the organization serve as a gatekeeper, determining whether your report is sent to decision makers? What watchdog audiences might read the report?

   For each of these audiences and for your initial audience (your professor), give the person's name, job title, and business address and answer the following questions:

   ■ What is the audience's major concern or priority?
   ■ What will the audience see as advantages of your proposal?
   ■ What objections, if any, is the reader likely to have?
   ■ How interested is the audience in the topic of your report?
   ■ How much does the audience know about the topic of your report?
   ■ What terms, concepts, equations, or assumptions may need to be explained?
   ■ How do your audiences affect the content, organization, or style of the report?

5. **Topics to investigate.** List the questions and subquestions you will answer in your report, the topics or concepts you will explain, and the aspects of the problem you will discuss. Indicate how deeply you will examine each of the aspects you plan to treat and explain your rationale.

Competing for Real Money*

When students compete for real money, the stakes are high and the learning curve steep. And the opportunities are increasing. The Venture Forward Business Plan Competition, a $50,000 competition modelled on such plans as the MIT Entrepreneurship Competition and the Munich Business Plan Competition, is one more economic development and academic tool to add to the mix listed on the Global Business Plan Competition Web site. Venture Forward targets plans designed to start and grow new enterprises in Saskatchewan.

Not only do participants gain valuable training and mentoring, but the winners win cash prizes to support their new ventures.

Even those who are not among the winners benefit from the experience, from the networking opportunities, and the invaluable feedback from judges.

*Based on Venture Forward Web site at www.venture forward.ca/ and Global Business Plan Competition Web site at http://50k.mit.edu/ global/global network.php.

Choosing Topics to Investigate*

No report investigates all possible topics. Choose the ones that decision makers care most about and will find most useful.

In addition to the specific topic of the report, general topics can include managerial, technical, and social criteria.

Managerial Criteria
- Cost (e.g., acquisition, maintenance, disposal; taxes)
- Market demand
- Staffing requirements
- Organizational impact (distribution of resources; effect on personnel, other projects, and image)
- Consistency with organizational goals

Technical Criteria
- Availability of technology, materials, parts
- Compatibility with existing systems
- Adaptability, flexibility, ability to be upgraded
- Reliability, longevity, repair record
- Compliance with legal codes (e.g., environment)

Social Criteria
- Human impact (jobs, morale, employment benefits)
- Environmental impact
- Safety
- Quality
- Ethical issues (e.g., conflict of interest, use of resources, impact on stakeholders)

*Based on Mary M. Lay, Billie J. Wahlstrom, Carolyn Rude, Cindy Selfe, and Jack Selzer, *Technical Communication*, 2nd ed. (Burr Ridge, IL: Irwin/McGraw-Hill, 2000), 510.

6. **Methods/procedure.** How will you get answers to your questions? Whom will you interview or survey? Provide a draft of your questions. What published sources will you use? Give the full bibliographic references.

7. **Qualifications/facilities/resources.** Do you have the knowledge and skills needed to conduct this study? Do you have adequate access to the organization? Do you have access to any equipment you will need to conduct your research (computer, books, etc.)? Where will you turn for help if you hit an unexpected snag?

　　You'll be more convincing if you have already scheduled an interview, checked out books, or printed out online sources.

8. **Work schedule.** List the date when you expect to finish each of the following activities:
   - Gathering information
   - Analyzing information
   - Preparing the progress report
   - Organizing information
   - Writing the draft
   - Revising the draft
   - Preparing the visuals
   - Editing the draft
   - Proofreading the report

   Organize your work schedule either in a chart or in a calendar. A good schedule provides realistic estimates for each activity, allows time for unexpected snags, and shows that you can complete the work on time.

9. **Call to action.** In your final section, invite any suggestions your professor may have for improving the research plan. Ask your professor to approve your proposal so that you can begin work on your report.

Figure 11.3 shows a student proposal for a long report.

Proposals for Action

You can write a proposal for action or change in your organization. Normally, proposals for action recommend new programs or ways to solve organizational problems.

Organize a proposal for action as a direct request (← p. 164). Explain in detail how your idea could be implemented. Be sure to answer your readers' questions and to overcome objections.

Sales Proposals

To sell goods, ideas, or services, you may be asked to submit a proposal.

Be sure that you understand the buyer's priorities. Don't assume that the buyer will understand why your product or system is good. Show the reader benefits (← p. 38) and present the benefits using you-attitude (← p. 43). Consider using psychological description (← p. 168) to make the benefits vivid.

Use language appropriate for your audience. Even if the buyers want a state-of-the-art system, they may not want the level of detail that your staff could provide; they may not understand or appreciate technical jargon (← p. 91).

In the case of long proposals, provide a one-page cover letter in a modified version of the sales pattern in Chapter 8:

1. Catch the reader's attention and summarize up to three major benefits.
2. Discuss each of the major benefits in the order they are listed in the first paragraph.

FIGURE 11.3   Proposal for a Student Report Using Survey, Online, and Library Research

To: Kitty O. Locker

From: Elizabeth Ryan   *ESR*

In subject line ①*Indicate that this is a proposal*
②*Specify the kind of report*
③*Specify the topic*

Date: July 19, 2005

Subject: Proposal to Write a Problem-Solving Report Recommending Ways to Increase Student
          Attendance Rates at University of Saskatchewan Huskies Women's Basketball Games

Summarize topic and purposes of report

University of Saskatchewan (U of S) Huskies men's basketball team is a crowd pleaser, selling out home games in good years. However, the women's basketball team suffers from low attendance figures, typically filling only one-quarter of the seating capacity of the Physical Activity Complex (PAC). Huskie Athletics would like to find ways to increase attendance. I will survey students, interview staff of Huskie Athletics, and read online and print sources to find solutions to the problem.

Some reports will need a "Background" section so that the reader can understand what led to the problem statement

Problem   *If "Problem" section is detailed and well written, you may be able to use it unchanged in your report*

The PAC holds 2,400 fans, but the highest attendance in the last two years at a women-only basketball game was 700; the figure was 1,500 at a double-header where the women's and men's teams played back to back (Tera Schneider, personal communication, June 28, 2005).

The 2004–05 attendance rate was the highest in the past two years—the first years in the new PAC with twice the capacity of the old venue. The women's team went 11–9 in overall conference play (7–3 at home) and made the conference playoffs for the second year running. Still, the figures remain disappointing, though they are at least 40% better than in the close to 20 years that the team missed the playoffs. The opportunity to build student attendance is great at a time when students represent only 30% of overall attendance (Tera Schneider, personal communication, June 28, 2005).

Huskie Athletics would like to increase attendance, particularly student attendance, at women's basketball games. Student attendance builds school spirit and the morale of student athletes.

Feasibility   *Convince your professor that you have a backup plan if your original proposal proves unworkable*

Since basketball is a popular sport, it seems likely that attendance can be increased. Certainly students respond to marketing appeals for sports and other products. If I am unable to demonstrate that possible strategies will increase attendance, I will show readers why the obvious solutions won't work and recommend that the university hire a professional sports marketing consulting firm.

Audience   *Show how your audiences will affect how you'll present information in your report*

All of my audiences are at least somewhat interested in increasing attendance. None of them is hostile, so I will be able to present information straightforwardly. The topic is not technical, so I don't expect to need a glossary.

List your major audiences
Identify their knowledge, interests, and concerns

(continued)

3. Deal with any objections or concerns the reader may have.
4. Mention other benefits briefly.
5. Ask the reader to approve your proposal; provide a reason for acting promptly.

Proposals for Funding

Proposals for funding include both **business plans** (documents written to raise capital for new business ventures) and proposals submitted to a foundation, a corporation, a government agency, or a religious agency. In a proposal for funding, stress the needs your project will meet and show how your project helps fulfill the goals of the organization you are asking for funds.

FIGURE 11.3 Proposal for a Student Report Using Survey, Online, and Library Research *(continued)*

Proposal to Write a Recommendation Report on Attendance at U of S Huskies Women's Basketball Games
July 19, 2005
Page 2

My primary audience will be Ross Wilson, director of Huskies Athletics. He has the power to accept or reject my recommendations. I know how interested he is in women's basketball, and I assume he is somewhat knowledgeable about sports marketing. He will look good if attendance increases.

Secondary audiences to this report include staffers in Huskies Athletics who will be asked to implement the recommendations. Director of Marketing Sean Gilchrist and the coaching staff of the basketball team may be asked to evaluate the report. Finally, players and students are part of the secondary audience. Players benefit from student support at games, and the students are the people being targeted for increased attendance. Only a few of these secondary audiences will be very interested in my report.

You will be my initial audience. You've told me that you like men's basketball but have never been to a women's basketball game, even though several of your friends have season tickets.

Topics to Investigate

Indicate what you'll discuss briefly and what you'll discuss in more detail. This list should match your audience's concerns

I plan to answer these questions in detail:

1. What factors affect student attendance?
    - Why do the students who attend women's basketball games do so?
    - Why do the students who don't attend stay away?
    - What promotions or publicity could make students more likely to attend?

All items in list must be grammatically parallel. Here, all are questions.

2. How can student awareness of the team be increased?
    - What short-term strategies exist?
    - What long-term strategies exist?
    - Does it make sense to market the team to female audiences?

3. Would a loyalty program help?
    - What programs are available, and what is involved?
    - What are some university examples of programs?

If it is well written, the "Topics to Investigate" section will become the "Scope" section of the report —with minor revisions

I will briefly discuss how attendance and newspaper publicity correlate to the win/loss record.

If you'll administer a survey or conduct interviews, tell how many subjects you'll have, how you'll choose them, and what you'll ask them.

I will not discuss the cost or the return on investment of my recommendations. I will not discuss how changes in coaching or recruiting might affect attendance.

Indicate any topics relevant to your report that you choose not to discuss

Methods

I expect to get data from four sources: (1) surveys of 50 to 100 students, (2) interviews with members of Huskie Athletics, (3) my observations of marketing tactics on campus and in Saskatchewan, and (4) library and online sources about attendance at basketball games.

A draft of my questionnaire is attached. I will distribute the survey to a convenience sample at the Students Union.

(continued)

Every funding source has certain priorities; some have detailed lists of the kind of projects they fund. The Voluntary Sector Initiative's *Canadian Directory to Foundations and Corporations* is a bilingual online directory listing funding resources relevant to those working in the voluntary sector.

Figuring the Budget and Costs

For a class research project, you may not be asked to prepare a budget. However, many proposals do require budgets, and a good budget is crucial to making the winning bid. Ask for everything you need to do a quality job. Asking for too little may backfire, leading the funder to think that you don't understand the scope of the project.

FIGURE 11.3 Proposal for a Student Report Using Survey, Online, and Library Research *(continued)*

Proposal to Write a Recommendation Report on Attendance at U of S Huskies Women's Basketball Games
July 19, 2005
Page 3

If you're using library or Web research, list sources you hope to use. Use full bibliographic citations.

I have already identified the following useful Web sites with additional links:

Canadian Association for the Advancement of Women and Sport and Physical Activity. (2005). Web site. Retrieved June 28, 2005, from http://www.caaws.ca/e.

Canadian Fitness and Lifestyle Research Institute. (2005). Retrieved June 28, 2005, from http://www.cflri.ca.

This list uses APA format

Canadian Interuniversity Sport. (2005) Web site. Retrieved June 28, 2005, from http://www.universitysport.ca.

Cite knowledge and skills from other classes, jobs, and activities that will enable you to conduct the research and interpret your data. If you've already done some of the work, say so.

Qualifications

I am a student majoring in Marketing at the University of Saskatchewan and a sports fan. I would like to see the student community offer more support to the Huskies. I know Tera Schneider, a College of Commerce graduate and the person responsible for Sports Information at Huskie Athletics. She can give me information about Huskie Athletics and the names of people I should talk to.

Work Schedule

The following schedule will enable me to finish this report by the end of the summer term.

Activity	Total Time	Completion Date	
Gathering information	15 hours	July 6	
Analyzing information	10 hours	July 19	*Time needed will depend on the length and topic of the report, your knowledge of the topic, and your writing skills*
Organizing information	7 hours	July 25	
Preparing the progress report	3 hours	July 30	
Writing the draft/creating visuals	15 hours	August 6	
Revising the draft/visuals	12 hours	August 10	
Editing the draft	5 hours	August 13	
Proofreading the report	3 hours *Allow plenty*	August 20	
Preparing PowerPoint slides	5 hours *of time!*	August 20	

Good reports need good revision, editing, and proofreading as well as good research.

Call to Action

Could we schedule a conference to discuss my proposal and survey draft? I would appreciate any suggestions you may have for strengthening my ideas and making the report better. Please approve my proposal so I may continue my research and begin the report.

It's tactful to indicate you'll accept suggestions. End on a positive note.

(continued)

Read the RFP to find out what is and isn't fundable. Talk to the program officer and read successful past proposals to find answers to the following questions:

- What size projects will the organization fund in theory?
- Does the funder prefer making a few big grants or many smaller grants?
- Does the funder expect you to provide in-kind or cost-sharing funds from other sources?

Think about exactly what you'll do and who will do it. What will it cost? What supplies or materials will be needed? Also think about indirect costs for using office space, retirement and health benefits, salaries, office supplies, administration, and infrastructure.

FIGURE 11.3 Proposal for a Student Report Using Survey, On-Line, and Library Research *(concluded)*

A catchy title can help

In your introductory ¶,
①Tell how to return the survey.
②Tell how the information will be used.

Survey: Why Do Students Attend Athletic Events?

The purpose of this survey is to determine why students attend sports events, and what might increase attendance. All information is to be used solely for a student research paper. Please return completed surveys to Elizabeth or Vicki in the Students' Union. Thank you for your assistance!

Start with easy-to-answer questions

1. Gender (Please circle one)   M   F

2. What is your rank? (Please circle)   1   2   3   4   Grad   Other

Seeing a response in a survey can make respondents more willing to admit to feelings they may be embarrassed to admit

The words below each number anchor responses, while still allowing you to average the data numerically

3. How do you feel about women's sports? (Please circle)

| 1 | 2 | 3 | 4 | 5 |
| I enjoy watching women's sports | | I'll watch, but it doesn't really matter | | Women's sports are boring/ I'd rather watch men's sports |

4. Do you like to attend U of S men's basketball games or listen on the radio? (Please circle)
   Y   N

5. How often do you attend U of S women's basketball games? (Please circle)

| 1 | 2 | 3 | 4 | 5 |
| All/most games | Few games a season | Once a season | Less than once a year | Never |

6. If you do not attend all of the women's basketball games, why not? (Please check all that apply. If you attend all the games, skip to #7.)

__I've never thought to go.
__I don't like basketball.
__I don't like sporting events.
__The team isn't good enough.
__My friends are not interested in going.
__I want to go, I just haven't had the opportunity.
__Game time (6:15 P.M.) is less convenient than for men's play (8:00 P.M.).
__The tickets cost too much for friends without U of S ID cards ($8).
__Other (please specify) _____

Think about factors that affect the problem you're studying, and write survey questions to get information about them.

7. To what extent would each of the following make you more likely to attend a U of S women's basketball game? (please rank all)

| 1 | 2 | 3 |
| Much more likely to attend | Possibly more likely | No effect |

__Increased awareness on campus (flyers, bulletin boards, more articles in *The Sheaf*)
__Marketing to students (giveaways, days for residence halls or student societies)
__Student loyalty program (awarding points towards free tickets, clothing, food for attending games)
__Education (pocket guide explaining the rules of the game provided at the gate)
__Other (please specify) _____

Thank you!
Please return this survey to Elizabeth or Vicki.

Repeat where to turn in or mail completed surveys

Make the basis of your estimates specific.

| Weak: | 75 hours of transcribing interviews | $1,500 |
| Better: | 25 hours of interviews; a skilled transcriber can complete 1 hour of interviews in 3 hours; 75 hours @ $20/hour | $1,500 |

Figure your numbers conservatively. For example, even if you think you might be able to train someone and pay only $12 an hour, use the going rate of $20 an hour. Then, even if your grant is cut, you'll still be able to do the project well.

Writing Progress Reports

When you're assigned to a single project that will take a month or more, you'll probably be asked to file one or more progress reports. A progress report reassures that you're making progress and allows for problems to be resolved as they arise.

Different readers may have different concerns. A professor may want to know whether you'll meet your deadline. A client may be more interested in what you're learning about the problem. Adapt your progress report to the audience.

A study of the progress reports in a large research and development organization found that poor writers tended to focus on what they had done and said very little about the value of their work. Good writers, in contrast, spent less space on details and much more space explaining the value of their work for the organization.[2]

Subject lines for progress reports are straightforward. Specify the project on which you are reporting your progress.

> Subject: Progress on Group Survey on Campus Parking

Make your progress report as positive as you honestly can. You'll build a better image of yourself if you show that you can take minor problems in stride and that you're confident of your own abilities.

Negative: I have not deviated markedly from my schedule, and I feel that I will have very little trouble completing this report by the due date.

Positive: I am back on schedule and expect to complete my report by the due date.

Progress reports can be organized in three ways: by *chronology*, by *task*, and to support a *recommendation*.

The **chronological** pattern of organization focuses on what you have done and what work remains.

1. **Summarize your progress in terms of your goals and your original schedule.** Use measurable statements.

   Poor: My progress has been slow.

   Better: The research for my report is about one-third complete.

2. **Under the heading "Work Completed," describe what you have done.** Be specific, both to support your claims in the first paragraph and to allow the reader to appreciate your hard work. Acknowledge the people who have helped you. Describe any serious obstacles you've encountered and tell how you've dealt with them.

   Poor: I have found many articles about Procter & Gamble on the Web. I have had a few problems finding how the company keeps employees safe from chemical fumes.

   Better: On the Web, I found Procter & Gamble's home page, its annual report, and mission statement. No one whom I interviewed could tell me about safety programs specifically at P&G. I have found seven articles about ways to protect workers against pollution in factories, but none mentions P&G.

3. **Under the heading "Work to Be Completed," describe the work that remains.** If you're more than three days late (for school projects) or two weeks late (for business projects) submit a new schedule, showing how you will be able to meet the original deadline. You may want to discuss "Preliminary Conclusions" if you want feedback before writing the final report or if your reader has asked for substantive interim reports.

4. **Either express your confidence in having the report ready by the due date or request a conference to discuss extending the due date or limiting the project.** If you are behind your original schedule, show why you think you can still finish the project on time.

The student progress report in Figure 11.4 uses this pattern of organization.

The Bullet-Proof Business Plan*

[D]escribe the business in an understandable fashion. . . .

[T]alk about your competitors in detail in your business plan: identify direct, indirect, and even potential competitors and describe their offerings, their percentage of the market, their funding, and their pricing, distribution, and promotion strategies. . . . [B]e crystal clear about how your own offering is different and why it gives customers a better value.

Some evidence that customers will buy your product—and buy it at the price you're charging—is essential. . . .

[I]nvestors expect to see a highly qualified management team in place. . . . At a minimum, you need an experienced and proven CEO. . . . [D]on't cut corners on the sales-and-marketing side. . . .

The path to profitability has to be both clear and short—a year to 18 months. . . . Savvy entrepreneurs will also want to include the slowing economy in their assumptions . . . [I]nvestors still want to cash out in five to seven years. Investors like to see potential acquirers named in the business plan because it shows knowledge of the market.

*Quoted from Emily Barker, "The Bullet-Proof Business Plan," *Inc.*, October 2001, 102–104.

FIGURE 11.4 A Student Chronological Progress Report

To: Kitty O. Locker

From: David G. Bunnel *DGB*

Date: November 10, 2005

Subject: Progress on Software Feasibility Study for the Architecture Firm Patrick and Associates, Inc.

¶ 1: Summarize results in terms of purpose, schedule

I have obtained most of the information necessary to recommend whether CADAM or CATIA is better for Patrick and Associates, Inc. (P&A). I am currently analyzing and organizing this information and am on schedule.

Work Completed   *Underline headings or bold*

Be very specific about what you've done

To learn how computer literate P&A employees are, I interviewed a judgment sample of five employees. My interview with Bruce Ratekin, the director of P&A's Computer-Aided Design (CAD) Department on November 3 enabled me to determine the architectural drafting needs of the firm. Mr. Ratekin also gave me a basic drawing of a building showing both two- and three-dimensional views so that I could replicate the drawing with both software packages.

Show how you've overcome minor problems

I obtained tutorials for both packages to use as a reference while making the drawings. First I drew the building using CADAM, the package designed primarily for two-dimensional architectural drawings. I encountered problems with the isometric drawing because there was a mistake in the manual I was using; I fixed the problem by trying alternatives and finally getting help from another CADAM user. Next, I used CATIA, the package whose strength is three-dimensional drawings, to construct the drawing. I am in the process of comparing the two packages based on these criteria: quality of drawing, ease of data entry (lines, points, surfaces, etc.) for computer experts and novices, and ease of making changes in the completed drawings. Based on my experience with the packages, I have analyzed the training people with and without experience in CAD would need to learn to use each of these packages.

Indicate changes in purpose, scope, or recommendations. Progress report is a low-risk way to bring the readers on board.

Work to Be Completed

Making the drawings has shown that neither of the packages can do everything that P&A needs. Therefore, I want to investigate the feasibility of P&A's buying both packages.

Specify the work that remains

As soon as he comes back from an unexpected illness that has kept him out of the office, I will meet with Tom Merrick, the CAD systems programmer for Mount Royal College, to learn about software expansion flexibility for both packages as well as the costs for initial purchase, installation, maintenance, and software updates. After this meeting, I will be ready to begin the first draft of my report.

Whether I am able to meet my deadline will depend on when I am able to meet with Mr. Merrick. Right now, I am on schedule and plan to submit my report by the December 10 deadline.

End on a positive note

In a **task** progress report, organize information under the various tasks you have worked on during the period. For example, a task progress report for a group report project might use the following headings:

Finding Background Information on the Web and in Print
Analyzing Our Survey Data
Working on the Introduction of the Report and the Appendices

Under each heading, the group could discuss the tasks it has completed and those that remain.

Recommendation progress reports recommend action: increasing the funding for a project, changing its direction, cancelling a project that isn't working out. When the recommendation will be easy for the reader to accept, use the direct request pattern of organization from Chapter 7 (p. 164). If the recommendation is likely to meet strong resistance, the problem-solving pattern (p. 165) may be more effective.

Research Strategies for Reports

Research for a report may be as simple as getting a computer printout of sales for the last month; it may involve finding published material or surveying or interviewing people. **Secondary research** retrieves information that someone else gathered. Library research and online searches are the best-known kinds of secondary research. **Primary research** gathers new information. Surveys, interviews, and observations are common methods for business reports.

Finding Information Online and in Print

You can save time and money by checking online and published sources of data before you gather new information.

Although there has been much talk of a paperless society, print sources—books, magazines, and journals—remain valuable resources. Not all published research is available online or is appropriate for online delivery. When you want an in-depth treatment of a subject, you will want to read a book.

To use a computer database efficiently, identify the concepts you're interested in and choose keywords that will help you find relevant sources. **Keywords** or **descriptors** are the terms that the computer searches for. If you're not sure what terms to use, check the ABI/Inform Thesaurus online for synonyms and the hierarchies in which information is arranged in various databases.

Specific commands allow you to narrow your search. For example, to study the effect of the minimum wage on employment in the restaurant industry, you might use a Boolean search (see Figure 11.5):

> (minimum wage) *and* (restaurant *or* fast food) *and*
> (employment rate *or* unemployment).

This descriptor would give you the titles of articles that treat all three of the topics in parentheses. Without *and*, you'd get articles that discuss the minimum wage in general, articles about every aspect of *restaurants*, and every article that refers to *unemployment*, even though many of these would not be relevant to your topic. The *or* descriptor calls up articles that use the term *fast food* but not the term *restaurant*. An article that used the phrase *food service industry* would be eliminated unless it also used the term *restaurant*. Google and some other Web search engines allow you to specify words that cannot appear in a source.

The Political Uses of Progress Reports

Progress reports can do more than just report progress. You can use progress reports to

- Enhance your image. Details about the number of documents you've read, people you've surveyed, or experiments you've conducted create a picture of a hardworking person doing a thorough job.

- Float trial balloons. Explain, "I could continue to do X [what you approved]; I could do Y instead [what I'd like to do now]." The detail in the progress report can help back up your claim. Even if the idea is rejected, you don't lose face because you haven't made a separate issue of the alternative.

- Minimize potential problems. As you do the work, it may become clear that implementing your recommendations will be difficult. In your regular progress reports, you can alert your boss or the funding agency to the challenges that lie ahead, enabling them to prepare psychologically and physically to act on your recommendations.

FIGURE 11.5 Example of a Boolean Search

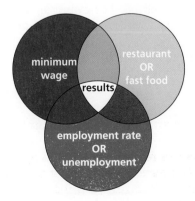

Insider Information*

You want to know how fast an F-16 flies, but your search engine spits back details on camera shutter speeds. To save yourself these detours, take a page from the book of Sergey Brin, co-founder of the search-engine Google: Think more like a programmer and ask yourself: What words do I want to come back in my response?

When Mr. Brin, who watches his waistline, wants to know how much protein is in a serving of chicken breast, he doesn't just type in "chicken breast" and "protein." He adds the word "grams."

Another of his winnowing tricks is to use the minus sign. To ensure that a search for "dolphins" doesn't bring up a slew of references to the Miami Dolphins football team, for instance, type dolphin –miami. (A space must be added before the minus sign, and the minus sign must go directly before the word to be removed.)

Mr. Brin has another secret. For local addresses and phone numbers, he uses Yahoo.

*Quoted from "Tricks of the Trade: Web Searching with a Pro," *The Wall Street Journal*, June 5, 2002, D1.

Many words can appear in related forms. To catch all of them, use the database's **wild card** or **truncated code** for shortened terms and root words.

Web search engines are particularly effective for words, people, or phrases that are unlikely to have separate pages devoted to them. For general topics or famous people, directories like E-Blast or Yahoo! are more useful, since they yield a smaller number of hits. Figures 11.6 and 11.7 list a few of the specialized sources available.

Evaluating Web Sources

Some of the material on the Web is excellent, but some of it is wholly unreliable. With print sources, the editor or publisher serves as a gatekeeper, so you can trust the material in good journals. To put up a Web page, all one needs is access to a server.

Use four criteria to decide whether a Web site is good enough to use for a research project:

1. **Authors.** What person or organization sponsors the site? What credentials do the authors have?
2. **Objectivity.** Does the site give evidence to support its claims? Does it give both sides of controversial issues? Is the tone professional?
3. **Information.** How complete is the information? What is it based on?
4. **Revision date.** When was the site last updated?

Answers to these questions may lead you to discard some of the relevant sites you find. For example, if you find five different Web pages about cell phones and car accidents that all cite the same Toronto study, you have one source, not five. Choose the most complete for your project.

Designing Questions for Surveys and Interviews

A **survey** questions a large group of people, called **respondents** or **subjects.** The easiest way to ask many questions is to create a **questionnaire,** a written

---

FIGURE 11.6   Sources for Electronic Research

CD-ROM databases are available in many university libraries. Check your college or university library to find additional sources.

ABI/Inform (indexes and abstracts 800 journals in management and business)

Business Index ASAP

Canadian Business & Current Affairs (CBCA) Complete

ComIndex (indexes and abstracts journals in communication)

Foreign Trade and Economic Abstracts

Gender Studies Database

Governments Canada Database

LEXIS/NEXIS Services

McGraw-Hill Encyclopedia of Science

Newspaper Abstracts

PAIS International—Public Affairs Information Service

Social Sciences Index

Wilson Business Abstracts

Women's Resources International

FIGURE 11.7 Sources for Web Research

Not Necessarily True*

Subject matter directories

Aboriginal Canada Portal
  www.aboriginalcanada.gc.ca
SmartPros Accounting
  www.pro2net.com
Canada Business/Enterprises Canada
  www.cbsc.org
Strategis: Canada's Business and Consumer Site
  www.strategis.ic.gc.ca
Education Index
  www.educationindex.com/
Resources for economists on the Internet
  http://rfe.wustl.edu/
FINWeb Homepage
  www.finweb.com/finweb.html
Human resource management resources on the Internet
  www.nbs.ntu.ac.uk/research/depts/hrm/links.php
Questia: Human Resource Management
  www.Questia.com
Global Edge
  www.globaledge.msu.edu
International Business Kiosk
  www.calintel.org/kiosk
Management and entrepreneurship
  www.lib.lsu.edu/bus/managemt.html
KnowThis.Marketing.com: Virtual Library
  www.knowthis.com
International Internet marketing resources
  www.lib.lsu.edu/bus/marketin.html

News sites

BusinessWeek
  www.businessweek.com
Canadian Business online
  www.canadianbusiness.com
CNN/CNNFN
  www.cnn.com (news)
  www.money.cnn.com (financial news)
CBC
  www.cbc.ca/newsworld
The Globe and Mail online
  www.globeandmail.com
Maclean's online
  www.macleans.ca

Information on the Web is not necessarily true.

Press releases from "Independent Financial Reports" touted an Internet stock. "Independent Financial Reports" did not exist; the press releases were fakes, designed to boost the price of the stock. (The SEC has filed suit.)

The satirical newspaper *The Onion* (http://www.theonion.com) posted an "interview" in which *Harry Potter* author J. K. Rowling "admitted" that she worshipped Satan. The interview was a spoof.

A Minnesota Web page showed a sunny beach where "thanks to a freak of nature: the Farr/Sclare Fissure" hot springs warmed water year round. The spoof caused so many people to ask for information on lodging that the page finally posted a disclaimer and was eventually removed.

For nearly a year in 2000–01, a Web site chronicled Kaycee Nicole Swenson's losing battle with leukemia. Only after her "death" did mourners realize that no one had ever met her. In fact, Kaycee was a fiction.

For information on Web frauds and hoaxes, see http://www.snopes.2.com or http://www.scambusters.org.

*Based on "Beware the Press Release," *BusinessWeek,* April 24, 2000, 153; "You Said It," *Reader's Digest,* April 2001, 18; Laura Gurak, "'Is This the Party to Whom I Am Speaking?' Women, Credibility, and the Internet," *The Women's Review of Books* 18, no. 5 (February 2001): 5; and Katie Hafter, "Friends Mourn a Life That Never Was," *The Columbus Dispatch,* July 9, 2001, E6.

FIGURE 11.7   Sources for Web Research *(concluded)*

The National Post online

    www.nationalpost.com

National Public Radio

    www.npr.org

NewsLink (links to U.S., Canadian, and international newspapers, magazines, and resources online)

    www.newslink.org

New York Times

    www.nyt.com

The Wall Street Journal

    www.wsj.com

Washington Post

    www.WashingtonPost.com

Canadian government information

Statistics Canada

    www.statcan.ca

Census of Population and Census of Agriculture

    www12.statcan.ca/english/census01/release/index.cfm

Consumer Price Index: Historical Summary

    www40.statcan.ca/l01/cst01/econ46.htm

The Daily

    www.statcan.ca/english/dai-quo/

Historical Statistics of Canada

    www.statcan.ca/english/freepub/11-516-XIE/sectiona/toc.htm

Print Research Sources

Accountants' Index

Business Periodicals Index

Canadian Business Index

Personnel Management Abstracts

Reader's Guide to Periodical Literature

list of questions that people fill out. An **interview** is a structured conversation with someone who will be able to give you useful information. Surveys and interviews can be useful only if the questions are well designed.

Good questions ask only one thing, are phrased neutrally, avoid making assumptions about the respondent, and mean the same thing to different people.

Phrase questions in a way that won't bias the response or lead the respondent. Words like *often* and *important* mean different things to different people. Whenever possible, use more objective measures:

Vague: Do you study in the library frequently?

Better: How many hours a week do you study in the library?

Questions can be categorized in several ways.

Closed questions have a limited number of possible responses. **Open questions** do not lock the subject into any sort of response. See Figure 11.8. Closed questions are faster for subjects to answer and easier for researchers to score.

InSite

erg.environics.net/

The Environics Research Group Web page posts questions and answers on leading issues in business and the public sector.

FIGURE 11.8 Closed and Open Questions

Closed questions

Are you satisfied with the city bus service? (yes/no)

How good is the city bus service?

Excellent 5 4 3 2 1 Terrible

Indicate whether you agree or disagree with each of the following statements about city bus service:

A D   The schedule is convenient for me.

A D   The routes are convenient for me.

A D   The drivers are courteous.

A D   The buses are clean.

Rate each of the following improvements in the order of their importance to you (1 = most important, 6 = least important)

_____ Buy new buses.

_____ Increase non-rush-hour service on weekdays.

_____ Increase service on weekdays.

_____ Provide earlier and later service on weekdays.

_____ Buy more buses with wheelchair access.

_____ Provide unlimited free transfers.

Open questions

How do you feel about the city bus service?

Tell me about the city bus service.

Why do you ride the bus? (or, Why don't you ride the bus?)

What do you like and dislike about the city bus service?

How could the city bus service be improved?

However, since all answers must fit into prechosen categories, they cannot probe the complexities of a subject.

Use an "Other, Please Specify" category when you want the convenience of a closed question but cannot foresee all the possible responses:

What is the single most important reason that you ride the bus?

_____ I don't have a car.

_____ I don't want to fight rush-hour traffic.

_____ Riding the bus is cheaper than driving my car.

_____ Riding the bus conserves fuel and reduces pollution.

_____ Other (Please specify) _____

When you use multiple-choice questions, make sure that any one answer fits only in one category. In the following example of overlapping categories, a person who worked for a company with exactly 25 employees could check either *a* or *b*. The resulting data would be unreliable.

Overlapping categories: Indicate the number of full-time employees in your company on May 16:

___ a. 0–25

___ b. 25–100

___ c. 100–500

___ d. over 500

Watch Your Language*

In two decades of writing and using surveys, psychologist Palmer Morrel-Samuels has seen that the wording of a survey question can affect responses. He recalls a survey that a maker of photographic equipment used to learn about the leadership skills of its managers. A question asked employees whether their manager "takes bold strides" and "has a strong grasp" of complicated issues. Male managers tended to outscore female managers. Morrel-Samuels noted that, in a literal sense, males on average take longer strides and have more muscle strength than females. The company changed the wording of the survey. "Has a strong grasp of complex problems" became "discusses complex problems with precision and clarity." After this change, the difference in ratings of female and male managers disappeared.

Another word-related bias is that respondents tend to agree more than disagree with statements. If a survey about managers asks employees whether their manager is fair, ethical, intelligent, knowledgeable, and so on, they are likely to assign all of these qualities to the manager—and to agree more and more as the survey goes along. To correct for this, some questions should be worded to generate the opposite response. For example, a statement about ethics can be balanced by a statement about corruption, and a statement about fairness can be balanced by a statement about bias or stereotypes.

*Based on Palmer Morrel-Samuels, "Getting the Truth into Workplace Surveys," *Harvard Business Review*, February 2002, 111–118.

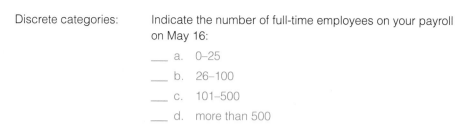

Discrete categories: Indicate the number of full-time employees on your payroll on May 16:

___ a.   0–25

___ b.   26–100

___ c.   101–500

___ d.   more than 500

Giving several options is more important the older your respondents are. Psychologist Cynthia Adams notes that older people are uncomfortable choosing between only two options. When asked "Are discounts important to you," more mature people want to answer, "It depends."[3] A good survey will specify the context or allow the respondent to do so.

Branching questions direct different respondents to different parts of the questionnaire based on their answers to earlier questions.

10. Have you talked to an academic adviser this year?   Yes   No
    (If "no," skip to question 14.)

Generally, put early in the questionnaire questions that will be easy to answer. Put questions that are harder to answer or that people may be less willing to answer (e.g., age and income) near the end of the questionnaire. Even if people choose not to answer such questions, you'll still have the rest of the survey filled out.

If subjects will fill out the questionnaire themselves, pay careful attention to the physical design of the document. Pretest the questionnaire to make sure the directions are clear. One researcher mailed a two-page questionnaire without pretesting it. Twenty-five respondents didn't answer the questions on the back of the first page.[4]

Conducting Surveys and Interviews

Face-to-face surveys are convenient when you are surveying a fairly small number of people in a specific location. In a face-to-face survey, the interviewer's sex, race, and non-verbal cues can bias results. Most people prefer not to say things they think their audience will find unacceptable. For that reason, women will be more likely to agree that sexual harassment is a problem if the interviewer is also a woman. Members of a minority group are more likely to admit that they suffer discrimination if the interviewer is a member of the same minority.

Telephone surveys are popular because they can be closely supervised. Interviewers can read the questions from a computer screen and key in answers as the respondent gives them. The results can then be available just a few minutes after the last call is completed.

The major limitation of phone surveys is that they reach only people who have phones and thus underrepresent poor people. To include people with unlisted numbers, professional survey-takers use automatic random-digit dialing. Since women are more likely to answer the phone than men are,[5] decide in advance to whom you want to speak, and ask for that person rather than surveying whoever answers the phone.

Mail surveys can reach anyone who has an address. Some people may be more willing to fill out an anonymous questionnaire than to give sensitive information to a stranger over the phone.

Online surveys deliver questions over the Internet. The researcher can contact respondents with e-mail containing a link to a Web page with the survey or can ask people by mail or in person to log on and visit the Web site with the survey. Another alternative is to post a survey on a Web site and invite the site's visitors to complete the survey. This approach does not generate a random sample, so the results probably do not reflect the opinions of the entire population.

Interactive technology makes it easy to use branching questions; the survey can automatically send respondents to the next question on a branch. However, many people worry about the privacy of online surveys, so they may be reluctant to participate. Researchers have found that a lower percentage of people are willing to complete online surveys than other kinds. To encourage participation, researchers should make online surveys as short as possible.[6]

A major concern with any kind of survey is the **response rate,** the percentage of people who respond. People who refuse to answer may differ from those who respond quickly, and you need information from both groups to be able to generalize to the whole population. To get as high a response rate as possible, good researchers contact non-respondents at least once to try to persuade them to participate in the survey.

Selecting a sample for surveys and interviews

To keep research costs reasonable, only a sample of the total population is polled. How that sample is chosen and the attempts made to get responses from non-respondents will determine whether you can infer that what is true of your sample is also true of the population as a whole. The **population** is the group you want to make statements about. Depending on the purpose of your research, your population might be all Top 1000 companies from the *Report on Business* annual listing, all business students at your college, or all consumers.

A **convenience sample** is a group of subjects who are easy to get: students who walk through the students' union, people at a shopping mall, workers in your own unit. Convenience samples are useful for a rough pretest of a questionnaire and may be acceptable for some class research projects. However, you cannot generalize from a convenience sample to a larger group.

A **judgment sample** is a group of people whose views seem useful. Someone interested in surveying the kinds of writing done on campus might ask each department for the name of a faculty member who cared about writing, and then send surveys to those people.

In a **random sample,** each person in the population theoretically has an equal chance of being chosen.

True random samples rely on random digit tables, published in statistics texts and books such as *A Million Random Digits* or computer-generated random numbers.

Conducting research interviews

Schedule interviews in advance; tell the interviewee about how long you expect the interview to take.

Interviews can be structured or unstructured. In a **structured interview,** the interviewer uses a detailed list of questions to guide the interview. Indeed, a structured interview may use a questionnaire just as a survey does. In an **unstructured interview,** the interviewer has three or four main questions. Other questions build on what the interviewee says. To prepare for an unstructured interview, learn as much as possible about the interviewee and the topic. Go into the interview with three or four main topics you want to cover.

Interviewers sometimes use closed questions to start the interview and set the interviewee at ease. The strength of an interview, however, is getting at a person's attitudes, feelings, and experiences. Situational questions let you probe what someone would do in a specific circumstance. Hypothetical questions that ask people to imagine what they would do generally yield less reliable answers than questions about **critical incidents** or key past events.

Ethical Issues in Interviewing

If you're trying to get sensitive information, interviewees may give useful information when the interview is "over" and the tape recorder has been turned off. Is it ethical to use that information?

If you're interviewing a hostile or very reluctant interviewee, you may get more information if you agree with everything you can legitimately agree to, and keep silent on the rest. Is it ethical to imply acceptance even when you know you'll criticize the interviewee's ideas in your report?

Most people would say that whatever public figures say is fair game: they're supposed to know enough to defend themselves. Many people would say that different rules apply when you'll cite someone by name than when you'll use the information as background or use a pseudonym so that the interviewee cannot be identified.

As a practical matter, if someone feels you've misrepresented him or her, that person will be less willing to talk to you in the future. But quite apart from practical considerations, interview strategies raise ethical issues as well.

Ethnographic research closely observes how people choose and use products. Videotapes showed that many customers bought only a few cuts of meat because they didn't know how to cook other cuts. As a result, many grocers are now rearranging meat products by cooking methods and offering simple, three-step instructions on packages.

Hypothetical question:	What would you say if you had to tell an employee that his or her performance was unsatisfactory?
Critical incident question:	You've probably been in a situation where someone who was working with you wasn't carrying his or her share of the work. What did you do the last time that happened?

A **mirror question** paraphrases the content of the last answer: "So you confronted him directly?" "You think that this product costs too much?" Mirror questions check that the interviewer understands what the interviewee has said and prompt the interviewee to continue talking. **Probes** follow up an original question to get at specific aspects of a topic:

Question:	What do you think about the fees for campus parking?
Probes:	Would you be willing to pay more for a reserved space? How much more? Should the fines for vehicles parked illegally be increased? Do you think fees should be based on income?

Observing Customers and Users

Answers to surveys and interviews may differ from actual behaviour—sometimes greatly. To get more accurate consumer information, many marketers observe users.

When she introduced Growing Healthy, a line of frozen baby foods, founder Julia Knight enlisted friends with kids to join her on research shopping trips.

She quickly realized that the frozen food section wasn't a good location. Kids didn't like the cold, and parents sped through as quickly as possible. So she persuaded supermarket managers to place cutaway freezers in the baby food section, and her company succeeded. Her observations also showed Knight why survey and interview data can be so unreliable: "What mother, especially in front of other mothers, would really tell you that she spent more on cat food than on baby food?"[7]

Using and Documenting Sources

In a good report, sources are cited and documented smoothly and unobtrusively. **Citation** means attributing an idea or fact to its source *in the body of the report*: "According to the 2006 Census . . .," "Jane Bryant Quinn argues that . . ." Citing sources demonstrates your honesty, enhances your credibility, directs readers to resources, and helps you avoid **plagiarism** charges. **Documentation** means providing the bibliographic information readers would need to go back to the original source.

While plagiarism, the unacknowledged use of another's ideas and/or expression, can be a deliberate act by desperate, cynical, or lazy people (concealing sources, handing in a report written by someone else), it is also often an act of omission. When students or professionals unintentionally recall and repeat exact wording from a source, forget to ensure quotation marks around exact quotations, use online material they thought was copyright free, or paraphrase or summarize a source's ideas without acknowledgment, they are guilty of plagiarism

High-profile cases like the 2002 suspension of 44 students at Simon Fraser University have kept plagiarism at the forefront and have caused many post-secondary institutions to develop programs and to use turnitin.com, a site with over 1 million previously submitted papers. University of Toronto is one of a number of Canadian universities using turnitin.com services, though the majority of students remain honest and "recognize that plagiarism threatens the value of their hard work."[8]

Journalistic plagiarism and firings have also made the news: reporter Jayson Blair admitted that he had faked or stolen material for 36 stories for *The New York Times*, a *Los Angeles Times* photographer acknowledged that in 2003 he had combined two pictures to make "a more dramatic image" of the war in Iraq, a *Toronto Star* reporter conceded that she had copied almost a third of a story about a US. Army deserter from *The Village Voice*, and *National Post* medical reporter Brad Evensen was fired for faking quotations in nine stories.[9]

Although poor training and inadequate resources have caused many plagiarism problems, the Internet has added to the challenges. At University of Toronto, plagiarism related to the Internet increased from 50% to 99% of cases between 2000–2001 and 2001–2002. Managing Editor Kirk LaPointe of the *Vancouver Sun* warns, "There is this great gateway to this exciting information that a reporter can steal, but on the other hand, there's a record of it and anybody who steals can be caught."[10]

Whether you are dealing with an online or print source, you will have to decide to quote or put it into your own words. You will choose to quote when

- The source's expression is especially effective, vivid, or original.
- The source depends on specialized or technical terms.
- You want to dispute the terms of the source's argument.

Be sure to integrate quotations into your own grammar/developing argument, varying introductory words (*Jennifer Barton agrees, argues, claims, responds, notes, suggests; from Jennifer Barton's point of view; according to Jennifer Barton*). Quote only those words necessary for document purposes and reader

Consumers in the Mist*

The 60-ish woman caught on the grainy videotape is sitting on her hotel bed, addressing her husband after a long day spent on the road. "Good job!" she exults. "We beat the . . . out of the front desk and got a terrific room!" . . . [T]he couple was part of the latest effort by marketers to figure out what consumers really think about their products. . . .

Best Western International . . . paid 25 over-55 couples to tape themselves on cross-country journeys. . . . [T]he effort convinced the hotel chain that it didn't need to boost its standard 10% senior citizen discount. The tapes showed that seniors who talked the hotel clerk into a better deal . . . were after the thrill of the deal. Instead of attracting new customers, bigger discounts would simply allow the old customers to trade up to a fancier dinner down the street somewhere[,] doing absolutely nothing for Best Western.

*Quoted from Gerry Khermouch, "Consumers in the Mist," *BusinessWeek*, January 26, 2001, 92–94.

needs; mark omissions with ellipses (spaced dots) and changes with square brackets (see the sidebar on p. 271).

If you paraphrase or summarize, be careful that you do not inadvertently repeat words or sentence structure from your source. For example:

Original: "There is a great gateway to this exciting information that a reporter can steal, but on the other hand, there's a record of it and anybody who steals can be caught" (LaPointe 4).

Plagiarism: The Internet is a great gateway to information that a reporter can borrow, but the record means that anybody who borrows can be found.

Acceptable paraphrases: If it gives access to information that reporters may use without credit, the Internet also supplies the evidence that will prove their theft (LaPointe 4).

According to Kirk LaPointe, the Internet is both a rich source of information for reporters and the source of evidence to catch them if they take without credit.

Note that citation and documentation are used in addition to quotation marks. If you use the source's exact words, you'll use the name of the person you're citing and quotation marks in the body of the report; you'll indicate the source in parentheses and a list of references, or works cited, or in a footnote or endnote. If you put the source's idea into your own words, or if you condense or synthesize information, you don't need quotation marks, but you still need to tell whose idea it is and where you found it.

You do *not* need to document historical dates or facts that are common knowledge ("More and more women are entering the workforce").

Long quotations (four typed lines or more) are used sparingly in business reports. Since many readers skip quotations, always summarize the main point of the quotation in a single sentence before the quotation itself. End the sentence with a colon, not a period, since it introduces the quotation. Indented quotations do not need quotation marks; the indentation shows the reader that the passage is a quotation.

The three most widely used formats for footnotes, endnotes, and bibliographies in reports are those of the American Psychological Association (APA), the Modern Language Association (MLA), and the University of Chicago *Manual of Style* format, which this book uses. The APA format uses internal documentation with a list of references; it does not use footnotes or endnotes. **Internal documentation** provides in parentheses in the text the work and the page number where the reference was found. The work may be indicated by the author's last name (if that isn't already in the sentence), or by the last name plus the date of the work. The full bibliographical citation appears in a list of references or works cited at the end of the report. Figures 11.9 and 11.10 show a portion of a report in APA and MLA formats, respectively, with the list of references (APA) or works cited (MLA). Figure 11.11 shows the APA and MLA formats for the sources used most often in reports.

If you have used many sources that you have not cited, you may want to list both works cited and works consulted. The term *bibliography* covers all sources on a topic.

If you use a printed source that is not readily available, consider including it as an appendix in your report. For example, you could copy an ad or include an organization's promotional brochure.

FIGURE 11.9 Report Paragraphs with APA Documentation

Does That Method Work?*

Heading, ¶ number help readers find material in Web site without page numbers

APA Format

Modern office buildings contain a surprising number of pollutants. Printing and copying documents creates particles that can be harmful to health. Office carpets and furniture emit chemical pollutants (Environmental Protection Agency, "Management of pollutant sources" section, ¶s 4–5). Indeed, the dyes and sealants used in many office chairs are considered hazardous waste. "Most people are sitting on chairs that are an amalgam of hundreds of chemicals that have never been [tested] . . . . The [more deeply] we look, [the more] we find . . . cancer-causing chemicals," says William McDonough, an architectural consultant who specializes in air-quality concerns (Conlin, 2000, p. 128).

Square brackets indicate a change from the original to make the quotation fit into the structure of your sentence

Ellipses (spaced dots) indicate some material has been omitted

An extra dot serves as the period of the sentence

The problem is compounded by inadequate ventilation. The American Society of Heating, Refrigeration, and Air-Conditioning Engineers recommends that a building's heating, ventilation, and cooling system deliver 20 cubic feet per minute of outside air for each occupant (Aerias, 2001, "Ventilation rates" section, ¶ 5). But, Conlin (2000) reports, some buildings provide only 5 cubic feet of fresh air per person a minute. And that "fresh air" may not be pure. Some buildings have fresh air vents over loading docks and parking garages. Revolving doors pull in second-hand smoke "like a chimney" (p. 117) from smokers who stand by the door.

All material from citation to end of ¶ is from a single source

Use page number for direct quotation (no need to repeat source when named earlier in ¶)

In the 1990s, responses to "sick buildings" often focused on the cost of solving the problem—a cost sometimes undertaken only after a lawsuit was filed (Nai, 1995). But recently several companies have found that improving air quality pays for itself. Pennsylvania Power and Light's remodelling paid for itself in just 69 days by cutting absenteeism 25%, increasing productivity 13%, and reducing energy costs 69% (Aerias, 2001, "Why indoor air quality should be improved," ¶ 4).

Place author, date in parentheses (use page numbers only for a direct quotation)

List all works (but only those works) cited in text

References

Don't abbreviate month

List sources alphabetically.

Aerias. (2001). Overview of IAQ problems in offices. Retrieved September 24, 2005 from the World Wide Web: http://www.aerias.org/office_overview.htm

List source only once, even when it's used more than once

Use URL of home page

Conlin, M. (with Carey, J.). (2000, June 5). Is your office killing you? *BusinessWeek*, 114–128.

Copyright/update date

Repeat hundreds

Environmental Protection Agency. (2001, July 19). An office building occupant's guide to indoor air quality. Retrieved September 19, 2005, from the World Wide Web: http://www.epa.gov/iaq/pubs/occupgd.html

No punctuation at the end of a URL

Nai, A. K. (1995, October 26). Squabbles delay cure of "sick" office building. *The Wall Street Journal*, pp. B1, B3.

[Some research methods don't really capture what they hope to capture. Consider, for example, the Nielsen TV diaries.] Nielsen's diaries divide an hour's worth of viewing into four 15-minute time blocks, under the impression, apparently, that viewers tend to watch at least a quarter of an hour of any given show. That's a misplaced assumption. . . . On any given morning, in one 15-minute Nielsen time block, I've typically surfed through four major networks, plus CNBC. That averages out to 3 minutes per station. Pathetic but true. So how did I account for such channel-surfing in the diary? I pretended to watch a half-hour of morning TV instead of 15 minutes, and knocked out the two stations I watched least. . . .

I also didn't jot down everything. Does anyone care that at 5 a.m. one morning my eyes were glued to Suzanne Somers and Patrick Duffy explaining what muscles the Torso Track targets? It's not as if I was really watching: I was simply too low on caffeine to begin my remote-control-pressing exercises.

*Quoted from Seema Nayyar, "Confessions of a Nielsen Household," *American*

Summary of Key Points

- **Information reports** collect data for the reader; **analytical reports** present and interpret data; **recommendation reports** recommend action or a solution.
- A good purpose statement must make three things clear:
  - The organizational problem or conflict.
  - The specific technical questions that must be answered to solve the problem.
  - The rhetorical purpose (to explain, to recommend, to request, to propose) in terms of audience benefits.
- A proposal must answer the following questions:
  - What problem will you solve?
  - How will you solve it?

FIGURE 11.10   Report Paragraphs with MLA Documentation

An extra dot serves as the period of the sentence

MLA Format

Modern office buildings contain a surprising number of pollutants. Printing and copying documents creates particles that can be harmful to health. Office carpets and furniture emit chemical pollutants (Environmental Protection Agency, "Management of Pollutant Sources" section, pars. 4–5). Indeed, the dyes and sealants used in many office chairs are considered hazardous waste. "Most people are sitting on chairs that are an amalgam of hundreds of chemicals that have never been [tested] . . . The [more deeply] we look, [the more] we find . . . cancer-causing chemicals," says William McDonough, an architectural consultant who specializes in air-quality concerns (Conlin 128).

Square brackets indicate a change from the original to make the quotation fit into the structure of your sentence

No comma between author, page number; no "p." before page number

The problem is compounded by inadequate ventilation. The American Society of Heating, Refrigeration, and Air-Conditioning Engineers recommends that a building's heating, ventilation, and cooling system deliver 20 cubic feet per minute of outside air for each occupant (Aerias, 2001, "Ventilation Rates" section, par. 5). But, Michelle Conlin reports, some buildings provide only 5 cubic feet of fresh air per person a minute. And that "fresh air" may not be pure. Some buildings have fresh air vents over loading docks and parking garages. Revolving doors pull in second-hand smoke "like a chimney' (117) from smokers who stand by the door.

Use only page number since author identified in sentence

In the 1990s, responses to "sick buildings" often focused on the cost of solving the problem—a cost sometimes undertaken only after a lawsuit was filed (Nai B1). But recently, several companies have found that improving air quality pays for itself. Pennsylvania Power and Light's remodelling paid for itself in just 69 days by cutting absenteeism 25%, increasing productivity 13%, and reducing energy costs 69% (Aerias, 2001, "Why Indoor Air Quality Should Be Improved," par. 4).

Heading, paragraph number helps reader find material in Web sites without page numbers

Give page number for facts, not just quotations

Works Cited   *Copyright/update date*

List all works cited in text   *Date you visited site*

Aerias. "Overview of IAQ Problems in Offices." 2001. 24 Sept. 2005 <http://www.aerias.org/office_overview.htm>.   *URL in angle brackets; period after angle bracket.*

List sources alphabetically

Conlin, Michelle with John Carey. "Is Your Office Killing You?" *BusinessWeek* 5 June 2000: 114–28.   *Don't repeat hundreds*

Environmental Protection Agency. "An Office Building Occupant's Guide to Indoor Air Quality." 19 July 2001. 19 Sept. 2005 <http://www.epa.gov/iaq/pubs/occupgd.html>.   *Use date month year; abbreviate month*   *If URL is too long to fit on one line, break after a punctuation mark*

Nai, Amal Kumar. "Squabbles Delay Cure of 'Sick' Office Building." *The Wall Street Journal* 26 October 1995: B1+.   *"+" indicates article continues*

- What exactly will you provide for us?
- Can you deliver what you promise?
- What benefits can you offer?
- When will you complete the work?
- How much will you charge?

- In a proposal for funding, stress the needs your project will meet. Show how your project will help fulfill the goals of the organization you are asking for funds.

- Progress reports may be organized chronologically, by task, or to support a recommendation.

- To decide whether to use a Web site as a source in a research project, evaluate the site's authors, objectivity, information, and revision date.

- A **survey** questions a large group of people, called **respondents** or **subjects**. A **questionnaire** is a written list of questions that people fill out. An **interview** is a structured conversation with someone who will be able to give you useful information.

FIGURE 11.11	APA and MLA Formats for Sources Used Most Often in Reports

APA Format

APA internal documentation gives the author's last name and the date of the work in parentheses in the text. A comma separates the author's name from the date (Gilsdorf & Leonard, 2001). The page number is given only for direct quotations (Cross, 2001, p. 74). If the author's name is used in the sentence, only the date is given in parentheses. (See Figure 11.9.) A list of References gives the full bibliographic citation, arranging the entries alphabetically by the first author's last name.

In titles of articles and books capitalize only
(1) First word
(2) First word of subtitle
(3) Proper nouns

comma *last name first*   *Year (period outside parentheses)*   *No quotation marks around title of article*

Article in a Periodical
Gilsdorf, J., & Leonard, D. (2001). Big stuff, little stuff: A decennial measurement of executives' and academics' reactions to questionable usage elements. *The Journal of Business Communication, 38,* 439–475. *no "pp." when journal has a volume number*   *Capitalize all major words in title of journal, magazine, or newspaper*
Italicize volume.

McCartney, S. (2000, December 27). Why a baseball superstar's megacontract can be less than it seems. *The Wall Street Journal*, p. B1, B3.
Separate discontinuous pages with comma and space

Article in an Edited Book *Ampersands join names of co-authors, co-editors*   *Editors'*
Killingsworth, M. J., & Jacobsen, M. (1999). The rhetorical construction of environmental *names* risk narratives in government and activist websites: A critique. In J. M. Perkins & N. *have last* Blyler (Eds.), *Narrative and professional communication* (pp. 167–177). Stamford, CT: *names* Ablex. *Repeat "1" in 177*   *last*
Editors before book title   *Give state or province when city is not well known*

Article from a Publication on the Web
Greengard, S. (2001, May). Scoring web wins. *Business Finance Magazine*. p. 37. Retrieved July 12, 2001, from http://www.businessfinancemag.com/archives/appfiles/Article.cfm? IssueID=348&ArticleID=13750 *← no punctuation after URL*
Initials only   *Italicize title of book*

Book
Cross, G. A. (2001). *Forming the collective mind: A contextual exploration of large-scale collaborative writing in industry*. Creskill, NJ: Hampton Press.
Put in square brackets information known to you

Book or Pamphlet with a Corporate Author *but not printed in document*
Citibank. (1994). *Indonesia: An investment guide*. [Jakarta:] Author.
Indicates organization authoring document also published it

E-Mail Message
[Identify e-mail messages in the text as personal communications (without mentioning e-mail addresses). Give name of author and as specific a date as possible. Do not list in References.]

Government Document
No abbreviations Senate Special Committee on Aging. (2001). *Long-term care: States grapple with increasing demands and costs*. Hearing before the Special Committee on Aging, Senate, One Hundred Seventh Congress, first session, hearing held in Washington, DC, July 11, 2001 (Doc ID: 75-038). Washington, DC: U.S. Government Printing Office.
Document number   *APA uses periods for "U.S."*

(continued)

- Good questions ask just one thing, are phrased neutrally, avoid making assumptions about the respondent, and mean the same thing to different people.
- **Closed questions** have a limited number of possible responses. **Open questions** do not lock the subject into any sort of response. **Branching questions** direct different respondents to different parts of the questionnaire based on their answers to earlier questions. A **mirror question** paraphrases the content of the last answer. **Probes** follow up an original question to get at specific aspects of a topic.

FIGURE 11.11   APA and MLA Formats for Sources Used Most Often in Reports *(continued)*

Copyright or update date

Government Document Available on the Web from the GPO Access Database
U.S. General Accounting Office. (2001, September 20.) Aviation security: Terrorist acts demonstrate urgent need to improve security at the nation's airports. Testimony before the Committee on Commerce, Science, and Transportation, U.S. Senate (GAO-01-1162T). Retrieved December 20, 2001, from General Accounting Office Reports Online via GPO Access: http://www.gao.gov/new.items/d011162t.pdf

Date you visited site

Keep "http://"

Interview Conducted by the Researcher
[Identify interviews in the test as personal communications. Give name of interviewee and as specific a date as possible. Do not list in References.]

Posting to a Listserv
[Identify messages on listservs to which one must subscribe in the text as personal communications. Give name of author and as specific a date as possible. Do not list in References.]

Web Site
American Express. (2001). Creating an effective business plan. Retrieved December 20, 2001, from http://home3.americanexpress.com/smallbusiness/ tool/biz_plan/ index.asp

Comma

No punctuation

Break long web address at a slash or other punctuation mark

MLA Format

MLA internal documentation gives the author's last name and page number in parentheses in the text for facts as well as for quotations (Gilsdorf and Leonard 470). Unlike APA, the year is not given, no comma separates the name and page number, and the abbreviation "p." is not used (Cross 74). If the author's name is used in the sentence, only the page number is given in parentheses. (See Figure 11.10.) A list of Works Cited gives the full bibliographic citation, arranging the entries alphabetically by the first author's last name.

First name first for second author

Put quotation marks around title of article

Article in a Periodical
Gilsdorf, Jeanette and Don Leonard. "Big Stuff, Little Stuff: A Decennial Measurement of Executives' and Academics' Reactions to Questionable Usage Elements." *The Journal of Business Communication* 38 (2001): 448–75.

Capitalize all major words in titles of articles, books, journals magazines, and newspapers

Omit "4" in "475"

Italicize title of journal, magazine, or newspaper

McCartney, Scott. "Why a Baseball Superstar's Megacontract Can Be Less Than It Seems." *The Wall Street Journal*, 27 Dec. 2000: B1+.

Indicates article continues past first page

Article from an Edited Book
Killingsworth, M. Jimmie and Martin Jacobsen. "The Rhetorical Construction of Environmental Risk Narratives in Government and Activist Websites: A Critique." *Narrative and Professional Communication*. Ed. Jane M. Perkins and Nancy Blyler. Stamford, CT: Ablex. 167–77.

Give authors', editors' names as printed in the source

Give state or province when city is not well known

Spell out editors' names. Join with "and."

(continued)

- A **convenience sample** is a group of subjects who are easy to get. A **judgment sample** is a group of people whose views seem useful. In a **random sample,** each person in the population theoretically has an equal chance of being chosen.

- **Citation** means attributing an idea or fact to its source in the body of the report. **Documentation** means providing the bibliographic information readers would need to go back to the original source. **Plagiarism** is the unacknowledged use of another's ideas and/or expression.

FIGURE 11.11	APA and MLA Formats for Sources Used Most Often in Reports *(concluded)*

Article from a Publication on the Web
> Greengard, Samuel. "Scoring Web Wins." *Business Finance Magazine*. May 2001. 12 July 2001. <http://www.businessfinancemag.com/archives/appfiles/Article.cfm? IssueID=348&ArticleID=13750>. *Don't add any extra*
> ◄ *Put Web address in angle brackets.* *hyphens when you break*
> *End entry with a period.* *a long Web address*

Book
> Cross, Geoffrey A. *Forming the Collective Mind: A Contextual Exploration of Large-Scale Collaborative Writing in Industry*. Creskill, NJ: Hampton Press, 2001.
> *Put in square brackets information known to you*

Book or Pamphlet with a Corporate Author *but not printed in source*
> Citibank. *Indonesia: An Investment Guide*. [Jakarta:] Citibank, 1994. *Date after city and publisher*

E-Mail Message
> Locker, Kitty O. "Could We Get a New Photo?" E-mail to Rajani J. Kamuth. 17 Dec. 2001. *Abbreviate long months*
> *Day month year*

Government Document
> United States. Sen. Special Committee on Aging. *Long-Term Care: States Grapple with Increasing Demands and Costs*. 107th Cong., 1st sess. Washington: GPO, 2001. *Abbreviate*
> *Omit state or province when city is well known!* *"Government Printing Office."*

Government Document Available on the Web from the GPO Access Database
> United States. General Accounting Office. *Aviation Security: Terrorist Acts Demonstrate Urgent Need to Improve Security at the Nation's Airports*. Testimony before the Committee on Commerce, Science, and Transportation, U.S. Senate (GAO-01-1162T). 20 Sept. 2001. 20 Dec. 2001 <http://www.gao.gov/new.items/d011162t.pdf>.

Interview Conducted by the Researcher
> Drysdale, Andrew. Telephone interview. 12 Apr. 1999.

Posting to a Listserv *Date of posting*
> Dietrich, Dan. "Re: Course on Report and Proposal Writing." Online posting. 14 Feb. 2000. BizCom Discussion Group. 23 Dec. 2001 <bizcom@ebbs.English.vt.edu>. *If discussion group*
> *Date you* *has a Web archive, give the Web address.*
> *accessed posting* *If it doesn't have a*

Web Site
> American Express. *Creating an Effective Business Plan*. 2001. 20 Dec. 2001. *Web page, give the*
> <http://home3.americanexpress.com/smallbusiness/tool/biz_plan/index.asp> *email address*
> *of the list.*

CHAPTER 11	Exercises and Problems

Getting Started

11.1   Identifying the Weaknesses in Problem Statements

Identify the weaknesses in the problem statements below. Use these criteria:

- Is the problem narrow enough?
- Can a solution be found in a term?
- What organization could implement any recommendations to solve the problem?
- Could the topic be limited or refocused to yield an acceptable problem statement?

1. One possible report topic I would like to investigate would be the differences in women's intercollegiate sports in our athletic conference.

2. How to market products effectively to university students.

3. Should Web banners be part of a company's advertising?

4. How can U.S. and Canadian students get jobs in Europe?

5. We want to explore ways our company can help raise funds for the Open Shelter. We will investigate whether collecting and recycling glass, aluminum, and paper products will raise enough money to help.

6. How can XYZ university better serve students from traditionally underrepresented groups?

7. What are the best investments for the next year?

11.2   Writing a Preliminary Purpose Statement

Answer the following questions about a topic on which you could write a formal report. (See Problems 12.3, 12.5, 12.6, 12.7, and 12.8.)

As Your Professor Directs,

a. Be prepared to answer the questions orally in a conference.

b. Bring written answers to a conference.

c. Submit written answers in class.

d. Give your professor a photocopy of your statement after it is approved.

1. What problem will you investigate or solve?
   a. What is the name of the organization facing the problem?
   b. What is the technical problem or difficulty?
   c. Why is it important to the organization that this problem be solved?
   d. What solution or action might you recommend to solve the problem?
   e. List the name and title of the person in the organization who would have the power to accept or reject your recommendation.

2. Will this report use information from other classes or from work experiences? If so, give the name and topic of the class and/or briefly describe the job. If you will need additional information (that you do not already have from other classes or from a job), how do you expect to find it?

3. List the name, title, and business phone number of a professor who can testify to your ability to handle the expertise needed for this report.

4. List the name, title, and business phone number of someone in the organization who can testify that you have access to enough information about that organization to write this report.

11.3   Choosing Research Strategies

For each of the following reports, indicate the kinds of research that might be useful. If a survey is called for, indicate the most efficient kind of sample to use.

a. How can XYZ store increase sales?

b. What is it like to live and work in [name of country]?

c. Should our organization have a dress code?

d. Is it feasible to start a monthly newsletter for students in your major?

e. How can we best market to mature adults?

f. Can compensation programs increase productivity?

g. What skills are in demand in our area? Of these, which could the local community college offer courses in?

11.4   Identifying Keywords for Computer Searches

As Your Professor Directs,

Identify the keyword combinations that you could use in researching one or more of the following topics:

a. Ways to evaluate whether recycling is working.

b. Safety of pension funds.

c. Ethical issues in accounting.

d. Effects of advertising on sales of automobiles.

e. What can be done to increase the privacy of personal data.

f. Accounting for intellectual capital.

g. Advantages and problems of Web advertising.

11.5   Comparing Web Search Engines

Using at least three different search engines, search for sources on a topic on which you could write a formal report. (See Problems 12.3, 12.5, 12.6, 12.7, and 12.8.) Compare the top 30 sources. Which sites turn up on all three search engines? Which search engine appears to be most useful for your project?

As Your Professor Directs,

a. Share your results orally with a small group of students.

b. Present your results to the class.

c. Write a memo to your professor summarizing your results.

d. With a small group of students, write a report recommending guidelines for using search engines.

11.6   Evaluating Web Sites

Evaluate 10 Web sites related to the topic of your report. For each, consider

- Authors.
- Objectivity.
- Information.
- Revision date.

Based on these criteria, which sites are best for your report? Which are unacceptable? Why?

As Your Professor Directs,

a. Share your results with a small group of students.

b. Present your results in a memo to your professor.

c. Present your results to the class in an oral presentation.

11.7   Choosing Subject Lines for Memo Reports

Identify the strengths and weaknesses of each subject line, and choose the best subject line(s) from each group.

1. A proposal to conduct research.
    a. Membership Survey
    b. Proposal to Survey Former Members to Learn Their Reasons for Not Rejoining
    c. Proposal to Investigate Former Members' Reasons for Not Rejoining

2. A survey to find out why former members did not renew their memberships.

a. 2003 Delinquency Survey

b. Results of 2003 Former Member Survey

c. Why Members Did Not Renew Their Memberships in 2003

3. A progress report.
    a. Progress Report
    b. Work Completed, October 15–November 5
    c. Status of the Survey of Former Members

Communicating at Work

As Your Professor Directs in Problems 11.8 and 11.9,

a. Create a document or presentation to achieve the goal.

b. Write a memo to your professor describing the situation at your workplace and explaining your rhetorical choices (medium, strategy, tone, wording, graphics or document design, and so forth).

11.8   Proposing a Change

No organization is perfect. Propose a change that would improve your organization. The change can affect only your unit or the whole organization; it can relate to productivity and profits, to quality of life, or to any other aspect your organization can control. Direct your proposal to the person or committee with the power to authorize the change.

11.9   Proposing to Undertake a Research Project

Pick a project you would like to study whose results could be used by your organization. (See Problem 12.3.) Write a proposal to your supervisor requesting time away from other duties to do the research. Show how your research (whatever its outcome) will be useful to the organization.

Memo and Letter Assignments

11.10   Writing a Report Based on a Survey

As Your Professor Directs,

a. Survey 40 to 50 people on some subject of your choice.

b. Team up with your classmates to conduct a survey and write it up as a group. Survey 50 to 80 people if your group has two members, 75 to 120 people if it has three members, 100 to 150 people if it has four members, and 125 to 200 people if it has five members.

c. Keep a journal during your group meetings and submit it to your professor.

d. Write a memo to your professor describing and evaluating your group's process for designing, conducting, and writing up the survey. (See Chapter 10 on working and writing in groups.)

For this assignment, you do **not** have to take a random sample. Do, however, survey at least two different groups so that you can see if they differ in some way. Possible groups are men and women, business majors and English majors, first-year students and seniors, students and non-students.

As you conduct your survey, make careful notes about what you do so that you can use this information when you write up your survey. If you work with a group, record who does what. Use complete memo format. Your subject line should be clear and reasonably complete. Omit unnecessary words such as "Survey of." Your first paragraph serves as an introduction, but it needs no heading. The rest of the body of your memo will be divided into four sections with the following headings: Purpose, Procedure, Results, and Discussion.

In your first paragraph, briefly summarize (not necessarily in this order) who conducted the experiment or survey, when it was conducted, where it was conducted, who the subjects were, what your purpose was, and what you found out. You will discuss all of these topics in more detail in the body of your memo.

In your **Purpose** section, explain why you conducted the survey. What were you trying to learn? What hypothesis were you testing? Why did this subject seem interesting or important?

In your **Procedure** section, describe in detail *exactly* what you did. "The first 50 people who came through the Students' Union on Wed., Feb. 2" is not the same as "The first 50 people who came through the south entrance of the Students' Union on Wed., Feb. 2, and agreed to answer my questions." Explain any steps you took to overcome possible sources of bias.

In your **Results** section, first tell whether your results supported your hypothesis. Use both visuals and words to explain what your numbers show. (See Chapter 12 on how to design visuals.) Process your raw data in a way that will be useful to your reader.

In your **Discussion** section, evaluate your survey and discuss the implications of your results. Consider these questions:

1. What are the limitations of your survey and your results?

2. Do you think a scientifically valid survey would have produced the same results? Why or why not?

3. Were there any sources of bias either in the way the questions were phrased or in the way the subjects were chosen? If you were running the survey again, what changes would you make to eliminate or reduce these sources of bias?

4. Do you think your subjects answered honestly and completely? What factors may have intruded? Is the fact that you did or didn't know them, were or weren't of the same sex relevant? If your results seem to contradict other evidence, how do you account for the discrepancy? Were your subjects shading the truth? Was your sample's unrepresentativeness the culprit? Or have things changed since earlier data were collected?

5. What causes the phenomenon your results reveal? If several causes together account for the phenomenon, or if it is impossible to be sure of the cause, admit this. Identify possible causes and assess the likelihood of each.

6. What action should be taken?

The discussion section gives you the opportunity to analyze the significance of your survey. Its insight and originality lift the otherwise well-written memo from the ranks of the merely satisfactory to the ranks of the above-average and the excellent.

The whole assignment will be more interesting if you choose a question that interests you. It does not need to be "significant" in terms of major political or philosophic problems; a quirk of human behaviour that fascinates you will do nicely.

11.11   Writing a Sales Proposal

Pick a project that you could do for a local company, non-profit, or government office. Examples include

- Creating a brochure or Web page.
- Revising form letters.
- Conducting a training program.
- Writing a newsletter or an annual report.
- Developing a marketing plan.
- Providing plant care, catering, or janitorial services.

Write a proposal specifying what you could do and providing a detailed budget and work schedule.

As Your Professor Directs,

a. Phone someone in the organization to talk about its needs and what you could offer.

b. Write an individual proposal.

c. Join with other students in the class to create a group proposal.

d. Present your proposal orally.

11.12   Writing a Progress Report for a Group Report

Write a memo to your professor summarizing your group's progress.

In the introductory paragraph, summarize the group's progress in terms of its goals and its schedule, your own progress on the tasks for which you are responsible, and your feelings about the group's work thus far.

Under a heading titled *Work Completed,* list what has already been done. Be most specific about what you yourself have done. Describe briefly the chronology of group activities: number, time, and length of meetings; topics discussed; and decisions made at meetings.

If you have solved problems creatively, say so. You can also describe obstacles you've encountered that you have not yet solved. In this section, you can also comment on problems that the group has faced and whether or not they've been solved. You can comment on things that have gone well and have contributed to the smooth functioning of the group.

Under *Work to Be Completed,* list what you personally and other group members still have to do. Indicate the schedule for completing the work.

In your last paragraph, either indicate your confidence in completing the report by the due date or ask for a conference to resolve the problems you are encountering.

12 Analyzing Information and Writing Reports

AN INSIDE PERSPECTIVE

Analyzing Information and Writing Reports

Trends in business (◀ Chapter 1) have impacted not only how workplaces are organized, but also how organizations communicate everything from routine messages to annual reports. In the early days of corporate reporting, annual reports were as short as one page and were targeted almost exclusively to analysts and regulators. Facts and figures were their stock in trade. In addressing the needs and knowledge of a much broader audience today, annual reports are much longer, packed with stories, and visually dramatic. In short, they have taken on a much more human face (◀ Figure 4.2, p. 86).

At a time when employee satisfaction is as important as client and investor satisfaction, and accountability and transparency are expected, new forms of reporting (triple bottom line, balanced score card, CSR, and sustainable development reports) are addressing new audiences and needs. The days when "the company might have simply had a list of directors and a bare-bones balance sheet," according to Bill Buchanan, former senior vice president of studies and standards at the Canadian Institute of Chartered Accountants, "were truly a disservice to investors. . . . In theory, today's investor seems to have access to almost everything, including the kitchen sink."

Since 1996 Bill Buchanan has been judging co-ordinator for the annual Canadian Institute of Chartered Accountants (CICA) Corporate Reporting Awards. Sometimes he longs for the days 53 years ago when the CICA began its awards and reports were eight or nine pages long. Now they can stretch to 75 or even 90 pages as companies respond to regulatory change and demands for transparency and accountability.

www.cica.ca/index.cfm/ci_id/24239/ la_id/1.htm

If consumer and employee interests are better served by new reporting measures, they are also bringing companies new rewards such as Canada's Chartered Accountants' Corporate Reporting Awards. For Buchanan they are an important means of encouraging reporting that is "not only informative and comprehensive, but understandable and meaningful." Award marks for electronic archiving of annual reports and presentations add even more value to stakeholders interested in comparing performance over time.

Quotations drawn from Robert Colapinto, "Worth Reporting," *CA Magazine* January/February 2005, 30–34; retrieved November 29, 2005, from http://www.camagazine.com/index.cfm/ci_id/24114/la_id/1.htm.

Careful analysis, smooth writing, and effective document design work together to make effective reports, whether you're writing a 2½-page memo report or a 250-page formal report complete with all the report components.

Chapter 11 covered the first two steps in writing a report:

1. Define the problem.
2. Gather the necessary data and information.

This chapter covers the last three steps:

3. Analyze the data and information.
4. Organize the information.
5. Write the report.

Other chapters that are especially useful for reports are Chapters 7, 10, and 13.

Using Your Time Efficiently

To use your time efficiently, think about your audience, purpose, and the parts of the report before you begin writing. Much of the introduction comes from your proposal, with only minor revisions. You can write six sections even before you've finished your research: Purpose, Scope, Assumptions, Methods, Criteria, and Definitions.

The background reading for your proposal can form the first draft of your list of references.

Save a copy of your questionnaire or interview questions to use as an appendix. As you tally and analyze the data, prepare an appendix summarizing all the responses to your questionnaire, your figures and tables, and a complete list of references. You can print appendices before the final report is ready if you number their pages separately. (Appendix A pages would be A-1, A-2, and so forth).

You can write the title page and the transmittal as soon as you know what your recommendation will be.

After you've analyzed your data, write the body, the conclusions, and recommendations. Prepare a draft of the table of contents and the list of illustrations. Write the executive summary last when you have clarified your core ideas.

When you write a long report, list all the sections (headings) that your report will have. Mark those that are most important to your reader and your logic, and spend most of your time on them.

Analyzing Data and Information for Reports

Analyzing the data you have gathered is essential to produce the tight logic needed for a good report. Analyze your data with healthy skepticism. Professor Raymond Panko (cited in Schrage) found that 30% of spreadsheets had errors, such as misplaced decimal points, transposed digits, and wrong signs, built into their rules.[1]

Check to be sure that your data come from a reliable source. Use the strategies outlined in Chapter 11 to evaluate Web sources (◄■ p. 264). When the source has a vested interest (◄■ p. 162) in the results, scrutinize them with special care. To analyze a company's financial prospects, use independent information as well as the company's annual report and press releases.

If your report is based upon secondary data from library and online research, look at the sample, the sample size, and the exact wording of questions to see what the data actually measure. According to Jakob Nielsen's research, a sample of just five people is enough to test the usability of a Web site. That conclusion is

Measure What Matters*

It sounds obvious: Find out whether your customers are satisfied, because satisfied customers will buy from you again and again, helping your profits grow. It sounds so obvious that big companies pay generous fees to researchers who create sophisticated measures of customer satisfaction.

It sounds obvious, but it's wrong. Frederick Reichheld compared consumers' answers to questions about customer satisfaction and loyalty with measures of their actual purchases and their memory of referring others to the company. He found little relationship between stated satisfaction and repeat purchases. Instead, the best predictor of repeat purchases was a favourable response to "How likely is it that you would recommend [company X] to a friend or colleague?" People who would recommend the company were also likely to buy from it again.

Responses fall into three clusters: promoters, defined as the customers who were extremely likely to recommend (choosing 9 or 10 on a 10-point scale), those who were less likely ("passively satisfied," at 7 or 8), and the remainder of the customers. The greater the share of customers who are promoters, the faster a company's revenues grow. . . . Reichheld's advice to companies looking for growth: Skip the fancy questionnaires, and just ask customers if they will recommend your company.

*Based on Frederick F. Reichheld, "The One Number You Need to Grow," *Harvard Business Review*, December 2003, 46–54.

Analyzing Numbers*

Beth Baldwin, Director of Marketing Information at Terra Lycos, the giant dotcom portal, knew the numbers didn't add up. Last November, New York–based Web audience measurement service Media Matrix reported that Lycos Zone—the portal's site for kids— had seen a 5 percent decline from the previous month. Baldwin's own numbers, however, showed that in fact the amount of traffic to the site had increased during that period.

Baldwin believed that her numbers, generated by Terra Lycos's site-metrics software, were probably right, but she had to prove it because Wall Street was more inclined to treat Media Matrix as the final word. It took two months, but she finally found the answer in a study, conducted by market research firm Roper Starch Worldwide, that reported on Web usage in schools and listed popular K–12 sites. Baldwin realized that many of the visitors to Lycos Zone were kids logging on from school, and that Media Matrix doesn't count those users. Her numbers were indeed correct.

*Quoted from Brian Caulfield, "Why Your Site Traffic Numbers Are Out of Whack," http://www.ecompany. com, March 2001, 122.

InSite

e-com.ic.gc.ca/epic/internet/ inecic-ceac.nsf/en/ h_gv00248e.html

The final report of the Task Force *Stopping Spam: Creating a Stronger, Safer Internet* presented in May 2005 is one of many reports available on federal government Web sites.

surprising, because for many kinds of research, a large sample is important for giving significant results. But other tests have led to similar conclusions.[2]

Identify exactly what the data measure. For example, using a Dun & Bradstreet database, many people claim that only 28% of small businesses survive for eight years. But that database counts a small business as "surviving" only if it remains under the same ownership. Researcher Bruce Kirchoff found that another 26% survive with ownership changes, for a total survival rate of 54%.[3]

If your data include words, try to find out what the words mean to the people who said them. Respondents to Whirlpool's survey of 180,000 households said they wanted "clean refrigerators." After asking more questions, Whirlpool found that what people really wanted were refrigerators that *looked* clean, so the company developed models with textured fronts and sides to hide fingerprints.[4] Also try to **measure words against numbers.** When he researched possible investments, Peter Lynch found that people in mature industries were pessimistic, seeing clouds. People in immature industries saw pie in the sky, even when the numbers weren't great.[5]

Look for patterns. If you have library sources, on which points do experts agree? Which disagreements can be explained by early theories or numbers that have now changed? Which are the result of having different values and criteria? In your interviews and surveys, what patterns do you see?

State accurately what your data show. Don't confuse causation with correlation. *Causation* means that one thing causes or produces another. *Correlation* means that two things happen at the same time. One might cause the other, but both might be caused by a third.

For example, suppose you're considering whether to buy PCs for everyone in your company, and suppose your surveys show that the people who currently have computers are, in general, more productive than people who don't use computers. Does having a computer lead to higher productivity? Perhaps. But perhaps productive people are more likely to push to get computers from company funds, while less productive people are more passive. Perhaps some other factor—experience in the company, education, or social background— leads both to increased productivity and to acquiring computers.

Consciously search for at least three possible causes for each phenomenon you've observed and at least three possible solutions for each problem. The more possibilities you brainstorm, the more likely you are to find good options. In your report, mention all of the possibilities; discuss in detail only those that you think are the real reasons and the best solutions.

When you have identified patterns that seem to represent the causes of the problem or the best solutions, check these ideas against the evidence. Can you find support in the quotes or in the numbers? Can you answer counterclaims? If you can, you will be able to present evidence for your argument in a convincing way.

Make the nature of your evidence clear to your reader. Do you have observations that you yourself have made? Or do you have inferences based on observations or data collected by others?

If you can't prove the claim you originally hoped to make, modify your conclusions to fit your data. Even when your market test is a failure or your experiment disproves your hypothesis, you can still write a useful report.

- Identify changes that might yield a different result. For example, selling the product at a lower price might enable the company to sell enough units.
- Divide the discussion to show what part of the test succeeded.
- Discuss circumstances that may have affected the results.
- Summarize your negative findings in progress reports to let readers down gradually and to give them a chance to modify the research design.

■ Remember that negative results aren't always disappointing to the audience. For example, the people who commissioned a feasibility report may be relieved to have an impartial outsider confirm their suspicions that a project isn't feasible.[6]

Choosing Information for Reports

Don't put information in reports just because you have it or just because it took you a long time to find it. Instead, choose the information that your reader needs to make a decision.

How much information you need to include depends on whether your audience is likely to be supportive, neutral, or skeptical.

You must also decide whether to put information in the body of the report or in appendixes. Put material in the body of the report if it is crucial to your proof or if it is short. (Something less than half a page won't interrupt the reader.)

Anything that a careful reader will want but that is not crucial to your proof can go in an appendix.

Organizing Information in Reports

Most sets of data can be organized in several logical ways. The following three guidelines will help you choose the arrangement that will be the most useful for your reader:

1. **Process your information before you present it to your reader.** The order in which you became aware of information usually is not the best order to present it to your reader.

2. **When you have lots of information, group it into three to seven categories.** The average person's short-term memory can hold only seven chunks, though the chunks can be of any size.[7] By grouping your information into seven categories (or fewer), you make your report easier to read.

3. **Work with the reader's expectations, not against them.** Introduce ideas in the overview in the order in which you will discuss them.

Basic Patterns for Organizing Information

Seven basic patterns for organizing information are useful in whole reports or in parts.

1. Comparison/contrast

Many reports use comparison/contrast sections within a larger report pattern. Comparison/contrast can also be the purpose of the whole report. Feasibility studies usually use this pattern. You can focus either on the alternatives you are evaluating or on the criteria you use. See Figure 12.1 for examples of these two patterns in a report.

Focus on the alternatives when

■ One alternative is clearly superior.

■ The criteria are hard to separate.

■ The reader will intuitively grasp the alternative as a whole rather than as the sum of its parts.

Focus on the criteria when

■ The superiority of one alternative to another depends on the relative weight assigned to various criteria. Perhaps Alternative A is better if we are most

Tripling the Bottom Line*

Since its one-page beginnings in 1823, the annual report has changed. In response to increasing expectations of corporate social responsibility (CSR), more and more businesses are reporting in ways variously titled:

■ Social reports

■ Green reports

■ Environmental reports

■ Sustainable development reports

■ Triple bottom line reports

The triple bottom line measures corporate or organizational performance in terms of social, environmental, and economic impacts.

While some commentators are skeptical about business motivation—detecting public relations rather than commitment to sustainability— a PriceWaterhouseCoopers Global CEO Survey indicates that 70% of CEOs believe CSR initiatives enhance profitability. They are among those increasingly making the business case for the triple bottom line.

*Based on Robert Colapinto, "Worth Reporting," *CA Magazine* January/February 2005, 30–34; Alison Arnot, "The Triple Bottom Line," *CGA Magazine* January/February 2004, retrieved from http://www.cga-canada.org/eng/magazine/jan-feb04/triple_line_e.htm; PriceWaterhouseCoopers(PwC), Corporate Social Responsibility and Long-Term Shareholder Value— Says PwC, retrieved June 24, 2005, from http://www.pwcglobal.com/Extweb/ncpressrelease.nsf/docid/CB5752E1DCB1BE9A80256E1B002BE744; Paul Hawken, *McDonald's and Corporate Social Responsibility?* 25 April 2002, retrieved January 25, 2005, from http://www.foodfirst.org/media.

FIGURE 12.1   Two Ways to Organize a Comparison/Contrast Report

Focus on alternatives	
Alternative A	Opening a New Store on Campus
Criterion 1	Cost of Renting Space
Criterion 2	Proximity to Target Market
Criterion 3	Competition from Similar Stores
Alternative B	Opening a New Store in the Suburban Mall
Criterion 1	Cost of Renting Space
Criterion 2	Proximity to Target Market
Criterion 3	Competition from Similar Stores

Focus on criteria	
Criterion 1	Cost of Renting Space for the New Store
Alternative A	Cost of Campus Locations
Alternative B	Cost of Locations in the Suburban Mall
Criterion 2	Proximity to Target Market
Alternative A	Proximity on Campus
Alternative B	Proximity in the Suburban Mall
Criterion 3	Competition from Similar Stores
Alternative A	Competing Stores on Campus
Alternative B	Competing Stores in the Suburban Mall

concerned about Criterion 1, cost, but worse if we are most concerned about Criterion 2, proximity to target market.

- The criteria are easy to separate.
- The reader wants to compare and contrast the options independently of your recommendation.

A variation of the divided pattern is the **pro-and-con pattern.** In this pattern, under each specific heading, give the arguments for and against that alternative. Whatever information comes second will carry more psychological weight. This pattern is least effective when you want to de-emphasize the disadvantages of a proposed solution, for it does not permit you to bury the disadvantages between neutral or positive material.

2. Problem-solution

Identify the problem, explain its background or history, discuss its extent and seriousness, identify its causes. Discuss the factors (criteria) that affect the decision. Analyze the advantages and disadvantages of possible solutions. Conclusions and recommendation can go either first or last, depending on the preferences of your reader. This pattern works well when the reader is neutral.

3. Elimination of alternatives

After discussing the problem and its causes, discuss the *impractical* solutions first, showing why they will not work. End with the most practical solution. This pattern works well when the solutions the reader is likely to favour will not work, while the solution you recommend is likely to be perceived as expensive, intrusive, or radical.

4. General to particular or particular to general

General to particular starts with the problem as it affects the organization or as it manifests itself in general and then moves to a discussion of the parts of the problem and solutions to each of these parts. Particular to general starts with the problem as the audience defines it and moves to larger issues of which the problem is a part. Both are good patterns when you need to redefine the reader's perception of the problem to solve it effectively.

5. Geographic or spatial

In a geographic or spatial pattern, you discuss problems and solutions in units by their physical arrangement. Move from office to office, building to building, factory to factory, province to province, region to region, etc.

6. Functional

In functional patterns, discuss the problems and solutions of each functional unit. For example, a report on a new plant might divide data into sections on the costs of land and building, on the availability of personnel, on the convenience of raw materials, and so on. A government report might divide data into the different functions an office performed, taking each in turn.

7. Chronological

A chronological report records events in the order in which they happened or are planned to happen. Many progress reports (◀ Chapter 11) are organized chronologically.

How to Organize Specific Varieties of Reports

Informative, feasibility, and justification reports will be more successful when you work with the readers' expectations for that kind of report.

Informative and closure reports

Informative and **closure reports** summarize completed work or research that does not result in action or recommendation.

Informative reports often include the following elements:

- Introductory paragraph summarizing the problems or successes of the project.
- Purpose and scope section(s) giving the purpose of the report and indicating what aspects of the topic it covers.
- Chronological account of how the problem was discovered, what was done, and what the results were.
- Concluding paragraph with suggestions for later action. In a recommendation report, the recommendations would be based on proof. In contrast, the suggestions in a closure or recommendation report are not proved in detail.

Figure 12.2 presents this kind of informative closure report.

Feasibility reports

Feasibility reports evaluate two or more alternatives and recommend one of them. (Doing nothing or delaying action can be one of the alternatives.)

Feasibility reports normally open by explaining the decision to be made, listing the alternatives, and explaining the criteria. In the body of the report, each alternative is evaluated according to the criteria using one of the two

FIGURE 12.2 An Informative Memo Report Describing How a
Company Solved a Problem

To: Kitty O. Locker

From: Sara A. Ratterman *SAR*

Date: March 14, 2005   *Informal short reports use
                                              letter or memo format*

*First
paragraph
summarizes*   Subject: Recycling at Bike Nashbar

*main
points*   Two months ago, Bike Nashbar began recycling its corrugated cardboard boxes. The program
           was easy to implement and actually saves money compared to our previous garbage pickup.

*Purpose
and scope
of report*   In this report, I will explain how, why, and by whom Bike Nashbar's program was initiated; how
             the program works and what it costs; and why other businesses should consider similar programs.

                              Bold headings
The Problem of Too Many Boxes and Not Enough Space in Bike Nashbar

           Every week, Bike Nashbar receives about 40 large cardboard boxes containing bicycles and other
           merchandise. As many boxes as possible would be stuffed into the garbage bin behind the building,
Cause of   which also had to accommodate all the other solid waste the shop produces. Boxes that didn't fit
problem   in the garbage bin ended up lying around the shop, blocking doorways, and taking up space needed
           for customers' bikes. The garbage bin was emptied only once a week, and by that time, even more
           boxes would have arrived.
                  *Triple space before
                  heading*
The Importance of Recycling Cardboard Rather Than Throwing It Away

           Arranging for more bins or more frequent pickups would have solved the immediate problem
           at Bike Nashbar but would have done nothing to solve the problem created by throwing away so
           much cardboard in the first place.
                        Double space between paragraphs within heading
           According to David Crogen, sales representative for Maritime Waste Management, Inc., 75% of
           all solid waste in Saint John goes to landfills. The amount of trash the city collects has increased
Further   150% in the last five years. Saint John's landfill is almost full. In an effort to encourage people
seriousness and businesses to recycle, the cost of dumping garbage in the landfill is doubling from $4.90 a cubic
of problem   metre to $9.90 a cubic metre next week and $12.95 a cubic metre next January. Crogen believes
           that the amount of garbage can be reduced by co-operation between the landfill and the power plant,
           and by recycling.

                                           Capitalize first letter of
How Bike Nashbar Started Recycling Cardboard   *major words in heading*

           After reading an article about how committed Maritime Waste Management, Inc., is to waste
Solution   reduction and recycling, I decided to see whether Maritime could recycle our boxes. Corrugated
           cardboard is almost 100% recyclable, so we seemed to be a good candidate for recycling.

           To get this service started, I contacted David Crogen to discuss the service. Maritime Waste
           Management, Inc., took care of the details. Two days later, Bike Nashbar was recycling its cardboard.

(continued)

comparison/contrast patterns. Discussing each alternative separately is better
when one alternative is clearly superior, when the criteria interact, and when
each alternative is indivisible. If the choice depends on the weight given to
each criterion, you may want to discuss each alternative under each criterion.

   Whether your recommendation should come at the beginning or the end of
the report depends on your reader and the culture of your organization. Most
readers want the "bottom line" upfront. However, if the reader will find your
recommendation hard to accept, you may want to delay your recommendation
until the end of the report when you have given all your evidence.

Justification reports

Justification reports recommend or justify a purchase, investment, hiring, or
change in policy. If your organization has a standard format for justification

FIGURE 12.2 An Informative Memo Report Describing How a Company Solved a Problem *(concluded)*

Reader's name, page number, and date

Kitty O. Locker   2   March 14, 2005

Talking heads tell reader what to expect in each section

How the Service Works and What it Costs

Details of solution

Maritime replaced our existing bin with two 4-metre bins picked up once a week: the contents of the white one marked "cardboard only" go to the recycling plant; those of the brown one for all other solid waste go to the landfill or power plant.

Since Bike Nashbar was already paying more than $60 a week for garbage pickup, our basic cost stayed the same. (Maritime can absorb the extra overhead only if the current charge is at least $60 a week). The cost is divided 80/20 between the two bins: 80% for landfill and powerplant bin; 20% for the cardboard pickup. Bike Nashbar actually receieves $5.00 for each ton of cardboard it recycles.

Double space between paragraphs

Employees must follow these rules when putting boxes in the recycling bin:

Indented lists provide visual variety

- The cardboard must have the word "corrugated" printed on it, along with the universal recycling symbol.

- The boxes must be broken down to their flattest form. More boxes means more money and space.

- Only corrugated cardboard can be put in the recycling bin. Other materials could break the recycling machinery or contaminate the new cardboard.

- The recycling bin is to be kept locked with a padlock provided by Maritime so that theft does not lose money for Maritime and Bike Nashbar.

Dis-advantages of solution

Minor Problems with Running the Recycling Program

The only problems have been minor violations of the rules. Sometimes employees at the shop forget to flatten boxes; sometimes people forget to lock the recycling bin. Cardboard has been stolen, and plastic cups and other solid waste dumped in the cardboard bin. I've posted signs reminding employees to empty and fold boxes and relock the bin.

Advantages of solution

Advantages of the Recycling Program

The program is a great success. Our company depends on a clean, safe environment for people to ride their bikes in. Now we have become part of the solution. By choosing to recycle and reduce the amount of solid waste our company generates, we can also save money while gaining a reputation as a socially responsible business.

Why Other Companies Should Adopt Similar Programs

Argues that her company's experience is relevant to other companies

Businesses and institutions in the region currently recycle less than 4% of their solid waste. David Crogen tells me he has over 8,000 clients in Saint John alone, and he acquires new ones every day. Many of these businesses can recycle a large portion of their solid waste at no additional cost. Depending on what they recycle, the may even get money back.

The environmental and economic benefits of recycling as part of a comprehensive waste reduction program are numerous. Recycling helps preserve our environment. We can use the same materials over and over again, saving natural resources such as trees, fuel, and metals, and decreasing the amount of solid waste in landfills. Crogen predicts that Saint John will be on a 100% recycling system by the year 2020. I hope he is right.

---

reports, follow that format. If you can choose your headings and organization, use this direct pattern when your recommendation will be easy for your reader to accept:

1. **Indicate what you're asking for and why it's needed.** Since the reader has not asked for the report, you must link your request to the organization's goals.
2. **Briefly give the background of the problem or need.**
3. **Explain each of the possible solutions.** For each, give the cost and the advantages and disadvantages.
4. **Summarize the action needed to implement your recommendation.** If several people will be involved, indicate who will do what and how long each step will take.
5. **Ask for the action you want.**

If the reader will be reluctant to grant your request, use this variation of the indirect, problem-solving pattern described in Chapter 8:

1. **Describe the organizational problem (which your request will solve).** Use specific examples to prove the seriousness of the problem.
2. **Show why easier or less expensive solutions will not solve the problem.**
3. **Present your solution impersonally.**
4. **Show that the disadvantages of your solution are outweighed by the advantages.**
5. **Summarize the action needed to implement your recommendation.** If several people will be involved, indicate who will do what and how long each step will take.
6. **Ask for the action you want.**

How much detail you give in a justification report depends on the corporate culture and on your reader's knowledge of and attitude toward your recommendation.

Presenting Information Effectively in Reports

The advice about style in Chapter 4 also applies to reports, with three exceptions:

1. **Use a fairly formal style, without contractions or slang.**
2. **Avoid the word *you*.** In a document with multiple audiences, it will not be clear who *you* is. Instead, use the company name.
3. **Include in the report all the definitions and documents needed to understand the recommendations.** The multiple audiences for reports include readers who may consult the document months or years from now; they will not share your special knowledge. Explain acronyms and abbreviations the first time they appear. Explain the history or background of the problem. Add as appendices previous documents on which you are building.

The following four points apply to any kind of writing, but they are particularly important in reports.

1. Say What You Mean.

Not-quite-right word choices are particularly damaging in reports, which may be skimmed by readers who know very little about the subject. Occasionally you can simply substitute a word.

Incorrect:	With these recommendations, we can overcome the solutions to our problem.
Correct:	With these recommendations, we can overcome our problem.
Also correct:	With these recommendations, we can solve our problem.

Putting the meaning of your sentence in the verbs will help you say what you mean.

Vague:	My report revolves around the checkout lines and the methods used to get price checks when they arise.
Better:	My report shows how price checks slow checkout lines and recommends ways to reduce the number of price checks needed.

2. Tighten Your Writing.

Eliminate unnecessary words, use gerunds and infinitives, combine sentences, and reword sentences to cut the number of words.

Wordy: Campus Jewellers' main objective is to increase sales. Specifically, the objective is to double sales in the next five years by becoming a more successful business.

Better: Campus Jewellers' objective is to double sales in the next five years.

No reader wants length for the sake of length. Even in a class report, the page requirement is an indication of the complexity of analysis that the professor expects.

Some repetition in reports is legitimate (➡ see sidebar p. 307). The conclusion restates points made in the body of the report; the recommendations appear in the transmittal, the abstract or executive summary, and the recommendations sections of the report. However, repetitive references to earlier material ("As we have already seen") may indicate that the document needs to be reorganized. Read the document through at a single sitting to make sure that any repetition serves a useful purpose. If the repetition is boring, eliminate it.

3. Introduce Sources and Visuals Gracefully.

The first time you cite an author's work, use his or her full name except in *APA* style: "Rosabeth Moss Kanter points out. . . ." In subsequent citations, use only the last name: "Kanter shows. . . ." Use active rather than passive verbs.

The verb you use indicates your attitude toward the source. *Says* and *writes* are neutral. *Points out, shows, suggests, discovers,* and *notes* suggest that you agree with the source. Words such as *claims, argues, contends that, believes,* and *alleges* distance you from the source. At a minimum, they suggest that you know that not everyone agrees with the source; they are also appropriate to report the views of someone with whom you disagree.

Use active verbs to refer to visuals, too:

As Table 1 shows, . . .

See Figure 4.

4. Use Blueprints, Transitions, Topic Sentences, and Headings.

Blueprints are overviews or forecasts that tell the reader what you will discuss in a section or in the entire report. Make your blueprint easy to read by telling the reader how many points there are and using bullets or numbers. In the following example, the first sentence in the revised paragraph tells the reader to look for four points; the numbers separate the four points clearly. This overview paragraph also makes a contract with readers, who now expect to read about tax benefits first and employee benefits last.

Paragraph without numbers: Employee stock ownership programs (ESOPs) have several advantages. They provide tax benefits for the company. ESOPs also create tax benefits for employees and for lenders. They provide a defence against takeovers. In some organizations, productivity increases because workers now have a financial stake in the company's profits. ESOPs are an attractive employee benefit and help the company hire and retain good employees.

Revised paragraph with numbers: Employee stock ownership programs (ESOPs) provide four benefits. First, ESOPs provide tax benefits for the company, its employees, and lenders to the plan. Second, ESOPs help create a defence against takeovers. Third, ESOPs may increase productivity by giving workers a financial stake in the company's profits. Fourth, as an attractive employee benefit, ESOPs help the company hire and retain good employees.

Transitions are words, phrases, or sentences that tell the reader whether the discussion is continuing on the same point or shifting points.

There are economic advantages, too.
(Tells the reader that we are still discussing advantages but that we have now moved to economic advantages.)
An alternative to this plan is . . .
(Tells reader that a second option follows.)
These advantages, however, are found only in A, not in B or C.
(Prepares reader for a shift from A to B and C.)

A topic sentence (see Chapter 4) introduces or summarizes the main idea of a sentence. Readers who skim reports can follow your ideas more easily if each paragraph begins with a clear topic sentence.

Hard to read (no topic sentence):   Another main use of ice is to keep the fish fresh. Each of the seven kinds of fish served at the restaurant requires 3.78 litres twice a day, for a total of 52.92 litres. An additional 22.68 litres a day are required for the salad bar.

Better (begins with topic sentence):   Seventy-six litres of ice a day are needed to keep food fresh. Of this, the biggest portion (52.92 litres) is used to keep the fish fresh. Each of the seven kinds of fish served at the restaurant requires 3.78 litres twice a day ($7 \times 7.56 = 52.92$ L). An additional 22.68 litres a day are required for the salad bar.

Headings (see Appendix A) are single words, short phrases, or complete sentences that indicate the topic in each section. A heading must cover all of the material under it until the next heading. For example, *Cost of Tuition* cannot include the cost of books or of room and board. You can have one paragraph under a heading or several pages. If you do have several pages between headings you may want to consider using subheadings. Use subheadings only when you have two or more divisions within a main heading.

Topic (or functional) headings focus on the structure of the report. As you can see from the following example, topic headings give very little information.

Topic headings are vague
Recommendation
Problem
Situation 1
Situation 2
Causes of the Problem
Background
Cause 1
Cause 2
Recommended Solution

Talking heads (or informative headings), in contrast, tell the reader what to expect. Talking heads, like those in the examples in this chapter, provide an overview of each section and of the entire report.

Talking heads are specific
Recommended Reformulation for Vibe Bleach
Problems in Maintaining Vibe's Granular Structure
Solidifying During Storage and Transportation
Customer Complaints about "Blocks" of Vibe in Boxes
Why Vibe Bleach "Cakes"
Vibe's Formula
The Manufacturing Process
The Chemical Process of Solidification
Modifications Needed to Keep Vibe Flowing Freely

In a very complicated report, you may need up to three levels of headings. Figure 12.3 illustrates one way to set up headings. Although the figure shows only one example of each level of headings, in an actual report you would not use a subheading unless you had at least two subsections under the next higher heading.

Avoid having a heading or subheading all by itself at the bottom of the page. Instead, have at least one line (preferably two) of type. If there isn't room for a line of type under it, put the heading on the next page. Don't use a heading as the antecedent for a pronoun. Instead, repeat the noun.

Writing Formal Reports

Formal reports are distinguished from informal letter and memo reports by their length and by their components. A full formal report may contain the following components (see Figure 12.4):

Cover
Title Page
Letter or Memo of Transmittal
Table of Contents
List of Illustrations
Executive Summary
Body

    Introduction (Orients the reader to the report.)

    Background or History of the Problem (Orients the reader to the topic of the report.)

    Body (Presents and interprets data in words and visuals.)

    Conclusions (Summarizes main points of report.)

    Recommendations (Recommends actions to solve the problem. May be combined with Conclusions; may be put at beginning of body rather than at the end.)

    Notes, References, or Works Cited (Document sources cited in the report.)

    Appendices (Provide additional materials that the careful reader may want: transcript of an interview, copies of questionnaires, tallies of all the questions, computer printouts, previous reports.)

Not every formal report necessarily has all these components. In addition, some organizations call for additional components or arrange these components in a different order.

FIGURE 12.3   Setting Up Headings in a Single-Spaced Document

Centre the title use bold and a bigger font

Typing Titles and Headings for Reports   *14-point type*

For the title of a report, use a bold font two point sizes bigger than the largest size in the body of the report. You may want to use an even bigger size or a different font to create an attractive title page. Capitalize the first word and all major words of the title.

Heading for main divisions

Two empty spaces (triple space)

Typing Headings for Reports   *12-point type.*

One empty space (double space)

11-point type for body text

Centre main headings, capitalize the first and all major words, and use bold. In single-spaced text, leave two empty spaces before main headings and one after. Also leave an extra space between paragraphs. You may also want to use main headings that are one point size bigger than the body text.

This example provides just one example of each level of heading. However, in a real document, use headings only when you have at least two of them in the document. In a report, you'll have several.

Two empty spaces (triple space)

Typing Subheadings   *Bold; left margin*

One empty space

Most reports use subheadings under some main headings. Use subheadings only if you have at least two of them under a given heading. It is OK to use subheadings in some sections and not in others. Normally you'll have several paragraphs under a subheading, but it's OK to have just one paragraph under some subheadings.

11-point type

Subheadings in a report use the same format as headings in letters and memos. Bold subheadings and set them at the left margin. Capitalize the first word and major words. Leave two empty spaces before the subheading and one empty space after it, before the first paragraph under the subheading. Use the same size font as the body paragraphs.

Period after heading

One empty space (normal paragraph spacing)

Typing Further Subdivisions. For a very long report, you may need further subdivisions under a subheading. Bold the further subdivision, capitalizing the first word and major words, and end the phrase with a period. Begin the text on the same line. Use normal spacing between paragraphs. Further subdivide a subheading only if you have at least two such subdivisions under a given subheading. It is OK to use divisions under some subheadings and not under others.

Title Page

The title page of a report usually contains four items: the title of the report, for whom the report is prepared, by whom it is prepared, and the release date.

The title of the report should be as informative as possible. Like subject lines, report titles are typically straightforward.

Poor title: New Plant Site

Better title: Why Woodstock, Ontario, Is the Best Site for the New Toyota Plant

Large organizations that issue many reports may use two-part titles to make it easier to search for reports electronically.

Small Business Administration: Steps Taken to Better Manage Its Human Capital, but More Needs to Be Done

In many cases, the title will state the recommendation in the report: "Why the United Nations Should Establish a Seed Bank." However, the title should omit recommendations when

- The reader will find the recommendations hard to accept.
- Putting all the recommendations in the title would make it too long.
- The report does not offer recommendations.

FIGURE 12.4 A Formal Report

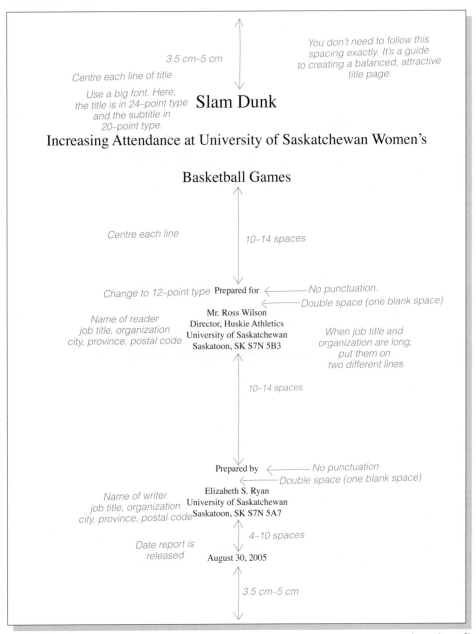

(continued)

If the title does not contain the recommendation, it normally indicates what problem the report tries to solve.

Eliminate any unnecessary words:

Wordy: Report of a Study on Ways to Market Life Insurance to Urban Professional People Who Are in Their Mid-40s

Better: Ways to Market Life Insurance to the Mid-40s Urban Professional

The *prepared for* section normally includes the name of the person who will make a decision based on the report, his or her job title, the organization's name, and its location.

The *prepared by* section will have the author's name, his or her title, the organization, and its location.

FIGURE 12.4 A Formal Report *(continued)*

2315 Lorne Avenue
Saskatoon, SK S7J 0S4
August 19, 2005

*You may also design
a letterhead for yourself,
especially if you're assuming
that you are doing the report
as a consultant*

*This letter uses block
format (see Figure 5.6, p. 119).
Modified block format is
also acceptable.*

Ross Wilson, Director
Huskie Athletics
University of Saskatchewan
87 Campus Drive
Saskatoon, SK S7N 5B3

*In paragraph 1, release the report.
Note when and by whom the report
was authorized. Note report's purpose.*

Dear Mr. Wilson:

Here is the report you authorized in July identifying why attendance at women's Huskies basketball games is low and recommending ways to increase student attendance at the games.

As you know, even though the team has been doing well, attendance at women's home games has not increased to expected levels since the opening of the Physical Activity Complex two years ago. When I surveyed a convenience sample of students, I found no season ticket holders and only two people who said they attended "a few" games each season. Fully 34% had never been to a Huskies women's basketball game.

Because most students do like basketball (62% follow the men's team), it's reasonable to think that some students could be persuaded to attend women's games as well. The two biggest reasons for not attending, according to my survey, were "I never thought to go" and "my friends aren't interested in going." I therefore recommend strategies that would remind students that the women's team exists and is playing, and would encourage groups of people to go to the games together.

Give recommendations or thesis

Short-term solutions that could be implemented this year include having team members visit the Memorial Union Building, Place Riel, or the Bowl to drum up support, and posting an abundance of signs about upcoming games around campus. Longer-term strategies include creating a calendar of special days for specific groups, offering giveaways, and cultivating sports writers. Because further research is needed, you might want to put a staff member in charge of marketing the women's basketball team and hire a student intern to do the legwork for this research.

Thank people who helped you

The information in this report came from print and online sources, a survey of U of S students, and interviews with several members of Huskie Athletics. Tera Schneider of Huskie Athletics' Athletic Sports Information office was particularly helpful.

Thank the reader for the opportunity to do the research

Thank you for the opportunity to conduct this research. I've enjoyed learning more about the basketball team, the workings of Huskie Athletics, and sports marketing strategies. If you have any questions about the material in this report, please call me.

*Offer to answer questions about the report.
Answers would be included in your fee—no extra charge!*

Sincerely,

Elizabeth Ryan

Elizabeth Ryan

*If used, centre page number
at the bottom of the page.
Use a lowercase Roman numeral.*

i

(continued)

The **release date,** the date the report will be released to the public, is usually the date the report is scheduled for discussion by the decision makers. The report is due four to six weeks before the release date so that the decision makers can review the report before the meeting.

If you have the facilities and the time, try using different sizes and styles of type, colour, and artwork to create a visually attractive and impressive title page. However, a plain typed page is acceptable. See Figure 12.4.

FIGURE 12.4 A Formal Report *(continued)*

*Headings or subheadings must
be parallel within a section.
Here, headings are nouns and
noun (gerund) phrases. Questions
and complete sentences can
also be used.*

*Table of
contents
does not
list itself.*

*Use lowercase
Roman numerals for
front matter.*

Table of Contents

*Intro
begins
on page
1*

*Capitalize
first letter
of each major
word in headings.*

*Indentations
show level or
heading at
a glance.*

Some reports have separate sections for "Conclusions" and "Recommendations"

*Line up right
margin (justify)*

*Add a "List of Illustrations" at the bottom
of the Table of Contents or on
a separate page if the
report has graphs and other
visuals. Omit "List of Illustrations"
if you have only tables.*

List of Illustrations

*Figures and Tables are numbered
independently, so you can have both
a "Figure 1" and a "Table 1"*

ii

(continued)

Letter or Memo of Transmittal

Use a letter of transmittal (see page i of Figure 12.4) if you are not a regular employee of the organization for which you prepare the report; use a memo if you are a regular employee.

The transmittal has several purposes: to transmit the report, to orient the reader to the report, and to build a good image of the report and of the writer.

FIGURE 12.4 A Formal Report *(continued)*

*Many readers read only the executive summary, not the report.
Include enough information to give the reader the key points you make.*

*Report
title*

**Slam Dunk
Increasing Attendance at University of Saskatchewan Women's Basketball Games**

Executive Summary

Start with recommendations or thesis

To increase student attendance at University of Saskatchewan women's basketball games, Huskie Athletics should implement short- and long-term marketing strategies and consider implementing a loyalty program.

Even though the team has been doing well, attendance at women's home games has failed to meet expectations over the last two years in the new Physical Activity Complex. Student attendance at games is especially important because there are close to 20,000 students; attending games is fun, promotes bonding with other students, and creates school spirit; and athletes do better when other students cheer them on.

*Provide
brief
support
for
recom-
mendations*

Because most students do like basketball (62% follow the men's team), it's reasonable to think that some students could be persuaded to attend women's games as well. The two biggest reasons for not attending, according to my survey, were "I never thought to go" and "My friends aren't interested in going." Students might be interested in going to the Huskies women's games if it occurred to them to go or if their friends went, too.

To increase attendance, the Athletic Department should

1. **Implement short-term marketing this fall.** Capitalize on the Huskies' winning streak last year to attract a higher attendance this year. Since basketball season is only weeks away, it might be smart to focus on increased awareness for the upcoming season.
   - Chalk and poster the Bowl before each home game.
   - Ask the women basketball players to host impromptu meet-and-greets at the Memorial Union Building or Place Riel or pickup games in the Bowl.
   - Provide information about the rules for women's basketball.

2. **Use students to develop a long-term marketing program and a formal publicity campaign.** Changing perceptions takes time and many messages.
   - Designate days for specific groups.
   - Offer deals and freebies. Ask sponsors to donate freebies or items to be raffled or auctioned.
   - Create an advertising campaign focusing on women students in student societies, women's floors in residence halls, and Women's Studies classes.
   - Buy more advertising space in *The Sheaf* and *The Saskatoon StarPhoenix*.
   - Try to persuade more reporters to write more stories in more prominent locations about the women's team.

3. **Consider adopting a loyalty program.** A loyalty program rewards students for behaviour Huskie Athletics wants to encourage. Further research is needed on the financial implications.

*Language in executive summary
can come from report. Make sure
any repeated language is well
written!*

*The abstract or executive summary
contains the logical skeleton of the
report: the recommendation(s)
and evidence supporting them*

iii

(continued)

An informal writing style is appropriate for a transmittal even when the style of the report is more formal.

Organize the transmittal in this way:

1. **Transmit the report.** Record the transmission (*Here is . . .*). Tell when and by whom it was authorized and the purpose it was to fulfill.

2. **Summarize your conclusions and recommendations.** If the recommendations will be easy for the reader to accept, put them early in the transmittal. If they will be difficult, summarize the findings and conclusions before the recommendations.

3. **Mention any points of special interest** in the report. Indicate minor problems you encountered in your investigation and show how you surmounted them. Thank people who helped you. These optional items can build goodwill and enhance your credibility.

FIGURE 12.4 A Formal Report *(continued)*

A running header is optional   *Also OK to omit*
          Slam Dunk: Increasing Attendance at U of S Women's Basketball Games   Page 1   *"Page"*
Here, the running heads and page numbers are
     one point size smaller than body   *Start with "Introduction"*   *Centre main headings. This*
     Spell out term the first time;   **Introduction**   *head uses bold (one point*
     put abbreviation in parentheses   *larger than body).*
                   University of Saskatchewan's (U of S) men's basketball team is a crowd pleaser, selling out home
                   games at the Physical Activities Complex (PAC) in good years. However, the U of S Huskies women's
                   basketball team suffers from low attendance figures, filling less than a quarter of the PAC.

"Purpose"
and "Scope"
can also   **Purpose and Scope**   *rhetorical purpose*
be separate
sections if The purpose of this report is to <u>recommend</u> ways to increase student attendance at Huskies women's
either is   basketball games.   *Tell what you discuss and how thoroughly*
long   *you discuss each topic*
                   In this report, I will focus on three topics: the factors that affect student attendance,   *Give*
                   student awareness of the women's team can be increased, and loyalty programs as a way of increasing   *topics*
                   attendance. I will briefly discuss how attendance and newspaper publicity correlate to the win/loss   *in*
                   record.   *"Scope" section should match report.*   *the order*
                          You may need to revise "Topics to Investigate" from the proposal.   *in which*
                   I will not discuss the cost of or the return on investment of my recommendations. I will not discuss   *you'll*
                   how changes in coaching or recruiting might affect attendance.   *discuss*
                          List any relevant topics you don't discuss   *them*

                   Assumption   *Assumptions cannot be proved. But if they are wrong,*
                                      the report's recommendation may no longer be valid.
                   My recommendations are based on the assumption that reasons for U of S student attendance at games
                   are similar to those of students at other universities.

Tell how and when you collected original data (surveys, interviews, or observations)

                   Methods

                   My information for this report comes from library and online sources, interviews with Huskies
                   Athletics staff, and a survey of 50 U of S students, using a convenience sample. I surveyed students
                   during the lunch hour in Louis' in the Memorial Union Building dining area on July 27, 2005. I walked
Sum-   around the room and asked everyone if he or she would be willing to answer the survey, until I had 50
marize   people.
respondent
demographic The students filling out my survey represent all academic ranks from undergraduate students (including
information   incoming first-year students) to graduate students. Sixty percent of the respondents are male, and 40%
                   are female. Sixty-eight percent of the people surveyed have never attended a women's basketball game,
                   although 62% watch men's games. (See Appendix A for the raw data.)

         Refer to your Appendices in
         the text of your report   *If your report has limitations, state them.*
                   Limitations   *Giving the number makes it easier for the reader to*
                                                  read the paragraph.
                   My research has <u>four</u> limitations. First, because I used a convenience survey, I cannot generalize from
                   the people I surveyed to all U of S students. Second, the timing of the survey was a problem. In the
                   summer, many of the people in Louis' are international students and incoming first-year students

                                                                                          (continued)

4. **Point out additional research that is necessary, if any.** Sometimes your recommendation cannot be implemented until further work is done. If you'd be interested in doing that research, or if you'd like to implement the recommendations, say so.

5. **Thank the reader for the opportunity to do the work and offer to answer questions.** Even if the report has not been fun to do, expressing satisfaction in doing the project is expected.

Table of Contents

The table of contents gives an overview of the report structure and is a useful resource for the busy professional. In the table of contents (page ii of Figure 12.4), list the headings exactly as they appear in the body of the report. If the report is fewer than 25 pages, you'll probably list all the levels of headings. In

InSite

**www.un.org/largerfreedom/
contents.html**

Tables of Contents for Web reports can have search boxes and clickable links for chapter titles and headings, as does this United Nations report on development, security, and human rights.

FIGURE 12.4   A Formal Report *(continued)*

10–point type   Slam Dunk: Increasing Attendance at U of S Women's Basketball Games   Page 2

11–point type   (or their parents) participating in orientation. However, incoming students will be here for at least four years, so they are the most interested in a long-term marketing program, such as a loyalty program. Third, 11 of my respondents circled "other." I cannot tell whether they are incoming first-year students, faculty, or visitors who are not students. Fourth, some interviewer error may have occurred. I was able to clarify questions for some students, but not all. I tried to be available to all students and answer all questions, but my words were not always consistent. I also found that the wording on my last question was not clear enough and caused some confusion.

Use Talking Heads. Note how much more specific this head is than "Background" would be.

12–point type   **Attendance at U of S Women's Basketball Home Games**

The PAC holds 2,400 fans, but the average general attendance at one of this past year's 10 women's home basketball games was only 600 (Tera Schneider, personal communication, June 26, 2005). This low attendance exists even though students with U of S I.D. cards pay no entry and adult tickets cost only $8.

Try for a mix of paragraph lengths (seven lines or less)

Begin most paragraphs with topic sentences

The 2004–05 attendance was the highest in the last three years because the team went 11–9 and made the conference playoffs for the second year running after almost 20 years of missing the playoffs. The highest attendance in the last two years at a women's-only basketball game was 700; the highest at a doubleheader where the women and men played back to back was 1,500. As Figure 1 shows, attendance has risen over the last two years, matching the increased success of the team. Still, attendance is disappointing given the enhanced capacity of the PAC, which has double the seating of the old venue.

APA format puts "Figure #" above the title of the Figure

Figure 1

U of S Women Win More Games …   But Attract Fewer Fans

Percentage of Games Won

Average Attendance at Each Women's Home Basketball Game

Still, the figures, though disappointing, are not unusual for women's Canadian Interuniversity Sport (CIS) basketball. Women's play routinely attracts fewer fans than men's play (Tera Schneider, personal communication, June 26, 2005).

Triple space before heading (two blank spaces)

The Importance of Increasing Student Attendance

Double space (one blank space) after

Students provide a promising audience for three reasons. First, there are a lot of them: 20,000. Second, attending games is fun and creates school spirit. Student attendance at sporting events (as well as theatrical performances and club meetings) brings students together and helps them realize common

In APA use "personal communication" for interviews, e-mails, and other information to which the reader has no access

(continued)

a very long report, pick a level and put all the headings at that level and above in the table of contents.

List of Illustrations

A list of illustrations enables readers to refer to your visuals.

Report visuals comprise both **tables** and **figures**. *Tables* are words or numbers arranged in rows and columns. *Figures* are everything else: bar graphs, pie charts, flow charts, maps, drawings, photographs, computer printouts, and so on. Tables and figures may be numbered independently, so you may have both a Table 1 and a Figure 1. In a report with maps and graphs but no other visuals, the visuals are sometimes called Map 1 and Graph 1. Whatever you call the illustrations, list them in the order in which they appear in the report; give the name of each visual as well as its number.

FIGURE 12.4 A Formal Report *(continued)*

Slam Dunk: Increasing Attendance at U of S Women's Basketball Games   Page 3

interests. Attending games is one way to make a large campus feel smaller. Third, student attendance helps the athletes. Student performance is better on the court when more people are cheering the team on. Athletes know their performance is enjoyed and like being watched.

In indented quote, period goes at end of quote. No punctuation after parenthesis.

In addition to all these benefits, increased student attendance can also translate into increased attendance by friends, family, and faculty. Nothing breeds success like success! Even with the family pack ($20 for 2 adults and up to 3 children), Huskie Athletics stands to gain financially too.

Increased attendance can also benefit the team in more tangible ways. When the Huskies competed for a qualifying spot in the CIS last season, Coach Lisa Thomaidis hoped for higher attendance rates so the women could play at home:

Indent quotations of 40 words or more

> The attendance that we have Sunday could ensure that we could host a championship game if we're fortunate enough to get there. The CIS wants to put [the championship game] on where the most interest is. ("Thomaidis," 2005, p. 2E)

Use first word of title in quotation marks for an article with no author

The quotation is itself a quotation. No extra quotation marks are necessary.

Factors Leading to Low Attendance at U of S Women's Basketball Games

At U of S, basketball is less popular than football. Women's basketball attracts fewer fans than does men's basketball. Few people I surveyed on the U of S campus could say they had been to a women's basketball game last year. Out of 50 surveys, 34 respondents—68%—say they have never been to a U of S women's basketball game. As Figure 2 shows, the two biggest reasons that students give for not attending the games is that they "have never thought to go" and their "friends are not interested" in attending the games.

Give both numbers and percentages

Refer to Figure in text before you give it. Tell what point it makes.

Quote to give the exact wording of survey question

Figure 2
Most Students Who Don't Attend Games "Never Thought" about Going

Use bars rather than columns when labels are long. Reorder bars in order of length— OK to shorten labels from survey questions.

Label both axes

Never thought to go
Friends not interested
Don't like basketball
No opportunity
Don't like sports
Team not good enough
Game time not convenient
Tickets cost too much

0   5   10   15   20   25
Number of students

(continued)

Executive Summary

An **executive summary** or **abstract** tells the reader what the document is about. It summarizes the recommendation of the report and the reasons for the recommendation or describes the topics the report discusses and indicates the depth of the discussion.

A good abstract is easy to read, concise, and clear. Edit your abstract carefully to tighten your writing and eliminate any unnecessary words.

Wordy: The author describes two types of business jargon, *businessese* and *reverse gobbledygook*. He gives many examples of each of these and points out how their use can be harmful.

Tight: The author describes and gives examples of two harmful types of business jargon, *businessese* and *reverse gobbledygook*.

Best Practices in Sustainable Development Reporting*

Avoiding technical jargon, acknowledging impact of industry trends and competition, making online disclosure user friendly (HTML rather than PDF downloading), educating the board, and matching graphic design and report content are some of the ways of meeting best practice objectives:

- Clear, concise articulation of key business risks and sustainability issues

- Communication of corporate vision for sustainability in terms of business strategy and decision-making

- Communication of corporate governance structure and management systems

- Comprehensive performance indicators for environment, regulatory compliance, product stewardship, community impacts, health and safety, and economic development

*Based on Robert Colapinto, "Worth Reporting," *CA Magazine* January/February 2005, 30–34, retrieved June 30, 2005, from http://www.camagazine.com/index.cfm/ci_id/24114/la_id/1.htm.

FIGURE 12.4   A Formal Report *(continued)*

10-point type

Slam Dunk: Increasing Attendance at U of S Women's Basketball Games   Page 4

11-point type

It's true that almost one-quarter of the respondents don't like basketball. But most do, and indeed, 62% watch men's games. Two people felt that the team wasn't "good enough." However, this past year, the team again made the CIS playoffs. It seems that perception, not reality, is likely the issue for these students. No one in my sample felt that the tickets cost too much. However, 2% found the game time of 6:15 P.M. inconvenient. It is obvious that the eight-dollar ticket price for those without U of S I.D. cards is not an issue.

12-point type

Summarize the point of a quotation before you give the quotation

Increasing Attendance through Marketing

Heading must cover everything under that heading until the next head or subhead at that level

Marketing sports events can increase attendance, as professors Clay Daughtrey and Andy Gillentine found in their research about marketing swim meets:

> Marketing techniques such as advertising, posters, word of mouth, and expanded ticket distribution were all identified as effective in increasing attendance. Making the meet more enjoyable for fans was also seen as imperative to increase fan attendance. This [goal] was achieved through music, giveaways, promotions, and fan participation exercises. Results could be useful to other Olympic or youth sport organizations that are attempting to market, increase public interest and generate funds for their sport (2000, p. A-118).

Use square brackets around words you add

Don't need authors' names in parentheses when they're in the sentence introducing the quote.

The three most promising options for U of S are short-term marketing to educate and increase awareness of games, long-term marketing programs, and loyalty programs. All of these methods should be used, but, as Table 1 shows, long-term marketing and a loyalty program are likely to have the greatest effect.

Tables and Figures are numbered independently, so you can have both a "Figure 1" and "Table 1"

Table 1
A Loyalty Program May Create Loyal Fans

Give question from survey

"To what extent would each of the following make you more likely to attend an U of S women's basketball game?"

Tell what numbers in a Likert-type scale mean

Average; N=50

Reorder from high to low

Rank	Option	(3 = Much more likely, 2 = Possibly more likely, 1 = No effect)
1	Loyalty Program	1.88
2	Long-Term Marketing	1.76
3	Increased Awareness	1.56
4	Education	1.28

"N" is the total number of people responding to the question. Use "n" to give the number of people giving a particular response.

Short-Term Marketing: Education and Increasing Awareness

Just walking across the U of S campus each day is a learning experience. Daily, groups pass out flyers, chalk the sidewalks, and set up booths with messages about credit cards, club meetings, textbook and class notes deals, Web sites, clothing sales, and parties. Most of this "publicity" takes place in the Bowl, the centre of campus.

Not every idea needs a source. Use your knowledge of people and of business.

Short-term marketing can be as simple as chalking messages on the sidewalk or tacking posters on the information poles near the library and administration buildings about upcoming games and when and where they will be held. If the team is not playing at home, the messages can remind students to listen to the radio for game coverage, to watch the nightly sports wrap-up on the local news, or to look for a report on the game's outcome the next morning in the university newspaper, *The Sheaf*, or the local *StarPhoenix*. Many of the

Italicize newspaper titles

(continued)

It's OK to use exactly the same words in the abstract and the report. Abstracts generally use a more formal style than other forms of business writing. Avoid contractions. Use second-person *you* only if the article uses the second person; even then, use *you* sparingly.

Summary or informative abstracts present the logical skeleton of the article: the thesis or recommendation and its proof. Use a summary abstract to give the most useful information in the shortest space.

> To market life insurance to mid-40s urban professionals, Fidelity Insurance should advertise in upscale publications and use direct mail.
>
> Network TV and radio are not cost efficient for reaching this market. This group comprises a small percentage of the prime-time network TV audience and a minority

FIGURE 12.4 A Formal Report *(continued)*

Limit claims you cannot prove with certainty

students surveyed say they've never thought to go to a game; maybe a friendly reminder in rather busy schedules would work.

Begin most paragraphs with topic sentences

A visit from the female basketball players in the Bowl is another way to attract fans. The Huskies could set up a booth to sell tickets in advance for a game, erect a temporary basketball hoop and play a pickup game, or host a shooting contest against interested students walking across the Bowl. Players might also visit the Memorial Union Building (MUB) or Place Riel and meet with students. Some respondents said they do not attend games because they do not know any players.

A lesson in the rules of the game may be in order. When the Western Hockey League (WHL) Saskatoon Blades wanted to increase attendance and bring in new fans, one of the sponsors, Credit Union Central, provided pocket-size pamphlets that unfolded into a cheat sheet with facts about the playing surface and players and explanations of the rules of the game. A pocket guide for women's basketball may be helpful to students who are new to women's CIS basketball, or in fact new to the game of basketball.

Divide a heading only when you have two or more subheads.

Long-Term Marketing

People like to do things in groups. The fact that U of S football games are "events" means that students want to go to the games whether they like football or not. Huskie Athletics needs to work to increase interest in women's basketball in general. As Figure 2 showed, the second most-common reason that students do not attend games is that their friends aren't interested.

Limit claims that you cannot prove with certainty

Huskie Athletics could designate days for specific groups: student societies, residential halls, and student organizations. Invite these groups to a game, seat them together in a certain spot in the arena, recognize them, and offer them a price break on food or merchandise for the game. Some of the students will invite friends from outside of the group to join in the fun. People who come just to be with their friends may enjoy the experience and return for other games.

APA does not capitalize words after a colon when the words are not a complete sentence

Offering freebies to the first so many fans attending a game will attract students. Besides shirts, other giveaways could include hats (which have been given away at a Huskies football game), ear coverings for the winter, drink and food coupons, promotional music CDs, signed posters of the team, or key chains. Fans also like raffles. The Orientation Days at the beginning of the year attract students because everyone hopes his or her ticket will be pulled for the term of free tuition. The campus bookstore could give away a gift certificate to be used towards textbooks, as most students know how expensive books are each term. Campus travel agents could donate a plane ticket to fly home or to be used for February Break travel.

Limit claims that you cannot prove with certainty

Men's basketball attracts many students, and men may always identify with the men's sport first. Therefore, it might make sense for Huskie Athletics to launch a campaign appealing to women students. Huskie Athletics could work with student societies, the advisers on women's residence hallfloors, and Women's Studies classes to find out what the students would like to see at games. It can create an advertising campaign for women, posting information on the floor bulletin boards, holding informational sessions throughout the year in the dorms with basketball players as speakers, and holding "Women's Nights" at the games. Once women students are recognized and catered to at games, they may attend more often and bring their male friends and classmates to games. Increasing women students' attendance will increase men's attendance.

(continued)

of most radio station listeners. They tend to discard newspapers and general-interest magazines quickly, but many of them keep upscale periodicals for months or years. Magazines with high percentages of readers in this group include *Architectural Digest, Bon Appetit, BusinessWeek, Canadian Gardening, Golf Digest,* and *Smithsonian.* Most urban professionals in their mid-40s are already used to shopping by mail and respond positively to well-conceived and well-executed direct mail appeals.

Any advertising campaign needs to overcome this group's feeling that they already have the insurance they need. One way to do this would be to encourage them to check the coverage their employers provide and to calculate the cost of their children's expenses through college or university graduation. Insurance plans that provide savings and tax benefits as well as death benefits might also be appealing.

FIGURE 12.4 A Formal Report *(continued)*

Slam Dunk: Increasing Attendance at U of S Women's Basketball Games   Page 6

APA calls for a capital letter after a colon when the words after the colon form a complete sentence

Last, Huskie Athletics could launch a formal publicity campaign: Buy more advertising space in *The Sheaf* and *The StarPhoenix*, and push for more articles to be written. In a search for articles over the past year about the women's basketball team in *The StarPhoenix*, I found approximately 50 articles. With an average of 537 words an article, a majority of the articles rehash the statistics of games or discuss injuries that plagued the team last season. Only 26% of the articles appeared on the front or inside front page of the Sports section. After the playoff win last season several Saskatoon residents wrote to the Sports editor to complain about the coverage of the team, or lack thereof:

> I understand that women's basketball usually doesn't produce the same crowds and therefore the same revenue that men's basketball produces. But one would think that they would deserve the same respect and praise that comes along with winning a championship. However, all that was awarded them was a passing mention on the TV news, and a small mention on the bottom of the front page of this newspaper and one article in the sports section compared with the multiple mentions that the men's team receives. . . . One of my co-workers didn't even know that the women's team was in a tournament. (Adams, 2005, p. 3D)

Use ellipses (3 spaces dots) when you omit part of a quote

Use author's name in parentheses when it isn't in the sentence introducing quote

Although the men's team did not win a tournament this past season, it had more and longer articles (averaging 603 words). Most of the articles built interest in the team, rather than simply rehashing the game. Almost twice as many articles about the men's team (49%) appeared on the front or inside front page of the Sports section. Several reporters wrote articles about the men's team, while one reporter wrote almost all the articles about women. Inviting more reporters for more interviews with the women's team and encouraging more reports on the front page would boost awareness of the team.

Reporters will write more stories if they know the team better. Daughtrey and Gillentine found "the most effective method used to generate media attention was to create a personal relationship with members of the media. Sponsorship was increased most when signage, hospitality, recognition through plaques/announcements, newspaper articles, and personal thank-you notes were offered" (2000, p. A-118).

When quote is part of your sentence, period goes after the parenthesis

Hire a College of Commerce student on an hourly salary to do the legwork for a long-term marketing program, contacting other university marketing programs, evaluating the financial expectations, and presenting a business plan to Huskie Athletics. In return, the student gains real-world experience that serves him or her well when interviewing for jobs later on.

Loyalty Program

Most Canadians today have at least one "club card" for the local grocery store. Many have three or four cards ranging from the supermarket to the drugstore and the video store that award points and give discounts on certain items each time the cards are swiped (as an ATM card is) and a purchase is made.

Short quotations (fewer than 40 words) go in your sentence

When author's name is in the sentence, it isn't repeated in the parentheses

In recent years, professional and collegiate athletic teams have joined the phenomenon. Joan Raymond explains, "Each time fans use their card, they rack up attendance points redeemable for promotional coupons or items such as food, drinks, and souvenirs. The more points they compile, the more 'rewards' they receive" (2001, p. 35). When fans sign up for the club cards, they provide basic information that the teams can use to tailor their offerings to the target audience. Customer relationship marketing (CRM) uses databases to track fan attendance and identify those most likely to buy season tickets.

When the original has a word in quotation marks, use single quotation marks (and double quotation marks for the whole quotation)

U of S can use the information that students give to create e-mail updates about the basketball team, give advance notice for tickets and giveaways, and attract more season ticket holders. The information can also clue the PAC in on what kind of concessions students want and what kind of merchandise penny-pinching university students will spend their money on.

(continued)

To write abstracts of business and government reports, conference papers, and published articles, write a sentence outline. A **sentence outline** not only uses complete sentences rather than words or phrases but also contains the thesis sentence or recommendation and the points that prove that point. Combine the sentences into paragraphs, adding transitions if necessary, and you'll have your abstract.

Descriptive abstracts indicate what topics the article covers and how deeply it goes into each topic, but they do not summarize what the article says about each topic. Phrases that describe the paper ("this paper reports," "it includes," "it summarizes," "it concludes") are marks of a descriptive abstract. An additional mark of a descriptive abstract is that the reader can't tell what the article says about the topics it covers. Descriptive abstracts are like elaborated tables

FIGURE 12.4 A Formal Report *(continued)*

Slam Dunk: Increasing Attendance at U of S Women's Basketball Games Page 7

Conclusions repeat points made in the report. Some companies ask for Conclusions and Recommendations are actions the readers should take. Recommendations at the beginning of reports

Conclusions and Recommendations

A majority of students like basketball and might be interested in going to the U of S women's games if it occurred to them to go or if their friends went, too. To increase attendance, the Athletic Department should

1. **Implement short-term marketing this fall.** Capitalize on the Huskies' winning streak last year to attract a higher attendance this year. Since basketball season is only weeks away, it might be smart to focus on increased awareness for the upcoming season.
   * Chalk and poster the Bowl before each home game.
   * Ask the women basketball players to host impromptu meet-and-greets at the MUB or Place Riel, or pickup games in the Bowl.
   * Provide information about the rules for women's basketball.

Numbering points makes it easy for readers

2. **Use U of S students to develop a long-term marketing program and a formal publicity campaign.** Changing perceptions takes time and many messages.
   * Designate days for specific groups.
   * Offer deals and freebies. Ask sponsors to donate freebies or items to be raffled or auctioned.
   * Create an advertising campaign focusing on women students in student societies, women's floors in residence halls, and Women's Studies classes.
   * Buy more advertising space in *The Sheaf* and *The StarPhoenix*.
   * Try to persuade more reporters to write more stories in more prominent locations about the women's team.

Make sure items in a list are parallel

3. **Consider adopting a loyalty program.** A loyalty program rewards students for behaviour Huskie Athletics wants to encourage. Further research is needed on the financial implications.

Because many readers turn to the "Recommendations" first, provide enough information so that the reason is clear all by itself. The ideas in this section must be logical extensions of the points made and supported **References** *in the body of the report.*   *APA Format*

Adams, E. (2005, April 8). U of S women deserved more attention from the media. *The StarPhoenix*, p. 3D.   *Use "p." when you don't have volume number*

Daughtrey, C., & Gillentine, A. (2000, March). The marketing of swim meets [Electronic Version]. *Research Quarterly for Exercise and Sport, 71*, A-118.   *No "p." when you give volume number*
Italicize volume number

University of Saskatchewan. (2005). Huskie Women's Basketball *Copyright/update date*
Retrieved July 3, 2005, from http://huskies.usask.ca/sports.php?s=7&g=2
Date you visited site

Raymond, J. (2001, April). Home field advantage. *American Demographics*, 34–36.

Start with the title of the article when no author is given
Thomaidis looks for U of S victory, big crowd. (2005, March 24). *The StarPhoenix*, p. 2E.
Month follows year. Period outside parentheses.

List all the printed and online sources cited in your report. Do not list sources you used for background but did not cite. Do not list interviews, phone calls, or other information to which the reader has no access.

(continued)

of contents, are typically shorter than summary abstracts, and explain the report in terms of its purpose and scope.

This report recommends ways Fidelity Insurance could market insurance to mid-40s urban professionals. It examines demographic and psychographic profiles of the target market. Survey results are used to show attitudes toward insurance. The report suggests some appeals that might be successful with this market.

A **mixed abstract** is a hybrid: part summary, part description. Mixed abstracts enable you both to comment about the kind of information and present the thesis and its proof.

FIGURE 12.4 A Formal Report *(concluded)*

Slam Dunk: Increasing Attendance at U of S Women's Basketball Games   Page A-1

Include a copy of your survey with the raw data. It's OK to change the format a bit to make room for the data

Appendix A: Raw Survey Data

N = 50.   *Tell how many people responded*

1. Gender   M   30 (60%)
              F   20 (40%)

2. Rank   First-Year   4 (8%)   *Give numbers*
            Second-Year   9 (18%)   *and percentages*
            Third-Year   13 (26%)
            Senior   5 (10%)
            Graduate student 7 (14%)
            Other   12 (24%)

3. How do you feel about women's sports?
   9 (18%)   1   I enjoy watching women's sports.
   10 (20%)   2
   20 (40%)   3   I'll watch, but it doesn't really matter.
   7 (14%)   4
   5 (10%)   5   Women's sports are boring/I'd rather watch men's sports.

4. Do you like to attend U of S men's basketball games or listen to them on radio?
   31 (62%) Y   19 (38%) N

5. How often do you attend U of S women's basketball games?
   0 (0%)   All/most games
   2 (4%)   Few games a season
   6 (12%)   Once a season
   8 (16%)   Less than once a year
   34 (68%)   Never

6. If you do not attend all of the women's basketball games, why not?
   22 (44%)   I've never thought to go.
   12 (24%)   I don't like basketball.
   3 (6%)   I don't like sporting events.
   2 (4%)   The team isn't good enough.
   14 (25%)   My friends are not interested in going.
   6 (12%)   I want to go, I just haven't had the opportunity.
   4 (8%)   Game time not convenient
   0 (0%)   The tickets cost too much ($8).

7. To what extent would each of the following make you more likely to attend an U of S women's basketball game? (3 = Much more likely, 2 = Possibly more likely, 1 = No effect)
   Increased awareness   1.56
   Long-term marketing   1.76
   Student loyalty program   1.88
   Education   1.28

Body

The **introduction** of the report always contains a statement of purpose and scope and may include all the parts in the following list.

- **Purpose.** The purpose statement (◄ p. 254) identifies the organizational problem the report addresses, the technical investigations it summarizes, and the rhetorical purpose (to explain, to recommend).
- **Scope.** The scope statement identifies how broad an area the report surveys. For example, Company XYZ is losing money on its line of radios. Does the report investigate the quality of the radios? The advertising campaign? The cost of manufacturing? The demand for radios? A scope statement allows the reader to evaluate the report on appropriate grounds. If the person who approved the proposal accepted a focus on advertising, then one cannot fault a report that considers only that factor.

- **Limitations.** Limitations make your recommendations less valid or valid only under certain conditions. Limitations usually arise because time or money constraints haven't permitted full research. For example, a campus pizza restaurant considering expanding its menu may ask for a report but not have enough money to take a random sample of students and non-students. Without a random sample, the writer cannot generalize from the sample to the larger population.

  Many recommendations are valid only for a limited time. For instance, a report on campus clothing recommendations will remain in force only for a short time: Three years from now, styles and tastes may have changed.

- **Assumptions.** Assumptions in a report are like assumptions in geometry: statements whose truth you assume, and which you use to prove your final point. If they are wrong, the conclusion will be wrong too.

  For example, to plan cars that will be built five years from now, an automobile manufacturer commissions a report on young adults' attitudes toward cars. The recommendations would be based on assumptions both about gas prices and about the economy. If gas prices radically rose or fell, the kinds of cars young adults wanted would change. If there were a major recession, people wouldn't be able to buy new cars.

  A good report spells out its assumptions so that readers can make decisions more confidently.

- **Methods.** If you conducted surveys, focus groups, or interviews, you need to tell how you chose your subjects, and how, when, and where they were interviewed.

  If your report is based solely on library or online research, simply cite your sources in the text and document them in notes or references. See Chapter 11 on how to cite and document sources.

- **Criteria.** The criteria section outlines the factors or standards that you are considering and the relative importance of each. If a company is choosing a city for a new office, is the cost of office space more or less important than the availability of skilled workers? Check with your audience before you write the draft to make sure that your criteria match those of your readers.

- **Definitions.** When you know that some members of your primary, secondary, or immediate audience will not understand technical terms, define them. If you have only a few definitions, you can put them in the Introduction. If you have many terms to define, use a **glossary** either early in the report or at the end. If the glossary is at the end, refer to it in the introduction so that readers know that you've provided it.

Formal reports usually have a section that gives the **background** of the situation or the *history of the problem*. Even though the current audience for the report probably knows the situation, reports are filed and consulted years later. These later audiences will probably not know the background, although it may be crucial for understanding the options that are possible.

In some cases, the history section may cover many years. For example, a report recommending that a Canadian hotel chain open hotels in Ukraine will probably give the history of that country for at least the last hundred years. In other cases, the history section is much briefer, covering only a few years or even just the immediate situation.

The rest of the **body** presents and interprets data in words and visuals. It analyzes causes of the problem and evaluates possible solutions, demonstrating the evidence that will support your conclusions and recommendations. Specific headings depend on the topic of the report and the organization that you have adopted to suit your purpose and audience.

Repeating with Style

The different parts of a formal report are designed to convey the same overall message, although they do not all include the same level of detail. The title page, transmittal document, table of contents, and executive summary (or abstract), for instance, prepare readers (who rarely read the report in its entirety) for what is to follow.

As a result, the parts often repeat key terms and concepts. Although some exact repetition is useful to reinforce important messages, too much cut-and-paste can give the impression of too much haste and insufficient attention to the needs of different readers.

To make your report as readable, memorable, and credible as possible, do the following:

- Quote sources when the phrasing is especially vivid or original.

- Learn the art of paraphrase.

- Increase level of detail in the body of the report.

- Include previews as well as reviews.

- Reinforce visually key verbal messages.

Conclusions and Recommendations

Conclusions summarize points you have made in the body of the report; **recommendations** are action items that would solve or ameliorate the problem. These sections are often combined if they are short: *Conclusions and Recommendations.*

No new information should be included in the conclusions.

Many readers turn to the recommendations section first. Number the recommendations to make it easy for people to discuss them. If the recommendations will seem difficult or controversial, give a brief paragraph of rationale after each recommendation. If they'll be easy for the audience to accept, you can simply list them without comments or reasons. The recommendations will also be in the executive summary and perhaps in the title and the transmittal.

Deciding When to Use Visuals

If the Information Age has proliferated sources of information, it has also produced added incentives—and aids—for readers eager to see what information means for them. We will focus here on how visuals can make numbers meaningful and messages memorable by replacing the proverbial 1,000 words (see Chapter 13 for visuals in oral presentations).

The 2005 Make Poverty History campaign, for instance, uses powerful visual effects to get across its message. From the white wristbands and shoelaces to the white bands wrapped around world landmarks on July 1, 2005, or Live 8 concert attracting 1 million spectators and 2 billion viewers around the world, the campaign uses visual display to reinforce messages about the 30,000 children who die every day as a result of extreme poverty.

A series of short videos make powerful statements: Bono snapping his fingers in *Make History 2005*, or celebrities in *Click* saying not a word but snapping their fingers to register someone dying every three seconds from extreme poverty, all urging us to make poverty history one by one.[8]

The ease of creating visuals by computer may make people use them uncritically. Use a visual only to achieve a specific purpose. Never put in numbers or visuals just because you have them; instead, use them to convey information the audience needs or wants.

"How thoughtful...a layoff notice in braille."

In your rough draft, use visuals

- **To see that ideas are presented completely.** A table, for example, can show you whether you've included all the items in a comparison.
- **To find relationships.** For example, charting sales on a map may show that the sales representatives who made quota all have territories on the East or the West Coast. Is the product one that appeals to coastal lifestyles? Is advertising reaching the coasts but not the Prairies, Ontario, or Quebec? Even if you don't use the visual in your final document, creating the map may lead you to questions you wouldn't otherwise ask.

In the final presentation or document, use visuals

- **To make points vivid.** Readers skim memos and reports; a visual catches the eye. The brain processes visuals immediately. Understanding words—written or oral—takes more time.
- **To emphasize material** that might be skipped if it were buried in a paragraph. The beginning and end are places of emphasis. Visuals allow you to emphasize important material, wherever it logically falls.
- **To present material more compactly and with less repetition** than words alone would require. Words can call attention to the main points of the visual, without repeating all of the visual's information.

The number of visuals you will need depends on your purposes, the kind of information, and the audience. You'll use more visuals when you want to show relationships and to persuade, when the information is complex or contains extensive numerical data, and when the audience values visuals.

Designing Visuals

Use the following six steps to create good visuals.

1. Check the Source of the Data.

Your chart is only as good as the underlying data. Check to be sure that your data come from a reliable source (see p. 283).

2. Determine the Story You Want to Tell.

Every visual should tell a story. Stories can be expressed in complete sentences that describe something that happens or changes. The sentence also serves as the title of the visual.

Not a story:	Canadian Sales, 2000–2005
Possible stories:	Forty Percent of Our Sales Were to New Customers.
	Growth Was Highest in Quebec
	Sales Increased from 2000 to 2005.
	Most Sales Representatives Have 2–5 Years' Experience.
	Sales Were Highest in the Areas with More Sales Representatives.

Stories that tell us what we already know are rarely interesting. Instead, good stories may

- Support a hunch you have
- Surprise you or challenge so-called common knowledge
- Show trends or changes you didn't know existed
- Have commercial or social significance
- Provide information needed for action
- Contain personal relevance for you and the audience

Why the Numbers Don't Add Up*

How many people work at home in Canada? That depends on who collected the data and how.

According to Statistics Canada, there was a decline from 8.2% in 1996 to 8.0% reporting the home as the workplace in the 2001 Census. But a 2001 survey (also by StatsCanada) shows that the home workforce increased from 16 to 17% between 1995 and 2000. That survey used different wording.

Statistics Canada warns that "users should be aware of [data] inaccuracies." In particular, StatsCanada stresses:

- Census returns are self-administered and depend on respondents understanding questions.
- Persons who did not check the Place of Work question could not be coded.
- Results differ from business and establishment surveys that report all workers as if they worked in one location.
- Census collects information on only one job; those with multiple jobs can report only the main one.
- Results may reflect two trends: increased working at home and decreased agricultural sector.

*Based on Statistics Canada, "Data Quality Measurement," retrieved July 2, 2005, from http://www12.statcan.ca/english/census01/release/release6.cfm; E. Akyeampong and R. Nadwodny, "Evolution of the Canadian Workplace: Work from Home," *Perspectives on Labour and Income* 2.9 (September 2001): 31.

To find stories,

1. **Focus on a topic** (purchases of cars, who likes jazz, etc.).
2. **Simplify the data** on that topic and convert the numbers to simple, easy-to-understand units.
3. **Look for relationships and changes.** For example, compare two or more groups: do men and women have the same attitudes? Look for changes over time. Look for items that can be seen as part of the same group. For example, to find stories about entertainers' incomes, you might compare the number of writers, actors, and musicians in three rankings.
4. **Process the data** to find more stories. Calculate the percentage change from one year to the next.

When you think you have a story, test it against all the data to be sure it's accurate.

Some stories are simple straight lines: "Sales Increased." But other stories are more complex, with exceptions or outlying cases. Such stories will need more nuanced titles to do justice to the story. Figure 12.5 tells a predictable story about growth in Alberta together with a powerful message about its unsustainability.

Almost every data set allows you to tell several stories. You must choose the story you want to tell. Dumps of uninterpreted data confuse and frustrate your audience; they undercut the credibility and goodwill you want to create.

3. Choose the Right Visual for the Story.

Visuals are not interchangeable. Good writers choose the visual that best matches the purpose of presenting the data.

■ Use a table when the reader needs to be able to identify exact values. (See Figure 12.6a.)

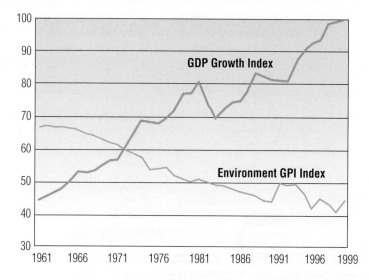

FIGURE 12.5 Alberta GPI Environmental Sustainability Index Compared with GDP Growth, 1961–1999.

Source: The Alberta GPI Accounts 1961–1999; rptd. from Mark Anielski & Mark Winfield, "A Conceptual Framework for Monitoring Municipal and Community Sustainability in Canada." Report prepared by the Pembina Institute for Environment Canada, June 17, 2002.

FIGURE 12.6 Choose the Visual to Fit the Story

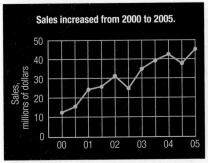

Canadian sales reach $44.5 million.

	Millions of dollars		
	1995	2000	2005
Atlantic	10.2	10.8	11.3
Southern Ontario	7.6	8.5	10.4
Quebec	8.3	6.8	9.3
Prairies	11.3	12.1	13.5
Totals	37.4	38.2	44.5

a. Tables show exact values.

Forty percent of our 2005 sales were to new customers.

Old customers 60%   New customers 40%

b. Pie charts compare a component to the whole.

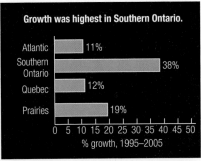

Growth was highest in Southern Ontario.

Atlantic 11%
Southern Ontario 38%
Quebec 12%
Prairies 19%

% growth, 1995–2005

c. Bar charts compare items or show distribution or correlation.

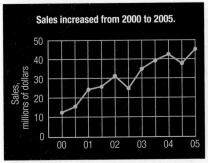

Sales increased from 2000 to 2005.

Sales, millions of dollars

d. Line charts compare items over time or show distribution or correlation.

Most sales representatives have 2-5 years' experience.

Number

Years' experience (or more)

e. Bar charts can show frequency.

Sales were highest in the areas with the most sales representatives.

2005 sales, millions of dollars

Number of sales reps. in region

f. Dot charts show correlation.

- Use a chart or graph when you want the reader to focus on relationships.[9]
  - To compare a part to the whole, use a **pie chart.** (See Figure 12.6b.)
  - To compare one item to another item, use a **map** or a **bar chart.** (See Figure 12.6c.)
  - To compare items over time, use a bar chart or a **line graph.** (See Figure 12.6d.)
  - To show frequency or distribution, use a line graph or bar chart. (See Figure 12.6e.)
  - To show correlations, use a bar chart, a line graph, or a **dot chart.** (See Figure 12.6f.)
- Use photographs to create a sense of authenticity or show the item in use. If the item is especially big or small, include something in the photograph that can serve as a reference point: a dime, a person.
- Use drawings to show dimensions or emphasize detail.
- Use maps to emphasize location.
- Use **Gantt charts** to show timelines for proposals or projects.

4. Follow the Conventions for Designing Typical Visuals.

Every visual should contain six components:

1. A title that tells the story that the visual shows.
2. A clear indication of what the data are. For example, what people *say* they did is not necessarily what they really did. An estimate of what a number

will be in the future differs from numbers in the past that have already been measured.

3.   Clearly labelled units.
4.   Labels or legends identifying axes, colours, symbols, and so forth.
5.   The source of the data, if you created the visual from data someone else gathered and compiled.
6.   The source of the visual, if you reproduce a visual someone else created.

Formal visuals are divided into tables and figures (See List of Illustrations p. 300).

Tables

Use tables only when you want the audience to focus on specific numbers. Graphs convey less specific information but are always more memorable.

- Round off to simplify the data (e.g., 35% rather than 35.27%; 44.5 million rather than 44,503,276).
- Provide column and row totals or averages when they're relevant.
- Put the items you want readers to compare in columns rather than in rows to facilitate mental subtraction and division.
- When you have many rows, screen alternate entries or double-space after every five entries to help readers line up items accurately.

Suppose you want to give investors information about various stocks' performance. Organizing the daily numbers into tables would be much more useful than paragraph after paragraph of statements. Tables of stock prices have been the norm until recently. Now, on the Internet, SmartMoney.com offers subscribers Market Map 1000, a graphics tool that helps them see the top performers. For 1,000 U.S. and international stocks, Market Map displays visual information about each company's performance. Each company is shown as a rectangle, and companies are clustered into industry groups. Users can click on industry groups for a more detailed view.[10]

Pie charts

Pie charts force the audience to measure area. Research shows that people can judge position or length (which a bar chart uses) much more accurately than they judge area. The data in any pie chart can be put in a bar chart.[11] Therefore, use a pie chart only when you are comparing one segment to the whole. When you are comparing one segment to another segment, use a bar chart, a line graph, or a map—even though the data may be expressed in percentages.

- Make the chart a perfect circle. Perspective circles distort the data.
- Limit the number of segments to no more than seven. If your data have more divisions, combine the smallest or the least important into a single "miscellaneous" or "other" category.
- Label the segments outside the circle. Internal labels are hard to read.

Bar charts

Bar charts (Figure 12.7) are easy to interpret because they ask people to compare distance along a common scale, which most people judge accurately. Bar charts are useful in a variety of situations: to compare one item to another, to compare items over time, and to show correlations. Use horizontal bars when your labels are long; when the labels are short, either horizontal or vertical bars will work.

FIGURE 12.7   Varieties of Bar Charts

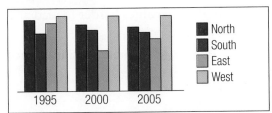

a. Grouped bar charts compare several aspects of each item, or several items over time.

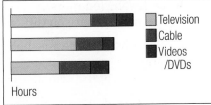

b. Segmented, subdivided, or **stacked bars** sum the components of an item.

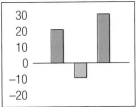

c. Deviation bar charts identify positive and negative values.

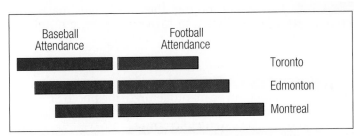

d. Paired bar charts show the correlation between two items.

e. Histograms or **pictograms** use images to create the bars.

- Order the bars in a logical or chronological order.
- Put the bars close enough together to make comparison easy.
- Label both horizontal and vertical axes.
- Put all labels inside the bars or outside them. When some labels are inside and some are outside, the labels carry the visual weight of longer bars, distorting the data.
- Make all the bars the same width.
- Use different colours for different bars only when their meanings are different: estimates as opposed to known numbers, negative as opposed to positive numbers.
- Avoid using perspective. Perspective makes the values harder to read and can make comparison difficult.
- **Grouped bar charts** allow you to compare either several aspects of each item or several items over time. Group together the items you want to compare.
- **Segmented, subdivided,** or **stacked bars** sum the components of an item. It's hard to identify the values in specific segments; grouped bar charts are almost always easier to use.
- **Deviation bar charts** identify positive and negative values, or winners and losers.
- **Paired bar charts** show the correlation between two items.
- **Histograms** or **pictograms** use images to create the bars.

Line graphs

Line graphs are also easy to interpret. Use line graphs to compare items over time, to show frequency or distribution, and to show correlations.

- Label both horizontal and vertical axes.
- When time is a variable, put it on the horizontal axis.

- Avoid using more than three different lines on one graph. Even three lines may be too many if they cross each other.
- Avoid using perspective. Perspective makes the values harder to read and can make comparison difficult.

Line graphs with the area below the line filled in are sometimes called **landscape graphs.**

Dot charts

Dot charts show correlations or other large data sets.

- Label both horizontal and vertical axes.
- Keep the dots fairly small. If they get too big, they no longer mark data "points"; some of the detail is lost.

Photographs

Photographs convey a sense of authenticity. The photo of a prototype helps convince investors that a product can be manufactured; the photo of a devastated area can suggest the need for government grants or private donations. You may need to **crop,** or trim, a photo for best results.

A growing problem with photos is that they may be edited or staged, purporting to show something as reality even though it never occurred.

Drawings

The richness of detail in photos makes them less effective than drawings for focusing on details. With a drawing, the artist can provide as much or as little detail as is needed to make the point; different parts of the drawing can show different layers or levels of detail. Drawings are also better for showing structures underground, undersea, or in the atmosphere.

Maps

Use maps to emphasize location or to compare items in different locations. Several computer software packages now allow users to generate municipal, provincial, national, or global maps, adding colour or shadings, and labels.

- Label cities, provinces, or countries if it's important that people be able to identify levels in areas other than their own.
- Avoid using perspective. Perspective makes the values harder to read and can make comparison difficult.

Gantt charts

Gantt charts are bar charts used to show schedules. They're most commonly used in proposals.

- Colour-code bars to indicate work planned and work completed.
- Use a red outline to indicate **critical activities,** which must be completed on time if the project is to be completed by the due date.
- Use diamonds to indicate progress reports, major achievements, or other accomplishments.

5. Use Colour and Decoration with Restraint.

Colour makes visuals more dramatic, but it creates at least two problems. First, readers try to interpret colour, an interpretation that may not be appropriate.

(Perhaps the best use of colour occurs in the weather maps printed daily in many newspapers. Blue seems to fit cold; red seems to fit hot temperatures.) Second, meanings assigned to colours differ depending on the audience's national background and profession.

As we have seen in Chapter 9, connotations for colour vary from culture to culture. Red is sometimes used to suggest danger or *stop* in Canada; it means *go* in China and is associated with festivities. Red suggests masculinity or aristocracy in France, death in Korea, blasphemy in some African countries, and luxury in many parts of the world. Yellow suggests caution or cowardice in Canada, prosperity in Egypt, grace in Japan, and femininity in many parts of the world.[12]

These general cultural associations may be superseded by corporate, national, or professional associations. Some people associate blue with IBM or Hewlett-Packard and red with Coca-Cola, communism, or Japan. People in specific professions learn other meanings for colours. Blue suggests *reliability* to financial managers, *water* or *coldness* to engineers, and *death* to health care professionals. Red means *losing money* to financial managers, *danger* to engineers, but *healthy* to health care professionals. Green usually means *safe* to engineers, but *infected* to health care professionals.[13]

Research also tells us that colour can be a powerful ally when you are trying to engage, inform, or persuade your audience. In particular, colour has these effects:

- Increases brand recognition by up to 80%
- Improves readership by 40%
- Speeds up learning from 55 to 78%
- Enhances comprehension by 73%
- Increases engagement by 42% (colour rather than black and white ads)[14]

When you do use colour in visuals, L. G. Thorell and W. J. Smith suggest these guidelines:[15]

- Use no more than five colours when colours have meanings.
- Use glossy paper to make colours more vivid.
- Be aware that colours on a computer screen always look brighter than the same colours on paper because the screen sends out light.

Resist the temptation to make your visual "artistic" or "relevant" by turning it into a picture or adding clip art. **Clip art** consists of predrawn images that you can import into your newsletter, sign, or graph. A small drawing of a car in the corner of a line graph showing the number of miles driven is acceptable in an oral presentation but out of place in a written report. Edward Tufte uses the term **chartjunk** for decorations that at best are irrelevant to the visual and at worst mislead the reader.[16] If you use clip art, be sure that the images of people show a good mix of both sexes, various races and ages, and various physical conditions.

6. Be Sure the Visual Is Accurate and Ethical.

Always double-check your visuals to be sure the information is accurate; many visuals have accurate labels but misleading visual shapes. Visuals communicate quickly; audiences remember the shape, not the labels. If the reader has to study the labels to get the right picture, the visual is unethical even if the labels are accurate.

Figure 12.8 is distorted by chartjunk and dimensionality. In an effort to make the visual interesting, the artist used a picture of a young man (presumably an engineer) rather than simple bars. By using a photograph rather than a bar, the chart implies that all engineers are young, nerdy-looking white men. The photograph also makes it difficult to compare the numbers. The number represented by the

FIGURE 12.8 Chartjunk and Dimensions Distort Data

How much is that engineer in the window?

Here's how much an employee in Silicon Valley was worth over the past year, determined by dividing the value of a sample acquisition by the number of employees acquired.

$5.6 million

$1.9 million

$1.3 million

GETTY IMAGES (3)

Nov. 2000   July 2001   Nov. 2001

Source: "Valley Horror Show: The Incredible Shrinking Engineer," Adam Lashinsky, *Fortune*, December 10, 2001, p. 40.

tallest figure is not quite 5 times as great as the number represented by the shortest figure, yet the tallest figure takes up 12 times as much space and appears even bigger than that. Two-dimensional figures distort data by multiplying the apparent value by the width as well as by the height—four times for every doubling in value. Perspective graphs are especially hard for readers to interpret and should be avoided.[17]

Even simple bar and line graphs may be misleading if part of the scale is missing, or truncated. **Truncated graphs** are most acceptable when the audience knows the basic data set well. For example, graphs of the stock market almost never start at zero; they are routinely truncated. This omission is acceptable for audiences who follow the market closely.

To make your visuals more accurate,

■   Differentiate between actual and estimated or projected values.

- When you must truncate a scale, do so clearly with a break in the bars or in the background.
- Avoid perspective and three-dimensional graphs.
- Avoid combining graphs with different scales.
- Use images of people carefully in histographs to avoid sexist, racist, or other exclusionary visual statements.

Integrating Visuals

Refer to every visual in your text. Normally one gives the table or figure number in the text but not the title. Put the visual as soon after your reference as space and page design permit. If the visual will not be immediately obvious to the reader, provide a page reference:

As Figure 3 shows (page 10), . . .

(See Table 2 on page 14.)

Summarize the main point of a visual *before* you present the visual itself. Then when readers get to it, they'll see it as confirmation of your point.

Weak: Listed below are the results.

Better: As Figure 4 shows, sales doubled in the last decade.

Visuals for presentations need to be simpler than visuals the audience reads on paper. You may want to cut out one of the columns, round off the data even more, or present the material in a chart rather than a table. Visuals for presentations should have titles but don't need figure numbers. Do know where each visual is so that you can return to one if someone asks about it during the question period. Decorative clip art, even though technically chartjunk, is acceptable in oral presentations as long as it does not obscure the story you're telling with the visual.

Rather than reading the visual to the audience, summarize the story and then elaborate on what it means for the audience. If you have copies of all the visuals for your audience, hand them out at the beginning of the talk.

Summary of Key Points

- *Causation* means that one thing causes or produces another. *Correlation* means that two things happen at the same time. One might cause the other, but both might be caused by a third.
- Reports use the same style as other business documents, with three exceptions:
  1. Reports use a more formal style than do many letters and memos.
  2. Reports rarely use the word *you.*
  3. Reports should be self-explanatory.
- To create good report style,
  1. Say what you mean.
  2. Tighten your writing.
  3. Introduce sources and visuals gracefully.
  4. Use blueprints, transitions, topic sentences, and headings.
- Organize the transmittal in this way:
  1. Release the report.

2. Summarize your conclusions and recommendations.

3. Mention any points of special interest in the report. Indicate minor problems you encountered in your investigation and show how you surmounted them. Thank people who helped you.

4. Point out additional research that is necessary, if any.

5. Thank the reader for the opportunity to do the work and offer to answer questions.

- **Summary or informative executive summaries or abstracts** present the logical skeleton of the article: the thesis or recommendation and its proof. **Descriptive abstracts** indicate what topics the article covers and how deeply it goes into each topic, but do not summarize what the article says about each topic. **Mixed abstracts** have some characteristics of both summary and descriptive abstracts.

- The **introduction** of the report always contains a statement of purpose and scope. The **purpose** statement identifies the organizational problem the report addresses, the technical investigations it summarizes, and the rhetorical purpose (to explain, to recommend). The **scope** statement identifies how broad an area the report surveys. The introduction may also include **limitations,** problems or factors that limit the validity of your recommendations; **assumptions,** statements whose truth you assume, and which you use to prove your final point; **methods,** an explanation of how you gathered your data; **criteria** used to weigh the factors in the decision; and **definitions** of terms readers may not know.

- A **background** or **history** section is included in the **body** because reports are filed and may be consulted years later.

- **Conclusions** summarize points made in the body of the report; **recommendations** are action items that would solve or ameliorate the problem. These sections are often combined if they are short.

- In the rough draft, use visuals to see that ideas are presented completely and to see what relationships exist. In the final report, use visuals to make points vivid, to emphasize material that the reader might skip, and to present material more compactly and with less repetition than words alone would require.

- You'll use more visuals when you want to show relationships and to persuade, when the information is complex or contains extensive numerical data, and when the audience values visuals.

- Pick data to tell a story, to make a point.

- Tables are numbers or words arrayed in rows and columns; figures are everything else. Formal visuals have both numbers and titles that indicate what to look for in the visual or why the visual is included and is worth examining.

- Visuals must present data accurately, both literally and by implication. **Chartjunk** denotes decorations that at best are irrelevant to the visual and at worst mislead the reader. **Truncated graphs** omit part of the scale and visually mislead readers. Perspective graphs and graphs with negative bases mislead readers.

- Summarize the main point of a visual before it appears in the text.

- Visuals for presentations need to be simpler than visuals on paper.

- How much discussion a visual needs depends on the audience, the complexity of the visual, and the importance of the point it makes.

| CHAPTER 12 | Exercises and Problems |

Getting Started

12.1 Identifying Assumptions and Limitations

Indicate whether each of the following would be an assumption or a limitation in a formal report.

a. Report on Ways to Encourage More Students to Join XYZ Organization

1. I surveyed a judgment sample rather than a random sample.

2. These recommendations are based on the attitudes of current students. Presumably, students in the next several years will have the same attitudes and interests.

b. Report on Car-Buying Preferences of Young Adults

1. These recommendations may change if the cost of gasoline increases dramatically or if there is another deep recession.

2. This report is based on a survey of adults ages 20 to 24 in Alberta, Newfoundland, British Columbia, Ontario, and Yukon.

3. These preferences are based on the cars now available. If a major technical or styling innovation occurs, preferences may change.

12.2 Revising an Executive Summary

The following executive summary is poorly organized and too long. Rearrange information to make it more effective. Cut information that does not belong in the summary. You may use different words as you revise.

In this report I will discuss the communication problems that exist at Rolling Meadows Golf Club. The problems discussed will deal with channels of communication. The areas that are causing problems are internal. Radios would solve these internal problems.

Taking a 15-minute drive on a golf cart in order to find the superintendent is a common occurrence. Starters and rangers need to keep in touch with the clubhouse to maintain a smooth flow of players around the course. The rangers have expressed an interest in being able to call the clubhouse for advice and support.

Purchasing two-channel FM radios with private channels would provide three advantages. First, radios would make the golf course safer by providing a means of notifying someone in the event of an emergency. Second, radios would make the staff more efficient by providing a faster channel of communication. Third, radios would enable clubhouse personnel to keep in touch with the superintendent, the rangers, and the starters.

During the week, radios can be carried by the superintendent, the golf pro, and another course worker. On weekends and during tournaments, one radio will be used by the golf professional. The other two will be used by one starter and one ranger. Three radios is the minimum needed to meet basic communication needs. A fourth radio would provide more flexibility for busy weekends and during tournaments.

Tekk T-20 radios can be purchased from Page-Com for $129 each. These radios have the range and options needed for use on the golf course. Radios are durable and easy to service. It is possible that another brand might be even less expensive.

Rolling Meadows Golf Club should purchase four radios. They will cost under $600 and can be paid for from the current equipment budget.

Communicating at Work

12.3   Recommending Action

Write a report recommending an action that your unit or organization should take. Possibilities include

- Buying more equipment for your department.
- Hiring an additional worker for your department.
- Making your organization more family friendly.

- Making a change that will make the organization more efficient.
- Making changes to improve accessibility for customers or employees with disabilities.

Address your report to the person who would have the power to approve your recommendation.

12.4   Evaluating a Report from Your Workplace

Consider the following aspects of a report from your workplace:

- How much information is included? How is it presented?
- Visuals and layout. Are visuals used effectively? Are they accurate and free from chartjunk? What image do the pictures and visuals create? Are colour and white space used effectively?
- Emphasis. What points are emphasized? What points are de-emphasized? What verbal and visual techniques are used to highlight or minimize information?

As Your Professor Directs,

a. Write a memo to your professor analyzing the report.

b. Join with a small group of students to compare and contrast several reports. Present your evaluation in an informal group report.

c. Present your evaluation orally to the class.

Report Assignments

12.5   Writing a Feasibility Study

Write a report evaluating the feasibility of two or more alternatives. Possible topics include the following:

1. Is it feasible for a local restaurant to open another branch? Where should it be?

2. Is it feasible to create a program to mentor women and minorities in your organization?

3. Is it feasible to produce a video yearbook in addition to or instead of a paper yearbook at your community college or university?

4. Is it feasible to create or enlarge a day care centre for the children of students?

5. Could your college or university host a regional meeting of the Association for Business Communication on or off campus?

Pick a limited number of alternatives, explain your criteria clearly, evaluate each alternative, and recommend the best course of action.

12.6   Writing an Informative or Closure Report

Write an informative report on one of the following topics.

1. What should a Canadian manager know about dealing with workers from _____ [you fill in the country or culture]? What factors do and do not motivate people in this group? How do they show respect and deference? Are they used to a strong hierarchy or to an egalitarian setting? Do they normally do one thing at once or many things? How important is clock time and being on time? What factors lead them to respect someone? Age? Experience? Education? Technical knowledge? Wealth? Or what else? What conflicts or miscommunications may arise between workers from this culture and other workers due to cultural differences? Are people from this culture similar in these beliefs and behaviours, or is there lots of variation?

2. What benefits do companies offer? To get information, check the Web pages of three companies in the same industry. Information about benefits is usually on the page about working for the company. For example, Eddie Bauer's Associate Benefits page is www.eddiebauer.com/about/company_info/careers_benefits.asp.

3. Describe an ethical dilemma encountered by workers in a specific organization. What is the background of the situation? What competing loyalties exist? In the past, how have workers responded? How has the organization responded? Have "whistle-blowers" been rewarded or punished? What could the organization do to foster ethical behaviour?

4. Describe a problem or challenge encountered by an organization where you've worked. Describe the problem, show why it needed to be solved, tell who did what to try to solve it, and tell how successful the efforts were. Possibilities include

■ How the organization is implementing work teams, downsizing, or a change in organizational culture.

■ How the organization uses e-mail or voice mail, statistical process control, or telecommuting.

■ How managers deal with stress, make ethical choices, or evaluate subordinates.

■ How the organization is responding to changing Canadian demographics or international competition and opportunities.

12.7   Writing a Library Research Report

Write a library research report.

As Your Professor Directs,

Turn in the following documents:

a. The approved proposal.

b. Two copies of the report, including
   Cover.
   Title Page.
   Letter or Memo of Transmittal.
   Table of Contents.
   List of Illustrations.
   Executive Summary or Abstract.
   Body (Introduction, all information, recommendations). Your professor may specify a minimum length, a minimum number or kind of sources, and a minimum number of visuals.
   References or Works Cited.

c. Your notes and rough drafts.

Choose one of the following topics.

1. **Making Money from Football.** Your boss, the athletic director at your college or university, is interested in increasing revenue. "CFL teams make money in lots of ways—and some of the teams that are successful financially don't have good teams. Look at what they're doing, and recommend whether we could copy any of their strategies. Also recommend ways to ensure that students aren't priced out of attending the games." Start with Sam Walker, "Pro Football: Scoring in a Slow Economy," *The Wall Street Journal,* September 7, 2001, W1, W4.

2. **Recommending a Dress Policy.** Your boss asks you to look into "business casual" dress. "Is it time to retire it? And what *is* 'business casual'? Recommend how our employees should dress, and why. Include some photos of what is and isn't appropriate." To start, read Laura Bogomolny and Andrew Wahl, "Suit Yourself," *Canadian Business,* November 10, 2003, 145.

   Hint: Choose a business, non-profit, or govern-ment agency you know well and recommend a dress policy for it.

3. **Accounting for Intellectual Capital.** You work for the Ontario Securities Commission. Your boss hands you a copy of Thomas A. Stewart, "Accounting Gets Radical," *Fortune,* April 1, 2001, 184–194. "Many experts believe that traditional, generally accepted accounting principles don't work well now that knowledge and intellectual property can be a firm's most important assets. Write a report summarizing proposals for alternate accounting schemes and explain the advantages and disadvantages of each."

4. **Evaluating Online Voting.** As an aide to a member of Parliament, you frequently research topics for legislation. You have been told, "Look into online voting. I want to know what the problems are and whether it's feasible for the next election." Start with Stephen H. Wildstrom, "Click and Be Counted," *BusinessWeek,* April 24, 2000, 22; and Thomas E. Weber, " 'Scalable' Ballot Fraud: Why One Tech Maven Fears Computer Voting," *The Wall Street Journal,* March 19, 2001, B1.

5. **Evaluating the Ethics of "Weblining."** You're an aide to a member of Parliament. You've been told, "I'm concerned that information on the Web allows companies to 'rank' customers and then charge rates and provide customer service based on how 'good' a customer is. Poor people and small businesses will be hurt. Find out how widespread the practice is. Especially consider the ethical implications. Should the federal government outlaw the practice?" Start with Marcia Stepanek, "Weblining," *BusinessWeek e.biz,* April 3, 2000, EB26–E34.

6. **Understanding Demographic Changes.** You work for a major political party. Your boss says, "As you know, the number of so-called minorities is growing. Moreover, they're increasingly middle class. I want you to analyze one ethnic group in our province. What issues are they interested in? Which party do they favour? What appeals might persuade them to vote for a candidate of the other party?" Andrew Wahl, "Leaders Wanted," *Canadian Business* March 1, 2004, 30–35; Kamal Dib,

"Diversity Works," *Canadian Business*
March 29–April 11, 2004, 53–54; Jill Mahoney,
"Visible Majority by 2017," *The Globe and Mail*,
March 23, 2005, A1 to A7.

7. **Improving Laptop Security.** Your boss hands you a copy of Charles C. Mann, "Where the Hell Is My Laptop?" www.ecompany.com, March 2001, 84–90. She says, "This article is frightening. Laptop theft is rising. My concern is not just the cost of the computers stolen, but the danger of data theft as well. Thieves can even re-create what's on a laptop screen in another room. Put together a report on how we can protect our data and our computers."

8. With your professor's permission, investigate a topic of your choice.

12.8   Writing a Recommendation Report

Write an individual or a group report.

As Your Professor Directs,
Turn in the following documents:

1. The approved proposal.
2. Two copies of the report, including
   Cover.
   Title Page.
   Letter or Memo of Transmittal.
   Table of Contents.
   List of Illustrations.
   Executive Summary or Abstract.
   Body (Introduction, all information, recommendations). Your professor may specify a minimum length, a minimum number or kind of sources, and a minimum number of visuals.
   Appendices if useful or relevant.
3. Your notes and rough drafts.
   Pick one of the following topics.

1. **Improving Customer Service.** Many customers find that service is getting poorer and workers are getting ruder. Evaluate the service in a local store, restaurant, or other organization. Are customers made to feel comfortable? Is workers' communication helpful, friendly, and respectful? Are workers knowledgeable about products and services? Do they sell them effectively? Write a report analyzing the quality of service and recommending what the organization should do to improve.

2. **Recommending Courses for the Local College or University.** Businesses want to be able to send workers to local colleges or universities to upgrade their skills; colleges and universities want to prepare students to enter the local workforce. What skills are in demand in your community? What courses at what levels should be offered?

3. **Improving Sales and Profits.** Recommend ways a small business in your community can increase sales and profits. Focus on one or more of the following: the products or services it offers, its advertising, its decor, its location, its accounting methods, its cash management, or any other aspect that may be keeping the company from achieving its potential. Address your report to the owner of the business.

4. **Increasing Student Involvement.** How could an organization on campus persuade more of the students who are eligible to join or to become active in its programs? Do students know that it exists? Is it offering programs that interest students? Is it retaining current members? What changes should the organization make? Address your report to the officers of the organization.

5. **Evaluating a Potential Employer.** What training is available to new employees? How soon is the average entry-level person promoted? How much travel and weekend work are expected? Is there a "busy season," or is the workload consistent year-round? What fringe benefits are offered? What is the corporate culture? Is the climate non-racist and non-sexist? How strong is the company economically? How is it likely to be affected by current economic, demographic, and political trends? Address your report to the Placement Office on campus; recommend whether it should encourage students to work at this company.

6. With your professor's permission, choose your own topic.

Visuals, Memos, and Report Assignments

12.9   Choosing Titles for Stories and Visuals

Which is the best title in each group? Why? Would the other titles ever be acceptable? Why or why not?

1. a. Single Women Are Buying More Computers than Are Single Men.
   b. More Women than Men Will Live Alone with Computers.
   c. What Do Single Women Want? Computers!

2. a. Lawyers in Private Practice Make More than Those in Public Practice.
   b. Lawyers Should Be Private in Choosing Their Salaries.

c. Private Practice Pays.

3. a. The Poor Give More.

   b. People Making under $11,000 a Year Gave a Larger Percentage of Their Incomes to Churches than Did People Making over $100,000 a Year.

c. People Making Least Give the Highest Percentage to Church.

12.10   Matching Visuals with Stories

What visual(s) would make it easiest to see each of the following stories?

1. Canada buys 25% of U.S. exports.

2. Undergraduate enrolment rises, but graduate enrolment declines.

3. Population growth will be greatest in the West and Southern Ontario.

4. Open communication ranks Number 1 in reasons to take a job.

5. Companies with fewer than 200 employees created a larger percentage of new jobs than did companies with more than 5,000 employees.

6. Men are more likely than women to see their chances for advancement as good.

12.11   Evaluating Visuals

Evaluate each of the following visuals.

■ Is visual's message clear?

■ Is it the right visual for the story?

■ Is the visual designed appropriately? Is colour, if any, used appropriately?

■ Is the visual free from chartjunk?

■ Does the visual distort data or mislead the reader in any way?

1.

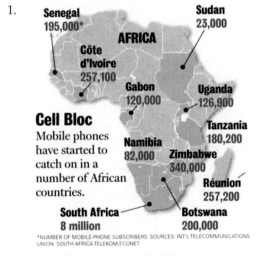

Source: Newsweek, August 27, 2001.

2.

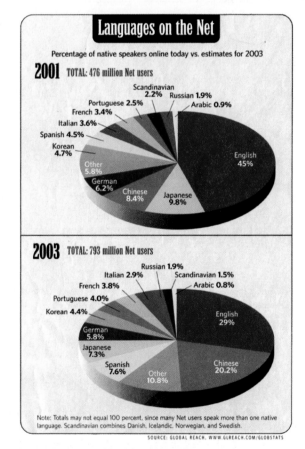

Source: Business 2.0, November 2001, 121.

3.

How My Time Will Be Used

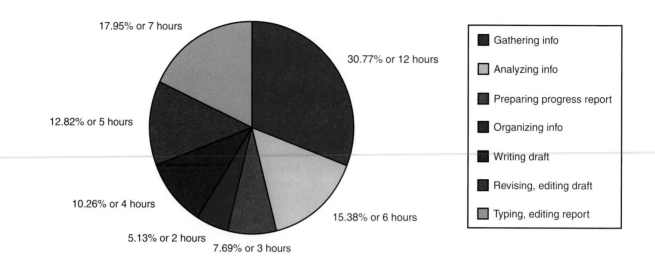

17.95% or 7 hours

30.77% or 12 hours

12.82% or 5 hours

10.26% or 4 hours

5.13% or 2 hours

7.69% or 3 hours

15.38% or 6 hours

■ Gathering info

□ Analyzing info

■ Preparing progress report

■ Organizing info

■ Writing draft

■ Revising, editing draft

■ Typing, editing report

4.   Historical Indian Treaties

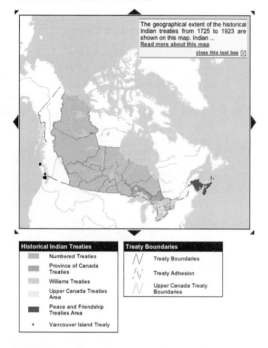

This map was taken from the Atlas of Canada http://atlas.gc.ca/
© 2005. Produced under licence from Her Majesty the Queen in
Right of Canada, with permission of Natural Resources Canada.

5.

Source: Cartoon by Susan Wheeler. Reprinted by permission of Ecotrust.

6.

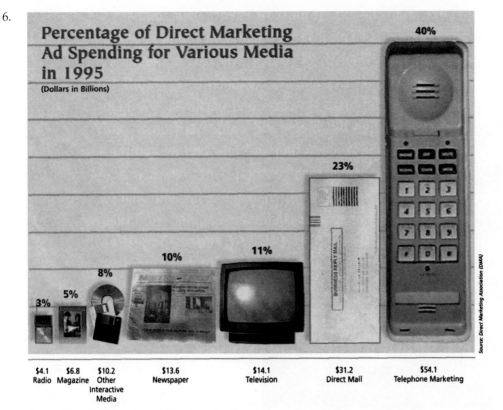

Source: *Direct Marketing*, Special Advertising Section, np.

12.12   Interpreting Data

As Your Professor Directs,

a. Identify at least seven stories in one or more of the following data sets.

b. Create visuals for three of the stories.

c. Write a memo to your professor explaining why you chose these stories and why you chose these visuals to display them.

d. Write a memo to some group that might be interested in your findings, presenting your visuals as part of a short report. Possible groups include career counsellors, radio stations, advertising agencies, and Mothers Against Drunk Driving.

e. Brainstorm additional stories you could tell with additional data. Specify the kind of data you would need. You may want to find comparative Canadian data in the case of Data on Tipping

1. Canadian Firms on Broadband Internet

Percentage of private firms using broadband, 2001–2003					
	Small firms		Medium firms		Large firms
	Low	High	Low	High	Low	High
2001	49.3	45.9	38.1	57.1	10.9	83.5
2002	39.1	55.7	26.0	70.9	10.5	83.6
2003	30.1	63.6	15.6	78.7	2.7	94.4

Source: Statistics Canada, "Broadband Internet: removing the speed limit for Canadian firms," 2003, Catalogue 11-621, No. 16, September 27, 2005.

2.   Data on Tipping

Tipping Made Easy

The vast majority (74 percent) of Americans tip their waiter or waitress a percentage of the final bill, about 17 percent on average. But 22 percent tip a flat amount instead, $4.67 on average.

	PEOPLE WHO TIP A PERCENTAGE OF THE BILL		PEOPLE WHO TIP A FLAT AMOUNT		PEOPLE WHO DON'T TIP
		AVG. PERCENT		AVG. AMOUNT	
Waiter or waitress	74%	17%	22%	$4.67	2%
Bartender	20%	16%	48%	$1.85*	18%
Barber, hair stylist, or cosmetician	26%	17%	52%	$4.21	18%
Cab or limousine driver	31%	14%	43%	$5.55	16%
Food delivery person	31%	15%	50%	$2.88	12%
Hotel maid	14%	14%	53%	$8.08**	26%
Skycap or bellhop	N/A	N/A	71%	$3.68***	10%
Masseuse	26%	16%	28%	$7.50	25%
Usher at theatre, sporting events, etc.	5%	13%	17%	$5.26	70%

*for one drink; ** for a two-night stay; *** for two bags*
Note: "No Answer/Refused" not shown

Source: Taylor Nelson Sofres Intersearch

Beauty Gets Bucks

While only 11 percent of all Americans say they give a bigger tip to service providers they find attractive, single people are twice as likely to make a habit of it (16 percent) than their married counterparts (8 percent).

PERCENTAGE OF AMERICANS WHO SAY THEY TIP MORE WHEN THEIR SERVICE PROVIDER IS:

	OVERALL	MEN	WOMEN	MARRIED	UNMARRIED	WHITE	BLACK
Older than others who usually do the job	20%	17%	22%	16%	24%	18%	30%
A student	25%	24%	27%	25%	26%	24%	36%
A parent	17%	14%	19%	17%	16%	16%	27%
Attractive	11%	17%	5%	8%	16%	11%	14%
Someone I know	38%	38%	38%	34%	42%	39%	29%
A female	6%	9%	3%	4%	9%	6%	8%
A male	3%	3%	3%	3%	4%	3%	6%
Disabled	33%	34%	32%	33%	34%	32%	47%
A racial minority	3%	3%	3%	2%	4%	2%	9%
Flirtatious	11%	17%	5%	7%	15%	11%	9%

Source: Taylor Nelson Sofres Intersearch

Source: American Demographics, May 2001, 11.

3. Alcohol Sales in Canada, 2003

Sales of alcoholic beverages

	2003			
	Beer	Wine	Spirits	Total
	in thousands of dollars			
Newfoundland and Labrador	169,778	30,169	89,491	289,437
Prince Edward Island	31,214	8,159	21,587	60,960
Nova Scotia	224,592	68,320	154,447	447,359
New Brunswick	192,437	49,447	84,470	326,354
Quebec	2,266,905	1,324,596	497,017	4,088,518
Ontario	2,903,075	1,267,618	1,542,766	5,713,459
Manitoba	212,687	73,726	179,015	465,429
Saskatchewan	201,988	36,904	152,028	390,920
Alberta	712,906	299,007	470,479	1,482,392
British Columbia	915,801	529,525	604,581	2,049,907
Yukon	12,363	4,141	7,645	24,151
Northwest Territories	17,977	4,233	16,267	38,477
Nunavut	2,715	211	899	3,824
Canada	**7,864,437**	**3,696,056**	**3,820,693**	**15,381,186**

Source: Statistics Canada, "The Daily," *Control and sale of alcoholic beverages*, Catalogue 11-001, Friday, October 29, 2004.

13 Making Oral Presentations

AN INSIDE PERSPECTIVE

Making Oral Presentations

Toronto presentations coach Jim Gray considers himself "an assistant storyteller." In a world of proliferating information that leaves some unable to disentangle their story from the data and detail, he aims to "help people cut through the information clutter to create stories that are clear, concise, and relevant."

If presentation nerves get the better of us, the "antidote is simple. We have to take our attention off ourselves and direct it to where it truly belongs, on the audience." Following these seven rules should take the pressure off and turn public speaking into a pleasure.

Preparation Is Key. If you know "your story cold," you are free to "engage others with self-assurance and enthusiasm."

Check Out the Venue. Test the technology and get to know the audio-visual personnel. Instead of fearing the unknown, you'll "luxuriate in the known."

A former journalist with *The Toronto Star* and the Canadian Broadcasting Corporation, Jim Gray, Principal of Media Strategy Inc., Toronto, is a regular *Globe and Mail* contributor and leading media strategist and presentations coach whose mission is to help "you tell your story."

www.mediastrategy.ca

Start Your Presentation Early. Reacquaint yourself with those you know, introduce yourself to those you don't, smile and connect with a few friendly faces in the crowd.

Go Easy on the Stimulants. Nervousness is both natural and energizing, but too much caffeine and too much food are not. Try room temperature water to soothe the vocal cords and have a rewarding meal afterward.

Have a Backup Plan. Bring hard copy in case of technology failures. Know your story so well that you can adapt to changed presentation times.

With PowerPoint, Less is More. Establish your relationship with the audience before the slides (at most one per minute) and make that personal connection again at the end.

Start Slowly. Take your time and keep sentences short and simple. Starting slowly means you begin and continue the journey together with your audience.

Source: Adapted from "Hint: It's not all about you," *The Globe and Mail*, June 11, 2003, retrieved December 7, 2005, from http://www.mediastrategy.ca.

Selling Your Message*

A lot of schools teach the "art" of advertising. But not one has a course or section devoted to the brutally important topic of presenting. Presentation skills are critical to an ad exec's career, especially in the creative department. And not just in pitches [selling a campaign to a client]. If you cannot sell yourself, how can you hope to sell anything? . . .

Being nervous is OK. It is not a sign of weakness. It's a sign of respect. Tell your clients that. I do this all the time. It works before speeches as well. People will warm up to you. Remember, some of the best performances begin with a healthy dose of stage fright. . . .

So many people try to cover up and play cool. . . . You know they know [you're afraid], and you end up stuttering and saying "basically" too much. Be honest about your nerves. Tell them this is the biggest meeting you've ever been in and of course you're nervous. Tell them it would be disrespectful if you weren't. Not only is it the truth, it's a great opener. . . .

When all is said and done, confidence tempered by respect is the most important trait a team can bring into the room. Second only to big ideas and a cashmere jacket from Barneys.

*Quoted from Steffan Postaer, "The Rules of Presenting," *Adweek*, February 24, 2003.

The power to persuade people to care about something you believe in is crucial to business and career success. Making a good oral presentation is more than just good delivery: it also involves developing a strategy that fits your audience and purpose, having good content, and organizing material effectively. The choices you make in each of these areas are affected by your purposes, the audience, and the situation.

Understanding Purposes in Oral Presentations

Oral presentations have the same three basic purposes that written documents have: to inform, to persuade, and to build goodwill. Like written messages, most oral presentations have to persuade to achieve their purposes. You need to gain and retain your audience's attention.

Informative presentations inform or teach the audience. Training sessions in an organization are primarily informative. Secondary purposes may be to persuade new employees to follow organizational procedures, rather than doing something their own way, and to help them appreciate the organizational culture (← p. 32).

Persuasive presentations motivate the audience to act or to believe. Giving information and evidence is an important means of persuasion. Stories, visuals, and self-disclosure are also effective. In addition, the speaker must build goodwill by appearing to be credible and sympathetic to the audience's needs. Presentations can persuade the audience to approve proposals, adopt ideas, buy products, change behaviour or attitudes, or reinforce existing attitudes. For example, a speaker at a meeting of factory workers may stress the importance of following safety procedures.

Goodwill presentations entertain and validate the audience. In an after-dinner speech, the audience wants to be entertained. Presentations at sales meetings may be designed to stroke the audience's egos and to validate their commitment to organizational goals.

Make your purpose as specific as possible.

Weak: The purpose of my presentation is to discuss saving for retirement.

Better: The purpose of my presentation is to explain how to calculate how much money someone needs to save in order to maintain a specific lifestyle after retirement.

Note that the purpose *is not* the introduction of your talk; it is the principle that guides your choice of strategy and content.

Comparing Written and Oral Messages

Giving a presentation is in many ways very similar to writing a message. Written messages make it easier to:

- Present extensive or complex financial data.
- Present many specific details of a law, policy, or procedure.
- Minimize undesirable emotions.

Oral messages make it easier to

- Use emotion to help persuade the audience.
- Focus the audience's attention on specific points.
- Answer questions, resolve conflicts, and build consensus.
- Modify a proposal that may not be acceptable in its original form.
- Get immediate action or response.

Oral and written messages have many similarities. In both, you should

- Adapt the message to the specific audience.
- Show the audience how they would benefit from the idea, policy, service, or product.
- Overcome any objections the audience may have.
- Use you-attitude and positive emphasis.
- Use visuals to clarify or emphasize material.
- Specify exactly what the audience should do.

Planning a Strategy for Your Presentation

A **strategy** is your plan for reaching your specific goals with a specific audience.

In all oral presentations, identify the one idea you want the audience to take home. Simplify your supporting detail so it's easy to follow. Simplify visuals so they can be taken in at a glance. Simplify your words and sentences so they're easy to understand.

Too complicated:	Information Storage Devices provides voice solutions using the company's unique, patented multilevel storage technique.
Simple:	We make voice chips. They're extremely easy to use. They have unlimited applications. And they last forever.[1]

An oral presentation needs to be simpler than a written message to the same audience. If readers forget a point, they can turn back to it and reread the paragraph. Headings, paragraph indentation, and punctuation provide visual cues to help readers understand the message. Listeners, in contrast, must remember what the speaker says. And good presenters allow for listening that is typically several times faster than talking (◄▬ Chapter 10) in order to stress key messages by repetition and emphasis.[2] Winston Churchill, for instance, knew that subtlety is not the best approach in the circumstances: "If you have an important point to make, don't try to be subtle or clever. Use a pile driver. Hit the point once. Then come back and hit it again. Then hit it a third time—a tremendous whack."

Analyze your audience for an oral presentation just as you do for a written message. If you'll be speaking to co-workers, talk to them about your topic or proposal to find out what questions or objections they have and therefore what they need to know and in what order. For audiences inside the organization, the biggest questions are often practical ones: Will it work? How much will it cost? How long will it take?

Think about where and when you'll be speaking. Is the room large or small, brightly lit or dark? Will the audience be tired at the end of a long day of listening? Sleepy after a big meal? Will the group be large or small? The more you know about your audience, the better you can adapt your message to them.

Choosing the Kind of Presentation

Although it is important to understand that presentation kinds are never as discrete as their titles suggest (monologues have interactive elements), most speakers choose one of three basic kinds: monologue, guided discussion, or interactive.

In a **monologue presentation,** the speaker speaks without interruption; questions are held until the end of the presentation, where the speaker functions as an expert. The speaker plans the presentation in advance and delivers it without deviation. This kind of presentation is often boring for the audience. Good delivery skills are crucial, since the audience is comparatively uninvolved.

Guided discussions offer a better way to present material and help an audience find a solution it can "buy into." Rather than functioning as an expert

---

Sharing the Stage with Visuals*

The audience can look at the speaker or the visual, but not both at the same time. An effective speaker directs the audience's attention to the visual and then back to the speaker, rather than trying to compete with the visual.

When Steve Mandel coaches clients on public speaking, he teaches them to use brief silences for visuals, so the audience has time to pay attention. For example, a speaker might say, "I've just talked to you about several problems you might experience. Now I'd like you to see a possible solution." Then the speaker shows the slide without talking for several seconds. This gives the audience time to absorb the contents of the slide. The presenter can regain attention by stepping toward the audience as he or she begins to speak again.

At its sales workshops, Communispond teaches a technique called "think-turn-talk." The presenter stands next to the visual and points to it with an open hand, thinking of what he or she intends to say. Then the presenter turns and makes eye contact with a person in the audience. Finally, the presenter talks. Communispond also teaches presenters to walk toward the audience when giving details from a visual. The connection is between presenter and audience, not presenter and slide.

*Based on Dave Zielinski, "Perfect Practice," *Presentations*, May 2003; and "Back to School," *Sales & Marketing Management*, July 2004, both downloaded from http://www.findarticles.com

with all the answers, the speaker serves as a facilitator to help the audience tap its own knowledge of questions or issues agreed on in advance.. This kind of presentation is excellent for presenting the results of consulting projects, when the speaker has specialized knowledge, but the audience must implement the solution if it is to succeed. Guided discussions need more time than monologue presentations, but produce more audience response, more responses involving analysis, and more commitment to the result.[3]

An **interactive presentation** is a conversation, even if the speaker stands up in front of a group and uses charts and overheads. Most sales presentations are interactive presentations. The sales representative uses questions to determine the buyer's needs, probe objections, and gain provisional and then final commitment to the purchase. Even in a memorized sales presentation, the buyer will talk at least 30% of the time. In a problem-solving sales presentation, the buyer may do 70% of the talking up until the action close (◀▥ p. 193).[4]

Adapting Your Ideas to the Audience

Measure the message you'd like to send against where your audience is now. If your audience is indifferent, skeptical, or hostile, focus on the part of your message the audience will find most interesting and easiest to accept.

Don't seek a major opinion change in a single oral presentation. If the audience has already decided to hire an advertising agency, then a good presentation can convince them that your agency is the one to hire. But if you're talking to a small business that has always done its own ads, limit your purpose. You may be able to prove that an agency can earn its fees by doing things the owner can't do and by freeing the owner's time for other activities. A second presentation may be needed to prove that an ad agency can do a *better* job than the small business could do on its own. Only after the audience is receptive should you try to persuade the audience to hire your agency rather than a competitor.

Make your ideas relevant to your audience by linking what you have to say to their experiences and interests. Showing your audience that the topic affects them directly is the most effective strategy. When you can't do that, at least link the topic (world hunger) to some everyday experience:

> When was the last time you were hungry? Maybe you remember being hungry while you were on a diet, or maybe you had to work late at a lab and didn't get back to the dorm in time for dinner.

Planning a Strong Opening and Close

The beginning and the end of a presentation, like the beginning and the end of a written document, are positions of emphasis. Use those key positions to connect with and interest the audience, emphasize your key point, and establish your credibility. You'll sound more natural and more effective if you talk from notes, but write out your opener and close in advance and memorize them. (They'll be short: just a sentence or two.)

Consider using one of the four modes for openers that appeared in ◀▥ Chapter 8: startling statement, narration or anecdote, question, or quotation. The more you can do to personalize your opener for your audience, the better. Recent events are better than things that happened long ago; local events are better than events at a distance; people they know are better than people who are only names.

Startling statement

> Twelve of our customers have cancelled orders in the past month.

This presentation to a company's executive committee went on to show that the company's distribution system was inadequate and to recommend a third warehouse located in the Atlantic provinces.

Narration or anecdote

A mother was having difficulty getting her son up for school. He pulled the covers over his head.

"I'm not going to school," he said. "I'm not ever going again."

"Are you sick?" his mother asked.

"No," he answered. "I'm sick of school. They hate me. They call me names. They make fun of me. Why should I go?"

"I can give you two good reasons," the mother replied. "The first is that you're 42 years old. And the second is *you're the school principal*."[5]

This speech to a seminar for educators went on to discuss "the three knottiest problems in education today." Educators had to face those problems; they couldn't hide under the covers.

Even better than canned stories are anecdotes that happened to you and that contain the point of your talk.

Question

Are you going to have enough money to do the things you want to when you retire?

This presentation to a group of potential clients discusses the value of using the services of a professional financial planner to achieve one's goals for retirement.

Quotation

According to Towers Perrin, the profits of Fortune 100 companies would be 25% lower—they'd go down $17 billion—if their earnings statements listed the future costs companies are obligated to pay for retirees' health care.

This presentation on options for health care for retired employees urges executives to start now to investigate options to cut the future costs.

Your opener should interest the audience and establish a rapport with them. Some speakers use humour to achieve those goals. However, an inappropriate joke can turn the audience against the speaker. Never use humour that's directed against the audience. In contrast, speakers who can make fun of themselves almost always succeed:

It's both a privilege and a pressure to be here.[6]

Humour isn't the only way to set an audience at ease. Smile at your audience before you begin; let them see that you're a real person and a nice one.

The end of your presentation should be as strong as the opener. For your close, you could do one or more of the following:

- Restate your main point.
- Refer to your opener to create a frame for your presentation.
- End with a vivid, positive picture.
- Tell the audience exactly what to do to solve the problem you've discussed.

The following close from a fundraising speech combines a restatement of the main point with a call for action, telling the audience what to do.

> Plain and simple, we need money to run the foundation, just like you need money to develop new products. We need money to make this work. We need money from you. Pick up that pledge card. Fill it out. Turn it in at the door as you leave. Make it a statement about your commitment . . . make it a big statement.[7]

When you write out your opener and close, be sure to use oral rather than written style. As you can see in the example close above, oral style uses shorter sentences and shorter, simpler words than writing does. Oral style can even sound a bit choppy when it is read by eye. Oral style uses more personal pronouns, a less varied vocabulary, and more repetition.

Planning Visuals and Other Devices to Involve the Audience

Visuals can give your presentation a professional image. One study showed that presenters using overhead transparencies were perceived as "better prepared, more professional, more persuasive, more credible, and more interesting" than speakers who did not use visuals. They were also more likely to persuade a group to adopt their recommendations.[8] Another study found that in an informative presentation, multimedia (PowerPoint slides with graphics and animation) produced 5% more learning than overheads made from the slides and 16% more learning than text alone. In sales presentations by two different banks, one bank's use of multimedia (PowerPoint slides with graphics, animation, and video) motivated 58% more students to choose that bank over the bank that used overheads only, and 50% more than text alone. Although the two banks offered identical fees and services, students said that the bank represented by the multimedia presentation "was more credible, was more professional, and offered better services and fees."[9]

To enhance visibility and readability, use at least 18-point type for visuals you prepare with a word processor. When you prepare slides with PowerPoint, Corel, or another presentation program, use at least 24-point type for the smallest words. You should be able to read the smallest words easily when you print a handout version of your slides.

Well-designed visuals can serve as an outline for your talk (see Figure 13.1), eliminating the need for additional notes. Visuals should highlight your main points, not give every detail.

Use these guidelines to create and show visuals for presentations:

PowerPoint slides aren't the only or necessarily the best way to involve the audience. Dan Leeber persuaded UPS to switch to Valeo clutches by completely disassembling the competitor's clutch and showing part by part why Valeo's product was better.

FIGURE 13.1 PowerPoint Slides for an Informative Presentation

- ■ Make only one point with each visual. Break a complicated point down into several visuals.
- ■ Substitute visuals for text when possible.
- ■ Give each visual a title that makes a point.
- ■ Limit the amount of information on a visual. Use 35 words or less on seven lines or less; use simple graphs, not complex ones.
- ■ Put your visual up when you're ready to talk about it.
- ■ Leave it up until your next point; don't turn the projector or overhead off.

See Appendix A for information on designing slides and ◄▪▪ Chapter 12 for information on how to present numerical data through visuals.

Visuals work only if the technology they depend on works. When you give presentations in your own office, check the equipment in advance. When you make a presentation in another location or for another organization, arrive early so that you'll have time not only to check the equipment but also to track down a service worker if the equipment isn't working. Be prepared with a backup plan to use if you're unable to show your slides or videotape.

Although students claim to be motivated by PowerPoint, close to 20 years after it appeared on the scene, a PowerPoint presentation may prove all too

InSite

www.norvig.com/Gettysburg/sld004.htm

Not every speech needs visuals. As Peter Norvig shows, Lincoln's Gettysburg Address is hurt, not helped, by adding bland PowerPoint slides.

Donovan Bailey, former World and Olympic Champion sprinter, is a powerful and passionate motivational speaker dedicated to charitable causes and to his foundation in support of Canada's most talented amateur athletes. www.donovanbailey.com

predictable for many professional audiences. Especially if it was written on the plane or in the airport! It can turn the most exciting initiative into a series of bulleted points. After e-mail, PowerPoint is the second most used communication tool, with an estimated 30 million presentations daily. An audience's number one peeve is being read to. Still, it is important to remember that "PowerPoint doesn't kill presentations: people kill presentations."[10]

Toronto presentations coach Jim Gray worries about the reasoning that led many to an addiction to PowerPoint: the belief that it offers protection from "the oppressive scrutiny of audiences by diverting at least some attention to visuals, away from the speaker." From his point of view, wrongly used PowerPoint "isolates and diminishes" the speaker. Yale professor Edward Tufte agrees, arguing that presentation programs can turn "everyone into bores" and prove "punishing to both content and audience," while turning "everything into a sales pitch" and reducing student writing to "infomercials."[11]

You might consider involving your audience in some of these ways:

- A student giving a presentation on English–French business communication demonstrated the differences in Canadian and French handshakes by asking a fellow class member to come up to shake hands with her.

- A student discussing the need for low-salt products brought in a container of salt, a measuring cup, a measuring spoon, and two plates. As he discussed the body's need for salt, he measured out three teaspoons onto one plate: the amount the body needs in a month. As he discussed the amount of salt the average diet provides, he continued to measure out salt onto the other plate, stopping only when he had 1¼ pounds of salt—the amount in the average diet. The demonstration made the discrepancy clear in a way words or even a chart could not have done.[12]

- Another speaker who was trying to raise funds used the simple act of asking people to stand to involve them, to create emotional appeal, and to make a statistic vivid:

> [A speaker] was talking to a luncheon club about contributing to the relief of an area that had been hit by a tornado. The news report said that 70% of the people had been killed or disabled. The room was set up [with] ten people at each round table. He asked three persons at each table to stand. Then he said, ". . . You people sitting are dead or disabled. You three standing have to take care of the mess. You'd need help, wouldn't you?"[13]

Choosing Information to Include in a Presentation

Choose the information that is most interesting to your audience and that answers the questions your audience will have. Limit your talk to three main points. In a long presentation (20 minutes or more) each main point can have subpoints. Your content will be easier to understand if you clearly show the relationship between each of the main points. Turning your information into a story also helps.

For example, a presentation about a plan to reduce scrap rates on the second shift can begin by setting the scene and defining the problem: Production expenses have cut profits in half. The plot unfolds as the speaker describes the facts that helped her trace the problem to scrap rates on the second shift. The resolution to the story is her group's proposal. One way to keep the choice of supporting information focused on what the audience needs to know is to start by writing the conclusion. Then move backward, identifying the main points that lead to this conclusion.

As part of choosing what to say, you should determine what data to present, including what to show in visuals. Any data you mention should be related to the points you are making. Databases and presentation software (such as PowerPoint) have given employees direct access to ready-made and easy-to-create slides. The temptation is to choose these and sprinkle them throughout the presentation, rather than starting with decisions about what the audience needs to know. Corporate trainer Pam Gregory observes, "What presentations are supposed to do is save the audience time in sifting through data themselves. But often presentations are overloaded with data; there may be an argument but it is buried."[14]

Statistics and numbers can be convincing if you present them in ways that are easy to hear. Simplify numbers by reducing them to two significant digits.

Hard to hear: If the national debt were in pennies, it would take 17,006,802,720 people, each carrying 100 pounds of pennies, to carry all of our debt.

Easier to hear: If the national debt were in pennies, it would take 17 billion people, each carrying 100 pounds of pennies, to carry all of our debt.[15]

In an informative presentation, link the points you make to the knowledge your audience has. Show the audience members that your information answers their questions, solves their problems, or helps them do their jobs. When you explain the effect of a new law or the techniques for using a new machine, use specific examples that apply to the decisions they make and the work they do. If your content is detailed or complicated, give people a written outline or handouts. The written material both helps the audience keep track of your points during the presentation and serves as a reference after the talk is over.

Quotations work well as long as you cite authorities whom your audience genuinely respects. Often you'll need to paraphrase a quote to put it into simple language that's easy to understand. Be sure to tell whom you're citing: "According to Jack Layton," "An article in *BusinessWeek* points out that," and so forth.

To be convincing, you must answer the audience's questions and objections.

> Some people think that women are less reliable than men. But the facts show that women take fewer sick days than men do.

However, don't bring up negatives or inconsistencies unless you're sure that the audience will think of them. If you aren't sure, save your evidence for the question phase. If someone does ask, you'll have the answer.

Organizing Your Information

Most presentations use a direct pattern of organization, even when the goal is to persuade a reluctant audience. In a business setting, the audience is in a hurry and knows that you want to persuade them. Be honest about your goal, and then prove that your goal meets the audience's needs too.

In a persuasive presentation, start with your strongest point, your best reason. If time permits, give other reasons as well and respond to possible objections. Put your weakest point in the middle so that you can end on a strong note.

Often one of five standard patterns of organization will work:

- **Chronological.** Start with the past, move to the present, and end by looking ahead.
- **Problem–causes–solution.** Explain the symptoms of the problem, identify its causes, and suggest a solution. This pattern works best when the audience will find your solution easy to accept.

Advice from the Pros*

Creation

1. Think of your last summary slide first—then make sure each of those key bullet points are clearly explained in the body of your presentation.

2. Use simple, clear graphics and pictures of familiar people to capture attention and build audience identification.

3. Get someone else to check spellings and the logical flow of your slide show. Another pair of eyes will often pick up an error that you have missed.

Presentation

1. Practice, Practice, Practice. Rehearse several times— aloud and standing up, with the same equipment you will use for your presentation.

2. Make eye contact with more than one audience member during the course of your presentation.

3. Always carry backup disks of your presentation program, your slide show, and any special fonts that were used in its creation.

*Quoted from Shonan Noronha and John Rhodes, "Power Presentations," *Presentations*, special advertising section, n.p.

- **Exclude alternatives.** Explain the symptoms of the problem. Explain the obvious solutions first and show why they won't solve the problem. End by discussing a solution that will work. This pattern may be necessary when the audience will find the solution hard to accept.
- **Pro–con.** Give all the reasons in favour of something, then those against it. This pattern works well when you want the audience to see the weaknesses in its position.
- **1–2–3.** Discuss three aspects of a topic. This pattern works well to organize short informative briefings. "Today I'll review our sales, production, and profits for the last quarter."

Make your organization clear to your audience. Early in your talk—perhaps immediately after your opener—provide an overview of the main points you will make.

> First, I'd like to talk about who the homeless in Halifax are. Second, I'll talk about the services The Open Shelter provides. Finally, I'll talk about what you—either individually or as a group—can do to help.

An overview provides a mental peg that hearers can hang each point on. It also can prevent someone from missing what you are saying because he or she wonders why you aren't covering a major point that you've saved for later.[16]

Offer a clear signpost as you come to each new point. A **signpost** is an explicit statement of the point you have reached. Choose wording that fits your style. The following statements are four different ways that a speaker could use to introduce the last of three points:

> Now we come to the third point: what you can do as a group or as individuals to help homeless people in Halifax.

> So much for what we're doing. Now let's talk about what you can do to help.

> You may be wondering, what can I do to help?

> As you can see, the Shelter is trying to do many things. We could do more things with your help.

Delivering an Effective Presentation

Audiences want the sense that you're talking directly to them and that you care that they understand and are interested. They'll forgive you if you get tangled up in a sentence and end it ungrammatically. They won't forgive you if you seem to have a "canned" talk that you're going to deliver no matter who the audience is or how they respond. You can convey a sense of caring to your audience by making direct eye contact with them and by using a conversational style.

Dealing with Fear

Feeling nervous is normal. But you can harness that nervous energy to help you do your best work. As Ralph Waldo Emerson said, "All the great speakers were bad speakers at first." And as one student said, "You don't need to get rid of your butterflies. All you need to do is make them fly in formation."

To calm your nerves before you give an oral presentation,

- **Be prepared.** Analyze your audience, organize your thoughts, prepare visual aids, practise your opener and close, check out the arrangements.
- **Use only the amount of caffeine you normally use.** More or less may make you jumpy.
- **Avoid alcoholic beverages.**
- **Relabel your nerves.** Instead of saying, "I'm scared," try saying, "My adrenaline is up." Adrenaline sharpens our reflexes and helps us do our best.

Just before your presentation,

- **Consciously contract and then relax your muscles,** starting with your feet and calves and going up to your shoulders, arms, and hands.
- **Take several deep breaths from your diaphragm.**

During your presentation,

- **Pause and look at the audience before you begin speaking.**
- **Concentrate on communicating well.**
- **Use body energy in strong gestures and movement.**

Using Eye Contact

Look directly at the people you're talking to. In one study, speakers who looked more at the audience during a seven-minute informative speech were judged to be better informed, more experienced, more honest, and friendlier than speakers who delivered the same information with less eye contact.[17] An earlier study found that speakers judged sincere looked at the audience 63% of the time, while those judged insincere looked at the audience only 21% of the time.[18]

The point in making eye contact is to establish one-on-one contact with the individual members of your audience. People want to feel that you're talking to them. Looking directly at individuals also enables you to be more conscious of feedback from the audience, so that you can modify your approach if necessary.

If you lose eye contact, audience members might wonder why you are not looking their way. They might question your honesty: *Why did the speaker look down when announcing the last quarter figures, for example? Why is she looking over my shoulder? Is she searching for someone more important?*

Building and maintaining respect and trust means mastering "the curriculum of eye contact." The best speakers know how to use "visual connectivity like a marvelously tuned instrument. They know that without it, even the best oratory will go flat." They know when to combine eye contact with a pause, the phrasing, and pacing that signals and supports a major message. But they also know that "unbroken eye contact" can be as ineffective or even as offensive as too little.[19]

Developing a Good Speaking Voice

People will enjoy your presentation more if your voice is easy to listen to. To find out what your voice sounds like, record it. Also record the voices of people on TV or on campus whose voices you like and imitate them. In a few weeks, record yourself again.

To find your best speaking voice, close your ears with your fingers and hum up and down the scale until you find the pitch where the hum sounds loudest or most vibrant to you. This pitch will be near your optimum pitch.[20]

When you speak to a group, talk loudly enough so that people can hear you easily. If you're using a microphone, adjust your volume so you aren't shouting. When you speak in an unfamiliar location, try to get to the room early so

InSite

www.toastmasters.org/pdfs/
top10.pdf

Toastmasters International suggests ways to deal with nervousness. The clubs provide forums where members can practise their speaking skills.

you can check the size of the room and the power of the amplification equipment. If you can't do that, ask early in your talk, "Can you hear me in the back of the room?"

The bigger the group is, the more carefully you need to **enunciate**, that is, voice all the sounds of each word. Words starting or ending with *f, t, k, v,* and *d* are especially hard to hear. "Our informed and competent image" can sound like "Our informed, incompetent image."

To enunciate, use your tongue and lips. Researchers have identified 38 different sounds, of which 31 are made with your tongue and 7 with your lips. None is made with the jaw, so how wide you open your mouth really doesn't matter. If the tongue isn't active enough, muscles in the throat try to compensate, producing sore throats and strained voices.[21]

Tongue twisters can help you exercise your tongue and enunciate more clearly. Stephen Lucas, author of *The Art of Public Speaking*, suggests the following:

- Sid said to tell him that Benny hid the penny many years ago.
- Fetch me the finest French-fried freshest fish that Finney fries.
- Three grey geese in the green grass grazed.
- Shy Sarah saw six Swiss wristwatches.
- One year we had a Christmas brunch with Merry Christmas mush to munch. But I don't think you'd care for such. We didn't like to munch mush much.[22]

You can also reduce pressure on your throat by fitting phrases to your ideas. If you cut your sentences into bits, you'll emphasize words beginning with vowels, making the vocal cords hit each other. Instead, run past words beginning with vowels to emphasize later syllables or later words:[23]

Choppiness hurts vocal cords:	*We must take more responsibility not*
	Only for
	Ourselves
	And
	Our families but for
	Our communities
	And
	Our country.
Smooth phrasing protects throat:	*We must take more*
	Responsibility
	Not only for our
	Selves and our
	Families but for our
	Communities and our
	Country.

You can reduce the number of *uhs* you use by practising your talk several times. Filler sounds aren't signs of nervousness. Instead, say psychologists, they occur when speakers pause searching for the next word. Searching takes longer when people have big vocabularies or talk about topics where many word choices are possible. Practising your talk makes your word choices automatic, and you'll use fewer *uhs*.[24]

Vary your volume, pitch, and speed. Inexperienced speakers are inclined to rush to the end. Speakers who speak quickly and who vary their volume during the talk are more likely to be perceived as competent.[25] Sound energetic and enthusiastic. If your ideas don't excite you, why should your audience find them exciting?

Standing and Gesturing

Stand with your feet far enough apart for good balance, with your knees flexed. Some speakers like to come in front of the lectern to remove that barrier between themselves and the audience. If you use slides or transparencies, stand beside the screen so that you don't block it.

Unless the presentation is very formal or you are on camera, movement will add to the energy and effectiveness of your presentation. We have the technology (wireless microphones and remote controls) to free us to engage our audiences through choreographed movement and gesture.

The best presenters know when to move and mesmerize their audiences: "Nothing engages audiences like passionate, well-prepared, assured presenters who move in tandem with their narrative." Indeed, the effect is to "communicate poise, panache and personality." Even though movement has the power to enhance credibility and persuasion, you need to understand when it won't work for you. Politicians announcing electrical power crises or CEOs announcing layoffs do not want to be seen to be restless and meandering. In short, the "more serious the situation, the less you should move."[26]

Since as much as 65% of our communication depends on body language, it's important to make the most of our gestures. Hand gestures "can help you say more in less time, show what you mean without having to resort to visuals, signal your conviction and confidence, and add texture and dimension to your material and ideas."[27]

Videotaping your presentation can help you see where gestures enhance your power and where they signal stage fright (clutching, clenching, fidgeting). Build on your natural style for gestures. Gestures usually work best when they're big and confident.

Using Notes and Visuals

Even experts use cards to keep their presentations focused and to avoid too many digressions. Put your notes on cards or on sturdy pieces of paper and number them. Most speakers like to use 10×15 cm or 12×17 cm cards. Your notes need to be complete enough to help you if you go blank, so use long phrases or complete sentences. Under each main point, jot down the evidence or illustration you'll use. Indicate where you'll refer to visuals.

Look at your notes infrequently. Most of your gaze time should be directed to members of the audience. Hold your notes high enough so that your head doesn't bob up and down like a yo-yo as you look from the audience to your notes and back again.

If you have lots of visuals and know your topic well, you won't need notes. Face the audience, not the screen. With transparencies, you can use coloured marking pens to call attention to your points as you talk. Show the entire visual at once: don't cover up part of it. If you don't want the audience to read ahead, prepare several visuals that build up. In your overview, for example, the first visual could list your first point, the second the first and second, and the third all three points.

Keep the room lights on if possible; turning them off makes it easier for people to fall asleep and harder for them to concentrate on you.

Handling Questions

Prepare for questions by listing every fact or opinion you can think of that challenges your position. Treat each objection seriously and try to think of a way to deal with it. If you're talking about a controversial issue, you may want to

Responding to Hostile Questions*

Presentation skills coach James Gray gives this advice for handling "the audience bully":

- Engage and make an ally of the know-it-all.

- Ask for his or her views, make the bully a co-presenter, and then re-establish your expertise.

- Freeze out if the bully persists in intervening (limit eye contact and your responses).

- Remind the whole group of the full agenda ahead.

- Silence the interrupter (chatting in the audience) by staring at the person while continuing to present—most get the message.

- Stop speaking if the interrupter does not; remain silent and look closely until the interrupter stops.

- Direct the question, "May I have your attention, please?" if all else fails (99.95% stop at this signal).

- Involve the whole group if interruption persists ("How should we handle this problem?").

- Establish ground rules (no shouting or insults) when you anticipate controversy.

*James Gray, "How to handle the audience bully," *The Globe and Mail*, January 16, 2004, C1.

Twice as Prepared*

Ralph Oliva made sales presentations for Texas Instruments. Each presentation to senior executives could, if successful, win a multimillion-dollar account for his company.

Oliva learned to prepare not one, but two presentations. In the first presentation, time didn't matter. He included every piece of support and tried to anticipate and respond to every possible objection. The second presentation hit just the main points in 10 to 15 minutes.

The second presentation is the one he actually gives. But because his preparation is so thorough, he isn't nervous. He can answer questions that may arise. The thorough preparation "makes me certain that the audience won't find me lacking in preparation. I can even say, 'I don't know' with confidence because I know I haven't done a sloppy job."

*Based on and quoted from "No Sweat: How to Deliver Winning Presentations for Million-Dollar Accounts," *Selling Power*, January/February 2000, 116.

save one point for the question period, rather than making it during the presentation. Speakers who have visuals to answer questions seem especially well prepared.

During your presentation, tell the audience how you'll handle questions. If you have a choice, save questions for the end. In your talk, answer the questions or objections that you expect your audience to have. Don't exaggerate your claims so that you won't have to back down in response to questions later.

During the question period, don't nod your head to indicate that you understand a question as it is asked. Audiences will interpret nods as signs that you agree with the questioner. Instead, look directly at the questioner. As you answer the question, expand your focus to take in the entire group. Don't say, "That's a good question." That response implies that the other questions have been poor ones.

If the audience may not have heard the question or if you want more time to think, repeat the question before you answer it. Link your answers to the points you made in your presentation. Keep the purpose of your presentation in mind, and select information that advances your goals.

If a question is hostile or biased, rephrase it before you answer it: "You're asking whether. . . ." Or suggest an alternative question: "I think there are problems with both the positions you describe. It seems to me that a third solution that is better than either of them is. . . ."

Occasionally someone will ask a question that is really designed to state the speaker's own position. Respond to the question if you want to. Another option is to say, "I'm not sure what you're asking," or even, "That's a clear statement of your position. Let's move to the next question now." If someone asks about something that you already explained in your presentation, simply answer the question without embarrassing the questioner. No audience will understand and remember 100% of what you say.

If you don't know the answer to a question, say so. If your purpose is to inform, write down the question so that you can look up the answer before the next session. If it's a question to which you think there is no answer, ask if anyone in the room knows. When no one does, your "ignorance" is vindicated. If an expert is in the room, you may want to refer questions of fact to him or her. Answer questions of interpretation yourself.

At the end of the question period, take two minutes to summarize your main point once more. (This can be a restatement of your close.) Questions may or may not focus on the key point of your talk. Take advantage of having the floor to repeat your message briefly and forcefully.

Making Group Presentations

Plan carefully to involve as many members of the group as possible in speaking roles.

The easiest way to make a group presentation is to outline the presentation and then divide the topics, giving one to each group member. Another member can be responsible for the opener and the close. During the question period, each member answers questions that relate to his or her topic.

In this kind of divided presentation, be sure to

- Plan transitions.
- Establish seating or standing arrangements to minimize disruption and audience distractions.
- Enforce time limits strictly.
- Coordinate your visuals so that the presentation seems a coherent whole.
- Practise the presentation as a group at least once; more is better.

The best group presentations are even more fully integrated: the group writes a very detailed outline, chooses points and examples, and creates visuals together.

Then, within each point, voices trade off. This presentation is most effective because each voice speaks only a minute or two before a new voice comes in. However, it works only when all group members know the subject well and when the group plans carefully and practises extensively.

Whatever form of group presentation you use, be sure to introduce each member of the team to the audience and use the opportunity to reinforce topics and messages: "Next, Raquel will discuss the project timelines." Pay close attention to each other and model behaviour for the audience. Smile at a play on words, for instance. If other members of the team seem uninterested in the speaker, the audience gets the sense that that speaker isn't worth listening to.

Evaluating Presentations

Whether presenting individually or in groups, giving and receiving feedback is critical to improvement and presentation success. Invite as much feedback when you are practising as when you present in formal situations. Learn from audiotapes and videotapes of your presentations. Learn from the informal and formal feedback, from the body language as well as the verbal feedback. Even if a listener has misheard or misunderstood your point, focus on the opportunity to be even clearer next time.

If you are assessing your own, your group's, or others' presentations, these criteria can be useful guides to success (➡ see also problems 13.6, 13.7, and 13.8):

- Verbal skills (enunciation, phrasing, pitch, projection, speed)
- Non-verbal skills (body language, eye contact, movement, gesture, dress)
- Readable, relevant, professional visuals
- Clear purpose, logical organization, appropriate evidence
- Engaging opener and compelling conclusion
- Signposts, transitions, previews, reviews, reinforcements
- Team identity, participation, cohesion, timing, enthusiasm
- Creativity, coherence, responsiveness, professionalism

Summary of Key Points

- **Informative presentations** inform or teach the audience. **Persuasive presentations** motivate the audience to act or to believe. **Goodwill presentations** entertain and validate the audience. Most oral presentations have more than one purpose.

- A written message makes it easier to present extensive or complex information and to minimize undesirable emotions. Oral messages make it easier to use emotion, to focus the audience's attention, to answer questions and resolve conflicts quickly, to modify a proposal that may not be acceptable in its original form, and to get immediate action or response.

- An oral presentation needs to be simpler than a written message to the same audience.

- In a **monologue presentation,** the speaker plans the presentation in advance and delivers it without deviation. In a **guided discussion,** the speaker presents the questions or issues that both speaker and audience have agreed on in advance. Rather than functioning as an expert with all the answers, the speaker serves as a facilitator to help the audience tap its own knowledge. An **interactive presentation** is a conversation using questions to determine the buyer's needs, probe objections, and gain provisional and then final commitment to the purchase.

- Use the beginning and end of the presentation to interest the audience, emphasize your key point, and establish/reinforce your credibility.
- Use visuals to seem more prepared, more interesting, and more persuasive.
- Limit your talk to three main points. Early in your talk—perhaps immediately after your opener—provide an **overview of the main points** you will make. Offer a clear signpost as you come to each new point. A **signpost** is an explicit statement of the point you have reached.
- To calm your nerves as you prepare to give an oral presentation,
  - Be prepared. Analyze your audience, organize your thoughts, prepare visual aids, practise your opener and close, check out the arrangements.
  - Use only the amount of caffeine you normally use.
  - Avoid alcoholic beverages.
  - Relabel your nerves. Instead of saying, "I'm scared," try saying, "My adrenaline is up." Adrenaline sharpens our reflexes and helps us do our best.

  During your presentation,
  - Pause and look at the audience before you begin speaking.
  - Concentrate on communicating well.
  - Use body energy in strong gestures and movement.
- Treat questions as opportunities to give more detailed information than you had time to give in your presentation. Link your answers to the points you made in your presentation.
- The best group presentations result when the group writes a very detailed outline, chooses points and examples, and creates visuals together. Then, within each point, voices trade off.
- Ongoing evaluation is critical to improvement and presentation success.

CHAPTER 13   Exercises and Problems

Getting Started

13.1   Analyzing Openers and Closes

The following openers and closes came from class presentations on information interviews.

- Does each opener make you interested in hearing the rest of the presentation?
- Does each opener provide a transition to the overview?
- Does the close end the presentation in a satisfying way?

a. Opener: I interviewed Mark Perry at CIBC.

   Close: Well, that's my report.

b. Opener: How many of you know what you want to do when you graduate?

Close: So, if you like numbers and want to travel, think about being a CMA. Ernst & Young can take you all over the world.

c. Opener: You don't have to know anything about computer programming to get a job as a technical writer at SaskTel.

Close: After talking to Raj, I decided technical writing isn't for me. But it is a good career if you work well under pressure and like learning new things all the time.

d. Opener: My report is about what it's like to work in an advertising agency.

Middle: They keep really tight security; I had to wear a badge and be escorted to Susan's desk.

Close: Susan gave me samples of the agency's ads and even a sample of a new soft drink she's developing a campaign for. But she didn't let me keep the badge.

13.2 Developing Stories

Think of personal anecdotes that you could use to open or illustrate presentations on the following topics:

1. Why people need to plan.
2. Dealing with change.
3. The importance of lifelong learning.
4. The value of good customer service.
5. The culture of an organization you know well.

As Your Professor Directs,

a. Share your stories with a small group of students.
b. Turn in your stories in a memo to your professor.
c. Make an oral presentation using one of the stories.

Presentation Assignments

13.3 Making a Short Oral Presentation

As Your Professor Directs,

Make a short (three- to five-minute) presentation with PowerPoint slides on one of the following topics:

a. Explain how what you've learned in classes, in campus activities, or at work will be useful to the employer who hires you after graduation.
b. Profile someone who is successful in the field you hope to enter and explain what makes him or her successful.
c. Describe a specific situation in an organization in which communication was handled well or badly.
d. Make a short presentation based on another problem in this book.
   i. Explain what a new hire in your unit needs to know to be successful.
   ii. Tell the class in detail about one of your accomplishments.
   iii. Explain one of the challenges (e.g., technology, ethics, international competition) that the field you hope to enter is facing.
   iv. Profile a company you would like to work for and explain why you think it would be a good employer.
   v. Share the results of an information interview.
   vi. Share the advice of students currently on the job market.
   vii. Share what you learn when you interview an interviewer.
   viii. Explain your interview strategy.

13.4 Making a Longer Oral Presentation

As Your Professor Directs,

Make a 5- to 12-minute presentation on one of the following. Use visuals to make your talk effective.

a. Show why your unit is important to the organization and either should be exempt from downsizing or should receive additional resources.
b. Persuade your supervisor to make a change that will benefit the organization.
c. Persuade your organization to make a change that will improve the organization's image in the community.
d. Persuade classmates to donate time or money to a charitable organization. (Read Chapter 8.)
e. Persuade an employer that you are the best person for the job.
f. Use another problem in this book as the basis for your presentation.
   i. Analyze an organization's culture.
   ii. Analyze a discourse community.
   iii. Describe the composing process(es) of a writer you've interviewed.
   iv. Evaluate the page design of one or more documents.
   v. Evaluate the design of a Web page.
   vi. Persuade your campus to make a change.
   vii. Analyze one or more sales or fundraising letters.
   viii. Analyze international messages that your workplace has created or received.
   ix. Summarize the results of a survey you have conducted.
   x. Summarize the results of your research.

13.5   Making a Group Oral Presentation

As Your Professor Directs,

Make a 5- to 12-minute presentation on one of the following. Use visuals to make your talk effective.

a. Explain the role of communication in one or more organizations.

b. Report on another country.

c. Present brochures you have designed to the class.

d. Describe the listening strategies of workers you have interviewed.

13.6   Evaluating Oral Presentations

Evaluate an oral presentation given by a classmate or given by a speaker on your campus. Use the following categories:

Strategy

1. Choosing an effective kind of presentation for the situation.
2. Adapting ideas to audience's beliefs, experiences, and interests.
3. Using a strong opening and close.
4. Using visual aids or other devices to involve the audience.

Content

5. Using specific, vivid supporting material and language.
6. Providing rebuttals to counterclaims or objections.

Organization

7. Providing an overview of main points.
8. Signposting main points in body of talk.
9. Providing adequate transitions between points and speakers.

Visuals

10. Using an appropriate design or template.
11. Using standard edited English.
12. Being creative.

Delivery

13. Making direct eye contact with audience.
14. Using voice and gestures effectively.
15. Handling questions effectively.
16. Maintaining appropriate stance, position (not blocking screen)

As Your Professor Directs,

a. Fill out a form indicating your evaluation in each of the areas.

b. Share your evaluation orally with the speaker.

c. Write a memo to the speaker evaluating the presentation. Send a copy of your memo to your professor.

13.7   Evaluating Team Presentations

Evaluate team presentations using the following questions:

1. How thoroughly were all group members involved?
2. Did members of the team introduce themselves or each other?
3. Did team members seem interested in what their teammates said?
4. How well was the material organized?
5. How well did the material hold your interest?
6. How clear did the material seem to you?

7. How effective were the visuals?
8. How well did the team handle questions?
9. What could be done to improve the presentation?
10. What were the strong points of the presentation?

As Your Professor Directs,

a. Fill out a form indicating your evaluation in each of the areas.

b. Share your evaluation orally with the speaker.

c. Write a memo to the speaker evaluating the presentation. Send a copy of your memo to your professor.

13.8 Evaluating the Way a Speaker Handles Questions

Listen to a speaker talking about a controversial subject. (Go to a talk on campus or in town, or watch a speaker on a TV show like *Hot Type* or *Marketplace*.) Observe the way he or she handles questions.

■ About how many questions does the speaker answer?

■ What is the format for asking and answering questions?

■ Are the answers clear? Responsive to the question? Something that could be quoted without embarrassing the speaker and the organization he or she represents?

■ How does the speaker handle hostile questions? Does the speaker avoid getting angry? Does the speaker retain control of the meeting? If so, how?

■ If some questions were not answered well, what (if anything) could the speaker have done to leave a better impression?

■ Did the answers leave the audience with a more or less positive impression of the speaker? Why?

As Your Professor Directs,

a. Share your evaluation with a small group of students.

b. Present your evaluation formally to the class.

c. Summarize your evaluation in a memo to your professor.

Job Hunting

14 Employment Communications

AN INSIDE PERSPECTIVE

Marketing Yourself

Learning how to manage and market yourself is not as natural or self-evident as it sounds. In fact, we are so close to our object of study that we often overlook the meaning and value of who we are and what we have done! Yet developing the complementary parts of the job search is a critical professional skill that we need to nourish so that we can land our dream job.

Know Yourself

Neils Lindhard has said that "until you know who you are, you cannot know what you can become." The basis of any good job search strategy is therefore to know yourself, to identify your strengths and weaknesses, values and goals, skills and abilities, education and experience. You can get help from career counsellors, business seminars and networking connections, and online and print resources.

Drina Nixon of Cenera Canadian Career Partners in Calgary is an accomplished human resource practitioner with 20 successful years coaching individuals and facilitating management development workshops. With her focus always on the client, Drina's energy and attentiveness support her personal objective: to help others realize their true potential.

www.career-partners.com/

Know the Job Market

Understand the major trends in the business world (◀ Chapter 1) and the range of skills and competencies that employers are looking for (see ◀ Conference Board of Canada Employability Skills on p. 25). Research the industry or profession as well as the particular businesses and organizations that you target. Know the trends, learn the language and culture, show your value by speaking in their terms. Nothing, not even your degree, speaks for itself.

Know the Job Search Process

The process is less sequential than simultaneous—repeated efforts at self-evaluation, targeting careers, researching, networking, calling, answering ads, writing résumés and cover letters—a set of complementary strategies designed to secure your job target. Learn how to access the hidden job market, how to make opportunities happen for you. Don't rely on luck: be proactive and get the information that will translate into opportunities—and the outcomes you want.

A **résumé** is a persuasive summary of your qualifications for employment. If you're on the job market, having a résumé makes you look well organized and prepared. When you're employed, having an up-to-date résumé makes it easier to take advantage of opportunities that may come up for an even better job. If you're several years away from job hunting, preparing a résumé now will help you become more conscious of what to do in the next two or three years to make yourself an attractive candidate. Writing a résumé is also an ego-building experience: The person who looks so good on paper is *you*!

This chapter covers paper, Web, and scannable résumés, job application letters (cover letters), interviews, and the communication after the interview. The focus is on job hunting in Canada. Conventions, expectations, and criteria differ from culture to culture: different norms apply in different countries.

All job communications must be tailored to your unique qualifications. Adopt the wording or layout of an example if it's relevant to your own situation, but don't be locked into the forms in this book. You've got different strengths; your application will be different, too.

A Timeline for Job Hunting

Informal preparation for job hunting should start soon after you arrive on campus. Join extracurricular organizations on campus and in the community to increase your knowledge and provide a network for learning about jobs. Find a job that gives you experience. Note which courses you like—and why you like them. If you like thinking and learning about a subject, you're more likely to enjoy a job in that field.

Formal preparation for job hunting should begin a full year *before you begin interviewing*. Visit the campus placement office to see what services it provides. Ask friends who are on the job market about their experiences in interviews; find out what kinds of job offers they get. Check into the possibility of getting an internship or a co-op job that will give you relevant experience before you interview.

The year you interview, write to any organization you'd like to work for that hasn't interviewed on campus.

Try to have a job offer lined up *before* you get the degree. People who don't need jobs immediately are more confident in interviews and usually get better job offers. If you have to job-hunt after graduation, plan to spend at least 30 hours a week on your job search. The time will pay off in a better job that you find more quickly.

Evaluating Your Strengths and Interests

A self-assessment is the first step in producing a good job search strategy. Each person could do several jobs happily. Personality and aptitude tests can tell you what your strengths are, but they won't say, "You should be a _____." You'll still need to answer questions like these:

- What achievements have given you the most satisfaction? *Why* did you enjoy them?

- Would you rather have firm deadlines or a flexible schedule? Do you prefer working alone or with other people? Do you prefer specific instructions and standards for evaluation or freedom and uncertainty? How comfortable are you with pressure? Are you willing to pay your dues for several years before you are promoted? How much challenge do you want?

- Are you willing to take work home? To travel? How important is money to you? Prestige? Time to spend with family and friends?

Jump-Starting Your Job Search*

While you're in college or university,

- Join the student organization in your specialty.

- Get summer internships before you're a senior.

- Use alumni connections. Mary E. Schilling, a director of career services says, "It isn't that these folks can give you a job, but they can give you some advice and pass along your résumé."

- "Treat e-mail as official correspondence, not as informal conversation," says Tom Wunderlich of Old Dominion University's career centre. Avoid goofy or suggestive e-mail addresses or phone messages. "No song of the day or joke of the week on your voicemail," Wunderlich advises.

*Based on "Get an Edge on Competition before School Lets Out," *Chicago Tribune Internet Edition*, December 19, 2001.

- Where do you want to live? What weather, geography, cultural and social life do you see as ideal?

- Do you see work as just a way to make a living? Or is it about values? Are the organization's culture and ethical standards important to you?

Once you know what is most important to you, analyze the job market to see where you could find what you want. For example, your greatest interest is athletics, but you aren't good enough for the pros. Studying the job market might suggest several alternatives. You could teach sports and physical fitness as a high school coach or a corporate fitness director. You could cover sports for a newspaper, a magazine, or a TV station. You could go into management or sales for a professional sports team, a health club, or a company that sells sports equipment.

How to Find Out about Employers and Jobs

The Internet is an invaluable source of advice and information on companies and on meeting *their* needs in your applications (see Figure 14.1). To adapt your job search strategy to a specific organization, you need information both about the employer and about the job itself (check Web listings and talk to your contacts). You'll need to know

- **The name and address of the person you should address.** Check the ad, call the organization, or visit its Web site. An advantage of calling is that you can find out what courtesy title (◀ pp. 53–54) a woman prefers and get current information.

- **What the organization does, and at least four or five facts about it.** Knowing the organization's larger goals enables you to show how your specific work will help the company meet its goals. Useful facts can include

FIGURE 14.1   Comprehensive Web Job Sites Covering the Entire Job Search Process

Canadian Association of Career Educators and Employers
    www.cacee.com
Canadian Careers.com
    www.canadiancareers.com
Career Beacon
    www.careerbeacon.com
Career Edge
    www.careeredge.org
FSIN Industry Canada Career PLACE
    fsin.careerplace.com
Human Resources and Skills Development Canada
    www.hrsdc.gc.ca
JobHuntersBible.com
    www.jobhuntersbible.com/
Monster.com
    www.monster.com
Public Service Commission of Canada
    www.jobs-emplois.gc.ca
Working.com
    www.working.canada.com
Workopolis.com
    www.workopolis.com

- Market share
- New products, services, or promotions
- Computer or manufacturing equipment it uses
- Plans for growth or downsizing
- Competitive position
- Challenges the organization faces
- The corporate culture (◀▥ p. 32).

To learn about new products, plans for growth, or solutions to industry challenges, read business newspapers such as *The Globe and Mail, The Wall Street Journal, The National Post,* or *The Financial Post;* business magazines such as *Canadian Business, Report on Business, Fortune, BusinessWeek;* and trade journals. Some sites are listed in Figure 14.1, for example.

In an **information interview** you talk to someone who works in the area you hope to enter to find out what the day-to-day work involves and how you can best prepare to enter that field. Here is what an information interview can do for you:

- Give you specific information that you can use to present yourself effectively in your résumé and application letter
- Create a good image of you in the mind of the interviewer who may remember you when openings arise

In an information interview, you might ask the following questions:

- What are you working on right now?
- How do you spend your typical day?
- Have your duties changed a lot since you started working here?
- What do you like best about your job? What do you like least?
- What do you think the future holds for this kind of work?
- How did you get this job?
- What courses, activities, or jobs would you recommend to someone who wanted to do this kind of work?

To set up an information interview, you can phone or write a letter like the one in Figure 14.2. If you do write, phone the following week to set up a specific time.

Many jobs are never advertised—and the number rises the higher on the job ladder you go. Over 60% of all new jobs come not from responding to an ad but from networking with personal contacts.[1] Some of these jobs are created especially for a specific person. These unadvertised jobs are called the **hidden job market.** Referral interviews, an organized method of networking, offer the most systematic way to tap into these jobs.

Referral interviews are interviews you schedule to learn about current job opportunities in your field. Sometimes an interview that starts out as an information interview turns into a referral interview.

A referral interview should refer you to other people who can tell you about job opportunities, and enable the interviewer to see that you could make a contribution to his or her organization. Therefore, the goal of a referral interview is to put you face to face with someone who has the power to hire you.

Then, armed with a referral from someone you know, you call Mr. or Ms Big and say, "So-and-so suggested I talk with you about job-hunting strategy." If the person says, "We aren't hiring," you say, "Oh, I'm not asking *you* for a job. I'd just like some advice from a knowledgeable person about the opportunities in banking [or desktop publishing, or whatever] in this city." If this person doesn't have

So Many Job Sites, So Little Time*

To use the Internet as the ultimate job-seeking tool, understand the kinds of employment sites it offers.

- Help-wanted sites are developed and maintained by employers and act as electronic versions of postings in store windows. They are informative and provide detailed job descriptions.
- Classified sites are online versions of local newspapers' want ads.
- Résumé sites showcase applicants' skills and experience rather than employer profiles.
- Industry sites locate jobs in a specific industry. Most feature searchable lists as well as profiles of major industry employers and employment statistics.
- Career sites are operated by independent companies and can advertise hundreds of thousands of job listings in their searchable databases.

*Based on Carolyn Gosselin, "Targeting a New Job: Where to Go in the Sea of Job Sites," *Chicago Tribune,* June 1, 2000, downloaded December 12, 2005, from http://www.chicagotribune.com.

FIGURE 14.2 Letter Requesting an Information Interview

72 E. 13th Avenue
Windsor, ON N9B 2P1

November 4, 2005

*Use the courtesy
title the reader
prefers*

Mrs. Kam Yuricich
Clary Communications
372 Sunset Avenue
Windsor, ON N9B 3P4

Dear Mrs. Yuricich: *If starting with the request seems too
abrupt, work up to it more gradually*

Could I schedule an information interview with you to learn more about how public
relations consultants interact with their clients?

*Refer to any
previous
contact
with
reader*

I was very interested in your talk at the University of Windsor last month about the
differences between working for a PR firm and being a PR staff person within an
organization. Last summer I had the chance to work as an intern at Management
Horizons. While many of my assignments were "gofer" jobs, my supervisor gave me the
chance to work on several brochures and to draft two speeches for managers. I enjoyed
this variety and would like to learn more about the possibility of working in a PR firm.

*Ask about
ways to
enter
the field*

Perhaps we could also talk about courses that would best prepare me for PR work. I have
a year and a half left before I graduate, and I have room for several free electives in my
schedule. I'd like to use them as productively as possible.

I'll call you early next week to set up an appointment. I look forward to your advice
as I attempt to find my niche in the workforce.

Sincerely,   *Mentioning your qualifications
and including a sample of your
work may help persuade the
reader to take time to see you*

Lee Tan
555-5932 *Even though you shouldn't depend on the reader to call
you, it's polite to give your phone number under your name*

Encl.: Marketing Brochure for the Cleary International Centre

the power to create a position, you seek more referrals at the end of *this* interview.
(You can also polish your résumé, if you get good suggestions.)

Some business people are cynical about information and referral interviewing. Prepare as carefully for these interviews as you would for an interview
when you know the organization is hiring. Think in advance of good questions;
know something about the general field or industry; try to learn at least a little
bit about the specific company.

Always follow up information and referral interviews with personal thank-
you letters. Use specifics to show that you paid attention during the interview,
and enclose a copy of your revised résumé.

Dealing with Difficulties

This section gives advice on how to highlight the positives of experience job
hunters often overlook or undervalue.

"All My Experience Is in My Family's Business."

In your résumé, simply list the company you worked for. For a reference, instead of a family member, list a supervisor, client, or vendor who can talk about
your work. Since the reader may wonder whether "Jim Clarke" is any relation
to the owner of "Clarke Construction Company," be ready to answer interview

questions about why you're looking at other companies. Prepare an answer that stresses the broader opportunities you seek but doesn't criticize your family or the family business. Remember too that those who work in the family business often amass a valuable range of diversity of experience.

"I've Been Out of the Job Market for a While."

You need to prove to a potential employer that you're up to date and motivated:

- Be active in professional organizations. Attend meetings; read trade journals.
- Learn the computer programs that professionals in your field use.
- Find out your prospective employer's immediate priorities. If you can show you'll contribute from day one, you'll have a much easier sell.
- Show how your at-home experience relates to the workplace. Dealing with unpredictable situations, building consensus, listening, raising money, and making presentations are transferable skills.
- Create a portfolio of your work—even if it's for imaginary clients—to demonstrate your expertise.[2] It may also get you Prior Learning Assessment and Recognition (PLAR) for post-secondary credits.

"I Want to Change Fields."

Have a good reason for choosing the field in which you're looking for work.

Think about how your experience relates to the job you want—and the benefits to the employer. Jack is an older-than-average student who wants to be a pharmaceutical sales representative. He has sold woodstoves, served subpoenas, and worked on an oil rig. A chronological résumé makes his work history look directionless. But a skills résumé could focus on persuasive ability (selling stoves), initiative and persistence (serving subpoenas), and technical knowledge (courses in biology and chemistry).[3]

"I Was Fired."

First, deal with the emotional baggage. You need to reduce negative feelings to a manageable level before you're ready to job-hunt.

Second, try to learn from the experience. You'll be a much more attractive job candidate if you can show that you've improved work habits, for example.

Third, suggests Phil Elder, an interviewer for an insurance company, call the person who fired you and say something like this: "Look, I know you weren't pleased with the job I did at _____. I'm applying for a job at _____ now and the personnel director may call you to ask about me. Would you be willing to give me the chance to get this job so that I can try to do things right this time?" All but the hardest of heart, says Elder, will give you one more chance. You won't get a glowing reference, but neither will the statement be so damning that no one is willing to hire you.[4]

"I Don't Have Any Experience."

If you have a year or more before you job-hunt, you can get experience in several ways:

- **Take a fast-food job—and keep it.** If you do well, you'll be promoted to a supervisor within a year. Use every opportunity to learn about the management and financial aspects of the business.
- **Volunteer.** If you work hard, you'll quickly get an opportunity to do more: manage a budget, write fundraising materials, and supervise other volunteers.

Putting Motherhood on Your Résumé*

When Barbara Mossberg was a candidate for president of Goddard College, Vermont, she listed as her greatest accomplishment "creating a nurturing structure in which to witness and guide the growth of unique human beings." She not only got the job but also had her answer posted on the college Web site.

Many professionals agree that parenting has made them "more proficient in their professions." Yet few list parenting among their credentials.

Anne Crittenden says it is time to see parenting as one more career of many in our lifetime. And her interviews suggest the time is right and attitudes are changing.

In an advertising profession desperate for talent, women face real employment opportunities. Still dominated by men at the top by a ratio of 2.77 to 1, the profession produces ads that 58% of women claim annoy them. So in advertising, as in many other professions, those parenting skills—people, organizational, and financial planning skills—are in high demand.

*Based on Ann Crittenden, "Time to put motherhood on your résumé," *Globe Careers*, March 25, 2005, B16; Keith McArthur, "Got itchy feet? You must be in the ad biz," *Globe Careers*, April 6, 2005, C1.

- **Freelance.** Design brochures, create Web pages, do tax returns for small businesses. Use your skills—for free, if you have to at first.
- **Write.** Create a portfolio of ads, instructions, or whatever documents are relevant for the field you want to enter. Ask a professional.

Pick something where you interact with other people, so that you can show that you can work well in an organization.

If you're on the job market now, think carefully about what you've really done. Complete sentences using the action verbs in Figure 14.4 (see p. 361). Think about what you've done in courses, in volunteer work, in unpaid activities. Especially focus on skills in problem solving, critical thinking, teamwork, and communication. Solving a problem for a hypothetical firm in an accounting class, thinking critically about a report problem in business communication, working with a group in a marketing class, and communicating with people at the senior centre where you volunteer are experience, even if no one paid you.

How Employers Use Résumés

Understanding how employers use résumés will help you create a résumé that works for you.

1. **Employers use résumés to decide whom to interview.** (The major exceptions are on-campus interviews, where the campus placement office has policies that determine who meets with the interviewer.) Since résumés are used to screen out applicants, omit anything that may create a negative impression.

2. **Résumés are scanned or skimmed.** At many companies, résumés are scanned into an electronic job applicant tracking system. Only résumés that match keywords are skimmed by a human being. A human may give a résumé 3 to 30 seconds before deciding to keep or toss it. You must design your résumé to pass both the "scan test" and the "skim test."

3. **Employers assume that your letter and résumé represent your best work.** Neatness, accuracy, and freedom from typographical errors are essential.

4. **Interviewers usually reread your résumé before the interview to refresh their memories.** Be ready to offer fuller details about everything on your résumé.

5. **After the search committee has chosen an applicant, it submits the applicant's résumé to people in the organization who must approve the appointment.** These people may have different backgrounds and areas of expertise. Spell out acronyms and explain unusual job titles or organizations that may be unfamiliar to the reader.

Guidelines for Résumés

Writing a résumé is not an exact science. If your skills are in great demand, you can violate every guideline here and still get a good job. But when you must compete against many applicants, these guidelines will help you look as good on paper as you are in person. You want a résumé with eye appeal!

A one-page résumé is sufficient, but do fill the page. Less than a full page suggests that you do not have very much to say for yourself.

The average résumé is now two pages. An experiment that mailed one- or two-page résumés to recruiters at accounting firms showed that even readers who said they preferred short résumés were more likely to want to interview the candidate with the longer résumé.[5]

Emphasize the things you've done that (a) are most relevant to the position for which you're applying, (b) show your superiority to other applicants, and (c) are recent (last three to five years):

- Emphasize problem-solving, organizational, interpersonal, and communications skills.
- Use action verbs (see Figure 14.4) to emphasize your contributions ("planned major trade show" or "trained five employees").
- Give details to support claims: "increased sales by 15% in first six months."
- List relevant technical skills and knowledge.
- List relevant course projects, activities, and jobs where you have done similar work. Marketing recruiters favoured résumés giving details about course projects, especially in the absence of work experience.[6]
- Emphasize promotions, honours and achievements, experience with computers or other technology, other languages, and so on.

Once you are pursuing a degree, omit high school jobs, activities, and honours unless you need them to fill the page. Briefly mention low-level jobs to show dependability.

Include full-time work after high school and during college or university. Present low-level jobs briefly or combine them:

2002–05	Part-time and full-time jobs to support family

You can emphasize material by putting it at the top or the bottom of a page, by giving it more space, and by setting it off with white space. The beginning and end—of a document, a page, a list—are positions of emphasis.

Weak order: Coordinated weekly schedules, assigned projects to five staff members, evaluated their performance, and submitted weekly time sheets.

Emphatic order: Coordinated weekly schedules and submitted weekly time sheets. Assigned projects to five staff members and evaluated their performance.

You can also emphasize material by presenting it in a bulleted list, using a phrase in a heading, and providing details.

Without sacrificing content, be as concise and concrete as possible.

Wordy: Member, Meat Judging Team, 2000–01
Member, Meat Judging Team, 2001–02
Member, Meat Judging Team, 2002–03
Captain, Meat Judging Team, 2003–04

Tight: Meat Judging Team, 2000–05; Captain 2003–05

Résumés normally use phrases and sentence fragments. Complete sentences are acceptable if they are the briefest way to present information. To save space and to avoid sounding arrogant, never use *I* in a résumé. *Me* and *my* are acceptable if they are unavoidable or if using them reduces wordiness.

Verbs or gerunds (the *-ing* form of verbs) create a more dynamic image than do nouns. In the following revisions, nouns, verbs, and gerunds are in bold type:

Nouns: Chair, Income Tax Assistance Committee, Winnipeg, MB, 2004–05. Responsibilities: **recruitment** of volunteers; flyer **design, writing,** and **distribution** for **promotion** of program; **speeches** to various community groups and nursing homes to advertise the service.

Verbs: Chair, Income Tax Assistance Committee, Winnipeg, MB, 2004–05. **Recruited** volunteers for the program. **Designed, wrote,** and **distributed** a flyer to promote the program; **spoke** to various community groups and nursing homes to advertise the service.

Templates: Use Caution

Many Web sites have templates for paper and online résumés. If you choose to use one of them, print out a copy before you submit your résumé. Less sophisticated programs use fixed spacing before headings. If you skip the objective, or have less experience than the template allows, you may get blank space—hardly a way to build a good impression.

Almost certainly, you can create a better résumé by adapting a basic style you like to your own unique qualifications.

Gerunds: Chair, Income Tax Assistance Committee, Winnipeg, MB, 2004–05. Responsibilities included **recruiting** volunteers for the program; **designing, writing,** and **distributing** a flyer to promote the program; and **speaking** to various community groups and nursing homes to advertise the service.

Note that the items in the list must be in parallel structure (◄ p. 97).

Experiment with layout, fonts, and spacing to get an attractive and readable résumé. Consider creating a letterhead that you use for both your résumé and your application letter. Use enough white space to make your résumé and its blocks of information easy to read.

Even if you pay someone else to produce your résumé, *you* must specify the exact layout: you cannot expect a paid typist to care as much about your résumé as you do or to understand what needs emphasis.

Laser print your résumé on standard white (or grey or cream) paper. Take advantage of different sizes of type and perhaps of rules (thin lines) to make your résumé look professional.

Kinds of Résumés

Although the job market has seen a proliferation of kinds and names, there are two broad kinds of résumés: chronological and skills. A **chronological résumé** summarizes what you did in a timeline (starting with the most recent events, and going backward in **reverse chronology**). It emphasizes degrees, job titles, and dates. It is the traditional résumé format (Figure 14.3).

Use a chronological résumé when

- Your education and experience are a logical preparation for the position for which you're applying.
- You have impressive job titles, offices, or honours.
- You have shown good and steady progress to your current position.

A **skills résumé** (or **functional résumé**) emphasizes the skills you've developed and used rather than the job you did or the dates when you used the skills. Figures 14.5 and 14.6 (➡ pp. 362–363 and 366) show examples of functional or skills résumés. A functional résumé stresses individual areas of competence and accomplishment, while subordinating work and educational experience.

A **targeted résumé** highlights abilities and achievements that relate to a specific job target. Like the functional or skills résumé, it puts the emphasis on what you can do, and it supplies evidence in the form of concrete achievements described in action verbs. This kind of résumé signals the value you attach to the job because you tailor the information to one position and employer.

Use a skills résumé when

- Your education and experience are not the usual route to the position for which you're applying.
- You're changing fields.
- You want to combine experience from paid jobs, activities or volunteer work, and courses to show the extent of your experience in administration, finance, speaking, and so on.
- Your recent work history may create the wrong impression (gaps, demotions, frequent changes).

The two kinds differ in what information is included and how that information is organized. You may assume that the advice in this chapter applies to both kinds of résumés unless there is an explicit statement that the two kinds of résumés would handle a category differently.

FIGURE 14.3 Chronological Résumé

Vary font sizes. The name is in 18–point, the main headings in 12–point, and the text in 11–point type.

Jerry A. Jackson

Campus Address
1636 Highland Street
Guelph, ON
(519) 555-5718
jackson.2495@guelphu.ca
www.guelphu.ca/students/jackson.2495/home.htm   *If you have a professional Web page, include its URL*

Permanent Address
45 East Main Street
Moncton, NB E1C 1E6
(506) 555-7793

Education
B.Comm. in Financial Management, June 2005, University of Guelph, Guelph, ON
"B" Average
   Give your grade average if it's good

Sports Experience
Intramural Hockey Team (Division Champions, Winter 2004)
Men's Division I Lacrosse (Provincial champions, 2003)

Work Experience

Financial Sales Representative, Primerica Company, Guelph, ON, February 2003–present.
   • Work with clients to plan investment strategies to meet family and retirement goals.
   • Research and recommend specific investments.

Ways to handle self-employment
Entrepreneur, Moncton, NB, and Guelph, ON, September 2002–January 2003.
   • Created a saleable product, secured financial backing, found a manufacturer, supervised production, and sold product–12 dozen T-shirts at a $5.25 profit each–to help pay for university expenses.

Landscape Maintenance Supervisor, Moncton, NB, Summers 1994–2002.
   • Formed a company to cut lawns, put up fences, fertilize, garden, and paint houses.
   • Hired, fired, trained, motivated, and paid friends to complete jobs.

Specify large sums of money
Collector and Repair Worker, ACN Inc., Moncton, NB, Summers 1994–2000.
   • Collected and counted up to $10,000 a day.
   • Worked with technicians troubleshooting and repairing electronic and coin mechanisms of video and pinball games, cigarette machines, and jukeboxes.

What to Include in a Résumé

Although the résumé is a factual document, its purpose is to persuade. In a job application form or an application for graduate or professional school, you answer every question even if the answer is not to your credit. In a résumé, you cannot lie, but you can omit anything that does not work in your favour.

Résumés commonly contain the following information. The categories marked with an asterisk are essential.

*Name and Contact Information
Career Objective
Summary of Qualifications

```
*Education
*Experience
 Honours
 Activities
 References
```

You may choose other titles for these categories and add categories that are relevant for your qualifications: COMPUTER SKILLS, FOREIGN LANGUAGES.

EDUCATION and EXPERIENCE always stand as separate categories, even if you have only one item under each head. Combine other headings so that you have at least two long or three short items under each heading. For example, if you're in one honour society, and two social clubs, and on one athletic team, combine them all under ACTIVITIES AND HONOURS.

If you have more than seven items under a heading, consider using subheadings. For example, a student who had a great many activities might divide them into STUDENT GOVERNMENT, OTHER CAMPUS ACTIVITIES, and COMMUNITY SERVICE.

Put your strongest categories near the top and at the bottom of the first page. If you have impressive work experience, you might want to put that category first after your name and contact information.

Name and Contact Information

Put your full name in big type. You may use an initial rather than spelling out your first or middle name.

If you use only one address, consider centring it under your name. If you use two addresses (office and home, campus and permanent, until _____ / after _____) set them up side by side to balance the page visually.

Include an e-mail address, Web page URL, and a complete phone and/or cell number, including the area code in parentheses, or separate the area code by a hyphen.

(250) 555-1212 or 250-555-1212

If you don't have a phone, try to make arrangements with someone to take messages for you—employers usually call to schedule interviews and make job offers.

Omit your age, marital status, race, gender, and health. Questions about these topics are illegal.

Career Objective

CAREER OBJECTIVE statements (immediately after your contact information) should sound like the job descriptions an employer might use in a job listing. Keep your statement brief—two or three lines at most. Tell what you want to do, what level of responsibility you want to hold.

Ineffective career objective:	To offer a company my excellent academic foundation in hospital technology and my outstanding skills in oral and written communication
Better career objective:	Selling state-of-the-art medical equipment

Good CAREER OBJECTIVES are hard to write. If you talk about entry-level work, you won't sound ambitious; if you talk about where you hope to be in 5 or 10 years, you won't sound as though you're willing to do entry-level work. You may omit this category and specify the job you want in your cover letter.

Summary of Qualifications

A section summarizing the candidate's qualifications seems to have first appeared in scannable résumés, where its keywords helped to increase the number of matches a résumé produced. But the section proved useful for human readers as well and now is a standard part of most résumés. The best summaries show your knowledge of the specialized terminology of your field and offer specific, quantifiable achievements.

Weak: Reliable

Better: Achieved zero sick days in four years with A&B Sound.

Weak: Presentation skills

Better: Gave 20 individual and 7 team presentations to groups ranging from 5 to 100 people.

Your real accomplishments should go in the SUMMARY section. Include as many keywords as you legitimately can.

The relevant section of a targeted résumé typically uses present-tense verbs to describe CAPABILITIES and past-tense verbs to demonstrate the evidence of what the writer has achieved to support the claims for the job target: Communications assistant, King Associates.

CAPABILITIES | Write, edit, design publishable work
Solicit articles and negotiate effectively
Master Microsoft Office 2003 and WordPerfect Office 2002
Succeed in independent and team settings
Meet deadlines and organize production

ACHIEVEMENTS | Wrote eight feature articles for *The Sheaf.*
Designed and implemented new production procedures at *The Sheaf*
Designed *The Sheaf* anti-racist supplement
Solicited, edited, and designed three issues of the community newsletter, *NutanaNews*
Strengthened communication skills in customer service at The Bay

Education

EDUCATION can be your first major category if you've just earned (or are about to earn) a degree, if you have a degree that is essential or desirable for the position you're seeking, or if you lack work experience. Put EDUCATION later if you need all of page 1 for skills and experience or if you lack a degree that other applicants may have.

Under EDUCATION, include information about your undergraduate and graduate degrees as well as certificate programs. You may also include selected courses and grades related to the career objective.

To punctuate your degrees, do not space between letters and periods:

B.B.A. in Office Administration

B.Comm. in Accountancy

Current usage also permits you to omit the periods:

MBA

PhD in Finance

There are two basic options for presenting your educational information.

Option I: List in reverse chronological order each degree earned, field of study, date, school, city, province of any graduate work, short courses and professional certification courses, university, community college, or school from which you transferred.

MSc in Management, May 2005, University of Manitoba, Winnipeg, MB
Bachelor of Commerce in Finance, May 2003, St. Mary's University, Halifax, NS

Plan to sit for the CMA exam November 2005

BComm in Business Management, June 2006, University of Calgary, Calgary, AB
BUIS in Business-Information Systems, June 2003, Georgian Community College, Barrie, ON

Option II: After giving the basic information (degree, field of study, date, school, city, province) about your degree, list courses, using short descriptive titles rather than course numbers. Use a subhead like "Courses Related to Major" or "Courses Related to Financial Management" that will allow you to list all the courses (including psychology, speech, and business communication) that will help you in the job for which you're applying. Don't say "Relevant Courses," as that implies your other courses were irrelevant.

Bachelor of Business Administration in Management, May 2005, St. Francis Xavier, Antigonish, NS

Courses Related to Management:
Personnel Administration   Business Decision Making
Finance   International Business
Management I and II   Marketing
Accounting I and II   Legal Environment of Business
Business Communications

Valedictorian, Westmount High School, June 2000, Montreal, QC

Honours and Awards

It's nice to have the word HONOURS in a heading where it will be obvious even when the reader skims the résumé.

Include the following kinds of entries in this category:

- Listings in recognition books (e.g., *Who's Who in Advertising*).
- Academic honour societies. Specify the nature of honour societies so the reader doesn't think they're just social clubs.
- Fellowships and scholarships, including honorary scholarships for which you received no money and fellowships you could not hold because you received another fellowship at the same time.
- Awards given by professional societies.
- Major awards given by civic groups.
- Selection to provincial or national teams; finishes in provincial, national, or Olympic meets; drama or music awards. (These could also go under ACTIVITIES but may look more impressive under HONOURS. Put them under one category or the other—not both.)

Experience

Under this section include the following information for each job you list: position or job title, organization, city and province (no postal code), dates of employment, and other details, such as full- or part-time status, job duties, special responsibilities, or the fact that you started at an entry-level position and were promoted. Use the verbs in Figure 14.4 to brainstorm what you've done. Include unpaid jobs and self-employment if they provided relevant skills (e.g., supervising people, budgeting, planning, persuading).

In a functional or skills résumé the subheadings under EXPERIENCE will be the *skills* used in or the *aspects* of the job you are applying for, rather than the title or the dates of the jobs you've held (as in a chronological résumé). For entries under each skill, combine experience from paid jobs, unpaid work, classes, activities, and community service.

Use headings that reflect the jargon of the job for which you're applying: *logistics* rather than *planning* for a technical job. Figure 14.5 shows a functional résumé for someone who is changing fields. The functions you perform produce the headings.

A job description can give you ideas for headings. Possible headings and subheadings for functional or skills résumés include

Administration	Communication
Alternates or Subheadings:	Alternates or Subheadings:
Budgeting	Conducting Meetings
Coordinating	Editing
Evaluating	Fundraising
Implementing	Interviewing
Keeping Records	Negotiating
Negotiating	Persuading
Planning	Presenting
Scheduling	Proposal Writing
Solving Problems	Report Writing
Supervising	

FIGURE 14.4 Action Verbs for Résumés

analyzed	directed	led	reviewed
budgeted	earned	managed	revised
built	edited	motivated	saved
chaired	established	negotiated	scheduled
coached	examined	observed	simplified
collected	evaluated	organized	sold
conducted	helped	persuaded	solved
coordinated	hired	planned	spoke
counselled	improved	presented	started
created	increased	produced	supervised
demonstrated	interviewed	recruited	trained
designed	introduced	reported	translated
developed	investigated	researched	wrote

I Do Good Work*

[Create an "I Do Good Work" folder to] back up your claims of top performance with solid evidence.

Before you leave the office this Friday, write down five things you—not necessarily others—believe you did well this week, even if they represent common tasks. Perhaps you returned all phone calls, leaving no loose ends to tie at the end of the week. Or maybe the details you provide in your sales reports enabled you to find additional product fits for the client. Any letters from happy customers or e-mails thanking you for solving a problem should go right in your folder. . . .

Tuck that list away and continue this weekly exercise for the entire month. At the end of the month, narrow the four or five lists to 10 accomplishments that stand out to you. At the end of the year, review the 120 items and cull them to 25. Formalize the language that describes those 25 achievements and print them out in an organized manner . . . along with your references.

"When someone asks, 'What do you bring to this organization?' you won't merely reply, 'I'm good with people,' you'll hand that sales manager or HR person proof," says professional trainer Carol Price.

*Quoted from Julie Sturgeon, "All About You," *Selling Power*, September 2000, 57.

FIGURE 14.5 A Functional Résumé for Someone Changing Fields

On the first page of a functional résumé, put skills directly related to the job for which you're applying

Marcella G. Cope

370 49th Avenue
Yellowknife, NT X1A 2R3
867-555-1997
mcope@shaw.ca

Objective
Put company's name in objective

To help create high quality CD-ROM products in Metatec's New Media Solutions Division

Editing and Proofreading Experience

An extra half space creates good visual impact

- **Edited** a textbook published by Simon and Schuster, revising with attention to format, consistency, coherence, document integrity, and document design.
- **Proofed** training and instructors ma nuals, policy statements, student essays and research papers, internal documents, and promotional materials.
- **Worked with authors** in a variety of fields including English, communication, business, marketing, economics, education, history, sociology, biology, agriculture, computer science, law, and medicine to revise their prose and improve their writing skills by giving them oral and written feedback.

Writing Experience

- **Wrote** training and instructor's manuals, professional papers, and letters, memos, and reports.
- **Co-authored** the foreword to a forthcoming textbook (Fall 2006) from NCTE press.
- **Contributed** to a forthcoming textbook (Fall 2006) from Bedford Books/St. Martin's press.

Computer Experience

- **Designed** a Web page using Dreamweaver (www.unbc.ca/english/People/Bracken.1/Sedgwick/)
- **Learned and used** a variety of programs on both Macintosh and PC platforms:
  Word Processing and Spreadsheets   Dreamweaver
  Microsoft Project   PageMaker
  E-Mail   PowerPoint *Computer experience*
  Aspects (a form for online synchronous discussion) *is crucial for almost every job.*
  Storyspace (a hypertext writing environment) *Specify the hardware and software you've worked with*

Other Business and Management Experience

- **Developed** policies, procedures, and vision statements.
- **Supervised** new staff members in a mentoring program.
- **Coordinated** program and individual schedules, planned work and estimated costs, set goals, and evaluated progress and results.
- **Member of team that directed** the nation's largest first-year writing program.

(continued)

Many jobs require a mix of skills. Try to include the skills that you know will be needed in the job you want. For example, one study identified the six top communication skills for jobs in finance and in management.[7] Applicants who had experience in some of these areas could list them as well as subject-related skills and knowledge.

You need at least three subheadings in a skills résumé. Give enough detail under each subheading so the reader will know what you did. Put the most important category from the reader's point of view first.

In a skills résumé, list your paid jobs under WORK HISTORY or EMPLOYMENT RECORD near the end of the résumé (see Figure 14.5). List only job title,

FIGURE 14.5 A Functional Résumé for Someone Changing Fields *(concluded)*

Marcella G. Cope

Page 2

If you use two pages be sure to put your name and "Page 2" on the second page. The reader may remove a staple.

Employment History

Most recent job first

Graduate Teaching Associate, Department of English, University of Northern British Columbia (UNBC), September 1999–Present. Taught Intermediate and First-Year Composition.

Writing Consultant, University Writing Centre, UNBC, January–April 2002

Program Administrator, First-Year Writing Program, UNBC, September 2000–January 2002

Honours

Explain honour societies that the reader may not know

Phi Kappa Phi Honour Society, inducted 2000. Membership based upon performance in top 10% of graduate students nationwide.

Letters of Commendation, 1999–2002. Issued by the Director of Graduate Studies in recognition of outstanding achievement.

Dean s List, University of Alberta, Edmonton, AB

Education

Master of Arts, June 2001, University of Northern British Columbia, Prince George, BC. Cumulative GPA: 4.0/4.0

Bachelor of Arts, June 1999, University of Alberta, Edmonton, AB. Graduated with Honours.

References

Marilyn Duffey
Director, UNBC University Writing Program
3333 University Way
Prince George, BC V2N 4Z9
205-960-5555
duffeymc@unbc.ca

James Bracken
Associate Professor, English and Library Science
University of Northern British Columbia
3333 University Way
Prince George, BC V2N 4Z9
205-960-6300
bracken@unbc.ca

Choose references who can speak about your skills for the job for which you're applying

Kitty O. Locker
Associate Professor, Business and Administrative Communication
The Ohio State University
421 Denney Hall, 164 W. 17th Ave.
Columbus, OH 43210
614-555-6556
locker.1@osu.edu

employer, city, province, and dates. Omit details that you have already used under EXPERIENCE.

Activities

Employers are very interested in your activities if you're a new graduate. If you've worked for several years or have an advanced degree (MBA, MSc), you can omit ACTIVITIES and include PROFESSIONAL ACTIVITIES AND AFFILIATIONS or COMMUNITY AND PUBLIC SERVICE.

Finding Your Flaws Online*

Ever file a workers' compensation claim? Wrecked a company car? Received a speeding ticket?

Prospective employers can find out if you did. And now, thanks to the Internet, they can do it almost instantly.

Informus Corp. makes a living giving curious employers information such as the names and phone numbers of your neighbours. Besides access to workers' compensation claims, Informus connects employers to credit bureaus and agencies that store financial and criminal information.

*Based on Tawn Nhan, "On-line Service Checks Out Job Applicants," *The Columbus Dispatch*, May 19, 1996.

Include the following kinds of items under ACTIVITIES:

- Volunteer work. Include important committees and leadership roles.
- Membership in organized student activities. Include important subcommittees, leadership roles.
- Membership in professional associations.
- Participation in organized activities that require talent or responsibility (e.g., sports, choir, new student orientation).

Major leadership roles may look more impressive if they're listed under EXPERIENCE instead of under ACTIVITIES.

References

Including references (with full contact information) anticipates the employer's needs and removes a potential barrier to your getting the job. To make your résumé fit on one page, you can omit this category. However, include REFERENCES if you're having trouble filling the page. Don't say "References Available on Request" since no job applicant will refuse to supply references. If you don't want your current employer to know you're job-hunting, omit the category in the résumé and say in the letter, "If I become a finalist for the job, I will supply the names of current references."

When you list references, provide at least three, including at least one professor and at least one employer or adviser—someone who can comment on your work habits and leadership skills. Don't use relatives or roommates, even if you've worked for them. If you're changing jobs, include your current superior. See Figure 14.5.

Always ask the person's permission to list him or her as a reference. Don't say, "May I list you as a reference?" Instead, say, "Can you speak positively about my work?" Jog the person's memory by taking along copies of work you did for him or her and a copy of your current résumé. Tell the person what points you'd like him or her to stress in a letter. Keep your list of references up to date. If it's been a year or more since you asked someone, ask again—and tell the person about your recent achievements.

How an Average Student Created an Excellent Résumé

Allyson was convinced that she had nothing to put on her résumé. In a conference, her professor asked Allyson to describe exactly what she'd done. Allyson's "baby-sitting" was actually house management and child care. But a summer job at Harvard had consisted of changing beds and cleaning rooms for conference guests.

Her five summers of work at a law firm sounded more promising. She went to the library, formulated medical and legal questions, and searched for answers. The information she found helped the firm win a $7 million out-of-court settlement. But Allyson was in advertising and wanted to go into copywriting, not market research. The experience was certainly worth putting on her résumé, but the kind of thinking she'd done as a law clerk wasn't the kind of thinking she needed to demonstrate to an ad agency.

Some of the items under ACHIEVEMENTS were interesting. The Locker Room was a restaurant in town where Allyson had had dinner. Its menu said the restaurant "had a long history." In fact, the restaurant was new; it was the *building* that was old. Allyson went up to the owner, told him several of the things that were wrong with the menu, and offered to rewrite it. The owner told her he'd pay her for doing that and also invited her to submit ideas for ads.

The professor was impressed. The whole anecdote might work in a job application letter, while the résumé could highlight the fact that Allyson had written menu and advertising copy for a real business (not just a class). "What you need," the instructor said, "is a skills résumé" (Figure 14.6).

Online Résumés

Most large companies scan résumés into an electronic job-applicant tracking system.[8] Creating a Web résumé is optional, but prepare a scannable version of your résumé to send any company that asks for it.

Hiring managers and recruiters now use e-mail for most of their correspondence. According to a survey by the Society for Human Resource Management, more than one-third of human resource professionals reported a preference for e-mailed résumés.[9] Here are some basic guidelines of e-mail job-hunting etiquette:

- Don't use your current employer's e-mail system for your job search. You'll leave potential employers with the impression that you spend company time on writing résumés and other non-work-related activities.

- Set up a free, Internet-based e-mail account using services such as Hotmail or Yahoo! to manage correspondence related to your job hunt.

- Avoid using silly or cryptic e-mail addresses. Instead of bubbles@aol.com, opt for something businesslike: yourname@yahoo.com.

- Understand that e-mail isn't confidential. Don't put an address or phone number on your e-résumé. Instead write "Confidential Résumé" and list a personal e-mail address where you can be reached.

- Send individual, targeted messages rather than mass mailings. You don't want a coveted employer to see that you're also sending your résumé to 20 other companies.

- Write a simple subject line that makes a good first impression: Résumé—Kate Sanchez. A good subject line will improve the chances that your résumé is actually read.

Prepare a résumé that looks good on a computer screen. Computer systems vary widely and have differently installed fonts, printer drivers, and word processing software.

Use a plain text résumé. Save your fully formatted résumé in your word processing program as "text" or "rich-text format" (rtf)—a document type that's compatible with all systems. It's important to heed the specific directions of employers that you are e-mailing. Also mention the types of files in a brief cover letter in your message. (See Figure 14.12 on p. 375.)

With the popularity of the Web, you may want to post your résumé online. If you don't know hypertext markup language (HTML), the behind-the-scenes programming that displays Web pages in your browser, you can save your résumé as HTML in Word or WordPerfect. However, be aware that the HTML editors in word-processing programs create messy codes that computer programmers deplore. If you're claiming the ability to code Web pages as one of your skills and abilities, use real HTML.

- Include an e-mail link at the top of the résumé under your name.

- Omit your street addresses and phone numbers. Employers who find your résumé on the Web will have the technology to e-mail you.

- Consider having links under your name and e-mail address to the various parts of your résumé. Use phrases that give the viewer some idea of what you offer: e.g., *Marketing Experience.*

Online "Salvaging"*

You post a résumé online and wait for the offers to come in. Then you get an e-mail—from the boss. Seems a sharp-eyed guy in personnel saw your résumé on Getajob.com. If you're lucky and the company has decided that you're worth "salvaging," you'll get a raise and a warning. If not, you'll be shown the door. . . .

Usually based in the human resources department, "salvagers" monitor online job-listing sites, which range from general ones like Monster.com to specialty sites for tax preparers. . . . [S]alvaging operations can range from a full-time staff of salvagers to "find and tell" policies that require any employee who finds a colleague's résumé online to inform a supervisor immediately. . . .

A quality control officer at a midsize telecom company posted his résumé in the "confidential" section of a highly specialized job site, which withheld his name and his employer's and blocked anyone logging in from his employer's domain name from seeing his résumé. The employee got several offers—including one from his employer. The personnel officer who smoked him out used a free Yahoo! account to avoid the job site's filters. . . . After a few sleepless nights, he came clean. The company gave him a small raise and warned that he would lose certain assignments if his résumé was found again within a year.

*Quoted from Richard Miniter, "Watch Out, or You Might Get 'Salvaged,'" *The Wall Street Journal,* November 1, 1999, A54.

FIGURE 14.6 A Skills Résumé for a Graduate Entering the Job Market

A border creates visual variety

Allyson Karnes

1629 Alexandre-Desève Street
Montreal, QC H2L 2V8
(514) 598-0444
karnes.173@concord.ca

She varies the usual "Summary of Qualifications" to make it specific to the job. This really is Allyson's philosophy—and it's one an agency will appreciate.

Qualifications for Writing Creative Ads That Make People Remember the Product

➤ Created headlines and print ads for a variety of audiences.
➤ Persuaded team members, business owners, and lawyers to accept my ideas.
➤ Self-starter who sees a project through from start to finish.

Skills résumé allows her to combine experience from classes and life

Education

B.A. in Advertising, June 2005, Concordia University, Montreal, QC
    Core courses: Copywriting, promotional strategies, magazine writing, graphics, media planning
    Harvard University Writing Program, Summer 2001, Boston, MA

Experience Creating Ads

Led the team that developed the winning promotional strategy for Max & Erma's Restaurants.
➤ Developed idea for theme for a year's campaign of ads.
➤ Wrote copy for radio spots, magazine ads, and billboards. One billboard ad had the headline "Multiple Choice" and boxes for burgers, chicken, and salads--with all the boxes checked.
➤ Presented creative strategy to Max & Erma's CEO and the Head of Advertising.
➤ Strategy won first place from among 17 proposals.

Details, wording demonstrate her ability

Wrote more than 15 ads for Copywriting class, including
➤ Ad for cordless phone: "Isn't It Time to Cut the Cord?"
➤ Slogan for Concordia's Jamboree: "In Short, It Jams"
➤ Billboard for Villa Maria School: "Who Said It's Lonely at the Top?"

Created ads and revised menu for The Locker Room (restaurant).

Allyson chooses unusual bullets rather than the standard dots or squares. In a résumé for an ad agency, the bullets work.

Other Writing Experience

Wrote "Commuter Flights" (humour).
Created more than 30 magazine articles as part of courses at Harvard University and Concordia.
Researched and wrote legal briefs as part of course at Harvard.
Summarized research on $7 million malpractice case for Garson and Associates.

Employment History

2001–04   Child care and house management, Laval, QC. Part-time daily during school year.

Summer 2001   Maid, Harvard Student Agency, Boston, MA. Part-time while attending Harvard University Writing Program.

Summers 1997–2000   Law Clerk, Garson and Associates, Montreal, QC. Did independent case research used by the firm to win $7 million malpractice out-of-court settlement for the client.

Reverse chronology

Portfolio Available on Request   *A position of emphasis*

- Link to other pages that provide more information about you (a list of courses, a document you've written), but not to organizations (your university, an employer) that shift emphasis away from your credentials.
- Be professional. Link to other pages you've created only if they convey the same professional image as your résumé.
- Put your strongest qualification immediately after your name and e-mail address. If the first screen doesn't interest readers, they won't scroll through the rest of the résumé.
- Specify the job you want. Recruiters respond negatively to scrolling through an entire résumé only to find that the candidate is in another field.[10]

- Specify city and province for educational institutions and employers.
- Use lists, indentations, and white space to create visual variety.
- Most commercial and many university sites offer lists of applicants, with a short phrase after each name. Craft this phrase to convince the recruiter to click on your résumé.
- Proofread the résumé carefully.

Be prepared during the job interview to create HTML or Java text or provide an in-office writing sample. Firms may want confirmation that the skills they represent indeed belong to the candidate.[11]

Increasingly, large companies scan paper résumés to search them by keyword to match job descriptions. See Figure 14.7. To increase the chances that the résumé is scanned correctly,

- Use a standard typeface: Helvetica, Futura, Optima, Times Roman, New Century Schoolbook, Courier, Univers, or Bookman.[12]
- Use 12- or 14-point type.
- Use a ragged right margin rather than full justification. Scanners can't always handle the extra spaces between words and letters that full justification creates.
- Don't italicize or underline words—even titles of books or newspapers that grammatically require such treatment.
- Check text to make sure letters are not touching; use Times New Roman or Helvetica to avoid the problem.
- Don't use lines, boxes, script, leader dots, or borders.
- Don't use two-column formats.
- Put each phone number on a separate line.
- Use plenty of white space.
- Don't fold or staple the pages.
- Don't write anything by hand on your résumé.
- Send a laser copy or a high-quality photocopy. Stray marks defeat scanners.

To increase the number of matches, or hits,

- Prepare a traditional chronological résumé. Don't be "creative." It doesn't matter where information is; the system can find it anywhere.
- Use a *Keywords* summary under your name, address, and phone. In it, put not only degrees, job field or title, and accomplishments but also personality traits and attitude: *dependable, skill in time management, leadership, sense of responsibility.*[13]
- Use industry buzzwords and jargon, even if you're redundant. For example, "Web page design and HTML coding" will "match" either "Web" or "HTML" as a keyword.
- Use conventional terms, even if they're a bit wordy.
- Use specific, concrete nouns. Some systems don't handle verbs well, and tracking systems "key in" primarily on nouns.
- Use common headings such as *Summary of Qualifications, Strengths, Certifications,* and so forth as well as *Education, Experience,* and so on.
- Use as many pages as necessary.
- Mention specific software programs (e.g., *Dreamweaver*) you've used.
- Be specific and quantifiable. "Managed $2 million building materials account" will generate more hits than "manager" or "managerial experience."

Unfiltered Résumés*

Companies are losing billions of dollars a year to the time wasted on spam, so they have installed filters to block spam. Unfortunately, some messages being blocked are legitimate messages containing résumés.

To lessen the chance of a résumé being blocked by a spam filter:

- Try not to use words that filters are likely to block, including *cash, expand, free, mortgage, singles,* and *trial.* Avoid exclamation points, too.

- Put the résumé in the body of the message instead of attaching it (unless the company requests an attachment).

- Avoid using coloured backgrounds.

- Send your résumé to one recipient per message. Avoid services that will "blast" your résumé to thousands of companies.

- Test your message and résumé by sending it to yourself, perhaps at a different address where you set filtering at various levels. Make sure it gets through your own filters before you send it to a company.

Also, just as companies may filter out your résumé, your own e-mail service may filter out important messages from recruiters. Read addresses and subject lines carefully before deleting anything in your spam folder.

*Based on Kris Maher, "Stringent Spam Filters Mistakenly Block E-Mailed Résumés," *The Wall Street Journal,* April 13, 2004, downloaded at http://online.wsj.com; and Sharon Gaudin, "False Positives: Spam's Casualty of War Costing Billions," Earthweb, August 7, 2003, downloaded at http://itmanagement. earthweb.com.

FIGURE 14.7 A Scannable Résumé

Jerry A. Jackson

Use 12– or 14–point type in a standard typeface. Here, Times Roman is used.

Keywords: family financial management; investment sales; computer modelling; competitive; self-starter; hard worker; responsible; collegiate athletics; sales experience; willing to travel

In keywords, use labels and terms that employers might use in a job listing

Campus Address
1636 Highland Street
Guelph, ON N1G 1W2
(519) 555-5718
E-mail address: Jackson.2495@guelphu.ca
Created a Web page on saving for life goals, such as a home, children's education, and retirement: http://www.guelphu.ca/students/Jackson.2495/home.htm

Permanent Address
45 East Main Street
Moncton, NB E1C 1E6
(506) 555-7793

Don't use columns. Scanners can't handle them.

Summary of Qualifications
High energy. Played sports during four years of university. Started two businesses.
Sales experience. Sold both clothing and investments successfully.
Presentation skills. In individual and group presentations, spoke to groups ranging from 2 to 75 people. Gave informative, persuasive, and inspirational talks.
Knowledgeable about stocks and bonds, especially energy and telecommunication companies.
Computer experience. Microsoft Word, Excel, SPSS, PowerPoint, and Dreamweaver. Experience creating Web pages.

Education
BBA. in Finance, June 2005, University of Guelph—Humber, Toronto, ON
"B" Grade Point Average
Comprehensive courses related to major provide not only the basics of family financial management but also skills in communication, writing, speaking, small groups, and computer modelling
Accounting I and II
Business and Professional Writing
Business Information Systems
Business Law
Computer Programming
Investment Finance
Economics I and II
Personal Financial Planning
Portfolio Management

Give as much information as you like. The computer doesn't care how long the document is.

(continued)

Weak: Microsoft Front Page

Better: Used Microsoft Front Page to design an interactive Web page for a national fashion retailer, with links to information about style trends, current store promotions, employment opportunities, and an online video fashion show.

- Put everything in the résumé rather than "saving" some material for the cover letter. While some applicant-tracking systems can search for keywords in cover letters and other application materials, most extract information only from the résumé, even though they store the other papers. The length of the résumé doesn't matter.

Experts differ on whether candidates should phone to follow up. Taunee Besson advises phoning the administrator or verifier of the tracking system just once to be sure that your résumé arrived.[14]

FIGURE 14.7 A Scannable Résumé *(concluded)*

Don't just justify margins. Doing so creates extra spaces, which confuse scanners.

Sports Experience
Intramural Hockey Team (Division Champions, Winter 1997)
Men's Division I Lacrosse (Provincial Champions, 2003)

Omit bold and italics. Some scanners can handle bullets, but they aren't needed in a scannable résumé.

Work Experience
Financial Sales Representative, Primerica Company, Guelph, ON, February 2003–present.
Work with clients to plan investment strategies.
Research and recommend specific investments, including stocks, bonds, mutual funds, and annuities.

Entrepreneur, Moncton, NB and Guelph, ON, September 2002–January 2003.
Created a saleable product, secured financial backing, found a manufacturer, supervised production, and sold product—12 dozen T-shirts at a $5.25 profit each—to help pay for university expenses.

Landscape Maintenance Supervisor, Moncton, NB, Summers 1994–2002.
Formed a company to cut lawns, put up fences, fertilize, garden, and paint houses.
Hired, fired, trained, motivated, and paid employees to complete jobs.

Collector and Repair Worker, ACN Inc., Moncton, NB, Summers 1994–2000.
Collected and counted up to $10,000 a day.
Worked with technicians troubleshooting and repairing electronic and coin mechanisms of video and pinball games, cigarette machines, and jukeboxes.

How Job Letters Differ from Résumés

The job application letter accompanies your résumé. Although the two documents overlap slightly, they differ in several ways:

- A résumé is adapted to a position; the letter is adapted to the needs of a particular organization.
- The résumé summarizes all your qualifications. The letter shows how your qualifications can help the organization meet its needs, how you differ from other applicants, and how much you know about the organization.
- The résumé uses short, parallel phrases (p. 97) and sentence fragments. The letter uses complete sentences in well-written paragraphs.

Writing a letter is good preparation for a job interview, since the letter is your first step in showing a specific company what you can do for it.

Content and Organization for Job Application Letters

In your letter, focus on

- Major requirements of the job for which you're applying
- Qualifications that separate you from other applicants
- Points that show your knowledge of the organization
- Qualities that every employer is likely to value: the ability to write and speak effectively, to solve problems, to get along with people

Two different hiring situations call for two different kinds of application letters. Write a **solicited letter** when you know that the company is hiring: you've seen an ad, you've been advised to apply by a professor or friend, you've read in a trade publication that the company is expanding. This situation is similar to a persuasive direct request (p. 164): you can indicate immediately that you are applying for the position. See Figure 14.9.

FIGURE 14.8   How to Organize a Solicited Job Application Letter

1. State that you're applying for the job (phrase the job title as your source phrased it). Tell where you learned about the job (ad, referral, etc.). Include any reference number mentioned in the ad. Briefly show that you have the major qualifications required by the ad: a degree, professional certification, job experience, etc. Summarize your other qualifications briefly in the same order in which you plan to discuss them in the letter.

2. Develop your major qualifications in detail. Be specific about what you've done; relate your achievements to the work you'd be doing in this new job. Remember that readers know only what you tell them. This is not the place for modesty!

3. Develop your other qualifications, even if the ad doesn't ask for them. (If the ad asks for a lot of qualifications, pick the most important three or four.) Show what separates you from the other applicants who will also answer the ad. Demonstrate your knowledge of the organization.

4. Ask for an interview; tell when you'll be available to be interviewed and to begin work. End on a positive, forward-looking note.

Sometimes, however, the advertised positions may not be what you want, or you may want to work for an organization that has not announced openings in your area. Then you write a **prospecting letter** to tap in to the hidden job market. (The metaphor is drawn from prospecting for gold.) The prospecting letter is like a problem-solving persuasive message (◀▦ p. 165). See Figure 14.11.

In both solicited and prospecting letters you should

- Address the letter to a specific person.
- Indicate the specific position for which you're applying.
- Be specific about your qualifications.
- Show what separates you from other applicants.
- Show a knowledge of the company and the position.
- Use the language of the ad, organization, and industry.
- Refer to your résumé (which you would enclose with the letter).
- Ask for an interview.

First Paragraphs of Solicited Letters

Note how the following paragraph picks up several of the characteristics of the ad:

Ad: Architectural Technology Professor at Mohawk College of Applied Arts and Technology. Candidate must possess a Bachelor's degree in Engineering or Architecture. Will be responsible for providing in-house leadership/training to professionals. . . . Candidate should have at least six months' experience. Prior teaching experience not required.

Letter: I am interested in your position in Architectural Technology. I will receive a Bachelor of Engineering degree from Carleton University in December. I have two years' experience teaching word processing and computer accounting courses to adults and have developed leadership skills in the volunteer guide program at the National Gallery of Canada.

Your **summary sentence** or **paragraph** covers everything you will talk about and serves as an organizing device for your letter.

I have a good background in standard accounting principles and procedures and a working knowledge of some of the special accounting practices of the oil industry.

FIGURE 14.9 A Solicited Letter from a Graduating Senior

Tracey has had only course work and one part-time job. But by being specific about what she's done in class and on the job, she creates a positive impression.

1072 Adams Street, Apt. 23
London, ON N4A 5B3
April 17, 2005

Mr. Robert H. Catanga, Senior Accountant
IBM Corporation
1717 Central
New York, NY 10021

Block format is good for letters of application

Dear Mr. Catanga:

Tell where you learned about the job. If the job has a number, provide it

I am applying for the Accounting position announced on IBM's Web site (jof17747). I will receive an Honours Business Administration degree from Richard Ivey School of Business this May and plan to take the CA exam next December. *In paragraph 1, show you have the qualifications the ad lists*

My courses in the accountancy curriculum at Ivey have given me not only the necessary theoretical background but also extensive practical experience in General Ledgers, Accounts Payable, and Travel Expenses. I have worked many cases and problems using computer data, including preparing simulated accounting records for hypothetical firms.

Many courses provide practice with simulated cases—you may be able to use Tracey's strategy, too

These terms come from the job listing

These true-to-life cases gave me the opportunity to interpret all sorts of data in order to prepare accurate financial statements. For instance, I've learned the best measures for fixed assets and property controls, how to figure inter/intra-company and travel expenses, and the best methods of matching revenues with expenditures. These I could then analyze and compare to past statements to identify trends and recommend ways that costs could be reduced so that the business could be run even more efficiently.

Referring to her Web page suggests her technological savvy

Courses in management communication have taught me how to communicate with various business audiences. This means that I would be able to provide reports, financial statements, and visuals to show how accounting information is related to management needs. I can use Excel and create computer graphics to provide the reliable accounting data that IBM needs to continue growing each year. Visit my Web page (www.ivey/business/ students/mckenna/report.htm) to see the report I wrote on choosing the best method to accelerate depreciation.

Relates what she has done to what she could do for the company

The ad asked for experience with spreadsheets and computer graphics

My three years of experience working for Imperial Insurance have also given me the opportunity to take leadership and show responsibility. Although I was hired as a part-time typist, my supervisor frequently asked for my recommendations of ways to get work done more efficiently. In fact, I developed a procedure for making out arbitration reports that saved so much time that I was asked to teach it to the other employees in my department.

She gets a lot of mileage out of her part-time job by being specific

Phrase from the CEO's letter in the annual report, which Tracey read on the Web

One way to refer to résumé

The enclosed résumé summarizes my qualifications. I can come to New York for an interview now that examinations are over. I can begin work in September and look forward to discussing with you ways in which I can help IBM continue its tradition of excellence.

Sincerely,

Nice allusion to inclusion of IBM in In Search of Excellence

Tracey McKenna

Tracey McKenna

Encl.: Résumé

You don't have to note the enclosure, but doing so is a nice touch if you have room at the bottom of the page

This working knowledge is based on practical experience in the oil fields: I've pumped, tailed rods, and worked as a roustabout.

Let me put my creative eye, artistic ability, and experience to work for McLean Design.

Good word choices can help set your letter apart from the scores or even hundreds of letters the company is likely to get in response to an ad. The following first paragraph of a letter in response to an ad by Imperial Insurance

FIGURE 14.10   How to Organize a Prospecting Letter

1. Catch the reader's interest.
2. Create a bridge between the attention-getter and your qualifications. Focus on what you know and can do. Since the employer is not planning to hire, he or she won't be impressed with the fact that you're graduating. Summarize your qualifications briefly in the same order in which you plan to discuss them in the letter. This summary sentence or paragraph then covers everything you will talk about and serves as an organizing device for your letter.
3. Develop your strong points in detail. Be specific. Relate what you've done in the past to what you could do for this company. Show that you know something about the company. Identify the specific niche you want to fill.
4. Ask for an interview and tell when you'll be available for interviews. (Don't tell when you can begin work.) End on a positive, forward-looking note.

Company shows a knowledge of the firm's advertising slogan and sets itself apart from the dozens of letters that start with "I would like to apply for. . . ."

> The Imperial Insurance Company is famous for its "Good Hands Policy." I would like to lend a helping hand to many Canadians as a financial analyst for Imperial, as advertised in *The Globe and Mail.* I have an Honours Business Administration degree from the Ivey School, University of Western Ontario, and I have worked with figures, computers, and people.

Note that the last sentence forecasts the organization of the letter, preparing for paragraphs about the student's academic background and (in this order) experience with "figures, computers, and people."

First Paragraphs of Prospecting Letters

In a prospecting letter, asking for a job in the first paragraph is dangerous: unless the company plans to hire but has not yet announced openings, the reader is likely to throw the letter away. Instead, catch the reader's interest. Then in the second paragraph you can shift the focus to your skills and experience, showing how they can be useful to the employer.

See the first two paragraphs of a letter applying to be a computer programmer for an insurance company:

> Computers alone aren't the answer to demands for higher productivity in the competitive insurance business. Merging a poorly written letter with a database of customers just sends out bad letters more quickly. But you know how hard it is to find people who can both program computers and write well.
>
> My education and training have given me this useful combination. I'd like to put my associate's degree in computer technology and my business experience writing to customers to work in FarmCredit's service approach to insurance.

Showing What Separates You from Other Applicants

Your knowledge of the company separates you from other applicants (Figure 14.11). You can also use coursework, an understanding of the field, and experience in jobs and extracurricular events to show that you're unique. Be specific but concise. Usually three to five sentences will enable you to give enough specific supporting details.

FIGURE 14.11 A Prospecting Letter from a Career Changer

FIGURE 14.11 A Prospecting Letter from a Career Changer

Marcella creates a "letterhead" that harmonizes with her résumé (see Figure 14.5 on p. 362)

Marcella G. Cope
370 49th Avenue
Yellowknife, NT X1A 2R3
867-555-1997
mcope@shaw.ca

August 23, 2005

Mr. John Harrobin
New Media Solutions
Metatec Corporation
618 5th Avenue SW
Calgary, AB T2P 0M7

Block format with justified margins lets Marcella get this letter on one page

Dear Mr. Harrobin:

In a prospecting letter, open with a sentence that (1) will seem interesting and true to the reader and (2) provides a natural bridge to talking about yourself

One way to refer to the enclosed résumé

Putting a textbook on a CD-ROM saves paper but does nothing to take advantage of the many possibilities the CD-ROM environment provides. Yet it can be a real challenge to find people who write well, proof carefully, and understand multimedia design. You will see from my enclosed résumé that I have this useful combination of skills.

Shows knowledge of the company

Rita Haralabidis tells me that Metatec needs people to design and develop high-quality CD-ROM products to meet business and consumer deadlines. Most of the writing and editing that I do is subject to strict standards and even stricter deadlines, and I know information is useful only if it is available when clients need it.

Shows she can meet company needs

When I toured Metatec this spring, members of the New Media Solutions Group shared some of their work from a series of interactive CD-ROM textbooks they were developing in tandem with Harcourt Brace. This project sparked my interest in Metatec because of my own experience with evaluating, contributing to, and editing university-level textbooks.

Relates what she's done to what she could do for this company

As a program administrator at University of Northern British Columbia, I examined dozens of textbooks from publishers interested in having their books adopted by the nation's largest First-Year Writing Program. This experience taught me which elements of a textbook—both content and design—were successful, and which failed to generate interest. Often, I worked closely with sales representatives to suggest changes for future editions. My own contributions to two nationally distributed textbooks further familiarized me with production processes and the needs of multiple audiences. My close contact with students convinces me of the need to produce educational materials that excite students, keep their attention, and allow them to learn through words, pictures, and sounds.

All of these terms fit Metatec's production of multimedia educational materials.

My communication and technology skills would enable me to adapt quickly to work with both individual clients and major corporations like CanWest Global and Nexen, Inc. I am a flexible thinker, a careful editor, a fluent writer, and, most important, a quick study. I will call you next week to find a mutually convenient time when we can discuss putting my talents to work for Metatec.

Names specific clients, showing more knowledge of the company.

When you're changing fields, learning quickly is a real plus

Sincerely,

Marcella G. Cope

Marcella G. Cope

Enclosed: Résumé

◼ This student uses both coursework and summer jobs to set herself apart from other applicants:

My university courses have taught me the essential accounting skills required to contribute to the growth of Monsanto. Since you recently adopted new accounting methods for fluctuations in foreign currencies, you will need people knowledgeable in foreign currency translation to convert currency exchange rates. In two courses in international accounting, I compiled simulated accounting statements of hypothetical multinational firms in countries experiencing different rates of currency devaluation. Through these classes, I acquired the skills needed to work with the daily fluctuations of exchange rates and at the same time formulate an accurate and favourable representation of Monsanto.

> A company as diverse as Monsanto requires extensive record keeping as well as numerous internal and external communications. Both my summer jobs and my coursework prepare me to do this. As Office Manager for Shaw Cable, I was in charge of most of the bookkeeping and letter writing for the company. I kept accurate records for each workday, and I often entered over 100 transactions in a single day. In business and technical writing I learned how to write persuasive letters and memos and how to present extensive data in reports in a simplified style that is clear and easy to understand.

In your résumé, you may list activities, offices, and courses. In your letter, give more detail about what you did and show how that experience will help you contribute to the employer's organization more quickly.

When you discuss your strengths, don't exaggerate. No employer will believe that a new graduate has a "comprehensive" knowledge of a field. Indeed, most employers believe that six months to a year of on-the-job training is necessary before most new hires are really earning their pay. Specifics about what you've done will make your claims about what you can do more believable and ground them in reality.

The Last Paragraph

In the last paragraph, indicate when you'd be available for an interview. If you're free anytime, you can say so. But it's likely that you have responsibilities in class and work. If you'd have to go out of town, there may be only certain days of the week or certain weeks that you could leave town for several days. Use a sentence that fits your situation.

> I could come to London for an interview any Wednesday or Friday.

> I'll be attending the Administrative Science Association's November meeting and will be available for interviews there.

Should you wait for the employer to call you, or should you call the employer to request an interview? In a solicited letter, it's safe to wait to be contacted: you know the employer wants to hire someone, and if your letter and résumé show that you're one of the top applicants, you'll get an interview. In a prospecting letter, call the employer. Because the employer is not planning to hire, you'll get a higher percentage of interviews if you're aggressive.

End the letter on a positive note that suggests you look forward to the interview and that you see yourself as a person who has something to contribute, not as someone who just needs a job.

> I look forward to discussing with you ways in which I could contribute to Big Rock's continued growth.

Interviewing in the 21st Century

Job interviews are scary, even when you've prepared thoroughly. But when you are prepared, you can harness the adrenaline to work for you, so that you put your best foot forward and get the job you want.

Interviews are changing as interviewers respond to interviewees who are prepared to answer the standard questions. Today, many employers expect you to

FIGURE 14.12   An E-Mail Application Letter

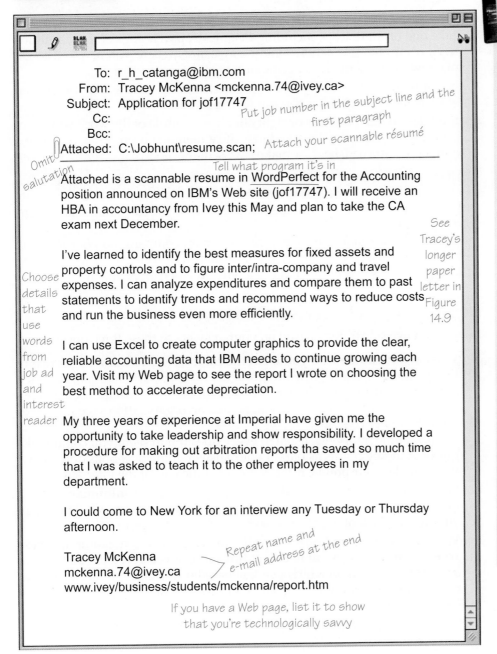

To: r_h_catanga@ibm.com
From: Tracey McKenna <mckenna.74@ivey.ca>
Subject: Application for jof17747
Cc:
Bcc:
Attached: C:\Jobhunt\resume.scan;

Put job number in the subject line and the first paragraph

Attach your scannable résumé

Omit salutation

Attached is a scannable resume in <u>WordPerfect</u> for the Accounting position announced on IBM's Web site (jof17747). I will receive an HBA in accountancy from Ivey this May and plan to take the CA exam next December.

Tell what program it's in

I've learned to identify the best measures for fixed assets and property controls and to figure inter/intra-company and travel expenses. I can analyze expenditures and compare them to past statements to identify trends and recommend ways to reduce costs and run the business even more efficiently.

Choose details that use words from job ad and interest reader

See Tracey's longer paper letter in Figure 14.9

I can use Excel to create computer graphics to provide the clear, reliable accounting data that IBM needs to continue growing each year. Visit my Web page to see the report I wrote on choosing the best method to accelerate depreciation.

My three years of experience at Imperial have given me the opportunity to take leadership and show responsibility. I developed a procedure for making out arbitration reports tha saved so much time that I was asked to teach it to the other employees in my department.

I could come to New York for an interview any Tuesday or Thursday afternoon.

Tracey McKenna
mckenna.74@ivey.ca
www.ivey/business/students/mckenna/report.htm

Repeat name and e-mail address at the end

If you have a Web page, list it to show that you're technologically savvy

- Be more assertive. One employer says he deliberately tells the company receptionist to brush off callers who ask about advertised openings. He interviews only those who keep calling and offer the receptionist reasons they should be interviewed.

- Follow instructions to the letter. The owner of a delivery company tells candidates to phone at a precise hour. Failing to do so means that the person couldn't be trusted to deliver packages on time.[15]

- Participate in many interviews. Candidates for jobs with Electronic Arts, a maker of computer games, first answer questions online. Then they have up to five phone interviews—some asking candidates to solve problems or program functions. Candidates who get that far undergo "the gauntlet": three days of onsite interviewing.[16]

- Have one or more interviews by phone, computer, or video.
- Take one or more tests, including drug tests, psychological tests, aptitude tests, computer simulations, and essay exams where you're asked to explain what you'd do in a specific situation.
- Be approved by the team you'll be joining. In companies with self-managed work teams, the team has a say in who is hired.
- Provide—at the interview or right after it—a sample of the work you're applying to do. You may be asked to write a memo or a proposal, calculate a budget on a spreadsheet, or make a presentation.

All the phoning required in 21st-century interviews places a special emphasis on phone skills. If you get voice mail, leave a concise message—complete with your name and phone number. Even if you've called 10 times, keep your voice pleasant.

If you get voice mail repeatedly, call the main company number to speak with a receptionist. Ask whether the person you're trying to reach is in the building. If he or she is on the road, ask when the person is due in.

Developing an Interview Strategy

Develop an overall strategy based on your answers to these three questions:

1. **What about yourself do you want the interviewer to know?** Pick two to five points that represent your strengths for that particular job. For each strength, think of a specific action or accomplishment to support it. For example, be ready to show how you helped an organization save money or serve customers better.

   Then at the interview, listen to every question to see if you could make one of your key points as part of your answer. If the questions don't allow you to make your points, bring them up at the end of the interview.

2. **What disadvantages or weaknesses do you need to minimize?** Expect that you may be asked to explain weaknesses or apparent weaknesses in your record: lack of experience, so-so grades, and gaps in your record.

3. **What do you need to know about the job and the organization to decide whether or not you want to accept this job if it is offered to you?** Plan *in advance* the criteria on which you will base your decision (you can always change the criteria).

Taking Care of the Details

Wearing inappropriate clothing or being late can cost you a job. Put enough time into planning details so that you can move on to substantive planning.

If you're interviewing for a management or office job, wear a business suit. What kind of suit? If you've got good taste and a good eye for colour, follow your instincts.

Take care of all the details. Check your heels to make sure they aren't run down; make sure your shoes are shined. Have your hair cut or styled conservatively. Jewellery and makeup should be understated. Personal hygiene must be impeccable. Avoid cologne and perfumed aftershave lotions.

Bring extra copies of your résumé. If your campus placement office has already given the interviewer a data sheet, present the résumé at the beginning of the interview: "I thought you might like a little more information about me."

Mirage Resorts sifted 75,000 applications to hire 9,600 workers in 24 weeks for a resort. Here, a staffer asks an applicant for permission to do a background check. Mirage checked for criminal records and looked at job, school, and credit histories; finalists also took drug tests. Showing applicants courtesy and consideration helped keep the best candidates interested. Because background checks took time, job offers came a few months after interviews. But only 3% of the people Mirage liked dropped out during the process.

Bring something to write on and something to write with. It's OK to bring in a small notepad with the questions you want to ask on it.

Bring copies of your work or a portfolio: an engineering design, a copy of a memo you wrote on a job or in a business writing class, an article you wrote for the campus paper. You don't need to present these unless the interview calls for them, but they can be very effective.

Bring the names, addresses, and phone numbers of references if you didn't put them on your résumé. Bring complete details about your work history and education, including dates and street addresses, in case you're asked to fill out an application form.

If you can afford it, buy a briefcase to carry these items. At this point in your life, an inexpensive vinyl briefcase is acceptable.

Rehearse everything you can: Put on the clothes you'll wear and practise entering a room, shaking hands, sitting down, and answering questions. Ask a friend to interview you. Saying answers out loud is surprisingly harder than saying them in your head.

During the Interview

Be yourself. There's no point in assuming a radically different persona. If you do, you run the risk of getting into a job that you'll hate (though the persona you assumed might have loved it). Furthermore, as interviewers point out, you have to be a pretty good actor to come across convincingly if you try to be someone other than yourself. Yet keep in mind that all of us have several selves. Be your best self at the interview.

Are You Pink or Blue?*

According to Ronna Lichtenberg, career advice columnist and author of *Pitch Like a Girl: How a Woman Can Be Herself and Still Succeed*, Carly Fiorina might have avoided being axed by Hewlett-Packard in February 2005 if she had been less blue.

The two colours—pink and blue—stereotypically distinguish men's and women's style of interacting with people. But executives need some of each style to succeed. Blue types value credentials, achievements, position, and directness; pink types want personal connection. More involvement with staff and board might have saved Fiorina.

If you have to pitch to a blue:

- Be direct and cover one topic at a time.
- Use numbers, graphs, and charts to support claims.
- Stress benefits in performance terms (5% sales increase)

If you have to pitch to a pink:

- Illustrate concepts with real examples and stories.
- Connect benefits to people.
- Use sound, colour, and images.
- Listen, show responsiveness, and expect a final decision after consultation with a trusted colleague.

* Based on Ronna Lichtenberg and Wallace Immen, "Colours of success: Are you pink or blue?" *The Globe and Mail*, February 16, 2005, C3.

Interviews can make you feel vulnerable and defensive; to counter this, review your accomplishments—the things you're especially proud of having done. You'll make a better impression if you have a firm sense of your own self-worth.

Every interviewer repeats the advice that your mother probably gave you: sit up straight, don't mumble, look at people when you talk. It's good advice for interviews. Be aware that many people respond negatively to smoking.

Office visits that involve meals and semi-social occasions call for sensible choices. When you order, choose something that's easy and unmessy to eat. Watch your table manners. At dinner or an evening party, decline alcohol if you don't drink. If you do drink, accept just one drink—you're still being evaluated, and you can't afford to have your guard down. Be aware that some people respond negatively to applicants who drink hard liquor.

In the **opening** (two to five minutes), good interviewers will try to set you at ease. Some interviewers will open with easy questions about your major or interests. Others open by telling you about the job or the company. If this happens, listen so you can answer questions later to show that you can do the job or contribute to the company that's being described.

The **body** of the interview (10 to 25 minutes) is an all-too-brief time for you to highlight your qualifications and find out what you need to know to decide if you want to accept a follow-up interview or office trip. Expect questions that give you an opportunity to showcase your strong points and questions that probe any weaknesses evident from your résumé. ("You were neither in school nor working last fall. What were you doing?") Normally the interviewer will also try to sell you on the company and give you an opportunity to raise questions.

In the **close** of the interview (two to five minutes), the interviewer will usually tell you what happens next: "We'll be bringing our top candidates to the office in February. You should hear from us in three weeks." One interviewer reports that he gives applicants his card and tells them to call him. "It's a test to see if they are committed, how long it takes for them to call, and whether they even call at all."[17]

Close with an assertive statement. Depending on the circumstances, you could say: "I've certainly enjoyed learning more about General Electric." "I hope I get a chance to visit your Mississauga office. I'd really like to see the new computer system you talked about." "This job seems to be a good match between what you're looking for and what I'd like to do."

Answering Traditional Interview Questions

First interviews seek to screen out less qualified candidates rather than to find someone to hire. Negative information will hurt you less if it comes out in the middle of the interview and is preceded and followed by positive information. If you blow a question near the end of the interview, don't leave until you've said something positive—perhaps restating one of the points you want the interviewer to know about you.

As Figure 14.13 shows, successful applicants use different communication behaviours than do unsuccessful applicants. Successful applicants are more likely to use the company name during the interview, support their claims with specific details, and ask specific questions about the company and the industry. In addition to practising the content of questions, try to incorporate these tactics.

The following questions frequently come up at interviews. Do some unpressured thinking before the interview so that you'll be able to come up with answers that are responsive, honest, and paint a good picture of you. Choose answers that fit your qualifications and your interview strategy.

FIGURE 14.13 The Communication Behaviours of Successful Interviewees

Behaviour	Unsuccessful interviewees	Successful interviewees
Statements about the position	Had only vague ideas of what they wanted to do; changed "ideal job" up to six times during the interview.	Specific and consistent about the position they wanted; were able to tell why they wanted the position.
Use of company name	Rarely used the company name.	Referred to the company by name four times as often as unsuccessful interviewees.
Knowledge about company and position	Made it clear that they were using the interview to learn about the company and what it offered.	Made it clear that they had researched the company; referred to specific brochures, journals, or people who had given them information.
Level of interest, enthusiasm	Responded neutrally to interviewer's statements: "OK," "I see." Indicated reservations about company or location.	Expressed approval of information provided by the interviewer non-verbally and verbally; "That's great!" Explicitly indicated desire to work for this particular company.
Non-verbal behaviour	Made little eye contact; smiled infrequently.	Made eye contact often; smiled.
Picking up on interviewer's cues	Gave vague or negative answers even when a positive answer was clearly desired ("How are your math skills?").	Answered positively and confidently—and backed up the claim with a specific example of "problem solving" or "toughness."
Response to topic shift by interviewer	Resisted topic shift.	Accepted topic shift.
Use of industry terms and technical jargon	Used almost no technical jargon.	Used technical jargon: "point of purchase display," "NCR charge," "two-column approach," "direct mail."
Use of specifics in answers	Gave short answers—10 words or less, sometimes only one word; did not elaborate. Gave general responses: "fairly well."	Supported claims with specific personal experiences, comparisons, statistics, statements of teachers and employers.
Questions asked by interviewee	Asked a small number of general questions.	Asked specific questions based on knowledge of the industry and the company. Personalized questions: "What would my duties be?"
Control of time and topics	Interviewee talked 37% of the interview time, initiated 36% of the comments.	Interviewee talked 55% of the total time, initiated subjects 56% of the time.

Source: Based on research reported by Lois J. Einhorn, "An Inner View of the Job Interview: An Investigation of Successful Communicative Behaviors," *Communication Education* 30 (July 1981), 217–228; and Robert W. Elder and Michael M. Harris, eds., *The Employment Interview Handbook* (Thousand Oaks, CA: Sage, 1999), 300, 303, 327–328.

1. **Tell me about yourself.**

   Don't launch into an autobiography. Instead, state the things about yourself that you want the interviewer to know. Give specifics to prove each of your strengths.

2. **What makes you think you're qualified to work for this company?** Or, **I'm interviewing 120 people for two jobs. Why should I hire you?**

   This question may feel like an attack. Use it as an opportunity to state your strong points: your qualifications for the job, the things that separate you from other applicants.

InSite

www.jobpostings.ca/resources/ interview_default.cfm

Visit JobPostings.ca, Canada's Student Job Network in Print and Online for advice on interviews and those difficult and even illegal questions you may be asked.

3. **What two or three accomplishments have given you the greatest satisfaction?**

    Pick accomplishments that you're proud of, that create the image you want to project, and that enable you to share one of the things you want the interviewer to know about you. Focus on the problem-solving and thinking skills that made the achievement possible.

4. **Why do you want to work for us? What is your ideal job?**

    Even if you're interviewing just for practice, make sure you have a good answer—preferably two or three reasons you'd like to work for that company.

    If you're interested in this company, do some research so that what you ask for is in the general ballpark of the kind of work the company offers.

5. **What college or university subjects did you like best and least? Why?**

    This question may be an icebreaker; it may be designed to discover the kind of applicant they're looking for. If your favourite class was something outside your major, prepare an answer that shows that you have qualities that can help you in the job you're applying for: "My favorite class was a seminar on the Canadian novel. We got a chance to think on our own, rather than just regurgitate facts; we made presentations to the class every week. I found I really like sharing my ideas with other people and presenting reasons for my conclusions about something."

6. **Why are your grades so low?**

    If your grades aren't great, be ready with a non-defensive explanation. If possible, show that the cause of low grades now has been solved or isn't relevant to the job you're applying for: "My father almost died last year, and my schoolwork really suffered." "When I started, I didn't have any firm goals. Once I discovered the field that was right for me, my grades have all been B's or better."

7. **What have you read recently? What movies have you seen recently?**

    These questions may be icebreakers; they may be designed to probe your intellectual depth. The term you're interviewing, read at least one book or magazine (regularly) and see at least one movie that you could discuss at an interview.

8. **Show me some samples of your writing.**

    Employers no longer take mastery of basic English for granted, even if the applicant has a degree from a prestigious university.

    The year you're interviewing, go through your old papers or reports and select the best ones, retyping them if necessary, so that you'll have samples if you're asked for them.

9. **Where do you see yourself in five years?**

    Employers ask this question to find out if you are a self-starter or if you passively respond to what happens. You may want to have several scenarios for five years from now to use in different kinds of interviews. Or you may want to say, "Well, my goals may change as opportunities arise. But right now, I want to. . . ."

10. **What are your interests outside work? What campus or community activities have you been involved in?**

    While it's desirable to be well rounded, naming 10 interests is a mistake: the interviewer may wonder when you'll have time to work.

    If you mention your fiancé, spouse, or children in response to this question ("Well, my fiancé and I like to go sailing"), it is perfectly legal for the interviewer to ask follow-up questions ("What would you do if your spouse got a job offer in another town?"), even though the same question would be illegal if the interviewer brought up the subject first.

Amy's Ice Cream stores sell entertainment. To find creative, zany employees, Amy Miller gives applicants a white paper bag and a week to do something with it. People who produce something unusual are hired.

11. **What have you done to learn about this company?**

    An employer may ask this to see what you already know about the company (if you've read the recruiting literature, the interviewer doesn't need to repeat it). This question may also be used to see how active a role you're taking in the job search process and how interested you are in this job.

12. **What adjectives would you use to describe yourself?**

    Use only positive ones. Be ready to illustrate each with a specific example of something you've done.

13. **What is your greatest strength?**

    Employers ask this question to give you a chance to sell yourself and to learn something about your values. Pick a strength related to work, school, or activities: "I'm good at working with people." "I'm good at solving problems." "I learn quickly." When I say I'll do something, I do it." Be ready to illustrate each with a specific example of something you've done.

14. **What is your greatest weakness?**

    Use a work-related negative, even if something in your personal life really is your greatest weakness. Interviewers won't let you get away with a "weakness" like being a workaholic or just not having any experience yet. Instead, use one of the following strategies:

    a. Discuss a weakness that is not related to the job you're being considered for and will not be needed even when you're promoted. (Even if you won't work with people or give speeches in your first job, you'll need those skills later in your career, so don't use them for this question.) End your answer with a positive that *is* related to the job:

    > [For a creative job in advertising:] I don't like accounting. I know it's important, but I don't like it. I even hire someone to do my taxes. I'm much more interested in being creative and working with people, which is why I find this position interesting.

    b. Discuss a weakness that you are working to improve:

In the past, I wasn't a good writer. But last term I took a course in business writing that taught me how to organize my ideas and how to revise. I may never win a Pulitzer Prize, but now I'm a lot more confident that I can write effective reports and memos.

15.   **Why are you looking for another job?**

Stress what you're looking for in a new job, not why you want to get away from your old one.

If you were fired, say so. There are three acceptable ways to explain why you were fired:

a.   It wasn't a good match. Add what you now know you need in a job, and ask what the employer can offer in this area.

b.   You and your supervisor had a personality conflict. Make sure you show that this was an isolated incident, and that you normally get along well with people.

c.   You made mistakes, but you've learned from them and are now ready to work well. Be ready to offer a specific anecdote proving that you have indeed changed.

16.   **What questions do you have?**

This question gives you a chance to cover things the interviewer hasn't brought up; it also gives the interviewer a sense of your priorities and values. Don't focus on salary or fringe benefits. Better questions are

- What would I be doing on a day-to-day basis?
- What kind of training program do you have? If, as I'm rotating among departments, I find that I prefer one area, can I specialize in it when the training program is over?
- How do you evaluate employees? How often do you review them? Where would you expect a new trainee (banker, staff accountant) to be three years from now?
- What happened to the last person who had this job?
- How are interest rates (a new product from competitors, imports, demographic trends, government regulations, etc.) affecting your company?
- How would you describe the company's culture?
- This sounds like a great job. What are the drawbacks?

You won't be able to anticipate every question you may get. (One interviewer asked students, "What vegetable would you like to be?" Another asked, "If you were a cookie, what kind of cookie would you be?"[18]) Check with other people at your community college or university who have interviewed recently to find out what questions are being asked in your field.

Behavioural, Situational, and Stress Interviews

Many companies, dissatisfied with hires based on responses to traditional questions, are now using behavioural or situational interviews. **Behavioural interviews** ask the applicant to describe actual behaviours, rather than plans or general principles. Thus instead of asking "How would you motivate people?" the interviewer might ask, "Tell me what happened the last time you wanted to get other people to do something." Follow-up questions might include, "What exactly did you do to handle the situation? How did you feel about the results? How did the other people feel? How did your superior feel about the results?"

In your answer, describe the situation, tell what you did, and what happened. Think about the implications of what you did and be ready to talk about whether you'd do the same thing next time or if the situation were slightly different. For example, if you did the extra work yourself when a team member didn't do his or her share, does that fact suggest that you prefer to work alone? If the organization you're interviewing with values teams, you may want to go on to show why doing the extra work was appropriate in that situation but that you can respond differently in other situations.

Situational interviews put you in a situation that allows the interviewer to see whether you have the qualities the company is seeking.

Situational interviews may also be conducted using traditional questions but evaluating behaviours other than the answers. Greyhound hired applicants for its customer-assistance centre who made eye contact with the interviewer and smiled at least five times during a 15-minute interview.[19]

A **stress interview** deliberately puts the applicant under stress. If the stress is physical (for example, you're given a chair where the light is in your eyes), be assertive: move to another chair or tell the interviewer that the behaviour bothers you.

Usually the stress is psychological. A group of interviewers fire rapid questions. A single interviewer probes every weak spot in your record and asks questions that elicit negatives. If you get questions that put you on the defensive, *rephrase* them in less inflammatory terms, if necessary, and then *treat them as requests for information.*

Q: Why did you major in physical education? That sounds like a pretty Mickey Mouse major.

A: You're asking whether I have the academic preparation for this job. I started out in physical education because I've always loved sports. I learned that I couldn't graduate in four years if I officially switched my major to business administration because the requirements were different in the two programs. But I do have 21 hours in business administration and 9 hours in accounting. And my sports experience gives me practical training in teamwork, motivating people, and management.

Respond assertively. The candidates who survive are those who stand up for themselves and who explain why indeed they *are* worth hiring.

After the Interview

What you do after the interview can determine whether you get the job. One woman wanted to switch from banking, where she was working in corporate relations, to advertising. The ad agency interviewer expressed doubts about her qualifications. Immediately after leaving the agency, she tracked down a particular book the interviewer had mentioned he was looking for but had been unable to find. She presented it to him—and was hired.[20]

After a first interview, make follow-up phone calls to reinforce positives from the first interview, to overcome any negatives, and to get information you can use to persuade the interviewer to hire you.

A letter after an onsite visit (Figure 14.14) is essential to thank your hosts for their hospitality as well as to send in receipts for your expenses. The letter should

- Remind the interviewer of what he or she liked in you.
- Counter any negative impressions that may have come up at the interview.
- Use the jargon of the company and refer to specific things you learned during your interview or saw during your visit.
- Be enthusiastic.

FIGURE 14.14 Follow-up Letter after an Office Visit

405 West College, Apt. 201
Antigonish, NS B2G 1L3
April 2, 2005

*Single-space your address
when you don't use letterhead*

Mr. Robert Land, Account Manager
Sive Associates
378 Norman Boulevard
Montreal, QC H3B 4A3

Dear Mr. Land:

After visiting Sive Associates last week, I'm even more sure that writing direct mail is the career for me.

Refers to things she saw and learned during the interview

I've always been able to brainstorm ideas, but sometimes, when I had to focus on one idea for a class project, I wasn't sure which idea was best. It was fascinating to see how you make direct mail scientific as well as creative by testing each new creative package against the control. I can understand how pleased Linda Hayes was when she learned that her new package for *Canadian Art* beat the control.

Reminds interviewer of her strong points

Seeing Kelly, Luke, and Gene collaborating on the Sesame Street package gave me some sense of the tight deadlines you're under. As you know, I've learned to meet deadlines, not only for my class assignments, but also in working on the *Antigonish Review*. The award I won for my feature on the provincial election suggests that my quality holds up even when the deadline is tight!

Thank you for your hospitality while I was in Montreal. You and your wife made my stay very pleasant. I especially appreciate the time the two of you took to help me find information about apartments that are accessible to wheelchairs. Montreal seems like a very livable city.

I'm excited about a career in direct mail and about the (possibility) of joining Sive Associates. I look forward to hearing from you soon!

Be positive, not pushy. She doesn't assume she has the job.

Refers to what will happen next

Sincerely,

Gina Focasio

Gina Focasio
(902) 555-2948

Writer's phone number

Puts request for reimbursement in P.S. to de-emphasize it; focuses on the job, not the cost of the trip

P.S. My expenses totalled $454. Enclosed are receipts for my plane fare from Halifax to Montreal ($367), the taxi to the airport in Montreal ($30), and the bus from Antigonish to Halifax ($57).

Encl.: Receipts for Expenses

- Refer to the next move, whether you'll wait to hear from the employer or whether you want to call to learn about the status of your application.

  Be sure the letter is well written and error free.

Summary of Key Points

- Informal preparation for job hunting should start soon after you arrive on campus. Formal preparation for job hunting should begin a full year before you begin interviewing.
- Use directories, annual reports, recruiting literature, business periodicals, trade journals, and the Web to get information about employers and jobs to use in your letter.

■ Information and referral interviews can help you tap into the **hidden job market**—jobs that are not advertised.

■ Employers skim résumés to decide whom to interview. Employers assume that the letter and résumé represent your best work. Interviewers normally reread the résumé before the interview. After the search committee has chosen an applicant, it submits the résumé to people in the organization who must approve the appointment.

■ A résumé must fill at least one page. Use two pages if you have extensive activities and experience.

■ A **chronological résumé** summarizes what you did in a timeline (starting with the most recent events, and going backward in **reverse chronology**). It emphasizes degrees, job titles, and dates.

■ A **skills** or **functional résumé** emphasizes the skills you've developed and used, rather than the job in which or the date when you used them.

■ A **targeted résumé** highlights abilities and achievements that relate to a specific job target.

■ To create a scannable résumé, create a "plain vanilla" text using industry jargon, buzzwords, and acronyms.

■ Résumés differ from letters of application in the following ways:

■ A résumé is adapted to a position. The letter is adapted to the needs of a particular organization.

■ The résumé summarizes all your qualifications. The letter shows how your qualifications can help the organization meet its needs, how you differ from other applicants, and how much you know about the organization.

■ The résumé uses short, parallel phrases and sentence fragments. The letter uses complete sentences in well-written paragraphs.

■ When you know that a company is hiring, send a **solicited job letter.** When you want a job with a company that has not announced openings, send a **prospecting job letter.**

■ Develop an overall interview strategy based on your answers to these three questions:

1. What two to five facts about yourself do you want the interviewer to know?

2. What disadvantages or weaknesses do you need to overcome or minimize?

3. What do you need to know about the job and the organization to decide whether or not you want to accept this job if it is offered to you?

■ **Behavioural interviews** ask the applicant to describe actual behaviours, rather than plans or general principles. **Situational interviews** put you in a situation that allows the interviewer to see whether you have the qualities the company is seeking.

■ To answer a behavioural question, describe the situation, tell what you did, and what happened.

■ In a **stress interview,** the interviewer deliberately creates physical or psychological stress. Change the conditions that create physical stress. Meet psychological stress by rephrasing questions in less inflammatory terms and treating them as requests for information.

■ Use follow-up phone calls to reinforce positives from the first interview, to overcome any negatives, and to get information you can use to persuade the interviewer to hire you.

| CHAPTER 14 | Exercises and Problems |

Getting Started

14.1   Analyzing Your Accomplishments

List the 10 accomplishments that give you the most personal satisfaction. These could be things that other people wouldn't notice. They can be things you've done recently or things you did years ago.

Answer the following question for each accomplishment:

1. What skills or knowledge did you use?
2. What personal traits did you exhibit?
3. What about this accomplishment makes it personally satisfying to you?

As Your Professor Directs,

a. Share your answers with a small group of other students.
b. Summarize your answers in a memo to your professor.
c. Present your answers orally to the class.

14.2   Remembering What You've Done

Use the following list to jog your memory about what you've done. For each, give three or four details as well as a general statement.

Describe a time when you

1. Used facts and figures to gain agreement on an important point.
2. Identified a problem that a group or organization faced and developed a plan for solving the problem.
3. Made a presentation or a speech to a group.
4. Won the goodwill of people whose continued support was necessary for the success of some long-term project or activity.
5. Interested other people in something that was important to you and persuaded them to take the actions you wanted.
6. Helped a group deal constructively with conflict.
7. Demonstrated creativity.
8. Took a project from start to finish.
9. Created an opportunity for yourself in a job or volunteer position.
10. Used good judgment and logic in solving a problem.

As Your Professor Directs,

a. Identify which job(s) each detail is relevant for.
b. Identify which details would work well on a résumé.
c. Identify which details, further developed, would work well in a job letter.

14.3   Developing Action Statements

Use 10 of the verbs from Figure 14.4 on p. 361 to write action statements describing what you've done in paid or volunteer work, in classes, in extracurricular activities, or in community service.

14.4   Changing Verbs to Nouns

Revise the action statements you created for Problem 14.3, changing the verbs to nouns so that you could use the same information in a scannable résumé.

14.5   Evaluating Career Objective Statements

None of the following career objective statements is effective. What is wrong with each statement as it stands? Which statements could be revised to be satisfactory? Which should be dropped?

1. To use my acquired knowledge of accounting to eventually own my own business.

2. A progressively responsible position as a MARKETING MANAGER where education and ability would have valuable application and lead to advancement.

3. To work with people responsibly and creatively, helping them develop personal and professional skills.

4. A position in international marketing that makes use of my specialization in marketing and my knowledge of foreign markets.

14.6 Deciding How Much Detail to Use

In each of the following situations, how detailed should the applicant be? Why?

1. Ron Leung has been steadily employed for the last six years while getting his degree, but the jobs have been low-level ones, whose prime benefit was that they paid well and fit around his class schedule.

2. Adrienne Barcus was an assistant department manager at a clothing boutique. As assistant manager, she was authorized to approve cheques in the absence of the manager. Her other duties were ringing up sales, cleaning the area, and helping mark items for sales.

3. Lois Heilman has been a clerk-typist in the Alumni Office. As part of her job, she developed a schedule for mailings to alumni, set up a merge system, and wrote two of the letters that go out to alumni. The merge system she set up has halved the time needed to produce letters.

4. As a co-op student, Stanley Greene spends every other term in a paid job. He now has six terms of job experience in television broadcasting. During his last co-op he was the assistant producer for a daily "morning magazine" show.

Résumé Assignments

For problems 14.7 and 14.8, write the kind of résumé (chronological, skills, functional, targeted, or a new creation) that best represents your qualifications.

14.7 Writing a Paper Résumé

Write a résumé on paper that you could mail to an employer or hand to an interviewer at an interview.

As Your Professor Directs,

a. Write a résumé for the field in which you hope to find a job.

b. Write two different résumés for two different job paths you are interested in pursuing.

c. Adapt your résumé to a specific company you hope to work for.

14.8 Writing a Scannable Résumé

Take the résumé you like best from problem 14.14, and create a scannable version of it.

E-Mail and Letter Assignments

14.9 Writing a Solicited Letter

Write a letter of application in response to an announced opening for a full-time job (not an internship) that a new graduate could hold.

Turn in a copy of the listing. If you use option (a), (b), or (d) below, your listing will be a copy. If you choose option (c), you will write the listing and can design your ideal job.

a. Respond to an ad in a newspaper, in a professional journal, in the placement office, or on the Web. Use an ad that specifies the company, not a blind ad. Be sure that you are fully qualified for the job.

b. Take a job description and assume that it represents a current opening. Use a directory to get the name of the person to whom the letter should be addressed.

c. If you have already worked somewhere, you may assume that your employer is asking you to apply for full-time work after graduation. Be sure to write a fully persuasive letter.

d. Respond to one of the listings below. Use a directory to get the name and address of the person to whom you should write.

1. Enterprise Rent-A-Car has an immediate opening for an entry-level **staff accountant.** Responsibilities will include but are not limited to A/P, A/R, Bank Recs, and journal entries. To qualify you must possess a four-year accounting degree, strong written and oral skills, and a strong desire to succeed.

2. KPMG seeks **international human resources trainees** to interact with corporate human resources, expatriates, payroll, relocation, and accounting functions. Bachelor's degree in an international field a plus. Personal expatriate experience preferred but not required. Must have computer skills. Please refer to job number MMGE-3W7LAY in your correspondence.

3. Roxy Systems (Roxy.com) seeks **Internet Marketing Coordinators** to analyze online campaigns and put together detailed reports, covering ad impressions and click-through rates. Must have basic understanding of marketing; be organized, creative, and detail oriented; know Microsoft Excel; have excellent communication skills; and be familiar with the Internet. Send letter and resume to mike@roxy.com.

4. Bose Corporation seeks **public relations/communications administrative associate** (Job Code 117BD). Write, edit, and produce the in-house newsletter using desktop publishing software. Represent the company to external contacts (including the press). Provide administrative support to the manager of PR by scheduling meetings, preparing presentations, tabulating and analyzing surveys, and processing financial requests. Excellent organizational, interpersonal, and communication skills (both written and oral) required. Must be proficient in MS Office and Filemaker Pro.

5. The Limited is hiring **executive development program trainees.** After completing 10-week training programs, trainees will become assistant buyers. Prefer people with strong interest and experience in retailing. Apply directly to the store for which you want to work.

6. A local non-profit organization seeks a **Coordinator of Volunteer Services.** Responsibilities for this full-time position include coordinating volunteers' schedules, recruiting and training new volunteers, and evaluating existing programs. Excellent listening and communication skills required.

7. Your province wants **assistant international trade managers** for offices in London, Paris, Tokyo, Hong Kong, and Buenos Aires. Duties include promoting provincial exports, promoting the province as a site for foreign business investment and branch plants, and representing the province to government officials. Candidate should know language and culture of target country.

8. Ogilvie & Mather is hiring **assistant account executives.** You will be assigned to a major client account, and will help develop strategies for marketing and advertising, with specific assignments in one of the following: creative, media, research, or production.

14.10   Analyzing First Paragraphs of Prospecting Letters

All of the following are first paragraphs in prospecting letters written by new college graduates. Evaluate the paragraphs on these criteria:

■ Is the paragraph likely to interest the reader and motivate him or her to read the rest of the letter?

■ Does the paragraph have some content that the student can use to create a transition to talking about his or her qualifications?

■ Does the paragraph avoid asking for a job?

1. For the past two and one-half years I have been studying turf management. On August 1, I will graduate from _____ University with a BA in Ornamental Horticulture. The type of job I will seek will deal with golf course maintenance as an assistant superintendent.

2. Ann Gibbs suggested that I contact you.

3. Whether to plate a two-inch eyebolt with cadmium for a tough, brilliant shine or with zinc for a rust-resistant, less expensive finish is a tough question. But similar questions must be answered daily by your salespeople. With my experience in the electroplating industry, I can contribute greatly to your constant need of getting customers.

4. What a set of tractors! The new 9430 and 9630 diesels are just what is needed by today's farmer with his ever-increasing acreage. John Deere has truly done it again.

5. Prudential Insurance Company did much to help my academic career as the sponsor of my National Merit Scholarship. Now I think I can give something back to Prudential. I'd like to put my education, including a B.Comm. degree in finance from _____ University, to work in your investment department.

6. Since the beginning of Delta Electric Construction Co. in 1993, the size and profits have grown steadily.

My father, being a stockholder and vice-president, often discusses company dealings with me. Although the company has prospered, I understand there have been a few problems of mismanagement. I feel with my present and future qualifications, I could help ease these problems.

14.11   Improving You-Attitude and Positive Emphasis in Job Letters

Revise each of these sentences to improve you-attitude and positive emphasis. You may need to add information.

1. I understand that your company has had problems due to the mistranslation of documents during international ad campaigns.

2. Included in my résumé are the courses in Finance that earned me a fairly attractive grade average.

3. I am looking for a position that gives me a chance to advance quickly.

4. Although short on experience, I am long on effort and enthusiasm.

5. I have been with the company from its beginning to its present unfortunate state of bankruptcy.

14.12   Evaluating Rough Drafts

Evaluate the following drafts. What parts should be omitted? What needs to be changed or added? What parts would benefit from specific supporting details?

1.

Dear _____:

There is more to a buyer's job than buying the merchandise. And a clothing buyer in particular has much to consider.

Even though something may be in style, customers may not want to buy it. Buyers should therefore be aware of what customers want and how much they are willing to pay.

In the buying field, request letters, thank-you letters, and persuasive letters are frequently written.

My interest in the retail field inspired me to read The Gap's annual report. I saw that a new store is being built. An interview would give us a chance to discuss how I could contribute to this new store. Please call me to schedule an interview.

Sincerely,

2.

Dear Sir or Madam:

I am taking the direct approach of a personnel letter. I believe you will under stand my true value in the areas of practical knowledge and promotional capabilities.

I am interested in a staff position with Darden in relation to trying to improve the operations and moral of the Olive Garden Restaurants, which I think that I am capable of doing. Please take a minute not to read my résumé (enclosed) and call to schedule an interview.

Sincerely,

3.

> Dear _____:
>
> I would like to apply for the opening you announced for an Assistant Golf Course Superintendent. I have the qualifications you are asking for.
>
> Every year the Superintendent must go before the greens committee to defend its budget requests. To prepare myself to do this, I took courses in accounting, business and administrative writing, and speech.
>
> I have done the operations necessary to maintain the greens properly.
>
> I look forward to talking with you about this position.
>
> Sincerely,

Interview Assignments

14.13   Gathering Information about an Industry

Use six recent issues of a trade journal to report on three to five trends, developments, or issues that are important in an industry.

As Your Profesor Directs,

a. Share your findings with a small group of other students.

b. Summarize your findings in a memo to your professor.

c. Present your findings to the class.

d. Join with a small group of other students to write a report summarizing the results of this research.

14.14   Gathering Information about a Specific Organization

Gather information about a specific organization, using several of the following methods:

- Check the organization's Web site.
- Read the company's annual report.
- Pick up relevant information at the Chamber of Commerce.
- Read articles in trade publications and *The Globe and Mail* or *National Post* that mention the organization (check the indexes).
- Get the names and addresses of its officers from a directory or the Web.

- Read recruiting literature provided by the company.

As Your Professor Directs,

a. Share your findings with a small group of other students.

b. Summarize your findings in a memo to your professor.

c. Present your findings orally to the class.

d. Write a paragraph for a job letter using (directly or indirectly) the information you found.

14.15   Preparing an Interview Strategy

Based on your analysis in problems 14.1 and 14.2, prepare an interview strategy.

1. List two to five things about yourself that you want the interviewer to know before you leave the interview.

2. Identify any weaknesses or apparent weaknesses in your record and plan ways to explain them or minimize them.

3. List the points you need to learn about an employer to decide whether to accept an office visit or plant trip.

As Your Professor Directs,

a. Share your strategy with a small group of other students.

b. Describe your strategy in a memo to your professor.

c. Present your strategy orally to the class.

14.16 Preparing Answers to Questions You May Be Asked

Prepare answers to 10 of the interview questions listed in this chapter and to any other questions that you know are likely to be asked of job hunters in your field or on your campus.

As Your Professor Directs,

a. Write down the answers to your questions and turn them in.

b. Conduct mini-interviews in a small group of students. In the group, let student A be the interviewer and ask five questions from the list. Student B will play the job candidate and answer the questions, using real information about student B's field and qualifications. Student C will evaluate the content of the answer. Student D will observe the non-verbal behaviour of the interviewer (A); student E will observe the non-verbal behaviour of the interviewee (B).

After the mini-interview, let students C, D, and E share their observations and recommend ways that B could be even more effective. Then switch roles. Let another student be the interviewer and ask five questions of another interviewee, while new observers note content and non-verbal behaviour. Continue the process until everyone in the group has had a chance to be "interviewed."

c. Assume that you are an independent behavioural psychologist hired to conduct screening interviews and interview yourself (silently, if you like). Then write a report to the organization considering the applicant, identifying each strength, weakness, and other characteristics. Support each claim with one or more behavioural examples. Write about yourself in the third person.

(Option c based on a problem written by William J. Allen, University of La Verne and University of Phoenix.)

A Designing Documents, Slides, and Screens

AN INSIDE PERSPECTIVE

Designing Documents, Slides, and Screens

Good document design focuses on the reader. Imagine a particular reader trying to do something with your document. Document design is not about decoration but rather about guiding the reader through a task.

To test a document, ask people to do something with it, such as fill out a form. Ask them how well it worked; they'll tell you what they understand and what they don't. Observe them; they'll show you when the instructions are unclear or when they can't find the right information.

Good document design is good business. Good design saves money by preventing errors and reducing the number of phone calls from customers who don't understand what they're supposed to do. Employees can be freed up to do other work—including providing better customer service. Good design shows customers that you care about their time and want to make tasks easier for them. Isn't that the best marketing a company can have?

John Paul Luisi, owner of Lulu Digital Design (http://www.luludigital.com) in Vaughan, Ontario, specializes in Web site design. To help his clients stand out in a crowded digital world, he gives each site a unique look. He takes as much care when he donates his design skills, matching his business with the right charity, whether it is the Gift of Life Walk for Leukemia, or Friends of Ferrari raising funds for the Alzheimer Society, Hospice Vaughan, or the Shining Through Centre for Children with Autism.

Standards continue to evolve for online documents. The Nielsen Norman Group, founded by two pioneers of usability (Donald Norman and Jakob Nielsen), offers advice on what works and what online documents should be able to achieve. You can find their Web site at www.useit.com. Then, for great examples of what doesn't work and a somewhat irreverent approach, look at www.webpagesthatsuck.com.

Good document design saves time and money, reduces legal problems, and builds goodwill. A well-designed document looks inviting, friendly, and easy to read. Effective design also groups ideas visually, making the structure of the document more obvious so the document *is* easier to read. Research shows that easy-to-read documents also enhance your credibility and build an image of you as a professional, competent person.[1] Good design is as important for short as for long documents: reports, Web pages, and newsletters as well as announcements and one-page letters and memos.

The Importance of Effective Design

When document design is poor, both organizations and society suffer.

The nuclear accident at Three Mile Island could have been prevented if safety guidelines recommended 17 months before the accident had been implemented.[2] But none of the 12 people who received the memo responded. The memo was ignored because the subject line was vague, the writing was ineffective, and the recommendations were on the second page. The *Challenger* space shuttle blew up because its O-rings failed in the excessive cold. Poor communication—including charts that hid, rather than emphasized, the data—contributed to the decision to launch. In 2000, the badly designed "butterfly ballot" confused enough voters to change the outcome of the U.S. presidential election.[3]

Design as Part of Your Writing Process(es)

Design isn't something to "tack on" when you've finished writing. Indeed, the best documents, slides, and screens are created when you think about design at each stage of your writing process(es).

- As you plan, think about your audience. Are they skilled readers? Are they busy? Will they read the document straight through or skip around in it?
- As you write, incorporate lists and headings. Use visuals to convey numerical data clearly and forcefully (← Chapter 12).
- Get feedback from people who will be using your document. What parts of the document do they find hard to understand? Do they need more information?
- As you revise, check your draft against the guidelines in this chapter.

Guidelines for Page Design

Use the eight guidelines in Figure A.1 to create visually attractive documents.

White space—the empty space on the page—makes material easier to read by emphasizing the material that it separates from the rest of the text. To create white space,

- Use headings.
- Use a mix of paragraph lengths (most no longer than seven typed lines). It's OK for a paragraph to be just one sentence. First and last paragraphs, in particular, should be short.
- Use lists.
  - Use tabs or indents—not spacing—to align items vertically.
  - Use numbered lists when the number or sequence of items is exact.
  - Use **bullets** (large dots or squares like those in this list) when the number and sequence don't matter.

Good Document Design Saves Money*

- Rewriting its policy and procedure manuals saved FedEx $400,000 in the first year in increased productivity. More searches for information were successful, and more of them could be completed in less than three minutes.

- A Sabre computer reservation manual was cut from 100 pages to 20, saving $19,000 just in producing the document.

- Improving its documentation for its products saved Fisher Controls more than $100,000 and enabled the company to ship a major new product three months early.

*Based on Jay Mead, "Measuring the Value Added for Technical Documentation: A Review of Research and Practice," *Technical Communication* 45, no. 3 (August 1998): 353–379.

FIGURE A.1   Guidelines for Page Design

1. Use white space to separate and emphasize points.
2. Use headings to group points and lead the reader through the document.
3. Limit the use of words set in all capital letters.
4. Use no more than two fonts in a single document.
5. Decide whether to justify margins based on the situation and the audience.
6. Put important elements in the top left and lower right quadrants of the page.
7. Use a grid of imaginary columns to unify visuals and other elements in a document.
8. Use highlighting, decorative devices, and colour in moderation.

When you use a list, make sure that all of the items in it are parallel (◀ p. 97) and fit into the structure of the sentence that introduces the list.

Faulty:	The following suggestions can help employers avoid bias in job interviews: 1. Base questions on the job description. 2. Questioning techniques. 3. Selection and training of interviewers.
Parallel:	The following suggestions can help employers avoid bias in job interviews: 1. Base questions on the job description. 2. Ask the same questions of all applicants. 3. Select and train interviewers carefully.
Also parallel:	Employers can avoid bias in job interviews by 1. Basing questions on the job description. 2. Asking the same questions of all applicants. 3. Selecting and training interviewers carefully.

Figure A.2 shows an original typed document. In Figure A.3, the same document has been improved by using shorter paragraphs, lists, and headings. These devices take space. When saving space is essential, it's better to cut the text and keep white space and headings. To see how to set up subheadings, see Figure 12.3 in Chapter 12, p. 294.

As George Miller has shown, our short-term memories can hold only seven plus or minus two bits of information.[4] Only after those bits are processed and put into long-term memory can we assimilate new information. Large amounts of information will be easier to process if they are grouped into three to seven chunks rather than presented as individual items.

Headings are words, short phrases, or short sentences that group points and divide your document into sections. Headings enable your reader to see at a glance how the document is organized, to turn quickly to sections of special interest, and to compare and contrast points more easily. Headings also break up the page, making it look less formidable and more interesting.

- Make headings specific.
- Make each heading cover all the material until the next heading.
- Keep headings at any one level parallel: all nouns, all complete sentences, or all questions.

Headings may be functional (or generic) or informative (or talking) heads. Functional headings (*Background, Budget, Recommendations*) describe general topics or functions; informative headings (*Employee Survey Supports New E-Mail Policy*) add information and interest. Functional headings make good sense in regular or routine reports (trip or progress, for instance) and in defusing

FIGURE A.2   A Document with Poor Visual Impact

Full capital letters make title hard to read

MONEY DEDUCTED FROM YOUR WAGES TO PAY CREDITORS

When you buy goods on credit, the store will sometimes ask you to sign a Wage Assignment form allowing it to deduct money from your wages if you do not pay your bill. When you buy on credit, you sign a contract agreeing to pay a certain amount each week or month until you have paid all you owe. The Wage Assignment Form is separate. It must contain the name of your present employer, your social insurance number, the amount of money loaned, the rate of interest, the date when payments are due, and your signature. The words "Wage Assignment" must be printed at the top of the form and also near the line for your signature. Even if you have signed a Wage Assignment agreement, Roysner will not withhold part of your wages unless all of the following conditions are met: 1. You have to be more than forty days late in payment of what you owe; 2. Roysner has to receive a correct statement of the amount you are in default and a copy of the Wage Assignment form; and 3. You and Roysner must receive a notice from the creditor at least twenty days in advance stating that the creditor plans to make a demand on your wages. This twenty-day notice gives you a chance to correct the problems yourself. If these conditions are all met, Roysner must withhold 15% of each paycheque until your bill is paid and give this money to your creditor.

Long paragraph is visually uninviting

If you think you are not late or that you do not owe the amount stated, you can argue against it by filing a legal document called a "defence." Once you file a defence, Roysner will not withhold any money from you. However, be sure you are right before you file a defence. If you are wrong, you have to pay not only what you owe but also all legal costs for both yourself and the creditor. If you are right, the creditor has to pay all these costs.

Important information is hard to find

emotions in response to documents addressing sensitive issues. Informative headings can help readers think about issues when they are clear and concrete. Vagueness (*Moving Forward in a New Era*) will do little to conjure images and clarify emphases.

In a letter or memo, type main headings even with the left-hand margin in bold. Capitalize the first letters of the first word and of other major words; use lowercase for all other letters. (See Figure A.3 for an example.) In single-spaced text, triple-space between the previous text and the heading; double-space between the heading and the text that follows.

If you need subdivisions within a head, use bold type and put a period after the subhead. Begin the paragraph on the same line. Use subheadings only when you have at least two subdivisions under a given main heading.

In a report, you may need more than two levels of headings. ◄▥ Figure 12.3 in Chapter 12, p. 294, shows levels of headings for reports.

We recognize words by their shapes.[5] (See Figure A.4.) In **capitals**, all words are rectangular; letters lose the descenders and ascenders that make reading go 19% more quickly.[6] Use full capitals sparingly.

Fonts are unified styles of type. Each font comes in several sizes and usually in several styles (bold, italic, etc.). Typewriter fonts are **fixed;** that is, every letter takes the same space. An *i* takes the same space as a *w*. Courier and Prestige Elite are fixed fonts. Computers usually offer **proportional** fonts as well, where wider letters take more space than narrower letters. Times Roman, Palatino, Helvetica, and Arial are proportional fonts.

Serif fonts have little extensions, called serifs, from the main strokes. (In Figure A.5, look at the feet on the *r*'s in New Courier and the flick on the top of the *d* in Lucinda.) New Courier, Elite, Times Roman, Palatino, and Lucinda

FIGURE A.3   A Document Revised to Improve Visual Impact

**Money Deducted from Your Wages
to Pay Creditors**

First letter of each main word capitalized— Title split onto two lines

When you buy goods on credit, the store will sometimes ask you to sign a Wage Assignment form allowing it to deduct money from your wages if you do not pay your bill.

Have You Signed a Wage Assignment Form?

Headings divide document into chunks

When you buy on credit, you sign a contract agreeing to pay a certain amount each week or month until you have paid all you owe. The Wage Assignment Form is separate. It must contain

- The name of your present employer
- Your social insurance number
- The amount of money loaned
- The rate of interest
- The date when payments are due
- Your signature

List with bullets where order of items doesn't matter

Single-space list when items are short

The words "Wage Assignment" must be printed at the top of the form and also near the line for your signature.

When Would Money Be Deducted from Your Wages to Pay a Creditor?

Headings must be parallel; here all are questions

Even if you have signed a Wage Assignment agreement, Roysner will not withhold part of your wages unless all of the following conditions are met:

White space between items emphasizes them

1. You have to be more than 40 days late in payment of what you owe;

2. Roysner has to receive a correct statement of the amount you are in default and a copy of the Wage Assignment form; and

Double space between items in list when most items are two lines or longer

Numbered list where number, order of items matter

3. You and Roysner must receive a notice from the creditor at least 20 days in advance stating that the creditor plans to make a demand on your wages. This 20-day notice gives you a chance to correct the problem yourself.

If these conditions are all met, Roysner must withhold fifteen percent (15%) of each pay-cheque until your bill is paid and give this money to your creditor.

What Should You Do If You Think the Wage Assignment Is Incorrect?

If you think you are not late or that you do not owe the amount stated, you can argue against it by filing a legal document called a "defence." Once you file a defence, Roysner will not withhold any money from you. However, be sure you are right before you file a defence. If you are wrong, you have to pay not only what you owe but also all legal costs for both yourself and the creditor. If you are right, the creditor has to pay all these costs.

Calligraphy are serif fonts. Serif fonts are easier to read since the serifs help the eyes move from letter to letter. Helvetica, Arial, Geneva, and Technical are **sans serif** fonts since they lack serifs (*sans* is French for *without*). Sans serif fonts are good for titles and tables.

Most business documents use just one font—usually Times Roman, Palatino, Helvetica, or Arial. You can create emphasis and levels of headings by using bold, italics, and different sizes. Bold is easier to read than italics, so use bolding if you need only one method to emphasize text. In a complex document, use bigger type for main headings and slightly smaller type for subheadings and text. If you combine two fonts in one document, choose one serif and one sans serif typeface.

FIGURE A.4   Full Capitals Hide the Shape of a Word

Full | capitals | hide | the | shape | of | a | word | and | slow | reading | 19% .

FULL | CAPITALS | HIDE | THE | SHAPE | OF | A | WORD | AND | SLOW | READING | 19% .

FIGURE A.5   Examples of Different Fonts

This sentence is set in 12-point Times Roman.

This sentence is set in 12-point Arial.

This sentence is set in 12-point New Courier.

This sentence is set in 12-point Lucinda Calligraphy.

This sentence is set in 12-point Broadway.

This sentence is set in 12-point Technical.

Eleven-point Times Roman is ideal for letters, memos, and reports. Twelve-point type is acceptable, especially for mature readers. Use 9- or 10-point type to get the effect of a printed book or brochure.

If your material will not fit in the available pages, cut one more time. Putting some sections in tiny type will save space but creates a negative response— a negative response that may extend to the organization that produced the document.

Computers often allow you to use **full justification** so that type on both sides of the page is evenly lined up. The paragraph above justifies margins. Margins justified only on the left are sometimes called **ragged right margins.** Lines end in different places because words are of different lengths. The sidebar columns in this book use ragged right margins.

Use full justification when you

- Can use proportional fonts
- Want a more formal look
- Want to use as few pages as possible
- Write to skilled readers[7]

Use ragged right margins when you

- Cannot use a proportional font
- Want an informal look
- Want to be able to revise an individual page without reprinting the whole document
- Use very short line lengths
- Write to poor readers

Readers of English start in the upper left-hand corner of the page and read to the right and down. The eye moves in a Z pattern.[8] (See Figure A.6.) Therefore, as Philip M. Rubens notes, the four quadrants of the page carry different

InSite

www.infomap.com/method/method.htm

Information Mapping uses grids and tables to present complex information in an easy-to-find format.

Cultural Differences in Document Design*

Cultural differences in document design are based on reading practices and experiences with other documents. For example, one laundry detergent company printed ads in the Middle East showing soiled clothes on the left, its box of soap in the middle, and clean clothes on the right. But, because people in that part of the world read not from left to right but from right to left, many people thought the ads meant that the soap actually soiled the clothes.

People in Canada focus first on the left side of a Web site. However, Middle Eastern people focus first on the right side. Web sites in Arabic and Hebrew orient text, links, and graphics from right to left.

*Based on David A. Ricks, *Blunders in International Business* (Cambridge, MA: Blackwell, 1993), 53; and Albert N. Badre, "The Effects of Cross Cultural Interface Design Orientation on World Wide Web User Performance," GVU Technical Report GIT-GVU-01-03, August 31, 2000, 8, retrieved September 1, 2001, from http://www.cc.gatech.edu/gvu/reports/2001.

FIGURE A.6   Put Important Elements in the Top Left and Bottom Right Quadrants

Eye movement on the page

Start

Stop

Scarlet quadrants are most important

Source: Based on Russel N. Baird, Arthur T. Turnbull, and Duncan McDonald, *The Graphics of Communication: Typography, Layout, Design, Production,* 5th ed. (New York: Holt, Rinehart, and Winston, 1987), 37.

visual weights. The top left quadrant, where the eye starts, is the most important; the bottom right quadrant, where the eye ends, is next most important.[9] Titles should always start in the top left; reply coupons or another important elements should be in the bottom right.

For years, graphic designers have used a **grid system** to design pages. In its simplest form, a grid imposes two or three imaginary columns on the page. In more complex grids, these columns can be further subdivided. Then all the graphic elements—text indentations, headings, visuals, and so on—are lined up within the columns. The resulting symmetry creates a more pleasing page[10] and unifies long documents.

Figure A.7 uses grids to organize a page with visuals and a résumé.

Many word processing programs have arrows, pointing fingers, and a host of other **dingbats** that you can insert. Clip art packages and presentation soft-

FIGURE A.7   Examples of Grids to Design Pages

Three-column grid.   Six-column grid.   Twelve-column grid.

ware allow you to insert more and larger images into your text. The revised Ford warranty booklet design uses icons as well as better page design. (See Figure A.8.) Used in moderation, highlighting and decorative devices make pages more interesting. However, don't overdo them. A page or screen that uses every possible highlighting device just looks busy and hard to read.

Colour works well to highlight points. Use colour for overviews and main headings, not for small points. Blue, green, or violet type is most legible for younger readers, but perception of blue diminishes for readers over 50.[11] Red is appropriate for warnings in North America. Since the connotations of colours vary among cultures, check ◄▥ Chapter 9 before you use colour with international or multicultural audiences.

When you use colour,

- Use glossy paper to make colours more vivid.
- Be aware that colours on a computer screen always look brighter than the same colours on paper because the screen sends out light.

Designing Presentation Slides

As you design slides for PowerPoint and other presentation programs, keep the following guidelines in mind:

- Use a big font size: 44 or 50 point for titles, 32 point for subheads, and 28 point for examples.
- Use bullet-point phrases rather than complete sentences.
- Use clear, concise language.

FIGURE A.8   "Before" and "After" Pages from Ford's Warranty Booklet

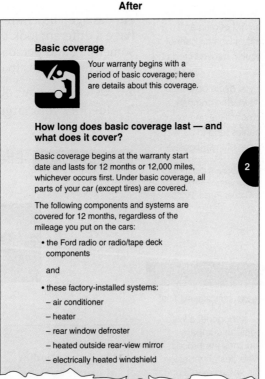

Source: Lee L. Gray, "Ford Offers a Readable Warranty Booklet," *Simply Stated … in Business*, no. 18 (March 1987): 12.

Say It with Colour*

In *Bulletproof Presentations*, consultant G. Michael Campbell says colour is a useful tool for coding information and affecting the reader's reaction. Here are some of his ideas for using colour:

- Identify ideas according to common associations with colour—red for stop or danger, green for go or money.

- Use distinctive colours when you need to refer to something: "In the graph, the green bar shows how much our water quality has improved since [Councillor] Jones took office."

- Match colours to the moods they tend to evoke. Red demands attention (but is easy to overuse); yellow is cheery. Blue and green tend to have a calming effect.

- Avoid colour combinations that would confuse people who are colourblind. About 10 percent of men and 0.5 percent of women cannot distinguish between red and green.

- When you use a corporate logo, follow the company's colour specifications exactly. Companies tend to be very protective of their logos.

*Based on G. Michael Campbell, *Bulletproof Presentations* (Franklin Lakes, NJ: Career Press, 2002), 190–193.

InSite

www.xenogene.com/xclients.html

Xenogene, a Web design company, outlines the process of Web design/redesign. Thumbnails show sample end products.

- Make only three to five points on each slide. If you have more, consider using two slides.
- Customize your slides with the company logo, charts, downloaded Web pages, and scanned-in photos and drawings.
- Use animation to make words and images appear and move during your presentation—but only in ways that help you control information flow and build interest. Avoid using animation just to be clever; it will distract your audience.

Use clip art only if the art is really appropriate to your points and only if you use non-sexist and non-racist images. In the 1990s, Marilyn Dyrud found the major clip art packages to be biased. Today, however, Internet sources have made such a wide variety of drawings and photos available that designers really have no excuse for failing to pick an inclusive and visually appealing image. Even organizations on tight budgets can find free public domain (not copyrighted) and low-cost resources.[12]

Choose a consistent template, or background design, for the entire presentation. Make sure that the template is appropriate for your subject matter. For example, use a globe only if your topic is international business and palm trees only if you're talking about tropical vacations. One problem with PowerPoint is that the basic templates may seem repetitive to people who see lots of presentations made with the program. For a very important presentation, you may want to consider customizing the basic template.

Choose a light background if the lights will be off during the presentation and a dark background if the lights will be on. Slides will be easier to read if you use high contrast between the words and backgrounds. See Figure A.9 for examples of effective and ineffective colour combinations.

Designing Brochures

To design brochures and newsletters, first think about audience and purpose. An "image" brochure designed to promote awareness of your company will have a different look than an "information" brochure telling people how to do something and persuading them to do it.

Use this process to create effective brochures.

1. Determine your objective(s).
2. Identify your target audience(s).

FIGURE A.9   Effective and Ineffective Colours for Presentation Slides

Effective

Use high contrast between words and background.

Repeat colours in words and design elements.

Ineffective

Limit the number of bright colours.

Dark colours disappear against a dark background.

Light colours disappear against a light background.

3. Identify a *central selling point*: one overarching reader benefit the audience will get.

4. Choose the image you want to project. (Clean and clear? Postmodern and trendy? Or what?)

5. Identify objections and brainstorm ways to deal with them (◀ Chapter 7).

6. When text is important, draft text to see how much room you need. Do tighten your writing (◀ Chapter 4). But when you really need more room, use a bigger brochure layout or a series of brochures.

7. Experiment with different sizes of paper and layout. Consider how readers will get the brochure—must it fit in a standard rack? Use thumbnail sketches to test layouts.

8. Make every choice—colour, font, layout, paper—a conscious one. The three-fold brochure shown in Figure A.10 is the most common, but many other arrangements are possible.

9. Polish the prose and graphics. Use you-attitude and positive emphasis.

Follow these design principles:

■ Use the cover effectively.

   ■ Put your central selling point on the cover.

   ■ Use a photo that tells a story. Remember that the photo has to work for the audience. A photo of a campus landmark may not mean much to an audience thinking about attending a summer program on campus.

■ Use a grid to align the elements within the panels. Make sure that the Z pattern emphasizes important points for each spread the reader sees. In a three-fold brochure, the Z pattern needs to work for the cover alone, for inside pages 1 and 2 (as the reader begins to unfold the brochure), and for inside pages 1, 3, and 4 (when the brochure is fully opened).

Making Your Web Page Accessible

Users with hearing impairments need captions for audio material on the Web.

Blind users need words, not images. Words can be voiced by a screen reader or translated into Braille text. Canadian screen reader programs go from left to right, then down line by line. Keystrokes can let users skip to a specific letter in a list. To make your Web page accessible for people with vision impairments,

■ Put a link to a text-only version of the site in the upper-left-hand corner.

■ Put navigation links, a site map, and search box at the top of the screen, preferably in the upper-left-hand corner.

■ Arrange navigation links alphabetically so that blind users can jump to the links they want.

■ Provide alternative text (an "Alt tag") for all images, applets, and submit buttons.

■ Provide a static alternative to flash or animation.

FIGURE A.10   Three-Fold Brochure on 8½-by-11-inch (22 × 28 cm) Paper

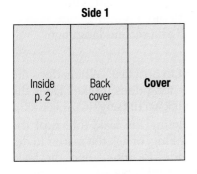
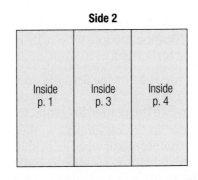
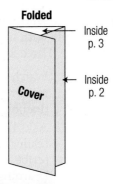

Well-Designed Web Sites Keep Customers*

Imagine going to a supermarket where three-fourths of the customers abandon their carts half full in the aisles because they are so frustrated they decide to shop somewhere else. It would be a lot like shopping online.

In a recent poll, almost half the online retailers said they don't know what percentage of their customers abandon shopping carts. Among the rest, 87 percent reported abandonment rates above 20 percent. Because the Internet makes it easy for shoppers to go to other sites, Jakob Nielsen says, "People don't have to use bad sites."

What keeps online shoppers happy? Other polls ask customers what they look for when they shop on the Internet. Recent answers indicate they want pages that load quickly and make it easy to find what they want. They like basics such as search tools and clear labels. Few online shoppers care about bells and whistles like personalized recommendations.

*Based on Robyn Greenspan, "E-Commerce Mainstream, Measurements Lacking," ClickZ Internet Marketing Statistics, April 9, 2004, downloaded at http://www.clickz.com; ClickZ Stats staff and Sharon Gaudin, "Personalization Not the Secret to E-Commerce," ClickZ Internet Marketing Statistics, November 14, 2003, downloaded at http://www.clickz.com; David Neal, "Interview: Good Design Pays Off," IT Week, May 19, 2003, downloaded at http://www.itweek.co.uk/articles/print/2086589; Reid Goldsborough, "Substance, Not Style, Draws Hits," Philadelphia Inquirer, May 20, 2004, downloaded at http://www.philly.com.

- Effective brochures not only repeat graphic elements (headings, small photos) across panels to create a unified look but also contain contrast (between text and images, and between a larger font for headings and a smaller one for text).
- Use colour effectively.
  - Restraint usually works best for informative brochures. To get the effect of colour with the least expense, use black print on coloured paper.
  - If you use four-colour printing, use glossy paper.
  - Readers over 50 may have trouble reading text in some shades of blue.
- Make the text visually appealing.
  - Use no more than two fonts—just one may be better.
  - Use proportional fonts.
  - Avoid italic type and underlining, which make text hard to read. To emphasize text, use bold (sparingly).
  - Most brochures use 8-, 9-, or 10-point type. Use 10-point rather than 8-point for readers over 40.
  - Use small tab indents.
  - Make sure that you have enough white space in your copy. Use lists and headings. Use short paragraphs with extra space between paragraphs.
  - Ragged right margins generally work better with short line lengths.
- If you use a reply coupon, make sure its back side doesn't have crucial information the reader needs to keep.

To make the brochure worth keeping, provide useful information. Make the text candid, believable, and human.

Testing the Design for Usability

A design that looks pretty may or may not work for the audience. To know whether your design is functional, test it with your audience.

Testing a draft with five users will reveal 85% of the problems with the document.[13] If time and money permit additional testing, revise the document and test the new version with another five users. Test the document with the people who are most likely to have trouble with it: very old or young readers, people with little education, people who read English as a second language.

Three kinds of tests yield useful information:

- Watch someone as he or she uses the document to do a task. Where does the reader pause, reread, or seem confused? How long does it take? Does the document enable the reader to complete the task accurately?
- Ask the reader to "think aloud" while completing the task, interrupt the reader at key points to ask what he or she is thinking, or ask the reader to describe the thought process after completing the document and the task. Learning the reader's thought processes is important, since a reader may get the right answer for the wrong reasons. In such a case, the design still needs work.
- Ask readers to put a plus sign (+) in the margins by any part of the document they like or agree with, and a minus sign (−) by any part of the document that seems confusing or wrong. Then use interviews or focus groups to find out the reasons for the plus and minus judgments.

Summary of Key Points

- An attractive document looks inviting, friendly, and easy to read. The visual grouping of ideas also makes the structure of the document more obvious so it is easier to read.
- Good document design can save time and money, and can prevent legal problems.
- The best documents are created when you think about design at each stage of the writing process.
    - As you plan, think about the needs of your audience.
    - As you write, incorporate lists, headings, and visuals.
    - Get feedback from people who will be using your document.
    - As you revise, check your draft against the guidelines in this chapter.
- Eight guidelines help writers create visually attractive documents:
    1. Use white space.
    2. Use headings.
    3. Limit the use of words set in all capital letters.
    4. Use no more than two fonts in a single document.
    5. Decide whether to justify margins based on the situation and the audience.
    6. Put important elements in the top left and lower right quadrants.
    7. Use a grid to unify visuals and other graphic elements.
    8. Use highlighting, decorative devices, and colour in moderation.
- As you design slides for PowerPoint and other presentation programs,
    - Use a big font.
    - Use bullet-point phrases.
    - Make only three to five points on each slide.
    - Customize your slides.
- To design brochures, first think about audience and purpose. Use a consistent design for a series of brochures or for issues of a newsletter.
- To test a document, observe readers, ask them to "think aloud" while completing the task, interrupt them at key points to ask what they are thinking, or ask them to describe the thought process after completing the document and the task.

APPENDIX A | Exercises and Problems

Getting Started

A.1 Evaluating Page Designs

Use the guidelines in this chapter to evaluate each of the following page designs. What are their strong points? What could be improved?

A.2   Evaluating PowerPoint Slides

Evaluate the following drafts of PowerPoint slides.

- Are the slides' background appropriate for the topic?
- Do the slides use words or phrases rather than complete sentences?
- Is the font big enough to read from a distance?
- Is the art relevant and appropriate?
- Is each slide free from errors?

a(1)

a(2)

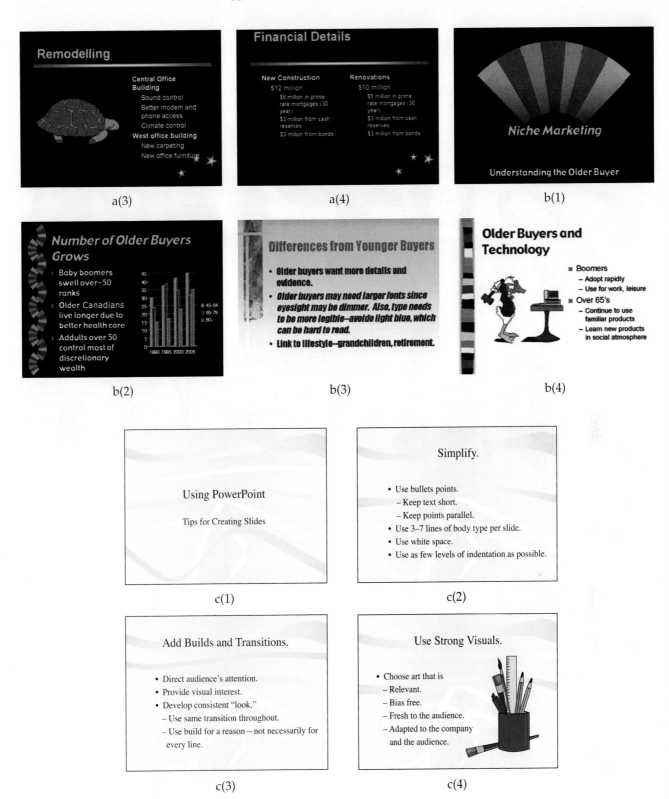

a(3)

a(4)

b(1)

b(2)

b(3)

b(4)

c(1)

c(2)

c(3)

c(4)

A.3   Recognizing Typefaces

Some companies commission a unique typeface, or wordmark, for their logos. Other companies use a standard font. When a logo is used consistently and frequently, it becomes associated with the organization. Can you name the brands that go with each letter of the alphabet below?

Source: "Alphabet Soup," *@Issue: The Journal of Business and Design* 3, no. 2 (Fall 1997): 24–25.

Source: "Alphabet Soup." Reprinted with permission from *@Issue: The Journal of Business & Design*, Vol. 1, No. 2 (Fall 1997) 24–25. Published by Corporate Design Foundation and sponsored by Potlatch Corporation.

A.4   Evaluating the Ethics of Design Choices

Indicate whether you consider each of the following actions ethical, unethical, or a grey area. Which of the actions would you do? Which would you feel uncomfortable doing? Which would you refuse to do?

1. Putting the advantages of a proposal in a bulleted list, while discussing the disadvantages in a paragraph.
2. Using a bigger type size so that a résumé visually fills a whole page.
3. Putting reasons to buy a product in the upper left and lower right quadrants, and the price in a part of the page that will get less emphasis.
4. Using a line at the bottom of the first page so it appears that the document is finished, and then putting the price and limitations on the back of that page.
5. Putting the services that are not covered by your health plan in full caps to make it less likely that people will read the page.

A.5   Using Headings

Reorganize the items in each of the following lists, using appropriate headings. Use bulleted or numbered lists as appropriate.

a. Rules and Procedures for a Tuition Reimbursement Plan

1. You are eligible to be reimbursed if you have been a full-time employee for at least three months.
2. You must apply before the first class meeting.
3. You must earn a "C" or better in the course.

4. You must submit a copy of the approved application, an official grade report, and a receipt for tuition paid to be reimbursed.
5. You can be reimbursed for courses related to your current position or another position in the company, or for courses that are part of a degree related to a current or possible job.
6. Your supervisor must sign the application form.
7. Courses may be at any appropriate level (high school, college, or graduate school).

b. Activities in Starting a New Business

- Getting a loan or venture capital
- Getting any necessary city or state licenses
- Determining what you will make, do, or sell
- Identifying the market for your products or services
- Pricing your products or services
- Choosing a location
- Checking zoning laws that may affect the location
- Identifying government and university programs for small business development
- Figuring cash flow
- Ordering equipment and supplies
- Selling
- Advertising and marketing

Communicating at Work

A.6   Analyzing Documents at Work

1. Collect several documents: letters and memos, newsletters, ads and flyers, and reports. Use the guidelines in this chapter to evaluate each of them.
2. Compare documents or pages produced by your competitors to those produced by your own organization in a specific category (for example, brochures, instructions, Web pages). Which documents are more effective? Why?

As Your Professor Directs,

a. Discuss the documents with a small group of classmates.

b. Write a memo to your professor evaluating three or more of the documents. Include originals or photocopies of the documents you discuss as an appendix to your memo.

c. Write a memo to your supervisor recommending ways the organization can improve its documents.

d. In an oral presentation to the class, explain what makes one document good and another one weak. If possible, use transparencies so that classmates can see the documents as you evaluate them.

Document Assignments

A.7   Evaluating Page Designs

Collect several documents that you receive as a consumer or a student: forms, letters, newsletters, announcements, ads, and flyers. Use the guidelines in this chapter to evaluate each of them.

As Your Professor Directs,

a. Discuss the documents with a small group of classmates.

b. Write a memo to your professor evaluating three or more of the documents. Include originals or photocopies of the documents you discuss as an appendix to your memo.

c. Write a letter to an organization recommending ways it can improve the design of the documents.

d. In an oral presentation to the class, explain what makes one document good and another one weak. If possible, use transparencies so that classmates can see the documents as you evaluate them.

A.8   Evaluating Web Pages

Compare three Web pages in the same category (for example, helping the homeless, organizations, car companies, university departments, sports information). Which page(s) are most effective? Why? What weaknesses do the pages have?

As Your Professor Directs,

a. Discuss the pages with a small group of classmates.

b. Write a memo to your professor evaluating the pages. Include URLs of the pages in your memo.

c. In an oral presentation to the class, explain what makes one page good and another one weak. If possible, put the pages on screen so that classmates can see the pages as you evaluate them.

d. Post your evaluation in an e-mail message to the class. Include the URLs so classmates can click to the pages you discuss.

A.9   Creating a Brochure

Create a brochure for a campus, non-profit, government, or business organization. Write a memo to your professor explaining your choices for content and design.

A.10   Creating a Web Page

Create a Web page for an organization that does not yet have one. Write a memo to your professor explaining your choices for content and design.

A.11   Testing a Document

Ask someone to follow a set of instructions or to fill out a form. (Consider consumer instructions, forms for financial aid, and so forth.)

- Time the person. How long does it take? Is the person able to complete the task?
- Observe the person. Where does he or she pause, reread, seem confused?
- Interview the person. What parts of the document were confusing?

As Your Professor Directs,

a. Discuss the changes needed with a small group of classmates.

b. Write a memo to your professor evaluating the document and explaining the changes that are needed. Include the document as an appendix to your memo.

c. Write to the organization that produced the document recommending necessary improvements.

d. In an oral presentation to the class, evaluate the document and explain what changes are needed. If possible, use a transparency of the document so that classmates can see it.

A.12   Improving a Financial Aid Form

You've just joined the financial aid office at your school. The director gives you the following form and asks you to redesign it. The director says:

> We need this form to see whether parents have other students in university besides the one requesting aid. Parents are supposed to list all family members that the parents support—themselves, the person here, any other kids in university, and any younger dependent kids.
>
> Half of these forms are filled out incorrectly. Most people just list the student going here; they leave out everyone else.
>
> If something is missing, the computer sends out a letter and a second copy of this form. The whole process starts over. Sometimes we send this form back two or three times before it's right. In the meantime, students' financial aid is delayed—maybe for months. Sometimes things are so late that they can't register for classes, or they have to pay tuition themselves and get reimbursed later.
>
> If so many people are filling out the form wrong, the form itself must be the problem. See what you can do with it. But keep it to a page.

As Your Professor Directs,

a. Analyze the current form and identify its problems.

b. Revise the form. Add necessary information; reorder information; change the chart to make it easier to fill out.

Hints:

- Where are people supposed to send the form? What is the phone number of the financial aid office? Should they need to call the office if the form is clear?
- Does the definition of *half-time* apply to all students or just those taking courses beyond high school?
- Should capital or lowercase letters be used?
- Are the lines big enough to write in?
- What headings or subdivisions within the form would remind people to list all family members whom they support?
- How can you encourage people to return the form promptly?

Please complete the chart below by listing all family members for whom you (the parents) will provide more than half support during the academic year (July 1 through June 30). Include yourselves (the parents), the student, and your dependent children, even if they are not attending university.

EDUCATIONAL INFORMATION, 200_–200_						
FULL NAME OF FAMILY MEMBER	AGE	RELATIONSHIP OF FAMILY MEMBER TO STUDENT	NAME OF SCHOOL OR UNIVERSITY THIS SCHOOL YEAR	FULL-TIME	HALF-TIME* OR MORE	LESS THAN HALF-TIME
STUDENT APPLICANT						

*Half-time is defined as 6 credit hours or 12 clock hours a term.

When the information requested is received by our office, processing of your financial aid application will resume.

Please sign and mail this form to the above address as soon as possible. Your signature certifies that this information and the information on the FAF is true and complete to the best of your knowledge. If you have any questions, please contact a member of the need analysis staff.

_____   _____
Signature of Parent(s)   Date

A

abstract A summary of a report, specifying the recommendations and the reasons for them. Also called an executive summary.

acknowledgment responses Nods, smiles, frowns, and words that let a speaker know someone is listening.

active listening Feeding back the literal meaning or the emotional content or both so that the speaker knows that the listener has heard and understood.

AIDA plan A four-part indirect persuasive pattern involving gaining **A**ttention, creating **I**nterest, building **D**esire, and motivating **A**ction. It is also referred to as the **AIRA** plan when the emphasis is on reducing Resistance before motivating action.

alliteration A sound pattern occurring when several words begin with the same sound.

AMS simplified format A letter format that omits the salutation and complimentary close and lines everything up at the left margin.

argument The reasons or logic offered to persuade the audience.

B

background (or history of the problem) Section of a report that explains factors leading to the problem addressed in the report. It is a useful record for later readers who may not have ready access to the situation that gave rise to the report.

bar chart A visual consisting of parallel bars or rectangles that represent specific sets of data.

behavioural interviews Job interviews that ask candidates to describe actual behaviours they have used in the past in specific situations.

bias-free language Language that does not discriminate against people on the basis of sex, physical condition, race, age, or any other category.

blind copies Copies sent to other recipients that are not listed on the original letter or memo.

block format In letters, a format in which inside address, date, and signature block are lined up at the left margin. In résumés, a format in which dates are listed in one column and job titles and descriptions in another. This format emphasizes work history.

blueprint An overview or forecast that tells the reader what will be discussed in a section or an entire report.

body The body of a report is the main part (after the front matter and before the conclusions and recommendations) that introduces the report, gives background or history, presents and interprets data, analyzes causes, and assesses solutions. Some organizations count the executive summary as part of the body, while others count as the body only the section after the introduction and background.

buffer A neutral or positive statement designed to allow the writer to bury, or buffer, the negative message.

build goodwill To create a good image of yourself and of your organization—the kind of image that makes people want to do business with you.

bullets Large round dots or squares that set off items in a list. When you are giving examples, but the number is not exact and the order does not matter, use bullets to set off items.

businessese A kind of jargon including unnecessary words. Some words were common 200–300 years ago but are no longer part of spoken English. Some have never been used outside business writing. All of these terms should be omitted.

bypassing Miscommunication that occurs when two people use the same symbol to mean different things.

C

central selling point A super reader benefit, big enough to motivate readers by itself, but also serving as an umbrella to cover other benefits and to unify the message.

chain The body of a direct mail letter, providing the logical and emotional links that move readers from interest to the action the writer wants.

channel The physical means by which a message is sent. Written channels include memos, letters, and billboards. Oral channels include phone calls, speeches, and face-to-face conversations.

channel overload The inability of a channel to carry all the messages that are being sent.

chartjunk Decoration that is irrelevant to a visual and that may be misleading.

chronological résumé A résumé that lists what you did in a timeline, starting with the most recent events and going backward in reverse chronology.

claim The part of an argument that the speaker or writer wants the audience to agree with.

clip art Predrawn images that you can import into your newsletter, sign, or graph.

closed body position Includes keeping the arms and legs crossed and close to the body. Suggests physical and psychological discomfort, defending oneself, and shutting the other person out. Also called a defensive body position.

cold list A list used in marketing of people with no prior connection to your group.

collection letter A letter asking a customer to pay for goods and services received.

colon A punctuation mark used primarily to introduce the words that follow it: a list, a formal quotation, or formal statement, for example.

comma A punctuation mark that introduces, coordinates, links, or inserts words, phrases, or clauses in a sentence.

comma splice or comma fault Using a comma to join two independent clauses. To correct, use a semicolon, subordinate one of the clauses, or use a period and start a new sentence.

communication theory A theory explaining what happens when we communicate and where miscommunication can occur.

community of practice A group of people who work together, share a sense of purpose, engage in learning together, produce meaning, develop identities, and add value to an organization. People may belong to more than one community of practice within an organization.

complex sentence Sentence with one main clause and one subordinate clause.

complimentary close The words after the body of the letter and before the signature. *Sincerely* and *Cordially* are the most commonly used complimentary closes in business letters.

compound sentence Sentence with two main clauses joined by a conjunction.

conclusions Section of a report that restates the main points.

confirmation bias The process whereby people who have formed stereotypes perceive examples that reinforce or confirm their biases, while overlooking examples that would disprove their biases.

connotations The emotional colourings or associations that accompany a word.

contact letter Letter written to keep in touch with customer or donor.

conversational style Conversational patterns such as speed and volume of speaking, pauses between speakers, whether questions are direct or indirect. When different speakers assign different meanings to a specific pattern, miscommunication results.

coordination The third stage in the life of a task group, when the group finds, organizes, and interprets information, and examines alternatives and assumptions. This is the longest of the four stages.

counterclaim In logic, a statement whose truth would negate the truth of the main claim.

credibility The audience's response to the source of the message as a believable one.

critical activities Activities that must be done on time if a project is to be completed by its due date.

crop To trim a photograph to fit a specific space. Photographs are also cropped to delete visual information that is unnecessary or unwanted.

cultural competence See *intercultural competence.*

culture The unconscious patterns of behaviour and beliefs that are common to a people, nation, or organization.

cycling The process of sending a document from writer to superior to writer to yet another superior for several rounds of revisions before the document is approved.

D

dangling modifier A phrase that modifies a word that is not actually in a sentence. To correct a dangling modifier, recast the modifier as a subordinate clause or revise the sentence so its subject or object can be modified by the now-dangling phrase.

data Facts or figures from which conclusions can be drawn.

decode To extract meaning from symbols.

defensive body position See *closed body position.*

demographic characteristics Measurable features of an audience that can be counted objectively: age, sex, race, education level, income, etc.

denotation A word's literal or "dictionary" meaning. Most common words in English have more than one denotation.

Context usually makes it clear which of several meanings is appropriate.

dependent clause See *subordinate clause.*

descriptive abstract A listing of the topics an article or report covers that tells how thoroughly each topic is treated but does not summarize what is said about each topic.

deviation bar charts Bar charts that identify positive and negative values, or winners and losers.

dingbats Small symbols such as arrows, pointing fingers, and so forth that are part of a typeface.

direct mail A form of direct marketing that asks for an order, inquiry, or contribution directly from the reader.

direct request pattern A pattern of organization that makes the request directly in the first and last paragraphs.

directed subject line A subject line that makes clear the writer's stance on the issue.

discourse community A group of people who share assumptions about what channels, formats, and styles to use for communication, what topics to discuss and how to discuss them, and what constitutes evidence.

dot chart A chart that shows correlations or other large data sets. Dot charts have labelled horizontal and vertical axes.

dot planning A way for large groups to set priorities; involves assigning coloured dots to ideas.

E

early letter A collection letter that is gentle. An early letter assumes that the reader intends to pay but has forgotten or has met with temporary reverses.

editing Checking the draft to see that it satisfies the requirements of good English and the principles of business writing. Unlike revision, which can produce major changes in meaning, editing focuses on the surface of writing.

emotional appeal Making the audience want to do what the writer or speaker asks.

empathy The ability to put oneself in someone else's shoes, to feel with that person.

enclosure A document that accompanies a letter.

encoding Putting ideas into symbols.

enunciate To voice all the sounds of each word while speaking.

ethnocentrism The tendency to assess other cultures by criteria specific to one's own culture and to believe other cultures are inferior.

evaluating Measuring the draft against your goals and the requirements of the situation and audience. Anything produced during each stage of the writing process can be evaluated, not just the final draft.

evidence Facts or data the audience already accepts.

executive summary See *abstract.*

expectancy theory A theory that argues that motivation is based on the expectation of being rewarded for performance and the importance of the reward.

external audiences Audiences who are not part of the writer's organization.

external documents Documents that go to people outside the organization.

extranets Web pages for customers and suppliers.

extrinsic motivators Benefits that are "added on"; they are not a necessary part of the product or action.

eye contact Looking another person directly in the eye.

essential clause A clause (that is not set off by commas) that gives necessary information that restricts or limits the noun it modifies.

F

feasibility report A report that evaluates two or more possible alternatives and recommends one of them. Doing nothing is always one alternative.

feedback The receiver's response to a message.

figure Any visual that is not a table.

fixed typeface A typeface in which each letter has the same width on the page. Sometimes called typewriter typeface.

form letter A prewritten, fill-in-the-blank letter designed to fit standard situations.

formal meetings Meetings run under strict rules, like the rules of parliamentary procedure summarized in *Robert's Rules of Order.*

formalization The fourth and last stage in the life of a task group, when the group makes and formalizes its decision.

formation The second stage in the life of a task group, when members choose a leader and define the problem they must solve.

frozen evaluation An assessment that does not take into account the possibility of change.

full justification Margins that end evenly on the right side of the page.

functional headings See *headings.*

functional résumé Stresses individual areas of competence and accomplishment, while subordinating work and educational experience.

fused sentence The result when two or more sentences are joined with neither punctuation nor conjunctions.

G

Gantt charts Bar charts used to show schedules. Gantt charts are most commonly used in proposals.

gatekeeper The audience with the power to decide whether your message is sent on to other audiences. Some gatekeepers are also initial audiences.

gathering Physically getting the background data you need. It can include informal and formal research or simply getting the letter to which you're responding.

generic headings See *headings.*

getting feedback Asking someone else to evaluate your work. Feedback is useful at every stage of the writing process, not just during composition of the final draft.

glossary A list of terms used in a report with their definitions.

good appeal An appeal in direct marketing that offers believable descriptions of benefits, links the benefits of the product or service to a need or desire that motivates the reader, makes the reader want to read the letter, and motivates the reader to act.

good mailing list A mailing list used in direct marketing that has accurate addresses and is a good match to the product.

good product A product that appeals to a specific segment of people, is not readily available in stores, is mailable, and provides an adequate profit margin.

good service or cause A service or cause that fills an identifiable need.

goodwill The value of a business beyond its tangible assets, including its reputation and patronage. Also, a favourable condition and overall atmosphere of trust that can be fostered between parties conducting business.

goodwill presentation A presentation that entertains and validates the audience.

grapevine An organization's informal informational network that carries gossip and rumours as well as accurate information.

grid system A means of designing layout by imposing columns on a page and lining up graphic elements within the columns.

grouped bar chart A bar chart that allows the viewer to compare several aspects of each item or several items over time.

guide headings The elements at the top of a memo or e-mail that introduce who the memo is from, to whom it is addressed, date, and subject. The order may be altered according to the preference of business, organization, or individual. Some organizations have special letterhead for memos; some use the memo templates in word-processing programs.

guided discussion A presentation in which the speaker presents the questions or issues that both speaker and audience have agreed on in advance. Instead of functioning as an expert with all the answers, the speaker serves as a facilitator to help the audience tap its own knowledge.

H

headings Words or short phrases that group points and divide a letter, memo, or report into sections. Topic, generic, or functional headings describe topics or functions (background, budget, recommendations); informative or talking heads add information and interest.

hearing Perceiving sounds. (Not the same thing as listening.)

hidden job market Jobs that are never advertised but that may be available or may be created for the right candidate.

hidden negatives Words that are not negative in themselves, but become negative in context.

histogram A bar chart using pictures, asterisks, or points to represent a unit of the data.

history of the problem See *background.*

I

impersonal expression A sentence that attributes actions to inanimate objects, designed to avoid placing blame on a reader.

independent clause See *main clause.*

indirect approach A pattern of organization that gives the reasons first to prepare the reader for and to explain negative messages. It is appropriate for bad news, unreceptive audiences, ideas requiring persuasion, and sensitive matter communicated to superiors.

inference A statement that has not yet been verified but whose truth or falsity could be established, either now or in the future.

infinitive The form of the verb that is preceded by *to*.

inform To explain something or tell the audience something.

informal meetings Loosely run meetings in which votes are not taken on every point.

information interview An interview in which you talk to someone who works in the area you hope to enter to find out what the day-to-day work involves and how you can best prepare to enter that field.

information overload A condition in which a human receiver cannot process all the messages he or she receives.

informative abstract See *summary* or *informative abstract*.

informational messages In a group, messages focusing on the problem, data, and possible solutions.

informative message Message to which the reader's basic reaction will be neutral.

informative presentation A presentation that informs or teaches the audience.

informative report A report that provides information.

inside address The reader's name and address; put below the date and above the salutation in most letter formats.

initial audience The audience that assigns the message and routes it to other audiences.

interactive presentation A conversation in which the seller uses questions to determine the buyer's needs, probe objections, and gain provisional and then final commitment to the purchase.

intercultural competence The ability to communicate sensitively with people from other cultures and countries, based on an understanding of cultural differences.

internal audiences Audiences in the writer's organization.

internal report Reports written by employees for use only in their organization.

interpersonal communication Communication between people.

interpersonal messages In a group, messages promoting friendliness, co-operation, and group loyalty.

interpret To determine the significance or importance of a message.

intranet A Web page just for employees.

intrapreneurs Innovators who work within organizations.

intrinsic motivators Benefits that come automatically from using a product or doing something.

introduction The part of a report that states the purpose and scope of the report. The introduction may also include limitations, assumptions, methods, criteria, and definitions.

J

jargon There are two kinds of jargon. The first kind is the specialized terminology of a technical field. The second is businessese, outdated words that do not have technical meanings and are not used in other forms of English.

Johnson box In the 1940s, in an effort to add impact to his sales letters, direct mail copywriter Frank H. Johnson developed the Johnson box. Placed before the salutation, the Johnson rectangular box highlights the offer without readers having to read masses of copy first.

judgment See *opinion*.

justification report Report that justifies the need for a purchase, an investment, a new personnel line, or a change in procedure.

K

knot The action close of a direct mail letter, which harnesses the motivation you have created and turns it into action.

L

landscape graphs Line graphs with the area below the line filled in are sometimes called landscape graphs.

late letter A collection letter that threatens legal action if the bill is not paid.

letter Short document using block, modified, or AMS simplified letter format that goes to readers outside an organization.

letterhead Stationery with the organization's name, logo, address, and telephone number printed on the page.

limitations Problems or factors that limit the validity of the recommendations of a report.

line graph A visual consisting of lines that show trends or allow the viewer to interpolate values between the observed values.

listening Decoding and interpreting sounds correctly.

M

main clause A group of words that can stand by itself as a complete sentence. Also called an independent clause.

memo Document using memo format sent to readers in an organization.

middle letter A collection letter that is more assertive than an early letter. Middle letters may offer to negotiate a schedule for repayment if the reader is not able to pay the whole bill immediately, remind the reader of the importance of good credit, educate the reader about credit, or explain why the creditor must have prompt payment.

minutes Record of a meeting, listing the items discussed, the results of votes, and the individuals responsible for carrying out follow-up steps.

misplaced modifier A word or phrase that appears to modify another element of the sentence than the writer intended.

mixed punctuation Using a colon after the salutation and a comma after the complimentary close in a letter.

modified block format A letter format in which the inside address, date, and signature block are lined up with each other one-half or one-third of the way over on the page.

modifier A word or phrase giving more information about another word in a sentence.

monochronic culture Culture in which people do only one important activity at a time.

monologue presentation A presentation in which the speaker speaks without interruption. The presentation is planned and is delivered without deviation.

Myers-Briggs Type Indicator A scale that categorizes people on four dimensions: introvert-extravert; sensing-intuitive; thinking-feeling; and perceiving-judging.

N

negative message A message in which basic information conveyed is negative; the reader is expected to be disappointed or angry.

noise Any physical or psychological interference in a message.

non-agist Refers to words, images, or behaviours that do not discriminate against people on the basis of age.

non-essential clause A clause that gives additional information that does not identify or restrict the meaning of the noun it modifies.

non-racist Refers to words, images, or behaviours that do not discriminate against people on the basis of race.

non-sexist Language that treats both sexes neutrally, that does not make assumptions about the proper gender for a job, and that does not imply that one sex is superior or takes precedence over the other.

non-verbal communication Communication that does not use words.

noun–pronoun agreement Having a pronoun be the same number (singular or plural) and the same person (first, second, or third) as the noun it refers to.

O

observation In semantics, a statement that you yourself have verified.

omnibus motion A motion that allows a group to vote on several related items in a single vote. Saves time in formal meetings with long agendas.

open body position Includes keeping the arms and legs uncrossed and away from the body. Suggests physical and psychological comfort and openness.

open punctuation Using no punctuation after the salutation and the complimentary close.

opinion A statement that can never be verified, since it includes terms that cannot be measured objectively. Also called a judgment.

organizational culture The values, attitudes, and philosophies shared by people in an organization that shape its messages and its reward structure.

orientation The first stage in the life of a task group, when members meet and begin to define their task.

outsourcing Going outside the company for products and services that once were made by the company's employees.

P

paired bar chart A bar chart that shows the correlation between two items.

parallel structure Putting words or ideas that share the same role in the sentence's logic in the same grammatical form.

paraphrase To repeat in your own words the verbal content of what the previous speaker said.

parentheses Brackets that set off words, phrases, or sentences used to explain or comment on the main idea. Also used to insert sources in in-text citations.

passive verb A verb that describes action done to the grammatical subject of the sentence.

perception The ability to see, hear, taste, smell, and touch.

persona The "author" or character who allegedly writes a letter; the voice that a writer assumes in creating a document.

personal space The distance someone wants between him- or herself and other people in ordinary, non-intimate interchanges.

persuade To motivate and convince the audience to act.

persuasive presentation A presentation that motivates the audience to act or to believe.

pie chart A circular chart whose sections represent percentages of a given quantity.

plagiarism (from Latin *plagiarius*: kidnapper) The unacknowledged use of another's ideas and/or expression. To plagiarize is to pass off as your own something borrowed from someone else.

planning All the thinking done about a subject and the means of achieving your purposes. Planning takes place not only when devising strategies for the document as a whole, but also when generating "miniplans" that govern sentences or paragraphs.

polite listening Listening that is mechanical and inattentive to the message because it is focused on the listener's own thoughts, speech, or response.

polychronic culture Culture in which people do several things at once.

positive or good news message Message to which the reader's reaction will be positive.

primary audience The audience who will make a decision or act on the basis of a message.

pro-and-con pattern A pattern of organization for reports that presents all the arguments for an alternative and then all the arguments against it.

problem-solving pattern A pattern of organization that describes a problem that affects the reader before offering a solution to the problem.

procedural messages Messages focusing on a group's methods: how it makes decisions, who does what, when assignments are due.

proofreading Checking the final copy to see that it's free from typographical errors.

proportional typeface A typeface in which some letters are wider than other letters (for example, *w* is wider than *i*).

prospecting letter A job application letter written to companies that have not announced openings but where you'd like to work.

psychographic characteristics Human characteristics that are qualitative rather than quantitative: values, beliefs, goals, and lifestyles.

psychological description Description of a product or service in terms of reader benefits.

psychological reactance Phenomenon occurring when a reader reacts to a negative message by asserting freedom in some other arena.

Q

questionnaire List of questions for people to answer in a survey.

R

ragged right margins Margins that do not end evenly on the right side of the page.

reader benefits Benefits or advantages that the reader gets by using the writer's services, buying the writer's products, following the writer's policies, or adopting the writer's ideas. Reader benefits can exist for policies and ideas as well as for goods and services.

rebuttal In logic, the refutation of a counterclaim.

recommendations Section of a report that specifies items for action.

reference line A subject line that refers the reader to another document (usually a numbered one, such as an invoice).

referral interview Interviews scheduled to learn about current job opportunities in a field and to get referrals to other people who may have the power to create a job. Useful for tapping into unadvertised jobs and the hidden job market.

release date Date a report will be made available to the public.

request To ask the audience to take an easy or routine action.

reverse chronology Starting with the most recent job or degree and going backward. Pattern of organization used for chronological résumés.

revising Making changes in the draft: adding, deleting, substituting, or rearranging. Revision can be changes in single words, but more often it means major additions, deletions, or substitutions, as the writer measures the draft against purpose and audience and reshapes the document to make it more effective.

rhyme Repetition of the final vowel sounds, and if the words end with consonants, the final consonant sounds.

rhythm The repetition of a pattern of accented and unaccented syllables.

rule of three The rule explaining that when a series of three items are logically parallel, the last will receive the most emphasis.

run-on sentence A sentence containing several main clauses strung together with *and*, *but*, or, *so*, or *for*.

S

salutation The greeting in a letter: "Dear Ms. Smith."

sans serif Literally, without serifs. Typeface whose letters lack bases or little extensions. Helvetica and Geneva are examples of sans serif typefaces.

secondary audience The audience affected by the decision or action. These people may be asked by the primary audience to comment on a message or to implement ideas after they've been approved.

segmented, subdivided, or stacked bars Bars in a bar chart that sum components of an item.

semantics or general semantics The study of the ways behaviour is influenced by the words and other symbols used to communicate.

sentence fragment A group of words that are not a complete sentence but that are punctuated as if they were a complete sentence.

sentence outline An outline using complete sentences that lists the sentences proving the thesis and the points proving each of those sentences. A sentence outline is the basis for a summary abstract.

serif The little extensions from the main strokes on the *r* and *g* and other letters. Times Roman and Courier are examples of serif typefaces.

semicolon A punctuation mark used to join closely related independent clauses not joined by a coordinating conjunction; before conjunctive adverbs (*consequently*, *however*, *indeed*); before transitional expressions (*in addition*, *as a result*) in compound sentences; and between items in a series when the items contain commas.

signpost An explicit statement of the place that a speaker or writer has reached: "Now we come to the third point."

simple sentence Sentence with one main clause.

situational interviews Job interviews in which candidates are asked to describe what they would do in specific hypothetical situations.

skills résumé A résumé organized around the skills you've used, rather than the date or the job in which you used them.

solicited letter A job letter written when you know that the company is hiring.

standard agenda A seven-step process for solving problems.

star The attention-getting opener of a direct mail letter.

star-chain-knot pattern A pattern of persuasion that consists of an attention-getting opener (star), a body with logical and emotional links (chain), and an action close (knot).

stereotyping Distorting unfair generalizations and labels to make people conform to unfair mental images.

storyboard A visual representation of the structure of a document, with a rectangle representing each page or unit. An alternative to outlining as a method of organizing material.

strategy A plan for reaching your specific goals with a specific audience.

stress Emphasis given to one or more words in a sentence.

stress interview A job interview that deliberately puts the applicant under stress, physical or psychological. Here it's important to change the conditions that create physical stress and to meet psychological stress by rephrasing questions in less inflammatory terms and treating them as requests for information.

subject line The title of the document, used to file and retrieve the document. A subject line tells readers why they need to read the document and provides a framework in which to set what you're about to say.

subordinate clause A group of words containing a subject and a verb but that cannot stand by itself as a complete sentence. Also called a *dependent clause*.

summary or informative abstract The logical skeleton of an article or report, containing the thesis or recommendation and its proof.

summary sentence or paragraph A sentence or paragraph listing in order the topics that following sentences or paragraphs will discuss.

T

table Numbers or words arrayed in rows and columns.

talking or informative headings See *headings*.

target audience The audience one tries to reach with a mailing: people who are likely to be interested in buying the product, using the service, or contributing to the cause.

thank-you note A note thanking someone for helping you.

targeted résumé Highlights abilities and achievements that relate to specific job targets.

tone The implied attitude of the author toward the reader and the subject.

tone of voice The rising or falling inflection that indicates whether a group of words is a question or a statement, whether the speaker is uncertain or confident, whether a statement is sincere or sarcastic.

topic sentence A sentence that introduces or summarizes the main idea in a paragraph. A topic sentence may be either stated or implied, and it may come anywhere in the paragraph.

transmit To send a message.

transitions Words, phrases, or sentences that show the connections between ideas.

truncated graphs Graphs with part of the scale missing.

U

umbrella sentence or paragraph A sentence or paragraph listing in order the topics that following sentences or paragraphs will discuss.

unity Using only one idea or topic in a paragraph or other piece of writing.

V

verbal communication Communication that uses words; may be either oral or written.

vested interest The emotional stake readers have in something if they benefit from keeping things just as they are.

vicarious participation An emotional strategy in fundraising letters based on the idea that by donating money, readers participate vicariously in work they are not able to do personally.

volume The loudness or softness of a voice or other sound.

W

watchdog audience An audience that has political, social, or economic power and that may base future actions on its evaluation of a message.

white space The empty space on the page. White space emphasizes material that it separates from the rest of the text.

wordiness Taking more words than necessary to express an idea.

writing The act of putting words on paper or on a screen, or of dictating words to a machine or a secretary.

Y

you-attitude A style of writing that looks at things from the reader's point of view, emphasizes what the reader wants to know, respects the reader's intelligence, and protects the reader's ego. Using *you* probably increases you-attitude in positive situations. In negative situations or conflict, avoid *you* since that word will attack the reader.

Chapter 1

1. Charles Rubin, "You Are What You Write," Guerrilla Marketing International. http://www.gmarketing.com/articles/print/103/, retrieved September 28, 2005.

2. Gillian Shaw, "'Soft skills' can pack a punch," The StarPhoenix, December 31, 2004, F16.

3. Anne Fisher, "Ask Annie," Fortune, March 1, 1999, 242.

4. Robyn D. Clarke, "A New Labor Day," Black Enterprise, February 2001, 98.

5. Anne Fisher, "The High Cost of Living and Not Writing Well," Fortune, December 7, 1998, 244.

6. Elaine Viets, "Voice Mail Converts Boss into a Secretary," The Columbus Dispatch, August 10, 1995, 3E; Rochelle Sharpe, "Work Week," The Wall Street Journal, September 26, 1995, A1.

7. Terrence Belford, "Engineers need 'soft' skills," The Globe and Mail, January 13, 2003, B10.

8. Paul Craig Roberts, "America's 'Savings Crisis' Is a Chimera," BusinessWeek, February 12, 1990, 20.

9. Henry Mintzberg, The Nature of Managerial Work (New York: Harper & Row, 1973), 32, 65.

10. Frederick K. Moss, "Perceptions of Communication in the Corporate Community," Journal of Business and Technical Communication 9.1 (January 1995): 67.

11. John Kotter, The General Managers (1982), summarized in Alan Deutschman, "The CEO's Secret of Managing Time," Fortune, June 1, 1992, 140.

12. "1996 Cost of a Business Letter" (Chicago: Dartnell/From 9 to 5, September 30, 1996), 1.

13. Dianna Booher, Cutting Paperwork in the Corporate Culture (New York: Facts on File, 1986), 24.

14. Claudia MonPere McIsaac and Mary Ann Aschauer, "Proposal Writing at Atherton Jordan, Inc.: An Ethnographic Study," Management Communication Quarterly 3 (1990): 535.

15. Elizabeth Allen, "Excellence in Public Relations & Communication Management," IABC/Dayton Awards Banquet, Dayton, OH, July 12, 1990.

16. Murray Raphel, "Comes the Revolution," Direct Marketing, May 2001, 61.

17. James R. Rosenfield, "Tackling the Tough Topics," Direct Marketing, June 2001, 4.

18. Nicholas G. Carr, "The Economics of Customer Satisfaction," Harvard Business Review, March–April 1999, 17–18.

19. Adapted from Andy Holloway, "Top CEO: WestJet's Clive Beddoe," Canadian Business 77.9, April 26–May 9, 2004, 43.

20. Adapted from Dr. Marie-Hélène Adrien, Suzanne Kirouac, and Alicia Sliwinski, 'Women's Entrepreneurship in Canada: All the Glitters Is Not Gold,' Universalia Occasional Paper, No. 38, Montreal, September 1999. http://www.universalia.com/files/occas38.pdf, retrieved March 10, 2005; CIBC report, Women Entrepreneurs: Leading the Charge, http://www.cibc.com/ca/womenentrepreneurs, retrieved September 10, 2005.

21. Adapted from Canadian Youth Business Foundation Web site, http://www.cybf.ca/ab_aboutus.html, retrieved March 8, 2005.

22. Adapted from Micro-Economic Policy Analysis Branch and Aboriginal Business Canada, Aboriginal Entrepreneurs in Canada: Progress and Prospects, http://www.strategis.ic.gc.ca/SSI/ab/440_ref_rep001_e.pdf, retrieved March 10, 2005.

23. Adapted from Canadian Centre for Social Entrepreneurship, Homepage, http://www.bus.ualberta.ca/ccse; Sherrill Johnson, "Literature Review on Social Entrepreneurship," http://www.bus.ualberta.ca/ccse/Publications/Publications/Lit. Review SE November 2000.rtf, retrieved March 10, 2005.

24. L. D. DeSimone, George N. Hatsopoulous, Charles P. Holt, et al., "How Can Big Companies Keep the Entrepreneurial Spirit Alive?" Harvard Business Review, November–December 1995, 183–192.

25. Doug Garr, "Inside Out-Sourcing," Fortune, Summer 2001, 85–92; and Susan Greco, "Fanatics," Inc., April 2001, 47.

26. Adapted from Jim Sutherland, "Unbeatable: Even After Cuts in Funding, BC Biomedical Is Our No. 1 Employer for the Third Year in a Row. Here's How They Do It." Report on Business, January 2005, 46–47.

27. Adapted from Kamal Dib, "Diversity Works," Canadian Business, March 29–April 11, 2004, 53.

28. Pet Engardio, "Smart Globalization," BusinessWeek, August 27, 2001, 132–136; Mickael Arndt and Pete Engardio, "Diebold," BusinessWeek, August 27, 2001, 138.

29. Adapted from Shannon Boklaschuk, "Internet Help for Arabian Firms," StarPhoenix December 31, 2003, posted Canadian Youth Business Foundation Web site, http://www.cybf.ca/cl_saskatoon2.html, retrieved September 8, 2005.

30. "On Trial," BusinessWeek, January 12, 2004, downloaded from Infotrac at http://www.businessweek.com/magazine; and Nanette Byrnes, "Reform: Who's Making the Grade," BusinessWeek, September 22, 2003, http://www. businessweek.com/magazine, retrieved November 4, 2005.

31. Byrnes, "Reform"; KPMG LLP, "KPMG Survey: More Organizations Detecting Fraud, Spurred by New Regulations and Investor Demands," news release, December 1, 2003, http://www.us.kpmg.com, retrieved November 4, 2005; KPMG Forensic, Fraud Survey 2003 (May 25, 2003, www.us.kpmg.com retrieved November 4, 2005); Brian Hindo, Teaching MCI Right from Wrong," BusinessWeek, November 3, 2003, http://www.businessweek.com/magazine, retrieved November 4, 2005; and Margaret M. Clark, "Corporate Ethics Programs Make a Difference, but Not the Only Difference," HRMagazine, July 2003, http://www.shrm.org/hrnews_published/archives/CMS_004611.asp, retrieved November 4, 2005.

32. Adapted from Matthew McClearn, "Did Anybody Even Read This?' Canadian Business, May 24–June 6, 2004, 14l; Steve Maich, "Selling Ethics at Nortel: The Company's Paens to Integrity Drip with Irony to Shareholders," Maclean's, January 24, 2005, 32.

33. Adapted from Jane Gadd, "Is ethics the new bottom line," The Globe and Mail, March 8, 2005, E6.

34. Clarke, "A New Labor Day," 96; Tony Schwartz, "While the Balance of Power Has Already Begun to Shift, Most Male CEOs Still Don't Get It," Fast Company, December 1999, 366; and Pamela Kruger, "Jobs for Life," Fast Company, May, 2000, 236–252.

35. Keith H. Hammonds, "Balancing Work and Family," BusinessWeek, September 16, 1996, 74.

36. J. McFarland, "Start spreading the (good) news, Conference Board tells business," The Globe and Mail, May 27, 2004, http://www.theglobeandmail.com/servlet/ArticleNews/TPPrint/LAC/, retrieved May 29, 2004.

37. Canadian Business for Social Responsibility (CBSR), Engaging small business in Corporate Social Responsibility: A Canadian small business perspective on CSR. L. Princic with M. Floyd & J. Bonham, http://www.cbsr.bc.ca/files/ReportsandPapers/EngagingSME_FINAL.pdf, retrieved October 23, 2004.

38. A. Arnot, "The Triple Bottom Line," *CGA Magazine* January/February 2004, http://www.cga-canada.org/eng/magazine/jan-feb04/triple_line_e.htm, retrieved November 24, 2004.

39. D. J. Manning, "Benefits of Environmental Stewardship," *Review of Business* 25.2 (2004), 9.

40. Arnot, "The Triple Bottom Line."

41. P. Raynard, "Coming Together: A Review of Contemporary Approaches to Social Accounting, Auditing, and Reporting in Non-Profit Organisations," *Journal of Business Ethics* 17.13 (1998), 1471–1479.

42. G. Monbiot; cited in R. Frost, "Corporate Social Responsibility and Globalization: A Reassessment, 2004, *CW Online*, International Association of Business Communicators, http://www.iabc.com/cw/private/cwb/2004/0204/reassessment.htm, retrieved July 16, 2004.

43. Turnbull and Stamnes presentations to Canadian Co-operative Association Congress, 2003.

44. Janet McFarland and Elizabeth Church, "Crisis management moving up on the boardroom agenda," *The Globe and Mail*, October 15, 2004, B1–B5.

45. Linda H. Heuring, "Patients First," *HR Magazine*, July 2003, http://www.shrm.org/hrmagazine/articles/0703/0703heuring.asp, retrieved November 4, 2005.

46. Jörgen Sandberg, "Understanding Competence at Work," *Harvard Business Review*, March 2001, 24–28.

47. Eric Abrahamson, "Change Without Pain," *Harvard Business Review*, July–August 2000, 75–79; and "Change Is Changing," *Harvard Business Review*, April 2001, 125.

48. "The List: Hit the Net, Then the Met," *BusinessWeek*, January 29, 2001, 8; Paul C. Judge, "How I Saved $100 Million on the Web," *Fast Company*, February 2001, 174–181.

49. Brian Caulfield, "Talk Is Cheap. And Good for Sales, Too," *Business 2.0*, April 2001, 114.

50. Jennifer Reingold and Marcia Stepanek, "The Boom," *BusinessWeek*, February 14, 2000, 116.

Chapter 2

1. ABC Canada Literacy Foundation, http://www.abc-canada.org/public_awareness/secrets_campaign.asp.

2. Audiences 1, 3, and 4 are based on J. C. Mathes and Dwight Stevenson, *Designing Technical Reports: Writing for Audiences in Organizations*, 2nd ed. (New York: Macmillan, 1991), 40. The fifth audience is suggested by Vincent J. Brown, "Facing Multiple Audiences in Engineering and R&D Writing: The Social Context of a Technical Report," *Journal of Technical Writing and Communication* 24, no. 1 (1994): 67–75.

3. Isabel Briggs Myers, *Introduction to Type* (Palo Alto, CA: Consulting Psychologists Press, 1980). The material in this section follows Myers's paper.

4. Isabel Briggs Myers and Mary H. McCaulley, *Manual: A Guide to the Development and Use of the Myers-Briggs Type Indicator* (Palo Alto, CA: Consulting Psychologists Press, 1985), 251, 248, respectively.

5. Matt Siegel, "The Perils of Culture Conflict," *Fortune*, November 9, 1998, 258.

6. Keith Naughton, "How Ford's F-150 Lapped the Competition," *BusinessWeek*, July 29, 1996, 74–76.

7. Gabrielle Sándor, "Attitude (Not Age) Defines the Mature Market," *American Demographics*, January 1994, 18–21.

8. SRIC-BI, "Representative VALS projects," SRIC-BI Web site, www.sric-bi.com, retrieved June 2, 2004.

9. Andy Holloway, Zena Olijnyk, Thomas Watson, "The Countdown Continues," *Canadian Business*, 88–89; cited in Kitty O. Locker, Stephen Kyo Kaczmarek, and Kathryn

Braun, *Business Communication: Building Critical Skills* (Toronto: McGraw-Hill Ryerson, 2005), 35.

10. Linda Driskill, "Negotiating Differences among Readers and Writers" (Paper presented at the Conference on College Composition and Communication, San Diego, CA, March 31–April 3, 1993).

11. Robyn D. Clarke, "More Than Money," *Black Enterprise*, June 2000, 89; and Charles Fishman, "Sanity Inc.," *Fast Company*, January 1999, 85–99.

12. Kevin Leo, "Effective Copy and Graphics," DADM/DMEF Direct Marketing Institute for Professors, Northbrook, IL, May 31–June 3, 1983.

13. Abraham H. Maslow, *Motivation and Personality* (New York: Harper & Row, 1954).

14. Cf. Tove Helland Hammer and H. Peter Dachler, "A Test of Some Assumptions Underlying the Path-Goal Model of Supervision: Some Suggested Conceptual Modifications," *Organizational Behavior and Human Performance* 14 (1975): 73.

15. Edward E. Lawler, III, *Motivation in Work Organizations* (Monterey, CA: Brooks/Cole, 1973), 59. Lawler also notes a third obstacle: people may settle for performance and rewards that are just OK. Offering reader benefits, however, does nothing to affect this obstacle.

16. Rachel Spilka, "Orality and Literacy in the Workplace: Process- and Text-Based Strategies for Multiple Audience Adaptation," *Journal of Business and Technical Communication* 4, no. 1 (January 1990): 44–67.

17. Sue Shellenbarger, "Companies Are Finding It Really Pays to Be Nice to Employees," *The Wall Street Journal*, July 22, 1998, B1.

18. Jim Collins, "Level 5 Leadership: The Triumph of Humility and Fierce Resolve," *Harvard Business Review*, January 2001, 66–76; Alan M. Webber, "Danger: Toxic Company," *Fast Company*, November 1998, 152–159.

19. Charles Burck, "Learning from a Master," *Fortune*, December 27, 1993, 144; Kathy Casto, "Assumptions about Audience in Negative Messages," Association for Business Communication Midwest Conference, Kansas City, MO, April 30–May 2, 1987; and John P. Wanous and A. Colella, "Future Directions in Organizational Entry Research," *Research in Personnel/Human Resource Management*, ed. Kenneth Rowland and G. Ferris (Greenwich, CT: JAI Press, 1990).

20. Annette N. Shelby and N. Lamar Reinsch, Jr., "Positive Emphasis and You-Attitude: An Empirical Study," *Journal of Business Communication* 32, no. 4 (October 1995): 303–327.

21. Alan Farnham, "Are You Smart Enough to Keep Your Job?" *Fortune*, January 15, 1996, 42.

22. Margaret Baker Graham and Carol David, "Power and Politeness: Administrative Writing in an 'Organized Anarchy,'" *Journal of Business and Technical Communication* 10, no. 1 (January 1996): 5–27.

23. John Hagge and Charles Kostelnick, "Linguistic Politeness in Professional Prose: A Discourse Analysis of Auditors' Suggestion Letters, with Implications for Business Communication Pedagogy," *Written Communication* 6, no. 3 (July 1989): 312–339.

24. For a fuller account, see Margery Fee and Janice McAlpine, *Oxford Guide to Canadian English Usage* (Don Mills, ON: Oxford University Press, 1997).

25. Brad Edmondson, "What Do You Call a Dark-Skinned Person?" *American Demographics*, October 1993, 9.

26. Michael J. Prince, "Canadian Disability Policy: Still a Hit-or-Miss Affair," *Canadian Journal of Sociology* 29.1 (2004), http://muse.jhu.edu/demo/Canadian_journal_of_sociology/vo29/29.1prince.pdf, retrieved March 10, 2005.

27. Marilyn A. Dyrud, "An Exploration of Gender Bias in Computer Clip Art," *Business Communication Quarterly* 60, no. 4 (December 1997): 30–51.

Chapter 3

1. See especially Linda Flower and John R. Hayes, "The Cognition of Discovery: Defining a Rhetorical Problem," *College Composition and Communication* 31 (February 1980): 21–32; Rose, *Writer's Block*; and the essays in two collections: Charles R. Cooper and Lee Odell, *Research on Composing: Points of Departure* (Urbana, IL: National Council of Teachers of English, 1978), and Mike Rose, ed., *When a Writer Can't Write: Studies in Writer's Block and Other Composing-Process Problems* (New York: Guilford Press, 1985).

2. Rebecca E. Burnett, "Content and Commas: How Attitudes Shape a Communication-Across-the-Curriculum Program," Association for Business Communication Convention, Orlando, FL, November 1–4, 1995.

3. W. Ross Winterowd and John Nixon, *The Contemporary Writer: A Practical Rhetoric,* 3rd ed. (San Diego: Harcourt Brace Jovanovich, 1989), 37.

4. Mike Rose, *Writer's Block: The Cognitive Dimension,* published for Conference on College Composition and Communication (Carbondale, IL: Southern Illinois University Press, 1984), 36.

5. Peter Elbow, *Writing with Power: Techniques for Mastering the Writing Process* (New York: Oxford University Press, 1981), 15–20.

6. See Gabriela Lusser Rico, *Writing the Natural Way* (Los Angeles: J. P. Tarcher, 1983), 10.

7. Rachel Spilka, "Orality and Literacy in the Workplace: Process- and Text-Based Strategies for Multiple Audience Adaptation," *Journal of Business and Technical Communication* 4, no. 1 (January 1990): 44–67.

8. Fred Reynolds, "What Adult Work-World Writers Have Taught Me About Adult Work-World Writing," *Professional Writing in Context: Lessons from Teaching and Consulting in Worlds of Work* (Hillsdale, NJ: Lawrence Erlbaum Associates, 1995), 18–21.

9. Raymond W. Beswick, "Communicating in the Automated Office," American Business Communication Association International Convention, New Orleans, LA, October 20, 1982.

10. Susan D. Kleimann, "The Complexity of Workplace Review," *Technical Communication* 38, no. 4 (1991): 520–526.

11. This three-step process is modelled on the one suggested by Barbara L. Shwom and Penny L. Hirsch, "Managing the Drafting Process: Creating a New Model for the Workplace," *Bulletin of the Association for Business Communication* 57, no. 2 (June 1994): 1–10.

Chapter 4

1. Robert L. Brown, Jr., and Carl G. Herndl, "An Ethnographic Study of Corporate Writing: Job Status as Reflected in Written Text," *Functional Approaches to Writing: A Research Perspective,* ed. Barbara Couture (Norwood, NJ: Ablex, 1986), 16–19, 22–23.

2. Linda Flower, *Problem-Solving Strategies for Writing,* 3rd ed., (New York: Harcourt Brace Jovanovich, 1989), 38.

3. James Suchan and Robert Colucci, "An Analysis of Communication Efficiency between High-Impact and Bureaucratic Written Communication," *Management Communication Quarterly* 2, no. 4 (May 1989): 464–473.

4. Hilvard G. Rogers and F. William Brown, "The Impact of Writing Style on Compliance with Instructions." *Journal of Technical Writing and Communication* 23, no. 1 (1993): 53–71.

5. Gretchen Glasscock, "My Favorite Bookmarks," *Fast Company,* October 1999, 62.

6. Myer Siemiatycki, Tim Rees, Roxana Ng, and Khan Rahi, "Integrating Community Diversity in Toronto: On Whose Terms?" CERIS Working Paper no. 14, 2001, at http://ceris.metropolis.net/Virtual%20Library/community/siemiatycki2.html, retrieved March 8, 2005; *The New Canada,* special issue of *Canadian Geographic,* January–February 2001.

7. George Bush, Washington, D.C., November 27, 2002, cited in Slate's *The Complete Bushisms,* retrieved November 4, 2005, from http://www.slate.com.

8. Sign in front of a Kentucky Fried Chicken franchise in Bloomington, IN, July 13, 1984.

9. Philip B. Crosby, *Quality Is Free: The Art of Making Quality Certain* (New York: New American Library, 1979), 79–84.

10. Jaguar ad, *The Wall Street Journal,* September 29, 2000, A20.

11. Erika L. Kirby and Lynn M. Harter, "Speaking the Language of the Bottom Line: The Metaphor of 'Managing Diversity,'" *Journal of Business Communication* 40.1, 28–49.

12. Richard C. Anderson, "Concretization and Sentence Learning," *Journal of Educational Psychology* 66, no. 2 (1974): 179–183.

13. Harris B. Savin and Ellen Perchonock, "Grammatical Structure and the Immediate Recall of English Sentences," *Journal of Verbal Learning and Verbal Behavior* 4 (1965): 348–353; and Pamela Layton and Adrian J. Simpson, "Deep Structure in Sentence Comprehension," *Journal of Verbal Learning and Verbal Behavior* 14 (1975): 658–664.

14. E. B. Coleman, "The Comprehensibility of Several Grammatical Transformations," *Journal of Applied Psychology* 48, no. 3 (1964): 186–190; Keith Rayner, "Visual Attention in Reading: Eye Movements Reflect Cognitive Processes," *Memory and Cognition* 5 (1977): 443–448; and Lloyd Bostian and Ann C. Thering, "Scientists: Can They Read What They Write?" *Journal of Technical Writing and Communication* 17 (1987): 417–427.

15. Arn Tibbetts, "Ten Rules for Writing Readably," *Journal of Business Communication* 18, no. 4 (Fall 1981): 55–59.

16. Thomas N. Huckin, "A Cognitive Approach to Readability," *New Essays in Technical and Scientific Communication: Research, Theory, Practice,* ed. Paul V. Anderson, R. John Brockmann, and Carolyn R. Miller (Farmingdale, NY: Baywood, 1983), 93–98.

17. Janice C. Redish and Jack Selzer, "The Place of Readability Formulas in Technical Communication," *Technical Communication* 32, no. 4 (1985): 46–52.

18. James Suchan and Ronald Dulek, "A Reassessment of Clarity in Written Managerial Communications," *Management Communication Quarterly* 4, no. 1 (August 1990): 93–97.

Chapter 5

1. Christopher B. Sullivan, "Preferences for Electronic Mail in Organizational Communication Tasks," *The Journal of Business Communications* 32, no.1 (January 1995): 46–64.

2. In a study of 483 subject lines written by managers and MBA students, Priscilla S. Rogers found that the average subject line was 5 words; only 10% of the subject lines used 10 or more words ("A Taxonomy for Memorandum Subject Lines," *Journal of Business and Technical Communication* 4, no. 2 [September 1990]: 28–29).

3. A 2004 study of 650 e-mail marketers found that lines under 50 text characters had open rates 12.5% higher than those over 50 text characters. *Daily News* for Monday, October 4, 2004, http://www.internetretailer.com/dailyNews.asp?id=13051, retrieved May 5, 2005.

4. Deborah Tannen, *That's Not What I Meant: How Conversational Style Makes or Breaks Your Relationships with Others* (New York: Morrow, 1986), 108.

5. Richard C. Whitely, *The Customer-Driven Company* (Reading, MA: Addison-Wesley, 1991), 39–40.
6. An earlier version of this problem, the sample solutions, and the discussion appeared in Francis W. Weeks and Kitty O. Locker, *Business Writing Cases and Problems* (Champaign, IL: Stipes, 1980), 40–44.
7. For more detailed advice, see the Postal Guide on the Canada Post Web site at http://canadapost.ca.

Chapter 6

1. Brent Jang, "Jetsgo ditches in red ink," *The Globe and Mail*, March 12, 2005, A1–A6; Brent Jang, "Jetsgo Sent Jets to Quebec for Safe Haven from Creditors," *Report on Business*, March 15, 2005, B1–B8; Brent Jang, "Leblanc on Sorrow, Remorse and His Little 'White Lie'," *Report on Business*, March 18, 2005, B1–B2; Keith MacArthur, "An Airline Addict Hits his Fourth Wall," *Report on Business*, March 12, 2005, B4; Richard Bloom and Colin Freeze, "Workers Find That Jobs Have Flown," *Report on Business*, March 12, 2005, B5.
2. Joann S. Lublin, "More Companies Cut Little Perks," *The Wall Street Journal*, January 4, 2001, B4.
3. Kitty O. Locker, "Factors in Reader Responses to Negative Letters: Experimental Evidence for Changing What We Teach," *Journal of Business and Technical Communication*, 13, no. 1 (January 1999): 21.
4. Jacquie McNish, "Compromise, or 'the Canadian way,' in Governance," *Report on Business*, March 25, 2005, B4.
5. Locker, "Factors in Reader Responses," 25–26.
6. Sharon S. Brehm and Jack W. Brehm, *Psychological Reactance: A Theory of Freedom and Control* (New York: Academic Press, 1981), 3.
7. "Tim Hortons Pulls Ad That Offended Family of Murder Victim," *Report on Business*, September 17, 2005, B7.
8. Jan Wong, "Fifteen minutes of shame," *The Globe and Mail*, May 7, 2005, F1–8; Jacquie McNish, "E-mails penetrate closed doors," *The Globe and Mail*, January 26, 2004, B1–4; Erin Pooley, "Not for Your Eyes Only," *Canadian Business*, January 31–February 13, 2005, 36.
9. Deborah Tannen, *Talking from 9 to 5: Women and Men in the Workplace: Language, Sex, and Power* (New York: Avon, 1994), 43–52.
10. Leslie N. Vreeland, "SEC 'Cop' Has Eye on Mutual Funds," *Columbus Dispatch*, July 21, 1987, 3F.
11. Frederick M. Jablin and Kathleen Krone, "Characteristics of Rejection Letters and Their Effects on Job Applicants," *Written Communication* 1, no. 4 (October 1984): 387–406; and Carlos Tejada, "Work Week," *The Wall Street Journal*, October 23, 2001, A1.
12. Elizabeth A. McCord, "The Business Writer, the Law, and Routine Business Communication: A Legal and Rhetorical Analysis," *Journal of Business and Technical Communication* 5, no. 2 (1991): 183.
13. Gabriella Stern, "Companies Discover That Some Firings Backfire into Costly Defamation Suits," *The Wall Street Journal*, May 5, 1993, B1.

Chapter 7

1. Alan Farnham, "You're So Vain," *Fortune*, September 9, 1996, 78–80.
2. Jay A. Conger, "The Necessary Art of Persuasion," *Harvard Business Review*, May–June 1998, 88.
3. Adapted from Andy Holloway, "Massaging the Message: A New Breed of Marketer Turns Conventional Brand Wisdom Upside Down," *Canadian Business*, March 15–28, 2004, 65–66; Keith McArthur, "Teens, moms targeted in oven-ready pizza war," *The Globe and Mail*, February 21, 2005, B4.
4. James Suchan and Ron Dulek, "Toward a Better Understanding of Reader Analysis," *Journal of Business Communication* 25, no. 2 (Spring 1988): 40.
5. Frances Harrington, "Formulaic Patterns versus Pressures of Circumstances: A Rhetoric of Business Situations," Conference on College Composition and Communication, New Orleans, LA, March 17–19, 1986.
6. Priscilla S. Rogers, "A Taxonomy for the Composition of Memorandum Subject Lines: Facilitating Writer Choice in Managerial Contexts," *Journal of Business and Technical Communication* 4, no. 2 (September 1990): 21–43.
7. Brian Morton, "Workplace fitness cited for bottom-line benefits," *Vancouver Sun*, reprinted in Saskatoon *StarPhoenix*, July 30, 2005, F11.
8. Karen Lowry Miller and David Woodruff, "The Man Who's Selling Japan on Jeeps," *BusinessWeek*, July 19, 1993, 56–57.
9. Daniel J. O'Keefe, *Persuasion* (Newbury Park, CA: Sage, 1990), 168; Joanne Martin and Melanie E. Powers, "Truth or Corporate Propaganda," *Organizational Symbolism*, ed. Louis R. Pondy, Thomas C. Dandridge, Gareth Morgan, and Peter J. Frost (Greenwich, CT: JAI Press, 1983), 97–107; and Dean C. Kazoleas, "A Comparison of the Persuasive Effectiveness of Qualitative versus Quantitative Evidence: A Test of Explanatory Hypotheses," *Communication Quarterly*, 41, no. 1 (Winter 1993): 40–50.
10. "Phoning Slow Payers Pays Off," *Inc.*, July 1996, 95.
11. An earlier draft of this problem and analysis appeared in Francis W. Weeks and Kitty O. Locker, *Business Writing Problems and Cases* (Champaign, IL: Stipes, 1980), 78–81.

Chapter 8

1. Adapted from "2004 Facts about Newspapers," Newspaper Association of America, http://www.naa.org/info/facts04/canada-allmedia.html, retrieved May, 6, 2005; Fraser Green, "Direct Mail," The FLA Group, http://www.theflagroup.com/new/news/, retrieved May 6, 2005.
2. Bill Bradley, Paul Jansen, and Les Silverman, "The Non-profit Sector's $100 Billion Opportunity," *Harvard Business Review*, May 2003, 94–103.
3. Sandra Yin, "Mail Openers," *American Demographics*, October 2001, 20–21.
4. This pattern is an adaptation of the Star-Chain-Hook pattern developed by Cy Frailey in the 1930s.
5. John D. Beard, David L. Williams, and J. Patrick Kelly, "The Long versus the Short Letter: A Large Sample Study of a Direct-Mail Campaign," *Journal of Direct Marketing* 4, no. 12 (Winter 1990): 13–20.
6. Ray Jutkins, "All about Post and Post Post Scripts—A Key Element in Direct Mail," *Direct Marketing*, January 1997, 44.
7. Eileen Daspin, "How to Give More," *The Wall Street Journal*, October 2, 1998, W1, W4.
8. Maxwell Sackheim, *My First Sixty-Five Years in Advertising* (Blue Ridge Summit, PA: Tab Books, 1975), 97–100.

Chapter 9

1. Brenda Arbeláez, statement to Kitty Locker, December 12, 1996.
2. Richard Blackwell, "Canadian Builds Global Ad Empire," *Report on Business*, March 14, 2005, B1.
3. Gail Edmondson. "See the World, Erase Its Borders," *BusinessWeek*, August 28, 2000, 113.
4. Mark Clifford and Manjeet Kripalani, "Different Countries, Adjoining Cubicles," *BusinessWeek*, August 28, 2000, 182–184.

5. Zena Olijnyk, et al, "Canada's Global Leaders: 40 Canadians Who've Become International Business Power Players," *Canadian Business*, March 28–April 10, 2005, 37–64.

6. Douglas Coupland, *Generation X: Tales for An Accelerated Culture* (New York: St. Martin's Press, 1991); "Generation X," *Wikipedia: The Free Encyclopedia*, retrieved May 13, 2005, from http://www.wikipedia.org/wiki/Generation_X; Barbara Moses, "Coddled, confident and cocky: The challenge of managing Gen Y," *The Globe and Mail*, March 11, 2005, C1–2.

7. Bureau of the Census, Press Releases, retrieved September 24, 2005, from http://www.census.gov.

8. Charles W. Holmes, "U.S. more diverse by the decade," *The Columbus Dispatch*, March 13, 2001, A1; and Nicholas Kulish, "Census Survey Uncovers More About U.S.," *The Wall Street Journal*, August 6, 2001, B4.

9. "Amazing Numbers," *Selling Power*, September 1996, 28.

10. Collector's Edition: The New Canada, *Canadian Geographic*, January/February 2001; Myer Siemiatycki, Tim Rees, Roxana Ng, and Khan Rahi, "Integrating Community Diversity in Toronto: On Whose Terms?" CERIS Working Paper no. 14, 2001, retrieved March 8, 2005, from http://ceris.metropolis.net/Virtual%20Library/community/siemiatycki.html; *The New Canada*, special issue of *Canadian Geographic*, January–February 2001; Jill Mahoney, "Visible majority by 2017," *The Globe and Mail*, March 23, 2005, A1; Jill Mahoney and Caroline Alphonso, "How the lines between races are blurring," *The Globe and Mail*, March 24, 2005, A3.

11. Karl Moore, "Multicultural Canada breeds managers with global outlook," *The Globe and Mail*, August 21, 2002, B9.

12. Terry Eagleton, *The Idea of Culture* (Oxford: Blackwell, 2000); Raymond Williams, *Keywords: A Vocabulary of Culture and Society* (London: Fontana, 1976).

13. Richard Davis, "The trouble with typecasting on the job," *The Globe and Mail*, July 23, 2004, C 1–2; Rosemary Barnes, "Encouraging diversity key to success," *The Globe and Mail*, September 11, 2004, B13; Virginia Galt, "Visible minorities build a diverse work force," *The Globe and Mail*, September 18, 2004, B9.

14. Edward T. Hall, *The Hidden Dimension* (Garden City, NY: Doubleday, 1966).

15. David Matsumoto, *The New Japan: Debunking Seven Cultural Stereotypes* (Yarmouth, ME: Intercultural Press, 2002), 28–29, 40–41, 144–45.

16. William Ruch, *Corporate Communication: A Comparison of Japanese and American Practices* (Westport, CT: Quorum Books, 1984), 5–6.

17. Laray M. Barna, "Stumbling Blocks in Intercultural Communication," in *Intercultural Communication*, ed. Larry A. Samovar and Richard E. Porter (Belmont, CA: Wadsworth, 1985), 331.

18. Kitty O. Locker, Stephen Kyo Kaczmarek, and Kathryn Braun, *Business Communication: Building Critical Skills*, 2nd Canadian Edition (Toronto: McGraw-Hill Ryerson, 2005), 56.

19. Carmen Judith Nine-Curt, "Hispanic-Anglo Conflicts in Nonverbal Communication," in *Perspectivas Pedagogicas*, ed. I. Abino et al. (Universidad de Puerto Rico, 1983), 235.

20. Laurence Wylie, *Beaux Gestes: A Guide to French Body Talk* (Cambridge, MA: Undergraduate Press, 1977), xi.

21. Marjorie Fink Vargas, *Louder than Words* (Ames: Iowa State University Press, 1986), 47.

22. Michael Argyle, *Bodily Communication* (New York: International University Press, 1975), 89.

23. Jerrold J. Merchant, "Korean Interpersonal Patterns: Implications for Korean/American Intercultural Communication," *Communication* 9 (October 1980): 65.

24. Argyle, *Bodily Communication*, 92.

25. Ray L. Birdwhistell, *Kinesics and Context: Essays on Body Motion Communication* (Philadelphia: University of Philadelphia Press, 1970), 30–31.

26. Glenna Dod and Gergana Kuneva, "*Yes* or *No*: Communication Barriers between Bulgaria and the United States," ABC Canadian, Eastern US, Southeastern US Joint Regional Conference, Nashville, TN, March 30–April 1, 2000.

27. Paul Ekman, Wallace V. Friesen, and John Bear, "The International Language of Gestures," *Psychology Today* 18, no. 5 (May 1984): 64.

28. Baxter, 1970, reported in Marianne LaFrance, "Gender Gestures: Sex, Sex-Role, and Nonverbal Communication," in *Gender and Nonverbal Behavior*, ed. Clara Mayo and Nancy M. Henley (New York: Springer-Verlag, 1981), 130.

29. Nine-Curt, "Hispanic-Anglo Conflicts," 238.

30. Brenda Major, "Gender Patterns in Touching Behavior," in *Gender and Nonverbal Behavior*, ed. Clara Mayo and Nancy M. Henley (New York: Springer-Verlag, 1981), 26, 28.

31. Mike McKeever to Kitty Locker, June 25, 2001.

32. Natalie Porter and Florence Gies, "Women and Nonverbal Leadership Cues: When Seeing Is Not Believing," in *Gender and Nonverbal Behavior*, ed. Clara Mayo and Nancy M. Henley (New York: Springer-Verlag, 1981), 48–49.

33. Robert C. Christopher, *Second to None: American Companies in Japan* (New York: Crown, 1986), 102–103.

34. Edward Twitchell Hall, *Hidden Differences: Doing Business with the Japanese* (Garden City, NY: Anchor-Doubleday, 1987), 25.

35. Lawrence B. Nadler, Marjorie Keeshan Nadler, and Benjamin J. Broome, "Culture and the Management of Conflict Situations," in *Communication, Culture, and Organizational Processes*, ed. William B. Gudykunst, Lea P. Stewart, and Stella Ting-Toomey (Beverly Hills, CA: Sage, 1985), 103.

36. Argyle, *Bodily Communication*, 90.

37. Carl Quintanilla, "Work Week," *The Wall Street Journal*, August 13, 1996, A1; Mary Ritchie Key, *Paralanguage and Kinesics* (Metuchen, NJ: Scarecrow, 1975), 23; Fred Hitzhusen, conversation with Kitty Locker, January 31, 1988; and William Horton, "The Almost Universal Language: Graphics for International Documents," *Technical Communication* 40, no. 4(1993): 687.

38. David Stipp, "Mirror, Mirror on the Wall, Who's the Fairest of Them All?" *Fortune*, September 9, 1996, 87.

39. Deborah Tannen, *That's Not What I Meant!* (New York: William Morrow, 1986).

40. Daniel N. Maltz and Ruth A. Borker, "A Cultural Approach to Male-Female Miscommunication," in *Language and Social Identity*, ed. John J. Gumperz (Cambridge: Cambridge University Press, 1982), 202.

41. Barbara Moses, "Still wanted: Female-friendly workplaces," *Globe Careers*, January 14, 2005, C1–2.

42. Muriel Saville-Troike, "An Integrated Theory of Communication," in *Perspectives on Silence*, ed. Deborah Tannen and Muriel Saville-Troike (Norwood, NJ: Ablex, 1985), 10–11.

43. A. Jann Davis, *Listening and Responding* (St. Louis: Mosby, 1984), 43.

44. Marilyn A. Dyrud, "An Exploration of Gender Bias in Computer Clip Art," *Business Communication Quarterly*, 60.4 (December 1997), 30–51.

45. Kitty O. Locker, Stephen Kyo Kaczmarek, and Kathryn Braun, *Business Communication: Building Critical Skills*, 2nd Canadian Edition (Toronto: McGraw-Hill Ryerson, 2005), 67; Lisa Tyler, "Communicating about People with Disabilities: Does the Language We Use Make a Difference?" *Bulletin of the Association for Business Communications* 53.3 (September 1990), 65.

Chapter 10

1. Tom Harris, "Listen Carefully," *Nation's Business*, June 1989, 78; L. K. Steil, L .I. Barker, and K. W. Watson, *Effective Listening: Key to Your Success* (Reading, MA: Addison-Wesley, 1983); and J. A. Harris, "Hear What's Really Being Said," *Management-Auckland*, August 1998, 18; qtd. in Mary Ellen Guffey, Kathleen Rhodes, and Patricia Rogin, *Business Communication: Process and Product*, 4th Canadian Edition. Toronto: Thomson Nelson, 2005, 72.

2. "Listening Factoids," International Listening Association, retrieved September 25, 2005, from http://www.listen.org/Templates/factoids.htm.

3. For a full account of the accident, see Andrew D. Wolvin and Caroline Gwynn Coakely, *Listening*, 3rd ed. (Dubuque, IA: William C. Brown, 1988), 10–11.

4. Thomas Gordon with Judith Gordon Sands, *P.E.T. in Action* (New York: Wyden, 1976), 83.

5. Thomas J. Knutson, "Communication in Small Decision-Making Groups: In Search of Excellence," *Journal for Specialists in Group Work* 10, no. 1 (March 1985): 28–37. The next four paragraphs summarize Knutson's analysis.

6. For a fuller listing of roles in groups, see David W. Johnson and Frank P. Johnson, *Joining Together: Group Theory and Group Skills,* 6th ed. (Englewood Cliffs, NJ: Prentice Hall, 1997), 20–21.

7. Beatrice Schultz, "Argumentativeness: Its Effect in Group Decision-Making and Its Role in Leadership Perception," *Communication Quarterly* 30, no. 4 (Fall 1982): 374–375; Dennis S. Gouran and B. Aubrey Fisher, "The Functions of Human Communication in the Formation, Maintenance, and Performance of Small Groups," in *Handbook of Rhetorical and Communication Theory,* ed. Carroll C. Arnold and John Waite Bowers (Boston: Allyn and Bacon, 1984), 640; Curt Bechler and Scott D. Johnson, "Leadership and Listening: A Study of Member Perceptions," *Small Group Research* 26, no. 1 (February 1995): 77–85; and Scott D. Johnson and Curt Bechler, "Examining the Relationship between Listening Effectiveness and Leadership Emergence: Perceptions, Behaviors, and Recall," *Small Group Research* 29, no. 3 (August 1998): 452–471.

8. H. Lloyd Goodall, Jr., *Small Group Communications in Organizations,* 2nd ed. (Dubuque, IA: William C. Brown, 1990), 39–40.

9. Nance L. Harper and Lawrence R. Askling, "Group Communication and Quality of Task Solution in a Media Production Organization," *Communication Monographs* 47, no. 2 (June 1980): 77–100.

10. Rebecca E. Burnett, "Conflict in Collaborative Decision-Making," in *Professional Communication: The Social Perspective,* ed. Nancy Roundy Blyler and Charlotte Thralls (Newbury Park, CA: Sage, 1993), 144–162.

11. Kimberly A. Freeman, "Attitudes Toward Work in Project Groups as Predictors of Academic Performance," *Small Group Research* 27, no. 2 (May 1996): 265–282.

12. Poppy Lauretta McLeod, Sharon Alisa Lobel, Taylor H. Cox, Jr., "Ethnic Diversity and Creativity in Small Groups," *Small Group Research* 27, no. 2 (May 1996): 248–264; and Leisa D. Sargent and Christina Sue-Chan, "Does Diversity Affect Efficacy? The Intervening Role of Cohesion and Task Interdependence," *Small Group Research* 32 (2001): 426–450.

13. David S. Jalajas and Robert I. Sutton, "Feuds in Student Groups: Coping with Whiners, Martyrs, Saboteurs, Bullies, and Deadbeats," *Mastering Management Education: Innovations in Teaching Effectiveness,* ed. Charles M. Vance (Newbury Park, CA: Sage, 1993), 217–227.

14. Nancy Schullery and Beth Hoger, "Business Advocacy for Students in Small Groups," Association for Business Communication Annual Convention, San Antonio, TX, November 9–11, 1998.

15. "Survey Finds Workers Average Only Three Productive Days per Week," March 15, 2005, retrieved September 25, 2005, from http://www.microsoft.com/presspass/press/2005/mar05/03-15ThreeProductiveDaysPR.mspx.

16. Frank Buchar, "Stifle yawns: Wake up your meetings," *Globe Careers*, June 4, 2004, C1.

17. Lisa Ede and Andrea Lunsford, *Singular Texts/Plural Authors: Perspectives on Collaborative Writing* (Carbondale, IL: Southern Illinois Press, 1990), 60.

18. Paul Benjamin Lowry, Aaron Curtis, and Michelle Rene Lowry, "Building a Taxonomy and Nomenclature of Collaborative Writing to Improve Interdisciplinary Research and Practice," *Journal of Business Communication*, January 2004, 66–99, downloaded from http://www.jobsagepub.com November 29, 2005.

19. Rebecca Burnett, "Characterizing Conflict in Collaborative Relationships: The Nature of Decision-Making During Coauthoring." PhD dissertation, Carnegie-Mellon University, Pittsburgh, PA, 1991.

20. Kitty O. Locker, "What Makes a Collaborative Writing Team Successful? A Case Study of Lawyers and Social Service Workers in a State Agency," in *New Visions in Collaborative Writing,* ed. Janis Forman (Portsmouth, NJ: Boynton, 1991), 37–52.

21. Ede and Lunsford, *Singular Texts/Plural Authors,* 66.

22. Jo Mackiewicz and Kathryn Riley, "The Technical Editor as Diplomat: Linguistic Strategies for Balancing Clarity and Politeness," *Technical Communication,* 50.1 (February 2003), 83–94, downloaded from http://www.ingentaconnect.com, November 29, 2005.

23. Meg Morgan, Nancy Allen, Teresa Moore, Dianne Atkinson, and Craig Snow, "Collaborative Writing in the Classroom," *The Bulletin of the Association for Business Communication* 50, no. 3 (September 1987): 22.

Chapter 11

1. For a useful taxonomy of proposals, see Richard C. Freed and David D. Roberts, "The Nature, Classification, and Generic Structure of Proposals," *Journal of Technical Writing and Communication* 19, no. 4 (1989): 317–351.

2. Christine Peterson Barabas, *Technical Writing in a Corporate Culture: A Study of the Nature of Information* (Norwood, NJ: Ablex Publishing, 1990), 327.

3. David B. Wolfe, "Targeting the Mature Mind," *American Demographics,* March 1994, 34.

4. Janice M. Lauer and J. William Asher, *Composition Research: Empirical Designs* (New York: Oxford University Press, 1986), 66.

5. Irving Crespi, quoted in W. Joseph Campbell, "Phone surveys becoming unreliable, pollsters say," *Columbus Dispatch,* February 21, 1988, 8F.

6. Palmer Morrel-Samuels, "Web Surveys' Hidden Hazards," *Harvard Business Review*, July 2003, 16–17; Jakob Nielsen, "Keep Online Surveys Short," *Alertbox,* http://www.useit.com, February 2, 2004.

7. Joshua Macht, "The New Market Research," *Inc.,* July 1998, 90–92.

8. Karen Birchard, Canada's Simon Fraser Suspends 44 students in Plagiarism Scandal," *The Chronicle of Higher Education,* October 2002, retrieved September 25, 2005, from http://chronicle.com/daily/2002/10/2002102404n.htm; Nicole Wahl, "Online database pinpoints plagiarism," *News @ University of Toronto,* retrieved September 25, 2005, from http://www.newsandevents.utoronto.ca/bin3/021121a.asp.

9. Stuart H. Loory and Petya Stoeva, "Journalism's Chronic Crisis: Corruption of Its Honesty," *Global Journalist Magazine*, 2004 Fourth Quarter, retrieved September 25, 2005, from http://www.globaljournalist.org/magazine/2004-4/chronic-crisis.html.

10. Wahl, 1. LaPointe quoted in Loory and Stoeva, 4.

Chapter 12

1. Michael Schrage, "Take the Lazy Way Out? That's Far Too Much Work," *Fortune*, February 5, 2001, 212.

2. Jakob Nielsen, "Risks of Quantitative Studies," *Alertbox*, March 1, 2004, http://www.useit.com

3. "The Incredible Shrinking Failure Rate," *Inc.*, October 1993, 58.

4. "Whirlpool: How to Listen to Consumers," *Fortune*, January 11, 1993, 77.

5. Peter Lynch with John Rothchild, *One Up on Wall Street: How to Use What You Already Know to Make Money in the Market* (New York: Fireside-Simon & Schuster, 2000), 189.

6. Patricia Sullivan, "Reporting Negative Research Results," and Kitty O. Locker to Pat Sullivan, June 8, 1990.

7. George A. Miller, "The Magical Number Seven, Plus or Minus Two: Some Limits on Our Capacity for Processing Information," *Psychological Review* 63, no. 2 (March 1956): 81–97.

8. *Make Poverty History* home page, retrieved July 2, 2005, from http://www.makepovertyhistory.org.

9. Gene Zelazny, *Say It with Charts: The Executive's Guide to Successful Presentations*, 4th ed. (New York: McGraw-Hill, 2001), 52.

10. Stephen H. Wildstrom, "A Picture is Worth 1,000 Charts," *BusinessWeek*, January 20, 2003, downloaded from http://www.businessweek.com on November 29, 2005; "Market Map 1000," SamartMoney.com, downloaded on August 30, 2004.

11. W. S. Cleveland and R. McGill, "Graphical Perception: Theory, Experiments, and Application to the Development of Graphic Methods," *Journal of the American Statistical Association* 79, nos. 3 & 7 (1984): 531–553; cited in Jeffry K. Cochran, Sheri A. Albrecht, and Yvonne A. Greene, "Guidelines for Evaluating Graphical Designs: A Framework Based on Human Perception Skills," *Technical Communication* 36, no. 1 (February 1989): 27.

12. L. G. Thorell and W. J. Smith, *Using Computer Color Effectively: An Illustrated Reference* (Englewood Cliffs, NJ: Prentice Hall, 1990), 12–13; William Horton, "The Almost Universal Language: Graphics for International Documents," *Technical Communication* 40, no. 4 (1993): 687; and Thyra Rauch, "IBM Visual Interface Design," *The STC Usability PIC Newsletter*, January 1996, 3.

13. Thorell and Smith, *Using Computer Color Effectively*, 13.

14. "Color Printing Center—Tips for Color Use," Hewlett-Packard Public Sector Web, retrieved July 2, 2005, from http://www.hp.com/united-states/public/color/use/tips.html.

15. Thorell and Smith, *Using Computer Color Effectively*, 49–51, 214–15.

16. Edward R. Tufte, *The Visual Display of Quantitative Information* (Cheshire, CT: Graphics Press, 1983), 113.

17. Thophilus Addo, "The Effects of Dimensionality in Computer Graphics," *Journal of Business Communication* 31, no. 4 (October 1994): 253–265.

Chapter 13

1. Dan Gilmore, "Putting on a Powerful Presentation," *Hemispheres*, March 1996, 31–32.

2. Florence L. Wolff, Nadine C. Marsnik, William S. Tracey, and Ralph G. Nicholas, *Perceptive Listening* (Englewood Cliffs, NJ: Prentice Hall, 1983), 154.

3. Linda Driskill, "How the Language of Presentations Can Encourage or Discourage Audience Participation," paper presented at the Conference on College Composition and Communication, Cincinnati, OH, March 18–21, 1992.

4. Anne Fisher, "Willy Loman Couldn't Cut It," *Fortune*, November 11, 1996, 210.

5. Roy Alexander, *Power Speech: Why It's Vital to You* (New York: AMACOM, 1986), 156.

6. Robert S. Mills, conversation with Kitty Locker, March 10, 1988.

7. Phil Theibert, "Speechwriters of the World, Get Lost!" *The Wall Street Journal*, August 2, 1993, A10.

8. "A Study of the Effects of the Use of Overhead Transparencies on Business Meetings," Wharton Applied Research Center, reported in Martha Jewett and Rita Margolies, eds., *How to Run Better Business Meetings: A Reference Guide for Managers* (New York: McGraw-Hill, 1987), 109–110; and Tad Simmons, "Multimedia or Bust," *Presentations*, February 2000, 44, 48–50.

9. University of Minnesota/3M Study, reported in Martha Jewett and Rita Margolies, eds., *How to Run Better Business Meetings: A Reference Guide for Managers* (New York: McGraw-Hill, 1987), 115.

10. Andrew Wahl, "PowerPoint of no return," *Canadian Business*, November 23, 2003, 131; Virginia Galt, "Glazed eyes a major peril of using PowerPoint," *Globe and Mail Report on Business*, June 4, 2005, B10; Ian Parker, "Absolute Powerpoint," *The New Yorker*, May 28, 2001, 76.

11. Jim Gray, ""The perils of PowerPoint slides," *The Globe and Mail*, September 6, 2002, retrieved October 3, 2005, from http://www.hrpao.org/HRPAO/KnowledgeCentre,; Edward Tufte, "PowerPoint is Evil," *Wired News*, 11.9, September 2003, retrieved October 3, 2005, from http://www.wired.com/wired/archive/11.09/ppt2_pr.html.

12. Stephen E. Lucas, *The Art of Public Speaking*, 2nd ed. (New York: Random House, 1986), 248.

13. Edward J. Hegarty, *Humor and Eloquence in Public Speaking* (West Nyack, NY: Parker, 1976), 204.

14. David Benady, "Look Who's Talking," *Marketing Week*, August 12, 2004, downloaded from Infotrac at http://www.findarticles.com.

15. The comparison is taken from Jim Martin, "National Debt: Pennies to Heaven," *The Wall Street Journal*, February 22, 1988, 18.

16. Some studies have shown that previews and reviews increase comprehension; other studies have found no effect. For a summary of the research see Kenneth D. Frandsen and Donald R. Clement, "The Functions of Human Communication in Informing: Communicating and Processing Information," *Handbook of Rhetorical and Communication Theory*, ed. Carroll C. Arnold and John Waite Bowers (Boston: Allyn and Bacon, 1984), 340–41.

17. S. A. Beebe, "Eye Contact: A Nonverbal Determinant of Speaker Credibility," *Speech Teacher* 23 (1974): 21–25; cited in Marjorie Fink Vargas, *Louder than Words* (Ames: Iowa State University Press, 1986), 61–62.

18. J. Wills, "An Empirical Study of the Behavioral Characteristics of Sincere and Insincere Speakers," Ph.D. diss., University of Southern California, 1961; cited in Vargas, *Louder than Words*, 62.

19. James Gray, "In a world of words, the eyes have it," *The Globe and Mail*, December 5, 2003, retrieved October 3, 2005, from http://www.hrpao.org/HRPAO/KnowledgeCentre, retrieved October 3, 2005.

20. George W. Fluharty and Harold R. Ross, *Public Speaking* (New York: Barnes & Noble, 1981), 162–163.

21. Ralph Proodian, "Mind the Tip of Your Tongue," *The Wall Street Journal,* May 4, 1992, A20.

22. Stephen E. Lucas, *The Art of Public Speaking,* 2nd ed. (New York: Random House, 1986), 243.

23. Ralph Proodian, "Raspy Throat? Read This, Mr. President," *The Wall Street Journal,* January 25, 1993, A14.

24. Michael Waldholz, "Lab Notes," *The Wall Street Journal,* March 19, 1991, B1.

25. George B. Ray, "Vocally Cued Personality Prototypes: An Implicit Personality Theory Approach," *Communication Monographs* 53, no. 3 (1986): 266–276.

25. Jim Gray, "The magic of movement," *The Globe and Mail,* September 5, 2003, retrieved October 3, 2005, from http://www.hrpao.org.

26. Speaking-Tips.com, "Hand Gestures," December 2003, retrieved October 3, 2005, from http://www.speaking-tips.com/Articles/Hand-Gestures.asp.

Chapter 14

1. Pierre Mornell, *Games Companies Play: The Job Hunter's Guide to Playing Smart & Winning Big in the High-Stakes Hiring Game* (Berkeley, CA: Ten Speed Press, 2000), 25.

2. Carl Quintanilla, "Coming Back," *The Wall Street Journal,* February 22, 1996, R10.

3. LeAne Rutherford, "Five Fatal Résumé Mistakes," *BusinessWeek's Guide to Careers* 4, no. 3 (Spring/Summer 1986): 60–62.

4. Phil Elder, "The Trade Secrets of Employment Interviews," Association for Business Communication Midwest Convention, Kansas City, MO, May 2, 1987.

5. Elizabeth Blackburn-Brockman and Kelly Belanger, "One Page or Two? A National Study of CPA Recruiters' Preferences for Résumé Length," *The Journal of Business Communication* 38 (2001): 29–45.

6. Davida H. Charney, Jack Rayman, and Linda Ferreira-Buckley, "How Writing Quality Influences Readers' Judgments of Résumés in Business and Engineering," *Journal of Business and Technical Communication* 6, no. 1 (January 1992): 38–74.

7. Vincent S. Di Salvo and Janet K. Larsen, "A Contingency Approach to Communication Skill Importance: The Impact of Occupation, Direction, and Position," *The Journal of Business Communication* 24, no. 3 (Summer 1987): 13.

8. Kitty O. Locker, Gianna M. Marsella, Alisha C. Rohde, and Paula C. Weston, "Electronic Résumés: Lessons from Fortune 500, Inc. 500, and Big Six CPA Firms," Association for Business Communication Annual Convention, Chicago, IL, November 6–9, 1996.

9. This section is based on Kirsten Dixon, "Crafting an E-Mail Résumé," *BusinessWeek,* November 13, 2001.

10. Locker, Marsella, and Rohde, "Electronic Résumés."

11. T. T. Sekine, "Employment Portfolios in the Nineties," Association for Business Communication Midwest Convention, Indianapolis, IN, April 20–22, 1995.

12. Beverly H. Nelson, William P. Gallé, and Donna W. Luse, "Electronic Job Search and Placement," Association for Business Communication Convention, Orlando, FL, November 1–4, 1995.

13. Resumix, "Preparing the Ideal Scannable Resume," [http://www.resumix.com] October 16, 1996.

14. Taunee Besson, *The Wall Street Journal National Employment Business Weekly: Résumés,* 3rd ed. (New York: John Wiley and Sons, 1999), 263.

15. Thomas Petzinger, Jr., "Lewis Roland's Knack for Finding Truckers Keeps Firm Rolling," *The Wall Street Journal,* December 1, 1995, B1.

16. Bill Breen and Anna Muoio, "PeoplePalooza," *Fast Company,* November 2000, 88.

17. Rachel Emma Silverman, "Why Are You So Dressed Up? Do You Have a Job Interview?" *The Wall Street Journal,* April 17, 2001, B1.

18. The Catalyst Staff, *Marketing Yourself* (New York: G. P. Putnam's Sons, 1980), 179.

19. Christopher Conte, "Labor Letter," *The Wall Street Journal,* October 19, 1993, A1.

20. *Marketing Yourself,* 101.

Appendix A

1. Linda Reynolds, "The Legibility of Printed Scientific and Technical Information," *Information Design,* ed. Ronald Easterby and Harm Zwaga (New York: John Wiley & Sons, 1984), 187–208.

2. For a review of the events and an analysis of the management problems, see J. C. Mathes, "Three Mile Island: The Management Communication Role," *Engineering Management International* 3 (1986): 261–268.

3. Bruch Tognazzini, "The Butterfly Ballot: Anatomy of a Disaster," *Ask Tog,* January 2001, retrieved September 4, 2001, from http://www.asktog.com/columns/042ButterflyBallot.html.

4. George A. Miller, "The Magical Number Seven, Plus or Minus Two: Some Limits on Our Capacity for Processing Information," *Psychological Review* 63, no. 2 (March 1956): 81–97.

5. Once we know how to read English, the brain first looks to see whether an array of letters follows the rules of spelling. If it does, the brain then treats the array as a word (even if it isn't one, such as *tweal*). The shape is processed in individual letters only when the shape is not enough to suggest meaning. Jerry E. Bishop, "Word Processing: Research on Stroke Victims Yields Clues to the Brain's Capacity to Create Language," *The Wall Street Journal,* October 12, 1993, A6.

6. David Matis, "The Graphic Design of Text," *Intercom,* February 1996, 23.

7. M. Gregory and E. C. Poulton, "Even versus Uneven Right-Hand Margins and the Rate of Comprehension of Reading," *Ergonomics* 13 (1970): 427–434.

8. Russell N. Baird, Arthur T. Turnbull, and Duncan McDonald, *The Graphics of Communication: Typography, Layout, Design, Production,* 5th ed. (New York: Holt, Rinehart & Winston, 1987), 37.

9. Philip M. Rubens, "A Reader's View of Text and Graphics: Implications for Transactional Text," *Journal of Technical Writing and Communication* 16, nos. 1–2 (1986): 78.

10. M. E. Wrolstad, "Adult Preferences in Typography: Exploring the Function of Design," *Journalism Quarterly* 37 (Winter 1960): 211–223; summarized in Rolf F. Rehe, "Typography: How to Make It Most Legible," Design Research International, Carmel, IN, 57.

11. Elizabeth Keyes, "Typography, Color, and Information Structure," *Technical Communication,* 40, no. 4 (November 1993): 652; and Joseph Koncelik, "Design, Aging, Ethics, and the Law" (Paper presented in Columbus, OH, May 6, 1993).

12. Marilyn A. Dyrud, "An Exploration of Gender Bias in Computer Clip Art," *Business Communication Quarterly* 60, no. 4 (December 1997): 30–51.

13. Jakob Nielsen, "Why You Only Need to Test With 5 Users," *Jakob Neilsen's Alertbox,* March 19, 2000, retrieved September 4, 2001 from www.useit.com/alertbox/20000319.html.

Chapter 1

Page 2: Courtesy of Myrna Bentley; p. 15: Courtesy of WestJet Airlines; p. 17: Michael Greenlar/The Image Works; p. 18: Courtesy of Amanah Tech Inc.; p. 23: Getty Images.

Chapter 2

Page 29: Courtesy of Patrick Scissons; p. 33: Courtesy of Vancity; p. 49: Kitty O. Locker, by permission of Joseph-Beth Booksellers; p. 56: Bill Sikes/AP/Wide World Photos.

Chapter 3

Page 63: Courtesy of Entre Vue Magazine.

Chapter 4

Page 84: Courtesy of Cheryl Stephens; p. 91: Courtesy of California Dried Plum Board.

Chapter 5

Page 106: Courtesy of Canadian Tire Corporation; p. 119: Photographer: Trevor Lush; p. 127: Courtesy of Siemens AG/ShareNet.

Chapter 6

Page 136: Courtesy of Rajani J. Kamath; p. 148: Courtesy of Schwinn Bicycle.

Chapter 7

Page 160: Courtesy of Chief Sophie Pierre; p. 163: Billboard advertisement provided courtesy of McCain Foods Canada and Target Marketing and Communications.

Chapter 8

Page 186: Courtesy of Germain Strengthening Brands, www.germaincommunications.com.

Chapter 9

Page 210: © Marvin Moore Photography 2005.

Chapter 10

Page 229: Photo provided courtesy of Itracks.

Chapter 11

Page 250: Photograph taken by Eric Mailloux and provided courtesy of Quebec chantier de l'economie sociale; p. 253: © Karen Moskowitz; p. 270: Rim Light/ PhotoLink/PhotoDisc, Volume 21 Retail, Shopping and Small Business.

Chapter 12

Page 282: Courtesy of the Canadian Institute of Chartered Accountants.

Chapter 13

Page 327: Janet Trost Photography; p. 332: © Junebug Clark/Photo Researchers; p. 334: CP/Fred Chartrand.

Chapter 14

Page 348: Courtesy of Drina Nixon; p. 377: © Rick Rickman/Matrix; p. 381: Copyright © Danny Turner. All rights reserved.

Appendix A

Page 392: Courtesy of Lulu Digital Design.